D1034519

THE POPE SPEAKS

The Teachings of Pope Pius XII

Compiled and edited
with the assistance of the Vatican Archives
by Michael Chinigo

PANTHEON

Imprimatur

Francis Cardinal Spellman
✠ Archbishop of New York

March 21, 1957

333 Sixth Avenue, New York 14, New York
Library of Congress Catalog Card Number: 57-7321
Manufactured in the U.S.A.

EDITOR'S PREFACE

WHILE I WAS GATHERING MATERIAL for a book on the Vatican, the necessity arose time and again to consult the Encyclicals, Apostolic Letters, and various Addresses of Pope Pius XII. Thus the idea of an anthology covering all the topics to which the Holy Father has dedicated attention was born.

In more than a year's work the Pontiff's Addresses, Encyclicals, and Apostolic Letters were sifted to select the material. Two basic criteria were applied to the selection: If one of several documents represented the most exhaustive treatment of a topic and the others were merely repetitive, then my choice fell on the principal pronouncement. In cases, however, where the Holy Father treated various aspects of a problem at different periods, I have taken the pertinent parts out of context and worked them into a harmonious whole in a single chapter, separating the excerpts by a line of space.

Many qualified advisers whose counsel I sought have made recommendations and helped me to realize this project. May I express the hope that this summary of the teachings of Pope Pius XII concerning the most crucial problems of our time will be useful to many.

These were the contents of an explanatory note which I sent with the manuscript to His Holiness Pope Pius XII. The manuscript was submitted to the Holy Father, who, in returning it, sent me through His Excellency Monsignor Angelo Dell'Acqua, Substitute of the Secretary of State, His Apostolic Blessing.

The English translations are my own, unless otherwise mentioned in the Acknowledgments. The religious and theological terms have been checked for accuracy by a qualified prelate. To him and to the Monsignori of the Vatican Secretary of State's Office, who helped me find him and otherwise encouraged me with this edition, go my heartfelt thanks.

MICHAEL CHINIGO

ACKNOWLEDGMENTS

GRATEFUL ACKNOWLEDGMENT is made to *Books On Trial,* Chicago, Ill., for permission to use "The Duty and Responsibility of the Literary Critic," in the translation of Father Joseph M. O'Leary, C.P., and to the *Catholic Messenger,* Davenport, Iowa, for permission to use "The Boarding School—Its Effects and Its Purpose," in the translation of Dom Celestine Cullen, O.S.B.

CONTENTS

LIST OF ILLUSTRATIONS

MAN

MAN

ON THE DAY when God formed man and crowned his brow with the diadem of His image and likeness, making him king of all living animals in the seas, in the skies, and on the land, on that day the Lord, Omniscient God, made Himself man's master. He taught him agriculture, how to cultivate and care for the delightful garden in which He had placed him; led to him all the beasts of the fields and all the birds of the air so that man might name them. And he gave to each of them its true and fitting name. But, even among that multitude of beings subject to him, man felt sadly alone and looked in vain for a brow which resembled his own and had a ray of that divine image with which the eye of every son of Adam sparkles. From man only could another man issue forth who would call him father and progenitor; and the helpmate given by God to the first man also comes from him and is flesh of his flesh, fashioned into a mate for him, named from man because she was derived from him. On the topmost rung of the ladder of the living, God placed man, endowed with a spiritual soul, to be the prince and sovereign of the animal kingdom. Manifold research in the fields of paleontology, biology, and morphology on various problems regarding the origin of man has not yet yielded anything positively clear and certain. We must therefore leave it to the future to answer the question as to whether someday science, illuminated and guided by revelation, will be able to reach certain and definitive results in such a momentous matter.

True science neither lowers nor humiliates man in his origin. Rather, it elevates and exalts him because it perceives, recognizes, and admires in every member of the great human family greater or lesser traces of the divine image and likeness stamped upon him.

Man's Dominion over Nature

Man is great. The progress he makes in the physical, natural, mathematical, and industrial sciences, eager for ever better, wider, and surer advancement, what is it but the effect of the domination he still exercises—even if limited and strenuously gained—over inferior nature? And when has human ingenuity ever searched, scrutinized, penetrated nature as at present, in order to get to know its forces and forms so as to dominate them, bend them in its instruments, and make use of them as it pleases?

Man is great, and he was still greater when created. If he fell from his original greatness, rebelling against the Creator, and went, an exile and wanderer, out of the Garden of Eden, gathering in the sweat of his brow the bread which the earth gave him, amid tribulations and thorns; if the sky and the sun, the cold and the heat, if refuges and forests, if so much other wear and tear and travail, so many discomforts due to environment and conditions of life debased his face and figure; if the remnants of the command once given to him over the animal world are nothing more than a fading recollection of his former power and a tiny fragment of his throne: even in his ruin he looms great because of that divine image and likeness he carries in his spirit, and on account of which God was so pleased with the human creature, the last work of His creative hand, that He did not disarm or abandon him when he fell. Rather, in order to elevate man again, He made Himself like unto man, and in His condition was recognized as a man, suffering from our infirmities, similarly tempted in all, except sin (Hebrews 4, 15).

Intellect and Will

Two gifts, which raise him very high between the world of celestial spirits and the world of bodies, make man great, even since his downfall: the intellect, whose view surveys the created universe and crosses the skies, yearning to contemplate God; and will, endowed with the power to choose freely, servant and master of the intellect, which makes us, in different degrees, masters of our own thoughts and of our actions before ourselves, before others, and before God.

The ingenuity, the will power, and the action of man with his machines and his tools, though they cannot upset the order of nature, may reveal it.

God is the sole commander and legislator of the universe. He is a sun that, in the infinite magnificence of its light, diffuses and multiplies its rays, resemblances of itself, in all the fields of creation; but no image can equal Him. Thus man too, when he does not find a word which alone can sufficiently express the concept of his mind, multiplies words in various ways. Similarly, in the multiplicity of creatures there is a diversity of natures and a different divine vestige, depending on how close they come to God in the resemblance of the being which is theirs.

God's Will Is the Primary Cause of All Nature

Does not the diversity of things demand that not all be equal but that a gradual order be resplendent there? In this order and in these gradations we see natures and forms differing in perfection and vigor, in action and object, in reaction and composition, in substance and quality, from which emerge different properties, operations, and agents with reciprocal impressions and diverse effects, which have their reason in the diversity impressed by the Creator in the nature of things, determined and directed to a particular end and action. In this natural necessity inherent in things, which is nothing but an impression produced by God, Who guides everything to an end, just as an archer directs his arrow to the target, lies the law of the nature of bodies, a law which is one with their very nature. Just as a man by his commandment impresses upon another man subject to him an internal principle of operation, so God impresses in all nature the principles of its own actions, and in this manner the Supreme Maker of the universe, God and Master of all sciences, *praeceptum posuit et non praeteribit*—He has made a law for the whole, and it shall not pass away. Hence—as the great Doctor of Aquino masterfully teaches—when one asks the wherefore of a natural effect, we may explain it by some near cause, such as the natural property of things, provided we trace everything back to the will of God as the primary cause, the wise instructor of all nature. Thus, if someone, on being asked why fire heats, replies because God wishes it, he would be replying correctly, if he wanted to reduce the question to the first cause; wrongly, however, if he intended to exclude all other causes.

In us, too, who are God's creatures, the first cause impressed a law, which is a sublime instinct wholly peculiar to man, to seek knowledge of the Creator; a desire which is a spiritual movement, and never ceases—until it reaches enjoyment of the object of its love. If our flesh comes from dust and will return to dust, our spirit is immortal; it comes from God and yearns to return to God by this world's ladder of science, which, however, does not succeed in fully satisfying the immense thirst for truth which animates us. The school of God, Master of every science, is the world; if its figure passes, we remain alone before the Master. Let us bow before His wisdom, unfathomable in its mysteries and in His decision to give humanity as its dwelling this globe so full of wonders and surrounded by millions of wonders even more resplendent and immeasurable; wonders which, as the Creator contemplated His work on the day He accomplished it, were all seen by Him to be very good.[1]

[1] Allocution to the Members of the Pontifical Academy of Sciences, November 30, 1941

LOVE

GOD IS LOVE, writes St. John, substantial and infinite love; He delights eternally, without desire and without satiety, in the contemplation of His infinite perfection; and, because He is the only absolute Being, beside Whom there is nothing, if He wishes to call into existence other beings, He can draw them only out of His own wealth. Every creature, being a more or less remote derivation of infinite love, is therefore the fruit of love and does not move except through love.

In the chaotic nebula, one day a first force of attraction, that is to say, a first symbol of love, grouped together around a nucleus the cosmic elements, which formed a star; then the attraction of this first one called forth a second; and because another was attracted in its turn, the marvellous procession of worlds began its course around the firmament. But God's masterpiece is man, and to this masterpiece of love He has given a power to love unknown to irrational creatures. Man's love is personal, that is to say, conscious; free, that is to say, subject to the control of his responsible will.

In giving man body and soul, God had endowed him with the full powers of human nature. Beyond that man could not hope to reach; but God's intentions reached further. He gave to the human creature a new and superhuman gift: grace; grace, inscrutable prodigy of the love of God, a marvel the mystery of which human intelligence cannot penetrate, and which man has called "supernatural," thus humbly confessing that it surpasses his nature.

Even purely sensible love has such tender touching beauty that the Lord compares Himself to the eagle which trains his young to fly and hovers over them. But human love is incomparably nobler, because here the soul participates, animated by the impulse of the heart, that delicate witness and interpreter of the union between body and soul, which harmonizes the material impressions of the one with the superior feelings of the other. The charm exercised by human love has been for centuries the inspiring theme of admirable works of genius, in literature, in music, in the visual arts; a theme always old and always new, upon which the ages have embroidered, without ever exhausting it, the most elevated and poetic variations.

But what new and unutterable beauty is added to this love of two human hearts, when its song is harmonized with the hymn of two souls vibrating with supernatural life! Here, too, there is a mutual exchange of gifts; and then, through bodily tenderness and its healthy joys, through natural affection and its impulses, through a spiritual union and its delights, the two beings who love each other identify themselves in all that is most intimate in them, from the unshaken depths of their beliefs to the highest summit of their hopes.

Christian Matrimony

Such is Christian matrimony, modelled, according to the famous expression of St. Paul, on the union of Christ with His Church. In the one as in the other, the gift of self is total, exclusive, irrevocable; in the one and in the other the husband is head of the wife, who is subject to him as to the Lord; in the one and in the other the mutual gift becomes a principle of expansion and a source of life (Ephesians 5).

Thus, married couples, in the providential mission assigned to them, are properly the collaborators of God and of Christ; something divine pertains to their achievements, so that they may call themselves *divinae consortes naturae*—partakers of the divine nature.

Is it surprising that these splendid privileges should entail grave duties? The nobility of the divine action obliges married Christians to considerable self-denial and to the performance of many acts of courage, so that matter may not hinder the spirit in its ascent toward truth and virtue and with its weight drag it down toward the abyss. But as God never commands what is impossible and with the order which He gives grants also the strength to fulfill it, matrimony, which is a great Sacrament, brings, together with its duties that may appear superhuman, help that shows itself to be supernatural.[1]

A mutual affection springing solely from the inclination which draws man toward woman, or from mere pleasure in the human gifts which one discovers with such satisfaction in one another; such an affection, however beautiful and deep it may prove to be, and however beautiful and deep may be its echo in the intimacy of the trusting conversations of the newly wed, would never be sufficient in itself. It could not even fully achieve the union of your souls in bringing you toward one another. Only supernatural charity, a bond of friendship between God and man, can tie knots strong enough to resist all the shocks, all the vicissitudes, all the inevitable trials of a long life spent together; only divine grace can make you rise superior to all the little daily miseries, all the nascent contrasts and disparities of tastes or of ideas, springing, like weeds, from the root of fallible human nature. And this charity and grace, is it not the strength and virtue which you went to ask of the great Sacrament you received? Divine charity, greater yet than faith and hope, is needed by the world, society, and the family!

Love, holy and sacred and divine: is it not—you will perhaps say —something too lofty for us? Will love so much above nature—you may even ask—still be that truly human love, which has been the beating of our hearts, which our hearts seek and in which they find peace, of which they have need and which they are so happy to have found? Set your minds at rest: God with His love neither destroys nor changes nature, but perfects it; and St. Francis de Sales, who well knew the human heart, concluded his beautiful page on the sacred character of conjugal love with this twofold advice: "Keep, O husbands, a tender, constant, and cordial love for your wives. . . . And you, wives, love tenderly, cordially, but with a love both respectful and full of deference, the husbands whom God has given you."

Cordiality and tenderness, then, from one side and from the other. "Love and faithfulness," he used to say, "always create intimacy and confidence; thus the saints were wont to give many demonstrations of affection in their marriages, demonstrations truly amorous, but chaste, tender, but sincere"; and he used to cite the example of the great king, St. Louis, no less stern toward himself than tender in his love for his wife, a man who knew how to bend his martial and brave spirit "to those littles duties necessary for the conservation of conjugal love," to those "little attestations of pure and frank friendship," which do so much to bring hearts together and make married life happy. What more and better than true Christian charity, devoted, humble, patient, which conquers and subdues nature, which is forgetful of itself and solicitous at all moments for the well-being and happiness of others, will know how to suggest and direct those thoughtful little attentions, those delicate signs of affection, and maintain them at the same time spontaneous, sincere, discreet, so that they may never seem irritating, but may always be welcomed with pleasure and appreciation? What better than grace, which is the fount and soul of that charity, will be your master and guide to make you choose almost by instinct the right moment for such human and divine tenderness?

Christian Love

However, you well understand that, if cordiality and tenderness have to be reciprocally exchanged by husband and wife and must adorn them both, they are nevertheless two flowers with a different beauty, springing as they do from a root somewhat different in man and woman. In man their root should be an uncompromising and inviolable faithfulness, which does not allow itself even the smallest deviation that would not be tolerated in his companion; as is fitting for him who is the head, it gives an open example of moral dignity and courageous frankness in never faltering from or shunning the full performance of his duty. In woman the root is wise, prudent, and watchful reserve, which removes and avoids even the shadow of anything that could soil the splendor of a spotless reputation or which could in any way endanger it.

From these two roots also springs that mutual trust which is the olive branch of perpetual peace in married life and in the flourishing of its love, for is it not true that without trust love faints, grows cold, freezes, dies, ferments, disrupts, tears and kills hearts? Therefore, observed St. Francis de Sales, "While I exhort you to grow always in that reciprocal love which you owe one another, take good care that it does not turn into a sort of jealousy; because it often happens that, as the worm is engendered in the most exquisite and ripest apple, so jealousy is born in the most ardent and devoted love, whose substance, however, it spoils and corrupts, provoking little by little disputes, dissensions, and divorces." No; jealousy, an exhalation and weakness of the heart, does not grow from a love that ripens and preserves the sap of true virtue, because "the perfection of friendship presupposes the certainty of that which is loved, while jealousy presupposes its uncertainty." Is not this the reason why jealousy, far from being a sign of the depth and true strength of a love, reveals instead its imperfect and base sides, which descend to suspicions that pierce innocent hearts and draw bitter tears? Is not jealousy, more often than not, perhaps a mitigated form of selfishness that alters the nature of affection; of selfishness bereft of that true gift, that self-forgetfulness, that faith unfraught with maligning thoughts, but trusting and benevolent, which, even here below, thus becomes the most profound and inexhaustible fount, no less than the safest guardian and preserver, of perfect love in a husband and wife? [2]

We detect true affection, without hardness as without weakness, true love, inspired and elevated by Christ, in those first families of Roman converts, such as the Flavii and the Acilii at the time of Domitian's persecution. We admire its splendor shining around a St. Paula and a St. Melania.

The secret of such a life? Always the same, that of all holy lives: Christ living and radiating with His sovereign grace in the soul, which meekly follows its inspirations and impulses. Our Lord alone was able to give birth in poor human hearts, wounded and led astray by original sin, to a love which stays pure and strong without stiffening and hardening, a love sufficiently deeply spiritual to unchain itself from the brutal stimuli of the senses and to dominate them, while preserving its warmth intact and its gentle tenderness unaltered. He alone, through example and the inward action of His heart inflamed with love, was able to keep the promise already made to Israel: *"Auferam cor lapideum de carne vestra, et dabo vobis cor carneum*—I shall tear from your flesh your heart of stone, and I shall give you a heart of flesh." He alone knows how to stir up and keep alive in souls a true affection, tender and at the same time strong, because He alone can, through His grace, free them from that inborn selfishness which, more or less unconsciously, poisons purely human loves.[3]

[1] Address to Newlyweds, October 23, 1940
[2] Address to Newlyweds, January 29, 1941
[3] Address to Newlyweds, July 30, 1941

CONJUGAL LOVE, ITS MEANING AND GOAL

"PERSONAL VALUES" and the need to respect them is a theme which for two decades has been treated more and more by writers. In many of their treatments also the specifically sexual act has a place assigned to it; it is presented as a means of personal completion of the married partners.

The proper and most profound meaning of the exercise of the conjugal rights would consist in this: that the union of bodies is the expression and realization of the personal affective union.

Articles, chapters, entire books, lectures, especially on the "technique of love," aim at propagating these ideas, at illustrating them with advice to the newly wed as a guide in marriage, in order that they may not forgo, through foolishness or misguided bashfulness, or through ungrounded scruples, that which God, Who has also created natural inclinations, offers them. If from this complete reciprocal gift of the couple there springs a new life, it is a result which remains outside, or at most as if on the outskirts of, the "personal values"; a result which is not denied, but which is not wanted as the center of married relations.

Now, if this one-sided estimate merely stressed the personal value of the partners rather than that of the offspring, it would, strictly speaking, be possible indeed to leave that problem aside; but here it is a question of a serious inversion of the scale of values and of the ends ordained by the Creator Himself. We find ourselves faced with the spread of a body of ideas and feelings in direct opposition to the clarity, the depth, and the seriousness of Christian thought.

The truth is that marriage, as a natural institution, by virtue of the will of the Creator, has not as a primary and intimate end the personal perfecting of the couple but the procreation and education of a new life. The other ends, though also intended by nature, do not occupy the same place as the first, and still less are they superior to it; rather, they are essentially subordinate to it. This is the same for every marriage, even if without issue; as of every eye it can be said that it is intended and formed to see, even if, in abnormal cases, owing to special internal and external conditions, it will never be in a position to lead to visual perception.

It was precisely in order to put an end to all the uncertainties and deviations which threatened to spread errors concerning the scale of value of the ends of marriage and their reciprocal relations, that some years ago (March 10, 1944) We drew up a declaration regarding the order of those ends as it appears from the natural disposition, showing what has been handed down by Christian tradition, what the Supreme Pontiffs have repeatedly taught, and what was afterward formulated in the Code of Canon Law. And again, shortly after, in order to correct conflicting opinions, the Holy See, in a public decree, proclaimed as inadmissible the stand of some recent authors who deny that the primary end of marriage is the procreation and upbringing of children, or teach that the secondary ends are not essentially subordinate to the primary end, but of equal value and independent thereof.

Does this mean, perhaps, that We want to deny or diminish what is good and just in personal values resulting from marriage and its realization? Certainly not, because for the procreation of new life the Creator has appointed in marriage human beings made of flesh and blood, endowed with soul and heart, and these are called upon, as men and not as irrational animals, to be the authors of their descendants. It is to this end that the Lord wills the union of husbands and wives. The Holy Scriptures do in fact say of God that He made man in His image and made him male and female, and it was His wish—as is repeatedly affirmed in the Sacred Books—that "man leave his father and mother, and cleave to his wife, and that they form one flesh."

All this is therefore true and willed by God; but it must not be separated from the primary function of matrimony, that is, from service for a new life. Not only the mutually shared material achievements, but also such personal riches as intellectual and spiritual growth, yes, even all that which is most spiritual and deepest in conjugal love as such, have been placed, by the will of nature and of the Creator, at the service of posterity. By its very nature, perfect conjugal life also means the total devotion of parents to the well-being of the children, and conjugal love in its strength and tenderness is itself a postulate of the sincerest care of offspring and a guarantee of its actuation.

The Conjugal Act

To reduce the life in common of married people and the conjugal act to a purely organic function for the transmission of the seed would be to convert the home, sanctuary of the family, into nothing but a biological laboratory. Therefore, in Our address of September 29, 1949, to the International Congress of Catholic Physicians, We expressly barred artificial insemination in marriage. The conjugal act, in its natural structure, is a personal action, a simultaneous and immediate co-operation of husband and wife, which, owing to the very nature of the agents and the propriety of the act, is the expression of the reciprocal gift, which, according to the word of Scripture, effects the union "in one flesh."

That is much more than the union of two genes, which can be effected even artificially, that is to say, without the natural union of the couple. The conjugal act, ordained and willed by nature, is a personal co-operation, to which the couple, in contracting marriage, exchange the right.

When, therefore, this performance in its natural form is, from the beginning and permanently, impossible, the object of the matrimonial contract is vitiated in its essence. And this is what We said: "Do not forget: only the procreation of a new life according to the will and the design of the Creator brings with it, in a stupendous degree of perfection, the realization of the intended ends. At the same time it conforms to the corporal and spiritual nature and to the dignity of the couple, to the normal and happy development of the child."

The personal values of married life, whether they belong to the sphere of the body and the senses or to the spiritual sphere, are genuine in themselves, but have been placed by the Creator not in the first but in the second degree of the scale of values.

Here is another consideration which there is risk of forgetting. All these secondary values in the generative sphere and activity come within the scope of the specific duty of married couples, which is to be the authors and educators of a new life. A high and noble duty indeed. It does not, however, belong to the essence of a complete human being; if the natural generative tendency fails to come to its realization, this does not imply, in some way and in some degree, a diminution of the human person. The renunciation of this realization—especially if made for the noblest motives—is not a mutilation of personal and spiritual values. Of such free renunciation for love of the Kingdom of God the Lord said: *"Non omnes capiunt verbum istud, sed quibus datum est*—All do not understand this doctrine, but only those to whom it is given."

To exalt the generative function beyond measure, as is not seldom done today, even in the rightful and moral form of conjugal life, is therefore not only an error and an aberration; it also entails the danger of an intellectual and affective deviation, apt to prevent and stifle good and elevated feelings, especially in young people without experience and ignorant of the delusions of life. For what normal man, healthy in body and soul, would want to belong to the number of those who are deficient in character and spirit?

The Sexual Instinct

Our present explanation would be altogether incomplete if We did not add a few words concerning the defense of human dignity in the use of the generative instinct.

On the Way to St. Peter's Basilica, Nov. 1, 1954

Easter Blessing *Urbi et Orbi,* April 10, 1955

The Pope at His Desk

This same Creator, Who in His goodness and wisdom desired the conservation and propagation of the human species to be served by the work of man and woman by uniting them in marriage, has also disposed that in this function the couple should experience pleasure and happiness in body and soul. The couple then, in seeking and enjoying this pleasure, do not do wrong. They accept what the Creator has destined for them.

Nevertheless, here too the couple must know how to keep themselves within the limits of just moderation. As in food and drink, so in sex they must not abandon themselves without restraint to the impulse of the senses. The golden rule is then this: The use of the natural generative instinct is morally licit only in marriage, in the service of and according to the order of the ultimate reason for marriage itself. From this it follows also that only in marriage, and by observing this rule, are the desire and the fruition of this pleasure and of this satisfaction licit. Because the pleasure is subordinate to the law of the action from which it derives, and not vice versa: the action is not subordinate to the law of pleasure. And this law, which is so reasonable, concerns not only the substance but also the circumstances of the action, so that, even when the substance of the act is not violated, it is possible to sin by the way it is performed.

The transgression of this norm is as ancient as original sin itself. But in our time there is a danger that people may lose sight of the fundamental principle itself. At present, in fact, it is usual to defend, in speeches and writings (and also by some Catholics), the necessary autonomy, the proper end, and the proper value of sensuality and its realization, independently of the scope of procreating a new life. There is a tendency to subject to a new examination and a new norm the very order established by God, to admit no other restraint to satisfying the instinct than observing the essence of the instinctive act itself. Thus for the moral obligation of dominating the passions one would substitute the license to serve blindly and without restraint the whims and impulses of nature; sooner or later this cannot but adversely affect morals, conscience, and human dignity.

If nature had aimed exclusively, or at least primarily, at a reciprocal gift and possession of couples in joy and delight, and if it had ordered this act only to make their personal experience happy in the highest possible degree, and not to stimulate them to the service of life, then the Creator would have adopted another design in the formation and constitution of the natural act. However, this is altogether subordinate to and ordered by that unique great law of the *"generatio et educatio proliis,"* that is to say, for the fulfillment of the primary scope of marriage as the origin and source of life.

Unhappily, incessant waves of the pleasure principle are invading the world and threaten to submerge in the growing tide of its thoughts, desires, and acts the whole of married life, not without serious dangers and grave prejudice to the primary duty of married couples.

Too often this anti-Christian hedonism does not blush to make of itself a doctrine, propagating the intensification of pleasure in the preparation and in the realization of the conjugal union; as if in matrimonial relations the whole moral law were reduced to the regular fulfillment of the act itself, and as if all the rest, no matter how it is done, is to be justified by the warmth of reciprocal affection, sanctified by the Sacrament of Matrimony, worthy of praise and mercy before God and conscience. For the dignity of man and the dignity of the Christian, which put a check on the excesses of sensuality, one does not care at all.

To this one must say "No." The gravity and sanctity of the Christian moral law do not permit an unrestrained satisfaction of the sexual instinct, which tends only to pleasure and enjoyment; they do not allow rational man to let himself be dominated up to that point, as to either the substance or the circumstances of the act.

Some would allege that happiness in marriage is in direct proportion to the reciprocal enjoyment in conjugal relations. This is not so; happiness in marriage is instead in direct proportion to the reciprocal respect between husband and wife, even in their intimate relations; not that they simply judge immoral and refuse what nature offers and the Creator has given, but because this respect, with the mutual esteem which it generates, is one of the most efficacious elements of a pure and therefore all the more tender love.

This teaching of Ours has nothing to do with Manichaeism or Jansenism, as some would like to have one believe in order to justify themselves. It is only a defense of the honor of Christian marriage and of the personal dignity of the spouses.[1]

[1] Address to Newlyweds, October 29, 1951

ON MARRIAGE

THE SACRAMENT OF MARRIAGE is a yoke of grace which, before the priest and the altar of Christ, unites two lives into one with an indissoluble bond.[1]

The conjugal bond is one. In the terrestrial paradise, the first image of the family paradise, the first bond was established by the Creator between man and woman, about which the Son of God incarnate will say one day: *"Quod Deus coniunxit, homo non separet*—What God has joined together, let no man put asunder"; because *"iam non sunt duo, sed una caro*—they are not two but one flesh." In that union of our progenitors in the garden of delights is the whole human species, all the future course of generations, which shall fill the earth and struggle to conquer it, and will dominate it in the sweat of their brows and make it yield them bread dampened by the bitterness of the original sin born from the stolen fruit of Eden. Why did God bring man and woman together in paradise? Not only that they might be custodians of that garden of happiness but also, in the words of the great Doctor of Aquino, because they were ordained for marriage to the end that they might generate and educate offspring, as well as for a common family life.

The seal of indissolubility is visibly stamped in the unity of the conjugal bond. Indeed, it is a bond to which nature tends, but one which is not necessarily caused by the principles of nature, being instead brought about by the exercise of free will. But the mere will of the contracting parties, though it can form the bond, cannot dissolve it. This holds not only for Christian nuptials but for every valid marriage contracted on earth through the mutual consent of the partners.

But if the will of the spouses, having contracted the matrimonial bond, cannot dissolve it, can the authority, which is above them and established by Christ for the religious life of man, do so? The bond of a Christian marriage is so strong that, if it has reached full stability by the use of conjugal rights, no power on earth, not even Our own, that is, that of the Vicar of Christ, is able to dissolve it. It is true that we may perceive and declare that a marriage, contracted as a valid one, was in reality void owing to some impediment, or an essential flaw in consent, or a substantial defect in the form. We can also in certain cases and for serious reasons dissolve marriages not having a sacramental character. We can even dissolve the bonds of a Christian marriage, rescind the "Yes" pronounced before the altar, if there is a just and proportionate cause, when it has been established that the marriage has not been brought to completion through realization of matrimonial cohabitation. But once that has taken place, no human agency may interfere with the bond. For has not Christ led the matrimonial common life back to the fundamental dignity which the Creator had given it at the dawn of the human race in paradise, to the inviolable dignity of marriage, one and indissoluble?

Jesus Christ, the Redeemer of fallen humanity, did not come to take away, but to fulfill and restore the divine law; to bring about, as a lawmaker above Moses, as a sage above Solomon, as a prophet above the prophets, what had been predicted of Him; heralded like unto Moses, and awaited eagerly by the people of Israel; from Whose lips the Lord would speak His word, while those who would not hear Him would be cast out of God's people. Therefore Christ, through His word which stands forever, elevated man in marriage and again raised up woman, who had been cast down by the ancients to the role of slave, and whom the most austere of the Roman censors had likened to "an unbridled nature and an unsubdued animal"; just as the Redeemer had exalted in Himself not only man but woman, taking human nature from a woman and sublimating His Mother, blessed among all women, to an immaculate mirror of virtue and grace for every Christian family throughout the centuries, crowned in Heaven Queen of the Angels and Saints.

Sanctification and Indissolubility

Through their presence, Jesus and Mary sanctified the wedding at Cana; it was there that the divine Son of the Virgin performed His first miracle, as if to show at the outset that He was beginning His mission in the world and the reign of God by the sanctification of the family and the conjugal union, which is the origin of life. It was there that began the elevation of marriage, which was to stand out in the supernatural world of symbols that produce sanctifying grace, to symbolize the union of Christ with the Church; an indissoluble and inseparable union fed by the absolute and endless love that flows from the heart of Christ. How could conjugal love represent and be called the symbol of such a union if it were deliberately limited, conditional, subject to dissolution, if it were a flame of love for a time only? No: having been elevated to the pure and sacred dignity of a Sacrament, imprinted and bound up in such close connection with the love of the Redeemer and the work of redemption, the marital union can only be indissoluble and perpetual.

In the face of this law of indissolubility, in all times human passions, curbed by it and repressed in the free satisfaction of their disordered appetites, have sought in every way to cast off its yoke, wanting to see in it only a hard tyranny arbitrarily weighing down conscience with an unbearable load, with a slavery repugnant to the sacred rights of the human being. It is true: a bond may sometimes constitute a burden, a coercion, like the chains which fetter a prisoner. But it may also be a powerful aid and a sure warranty, like the rope which binds the mountain climber to his companions in the ascent, or like the ligaments which unite the parts of the human body, making movement free and easy; and this is clearly the case with the indissoluble bond of marriage.

This law of indissolubility will appear and will be understood as a manifestation of vigilant motherly love, especially if viewed in the supernatural light in which it has been placed by Christ. In the midst of the difficulties, shocks, and covetous desires which life will perhaps sow in their path, two souls so inseparably linked will feel they are neither alone nor disarmed: the all-powerful grace of God, fruit of the Sacrament, will be with them constantly, to sustain their weaknesses at every step, to sweeten every sacrifice, to comfort and console them during even the hardest and longest trials. If, in obedience to the divine law, it may be necessary to refuse the promise of earthly joys glimpsed in the hour of temptation, to forgo "starting life anew," God's grace will still be there to put in full relief the teachings of faith: that the only true life, which must never be endangered, is life in Heaven, precisely the life which is assured by such renunciations, painful as they may be; these being, like all the events of our present life, something temporary, only meant to prepare the permanent state of the future life which will be the more happy and radiant as the inevitable afflictions met with along our way here below will have been accepted with greater courage and generosity.[2]

Marital Fidelity

As an indissoluble contract, marriage has the power to constitute and bind the wedded pair in a social and religious state having a legitimate and perpetual character, superior to all other contracts in this respect: that no power on earth—within the meaning and scope of Our previous declarations—is able to dissolve it. One of the parties would in vain attempt to free himself from it: the refuted contract, even if violated, disowned, torn up, does not loosen its grip; it continues to obligate with the same vigor as on the day when the consent of the contracting parties sealed it before God: not even the victim can be freed from the sacred tie which binds him or her to the one who has betrayed. That tie is not unknotted, or rather broken, except by death.

All this notwithstanding, fidelity says something still stronger, still deeper, but at the same time more tender and infinitely sweet. For, as the marriage contract unites the wedded couple in a community of social and religious life, it has to determine the precise limits within which it binds them, to refer to the possibility of external authority to which one of the parties may resort to force the other party to fulfill the duties which have been freely accepted. But, while these juridical particulars, which are, as it were, the material body of the contract, necessarily give it, so to speak, a cold, formal aspect, fidelity is like the heart and soul of the contract, its open proof, its clear witness.

Though it is more exacting, fidelity turns into sweetness the elements of rigor and austerity which juridical precision seemed to stamp on the contract. More exacting, yes; because fidelity considers faithless and a perjurer not only whoever makes an attempt through divorce—vain and ineffectual, anyhow—against the indissolubility of marriage, but also whoever, though not materially destroying the home he has founded and continuing the communion of conjugal life, yet takes the liberty of forming and maintaining another criminal relationship. He also is deemed unfaithful and a perjurer who, though not maintaining an illicit relationship for any length of time, makes use, be it once only, for someone else's pleasure or for his own selfish and sinful satisfaction, of a body to which—in the words of St. Paul—only the legitimate husband or wife has a right. True Christian fidelity, still more exacting and particular than strict natural fidelity, dominates and goes further; it rules and reigns, lovingly sovereign, over the whole expanse of the kingdom of love.

Indeed, what is fidelity if not religious respect for the gift that each mate has made to the other, of self, body, mind, and heart for the full course of life, with no other reserve save the sacred rights of God?

The freshness of youth in flower, modest elegance, the spontaneity and delicacy of her ways, the inner goodness of her soul, all these good and beautiful attractions which go to form the indefinable charm of a pure and innocent girl, have won the heart of a young man and have so drawn him toward her with the rapture of an ardent and chaste love that one would vainly seek elsewhere in nature for an image which could express so delightful an enchantment. . . .

Love and Resignation

But the years, passing over handsomeness and beauty and the dreams of youth, take away some of love's freshness and give it in exchange a more thoughtful and austere dignity. The growing family adds to the burden which weighs on the father's shoulders. Maternity, with its cares, its sufferings, and its risks, calls for and exacts courage: the wife, in the field of honor of conjugal duty, must be no less heroic than her husband in the field of honor of civic duty, where he makes the gift of his life to his country. And if distance, absence, and forced separations, and other delicate circumstances, should intervene, obliging a husband and wife to live in continence, then the wedded couple, remembering that the body of each belongs to the other, will, without any hesitation, accept their duty, with all its claims and consequences, and will, with a generous heart and without weaknesses, maintain the stern discipline which virtue enjoins.

And when, with the advent of old age, there comes a multiplication of ailments and infirmities, and of the humiliating and painful consequences of bodily decay, a host of afflictions which, without love's strength and support, would make repugnant the body which had formerly been so attractive, the most tender cares will be lovingly lavished on that body. This is fidelity in the mutual gift of the bodies.

In their first meetings, during the time of their engagement, everything seemed enchanting: each gave to the other, with sincerity as much as innocent illusion, a tribute of admiration that aroused indulgent smiles in those who witnessed it. . . . The expansion of joy and love gave to the conversations a candor, a vivacity, and a liveliness which lent sparkle to the minds and added a pleasing glitter to the treasure of knowledge each happened to possess; a very small treasure sometimes, but one which everything contributed to show off to the best advantage. This is attraction, enthusiasm; but it is not yet fidelity.

That season passes; failings are not slow in appearing, differences in character in coming forth and growing, and perhaps a limited intellect becomes more noticeable. The fireworks have died out, blind love opens its eyes, it suffers delusion. Then, for true and faithful love, begins the struggle, and at the same time the challenge. No longer blind, it becomes perfectly aware of these failings but accepts them with affectionate patience, conscious as it is of its own defects. And with the growth of discernment, it now goes on to discover and appreciate, under the rough surface, the qualities of judgment, good sense, and solid piety, rich treasures which, though hidden, are sound. While eager to bring to light and make the best of these spiritual gifts and virtues, love is no less clever and watchful in shielding from the eyes of others any gaps and blanks in intelligence or knowledge, as well as any eccentricities or asperities of character. . . . Love is ready to perceive what brings together and unites, and not what divides; ready to rectify an error or dissipate an illusion, with so much good grace as never to irritate or offend. Far from showing off its own superiority, it tactfully asks advice of the partner, letting it appear that if it has something to give, it is also happy to receive. It is in this way, evidently, that a spiritual union is established in the wedded couple, an intellectual and practical co-operation which makes them both rise toward the truth in which there is unity, toward the supreme truth, toward God. What else is this but fidelity in the mutual gift of their minds? [3]

Rights Without Duties

Those times are gone when girls often approached marriage in a state of virtual ignorance; but unfortunately, the time still endures when there are newly-wed couples who believe they can allow themselves at first a period of moral license and enjoy their rights without any concern for their duties. This is a grave sin which provokes the divine wrath; a source of unhappiness, even here on earth, whose consequences should instill fear in everybody. The duty which is disavowed or scorned at the start will continue to be neglected for so long that it becomes at last almost forgotten, and with it the joys which come from its courageous observance. And when it returns to memory and there comes repentance, it is sometimes realized, with useless tears, that it is too late: the couple which has been unfaithful to its mission has nothing left but to wither without hope, in the desert of its sterile selfishness.[4]

Happiness in Married Life

An open heart is a source of happiness in the common life of a wedded couple, while a closed heart lessens its joy and peace. Do not make a mistake when you speak about the heart: it is a symbol and image of the will. As the physical heart is the principle of all bodily movement, so is the will the principle of all spiritual movements. . . .

This mutual trust, this reciprocal opening of the heart, this mutual simplicity in sharing thoughts, aspirations, worries, joys, and sorrows, is a necessary condition, an element, indeed, an essential nourishment of happiness.

We do not wish to say that this reciprocal opening of the heart must be limitless. There are inviolable secrets which their nature, a promise, or their confidential communication cause to remain voiceless. A husband who is a doctor, a lawyer, an officer, a government official, an employee in some concern, will know or will come to know many things which professional secrecy does not allow him to divulge to anyone, not even to his wife, who, if she is wise and prudent, will show him her trust by respecting and admiring his silence, without doing or trying to do anything to pierce it.

Apart from these personal and sacred secrets of the inner and outer life, however, the souls of husband and wife should be put in common, as if to form of two souls one soul only.[5]

In sanctity, through grace, the wedded pair are equally and immediately united with Christ.

Present-day living conditions tend to engender and practically introduce widespread levelling in male and female activities, so that not infrequently a husband and a wife come to find themselves in a situation which almost approaches equality.

And yet, the Christian conception of marriage which St. Paul taught his disciples at Ephesus, like those of Corinth, could not be clearer and more explicit: "Women shall be subject to their husbands as to the Lord, because man is the master of woman as Christ is the head of the Church. . . . As the Church is subject to Christ, so are women subject to their husbands in everything. Men, love your wives as Christ loved the Church and gave Himself up for it. . . . Let each man love his wife as himself, and let the wife respect her husband."[6]

Now—see what a strange thing it is—while nobody would ever think of suddenly becoming, without any preparation or training, a mechanic or engineer, or a doctor or lawyer, every day not a few young men and women marry and form a union without having thought for a moment about preparing themselves for the arduous tasks that await them in the education of their children.[7]

Temptations

It is not necessary to have great knowledge and experience with regard to family life to know how frequent are the lamentable falls which overthrow and destroy a love that had originally been pure and sincere and, still less, to understand those weaknesses, fickle as passion but whose wounds leave a stinging scar deep down in two hearts, even after they have been forgiven and reparation has been made. . . .

Consider, on the one hand, the husband who is not able to meet all the expenses of a life of luxury; and, on the other hand, the wife who, with her mind full of thoughts for her many children, and with limited economic means, cannot change her modest household, with a wave of a magic wand, into one of the castles described in fairytales; and then say whether it will not seem to this married couple, whose days are monotonous and uneventful, that those days are paltry as compared with the romantic fantasies of novels and movies. Too bitter is the awakening for anyone who lives continually in a gilded daydream; too lively is the temptation to prolong and continue it in real life. How many tragedies of unfaithfulness have had no other origin than this! And if either of the partners, having remained faithful, weeps, uncomprehendingly, over the straying of the guilty one, still dear and loved, he or she is far from suspecting the personal share of responsibility in the slipping and final fall of the other. He or she does not know that conjugal love, as soon as it loses its healthy sereneness, its strong tenderness, its holy fecundity, and resembles selfish and profane love, is easily tempted to seek full enjoyment elsewhere.

Nor is the husband less imprudent who, in order to please his wife or to satisfy his own vanity, encourages her to abandon herself to all the whims and the most audacious extravagances of fashion in her dress and manner of living. Thoughtless young women do not perhaps even imagine the dangers to which they expose themselves and others. . . .

Moderation

Virtue lies midway; as against excessive compliance, it is possible to fall into the opposite excess of too much austerity. This is undoubtedly a rare case, but not without its examples. Exaggerated strictness, which would transform the home into a place of sadness, with neither gaiety nor light, with no wholesome and Godly relaxations, without a wide scope for action, might lead to the same disorders as a too easy hand. Who does not foresee that the more rigorous the constraint, the more violent may perhaps be the reaction? The victim of this tyranny—the man or the woman, maybe even the oppressor himself—will be tempted at some time or other to put an end to married life. But if the ruinous consequences of frivolity frequently help to open people's eyes and lead them back to better counsels and more sobriety, the straying caused by an exasperating severity is, on the other hand, often ascribed to a lack of sufficient rigor, which leads to still greater harshness and provokes further harm.

Far from these two extremes—excessive indulgence and excessive severity—let there reign among you moderation, which simply means the virtuous sense of measure and of what is fitting. Let the husband wish to see, and enjoy seeing, his wife dressing and acting with becoming elegance according to his means and social standing, encouraging and cheering her occasionally by some thoughtful gift, by praise for her looks and charm. In turn, let the wife banish from her home all that is unfitting and offensive to the Christian eye and the sense of beauty, and likewise any severity that would wither the heart. Let both enjoy reading, maybe together, good, beautiful, useful books that can instruct them, broaden their knowledge of things and achievements and the horizons of their art or work, inform them of the course of events, and keep them firm and better indoctrinated in faith and in virtue. Let them freely, but moderately, indulge in healthy and decent amusements that bring relaxation and cheer the mind. Let each be happy to see the other excel in his or her professional or social activities, in making himself liked for his smiling pleasantness among their mutual friends; and let them never be envious of each other.

Jealousy

And lastly, a great stumbling block to be avoided is jealousy, which can spring from indulgence or be caused by too much severity; a most dangerous stumbling block to faithfulness. That incomparable psychologist, St. John Chrysostom, described it with masterly eloquence: "Everything that can be said of this evil can never sufficiently describe its gravity. Once a man begins to suspect the person he loves most in the world, the person he would gladly give his life for, in what may he then find comfort . . . ? But if a husband is anxiously tossed by these evils, even when they have no foundation or reason, the poor, wretched wife is still more gravely tormented. He who should be her comforter in all her sufferings and her prop, is cruel to her and shows her only hostility . . . a soul thus prejudiced and struck by this disease is ready to believe everything, to accept all accusations, without discerning the true from the false, and more inclined to listen to one who confirms his suspicions than one who would dissipate them. . . . Exits, entrances, words, glances, the smallest sighs, all is spied; the poor woman must bear everything in silence; chained, so to speak, to the conjugal bed, she cannot even allow herself a step, a word, or a sigh without having to give account thereof to the very servants." May not such a life become almost intolerable? And is there cause to wonder then if, when the light and support of true Christian virtue are lacking, an endeavor is made to break loose from that life and escape from it through the shipwreck of unfaithfulness? [8]

[1] Address to Married Couples, March 18, 1942
[2] Address to Married Couples, April 22, 1942
[3] Address to Married Couples, October 21, 1942
[4] Address to Married Couples, July 24, 1940
[5] Address to Married Couples, November 12, 1941
[6] Address to Married Couples, September 10, 1941
[7] Address to Women of Catholic Action, October 26, 1941
[8] Address to Married Couples, November 10, 1942

THE FAMILY

IN THE ORDER OF NATURE, among social institutions there is none that is dearer to the Church than the family. Christ elevated marriage, which is, as it were, its root, to the dignity of a Sacrament. The family has found and will always find in the Church defense, protection, and support, in all that concerns its inviolable rights, its freedom, the exercise of its lofty function.

We have often and on the most varied occasions spoken in favor of the Christian family, and in most cases to come, or to call others, to its help, to save it from the gravest perils. Above all, to succor it in the calamities of war. The damage wrought by the First World

War was far from being completely repaired when the second and even more terrible conflagration came to fill the measure. Much time and effort will still be required, and also greater divine assistance, before the deep wounds that these two wars have inflicted on the family begin to heal properly. Another evil, also due in part to the devastation of war, but a consequence as well of overpopulation, is the housing crisis; all those, legislators, statesmen, members of social welfare institutions, who are seeking to find a remedy for this, are accomplishing, even if only indirectly, an apostolate of eminent value. The same is true of the struggle against the scourge of unemployment, for an adjustment in the matter of adequate family wages, so that a mother need not be obliged, as too often happens, to look for work outside the home, but may devote more of her time to her husband and children. To work for schools and religious education: that is another valuable contribution to the welfare of families, as is also to encourage in the family a healthy naturalness and simplicity of manners, to strengthen religious beliefs, fostering in the home an atmosphere of Christian purity, able to protect it from harmful outside influences and all the morbid excitement that arouses unregulated passions in an adolescent's mind. . . .

Conjugal Morality

Another danger threatens the family, not by any means recent, but of long standing, which, though, growing visibly as it is at present, may become fatal to it, because it attacks it in its very root; We mean the disrupting of conjugal morality in all its extension.

In the course of the last few years, We have taken every opportunity of emphasizing one or other of the essential points of that morality, and more recently of expounding it as a whole, not only confuting the errors that corrupt it, but also showing positively its meaning, function, and importance, its value for the happiness of a married couple, their children, and the whole family, and for stability and greater social welfare, ranging from the home to the State and the Church itself.

At the center of this doctrine marriage appeared as an institution in the service of life. In close connection with this principle, We, in accordance with the constant teaching of the Church, expounded a thesis which is one of the essential foundations not only of conjugal morality but also of the morality of society at large: that is, that a direct attempt on innocent human life, as means to an end—in the present case the end being to save another life—is illicit.

Which Life Is More Precious?

Innocent human life, in whatever condition it may be, is, from the first instant of its existence, to be preserved from any direct voluntary attack. This is a fundamental right of the human person, of general value in the Christian conception of life; valid both for the life still hidden in the mother's womb and for the life that has already left it; equally so against the causing of abortion and the direct killing of the child before, during, or after birth. However justified the distinction may be between those different moments of the development of the life, already born or not yet born, for profane and ecclesiastical law and with respect to certain civil and penal consequences, according to the moral law all these are cases of a serious and illicit attempt on inviolable human life.

This principle holds good for the life of the child as for that of the mother. Never and in no case has the Church taught that the child's life must be preferred to that of the mother. It is a mistake to formulate the question with this alternative: either the child's life or the mother's. No; neither the mother's life nor the child's may be submitted to an act of direct suppression. For the one and for the other the requirement can be only this: to make every effort to save the life of both the mother and the child.

One of the finest and noblest aspirations of medicine is this constant seeking for new methods of safeguarding the lives of both. And if, in spite of all the progress of science, there still remain, and will still remain in future, cases in which the mother's death must be reckoned with, when she wants to carry to birth the life she bears within her and not to destroy it in violation of God's commandment: "Thou shalt not kill!" man, while endeavoring up to the last moment to help and to save, has no alternative but to bow in awe to the laws of nature, and the dispositions of divine Providence.

Preservation of the Mother's Life

But—it is objected—the mother's life, especially if she is the mother of a numerous family, is of far greater value than that of a child yet unborn. The application of the theory of the scale of values to the case with which we are here concerned has already found support in juridical discussions. The answer to this much debated objection is not difficult. The inviolability of the life of an innocent being does not depend on its greater or lesser value. More than ten years ago the Church formally condemned the killing of a life deemed "worthless"; and anyone who knows the pitiful antecedents that called forth this condemnation, anyone who can ponder the deadly consequences that would follow if the intangibility of an innocent life were to be measured by its value, can well appreciate the motives that led up to it.

Besides, who can judge with certainty which of the two lives is really more valuable? Who can tell what path that child will take and what heights of achievements and perfection it may reach? Here, two quantities are compared, about one of which nothing is known.

We have always used, in this connection, the expressions "direct attempt on the life of the innocent creature," "direct killing." For if, for example, the safeguarding of the life of the future mother, independently of her state of pregnancy, were to call for an urgent surgical intervention, or any other therapeutic application, which would have as an accessory consequence, in no way desired or intended but unavoidable, the death of the fetus, this could not be termed a direct attempt on innocent life. In these conditions the operation can be licit, like other similar medical interventions, provided the stake at issue is a high one, such as a life, and that it is not possible to postpone it until after the birth of the child or to have recourse to any other efficacious remedy.

Since, then, the primary function of marriage is to be at the service of life, Our special congratulations and Our paternal gratitude go to those generous married couples who, for love of God, and trusting in Him, courageously bring up a numerous family.

Legitimate Regulation of Progeny

On the other hand, the Church looks with sympathy and understanding at the real difficulties of matrimonial life in our days. We have, therefore, affirmed the legitimacy and at the same time the limits—which are indeed very wide—of a regulation of offspring, which, unlike what is termed "birth control," is compatible with the law of God. It may even be hoped (but in such a field the Church, of course, leaves judgment to medical science) that the latter will succeed in giving this legitimate method a sufficiently sure basis, and the most recent information seems to confirm such a hope.

However, to overcome the numerous trials of married life nothing is more efficacious than a lively faith and a frequent use of the Sacraments, from which spring the torrents of strength of which it is hardly possible for those living outside the Church to form a clear notion.[1]

[1] Address to the "Family Front" Congress, November 27, 1951

TO THE FATHERS

WHAT ELSE IS FATHERHOOD if not to communicate being; still more, to put into that being the mysterious ray of life? God is the Father of the Universe: *"Nobis unus est Deus, Pater, ex quo omnia*—for us there is only one God, the Father from Whom are all things." God is the Father Who creates the heavens, the sun, and the stars that shine in His presence and announce His glory; God is the Father Who has created and shaped this world, Who has planted its flowers and forests, Who has multiplied and rendered prolific the airy nests of birds, the inaccessible haunts of fish, and the coral banks in the oceans, sheep- and cattle-folds, the lairs of wild beasts, the dens of roaring lions, alert and quick to fall upon their prey; all this multifarious, countless life is the child of God's love, directed, sustained, and enveloped in its growth and evolution by his Fatherly Providence. . . .

But the boundless love of a God, which is charity, has superior and very lofty means of pouring out its light and its flame by communicating, as a Father, a life similar to His own.

Angel and man are the children of God and they reveal it by the image and resemblance which, in the natural order of simple creatures, they have received from Him; but God has a more sublime Fatherhood that begets children of adoption and of grace, in an order that stands above the human and angelic natures and that makes them partakers of, and sharers in, the divine nature itself, calling on them to share His own happiness in the vision of His essence, in that inaccessible light, wherein He reveals to the children of grace Himself and the innermost secret of His incomparable Fatherhood, together with the Son and the Holy Ghost. In that great light rules God, creator, sanctifier, and glorifier Who, out of predilection for the last of His intelligent creatures, man, regenerates him, from son of His wrath, because born from his guilty progenitor Adam, and causes him to be born again here on earth, with water and the Holy Ghost, as a child of grace, brother to Christ, a new spotless Adam, making him joint heir to His glory in Heaven. And He wished that man himself might be the parent of such glory and of supernatural life as well as natural life, by co-operating with God; that he might be a parent to its transmission and to its preservation and perfection. This is the incomparable mystery into the heart of which man is led by marriage.

A Life of Comfort and Pleasure?

How beautiful and worth recalling is the blessing that Rachel gives to young Tobias when she hears whose son he is: *"Benedictio sit tibi fili, quia boni et optimi viri filius es*—Blessed be thou, my son, because thou art the child of a good and honest man." Old Tobias was no longer rich in earthly possessions; the Lord had put him to the test through the ordeal of his exile and his blindness; but he was rich in something more valuable, that is, the admirable example of his virtue and the wise advice he gave to his son. We, too, are living in difficult times: perhaps it will not always be possible to give children the comfortable, pleasant life that one dreams of for them or to make them peaceful and satisfied through the goods one would like to secure for them, in addition to their daily bread, which we trust, with the help of divine Providence, they will not be lacking. But, more than any earthly goods, which cannot, even for the powerful and the feasters, ever transform this valley of tears into a heaven of delight, it is the parents who must give their children and heirs more valuable things, the bread and wealth of faith, the atmosphere of hope and charity, the incentive to a courageous and steadfast Christian life in which the sacred duties of fathers and mothers, conscious of the loftiness of the parenthood granted to them by Heaven, will make them grow up and improve before God and their fellow creatures.[1]

[1] Address to Newlyweds, March 19, 1941

THE DUTIES OF HUSBAND AND WIFE

THE RESPONSIBILITY of man before his wife and children springs primarily from his obligations for their lives and involves his profession, his art, or his craft. With his professional labor he must procure for them a home, daily bread, the necessary means for a secure livelihood and sufficient clothing. His family must feel happy and safe under the protection he offers and gives with thoughtful foresight and the constructive activity of his hands.

The position of the man without a family is markedly different from that of a man with a wife and children for whom to provide. He is often confronted with hazardous undertakings, made attractive by the hope of large gains, but which too easily lead to ruin along unsuspected paths. Dreams of fortune often deceive the mind and unsettle calm judgment: moderation of the heart and its dreams is a virtue which never brings harm, because it is the daughter of prudence. Hence, the married man, even when there are no moral considerations involved, must not surpass the proper limits—limits imposed by his obligation to refrain, without grave reason, from exposing to danger the secure subsistence of his wife and children, those already born and those expected. It is another thing if the happiness of his family is jeopardized by circumstances beyond his control, as so often happens in times of great political and social upheaval which spreads throughout the world in millions of homes, carrying with it the malignant seeds of fear, misery, and death. However, in action or omission, undertaking or daring, he must always ask himself: May I assume this responsibility before my family?

In addition to being linked to his family by moral bonds, the married man is bound to society. These bonds are loyalty in the exercise of his profession, art, or craft; trustworthiness upon which his superiors may count unconditionally; correctness and integrity in conduct and action which earn him the trust of all those who deal with him; are not these bonds outstanding social virtues? And do not such splendid virtues constitute the outer defensive walls of domestic happiness and peaceful existence of the family, whose security, according to the law of God, is the first duty of the Christian father?

A Woman's Honor

We could add that since a woman's honor and social standing correspond to the public esteem of her husband, out of consideration for her, the man must strive to exceed his equals and rise above them in his own field of endeavor. Every woman as a rule wants to be proud of her life's companion. Is it not therefore praiseworthy that the husband, activated by noble feelings and affection for his wife, exert himself to furnish his best endeavor and, within the limits of his ability, reach for the highest aim?

For if by elevating himself creditably and honestly in society by means of his profession and labor the man confers esteem and security on his wife and children—since the pride of children is their father—the man must not forget how much he contributes to a happy domestic life if, in every circumstance, he shows, in his own heart as well as in his exterior behavior and speech, regard and respect for his wife, the mother of his children. The woman is not only the sun but also the sanctuary of the family; she is the little ones' refuge from tears; she guides the steps of the older ones, comforts their anxiety, resolves their doubts, and gives them faith in the future. Dispensing warmth and kindness, she is also mistress of the household. May it never happen, as is sometimes said, that married couples are distinguished from unmarried couples by the indifferent, less considerate, even rude behavior of the man toward his wife. No; the entire behavior of the husband toward his wife must never lack natural, noble, and dignified kindness and warmth, as is fitting in men of sound temperament and God-fearing soul; men who with their intellect perceive the inestimable value that mutually virtuous, kindly behavior between husband and wife has for the education of the children. The example of the father has a powerful effect: it is a vigorous, living stimulus which encourages the children to regard the mother—and the father—with respect, veneration, and love.

Marital Crises

But man's contribution to the happiness of the home must not stop at nor limit itself to kindness and consideration toward the consort of his life; it must advance to understand, appreciate, and recognize the work and effort of her who silently and assiduously dedicates herself to making the common home more comfortable, more pleasant, more gay. With what loving care, for example, a young woman has arranged everything to celebrate, as joyously as the circumstances permit, the anniversary of the day in which she was united before the altar with him who was to become the companion of her life and happiness, and who is now about to return from his office or workshop! But the man arrives, weary from the long hours of work, perhaps more exhausted than usual, nervous because of unforeseen vexations. He returns later than usual, somber and worried about other thoughts; the happy, affectionate words that greet him go unheeded and he remains silent; he appears unaware of the meal prepared with so much love: he only looks and notes that the dish which was selected especially to make him happy has been cooking too long, and he grumbles, without thinking that the reason was his own delay and the long wait. He eats hurriedly, since, he says, he must go out immediately after dinner. When the meal is over, the poor young woman, who had dreamed of the joy of a pleasant evening together with him, finds herself alone in the deserted room; she needs all her faith and courage to keep back her tears.

Such scenes are likely to occur in every life. A maxim laid down by the great philosopher Aristotle says that things appear to a man according to what he is in himself: in other words, things appear welcome to man or not according to his natural disposition or the passions which move him. And you see how even the most innocent concerns, such as business affairs and events, and their effects, change our thoughts and moods, cause us to forget the rules of propriety and courtesy, and to reject and disregard kindness and charm. Undoubtedly, the husband could give as his excuse the excessive fatigue of the day's work, aggravated by obstacles and worries. But does he believe that his wife neither feels nor experiences fatigue, nor encounters obstacles? True, deep love, in one or the other, must be stronger and show itself to be stronger than fatigue and boredom, stronger than the variations of personal humor or unforeseen misfortune. . . . When, therefore, you find yourselves at home where conversation and repose restore your strength, do not be quick to search for the little defects inevitable in every human endeavor; be mindful, rather, of all that is good, be it much or little, which is offered to you as the fruit of toil, vigilant attention, affectionate feminine intuition, to make your home, no matter how modest it may be, a little paradise of happiness and joy. Do not be content to contemplate and love such goodness only in the recesses of your thoughts and heart; let your wife know it and feel it, since she has not spared herself in procuring it for you; for her the best and sweetest recompense is a loving smile, a gentle word, an appreciative glance, which makes her aware of your gratitude.[1]

A Happy Family Life

God has given woman the sacred, painful mission of maternity, which is also a fountain of pure joy, and the mother, above all others, has been entrusted with the early upbringing of the child in its first months and years.

Certainly a woman can do more than a man to contribute to the happiness of home life. The husband's first duty is to assure the subsistence and the future of the family and the home through decisions which bind him and his children for the future: woman must apply vigilant diligence to caring for those thousand particulars, those intangible daily attentions which create the elements of the internal family atmosphere. And according to whether her diligence is correctly applied, or misdirected, or lacking, the atmosphere is rendered salutary, fresh, and bracing, or oppressive, spoiled, unbreathable. The actions of the wife in the home should always be like the work of the valiant woman exalted in Holy Scriptures: a woman in whom the heart of her husband trusteth, a woman who will render him good and not evil for all the days of his life.

Is it not an ancient yet always new truth—a truth rooted in the physical condition of a woman's life, an inexorable truth proclaimed not only by the experience of remote centuries, but even more so in our own times—that the woman makes the home and cares for it, and that the man can never supplant her in this? Is it not the destiny which nature and her union with man have imposed on her for the good of society? Draw her away from her family with one of the many lures employed to win and bind her, and you will see the woman neglect her hearth; without this fire her home will become cold; in practice the hearth will cease to exist, and be changed into the precarious refuge of a few hours; the center of daily life will shift elsewhere for her husband, for her, and for her children.

Whether you like it or not, for whoever, man or woman, is married and firmly resolved to remain faithful to the duties of such a condition, the edifice of happiness can be raised only on the solid foundation of family life. But where can there be true family life without a hearth, without a visible center, a genuine meeting place, where the family may gather, collect, put down roots, maintain itself, deepen, unfold, and flower? Do not say that the hearth is created on the day in which the rings are placed on the two clasped hands and the newlyweds share a common room under the same roof, in their own apartment, their own residence, large or small, rich or poor. No, a material hearth is not enough for the spiritual structure of happiness. It is necessary to elevate matter to a spiritual realm and transform earthly fire into the living, life-giving flame of the new family. This is not the work of a day, especially if the new couple does not dwell in a home prepared by the preceding generations but rather—as is the case most frequently today, especially in the cities—in a temporary, rented domicile. Who, then, little by little, day by day, will create the true home, if not the woman who has become the "mistress of the house"? Whether the husband is a workman, farmer, professional worker, man of letters or science, artist, white-collar worker, or executive, it is inevitable that he spend the major part of his time away from his house, or, if he works at home, that he confine himself to the silence of his study away from the life of the family. The domestic hearth will become for him the place where at the end of the day's labor he will be restored physically and morally in repose, calm, and intimate joy. However, for the woman, this home will be her principal creation; through her labor it will develop into a refuge, no matter how poor, into a happy, tranquil residence adorned not by furniture and objects without personal touch, without individual expression, but rich in memories and objects that recall the events of a life lived together, the tastes, the thoughts, the joys, the shared suffering, from whose traces and signs, sometimes visible, at other times hardly perceptible, the material hearth in the course of time will take its soul. And the animating spirit of it all will be the feminine hand and heart which the wife employs to make every corner of the house attractive, if only through care, order, neatness, keeping everything ready to be used when needed and at the moment desired; making meals a comfort after work, and preparing the bed for repose. To woman more than man, the Lord has granted, with the sense of grace and harmony, the gift of lending attraction to the simplest things, precisely because she, made similar to man to help him establish the family, is born to spread gentleness and sweetness in the home of the family, and to ensure that their life together finds in the home its nucleus from which it grows, becomes fruitful, and flowers in its true unfolding.

Motherhood: A Life of Sacrifice

And when the Lord in His goodness has granted to the wife the dignity of motherhood beside a cradle, the cry of the newborn child will not lessen or destroy happiness in the home; rather, it will cause it to grow and infuse it with the sublimity of that divine halo which radiates around the angels in Heaven, and from which descends the ray of life, which conquers nature and transforms the sons of men into children of God. This is the sanctity of the nuptial bed. This is the loftiness of Christian motherhood. This is the salvation of the married woman. Because woman, according to the great Apostle Paul, shall be saved through her mission as a mother, as long as she remains in faith, and in charity, and in holiness with modesty. Now you will understand how "piety is useful for everything, since it contains the promise of life in the present and hereafter," and is, according to the teachings of St. Ambrose, the foundation of all virtues.

A cradle consecrates the mother of the family; and more cradles sanctify and glorify her before her husband and children, before Church and homeland. The mother who complains because a new child presses against her bosom seeking nourishment at her breast is foolish, ignorant of herself, and unhappy. The enemy of happiness in the home is complaint over the blessing of God, which fosters it and makes it grow. The heroism of motherhood is the exaltation and glory of the Christian bride: in the desolation of her home, if it is without the joy of an infant, her solitude becomes a prayer and invocation to Heaven; her tears flow with those of Anna, who supplicated the Lord at the gate of the temple for the gift of Samuel.[2]

O wives, this is your share of responsibility for the harmony of domestic happiness. If your husband's task is to procure and establish with his toil the life of the hearth, it is for you and your gifts to arrange for his well-being and to assure the peaceful serenity of your lives together. For you, this is not only a law of nature, but also a religious duty and an obligation of Christian virtue, through the strength of whose acts and merits you grow in love and the grace of God.

"But," some of you may say, "you are asking of us a lifetime of sacrifices!" Yes; yours is a life of sacrifice, but not of sacrifice only. Do you believe that here on earth you can enjoy true, solid happiness without winning it through some privation and renunciation, that some corner of this world contains the full, perfect beatitude of a terrestrial paradise? And do you think that your husband must not also make sacrifices, at times many and grave ones, in order to procure honored and secure bread for the family? It is these mutual sacrifices, brought together for common advantage, which give to marital love and family happiness their warmth and stability, their holy depth and that exquisite nobility which spells reciprocal respect of husband and wife and exalts them in the affection and gratitude of their children. If maternal sacrifice is more acute and painful, virtue from on high tempers it. It is through her sacrifice that woman learns pity for the afflictions of others. Love for the happiness of her home does not close her within herself; the love of God, which through her sacrifice raises her above herself, opens her heart to all piety and sanctifies her.

The Married Career Woman

"But," others may also object, "the modern social structure of labor, industry, and the professions demands that a large number of women, wives included, enter the fields of work and public life." We are not unaware of this. But it is doubtful that such a condition is the social ideal for the married woman. However, the fact must be kept in mind. Providence, which is constantly watchful in its government of humanity, has given to the spirit of the Christian family superior powers to mitigate and conquer such a social state and to avoid the perils which are doubtless hidden in it. Have you not observed how the sacrifice of a mother who, for special motives, must, beyond her domestic duties, also work to provide with hard daily toil for the upkeep of her family, not only conserves her children's love but makes it increase; and when religious sentiment and faith in God are the foundation of family life, their recognition of her difficulties and labor is even stronger. If such is the case in your marriage, in addition to faith in God, Who always aids those who fear and serve Him, during the hours and days which you can dedicate entirely to your dear ones, add zealous attention to redoubled love, not only to assure the indispensable minimum for true family life, but also to transmit from yourself to the hearts of your husband and children those luminous rays of the sun which, even during the hours of exterior separation, comfort, foment, and nourish the spiritual framework of the hearth.[3]

[1] Address to Newlyweds, April 8, 1942
[2] Address to Women of Catholic Action, October 26, 1941
[3] Address to Newlyweds, February 25, 1944

THE MODERN WOMAN

IN ACCORDANCE with very ancient traditions, the woman's mode of life and the form given to her education used to be inspired by her natural instinct which made the family her field of endeavor, when she did not, for the love of Christ, prefer virginity. Kept away from public life and outside the public professions, a young woman, like a growing flower, tended and sheltered, was destined by her vocation to become a wife and mother. At her mother's side she learned womanly tasks and the care of the home and housework, and helped to look after her younger brothers and sisters, thus employing her strength and ingenuity and learning the art of governing the domestic hearth. The simple, natural forms which the lives of the people took, the homely and practical religious education which inspired all their activity until the late nineteenth century, the custom of marrying early, which was still possible under the economic and social conditions then existing, the pre-eminence of the family in the life of the people, all this and other circumstances, which have meanwhile radically changed, constituted the primary nourishment and support for that character and that kind of education of woman.

Today, by contrast, the old type of womanhood is rapidly changing. You now see women, especially the young women, leaving their retired position and entering nearly all the professions, hitherto fields of livelihood and action belonging exclusively to men. The first timid beginnings of this revolution had been manifest for a fairly long time, being due principally to the development of industry bound up with modern progress.

But for some years now, like a flood which, having overthrown its dams, breaks through every resistance, the march of women seems to have been penetrating into the whole area of public life. And, if this current is not as yet spread equally everywhere, it is not unusual to encounter its course in even the remotest mountain villages; while, in the labyrinth of large cities, such as in workshops and factories, ancient customs and trends have been forced to surrender unconditionally to the modern movement.[1]

Woman's Dignity

Let Us make it clear at once that for Us the problem of women, both in its general aspect and in each one of its multiple details, consists entirely in the conservation and increase of the dignity woman has received from God. For Us, therefore, it is not a problem of a purely legal or economic, educational or biological, political or demographic order; but one which, in all its complexity, nevertheless always gravitates around the question: How to maintain and strengthen the dignity of woman, especially today, in the circumstances in which Providence has placed us? To look at the problem in any other way, to consider it unilaterally under any one of the above-mentioned aspects, would be the same as evading it, without benefit to anyone, least of all woman herself. To separate it from God, from the Creator's wise ordering, from His holy will, is to distort the essential point of the question, that is, the true dignity of woman, the dignity which she possesses only from God and in God.

It follows from this, that those systems which exclude God and His law from social life, and allow the precepts of religion a humble place, at most, in the private life of man, are not in a position justly to consider the problem of woman.

In what, then, does this dignity which woman has received from God consist?

Ask it of human nature, as God formed, elevated, and redeemed it in Christ's blood.

In their personal dignity as children of God, man and woman are absolutely equal, also in regard to the ultimate end of human life, which is eternal union with God in the bliss of Heaven. It is an imperishable glory of the Church to have reinstated that truth and to have freed woman from a degrading bondage contrary to nature. But man and woman cannot maintain and perfect their equal dignity except by respecting and putting to use the peculiar qualities which nature has bestowed upon the one and the other, indestructible spiritual and physical qualities, whose order cannot be deranged without nature herself moving to re-establish it. These peculiar characteristics which distinguish the two sexes reveal themselves so clearly to the eyes of all, that only obstinate blindness or doctrinarianism, not less baneful than utopian, could, in a social organization, misunderstand or disregard its value.

The two sexes, through their peculiar qualities, themselves are co-ordinated in such a manner that their mutual co-ordination exercises its influence in all the multiple manifestations of human social life. We will be content here with recalling two of these because of their special importance: the state of matrimony and the state of voluntary celibacy according to the evangelical counsel.

Voluntary Renunciation of Married Life

In order to follow the counsel of Christ, for nearly twenty centuries now, in every generation, thousands and thousands of men and women among the best have been freely denying themselves a family and renouncing the holy duties and sacred rights of wedded life. Is the common good of peoples and of the Church perhaps exposed to danger on that account? On the contrary! Such generous spirits do indeed see that the association of the two sexes in matrimony is a great good. But when they leave the usual way, the beaten path, far from deserting humanity they devote themselves to its service through a complete detachment from self and from their own interests, in an incomparably wider, all-embracing, universal action. See them devoted to prayer and penitence; applying themselves to the instruction and education of youth and the ignorant; bending over the bedside of the sick and agonizing; with their hearts open to all afflictions and all weakness to rehabilitate them, comfort them, raise them up, sanctify them.

If one turns one's thoughts to the girls and women who voluntarily renounce matrimony in order to devote themselves to a higher life of contemplation, sacrifice, and charity, a luminous word comes to the lips immediately: Vocation! It is the only word that befits such an elevated sentiment. This vocation, this call of love, makes itself felt in the most diverse manners, as infinitely varied as are the modulations of the divine voice: irresistible invitations, affectionately soliciting inspirations, gentle impulses. But also the young Christian woman who has against her will remained unwedded, but firmly believes in the heavenly Father's Providence, recognizes the voice of the Master in the vicissitudes of life: *Magister adest et vocat te*—the Master is here and calls you! She responds; she renounces the fond dream of her adolescence and youth: to have a faithful companion in life, to form a family, and in the impossibility of marriage she espies her calling; then with a broken but submissive heart, she likewise gives her whole self to the works of charity.

In one state as in the other, the office of woman appears clearly traced by the features, by the inclinations, and by the faculties peculiar to her sex. She collaborates with man, but in accordance with her natural tendency. Now, the office of woman, her manner, her innate inclination, is motherhood. Every woman is destined to be a mother; mother in the physical sense of the word, or in a more spiritual and higher but no less real meaning.

The Creator has disposed to this end the entire being of woman, her organism, and even more her spirit, and above all her exquisite sensibility. So that a true woman cannot see and fully understand all the problems of human life otherwise than under the family aspect. For this reason, a sense of her own dignity makes her apprehensive whenever the social or political order threatens to be detrimental to her maternal mission and the good of the family.

Such are, unfortunately, the social and political conditions today; they might become even more unsettling for the sanctity of the domestic hearth and therefore the dignity of woman. Your hour has struck, Catholic women and girls; public life needs you: to each of you it can be said: *Tua res agitur*—Your interest is at stake.

The Working Mother

That for a long time now public trends have been developing in a manner not favorable to the true benefit of the family and of women is an undeniable fact.

Here is a woman who, in order to add to her husband's wages, also goes to work in a factory, leaving her home uncared for during her absence; and this home, perhaps squalid and small, becomes even more wretched because of lack of care; the various members of the family work each separately in the four corners of the city and at different hours; they are hardly ever together, either for meals or for a rest after the day's labor, much less for common prayers. What remains of family life? And what attraction can it have for the children?

To these painful consequences of the absence of the woman and mother from the home is added another even more deplorable; it concerns the education of the young girl especially, and her preparation for life.

Used to seeing her mother always absent and the home dismal in its abandonment, she will find no attraction in it, she will not feel the slightest inclination for domestic occupations, and she will be unable to understand their nobleness and beauty or desire to devote herself to them someday as a wife and mother.

This is true in all social strata, and in all conditions of life. The daughter of a woman of fashion, who sees the supervision of the home left to strangers and her mother engrossed in frivolous occupations and futile amusements, will follow her example, will want to emancipate herself as early as possible and, according to a truly sad expression, "live her own life." How could she conceive the desire to become someday a real *"domina,"* that is, the mistress of the house, in a happy, prosperous, worthy family? As for the working classes, obliged to earn their daily bread, the woman, if she were to reflect properly, would probably realize that the extra earnings which she secures by working outside of her home are easily devoured by other expenses or even by waste, which is ruinous for the economy of the family.

In the face of theories and methods which, from different approaches, strip woman of her mission and, with the mirage of unbridled emancipation, or in the reality of a hopeless misery, divest her of her personal dignity, her woman's dignity, we have heard a cry of apprehension which invokes, as much as possible, her active presence at the domestic hearth.

In truth, woman is kept away from her home not only by her proclaimed emancipation, but often also by the necessities of life, by the goading thought of daily bread. Therefore, it serves no purpose to preach her return to the hearth, as long as the conditions which force her to remain away continue. And thus becomes manifest the first aspect of your mission in social and political life, which opens up before you. Your entry into public life has come about suddenly, as an effect of the social events of which we are being spectators; that does not matter! You are called to take part in it; would you perhaps leave to others, to those who are the promoters and accomplices of the ruin of the domestic hearth, the monopoly of social organization, of which the family is the chief element in its economic, judicial, spiritual, and moral unity? The fortunes of the family, the fortunes of human coexistence, are at stake; they are in your hands, *tua res agitur!* Every woman, then, without exception, is strictly bound in conscience not to stand aloof but to come into action (in the forms and in the ways suited to the condition of each), in order to stem the currents which threaten the home and to fight the doctrines which undermine its foundations, to prepare, organize, and achieve its restoration.

To this impelling motive for the Catholic woman to enter the life which today opens up to her activity, yet another is added: her woman's dignity. She must compete with man for the good of civic life, in which she is, in dignity, equal to him. Each of the two sexes must take the part which belongs to it according to its nature, its characteristics, its physical, intellectual, and moral habits. Both have the right and the duty to co-operate for the total good of society and the nation, but it is clear that, if the man is by temperament more inclined to handle outside business and public affairs, the woman has, generally speaking, more perspicacity and greater tact to help her understand and solve the delicate problems of domestic and family life, which is the foundation of all social life; though this does not alter the fact that some women furnish an example of great skill in every field of public activity.

Woman's Role in Social Welfare

All this is not so much a question of distinct attributes as of the manner of judging and arriving at concrete, practical applications. Let us take the case of civil rights: at present they are the same for both. But with how much more discernment and efficacy will they be utilized, if man and woman come to each other's help. The sensibility and delicacy of feeling peculiar to woman, which might tempt her to be swayed by emotions and thus blur the clearness and breadth of her view and be detrimental to the calm consideration of future consequences, are, on the contrary, of valuable help in bringing to light needs, aspirations, and dangers in the domestic, welfare, and religious fields.

This effective collaboration in social and political life in no way alters the special character of the normal action of woman. Associating herself with man in his work in the area of civil institutions, she will apply herself principally to tasks which call for tact, delicate feelings, and maternal instinct, rather than administrative rigidity.

Who, better than she, can understand what is required by the dignity of woman, the integrity and honor of girlhood, the protection and education of the child? And in all these questions how many problems require the attention and action of those who govern and legislate! Only woman will know, for example, how, without detriment to efficacy, to temper with kindness the repression of loose morals; only she will know how to preserve from humiliation and educate in decency and in the religious and civil virtues delinquent youth; only she will be able to render fruitful service in the rehabilitation of discharged prisoners and of delinquent girls.[2]

[1] Address to Young Women of Catholic Action, April 24, 1943
[2] Address to Women of Catholic Action, October 21, 1945

FASHION AND VIRTUE

THERE'S NOTHING WRONG, intrinsically, in keeping up with fashion. It springs spontaneously from human sociability, from the impulse which tends to be in harmony with one's fellow men and the customs of the people among whom one lives.

God does not ask us to live outside our times, to ignore the dictates of fashion to the point of becoming ridiculous, dressing contrary to the tastes and habits common to our contemporaries, without ever worrying about their likes and dislikes. Hence, even the Angelic St. Thomas affirms that there is no vice in the outward things man uses, but that vice results when man makes immoderate use of them, either by making himself strangely different from the others, for his own sake and without regard for the customs of those with whom he lives, or by using these things—in harmony with or in excess of the use of others—with an inordinate attachment for an overabundance of clothes, for a luxury too frantically pursued, when humility and simplicity would have been sufficient to satisfy the requirements of dignity. And the same Holy Doctor goes so far as to say that feminine adornment may be a meritorious act of virtue, when it is in conformity with custom, with a woman's place in the world, and chosen with good intention, and when women wear ornaments in keeping with their station and dignity, and are moderate in adapting themselves to current fashion. Then even the act of adorning themselves will be the expression of that virtue of modesty which sets the style of walking, standing, dressing, and all the exterior movements.

In following fashion, too, virtue lies in the golden mean. What God asks is always to bear in mind that fashion is not, and cannot be, the supreme rule of conduct; that above fashion and its dictates there are higher and more imperious laws, superior and immutable principles, that can in no case be sacrificed to the whim of pleasure or caprice, and before which the idol of fashion must be ready to abdicate its fleeting omnipotence. These principles have been proclaimed by God, by the Church, by the Saints, by Christian reason and morals, as marking the borderline beyond which no lilies and roses can grow and blossom, where neither purity, modesty, decency, nor feminine honor can spread their radiance, but where there prevails and dominates an unhealthy atmosphere of superficiality, insincere talk, bold vanity, vainglory no less of the soul than of clothing. These are the principles which St. Thomas Aquinas points out for feminine adornment and which he recalls when he teaches what should be the order of our charity, or our affections: the good of the soul must precede that of our body, and to the advantage of our own body we must prefer the welfare of our neighbor's soul. Is it not, then, clear that there is a limit which no style of fashion can make us overstep, and beyond which fashion works the ruin of one's own soul and those of others?

Some young women may say perhaps that a certain style of clothing is more convenient, and also more healthful; but if it becomes a serious and imminent danger to the salvation of the soul, it is certainly not healthy for the spirit: it becomes a duty to renounce it. . . .

If, for mere personal pleasure, one has not the right to endanger the physical health of others, is it not perhaps still less permissible to compromise the health, nay, the very life, of their souls? If, as some women claim, bold fashions do not have a pernicious influence on them, what do they know of the effect they may have on others? What assurance have they that they do not arouse evil incentives?. . .

If some Christian women suspected the temptations and the downfalls they cause in others by their dress and overfamiliarity, to which, in their levity, they give such scant importance, they would be horrified by their responsibility.[1]

[1] Address to the Delegation of Young Women of Catholic Action, May 22, 1941

MATRIMONIAL TRIALS IN ECCLESIASTICAL COURTS

The Sole Aim in the Handling of Matrimonial Cases

IN PRINCIPLE it must be stated that the unity of human action results from the following elements: a single aim, a common course by all toward this single aim, a juridical-moral obligation to take and preserve such direction. You understand well that of these elements the single aim constitutes the formal beginning and end, from the objective standpoint as well as the subjective. For, as every movement receives its direction from the end to which it tends, so also every conscious human activity is conditioned by the goal at which it aims.

In a matrimonial trial the sole aim is to arrive at a decision which conforms to truth and law, concerning, in the procedure for annulment, the asserted inexistence of the conjugal bond, and in the informative procedure *de vinculo solvendo,* the existence or non-existence of the necessary prerequisites for the dissolution of the bond. In other words, the aim is to ascertain authoritatively and to enforce the truth and the law corresponding to truth, relative to the existence or the continuation of a matrimonial bond.

The personal direction is established by the will of the individuals who have a part in handling the case, since they direct and subordinate their every thought, wish, and action on the facts of the case to the achievement of that end. Therefore, if all the participants constantly follow this course, their unity of action or co-operation will come as a natural consequence.

Finally, the third element, that is the juridical-moral obligation to maintain such a course, in matrimonial cases, derives from divine law. The nuptial contract, by its very nature, and between baptized persons, by its elevation to the dignity of Sacrament, is ordered and determined not by the will of man, but by God. It suffices to recall the words of Christ: "That which God has joined together, let no man put asunder," and the teachings of St. Paul: *"Sacramentum hoc magnum est, ego autem dico in Christo et in Ecclesia*—This is a great mystery—I mean in reference to Christ and to the Church." The gravity of this obligation, originating in divine law as if from a supreme and inexhaustible fount, must be strongly affirmed and stressed in the service of truth at the matrimonial trial. May it never happen that in matrimonial cases before the ecclesiastical tribunals there should appear deceit, perjury, subornation, or fraud of any sort! Therefore, all those who have any part in the trial must keep vigilant watch over their conscience and, if need be, rouse it and revivify it, in order to remember that these cases are conducted not before the tribunal of men but before that of the omniscient Lord, and that, consequently, the relative decisions, should some fraud which concerns the substance falsify them, are not valid before God and in the field of conscience.

The Unity of Aim and Action of Individual Participants in Matrimonial Cases

Unity and collaboration in matrimonial cases are effected, then, through the unity of aim, the direction toward the goal, the obligation of subordination to the goal. This triple element imposes essential demands on the personal action of the individual participants and marks it with a particular stamp.

The Judge

The judge, who is, as it were, the personification of justice, reaches the culmination of his work in pronouncing the sentence. Juridically it certifies and fixes the truth and gives it legal value, in all that concerns the actual fact under judgment as well as in all that refers to the law to be applied in the case. To this clarification and service of truth the whole trial is directed. Therefore, by the objective direction toward this goal, the judge finds a sure directive norm in every personal inquiry, judgment, prescription, prohibition, which the unfolding of the case brings with it. From this it becomes evident that the juridical-moral obligation to which the judge is subject is identical with the obligation already mentioned as deriving from divine law, that is to say, to search and determine according to the truth whether a bond which has been contracted by external signs exists in reality, or whether the necessary prerequisites for its dissolution exist. Once the truth is established, the judge has to pronounce the sentence in conformity with it. In this resides the great importance and personal responsibility of the judge in the direction and conclusion of the trial.

The Defender of the Bond

To the Defender of the bond falls the duty of sustaining the existence, or the continuation, of the conjugal bond, not, however, in the absolute sense, but in subordination to the aim of the trial, which is the search for and establishment of objective truth.

Hence, the Defender of the bond must collaborate toward the common goal, by investigating, explaining, and throwing light on whatever can be adduced in favor of the bond. So that he, who must be considered as *Pars necessaria ad iudicii validitatem et integritatem*—a party necessary for the validity and integrity of the trial, may effectively fulfill his office, the trial procedure has attributed to him particular rights and assigned him definite duties. And just as it would not be compatible with the importance of his position and the careful and faithful performance of his duty, if he were to content himself with a cursory survey of the facts and with a few superficial observations, similarly, it is not proper that such an office be entrusted to those who lack experience in life and maturity of judgment. The fact that the observations of the Defender of the bond are subjected to the examination of the judges is no exemption from this rule, since the judges must find in the accuracy of his efforts an aid and a complement to their own activity; nor can it be expected that they repeat the labor and the investigation of the Defender; rather must they be able to trust his findings.

On the other hand, one cannot demand of the Defender of the bond that he compose and prepare, at all costs, an artificial defense, without regard to the serious foundation of his affirmations. Such a demand would be contrary to reason; it would place on the Defender of the bond the burden of fruitless labor; it would bring no clarification, but rather confuse the issue; it would be damaging by dragging out the trial indefinitely. In the interest of truth itself and because of the dignity of his office, one must grant to the Defender of the bond, should the case require it, the right to declare: that after diligent, accurate, and conscientious examination of the facts, he has found no reasonable objection to raise against the request of the plaintiff or the petitioner.

This fact and this consciousness, of not having to sustain unconditionally a thesis imposed upon him, but to be at the service of the truth as existing, will preserve the Defender of the bond from proposing questions which suggest one-sidedly the answer or set traps; from exaggerating and turning possibilities into probabilities or even accomplished facts; from affirming or construing contradictions, where sound judgment does not see them or easily dissolves them; from impugning the veracity of witnesses because of discrepancies or inexactness in nonessential points, or without importance for the object of the case—discrepancies or inexactitudes which, as the psychology of the depositions of witnesses teaches, are within the limits of the normal margin of error and do not detract from the value of the substance of the deposition itself. The consciousness of having to serve the end of truth will prevent the Defender of the bond from asking for new evidence when that on hand is already fully sufficient to establish the truth: on another occasion We have designated this as not to be approved.

Nor should it be objected that the Defender of the bond must put his animadversions on record not *pro rei veritate* but *pro validate matrimonii*. If by this one means that he, on his part, must emphasize all that speaks in favor and not that which is against the existence or the continuation of the bond, that is entirely correct. If, instead, it is meant to affirm that the Defender of the bond, in the performance of his task, is not also required to serve, as his ultimate goal, the ascertaining of the objective truth, but should unconditionally and independently from the evidence and the outcome of the trial sustain the obligated thesis of the existence, or of the necessary continuation, of the bond, this assertion must be considered false. In this sense, all those who take part in the trial must without exception make their action converge on the only goal: *pro rei veritate!*

The Promoter of Justice

We would not wish to omit some brief observations also concerning the Promoter of justice. It is possible that the public good requires a declaration of the nullity of a marriage and that the Promoter of justice makes a regular petition to the competent tribunal. At no other point would one be so much inclined to place in doubt the unity of purpose and collaboration of everyone involved in the matrimonial trial as here, where two public officers appear to take positions against each other before the tribunal: one, the Defender of the bond, must because of his office deny that which the other, also by his office, is called upon to promote. Instead, it is precisely here that the unity of purpose and the joint effort of all toward this end becomes most evident; for both, despite their apparent opposition, place before the judge basically the same request: to pronounce a verdict according to the truth and reality of the objective fact itself. The unity of purpose and collaboration would be broken only if the Defender of the bond and the Promoter of justice were to consider their own immediate and opposing aims as absolutes and were to free and separate them from their connection and subordination to the final common goal.

The Lawyer

But the unity of purpose, the direction toward the goal, and the obligation of subordination to the goal of the matrimonial trial must be considered and pondered with particular attention as regards the legal consultant or lawyer who serves the plaintiff, the defendant, or the petitioner, because more than anyone else he is in danger of losing sight of them.

The lawyer assists his client in formulating the introductory petition of the case; in clearly determining the object and the foundation of the controversy; in highlighting the decisive points of the fact to be judged; he indicates to him the evidence to put forward, the documents to exhibit; he suggests to him which witnesses are to be summoned to the trial and what points in the deposition of witnesses are unassailable; during the trial he helps him justly to evaluate the exceptions and counterarguments and to confute them; in a word, he brings together and puts forward everything that may be adduced as evidence in favor of the request of his client.

In this manifold activity the lawyer may well make every effort to win the case for his client; but in all his action he cannot evade the single and common final aim: the legal discovery, the ascertainment and affirmation of truth, and of the objective fact. The consciousness of such subordination must guide the lawyer in his reflections, in his counsels, in his assertions, and in his proofs. It not only cautions him against artificially constructing or taking on a case without any serious foundation, from employing fraud or deceit, from inducing the parties and the witnesses to make false depositions, from having recourse to any other dishonest expedient, but it also positively causes him to proceed, in the entire series of the acts of the trial, according to the dictates of conscience. To the supreme end of making truth manifest, it is necessary that the efforts of the lawyer as well as the Defender of the bond develop in convergence, because both, though moving from opposite points with different immediate objectives, must tend toward the same final goal.

From this is apparent what must be thought of the principle unfortunately frequently affirmed or, in fact, followed. "The lawyer," it is said, "has the right and the duty to produce all that helps his thesis, no less than the Defender of the bond does in respect to the opposite thesis; for neither of the two is the norm *pro rei veritate* valid. The appraisal of the truth is exclusively the office of the judge; to burden the lawyer with such a task would mean impeding or even completely paralyzing his activity." Such an observation is based on a theoretical and practical error; it fails to recognize the innate nature and the essential final objective of the juridical controversy. In matrimonial cases this cannot be compared to a contest or a joust where the two contestants do not have a common final objective, but where each follows his particular and absolute aim, without regard, and actually in opposition, to that of his antagonist; the sole aim is to defeat the adversary and win a victory. In such a case the victor, by the success which crowns his struggle, creates the objective fact, which for the judge of the combat or the contest is the determining motive for conferring the prize, because for him it is law; to the winner, the prize. Quite the opposite occurs in the juridical contention of a matrimonial trial. Here one does not seek to create a fact with eloquence or dialectics, but to place in evidence and give value to an already existing fact. The above-mentioned principle attempts to separate the activity of the lawyer from the service of objective truth, and would somehow attribute to able argumentation the power to create a right, such as the victorious participant in a contest acquires.

The same consideration of the unconditional obligation to the truth also applies in the simple informative procedure following a request for the dissolution of the bond. The hearing of the case in the ecclesiastical forum does not provide for the intervention of a legal defender of the petitioner; but it is the natural right of the latter to make use on his own of the advice and assistance of a jurist in the preparation of the motivation of the petition, in the selection and presentation of witnesses, and in the overcoming of any difficulties that may arise. The legal consultant or the lawyer may put into operation here also all his knowledge and ability in favor of his client; but even in this extrajudicial activity he must bear in mind the obligation which binds him to the service of truth, his subjection to the common objective and to his part in obtaining it, as he participates in the common effort for the attainment of this objective.

From what We have expounded it appears clear that, in the handling of matrimonial cases in the ecclesiastical forum, the judge, the Defender of the bond, the Promoter of justice, and the lawyer must, as it were, make common cause and collaborate together, without interfering with the specific duty of each, but in conscious and desired union, and in submission to the same purpose.

The Parties, the Witnesses, the Experts

It is superfluous to add that the same fundamental law—to investigate, to clarify, and to give legal value to the truth—is also binding for the other participants in the trial. In order to assure attainment of this goal they are placed under oath. In this subordination to the end they find a clear norm for their interior orientation and their external action, and derive from it certainty of judgment and peace of conscience. Neither to the parties, the witnesses, nor the experts is it permissible to fabricate nonexistent facts, give to existent ones an unfounded interpretation, deny them, confuse them, or hide them. All this would be in contrast with the service they owe to truth, to which they are obligated by the law of God and the oath they have taken.

The Matrimonial Trial in Its Disposition and Subordination to the Universal Aim of the Church: the Salvation of the Soul

If we now pass in review what has already been said, we perceive clearly how the matrimonial trial represents a unity of purpose and action, in which the individual participants must exercise their particular office in reciprocal co-ordination and in common direction toward the same end; like the members of a body each of which, to be sure, has its own function and its own activity, but all of which are reciprocally co-ordinated and arranged together for the attainment of the final design, which is that of the entire organism.

Still, this consideration of the intimate nature of the matrimonial trial would remain incomplete without a look at its external relations.

The matrimonial trial in the ecclesiastical forum is a function of the juridical life of the Church. In Our Encyclical on the mystical body of Christ We expounded how the so-called "Juridical Church" is assuredly of divine origin, but is not the whole Church; how, in a way, she represents only the body, which must be vivified by the spirit, that is to say the Holy Ghost and Its grace. In the same Encyclical We explained likewise how the entire Church, in her body and her soul, as to the participation in goods and the profit which derives from them, is constituted exclusively for the "salvation of souls," according to the words of the Apostle: *"Omnia vestra sunt*—All are yours." With that is indicated the superior unity and the superior aim toward which are destined and directed the juridical life and every juridical function of the Church. It follows that also the thought, will, and personal effort in the exercise of such activity must tend toward the innate purpose of the Church: the care of souls. In other words, the superior purpose, the superior principle, the superior unity mean nothing other than "care of souls," just as all the labor of Christ on earth was the care of souls, and the care of souls was and is the entire action of the Church.

But the jurist who, as such, looks at naked law and rigid justice, is wont to show himself almost instinctively alien to the ideas and the intentions of the care of souls, and advocates a clear separation between the two forums, the forum of conscience and that of external juridico-social coexistence. Up to a certain point, this tendency toward a clear-cut division between the two fields is legitimate, inasmuch as the judge and his collaborators in the judicial procedure do not have pastoral care as their direct and particular duty. However, it would be a fatal error to affirm that in the final and definitive analysis they, too, are not in the service of souls. Thus they would be placing themselves, in the ecclesiastical judgment, outside the scope and the unity of action proper to the Church by divine institution; they would be like the members of a body which no longer fit themselves into its whole and no longer wish to submit and order their actions to the functioning of the entire organism.

The Effectiveness of Such Disposition and Subordination on Juridical Activity

Juridical activity, and particularly the judiciary, has nothing to fear from such disposition and subordination; rather, it is fecundated and promoted by it. The necessary breadth of vision and decision is assured by it, since, while unilateral juridical effort always hides within itself the danger of exaggerated formalism and adherence to the letter, the care of souls guarantees a counterweight, keeping awake in the conscience the maxim: "*Leges propter homines, et non homines propter leges*—Laws are instituted for men, and not men for laws." For this reason, on another occasion We warned that where the letter of the law might be an obstacle to the attainment of the truth, the way must always be open for appeal to the law maker.

The idea of being at the service of the purpose of the Church, furthermore, confers on all those who participate in her juridical activity the necessary independence and autonomy before the civil judiciary power. Between Church and State, as We pointed out in the aforementioned Encyclical on the mystical body of Christ, although both are, in the full meaning of the word, perfect societies, there is nevertheless a profound difference. The Church has her own particular character of divine origin and divine imprint.

From this there derives also, in her juridical life, a trait particular to herself, an orientation, right to the final consequences, toward thoughts and goods of a higher order, supraworldly, eternal. Therefore, rather than an opinion, for various reasons it must be considered an erroneous judgment to say, as some do, that the ideal of ecclesiastical juridical practice consists in its greatest possible assimilation and conformity to the civil judiciary order. This stand, however, does not exclude the Church from taking advantage of true progress in the science of law even in this field.

Finally, the thought of belonging to this superior unity of the Church and subordination to her universal aim, the *salus animarum,* the salvation of souls, communicates to juridical activity the firmness to proceed on the sure path to truth and right, and preserves it no less from a weak condescension toward the disordinate covetousness of the passions than from a hard and unjustified inflexibility. The salvation of souls possesses as a guide a supreme, absolutely certain norm: the law and the will of God. To this same law and will of God juridical activity, which recognizes and is conscious of having no other aim save that of the Church, will direct itself firmly in handling the particular cases submitted to it, and will thus see confirmed in a superior order that which was already, in its own field, its fundamental maxim: service and affirmation of the truth in ascertaining the true fact and in applying to it the law and the will of God.[1]

[1] Message for the Inauguration of the Juridical Year of the Sacred Roman Rota, October 2, 1943

STRENGTH AND WEAKNESS, CHILDREN AND THE AGED

THE WORD "INFIRM"—from the Latin *in-firmus,* not firm, not strong—indicates a being without strength, without firmness. Now in every family there are generally, first of all, two categories of beings that are weak and therefore stand in greater need of attention and affection: children and old people.

Instinct gives even irrational animals tenderness for their young.

How, then, could it be necessary to inculcate it in you, young married couples and future Christian parents? It may happen, however, that too much severity, lack of understanding, may raise a sort of barrier between the hearts of children and those of their parents. St. Paul said: "To the weak I became weak . . . ; I became all things to all men, that I might save all." It is a great quality to be able to become small with the small, a child with children, without compromising, by so doing, paternal or maternal authority. Then it will always be fitting within the family circle to ensure the old the respect, the tranquillity, the delicate attentions, as it were, which they need.

The aged! People are sometimes, perhaps unconsciously, hard with regard to their little demands, their innocent manias, wrinkles that time has impressed on their souls, like those that furrow their faces, but that should make them more venerable in the eyes of others. People are easily inclined to reprove them for what they no longer do, instead of reminding them again, as they deserve, of what they *have* done. One smiles, perhaps, at their weakening memory, and one does not always recognize the wisdom of their judgments. In their eyes, blurred by tears, you will look in vain for the flame of enthusiasm, but you can see the light of resignation in which there already burns the desire of eternal splendor. . . .

However, when people speak of compassion for the weak, they usually mean persons of every age, afflicted with a physical infirmity, temporary or chronic.

In the garden of humanity, ever since it ceased to be called the earthly paradise, there has ripened and will always ripen one of the bitter fruits of original sin: pain. Instinctively man abhors it and avoids it; he would like to lose even the recollection and sight of it. But after Christ in the Incarnation "emptied" Himself, taking the form of a servant; after He chose to "elect the weak things of the world, to confound the strong"; after "Jesus, for the joy set before him, endured a cross, despising shame"; after He revealed to men the meaning of pain and the intimate joy of the gift of one's self to those who suffer, the human heart has discovered in itself unsuspected depths of tenderness and pity. Strength, it is true, is still the unchallenged ruler of unreasoning nature in the pagan souls of today, similar to those whom the Apostle St. Paul called in his time *sine affectione,* heartless, and *sine misericordia,* without pity for the poor and the weak. But for genuine Christians weakness has become a title claiming their respect, and infirmity a title claiming their love. For charity, unlike self-interest and selfishness, does not seek itself, but makes a gift of itself; and the weaker, the more miserable, the more needy and eager to receive is a being, the more it appears to the benevolent eye of charity to be an object of predilection.[1]

[1] Address to Married Couples, July 14, 1940

FAITH, HOPE, AND CHARITY

IF THREE NOTES are sufficient to fix with their harmony the tonality of a musical composition, the song of spring for the Christian could be condensed into three notes, the harmony of which brings his soul in tune with God Himself: faith, hope, and charity.

Faith is a theological virtue, through which we believe in God, Who cannot be seen with the eyes of the body; in His infinite goodness, which His justice veils sometimes from human shortsightedness; in His omnipotence, which seems, to the premature reasoning of men, to be in contradiction with His mysterious long-suffering.

God, if He sometimes seems changeable, is actually unchangeable, because He is eternal; each of His dispositions arrives in its turn; each of His designs is accomplished at the time fixed by His Providence.

In the supernatural order, hope is, like faith, a theological virtue, that is, it links man personally with God. It does not yet raise the veil of faith, to show our eyes the eternal and divine object of celestial contemplations. But it brings the soul that co-operates with grace the assurance of its future possession, in the infallible promise of the Redeemer. It gives it a pledge and, as it were, a foretaste in the resurrection of God made man, which took place in a spring dawn.

Charity is above all a hymn of love. Real, pure love is the gift of oneself; it is the desire of diffusion and complete donation that is an essential part of goodness, and because of which God, infinite goodness, substantial charity, was moved to diffuse Himself in creation. This expansive force of love is so great that it admits of no limits. As the Creator has loved for eternity the creatures that He wants, by an omnipotent aspiration of His divine mercy, to call in time from nothingness into being: *"In caritate perpetua dilexi te; ideo attraxi te, miserans*—I have loved thee with an everlasting love; therefore have I drawn thee, taking pity on thee," so also the Word Incarnate, come among men, *"cum dilexisset suos, qui erant in mundo, in finem dilexit eos*—Having loved His own who were in the world, He loved them unto the end." [1]

[1] Address to Married Couples, April 3, 1940

POVERTY AND CHARITY

FATHER OF ALL THE FAITHFUL, We turn on humanity Our look of deep commiseration, moved by the many ills which today are added to its century-long sufferings. But We see, too, that to the trials and tribulations God permits in order to purify the guilty world, He opposes, as a remedy, new and ever more ingenious forms of charity.

The Apostle St. James noted it, one might say, not without a certain amount of irony: "What is the use of saying to those in need: warm yourselves and eat your fill, yet give not the things necessary to life?" And Jesus declares that on the last day all men will be judged on this practical exercise of charity. True charity is not limited to giving; it gives itself. Now, to visit the poor, one must leave one's home, one's comfort, and often renounce the habits and the spirit of the world. The Apostle St. John provides the warning: "If any man love the world, the charity of the Father is not in him."

The poor man, who has a soul just like the rich man's, has, like him, also a heart; and how little is needed sometimes to console him in his distress or assuage the bitterness of his rebellion! In many a hovel into which a person of active and cheerful dedication has entered, even if with but modest material assistance, the words of

Wisdom will come true: *"Melius est vocari ad olera cum caritate, quam ad vitulum saginatum cum odio*—It is better to be invited to herbs with love, than to a fatted calf with hatred." Therefore, stimulating you to translate your feeling of pity into acts of benevolence, the poor man makes you realize at the same time the necessity of accompanying the acts by feeling, without which the gesture would remain cold and the word indifferent. Furthermore, the poor man unites you again to God by his example. Sometimes wonderful virtues blossom under miserable roofs.

O charity! Virgin with shining eyes, consoling Mother, Sister with soothing hands. You alone make this earth inhabitable for the unhappy, the orphans, the oppressed, the homeless. You reveal to man the intimate goodness of his heart, and show the earth the best image of God, which is substantial "charity." The only eternal virtue, it will triumph in glory, when faith and hope no longer exist. May it triumph now also in the world! How beautiful it seems, and more desirable than ever at this time in which violence, the daughter of hatred, seems to want to banish it! How good it seems, and more than ever necessary, to this agitated and tormented humanity, which does not want to believe in truth, no longer dares believe in justice, but cannot reconcile itself to denying charity!

Woe to the madmen whose fury is bent on destroying this immortal virtue! Woe to the Pharisees with arid souls and empty looks, who do not see the splendor in its face! Woe to the learned, with deaf hearts, who hear not the echo of its voice alleviating the sorrows of humanity! Woe to the false prophets of universal happiness, whose eyes consume themselves in a vision of the phantasm of complete and definitive justice on earth, and see in charity nothing but an importunate and intruding defamer of her regal sister!

Because it has failed to recognize charity, the world has lost true peace, nor will it find it again until it has once more raised, on the indispensable foundations of justice, the throne of charity. Threatened by a new flood, humanity is anxiously awaiting the return of the dove, herald of the rainbow of peace. But the winged messenger will not bring universal peace to individuals and nations unless it can gather once more on earth the green branch of the olive tree, with soothing salves, which requires, to grow and bear its fruit, the sunshine of charity.[1]

[1] Address to the Ladies of St. Vincent, March 13, 1940

MAN THE MACHINE

ONE MIGHT SAY that present-day humanity, which has known how to build the admirable, complex machine of the modern world, harnessing massive forces of nature to its service, still shows itself incapable of dominating their course, almost as if the rudder had slipped from its hand and, therefore, it runs the risk of being overwhelmed and crushed by them. Such inability to control should, of itself, suggest to men, who are its victims, not to seek salvation solely from the technicians of production and of organization. Their accomplishments can contribute, and notably so, to resolving the grave and extended problems which afflict the earth, only if bound and directed to bettering and strengthening true human values; but in no case—oh, how We wish that all, on both sides of the ocean, recognize this!—can it succeed in forming a world without misery.

One knows where to search for technology in social thinking: in the giant undertakings of modern industry. We have no intention here to pronounce a judgment on the necessity, the utility, and the conveniences of similar forms of production. Without doubt they are the marvellous realizations of the inventive and constructive power of the human spirit; very rightly these enterprises which, through carefully thought-out norms, succeed in production and administration, in co-ordinating and pooling the action of men and things, are held up to universal admiration; there is no doubt likewise that their solid order and quite frequently the completely new and unique beauty of their external forms are reason for legitimate pride at the present time. However, what We must deny is that they can and must be used as a general model for the conformation and organization of modern social life.

First of all, it is a clear principle of wisdom that every progress is truly such if it knows how to add new conquests to the old, new advantages to those acquired in the past, in short, if it knows how to store up experience. Now, history teaches that other forms of national economy have always had a positive influence on the entire social life; an influence of which both essential institutions such as the family, the State, private property, and those institutions formed through free association, have taken advantage. We cite as an example the indisputable advantages which appear wherever agricultural enterprise and the crafts predominated.

Without doubt, modern industrial enterprise also has had beneficial effects; but the problem which presents itself today is this: Will a world which recognizes only the economic forms of an enormous productive organization be capable of exercising a happy influence on social life in general, and on those three fundamental institutions in particular? We must answer that the impersonal character of such a world contrasts with the completely personal tendency of those institutions, which the Creator has given to human society. In fact, matrimony and the family, the State, and private property tend by nature to form and develop man as a person, to protect him, and render him capable of contributing, by his voluntary collaboration and personal responsibility, to the maintenance and development, personal also, of social life. The creative wisdom of God, therefore, remains foreign to that system of impersonal unity which makes attempts on the human person, fount and aim of social life, image of God in His most intimate being.

The Demon of Organization

Unfortunately, We are not dealing here with hypotheses or forecasts; this sad reality is already in being. Wherever the demon of organization invades and tyrannizes the human spirit, signs of false and abnormal orientation of social development come to light at once. In not a few countries the modern State is becoming a giant administrative machine. Its hand reaches into practically all facets of life: it attempts to make the entire scale of political, economic, social, and intellectual sectors its field of administration, even birth and death. No wonder, therefore, if in this impersonal climate which tends to penetrate and envelop all life, the sense of the common good becomes dull in the conscience of individuals, and the State loses more and more its primordial character of a moral community of citizens.

Thus is revealed the origin and the point of departure of the current which sweeps modern man into a state of anguish; his "depersonalization." His face and name have been taken away from him to a large extent; in many of the most important activities of life he has been reduced to a mere object of society, since society, in turn, is transformed into an impersonal system, a cold organization of forces.

Unemployment

Whoever still nourishes doubts about this state of affairs, let him turn his attention to the populous world of misery, and ask the various categories of the needy what answer society usually is wont to give them, oriented as it is toward nonrecognition of the person. Ask the ordinary poor, deprived of all resources, who are certainly not rare to encounter in the cities as in the towns and the country; ask the father of a needy family, assiduous client of the bureau of social assistance, whose children cannot wait for the vague, distant deadlines of a golden era always still to come. Ask also an entire people on an inferior or extremely low level of existence who, while taking a place in the family of nations beside their brothers who live in sufficiency or even abundance, wait in vain from one international conference to the other for a stable improvement of their plight. What is the answer which present-day society gives to the unemployed person who presents himself at the windows of the Unemployment Office, prepared, perhaps, through habit to be disappointed anew, but still unresigned to the unmerited destiny of considering himself a useless being? And what is the answer given to a whole people which, no matter how much it tries or struggles, does not succeed in freeing itself from the atrophying grip of mass unemployment?

To all of them for a long time now, it has been incessantly repeated that their case cannot be treated as personal or individual; that the solution must be found in an order yet to be established, in a system which will be all-embracing and which, without basic prejudice to liberty, will lead men and things to a more united and growing force of action, making use of an ever more profound exploitation of technical progress. When such a system shall be arrived at, salvation for all—it is said—shall gush forth automatically, ever improving living conditions and providing full employment everywhere.

The Standard of Living

Far from believing that the persistent deferring of men and things to the future powerful organization is a despicable diversion invented by those who do not wish to help; believing instead that it is a solid, sincere promise, intended to instill faith—one still cannot see, however, on what serious foundations it can rest, since the experiences to date induce rather to skepticism toward the chosen system. This skepticism is justified also by a sort of vicious circle, in which the end established and the means adopted pursue one another without ever coming together or reaching an accord; in fact, where there is an attempt to assure full employment by a continuous improvement of living standards, there is reason to ask oneself with anxiety up to what point it can increase without provoking a catastrophe, and, above all, without causing mass unemployment. It seems, therefore, that the effort should be toward the highest possible level of employment, but with a simultaneous attempt to guarantee its stability.

No faith, therefore, can illuminate a similar scene, dominated by the specter of that insoluble contradiction, nor can its spiral be evaded if men persist in counting on the sole element of top productivity. It is necessary to consider the concepts of living standards and employment of labor no longer as purely quantitative factors but rather as human values in the full sense of the word.

Hence, whoever wants to bring succor to the needs of individuals and peoples cannot await salvation from an impersonal system of men and things, even though it may be strongly developed from the technical standpoint. Every plan or program must be inspired by the principle that man, as a subject, custodian, and promoter of human values, is above things, even above the application of technical progress, and that it is necessary, above all, to preserve from unhealthy "depersonalization" the fundamental forms of social order and utilize them to create and develop human relations. If the social forces should be directed to this end, they will not only fulfill one of their natural functions, but will also be a powerful contribution toward satisfying present necessities, because to them belongs the mission of promoting the full, reciprocal solidarity of men and peoples.

We invite you to erect society on the basis of this solidarity, and not on vain and unstable systems. It requires that the strident, irritating disproportions in the living standards of different groups of people disappear. Rather than external compulsion, it is preferable to exert for this urgent purpose the effective action of conscience, which will impose limits on luxury spending and at the same time induce those who are less well off to think, above all, of the necessary and useful, and then to save the rest, if there is any.

The solidarity of men among themselves demands, not only in the name of fraternal sentiment but also for reciprocal convenience itself, that all possibilities be employed to preserve existing jobs and create new ones. Therefore, those who can invest capital should consider, in view of the common good, whether, within the proportion and limits of their economic possibilities, and at opportune moments, they can reconcile with their conscience not making such investments and, through vain caution, withdraw into inactivity. On the other hand, those who, egotistically exploiting their occupations, prevent others from finding work and cause them to join the ranks of the unemployed, act against conscience. Wherever, also, private enterprise is inoperative or insufficient, the public powers are obliged to provide jobs to the largest extent possible by undertaking projects of general utility and to facilitate with recommendations and other help the employment of those who seek it.

But our invitation to fortify the sentiment and obligation of solidarity extends also to peoples as such; each of them should, in the matter of living standards and employment of labor, develop its own possibilities and contribute to the corresponding progress of other peoples who are less favored. Although even the most perfect realization of international solidarity could hardly bring about absolute equality of peoples, nevertheless it must be practiced at least to the extent of noticeably modifying present conditions, which are far from representing harmonious proportions. In other words, the solidarity of peoples demands the end of the notable disproportions in living standards, and also in investments and the degree of productivity of human labor.

However, such a result cannot be obtained through a mechanical arrangement. Human society is not a machine, and must not become one, not even in the economic field. On the contrary, the contribution of the human being and the individuality of peoples must be employed constantly as a lever against the natural and primordial fulcrum from which one must always start toward the goal of public economy, that is to say, to assure permanent satisfaction in material goods and services, which in turn are directed toward strengthening moral, cultural, and religious conditions.[1]

[1] Address to the Sacred College, December 24, 1952

EDUCATION
THE SCIENCES
THE ARTS

THE EDUCATION OF THE CHILD

OUR SPIRIT looks upon the innumerable ranks of adolescents, seeing them as buds opening at the first light of dawn. Prodigious and enchanting is this thronging of youth from a generation which seemed almost condemned to extinction; new youth, throbbing with its freshness and vigor, with eyes fixed on the future, with an unswerving impulse toward higher goals, resolved to improve upon the past and to assure more lasting and more valuable conquests for man's journey on earth. Of this unrestrainable and perennial current toward human perfection, directed and guided by divine Providence, the educators are the most direct and responsible moderators, associated with this same Providence to carry out its designs. It depends on them, in great part, whether the tide of civilization advances or retrogresses, whether it strengthens its impetus or languishes from inertia, whether it goes swiftly toward the mouth of the river or, on the contrary, pauses, at least momentarily, in useless byways, or worse, in unhealthy and swampy backwaters.

We Ourselves, by divine disposition Vicar, and thus invested with the same offices as He Who on earth loved to be addressed as "Master," We include Ourselves in the number of those who, in various measure, represent the hand of Providence in leading man to his appointed end.

Is not indeed this See of Ours principally a teaching platform? Is not Our first office that of teaching? Did not the Divine Master and Founder of the Church give to Peter and the Apostles the fundamental precept: Go forth and teach, make disciples?

We feel Ourselves to be, and We are, educators of souls. The Church is no less a sublime school, for a great part of the priest's office consists in teaching and educating. Nor could it be otherwise in the new order established by Christ, which is founded entirely on the relationship of the Fatherhood of God, from which all other paternity in Heaven and on earth is derived, and from which, in Christ and through Christ, Our paternity toward all souls extends. Now, a father is an educator by the very fact of being a father since, as the Angelic Doctor so luminously explains, the basic right to teach is based on no other title but that of fatherhood.

Immense is the responsibility we share together; even if in varying degree, but not in entirely different fields: the responsibility for souls, for civilization, for the betterment and the happiness of man on earth and in Heaven.

If at this moment We have turned Our discourse to a wider field, such as that of education, We have done so with the thought that the erroneous doctrine which used to separate the formation of the intellect from that of the heart may by now be said to be surpassed, at least in principle. In fact, We must deplore that in recent years the limits of what is right have been overstepped in interpreting the norm which identifies teacher with educator, and school with life. Having recognized the potent formative value of the school on the conscience, some governments, regimes, and political movements have found in the school one of the most efficient means for winning over to their side that mass of supporters which they need for the triumph of certain conceptions of life. With a tactic as astute as it is insincere, and for reasons which contrast with the natural ends of education itself, some of the movements of the past and present century have pretended to subtract the school from the supervision of those institutions which, besides the State, had a primordial right—the family and the Church—and have attempted, or attempt, to gain exclusive possession of it, imposing a monopoly which is, among other things, gravely damaging to one of the fundamental human liberties.

But this See of Peter, vigilant guardian of the good of souls and of true progress, just as it has never in the past abdicated this essential right, besides admirably exercising it at all times through its institutions, which were often alone in dedicating themselves to it, will never surrender it in the future, either for hope of earthly advantages or through fear of persecution. It will never consent that either the Church, which has received it through divine mandate, or the family, which claims it through natural justice, be deprived of the effective exercise of their native right. The faithful throughout the world are witnesses of the firmness of this Apostolic See in defending the liberty of the school among a great variety of lands, circumstances, and men. For the school, and at the same time for the cult and the sanctity of marriage, the Holy See has not hesitated to face every difficulty and danger with the serene conscience of one who serves a just, holy cause, according to God's will, and with the certainty of performing an inestimable service to civil society itself.

On the other hand, in those countries where the freedom of the school is guaranteed by just laws, it is up to the teachers to know how to make effective use of them, insisting upon their actual application.

The Modern School

If it is excellent practice to prize those systems and methods which have been proven by experience, then it is necessary to weigh with every care the theories and usages of modern teaching institutions before accepting them. The good results which may perhaps have been obtained in countries whose populations have a different outlook and a different level of culture from yours, do not always give sufficient guarantee that those same doctrines may be applied everywhere without distinction.

The school cannot be compared to a chemical laboratory, in which the risk of wasting more or less costly substances is compensated by the probability of a discovery; for every single soul in the school salvation or ruin is at stake. Therefore, those innovations which will be judged opportune will involve, to be sure, the selection of secondary pedagogical means and directions without touching the end and substance, which will always be the same, as the final end of education, its subject, its principal author and inspiration are always identical—namely God our Lord.

The Teacher

The teacher, the educator who draws inspiration from the role of fatherhood, whose final end is the generation of human beings similar to ourselves, will form his students with the example of his life no less than with precepts. If he does not do so, his work will be —in St. Augustine's terms—that of a "merchant of words" and not of a shaper of souls. Moral teachings themselves have only a superficial effect upon the spirit unless they are buttressed by acts. Indeed, the very exposition of school disciplines will not be fully assimilated by the young unless it comes forth from the teacher's lips as live, personal expression: no subject will be profitably received by the student when it is presented without enthusiasm, as a matter extraneous to the life and interests of the person who teaches it.

Educators of the present day, who draw sure guidance from the past, what ideal image of man must you prepare for the future? You find it basically delineated in the perfect Christian. And in saying perfect Christian, We have in mind the Christian of today, a man of his times, who knows and admires all the progress brought about by science and technology, a citizen who is not a stranger to life as it unfolds today in his own country. The world will not regret it if an increasingly large number of such Christians occupy positions in every department of private and public life. It depends largely upon teachers to prepare the ground for this beneficial introduction by directing their students to a discovery of the inexhaustible energies of Christianity in the work of the improvement and renewal of peoples.

The Students

Let the students become accustomed to the difficult work of the intellect, and let them learn the severity and the necessity of work in order to enjoy the rights of living in society in the very same way as the manual laborer does. It is time to enlarge their views on a world less ridden with reciprocally envious factions, with extreme nationalisms and desires for hegemony, for which the present generations have suffered so much. Let the new youth open itself to the spirit of Catholicism, and let it feel the power of that universal love which gathers together all the peoples of the world in the One Lord. Conscious of their personality, and therefore of the greater treasure of freedom; healthily critical; but at the same time, with a sense of Christian humility, rightly subject to the laws and to the duties of solidarity; religious, honest, cultured, open-minded, and enterprising: this is how We would like to see youth come forth from the schools.[1]

[1] Address to Catholic Action, September 4, 1949

THE BOARDING SCHOOL–ITS EFFECTS AND ITS PURPOSES

WE FEEL that it is impossible in the education of youth to be satisfied simply with good results, without a reasonable effort being made to strive after perfection with the help of God's grace. Well, then, as One who has a particular love for youth at study, We should like to take this opportunity to set before you some thoughts on the educative work of schools. This We do for your benefit and also for that of so many other young people whose future, and that of society itself, depends upon the few short years spent at school.

Boarding school education has given good results in the past and is still doing so. Recently, however, it has been the object of severe criticism on the part of certain experts in pedagogy. These would like to see it abolished as though it were totally inept. But their criticisms, even when backed by this or that manifest defect, do not constitute a sufficiently good reason for a sweeping condemnation of this type of education in itself.

It is certainly true that the natural milieu of the home, when helped by the Church and its deficiencies made good by the school, is best suited to assure a good and even perfect education. Frequently, however, circumstances of place, of work, or the persons concerned prevent the family from fulfilling this difficult task on its own. In such cases the boarding school becomes a providential institution without which countless young people would be deprived of a great good.

Parents Still Responsible

But parents are not freed from the duty of caring for their children; rather must their influence be allowed to penetrate the boarding school itself, for they too have their part to play in that general formation which is the objective of the school. Between education within the family circle, which is often impracticable, and full-time education at a boarding school we have the system of part-time board, which combines the advantages of education at home with those proper to boarding schools.

The chief advantages of the latter are that it develops in the character a more rigorous sense of duty, a spirit of discipline and precision, as well as the habit of organizing one's own activity.

To these must be added a sense of responsibility for one's actions. In school a boy in time learns to live in society, thanks to the variety of relations he has with his superiors, his fellow pupils, and those junior to him in age. He is incited to a healthy emulation, a right sense of honor, and the acceptance of inevitable sacrifices. Such dispositions acquired when he is still young will doubtless help him to face life's vicissitudes and will help him to fulfill the duties of his own particular state. Excess and defect in method, however, can compromise the attainment of these results to such an extent that the outcome may be quite the contrary and so give rise to the charge that boarding school education is fruitless and harmful.

Too Rigid Discipline

A communal life away from one's environment, especially if discipline is so rigid as not to distinguish one individual from another, undoubtedly has its dangers. Even small errors in method can produce boys who will have anything but a sense of personal responsibility. Because of their mechanical discharge of their duties, their study, discipline, and prayer unconsciously become mere matters of form. Strict uniformity tends to suffocate personal initiative; a secluded life to restrict a wide vision of the world. An inflexible insistence on rules sometimes gives rise to hypocrisy, or imposes a spiritual level which for one will be too low and for another, on the contrary, unattainable. Excessive severity ends by making rebels of strong characters, while the timid become depressed and secretive.

It is possible and indeed imperative that these dangers be obviated by means of discernment, moderation, and kindness. In the first place one must learn to regard each boy as an individual of specific character. So-called mass education, as likewise mass teaching, is certainly less costly in effort but runs the risk of being of use to only some boys, while all have the right to profit by it.

It is one of the laws of life that children are never quite alike, either in intelligence or in character or in other spiritual qualities. When, therefore, one is arranging their way of life, or correcting or judging them, this individuality must be borne in mind. At least one must avoid that excessive uniformity which sometimes requires hundreds of boys of different ages to study, sleep, dine, and play in the same building—with the same timetable and rules for all.

Individual Attention

One way of obviating the disadvantages of such an arrangement is to divide the boys into homogeneous groups of such proportions as not to make it impossible for those in charge to have a paternal interest in each individual. Each group would have the timetable, rules, and activity best suited to it. It is true that from the complex of moral and spiritual values of which he is made aware through the education he receives at his school, through a judicious choice of books and through good example, the normal youth will choose what he needs for his right formation.

Yet this is not enough. He must further feel himself the object of a special attention on the part of the educator. He should never have the impression of being lost and forgotten in the mass—his own particular requirements disregarded, his needs and weaknesses overlooked—as if only his mere physical presence were of account. This individual attention will stimulate the boy to mold and develop his own personal character. It will develop a spirit of enterprise and a sense of responsibility toward his superiors and his fellows, just as if he were living in the bosom of a large and well-ordered family.

Moderation Necessary, Even in Pious Practices

The second characteristic of school life should be moderation. The old precept *"ne quid nimis,"* which is the same as the other *"in medio stat virtus,"* must inspire every act of the educator, be it when he draws up a rule or insists on its observance. An enlightened sense of discretion should determine the length of study time and of recreation. This same discretion should be in evidence when awarding prizes and when taking disciplinary action, when finding the balance between personal freedom and the enforcement of rules.

Even pious practices must know the right measure, so that they do not become insupportable or tedious to the soul. Not infrequently have deplorable results been noted from an excessive zeal in this matter. Boys of Catholic boarding schools where moderation has not been a guiding principle, but which have sought to impose a tenor of religious practices hardly suitable for young clerics, have been seen to neglect, on their return to their families, the most elementary duties of a Christian, such as going to Mass on Sunday. One should, indeed, help and exhort young men to pray but always in such measure that prayer remains a refreshing need of the soul.

Gentleness with the Young

Thirdly, an aura of gentleness should prevail in every school, of a kind, however, that will not undermine the formation of strong characters. Young people, especially those of good family background, are formed to a sense of duty through personal persuasion, rational arguments, and affection. A boy who is convinced of the love his parents and superiors have for him will not fail to respond, sooner or later, to their solicitude.

Therefore the command which cannot be reasonably justified, the reproof which betrays personal rancor, as also purely vindictive punishment, must be rejected.

Gentleness is to be abandoned only as a last resort, for a short time, and in individual cases. It must control our judgment and override strict justice because a boy is rarely mature enough to understand evil fully or so set upon it as not to be able to return to the path of righteousness when once this has been shown him.

Your work in education cannot fail to show excellent results if these general, though practical, norms are diligently applied.

You should also bear in mind the helpful recommendations which your knowledge of pedagogy will suggest to you.[1]

[1] Address to Students and Faculty of the Convitto Nazionale Maschile di Roma, April, 1956

CONSCIENCE AND EDUCATION

THE OBJECT OF EDUCATION and its role in the natural order is the development of a child to make a complete man of him; the role and object of Christian education is the formation of a new human being, reborn in baptism, into a perfect Christian.

We would now draw attention to an element which, though it is the basis and lever of education, especially of Christian education, seems to some people, at first sight, almost extraneous thereto. We would like to speak of that which is deepest and most intrinsic in man: conscience. We are led to do this by the fact that some currents of modern thought are beginning to alter its conception and question its value. We will therefore treat of conscience in so far as it forms the subject matter of education.

Conscience is, so to speak, the innermost and most secret nucleus in man. It is there that he takes refuge with his spiritual faculties in absolute solitude: alone with himself or, rather, alone with God—Whose voice sounds in conscience—and with himself. There it is that he decides for good or evil; there it is that he chooses between the way of victory and that of defeat. Even if he should wish to do so, a man could never shake off conscience; with it, whether it approves or condemns, he will travel along the whole way of his life, and likewise with it, a truthful and incorruptible witness, he will come up for God's judgment. Hence conscience, to express it with an image as old as it is fitting, is a sanctuary on the threshold of which all must halt, even, in the case of a child, his father and mother. Only the priest enters there, as entrusted with the care of souls and as minister in the Sacrament of Penance; nor for this reason does conscience cease to be a jealous sanctuary of which God Himself wishes the secrecy to be preserved through the seal of the most sacred silence.

In which sense can one then talk of the education of conscience?

It will be necessary to call to mind some of the fundamental Catholic doctrinal conceptions in order to understand well that conscience can and must be educated.

Our divine Savior has brought to ignorant and feeble man His truth and grace: truth, to show him the way toward his goal; grace, to give him the strength to reach it.

To go along that way means, in practice, to accept the will and the commandments of Christ and to conform one's life to them, i.e., each single act, inner or exterior, which the free human will chooses and decides upon. Now, what is the spiritual faculty, if not conscience, that, in each particular case, gives guidance to the will so that it may choose and determine its actions in conformance to the divine will? Conscience, then, is the faithful echo, the clear reflection of human action's divine pattern. Therefore, expressions such as "the judgment of the Christian conscience" or, "to judge according to the Christian conscience," mean this: that the pattern of the ultimate and personal decision for a moral action must be taken from the word and will of Christ. In fact, He is the way, the truth, and the life, not only for all men collectively, but for each single one; the mature man, the child, and the youth.

Formation of the Conscience and Christian Morality

From this it follows that the formation of the Christian conscience of a child or a youth consists above all in illuminating his mind with respect to Christ's will, law, and way; acting, besides, on his mind as much as this can be done from outside, so as to induce him freely and constantly to execute the divine will. This is the highest task of education.

But where shall the educator and the youth find in each individual case with ease and certainty the Christian moral law? They will find it in the law of the Creator imprinted in the heart of each one as well as in revelation, that is, in all the truth and precepts taught by the divine Master. Both the law written in the heart, that is, the natural law, and the truth and precepts of supernatural revelation, have been given by Jesus the Redeemer into

Friend of Animals

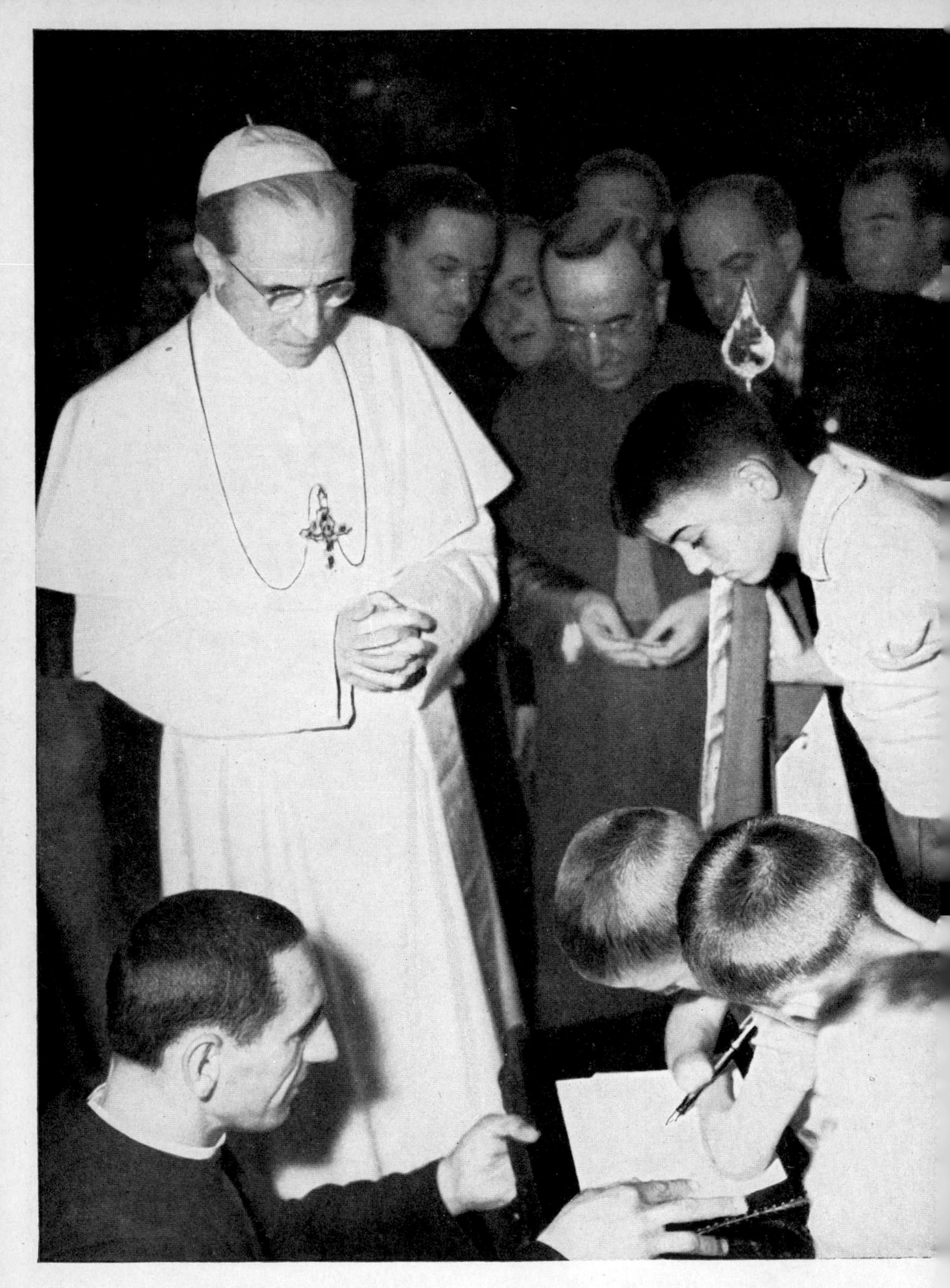

Reception of Children Maimed in World War II, July 11, 1948

the hands of His Church as humanity's moral treasure, so that the Church may preach them, intact and protected against any contamination and error, to all creatures, from one generation to another.

Against this doctrine, uncontroverted for many centuries, there are now emerging difficulties and objections which call for clarification.

For dogmatic doctrine as well as for the Catholic moral order the application of an almost radical revision is being advocated, with a view to deducing a new scale of values from it.

The primary step or, rather, the first blow against the edifice of Christian moral canons should be—as is pretended—the redeeming of these rules from the narrow and oppressive guardianship of the authority of the Church, so that, freed from the sophistic subtleties of the casuistic method, morality may be brought back again to its original form and left to the individual's intelligence and determination. Anyone can see to what baneful results such overturning of the very foundations of education would lead.

Omitting to point out the obvious inexperience and immaturity of judgment of those who maintain such opinions, it will be well to bring into light the central flaw of this "new morality." By leaving all ethical judgment to the conscience of the individual, jealously closed in itself and made sole arbiter of its determinations, this morality, far from smoothing the way for it, would make it stray from the main road which is Christ.

The divine Redeemer has given His relevation, of which moral obligations are an essential part, not to individual men but to His Church, with the mission to lead men faithfully to accept that sacred deposit.

Likewise, divine assistance, intended to preserve revelation from errors and distortions, was promised to the Church and not to individuals. A wise provision, because the Church, a living organism, may thus illustrate and probe truths, even moral truths, with certainty and flexibility, and apply them to the variable conditions of times and places without altering their substance.

How then is it possible to reconcile the Savior's providential disposition, through which the Church was entrusted with the Christian moral heritage, with a sort of individualistic autonomy of conscience?

Purity of Soul and Body

The "new morality" affirms that the Church, instead of urging the law of human liberty and of love, and enforcing it as the worthy dynamic force of moral life, leans instead almost exclusively and with excessive rigidity on the firmness and the irrevocability of Christian moral laws, resorting frequently to the admonitions "you must" and "it is not lawful," smacking all too often of demeaning pedantry.

The Church wishes instead—and this is expressly emphasized with regard to the forming of consciences—that a Christian should be introduced to the infinite riches of faith and grace in a persuasive manner, so that he may feel inclined to penetrate deeply into them.

The Church, however, cannot give up admonishing the faithful that these riches cannot be acquired and kept without observing some precise moral obligations. A different behavior would only end by putting into oblivion a dominant principle which Jesus, its Lord and Master, always insisted upon. Jesus did in fact teach that it is not enough to say "Lord! Lord!" in order to enter the Kingdom of Heaven, but that it is necessary to do the will of our heavenly Father. He spoke of the "strait gate," of the "narrow way," which leads to life and added: "Strive to enter by the narrow gate; for many shall seek to enter, and shall not be able." He gave as a touchstone and hallmark of love for Himself, Christ, the observance of the commandments. Likewise, to the rich young man questioning Him, He said: "If thou wouldst enter into life, keep the commandments," and to the further question: "Which?" He replied: "Thou shall not kill, thou shalt not commit adultery, thou shalt not steal, thou shalt not bear false witness, thou shalt honor thy father and thy mother, and love thy neighbor as thyself." He has put as a condition to those who want to follow Him that they have to renounce themselves and take up His Cross daily. He demands that man be ready to forsake for Him and for His sake his most cherished possessions, his father, his mother, and his own children, up to his ultimate wealth, his own life. Because, He added: "I say unto ye, my friends; fear not those who kill the body and can do no more. I shall show ye whom ye shall fear: fear Him who, when life has been taken away, has the power to cast into hell."

Thus spoke Jesus Christ, the divine Teacher, Who certainly knew better than men how to penetrate into souls and attract them to His love, with the infinite perfection of His heart, *bonitate et amore plenum*—full of goodness and love.

Therefore, taking the words of Christ strictly as a standard, should it not perhaps be said that the Church of today is inclined to lenience rather than to severity? Thus, the accusation of oppressive harshness which the "new morality" raises against the Church in reality attacks first and foremost the Person of Christ.

The Moral Obligations of Youth

Therefore, being conscious of the right and of the duty of the Apostolic See to intervene authoritatively, when necessary, on moral questions, We declare to educators and to youth: the divine commandment to be pure in soul and body applies without diminution also to today's youth. The youth of today has also the moral obligation and the possibility of keeping itself pure with the aid of grace. We reject, therefore, as erroneous the claim of those who consider inevitable the failings of the age of puberty, considered by them of no great import and almost as if they were not a grave fault, because, they add, passion cancels the liberty which is required to make a person morally responsible for an act.

On the contrary, it is required from a wise educator that, without neglecting to impress on his youthful charges the noble qualities of purity so as to induce them to love and desire it for its own sake, he should at the same time clearly inculcate the commandment as it stands, in all its gravity and earnestness as a divine order. He will thus urge them to avoid immediate occasions, he will comfort them in the struggle, of which he shall not hide the hardness, he will induce them to embrace courageously the sacrifices demanded by virtue, and he will exhort them to persevere and not to fall into the danger of surrendering from the very beginning and thus succumbing passively to perverse habits.

General Validity of Christian Moral Laws

Even more than from the field of private behavior many today would like to exclude the dominion of moral law from public, social, and economic life, from the action of internal and external public powers, in war and in peace, as if God had nothing to say there, at least nothing binding.

The emancipation of outward human activities such as the sciences, politics, and art from morality is sometimes motivated from a philosophical point of view by the autonomy which belongs to them, in their own field, to be governed exclusively by their own laws, although it is admitted that, as a rule, these laws agree with the moral laws. The example usually given is art, for which not only any dependence but also any connection with morality is denied since "Art is only art and not morality or anything else, and is subject therefore only to aesthetic laws; these, however, if truly aesthetic, will not lend themselves to serve lust." In a similar way one speaks of politics and economy, which do not require the counsel of other sciences and therefore of ethics, but, being guided by their own laws, are for that very reason good and just.

This evidently is a subtle way of removing consciences from the dominion of moral laws. One cannot deny that such autonomies are justified, inasmuch as they express the method peculiar to each activity and the boundaries which separate their various forms in theory. But the separation of method should not signify that the scientist, the artist, the politician, are independent from moral responsibilities in the carrying out of their activities, especially if these have an immediate repercussion in the field of ethics, as in the case of art, politics, and economy. A clear-cut and theoretical separation has no sense in life, which is always a synthesis, because the sole subject of any kind of activity is man himself, whose free and conscious acts cannot avoid moral evaluation. Furthermore, considering the problem from a wide and practical viewpoint which is sometimes wanting even in outstanding philosophers, it can be said that such distinctions and autonomies are perverted by decadent human nature in such a way as to make appear as the laws of art, politics, and economy what in reality serves lust, selfishness, and greed. Thus, the theoretical independence from morality becomes, in practice, rebellion against morality and the harmony inherent in the sciences and arts, which even the philosophers of that school of thought clearly detect but call accidental, is thereby destroyed, while, instead, it is essential when considered in relation to the subject, which is man, and to its Creator, which is God.

We have never ceased to insist on the principle that the order of God embraces the whole of life, with the inclusion of public life, in all of its manifestations, being convinced that in this principle there is no restriction of genuine human freedom or any intrusion into the province of the State, but a shield against errors and abuses from which Christian morality, if rightly applied, is able to protect. These truths must be taught to youth and inculcated in the youthful consciences by those who, in the family or in the school, have the obligation to attend to their education, sowing thus the seed of a better future.[1]

[1] Broadcast on "Family Day," March 24, 1952

FUNDAMENTAL RIGHTS OF THE CHRISTIAN FAMILY

TIME AND TIME AGAIN We have insisted—in connection with various problems—on the sanctity of the family, on its rights, on its tasks as the fundamental cell of human society. Its life, its health, its vigor, its activities ensure the life, health, vigor, and activities of society as a whole. For its existence, its dignity, its social function derived from God, the family must answer to God. Its rights and privileges are inalienable, intangible; it is its duty, above all before God, and in the second place before society, to defend, to claim, to promote effectively these rights and privileges, not only for its own benefit but for the glory of God, for the welfare of the community at large.

How often have been sung the praises of the mother, considered the very heart, the sun of the family! But if the mother is its heart, the father is its head; the health and efficiency of the family depend, therefore, first of all upon the ability, the virtues, the activities of the father.

For the Christian there is a rule which enables him to determine with certitude the extent of the rights and duties of the family within the community of the State. This is the rule: The family does not exist for society, but society exists for the family. The family is the fundamental cell, the element which constitutes the community of the State, since, to use the very expressions of Our predecessor Pius XI, of happy memory, "The State is such as the families and the men by whom it is formed make it, as the body is formed by its members." By virtue, so to speak, of the instinct of preservation, the State should consequently fulfill what is, essentially and according to the design of God, Creator and Savior, its first duty: to guarantee fully those values which ensure for the family order, human dignity, health, happiness. These values, which are the very elements of common welfare, can never rightly be sacrificed to what might, in appearance, seem to be a common good. Let us mention as examples, some of which are greatly threatened at the present day: the indissolubility of marriage; the protection of human life before birth; sufficient housing for the family, not that composed of one or two children or the childless family, but for the normal more numerous type of family; the possibility of working, because unemployment in the case of the father is the bitterest of hardships for the family; the rights of parents over their children with respect to the State; the full freedom of parents to educate their children in the true faith and therefore the right of Catholic parents to Catholic schools; social conditions that will guarantee that families, and particularly young people, need not have the moral certainty of being subjected to corruption.

In these and yet other points which more closely affect family life there is no difference whatsoever between families; as regards some other economic and political questions, however, they may find themselves in very different and unequal conditions, and sometimes in competition or even in conflict. Particularly here, every effort should be made—and Catholics will wish to give a good example—to promote an equilibrium, even at the cost of sacrificing particular interests, for the sake of internal peace and a healthy economy.

But, with regard to the essential rights of families, true followers of the Church will do their utmost to defend them. Perhaps here or there, on some points, it may be necessary to yield before the superiority of political forces, but in such cases there will be no surrender, only the exercise of patience. Moreover, in cases of this sort, it is necessary that doctrine be safe, that all efficient means be adopted to achieve step by step the end that has never been forgone.

Among such efficacious means, though not of immediate effect, one of the most powerful is the union of fathers, firm in the same convictions, in the same will.

Another means which, even though it may not bring immediately the desired results, is never wasted and always bears fruit, is the care taken by this coalition of fathers to endeavor to enlighten public opinion, to persuade it little by little to favor the triumph of truth and justice. No effort to act upon that public opinion should be spared or neglected.

Literature on Sexual Initiation

There is a field where the necessity for this education and a healthy influencing of public opinion is making itself felt with tragic urgency. In that field it has been perverted by propaganda which might unhesitatingly be called evil.

We refer to writings, books, and articles concerning sexual initiation, which nowadays often reach enormous sales and flood the whole world, invading infancy, submerging the new generation, disturbing the minds of those engaged to be married and of young married couples.

The Church has treated, with all the gravity, attention, and dignity which the question requires, the problem of instruction in this subject as made advisable or needful by the normal physical and psychic development of adolescents as well as in specific cases demanded by special conditions. The Church may with good reason proclaim that, with the deepest respect for the sanctity of matrimony, in theory and practice, she has granted freedom to husband and wife in what is permitted by the impulse of a healthy and decent nature, without offending the Creator.

The intolerable impudence of such literature is appalling: whereas the pagan world itself seemed to halt with respect before the secret intimacy of married life, today we witness the violation of that mystery, which is offered to the public at large, even to the young, as a vivid, sensual spectacle. There is truly reason to wonder whether there still remains a sufficiently clear-cut borderline between this initiation—so-called Catholic—and the erotic or obscene literature and illustrations which aim deliberately at corruption or which, for base motives of interest, shamefully exploit the basest instincts of fallen nature.

But there is more. Such propaganda also threatens the Catholic world with a twofold calamity, not to use a stronger expression. First of all it exaggerates beyond measure the importance and significance, in life, of the sexual element. Even if it be admitted that these authors, purely theoretically speaking, keep within the limits of Catholic ethics, it is, however, no less true that their manner of explaining sexual life is such that it acquires, in the mind of the reader and in his practical judgment, the meaning and value of something which is an end in itself. It makes him lose sight of the true original aim of matrimony, which is the procreation and the education of children, and the serious duty of husband and wife with regard to this end; the literature of which we are speaking leaves this too much in the background.

Furthermore, this so-called literature seems not to take into account the universal experience which is of yesterday, of today, and of all times, because it is based on nature itself, and which attests that in moral education neither initiation nor instruction brings of itself any advantage; that it is in fact seriously harmful and detrimental if not firmly supported by constant discipline, by strong self-control, and, above all, by resort to the supernatural force of prayer and the Sacraments. All Catholic educators worthy of the name and of their mission are fully conscious of the preponderant importance of supernatural energies in the sanctification of the individual, young or adult, unmarried or married. In writings of the kind mentioned, barely a word is said about all this when it is not altogether passed over in silence. The very principles so wisely illustrated by Our predecessor Pius XI in his Encyclical *Divini Illius Magistri* on the subject of sexual education and its interrelated problems, are set aside—sad sign of the times!—with a simple wave of the hand or with a smile. Pius XI, it is said, wrote these things twenty years ago for his own times; much ground has been covered since then!

Fathers, join together, under the guidance of your Bishops, of course; call to your help all Catholic women and mothers to fight together, without any wavering or false shame, in order to thwart and disrupt these movements, whatever may be the name or the authority with which they cloak themselves or which may have been lent to them.[1]

[1] Address to French Fathers, September 18, 1951

IMMORALITY

JUST AS ANY CHRISTIAN, any person endowed with decency and natural common sense is astonished and appalled at the sight of the rising tide of immorality which, even in these exceptionally grave times, threatens to submerge society. No one hesitates to recognize the cause of it, particularly in the licentious publications and the indecent shows which are offered to the eyes and ears of adolescents and adults, of the young and old, of mothers and daughters. And what should be said about art, fashions, the public and private behavior of both men and women? One can hardly believe that writers, publishers, artists, managers, and promoters of certain artistic and theatrical displays do not hesitate to sink to such low levels of corruption, converting the use of the pen and art itself, the industrial progress and the wondrous modern inventions, into tools, weapons, and allurements of immorality. Writings and stage productions, though unworthy of the honor due to art and literature, find, nonetheless, readers and spectators by the thousands. And you see teen-agers throw themselves at such a diet of the mind and eye with all the impulsiveness of the awakened passions; you see parents taking with them to such sorry spectacles boys and girls, in whose tender hearts and eyes are impressed fatal images and cravings, which often are never erased, instead of innocent and pious visions.

What, then, should we think? That human nature is universally and profoundly depraved and that its craving for scandal is without remedy? Certainly not. As a foundation, God has placed, in the human heart, righteousness which, however, is threatened by the Spirit of Evil and unbridled concupiscence. Except for a small minority, people would not spontaneously seek, and still less demand, unwholesome entertainment, if it were not offered to them and sometimes almost imposed upon them by surprise.

On Art

Consequently, it is extremely important to take the field in defense of public and social morals. It is not a battle waged with material weapons and bloodshed, but a conflict of ideas and feelings, between good and evil. It is proper that all who can do so should direct all their efforts and employ all their talents toward creating and promoting a type of literature, theater, and motion picture which constitutes genuine art, in concept and content elevating, wholesome, and at the same time interesting and attractive. We could never adequately commend and encourage the well-deserving intellectuals who devote themselves to this task like apostles of righteousness. It is evident, however, that not all can shoulder the burden of such an apostolate.

Is there, then, anything the others should do? Are they simply to lull themselves with the hope that the attractiveness of good and beautiful works will universally succeed in arousing and spreading an invincible disgust and repudiation of all turpitude? None is so naïve on this point as to cherish such vain hopes. In the face of the unscrupulous exploiters of the press, of stage and screen, shall decent people simply stand helplessly aside? This would be unjust, and so it would appear to whoever knows and considers the laudable legislation which honors the country. To respectable citizens, heads of families, and educators the way is open to ensure the enforcement of these provident laws and of the effective sanctions they envisage, by submitting to the civil authorities, in the prescribed form, reports based on facts and accurate in their references to persons, things, or expressions, so that whatever of an objectionable nature should be presented to the public may be prevented and suppressed.

We do not conceal that this is a vast and varied task. Because of its vastness, it offers a wide field to all people of good will; and because of its variety, it is suitable for people of varying aptitudes. But its amplitude, though it may frighten and discourage the fainthearted, serves also to kindle ever more vividly the ardor of generous souls.[1]

Eyes and Ears Are Broad Avenues

And now let us examine our subject more closely, because much remains to be done and much is expected by the Church.

Ever louder and more urgently resound from the soil of Europe and from beyond the seas the pleas for help in the unfortunate conditions of the family and of the young generation.

That war bears the major burden of guilt is well known. It is responsible, above all, for the violent and sorrowful separation of millions of couples and families and for the destruction of innumerable homes.

But it is equally certain that the real and true cause of such a great evil is even more profound. It must be sought in what, by a composite term, is called materialism, in the negation or at least in the neglect and contempt of all that is religion, Christianity, submission to God and to His law, the life to come, and eternity. Like a pestiferous breath, materialism pervades more and more the entire life and produces its evil fruits in matrimony, in the family, and in the youth.

It may be said that according to unanimous judgment the morality of youth in general is in continuous decline. And not only of youth in the cities. In that of the country also, where once a robust and healthy respect for morality flourished, the moral degradation is hardly less pronounced, while much of what spurs to luxury and pleasure in the city has obtained free entry in the village, too.

It is superfluous to recall how much the radio and the movies have been used and abused in the spreading of that materialism, and how much they, the bad book, the licentious illustrated periodical, the indecent show, the immoral dance, and immodesty on the beaches, have contributed to increase superficiality, worldliness, and the sensuality of youth. Reports coming from the most diverse regions signal those areas as centers of youth's religious and moral abandonment. But primarily responsible is the breakup of marriage, of which the moral debasement of youth is the hallmark and deplorable consequence.[2]

Movies and Morality

One wonders at times if the leaders of the motion picture industries fully appreciate the vast power they wield in affecting social life, whether in the family or the larger civic groups. The eyes and ears are like broad avenues that lead directly to the soul of man; and they are opened wide, most often without challenge, by the spectators of your films. What is it that enters from the screen into the inner recesses of the mind, where youth's fund of knowledge is growing and where norms and motives of conduct that will mold the definitive character are being shaped and sharpened? Is it something that will contribute to the formation of a better citizen, industrious, law-abiding, God-fearing, who finds his joy and recreation in wholesome pleasure and amusement? St. Paul was quoting Menander, an ancient Greek poet, when he wrote to the faithful of his church in Corinth that "bad conversation corrupts good manners." What was true then is no less true today; because human nature changes little with the centuries. And if it is true, as it is, that bad conversation corrupts morals, how much more effectively are they corrupted by bad conversation when accompanied by conduct, vividly depicted, which flouts the laws of God and civilized decency? Oh, the immense amount of good the motion picture can effect! That is why the evil spirit, always so active in this world, wishes to pervert this instrument for his own impious purposes; and it is encouraging to know that your committee is aware of the danger, and more and more conscious of its grave responsibility before society and God. It is for public opinion to sustain wholeheartedly and effectively every legitimate effort made by men of integrity and honor to purify the movies and keep them clean, to improve them and increase their usefulness.[3]

[1] Address to Catholic Women, February 20, 1942
[2] Address to Women of Catholic Action, July 24, 1949
[3] Address to U. S. Movie Producers, July 14, 1945

THE ESSENCE AND MISSION OF ART

So much has been said about art, an inexhaustible subject! The agitations of a world shaken in its very foundations, the divergencies of minds, the conflict of interests, the suspiciousness of a hypersensitive individualism have accentuated individual isolation and extended and deepened moral distances despite the multiplying of material contacts. Little by little, the excess of this evil has ended in placing the spotlight on the need for uniting in a common action all the isolated forces of nations and peoples earnestly desiring peace.

Persevering and discerning attempts to reach an understanding or co-operation between the different countries are neither of today nor of yesterday. Current events have underlined not, indeed, their inconsistency and uselessness, but rather their insufficiency and instability. All have therefore endeavored with praiseworthy eagerness to promote, notwithstanding all sorts of difficulties, international unions of a political, juridical, economic, and social nature. Very soon, however, it became evident that something more intimate and more human was still needed, and so, in the fields of engineering, science, and culture, there have begun to come into being, if not a union, at least partial associations.

In the intellectual order, the union of Catholic artists occupies one of the foremost positions. This is natural because, to begin with, art is, under certain aspects, the most vivid and synthetic expression of the human mind and human feelings, and also the most widely intelligible, since, speaking directly to the senses, art knows no diversity of languages, but only the extremely attractive diversity of temperaments and mentalities.

Moreover, with their persuasiveness and delicacy, the auditive and visual arts penetrate the intelligence and the sensitiveness of the spectator or of the listener to depths which the written or spoken word with its insufficiently colored analytical precision could never reach.

For these two reasons art helps men, notwithstanding all the differences of character, education, and civilization, to become acquainted with and understand each other, or at least to get an intuitive knowledge of one another, and consequently to pool their respective resources in order to complement one another.

In order that art may produce so desirable a result, it is necessary in the first place for it to have an expressive value, without which it ceases to be true art. This remark is not superfluous these days when, too often, in certain schools, a work of art is not sufficient of itself to express the thought, to disclose the sentiment, to reveal the soul of its author. But when a work of art needs to be explained verbally, it loses its peculiar value and only serves to give to the senses purely physical enjoyment and to the spirit the enjoyment of a subtle and empty game. Another condition, if art is to accomplish with dignity and fruitfulness its glorious mission consisting in the promotion of understanding, harmony, and peace, is that through art the senses, far from weighing down the soul and nailing it to the earth, should serve it as wings on which to rise above transient trifles and paltriness toward that which is eternal, true, beautiful, toward the only real good, the only center where union is accomplished, where unity is achieved, toward God. Is it not here that the splendid vision of the Apostle, *"Invisibilia enim ipsius a creatura mundi per ea quae facta sunt, intellecta conspiciuntur, sempiterna quoque eius virtus et divinitas* —For the invisible things of Him, from the creation of the world, are clearly seen, being understood by the things that are made; His eternal power also, and divinity," literally applies?

All the maxims which bring art down from its sublime office profane it, therefore, and make it barren. "Art for art's sake": as if art could be an end in itself, condemned to move, to crawl, at the level of sensible and material things; as if through art man's senses did not follow a call going beyond the simple knowledge of material nature, the call to awaken in his intellect and soul, because of the transparency of this nature, the wish for "things that the eye hath not seen, nor the ear heard and that have not reached his heart."

We will say nothing here about an immoral art which aims to debase and enslave the spiritual powers of the soul to the passion of the flesh. Furthermore, "art" and "immoral" are two terms in strident contradiction. Therefore, make the reflection of the divine beauty and light smile upon the earth, upon humanity; helping man to love "all that which is true, pure, just, saintly, lovable," and you will have made a great contribution to peace *"et Deus pacis erit vobiscum*—and the God of Peace will be with you."[1]

[1] Address to the First Congress of Catholic Artists, March 9, 1950

THE DUTY OF PHYSICIANS

THE CHRISTIAN PHYSICIAN never loses sight of the fact that his ailing or wounded patient, who, thanks to his care, will continue to live for a time either short or longer, or, notwithstanding his attention, will die, is on the way toward immortal life, and that his misery or eternal happiness is also dependent upon him.

Compounded of matter and spirit, himself an element in the universal order of beings, man on his journey here is in reality moving toward an end exceeding the limits of time, toward a goal set above nature. Because of this interpenetration of matter and spirit in the perfectly compounded unity of man, because of this participation in the movement of all visible creation, it follows that the physician is often called upon to give advice, to make decisions and formulate principles which, though aiming directly at the cure of the body, its members and organs, nevertheless have their bearing upon the spirit and its faculties, the supernatural destiny of man and his social mission.

Now, if he does not always take into account this composition of man, his place and his function in the universal order of beings, and his spiritual and supernatural destiny, the physician easily runs the risk of becoming entangled in more or less materialistic prejudices, of following the fatal consequences of utilitarianism, of hedonism, and absolute autonomy in respect to moral law.

Man Is Only the Usufructuary of His Body

The complexity of this compound of matter and spirit, and of the universal order as well, is such that man cannot guide himself toward the total and unique goal of his being and his personality except by the harmonious action of his multiple corporal and spiritual faculties, and he cannot maintain his place either by isolating himself from the rest of the world or by losing himself as thousands of identical molecules lose themselves in an amorphous agglomeration. Now, this very real complexity and this necessary harmony present their difficulties and dictate his duty to the physician.

In shaping man, God regulated each of his functions; He distributed them among his various organs; He established the distinction between those which are essential to life and those which concern only the integrity of the body, however precious may be its activity, its well-being, and its beauty. At the same time, He fixed, prescribed, and limited the use of each function. Therefore, man is not permitted to order his life and the functions of his organs according to his desire, in a way contrary to the internal and inherent purposes assigned to them. Actually, man is not the owner and absolute lord of his body, but only its usufructuary. From this fact is derived a whole series of principles and rules which regulate the use and the right to dispose of the organs and members of the body, and which are equally binding to the interested person himself and the physician called to advise him. . . .

The same rules should, moreover, guide the solution of conflicts between divergent interests, according to the scale of values, save, always, the Commandments of God. Therefore, man is never allowed to sacrifice his eternal interests to temporal goods, even the most highly valued, nor is he permitted to cast aside these goods in favor of vulgar caprice and the exigencies of passion. In such —sometimes tragic—crises the physician is often the counsellor and almost the final arbiter.

Though circumscribed and restricted to the person himself, complex as he is in his unity, the inevitable conflicts among divergent interests give rise to extremely delicate problems. How much more difficult are those, then, which society poses when it asserts its rights upon the body, its integrity, and upon the life of man itself! Now, it is sometimes quite difficult to determine the limits in theory; in practice, the physician, no less than the individual directly concerned, may find himself in the necessity of examining and analyzing such exigencies and claims, of measuring and evaluating their morality and binding ethical force. . . .

The Integrity of the Body

Here reason and faith equally draw the line between the respective rights of society and the individual. There is no doubt that man by his own nature is destined to live in society; but even as reason alone teaches us, in principle society is made for man and not man for society. Not from society but from the Creator Himself has he the right to his body and his life, and to the Creator he is responsible for the use he makes of them. From this it follows that society cannot directly deprive him of that right, until he has rendered himself punishable with such a privation by a grave and proportionate crime.

Regarding the body, the life, and the bodily integrity of single individuals, the juridical position of society is essentially different from that of the individuals themselves. Though it is limited, man's power over his members and organs is a direct power, as they are constitutional parts of his physical being. Indeed, it is clear that since their differentiation in a perfect unity has no other purpose than the good of the entire organism, each of these organs and members may be sacrificed, if it places the whole in a danger which cannot otherwise be avoided. Quite different is the case of society, since it is not a physical being whose parts would be the individual men, but a simple community of purpose and action; for which reason it may demand of those who compose it, and who are called its members, all the services necessary to the common good.

These are the bases upon which must be founded every judgment which concerns the moral value of the acts or interventions permitted or imposed by public power upon the human body, the life, and the integrity of the person. . . .

Suffering and Death

The truths so far set forth may be known only by the light of reason. But there is a fundamental law which presents itself more to the attention of the physician than the others, and whose integral meaning and purpose can be clarified and made manifest only by the light of revelation: We mean to say suffering and death.

Undoubtedly, physical pain has also a natural and salutary function: it is a signal of alarm which reveals the beginning and development, often insidious, of a hidden disease and induces and urges the search for a remedy. But the physician inevitably encounters pain and death in the course of his scientific research, as a problem to which his spirit does not possess the key, and in the exercise of his profession, as an ineluctable and mysterious law, before which his skill often remains impotent and his compassion sterile. He can indeed establish his diagnosis according to all laboratory and clinical findings and formulate his prognosis according to all the dictates of science; but in the depths of his conscience, of his heart of man and scientist, he feels that the explanation of that enigma persists in escaping him. He suffers because of it; anguish holds him inexorably in its viselike grip until he asks faith for an answer which, even if incomplete, as it is in the mystery of God's design and will be revealed only in eternity, nevertheless serves to pacify his soul.

Here is the reply. God, in creating man, had exempted him, through the gift of grace, from that natural law of every living and sensitive body, and had not designed to include pain and death in his destiny. It was sin that brought them upon him. But He, the Father of mercy, took them into His hands and caused them to pass through the body, the veins, and the heart of His beloved Son, Who was God like unto Himself, made into man to be the Savior of the world. Thus pain and death have become the means of redemption and sanctification for every man who does not deny Christ. Thus the path of the human race, which unfolds in its entire length under the Sign of the Cross and under the law of pain and death, while it matures and purifies the soul here on earth, leads it to unlimited happiness of a life without end.

To suffer, to die: it is really, to use the daring expression of the Apostle of all nations, the "foolishness of God," a foolishness wiser than all the wisdom of men. . . . In the light of revelation the pious author of *The Imitation of Christ* was able to write the sublime twelfth chapter of his second book, *"De regia via sanctae Crucis*—Of the Royal Road of the Cross," all resplendent with the most admirable understanding and the highest Christian wisdom of life.

In the face of the imperious problem of pain, what reply, then, can the physician give to himself? And what to the unfortunate man whom sickness has reduced to a gloomy torpor, or who rises in vain rebellion against suffering and death? Only a heart imbued with a vivid and profound faith can find accents of intimacy, sincerity, and conviction capable of making acceptable the reply of the divine Master Himself: It is necessary to suffer and die, in order to enter this way into glory. He will fight with all the means and resources of his science and his ability against sickness and death, not with the resignation of a desperate pessimism, nor with the exasperated resoluteness which a modern philosophy believes it must exalt, but rather with the calm serenity of one who sees and knows what pain and death represent in the designs of salvation of the omniscient and infinitely good and merciful Lord.

Is There Such a Thing as Christian Medical Science?

It is manifest, therefore, that the person of the physician and all his activities move constantly in the sphere of moral order and under the dominion of its laws. In no statement, in no advice, in no action, in no intervention may the physician keep outside the sphere of morals, free and independent from the fundamental principles of ethics and religion; nor is there any act or word for which he is not responsible before God and his own conscience.

It is true indeed that there are some who reject as an absurdity and a chimera the concept of a "Christian medical science," in theory and in practice. In their opinion there cannot be a Christian medicine, just as there is not a Christian physics or a Christian chemistry, theoretical or applied. The realm of the exact and experimental sciences—they say—extends beyond the religious and ethical area, and therefore they know and recognize only their own immanent laws. Strange and unjustified contraction of the field of vision of the problem! Do they not see that the objects of those sciences are not isolated in space, but are a part of the universal world of creatures; that they have a definite place and level in the order of goods and values; that they are in permanent contact with the objects of the other sciences, and in a special way they come under the law of immanent and transcendent finality which binds them into an ordered whole? Let us admit, though, that when one speaks of the Christian orientation of science, one has in mind not so much science in itself as its representatives and devotees, in whom it lives, develops, and becomes manifest. Physics and chemistry also, which conscientious scientists and professional men put to use to the advantage and benefit of individuals and society, can become agents and instruments of corruption and ruin in the hands of perverse men. It is therefore all the more obvious that in medicine the supreme interest of truth and good is opposed to a presumed objective or subjective freedom from the many relations and ties which relate it to the general order. . . .

Death and Capital Punishment

The Fifth Commandment—*Non occides*—Thou shalt not kill—this synthesis of the duties regarding the life and the integrity of the human body, is rich in lessons both for the teacher in his university chair and for the practicing physician. As long as a man is not guilty, his life is intangible, and, therefore, any act directly tending to destroy it is illicit, whether it be in embryonic form or in its full development, or even at its conclusion. Only God is the lord of the life of a man not guilty of a crime punishable by death! The physician does not have the right to dispose of the life of either a child or its mother; and no one in the world, no private person, no human authority, may authorize him to proceed to its direct destruction. His office is not to destroy lives but to save them. These are fundamental and immutable principles which the Church, in the course of the last ten years, has found it necessary to proclaim repeatedly and with every clarification against opposing opinions and methods. The Catholic physician finds a secure guide in this regard, for his theoretical judgment and his practical conduct, in the resolutions and decrees of the teaching authority of the Church.

But there is in the moral order a vast field which requires of the physician particular clearness of principle and security of action: that in which ferment the mysterious energies immersed by God in the organism of man and woman for the procreation of new lives. It is a natural power, of which the Creator Himself has determined the structure and the essential forms of activity, with a precise purpose and with corresponding duties, to which man is subjected in every conscious use of that faculty. Nature's primary purpose (to which the secondary ends are essentially subordinated) in this use is the propagation of life and the education of the offspring. Only matrimony, regulated by God Himself in its essence and in its properties, assures both of these things in accordance with the welfare and the dignity of the parents no less than the children. This is the only norm which illuminates and supports all this delicate material; the norm to which in all concrete cases, in all special questions, it is necessary to refer; the norm, finally, whose faithful observance guarantees in this matter the moral and physical health of individuals and of society.

The Physician and Temptations

It should not be difficult for the physician to understand this immanent finality profoundly rooted in nature, to affirm it and apply it with intimate conviction in his scientific and practical activity. People often listen to him with more belief than to the theologian himself, when he admonishes and advises that whoever offends and transgresses the laws of nature sooner or later will have to suffer the distressing consequences in his personal value and in his physical and psychical integrity.

There is the youth who, under the impulse of newborn passions, appeals to the physician; here, the betrothed, who on the eve of their approaching marriage ask advice, which all too often they want to be contrary to nature and virtue; here, married couples, who seek from him enlightenment and assistance, or, even more, connivance, because they pretend they can find no other solution or way out of the conflicts of life excepting the willful infraction of the ties and duties inherent in the use of matrimonial relations. They try, then, to give weight to all the possible arguments or pretexts (medical, eugenic, social, and moral) to induce the physician to give advice or offer help, which will permit the satisfaction of the natural instinct, but deprive it of the possibility of achieving the aim of the generating force of life. How can he remain firm before all these assaults if he himself should be lacking clear knowledge and conviction that the Creator Himself for the good of mankind has linked the voluntary use of those natural energies to their immanent purpose with an indissoluble bond which admits of no relaxation or rupture?

Is It Permitted to the Physician to Lie?

The Eighth Commandment also has its place in the duty of physicians. Falsehood is permitted to no one according to moral law. There are, however, cases in which the physician, even if questioned, though never saying anything positively false, still cannot crudely expose the whole truth, especially when he knows that the patient would not have the strength to bear it. But there are other cases in which he has, without doubt, the duty to speak clearly; a duty before which every medical or humanitarian consideration must give way. He is not permitted to lull the patient or his relatives in an illusory security, with the danger of compromising in this way the eternal salvation of the patient or the fulfillment of obligations of justice or charity. Anyone would be in error who attempted to justify or excuse such conduct under the pretext that the physician always expresses himself in the way he considers best in the personal interest of the patient and that it is the others' fault if they take his words too literally.

The Professional Secret

Among the duties deriving from the Eighth Commandment one must also list the observance of the professional secret, which should serve and does serve not private interests only but, even more so, the common good. Conflicts may arise in this field, also, between private and public good, or among the various elements and aspects of common welfare; conflicts in which it may become extremely difficult to measure and weigh justly the pros and cons of the reasons for speaking or keeping silent. In such perplexity, the conscientious physician asks of the fundamental principles of Christian ethics the rules which will help him to choose the right path. Indeed, these, while clearly affirming the obligation of the physician to maintain professional secrecy, especially in the interests of the common good, do not, however, recognize in this an absolute value. In fact, it would not be consistent with the common good if this secrecy should be placed at the service of crime or fraud.[1]

[1] Address, Micro-Biological Union of San Luca, November 12, 1943

BIRTH CONTROL

GOD HAS MADE all the other things on earth for man, and man, as regards his being and his essence, has been created for God and not for any other creature, though as to his actions he has obligations toward the community as well. Now, the child is "man," even if he is not yet born, in the same degree and by the same title as his mother.

Furthermore, every human being, even a child in his mother's womb, has the right to life directly from God and not from his parents, from any human society or authority. Therefore, there is no man, no human authority, no science, no "indication" whatsoever, medical, eugenic, social, economic, moral, that may lend a valid juridical right for the deliberate direct disposal of an innocent human life, that is, a disposal aiming at its destruction, either as an objective or as a means to another objective, in no way, perhaps, illicit of itself. Thus, for example, to save a mother's life is a very noble aim; but the direct killing of the child as a means to that end is not licit. The direct destructions of so-called "worthless lives," before or after birth, practiced in great numbers a few years ago, cannot in any way be justified. Consequently, when that practice began, the Church expressly declared it to be contrary to natural, divine, and positive law, and therefore illicit to kill—even by order of a public authority—those who, though innocent, are nevertheless, on account of a physical or psychical deficiency, not useful to a people, but will, rather, become a burden to it. The life of an innocent creature is intangible, and any direct attempt or aggression against it is a violation of one of the fundamental laws without which safe social living is not possible.

Pains of Childbirth

Even the pains that, since original sin, a mother has to suffer to give birth to her child only draw tighter the bond that binds them: she loves it the more, the more pain it has cost her. This was expressed with a great and touching simplicity by Him Who has molded mothers' hearts: "The woman, when delivering, is in pain because her hour has arrived; but when she has given birth to her child she will not even remember the anguish suffered, because of the joy that a man was born into the world." Moreover, the Holy Ghost, through the pen of St. Paul the Apostle, also emphasizes the greatness and joy of maternity. God gives the child to the mother, but along with the gift, He makes her co-operate effectively in the opening of the flower of which He had deposited the germ in her womb, and this co-operation becomes a life which will conduct her to eternal salvation: "Women will be saved by child-bearing."

Our predecessor Pius XI, of happy memory, in his Encyclical Letter *Casti connubii,* of December 31, 1930, once again solemnly proclaimed the fundamental law governing the matrimonial act and relations between husband and wife: that any attempt on their part in the performance of the matrimonial act or in the development of its natural consequences, aiming at depriving it of its innate force and hindering the procreation of a new life, is immoral; and that no "indication" or necessity can change an intrinsically immoral act into a moral and licit act.

This precept is in full force today, as it was yesterday, and it will be so tomorrow too, and always, because it is not a simple injunction by a human law, but the expression of a natural and divine law.

Sterilization

It would be much more than a simple want of diligence in the service of life if such human attempts did not regard a single act but touched the organism itself with the intention of depriving it, by means of sterilization, of the faculty to procreate a new life.

Direct sterilization—to wit, that aiming, as a means or as an objective, to render procreation impossible—is a serious infringement of the moral law and is therefore illicit. Even the public authority has no right, on the plea of any "indication," to permit, and much less to enjoin it or have it achieved, to the prejudice of innocent beings. This principle is already asserted in the Encyclical of Pius XI concerning marriage, just referred to. Hence, when, some ten years ago, sterilization began to be ever more widely applied, the Holy See found it necessary expressly and publicly to declare that direct sterilization, permanent or temporary, of either a man or a woman, is illicit, in virtue of the natural law, from which the Church herself, as you know, has not the authority to dispense.

Natural Sterility

Nowadays, another grave problem presents itself, that is, whether, and to what extent, the obligation of being ready for the service of maternity is reconcilable with a constantly spreading recourse to the natural periods of sterility (the so-called "agenesic" periods in woman), which seems to be a clear expression of a will contrary to that precept.

Before anything else, two hypotheses have to be taken into consideration. If the application of that theory does not mean anything beyond the fact that husband and wife may make use of their matrimonial right also during the days of natural sterility, there is nothing to object to; for it is true that, by so doing, they do not prevent or jeopardize in any way the consummation of the natural act and its further natural consequences. It is precisely in this that the application of the theory of which we speak differs essentially from the abuse already mentioned, which consists in the perversion of the act itself. If, instead, one goes further, that is, permitting the performance of the matrimonial act exclusively on those days, then a husband's and wife's conduct has to be examined more attentively. Here again two hypotheses come up for our consideration. If, when contracting marriage, at least one of the couple already had the intention of restricting to the periods of sterility the matrimonial right itself, and not merely its use, so that during the other days the other partner would not even have the right to request the act, then this would imply an essential defect in the marriage consent, which would bring with it invalidation of the marriage itself, because the right deriving from the marriage contract is a permanent one, uninterrupted and not intermittent, in each of the partners with respect to the other.

If, on the other hand, the limitation of the act to the days of natural sterility refers not to the right itself but only to the use of that right, the validity of the marriage is unquestionable; however, the lawfulness of such conduct on the part of a husband and wife should be admitted or denied, according as the intention constantly to observe those periods is or is not based on sufficient and reliable moral motives. The mere fact that the partners do not vitiate the nature of the act and are also ready to accept and to bring up the child that, notwithstanding their precautions, might be born, would not of itself be sufficient to guarantee the uprightness of their intention and the unquestionable morality of their motives.

The reason is that marriage imposes a state of life which, while it confers certain rights, likewise enjoins the accomplishment of a positive task concerning that state. This being so, the general principle may be applied that a positive service may be omitted if grave motives, beyond the control of the good will of those who are under the obligation to perform it, show that its performance is inadvisable and prove that the petitioner (in this case mankind) cannot equitably claim it.

The marriage contract, which confers on husband and wife the right to satisfy the natural inclination, sets them in a specific state of life, the matrimonial status. Now, on husbands and wives, who make use of it through the specific act of their status, nature and the Creator impose the function of providing for the preservation of the human race. That is the characteristic service which gives to their status its peculiar value, the *bonum prolis*—the good of posterity. The individual and society, the people and the State, the Church itself, depend for their existence, in the order established by God, on prolific marriages. Hence, to embrace the matrimonial state, to make use continually of the faculty peculiar to it and licit only therein, and, on the other hand, to avoid its primary duty, always and deliberately, without a serious motive, would be to sin against the very meaning of married life.

Medical, Eugenic, and Social "Indications"

Serious motives, such as those not seldom appearing in medical, eugenic, and social so-called "indications," may exempt some from the positive, obligatory act for a long time and even, if necessary, for the whole duration of marriage. It follows from this that observance of the sterile periods may be licit from the moral standpoint; and in the conditions mentioned it is so indeed. If, however, according to a reasonably and equitably formed judgment, there are no such serious reasons, personal or deriving from external circumstances, the will habitually to avoid the fecundity of their union, though continuing fully to satisfy their sensuality, may only derive from a false evaluation of life and from motives not harmonizing with sound ethical canons.

Abstention

In some very delicate cases, where it cannot be pretended that the risk of maternity should be run, where it has indeed to be absolutely avoided, and where, on the other hand, observance of the agenesic periods either does not afford sufficient guarantee or has to be discarded for other reasons, any preventive manipulation and any direct attempt on the life and development of the seed is in conscience prohibited and excluded, and one course only remains, that is, abstention from any complete exercise of the natural faculty.

It will be objected that such abstention is impossible, that such heroism cannot be put into practice. Nowadays you will hear this objection, you will read it, everywhere raised even by those who, in view of their duties and qualification, ought to be able to judge very differently. The following argument is brought up as a proof: "No one is obliged to do what is impossible, and it is presumable that no reasonable legislator can want to force people by his law to do that which is impossible. For a husband and wife abstention over long periods of time is impossible. Therefore, they are not obliged to abstain; the divine law cannot have this meaning."

In this way, from partially true premises, a false conclusion is made. In order to persuade oneself of this it is sufficient to invert the terms of the argument: "God does not oblige people to do what is impossible. But God enjoins abstinence to a husband and wife if their union cannot be completed according to the rules of nature. Therefore, in these cases abstinence is possible." As confirmation of this argument we also have the doctrine of the Council of Trent, which, in the chapter on the observance, necessary and possible, of the Commandments, referring to a passage from St. Augustine, teaches: "God does not command impossible things, but while commanding, He warns you to do what you can and to ask what you cannot do, and He helps you so that you may be able."[1]

[1] Address to Obstetricians, October 29, 1951

HEREDITY, EUGENICS, AND PAINLESS BIRTH

THE LAWS OF HEREDITY are full of meaning for man. From the first moment and at the first stage of its existence, the initial cell of the new man is already astonishing in its structure and incredibly rich in the specificity of its dispositions. It is full of teleological dynamism governed by the genes, and these genes are the bases of so much happiness or unhappiness, of vitality or weakness, of achievement or failure. This consideration explains why research on heredity meets with more and more interest and points of application. An attempt is made to preserve what is good and sound, to strengthen it, promote it, and perfect it. Deterioration of hereditary factors must be prevented; deficiencies already present must, as far as is possible, be corrected, and care must be taken to prevent hereditary factors of a negative character from becoming accentuated by combination with those of a similarly oriented inferior tendency in the partner. Vice versa, factors of a positive character should be united with a similar hereditary patrimony.

Genetics

The science of genetics does not have a merely theoretical importance; it is also extremely practical. It aims at contributing to the welfare of individuals and to that of the community, to the common good. It seeks to carry out this task in two fields, genetic physiology and genetic pathology.

Experience has demonstrated that natural dispositions, good or faulty, have great influence on the upbringing of man and his future behavior. Doubtless the body with its aptitudes and organs is only the instrument, whereas the soul is the artist who plays the instrument; doubtless the skill of the artist may compensate for many a defect in the instrument; but it is better and easier to play on a perfect instrument; and when its quality falls below a set limit, it becomes quite impossible to use it—without taking into consideration the fact that, leaving comparisons aside, matter and spirit are joined into a substantial unity in man.

But, to take up this comparison once again, the science of genetics does enable us better to understand the structure and variations of the instrument and hence improve the playing. An examination of a man's lineage makes it possible, within certain limits, to diagnose the dispositions he has received in his patrimony and to prognosticate the inherited positive characteristics and, more important still, those, too, which reveal some hereditary blemish.

However limited direct influence may be on the hereditary patrimony, practical genetics is not at all reduced to the role of passive spectator. Daily life already demonstrates the extremely harmful effects of certain practices of parents in the natural transmission of life. Such proceedings, with the poisonings and the infections they cause, are to be forbidden as far as possible, and genetics looks for and points out the means of reaching this goal. Its conclusions deal particularly with combinations of patrimonies of different origins: it points out those to be encouraged, those that can be tolerated, and those that should be rejected from the point of view of genetics and eugenics. Permit Us to quote the declarations of one of the most important geneticists of the present time: in a letter that he has just sent Us, he expresses his regret that, in spite of the enormous progress it has made, genetics "from the technical and analytical point of view is floundering in a mire of doctrinal errors, such as racism, mutationism applied to phylogenesis to explain in modern terms the evolutionism of Darwin, birth control in the case of all those who have, or are presumed to have, diseases or grave defects that are hereditary, either by preventive means or by abortive practices, the compulsory prenuptial certificate, etc."

There are, in fact, certain genetic and eugenic defense measures that common morality, and Christian morality especially, must reject in principle and in practice.

Eugenic Sterilization and the Right to Marry

Among the measures that are offensive to morality is the "racism" already mentioned: *eugenic sterilization*. Our predecessor Pius XI and We Ourselves have expressly declared contrary to natural law not only eugenic sterilization, but all sterilization whatsoever of an innocent person, whether it be temporary or final, of a man or woman. Our opposition to sterilization was and remains unchangeable, for the aim and desire to suppress by sterilization a lineage bearing hereditary diseases has not disappeared with the end of "racism."

Another path leads to the same goal: *forbidding marriage,* or making it a physical impossibility, by interning those with undesirable hereditary factors. It likewise is to be rejected. The end in view is good in itself, but the means of obtaining it is an attack on the right of the individual to contract and enjoy marriage. When the bearer of some hereditary disease or deficiency is unable to conduct himself as a human being, and consequently to contract marriage, or when later he has become incapable of claiming by an act of free will the right acquired by a valid marriage, he can legitimately be prevented from begetting a new life. Outside of these cases, the forbidding of marriage and matrimonial intercourse for biological, genetic, and eugenic motives is an injustice, no matter who does the forbidding, whether an individual or public authority.

It is certainly right, and in most cases an obligation, to point out to those who are bearers of extremely undesirable hereditary factors what a burden they are about to impose on themselves, their mates, and their offspring; a burden which might become intolerable. But to advise against something is not to forbid it. There may be other reasons, especially moral and personal ones, which are so imperious that they give the right to contract and enjoy marriage even in the circumstances indicated.

To justify direct eugenic sterilization, or the alternative of internment, it is claimed that the right to marriage and to the acts which it implies is not interfered with by sterilization, even when it is prenuptial, total, and certainly final. This attempt at justification is doomed to failure. If, for a person of common sense, the fact in question is doubtful, the unfitness for marriage is also doubtful; that is the time to apply the principle that the right to marry persists as long as the contrary is not proved beyond all doubt. And so, in this case, the marriage must be permitted; but the question of its objective validity remains open. If, on the other hand, there is no doubt whatsoever as to the above-mentioned fact of sterilization, it is premature to affirm that the right to marriage is not thereby called in question and, in any case, there are good grounds for challenging the truth of this assertion.[1]

Painless Childbirth

The laws, the theory, and the technique of natural childbirth, without pain, are undoubtedly valid, but they have been elaborated by scholars who, to a great extent, profess an ideology belonging to a materialistic culture; this latter is not valid simply because the scientific results mentioned above are. It is even much less accurate to say that the scientific results are true and demonstrated as such, because their authors and the cultures from which they derive have a materialistic orientation. The criteria of truth lie elsewhere.

The convinced Christian finds nothing in his philosophical ideas and his culture that prevents him from occupying himself seriously, in theory and in practice, with the psychoprophylactic method.

There are two points which deserve to be emphasized here: Christianity does not interpret suffering and the Cross in a merely negative fashion. If the new technique spares her the sufferings of childbirth, the mother can accept it without any scruple of conscience; but she is not obliged to do so. In the case of partial success or failure, she knows that suffering can be a source of good, if she bears it with God and in obedience to His will. The life and sufferings of Our Savior, the pains which so many great men have borne and even sought and through which they have matured and risen to the summits of Christian heroism, the daily examples we see of acceptance of the Cross with resignation: all this reveals the meaning of suffering, of the patient acceptance of pain in the present plan of salvation, for the duration of this earthly life.[2]

[1] Address to the Participants of the Primum Symposium Geneticae Medicae, September 8, 1953

[2] Address to a Group of Physicians of the International Secretariat of Catholic Physicians and of the AMCI, January 8, 1956

ARTIFICIAL INSEMINATION

WHETHER HE IS CONCERNED with the human body or with man as a whole, the Christian doctor must always beware of the fascination of technology, of the temptation to use his own science and ability for purposes other than the curing of the patients entrusted to him. He will also have to guard against another temptation—this one criminal—to make the gifts of God hidden in the depth of nature subservient to ignoble interests, unavowable passions, or inhuman experiments. Unfortunately, we need not reach back very far in time to find concrete proof of these deplorable abuses.

For example, the disintegration of the atom and the production of atomic energy is one thing; quite another is its use as destroyer, which is kept beyond any control. The magnificent technical progress of modern aviation is one thing, quite another the mass use of squadrons of bombers when there is no possibility of limiting their action to strategic and military objectives. One thing, above all, is the respectful research which reveals the beauty of God in the mirror of His works, and His power in the forces of nature; quite another thing, the deification of this nature and of material forces in the negation of their Author.

The Duties of the Physician

What, instead, does the doctor who is worthy of his vocation do? He gains possession of these same forces, of these properties of nature, in order to procure with them healing, health, vigor, and

Greeting Prince Fahad al Salim al Sabah of Kuwait, June 15, 1955

Reception of Pandit Nehru and His Daughter Indira Gandhi, July 8, 1955

Cardinal Agagianian, Archbishop of Beirut, the only Cardinal to Be Born in Russia

The Greek College Presents Blessed Candles on Candlemas Day, 1955

often, what is still more precious, to prevent disease, contagion, and epidemics. In his hands the terrifying force of radioactivity is imprisoned, aimed at healing ills rebellious to any other treatment; the properties of the most virulent poisons serve to prepare efficacious remedies; better still, the germs of the most dangerous infections are variously used in serum therapy and in vaccination.

Natural and Christian morals, finally, keep their own incontrovertible rights and from them, and not from considerations of sentiment, of materialistic, naturalistic philanthropy, are derived the essential principles of medical deontology: dignity of the human body, pre-eminence of the soul over the body, brotherhood among all men, sovereign rule of God over life and destiny. An important problem which requires, no less urgently than the others, the light of Catholic moral doctrine is artificial insemination. We cannot let this occasion pass without indicating briefly, along general lines, the moral judgment which is called for on this subject.

The practice of artificial insemination, when it refers to man, cannot be considered, either exclusively or principally, from the biological and medical point of view, ignoring the moral and legal one.

Artificial insemination, outside of marriage, must be condemned as essentially and strictly immoral.

Natural law and divine positive law establish, in fact, that the procreation of a new life cannot but be the fruit of marriage. Only marriage safeguards the dignity of the spouses (principally of the wife in the present case) and their personal good. It alone provides for the well-being and education of the child.

It follows that no divergence of opinion among Catholics is admitted on the condemnation of artificial insemination outside of marriage. The child conceived in those conditions would be, by that very fact, illegitimate.

Artificial insemination produced in a marriage by the active element of a third party is equally immoral and consequently to be condemned without appeal.

Only the spouses have a reciprocal right upon each other's body to generate a new life: an exclusive, inalienable right, which cannot be ceded. And so it must be, even out of consideration for the child. On whoever gives life to a small being, nature imposes, by the very strength of that tie, the duty to keep and educate it. But no ties of origin, no moral or legal bonds of conjugal procreation, exist between the legitimate husband and the child who is the fruit of the active element of a third party (even if the husband has given his consent).

As far as the legitimacy of artificial insemination in marriage is concerned, it suffices, for the moment, to recall these principles of natural law: the simple fact that the result desired is obtained by this means does not justify the use of the means itself; nor does the desire of the husband and wife, in itself perfectly legitimate, to have a child, suffice to establish the legitimacy of resorting to the artificial insemination which would satisfy this desire.

It would be erroneous, therefore, to think that the possibility of resorting to this means might render valid a marriage between persons unable to contract it because of the *impedimentum impotentiae.*

On the other hand, it is superfluous to mention that the active element can never be obtained legitimately by means of acts against nature.

Although new methods cannot be ruled out a priori for the sole reason of their novelty, nonetheless, as far as artificial impregnation is concerned, extreme caution is not enough; it must be absolutely excluded. Saying this does not necessarily proscribe the use of certain artificial means destined only to facilitate the natural act, or to assure the accomplishment of the end of the natural act regularly performed.

Let it never be forgotten that only the procreation of a new life according to the will and the designs of the Creator brings with it, to a marvellous degree of perfection, the accomplishment of the proposed ends. It is at the same time in conformity with corporeal and spiritual nature and the dignity of the married couple, as well as with the healthy, normal development of the child.[1]

[1] Address to Physicians, September 29, 1949

MORAL OBLIGATIONS OF CATHOLIC JURISTS

WITHOUT DOUBT THE JURIST is not called upon by his profession to dedicate himself to theological speculation in order to know the object of his study; but if he knows not how to rise to the vision of supreme and transcendent reality, from whose will is derived the order of the visible universe and of that small part of it which is the human race with its immanent and morally necessary laws, it will be impossible for him to see in all its admirable unity and its most intimate spiritual depths the intricate pattern of social relationships, over which law presides, and the norms which regulate them. As the great Roman jurisconsult and orator affirmed, "*natura iuris . . . ab hominis repetenda (est) natura*—nature and the essence of law cannot but be derived from the nature of man himself." On the other hand, this nature of man cannot be known, even approximately, in its perfection, dignity, and loftiness, and in the ends which command and subordinate its actions to themselves, without recognition of the ontological connection by which it is bound to its transcendent cause. It is therefore clear that it will not be possible for the jurist to arrive at a sound conception of law, nor to achieve his own systematic arrangement of it, unless he ceases regarding man and human things without the light emanating from divinity to illuminate for him the arduous path of his research.

The error of modern rationalism has consisted precisely in the pretension to want to build the system of human laws and the general theory of law, considering the nature of man as an independent entity, which lacks every necessary reference to a superior Being, on Whose creative and controlling will he depends, in essence and action. One knows in what an inextricable maze of difficulties contemporary juridical thought has become entangled because of this initial deviation, and how the jurist who conformed to the canon set up by the so-called positivism has failed in his task, losing, with the proper knowledge of human nature, a sound conception of law, which came to lack that compelling power on man's conscience which is its primary and principal effect. Divine and human matters, which, according to Ulpian's definition, form the most general object of jurisprudence, are so closely linked that it is impossible to ignore the former without losing the exact notion of the latter.

The Specific Object of Jurisprudence

This is all the more true in that the more specific object of jurisprudence is justice and injustice, "*iusti atque iniusti scientia,*" or justice, in its high function of preserving the balance between individual and social exigencies within the bosom of the human family. Justice is not only an abstract concept, an exterior ideal, which institutions must seek to embody as far as is possible at a given historical moment; it is also and above all something immanent to man, to society and its fundamental institutions, because of that sum total of practical principles that it dictates and imposes, of those more universal rules of conduct which form part of the objective, human, and civil order established by the lofty mind of the first Maker. The knowledge of justice and injustice presupposes, therefore, a higher wisdom, which consists in knowing the order of creation and consequently its Ordainer. Law, as Thomas Aquinas taught, *est obiectum iustitiae,* is the norm in which the great fruitful idea of justice takes concrete form and expression, and as such, if it leads to God, eternal and unchangeable justice in His essence, receives from God light and clarity, vigor and strength, meaning and content.

In the exercise of his profession, the jurist moves, therefore, between the infinite and the finite, between the divine and the human, and in this necessary movement lies the nobility of the science he cultivates. His other claims to respect in the eyes of human society can be regarded as the consequence of the one already mentioned.

The Subject of Jurisprudence: Man

If the objects of his investigations are juridical norms, the subject for whom these are intended is man, the human being, who thus falls into his field of competence. And, let it be noted, not man in his lower and less noble part, who is studied by other sciences, also useful and worthy of admiration, but man in his specific capacity as a rational agent who, in order to conform to the laws of his rationality, must act guided by certain rules of conduct, either directly dictated to him by his conscience—reflection and herald of a higher law—or prescribed for him by the human authority that regulates the life of society. It is true that man does not always present himself to the jurist in the higher aspects of his rational nature, but often offers for his study his least commendable sides, his bad inclinations, his wicked perversities, guilt, and crime;

yet even where the splendor of his rationality appears tarnished, the real jurist must always see that ground of humanity from which guilt and crime can never erase the seal stamped on it by the Creator's hand.

If, then, we look at the subject of law with the eyes of the Christian faith, what a crown of light we see round his head, that crown set on him by the redemption of Christ, the blood shed to redeem him, supernatural life, to which it restored him and of which it made him a participant, and the final goal assigned to him as the end of his journey on earth. In the light of Christian faith, the subject of law is not man in his pure nature, but man raised by the Savior's grace to the supernatural order, and therefore in contact with divinity through a new life, which is the very life of God, in which man shares. His dignity, therefore, grows to infinite proportions and, in like measure, increases the nobility of the jurist who makes him the object of his science.

Conflicts of Conscience

The irreconcilable contrasts between the lofty conception of man and of law according to the Christian principles, which We have attempted to expound briefly, and juridical positivism may become the source of inner bitterness in professional life. We know well how conflicts not infrequently arise in the conscience of the Catholic jurist, desirous of remaining true to the Christian conception of law, especially when he finds himself in the position of having to apply a law which his conscience condemns as unjust. As a matter of fact, from the end of the eighteenth century—especially in the regions where persecution of the Church was rife—there have been numerous cases of Catholic magistrates who found themselves faced with the painful problem of the application of unjust laws. Therefore, We take this opportunity to enlighten the conscience of Catholic jurists by enunciating some fundamental norms.

For every sentence passed, the principle holds good that the judge cannot purely and simply disclaim all responsibility for his decision, placing it totally on the law and on its authors. These are certainly principally responsible for the effects of the law itself. But the judge, who with his sentence applies it to the particular case, is a party to it, and therefore shares the responsibility for those effects.

The judge may never with his decision oblige anyone to commit any intrinsically immoral act, that is, an act which is by its nature contrary to the law of God and of the Church.

He may in no case expressly recognize and approve of an unjust law (which, in any case, would never constitute the basis of a valid judgment before his conscience and before God). He cannot therefore pronounce a penal sentence which would be tantamount to such an approval. His responsibility would be even more grave if his sentence were to cause a public scandal.

However, not every application of an unjust law is equivalent to recognizing and approving it. In this case, the judge may—and sometimes, perhaps, must—let the unjust law take its course, when that is the only way to avoid a still greater evil. In order to avoid harm or to ensure a good of much greater importance, he may inflict a penalty for the transgression of an unjust law if it is of such a nature that the person involved is reasonably disposed to endure it, and provided the judge knows and can prudently suppose that such a sanction will be readily accepted by the transgressor, for superior reasons. In times of persecution, both priests and laymen have permitted themselves to be sentenced, without putting up any resistance, and even by Catholic magistrates, to pay fines or be deprived of their personal freedom, for infraction of unjust laws, when by so doing it was possible to preserve for the people an honest magistrature and ward off from the Church and from the faithful much more terrible calamities.

Capital Punishment and Divorce

Of course, the more gravid of consequences is the judicial sentence, the more important and general must be the good it aims to protect or the evil it aims to avoid. There are, however, cases in which the idea of compensation through the attainment of superior benefits or the banishment of greater evils cannot apply, as for instance in the death sentence. In particular, the Catholic judge may not pronounce, unless for motives of great moment, a sentence of civil divorce (where it exists) for a marriage which is valid before God and the Church. He must not forget that such a sentence, in practice, has not civil effects only, but in reality leads rather to the erroneous belief that the present bond is broken and the new one valid and binding.[1]

[1] Address to the First National Congress of Italian Catholic Jurists, November 6, 1949

SCIENCE AND RELIGION

THE MARVEL OF CREATION has challenged the admiration and intellect of all peoples for centuries. . . . The ways and means of deciphering it have caused heated arguments between the learned investigators of nature, matter, and spirit. These efforts and arguments are nothing other than the search for the truth hidden within the enigma of creation. What else, what more, does the human soul desire than truth?

Just as we do not create nature, neither do we create the truth: our doubts, our opinions, our assertions or denials do not change it. We are not the measure of truth in the world, nor of ourselves, nor of the high objective to which we are destined. Our sagacious art measures the reliability of our tools and instruments, of our apparatus and contrivances, transforms and fetters and subdues the materials which nature offers us, but it does not create them; and it must be satisfied to follow nature as the disciple follows the master whose work he imitates. When our intellect does not conform to the reality of things or is deaf to the voice of nature, it wanders in the illusion of dreams and pursues a phantom.

The Church and Scientific Progress

But not only our technical arts come from God, but also the perception of truth in our intellect, since, in the scale of creation, it stands, as it were, on the third degree in descending order, below nature and below God.

As a friend of truth, the Church admires and loves the progress of knowledge, as she does that of the arts and of everything connected with learning.

Is not the Church herself the divine progress in the world and the mother of the highest intellectual and moral progress of mankind and the civilized life of the peoples of the earth? She advances through the centuries, teacher of truth and virtue, contending against error and not against those who have wandered from the fold, not destroying but constructing. . . .

As with every art, every science serves God, because God is *scientiarum dominus*—Master of sciences—and *docet hominem scientiam*—Teacher of sciences to mankind. In His school, man has two textbooks. In the book of the universe, human reason in search of the truth studies the good things made by God; in the book of the Bible, the human intellect and good will search for a truth higher than reason, sublime as the intimate mystery of God, known only to Him. The school of God is the meeting place of philosophy and theology, of the divine word and paleontology, of the division of the light from darkness and astronomy, of the earth set in its appointed place and its rotation around the sun, of the view of God and the view of man. God's goodness, like a mother's, takes on, as it were, the hesitations of the human language to help man retain the lofty truth which He reveals to him in order to exalt him and in his study of nature and faith make him a disciple of God. The Church has also made this school her school and the platform from which she teaches. . . .

Reason and Faith

No, the homage which reason renders faith does not humiliate reason but honors it and exalts it, for the highest achievement of the progress of human civilization is that it facilitates the path of faith as it evangelizes the world. Faith is not proud, it is not a lord that tyrannizes over reason, nor does it contradict it: the seal of truth is impressed by God no differently upon faith than upon reason. Indeed, not only do they not dissent, but they help one another in turn, as We have already pointed out, since clear reason demonstrates the foundations of faith and clarifies its terms with its light, while faith preserves reason from error, widens its horizon, and enlarges it with various knowledge.[1]

It is a fact that a considerable number of men of great culture are separated from Christian thought. The universities and the general studies are not of today or of yesterday; they were born in the Middle Ages in the bosom and under the protection of the Church. Even then one sometimes found errors, heresies, antisocial theories; however, in those days, Christian thought spread its wings at the universities, forming and directing the mind. The torch of faith radiated its light, a faith that does not humiliate the intellect, and when it makes it kneel down in reverence, rather exalts it before the truth and truthfulness of God. For it is God Who, in the admirable accord of the science of reason with divine science, renders the human intellect angelic. But what have been the results of the slow work of spiritual dissolution originating in pagan humanism, in the Enlightenment, in the philosophies of the eighteenth century, in the idealism and positivism of the nineteenth, against which the reality of the world and of man cries out? What advantages and progress have society, the family, and the human individual derived from them? Look at university culture. How many fields of study and scientific research have developed and expanded without any contact with Catholic thought, without taking into account the great fact of supernatural revelation, expanding in a sphere which, if not always antireligious, at least ignores religion? Out of them has come a de-Christianization of the spirit in many of the older generation who are called upon to guide their brothers, to enlighten others, to think for them and direct them in life, a de-Christianization of which we taste today the bitter fruit.

By this divorce and antagonism between science and religion, truth cannot be obscured or cast down from her throne of light, because she herself is light and throne, vestige and radiance of the inaccessible light in which God has His throne, and from which, like two streams from the same source, the truths of reason and the truths of faith descend to man. There is never a quarrel between them, they are sisters of unequal beauty. They do not disdain, nay, they love to show themselves friends in the human mind, eager for all flashes of truth, manifest and hidden: thus the great and sublime geniuses of the Christian centuries were content to make their intellects the handmaid of faith and bow their heads before "the shame that was Golgotha."[2]

Rediscovery of God Through Science

Contrary to rash statements in the past, the more true science advances, the more it discovers God, almost as though He were standing, vigilant and waiting, behind every door which science opens. Furthermore, We wish to say that not only does the philosophical thinker benefit from this progressive discovery of God, achieved in the increase of knowledge—and how could he do otherwise?—but those also profit who participate in the new discoveries or who make them the object of their considerations. The genuine philosophers especially benefit from it, since, by using the scientific advances as a springboard for their rational speculations, they can achieve greater security in their conclusions, clearer illustrations in possible obscurity, more convincing support in finding ever more satisfactory answers to difficulties and objections.

Nature and Basis of Proofs for the Existence of God

Thus directed and guided, the human intellect moves to meet that demonstration of the existence of God, which Christian wisdom recognizes in the philosophical arguments weighed through the centuries by giants of learning and, which is well known in the presentation of the "five paths" which the Angelic Doctor St. Thomas offers as the sure and expeditious itinerary of the mind to God. Philosophical arguments, We have said; but not for that aprioristic, as an ungenerous and self-contradictory positivism has accused them of being. They are based upon concrete realities ascertained by the senses and sciences, even if they acquire conclusive strength only from the vigor of natural reason.

In this manner, philosophy and the sciences develop with analogous and compatible methods, taking advantage of empirical and reasonable elements in differing measures and working together in harmonious unity toward the discovery of the truth.

But if the primitive experience of the ancients was able to offer sufficient arguments to reason to demonstrate the existence of God, now, with the amplification and deepening of the field of experience itself, the imprint of the Eternal upon the visible world is all the more splendid and radiantly visible. It seems profitable, therefore, to re-examine the classical proofs of St. Thomas on the basis of the new scientific discoveries, especially those based upon the movement and order of the universe; to consider, that is, if and to what extent the more profound knowledge of the structure of the macrocosm and the microcosm contributes to the reinforcement of philosophic arguments. On the other hand, it is not unprofitable to see if and to what point these arguments, as is not infrequently affirmed, have been shaken by the fact that modern physics has formulated new fundamental principles, abolished or modified ancient concepts, whose meaning was perhaps in the past adjudged fixed and definite, as, for example, time, space, movement, causality, substance, concepts of the greatest importance for the question that now holds our attention. Rather than a revision of the philosophic proofs, it is a question of scrutinizing the physical bases from which those arguments derive—and We must necessarily limit Ourselves to only a few for reasons of space. But there is no fear of surprises: science itself remains firmly grounded in that world which today, as yesterday, presents itself in those five "modes of being" from which the philosophic demonstration of the existence of God takes its motives and force.

Two Essential Hallmarks of the Cosmos

Of these "modes of being" of the world which surrounds us, perceived with more or less understanding, but with equal evidence, by the philosopher and the common intelligence, there are two which the modern sciences have sounded, verified, and probed wonderfully and beyond all expectation:

The mutability of things, including their beginning and their end.

The order of finality which shines in every corner of the cosmos.

The contribution made by the sciences to the two philosophical demonstrations is truly notable; and upon them hinge and are constituted the first and fifth ways. Physics especially has contributed to the first an inexhaustible mine of experience, revealing the fact of mutability in the profound recesses of nature, where before now no human mind could ever even suspect its existence and amplitude, and furnishing a multiplicity of empirical facts which gave highly valid support to the philosophical reasoning.

We say support, because the very direction of these transformations, while verified by modern physics, seems to Us to surpass the value of a simple confirmation and almost attains the structure and the level of physical argument which is largely new, and more acceptable, persuasive, and agreeable to many minds.

With equal richness, the sciences, especially astronomy and biology, have recently supplied to the argument of order such a wealth of knowledge and such an intoxicating vision, as it were, of the conceptual unity which animates the cosmos, and of the finality which directs its march, as to give to modern man in advance that joy which Dante imagined in the empyrean Heaven when he saw how "all that is dispersed through the universe is united by love in the mind of God."

Providence has disposed that the idea of God, so essential to the life of each man, while it can be easily grasped by a simple glance at the world so that not to comprehend the voice of nature is sheer foolishness, shall receive confirmation from every deepening of the understanding and progress in the field of scientific knowledge.

We wish, therefore, to give a few rapid examples of the precious service which modern sciences render to the demonstration of the existence of God. We limit Ourselves first to the fact of mutations, revealing principally the amplitude, the vastness, and, as it were, the totality which modern physics meets with in the inanimate cosmos. Then we shall pause for a look at the significance of their direction, which has been also ascertained. It will be as though one listened to a concerto within the immense universe, which sings "the glory of Him Who moves all things."

The Mutability of the Cosmos

It is truly astonishing at first glance to see how the knowledge of the fact of mutability has steadily gained ground in both the macrocosm and the microcosm as the sciences have gradually progressed, almost confirming with new proofs the theory of Heraclitus: "Everything flows."

Daily experience demonstrates the enormous quantity of transformations in the world, near and far, which surrounds us, especially the local movements of bodies. But in addition to these true and actual local motions, multiform chemicophysical changes are equally easy for us to see, as, for example, the mutation of the physical state of water in its three phases of vapor, liquid, and ice; the profound chemical effects brought about by the use of fire, the knowledge of which goes back to prehistoric ages; the disintegration of stone and the corruption of vegetable and animal bodies. To this common experience natural science was added, which teaches us to understand these and other similar events as processes of destruction or construction of corporeal substances in their chemical elements, that is to say, in their smallest parts, the chemical atoms. It further teaches us that this chemicophysical mutability is in no way restricted to terrestrial bodies, according to the belief of the ancients, but is extended to all bodies of our solar system and the great universe, which the telescope, and, even more, the spectroscope, have shown to be formed of the same kind of atoms.

Against the indisputable mutability of nature, including inanimate beings, there arose the enigma of the unexplored microcosm. It seemed, indeed, that inorganic matter, as opposed to the animated world, was in a certain sense immutable. Its smallest parts, the chemical atoms, could certainly unite among themselves in the most various ways, but it seemed that they enjoyed the privilege of an eternal stability and indestructibility, issuing unchanged from every chemical synthesis and analysis. A hundred years ago, elementary particles were still believed to be simple, indivisible, and indestructible. The same was thought of the energies and material forces of the cosmos, especially on the basis of the fundamental laws of the conservation of mass and energy. Some naturalists considered themselves authorized to the extent of formulating in the name of their science a fantastic monistic philosophy, the inglorious memory of which is bound to the name of Ernst Haeckel, among others. But during his own times, toward the end of the last century, this oversimplified conception of the chemical atom was also upset by modern science. The growing knowledge of the periodical system of chemical elements, the discovery of the corpuscular irradiation of radioactive elements, and many other similar facts have demonstrated that the microcosm of the chemical atom with dimensions in the order of one ten-millionth of a millimeter is a theater of continual mutation, no less than the macrocosm.

Mutability in the Electronic Sphere

The character of mutability was first verified in the electronic sphere. From the electronic structure of the atom, irradiations of light and heat emanate, which are absorbed by external bodies in a manner corresponding to the level of energy of the electronic orbits. In the exterior parts of this sphere the ionization of the atom is carried out as well as the transformation of energy and the analysis of chemical combinations. It was supposed, however, that these chemicophysical transformations still left one refuge for stability, because they had not reached the nucleus itself of the atom, home of the mass and the positive electric charge, by which the place of the chemical atom in the natural system of the elements is determined; and it almost seemed that the type of the absolutely stable and invariable had been met.

Mutability in the Nucleus

But already in the early days of the twentieth century, the observation of radioactive processes which are referable, in a last analysis, to the spontaneous dissolution of the nucleus, indicated that such a type did not exist. With the instability of the known aspects of nature verified as far as its most profound recesses, there was one fact which left investigators perplexed, because it seemed that the atom was impregnable at least to human forces, since in principle all the attempts to accelerate or arrest the natural radioactive dissolution, even the splitting of the nonactive nuclei, had failed. The first rather modest splitting of a nucleus (of nitrogen) goes back a bare three decades, and only for the past few years has it been possible, after great efforts, to bring about, in considerable quantities, processes of formation and decomposition of nuclei. Although this result, which, in so far as it serves the purposes of peace, will certainly be a matter of pride for our century, can be considered only a first step in the field of practical nuclear physics, nevertheless, it lends weight to our consideration: the atomic nuclei are certainly, for many orders of magnitude, less active and more stable than the ordinary chemical compositions, but notwithstanding that, they are also in general subject to similar laws of transformation, and therefore mutable.

At the same time, it has been discovered that such processes have the greatest importance in the economy of the energy of the fixed stars. At the center of our sun, for example, according to Bethe, a temperature which averages around twenty million degrees centigrade is reached, a recurring chain reaction in itself in which four nuclei of hydrogen are joined to a nucleus of helium. The energy which is thus freed compensates for the loss due to the irradiation of the sun itself. In modern physics laboratories also, it is possible to bring about transformations of nuclei by means of a bombardment with particles furnished with great energy, and with neutrons. This has been accomplished with the uranium atom, for example. In this connection, the effects of cosmic radiation should be mentioned, which can split the heaviest atoms, not infrequently giving off entire swarms of subatomic particles.

We wished to cite only a few examples, enough to place beyond doubt the definite mutability of the inorganic world, large and small: the thousandfold transformations of the forms of energy, especially in the chemical decomposition and combinations in the macrocosm, and no less the mutability of the chemical atoms as far as the subatomic particles of their nuclei.

The Eternally Immutable

The scientist of today, penetrating with his investigations more deeply into nature than his predecessor of a hundred years ago, knows that inorganic matter in its very marrow, in a manner of speaking, is stamped with the mark of mutability and therefore its being and its existence demand an entirely different reality and one that is by its nature immutable.

As in a painting in chiaroscuro the figures stand out from the dark background, obtaining in this manner alone the full effect of modelling and of life, so the image of the eternally immutable emerges clear and resplendent from the torrent that carries away with it all the material things in the macro- and microcosms and whirls them into an intrinsic mutability which never stops. The scientist who stands on the edge of this immense torrent finds relief in that cry of truth with which God defines Himself: "I am Who am," and Whom the Apostle praises as *"Pater luminum, apud quem non est transmutatio neque vicissitudinis obumbratio*—the Father of lights, with whom there is no change nor shadow of alteration."

The Direction of the Transformations

But modern science has not only enlarged and deepened our knowledge of the reality and magnitude of the mutability of the cosmos; it has also offered us valuable indications concerning the direction according to which the processes of nature are carried out. While a hundred years ago, especially after the discovery of the law of constants, it was thought that the natural processes were reversible and therefore, according to the principles of strict causality—or, rather, determination—an ever recurring renewal and rejuvenation of the cosmos was considered possible. With the law of entropy, discovered by Rudolf Clausius, it became known that the spontaneous natural processes are always related to a diminution of the free and utilizable energy, which in a closed material system must finally lead to a cessation of the processes on the macroscopic scale.

This fatal destiny, which only hypotheses, sometimes far too gratuitous ones such as that of the continuous renewal of creation, forcibly try to deny, but which instead comes from positive scientific experience, eloquently postulates the existence of a necessary Being.

In the microcosm, this law, which is actually statistical, is not applicable, and furthermore, at the time of its formulation, hardly anything was known of the structure and behavior of the atom. However, the most recent investigations of the atom and the quite unexpected development of astrophysics have made surprising discoveries possible in this field. Results can be mentioned here only briefly; they indicate that in the atomic and intra-atomic development a sense of direction is clearly noticeable.

In order to illustrate this fact it suffices to recall the already mentioned example of the behavior of solar energy. The electronic structure of the chemical atoms in the photosphere of the sun gives off each second a gigantic quantity of radiant energy into the surrounding space, an energy that does not return. The loss is compensated for from the interior of the sun by means of the formation of helium from hydrogen. The energy which is thus liberated derives from the mass of hydrogen nuclei, of which in this process a small part (seven per cent) is converted into equivalent radiation. The process of compensation is carried out, therefore, at the expense of the energy which originally existed as mass in the nuclei of hydrogen. Thus this energy, in the course of billions of years, is slowly but irreparably transformed into radiation. A similar phenomenon occurs in all radioactive processes, whether natural or artificial. Here too, then, in the narrow confines of the microcosm itself, we meet with a law which indicates the direction of evolution and which is analogous to the law of entropy in the macrocosm. The direction of spontaneous evolution is determined by means of the diminution of the energy utilizable in the structure and the nucleus of the atom, and up to now no processes have been noted which could compensate or cancel this diminution by means of spontaneous formation of nuclei of high energetic value.

The Universe and Its Development

If, then, the scientist turns his gaze from the present state of the universe to the future, however far off, he will be forced to realize that the world is growing old, both in the macrocosm and in the microcosm. In the course of billions of years, even the quantity of atomic nuclei, which is apparently inexhaustible, loses its utilizable energy and matter approaches, to speak figuratively, the state of a spent and scorified volcano. And the thought presents itself inescapably: if the present cosmos, today so pulsating with rhythm

The State and Quality of Original Matter

With equal earnestness and freedom of investigation and verification, learned men, in addition to the question of the age of the cosmos, have applied their audacious talents to another question which we have already mentioned and which is certainly much more difficult, and that is the problem concerning the state and quality of primitive matter. According to the theories which are taken as a basis, the relative calculations differ considerably one from the other. Nevertheless, the scientists agree in holding that not only the mass but also the density, the pressure, and the temperature must have attained degrees of enormous intensity, as can be seen in the recent work of A. Unsöld, director of the Observatory in Kiel. Only under these conditions can one comprehend the formation of the heavy nuclei and their relative frequency in the periodical system of the elements.

On the other hand, the eager mind, in its search for truth, rightfully insists upon asking how matter came to be in a state so unlike that of our common experience of today, and what preceded it. One waits in vain for an answer from natural science, which honestly declares that this is an insoluble enigma. It is true that this is asking too much of natural science as such; but it is also true that the human spirit versed in philosophical speculation is able to penetrate the problem more profoundly.

It is undeniable that a mind illuminated and enriched by modern scientific knowledge, which calmly evaluates this problem, is led to break the circle of a matter preconceived as completely independent and autochthonous—either because uncreated or self-created—and to acknowledge a Creative Spirit. With the same clear and critical gaze with which he examines and judges facts, he also catches sight of and recognizes the work of the omnipotent Creator, Whose power, aroused by the mighty "fiat" pronounced billions of years ago by the Creative Spirit, unfolded itself in the universe and, with a gesture of generous love, called into existence matter, fraught with energy. Indeed, it seems that the science of today, by going back in one leap millions of centuries, has succeeded in being a witness to that primordial *Fiat Lux,* when, out of nothing, there burst forth with matter a sea of light and radiation, while the particles of chemical elements split and reunited in millions of galaxies.

It is true that the facts verified up to now are not arguments of absolute proof of creation in time as are those which are drawn from metaphysics and revelation, in so far as they concern creation in its widest sense, and from revelation alone in so far as they concern creation in time. The facts pertinent to natural sciences, to which We have referred, still wait for further investigation and confirmation, and the theories founded upon them have need of new developments and proofs, in order to offer a secure basis to a line of reasoning which is, of itself, outside the sphere of the natural sciences.

Notwithstanding this, it is worth noting that modern exponents of the natural sciences consider the idea of the creation of the universe entirely reconcilable with their scientific conception, and indeed they are spontaneously brought to it by their researches, though only a few decades ago such a "hypothesis" was rejected as absolutely irreconcilable with the present status of science. As late as 1911, the celebrated physicist Svante Arrhenius declared that "the opinion that something can proceed from nothing is in contrast with the present status of science, according to which matter is immutable." Similar to this is Plate's affirmation: "Matter exists. Nothing proceeds from nothing: in consequence matter is eternal. We cannot admit the creation of matter."

Conclusion

What, then, is the importance of modern science in the argument for the existence of God drawn from the mutability of the cosmos? By means of exact and detailed investigations into the macrocosm and the microcosm, it has widened and deepened to a considerable extent the empirical foundation upon which the argument is based and from which we conclude a self-existent Being immutable by nature. Further, it has followed the course and the direction of cosmic developments, and just as it has envisioned the fatal termination, so it has indicated their beginning in time at a period about five billion years ago, confirming with the concreteness of physical proofs the contingency of the universe and the well-

extremely small, it was never seriously thought that they might become important even from a practical point of view. Today, on the other hand, this question has taken on an unexpected aspect as a consequence of the results of artificial radioactivity. It has in fact been established that in the splitting a uranium atom undergoes if it is bombarded by a neutron, two or three neutrons are freed, each of which may meet and smash another uranium atom. In this way the effects are multiplied, and it may happen that the growing number of collisions of neutrons with uranium atoms increases in a short time the number of freed neutrons and, proportionally, the sum of energy developed from them, to an extent so great that it is almost inconceivable. A special calculation shows that, by this reaction, a cubic meter of uranium oxide powder, in less than a hundredth of a second, develops enough energy to lift a weight of a billion tons to a height of 27 kilometers: an amount of energy which could supplant for many years the activity of all the great electric power stations in the world. Planck ends with the observation that, although the technical utilization of such a tempestuous process cannot yet be envisaged, it nevertheless opens the way to serious possibilities, so that the thought of the construction of a uranium machine cannot be regarded as merely utopian. It is important above all, however, to prevent this reaction from taking place as an explosion, and to brake its course by apt precautionary chemical means. Otherwise, a dangerous catastrophe might occur, not only in the locality itself but also for our whole planet.

The Higher Laws of Life

If now from the boundless realm of the inorganic we elevate ourselves to the spheres of vegetative and sensitive life, we find there a new world of laws in the property, the multitude, the variety, the beauty, the order, the quality, and the utility of the various forces of nature that are part of our globe. Beside many laws of the inorganic world, we meet also special higher laws, laws peculiar to life, which cannot be reduced to the purely physicochemical ones, so that it is impossible to consider living beings as mere sums of physicochemical components. Nature opens up to us here a marvellous new horizon; let it be enough for Us to mention as examples: the laws of the development of organisms, the laws of external and internal sensations, and, above all, the fundamental pyschophysical law. Higher spiritual life, too, is regulated by natural laws, for the most part of such a quality that to define them precisely becomes more difficult the higher they stand in the order of being.

The Hidden Laws of Nature

This admirable and ordered system of qualitative and quantitative, particular and general laws of the macrocosm and the microcosm, is today largely unveiled in its intricacy to the scientist's eyes. And why do We say unveiled? Because it is not projected or constructed by us into nature, thanks to some innate subjective form of consciousness or of the human intellect, nor is it created purposely on behalf and for the use of such an economy of thought and study, that is, to facilitate our knowledge of things; nor is it, finally, the fruit or the conclusion of agreements or understandings among scientists studying nature. Natural laws exist, so to speak, incarnate and secretly operative within nature, and we, by observation and experiment, look for them and discover them.

It cannot be said that matter is not a reality, but an abstraction fashioned by physics; that nature is in itself unintelligible and that the world that can be apprehended by the senses is a world apart, where the phenomenon, which is appearance of the exterior world, gives us a vague notion only of the reality of the things it hides. No: nature is reality, recognizable reality. If things seem to be and are mute, they have, however, a language that speaks to us, that emerges from their bosom, like water from a perennial spring. This language is their causality which reaches our senses with the sight of colors and movement, with the sound of metals, the roar of whirlwinds, and the cries of animals, with the sweetness and the bitterness of honey and gall, with the scent of flowers, with the weight and temperature of their material substance, impressing upon us an image or likeness which is the vehicle for our intellect to lead us to the reality of things. Hence we speak not of the image or likeness of our intellect, but of the things themselves; and we can distinguish the phenomenon of the world of the senses from the substance of things, the appearance of gold from the gold itself, as the appearance of bread from bread itself, from whose substance we make food in order to assimilate and identify it with the substance of the body itself. The movement of things toward us calls forth an image in us; without an image there can be no conformity of our intellect with real things, and without an image knowledge becomes impossible; and we cannot call anything true unless it has some equivalent in our intellect. The things from which our mind takes its knowledge provide measurements to our mind and to the laws we find in them and take from them; but they, in turn, are measured by that eternal divine intellect which embraces all things created, as the mind of the craftsman embraces every work of his art. What do the hand and the brain of the scientist do? They discover them, reveal them, distinguish them, and classify them, not like one who follows flying birds, but like one who is in possession of them, and is investigating their nature and intrinsic properties.

When, in 1869, Lothar Meyer and Mendeleev arranged the chemical elements in that simple scheme which today is recognized as the natural system of the elements, they were deeply convinced that they had found a regular order, based on their properties and internal tendencies, a classification suggested by nature, the progressive development of which promised the most penetrating discoveries regarding the structure and essence of matter. In fact, modern atomic research began from that point. . . . This is only one example among many, and therefore the most inspired scientists of the past and present have come to the lofty conclusion that they are heralds of a truth identical and the same for all peoples and races that walk the earth and look up at the sky; a truth resting, in its essence, on an *adaequatio rei et intellectus,* which is nothing but the acquired conformity, more or less perfect, more or less complete, of our intellect with the objective reality of natural things, in which the truth of our knowledge consists.

But do not be mistaken, like those philosophers and scientists who thought that our cognitive faculties know only their own mutations and sensations, so that they were induced to say that our intellect arrived at knowledge only from the images of things, and, therefore, that only the images of things, and not the things themselves, were the object of our science and of the laws we formulate with respect to nature. A manifest error!

Science, exalted by a Copernicus and a Galileo, a Kepler and a Newton, a Volta and a Marconi, and other famous and distinguished investigators of the physical world that surrounds us externally, would accordingly amount to a beautiful creation of daydreaming and a beautiful phantasm of physical knowledge; appearance would take the place of the reality and truth of things; and it would be just as true to assert as to deny the same thing. But no; science knows not dreams or images of things, but the things themselves through the images we receive from them, because, as the Angelic Doctor, following Aristotle, has taught, a stone cannot be in our mind, but the image or figure of the stone can—the image which it produces, a true likeness, in our senses and then in our intellect, so that by this likeness it can be, and is, in our mind and in our study and make us return to it and to reality. Even recent research in experimental psychology testifies, or rather confirms, that these likenesses are not the mere product of autonomous, subjective activity, but psychic reactions to stimuli independent of the subject, coming from the things themselves; reactions in conformity with the different qualities and properties of things, which vary with the variation of the stimulus.

The images, therefore, which natural things, by way of light and heat, or by way of sound, taste, and smell, or by any other means, impress on the organs of our senses and which, through the inner senses, arrive at our intellect, are nothing but the instrument provided us by nature, our first teacher of knowledge, to make herself known to us; but it is no less true that we can examine, study, investigate this instrument and think about these images and how much they present to us of nature, and the way in which they become our sources of knowledge of the world which surrounds us. From the act of cognition by which our intellect understands a stone, we pass on to the act of understanding how our intellect understands a stone: an act which follows the first, since man, born without innate ideas and without recollections of a previous life, enters the world devoid of images and knowledge—born and created, as We have already recalled, "with his senses only, to learn what he later will do in the light of reason."

The Spectacle of the Earth

Admire, O probers of nature and of the laws that govern it, in the center of the material universe the greatness of man, to whose first encounter with light, greeted by his infant wailing, God holds open the spectacle of the earth and the firmament with all the marvels to enchant him and attract his innocent eyes! What is this spectacle if not the fundamental and first object of all human knowledge, which embarks from there with thousands upon thousands of inquiries with which the teacher nature entices again and again the avidity of our senses?

You wonder at yourselves; you scrutinize your inner acts, you withdraw within yourselves to seek their sources, and you find them in these internal senses, in these powers and faculties, which you make the object of a new science of yourselves, of your intimate rational nature, of your feeling, your intellect, and your will. And so we have the science of man and of his corporal and psychic laws, anatomy, physiology, medicine, psychology, ethics, politics, and that sum total of sciences which, even with all its errors, is a hymn to God Who, when He molded man, breathed into him a vital spirit, superior to that of other living beings, making him into His image and likeness. Thus the material extrinsic macrocosm has a great deal to say to the spiritual intrinsic microcosm: one and the other in their operating power are supremely regulated by the Author of the laws of matter and spirit. But the changes of the spirit, which listens to the voice and the marvels of the universe, are sometimes terrible, sometimes give it vertigo, sometimes raise it powerfully and make it take strides, also in the progress of science, which are more gigantic than the regular movements of the planets and the constellations in the heavens, to the point of sublimating it from the material physical world of its study to the spiritual world beyond the created one to praise "Love that moves the sun and all the other stars."

This love, which has created, moves, and governs the universe, also rules and directs the history and progress of all humanity, and guides everything toward an end, hidden from our thought by the mist of time, but fixed forever by Him for that glory which the heavens show forth and which He awaits from the love of man, whom He has permitted to fill the earth and subdue it with his labor. May this love arouse and direct the desire and the good will of the powerful and of all men to become brethren, to act in peace and justice, to be inflamed by the fire of the immense, beneficial charity of God, and cease drenching in blood and filling with devastation and tears this earth, on which all of us, under whatever sky, have been placed to struggle as the children of God, for an eternal life of happiness.[1]

[1] Address at the Inauguration of the Seventh Year of the Pontifical Academy of Sciences, February 22, 1943

THE ATOMIC AGE

ON OUR GLOBE, under our eyes, man appears master and potent above all the natural living creatures—man, to whom God assigned the duty to multiply and to populate the earth and procure the bread on which he lives; therefore, it is not astonishing that the great philosopher Aristotle should compare the human soul to the hand, the organ before all other organs. Everything, in fact, we owe to the hand: cities and fortresses, monuments, books of knowledge, of science, of art and poetry, the inheritance and patrimony of libraries and of human civilization. Similarly, the soul has been given to man, one might say, in place of all sorts of things so that he might procure, in some way, all these things, inasmuch as our soul can receive through the senses and intellect all the shapes or images of the things themselves.

Knowledge of Natural Laws and Domination of Natural Forces

The genuine law of nature which the scientist formulates with patient observation and diligence in his laboratory is much more and better than a mere description or intellectual calculation, which considers only phenomena and not the real substances with their properties. It does not stop at, nor is it satisfied by, the appearance and the image of senses, but penetrates into the depths of reality, searches and discovers the intimate hidden forces of the phenomena, manifests their activity and relationships.

It is therefore easy to understand that the knowledge of the laws of nature makes it possible for man to dominate the natural forces and place them at his service in the highly advanced modern technology. Only in this way can human thought elevate itself to understand how the regular order of the spectroscopic lines, which the physicist observes and distinguishes today in his laboratory, will disclose perhaps tomorrow to the astrophysicist a deeper vision and knowledge of the mysteries of the composition and development of the celestial bodies.

Thus, from the foundation of the law of nature, with the active help of modern technological means, and by the positive and true knowledge of the internal tendencies of the elements and of their effects in the natural phenomena, the scientist proceeds, against all difficulties and obstacles, to further discoveries, pursuing his research with constancy and perseverance.

The most grandiose example of the results of such intense activity seems to be found in the fact that man's relentless efforts have finally succeeded in reaching a deeper knowledge of the laws which concern the formation and disintegration of the atom, and in that way to master experimentally, up to a certain point, the release of the powerful energy which emanates from many such processes, and all this not in submicroscopic quantity, but in truly gigantic measure.

The use of a great part of the internal energy of the nucleus of uranium has become a reality and has had its application in the making of the "atom bomb" or "nuclear energy bomb," the most terrible weapon which human mind has conceived up to date.

In this state of affairs We cannot refrain from expressing a thought which constantly weighs upon Our soul, as well as upon that of all who have a true sense of humanity; and in this connection We recall the words of St. Augustine in his treatise *De Civitate Dei,* where he talks about the horrors of war, even of a just war: "Of which evils"—he writes—"if I were to narrate, as it should be, the many and manifold devastations, the harsh and cruel sufferings, although it would be impossible to do justice to the subject, when would we reach the end of the long dispute? Whoever considers with sorrow these horrible and fatal evils, must confess their misery; but whoever endures them and thinks of them without anguish in his soul, much more miserably believes himself to be happy, because he has also lost human feeling." But if the wars of that period already justify such a severe judgment of the Great Doctor, with what words should We judge at present those which struck our generations and bent to the service of their work of destruction and extermination a technology incomparably more advanced? What misfortunes should humanity expect from a future conflict, if it should prove to be impossible to arrest or curb the use of ever newer and ever more surprising scientific inventions?

Conquests of the Human Intellect

But putting aside, for the moment, the use of atomic energy in war, and in the confident hope that it be directed instead solely to projects of peace, it must be considered as a truly inspired investigation and application of those laws of nature which regulate the intimate essence and activity of inorganic matter.

In truth, properly speaking, this involves only one single great law of nature, which manifests itself above all in the so-called "periodic system of the elements."

Up to a short time ago, science and technology had been interested almost exclusively in the problems regarding the synthesis and analysis of molecules and chemical compounds; now, instead, the interest is concentrated on the analysis and synthesis of the atom and of its nucleus. Above all, furthermore, the work of the scientists will have no rest until it finds an easy and sure way to govern the process of splitting the atomic nucleus, in order to make its very rich sources of energy serve the progress of civilization.

Amazing conquests of the human intellect, which scrutinizes and investigates the laws of nature, carrying humanity with it along new paths! Can one envisage a more exalted concept?

Idea and Design of God

But law means order; and universal law means order in great things as well as small. It is an order deriving immediately from the intimate tendencies innate in natural things; an order that nothing can create by itself or give of itself to itself, as no being can give itself to itself; an order that signifies the Order of Reason in a Spirit which has created the universe and on which "depend Heaven and the whole of nature"; an order which those tendencies and energies received as they came into being and through which both collaborate for a well-ordered world.

This marvellous assemblage of natural laws, which the human spirit, with tireless observation and accurate study, discovered, adding victories upon victories over the occult resistances of the forces of nature, what else is it but an image, though pale and imperfect, of the great idea and of the great divine design, which in the mind of God the Creator is conceived as a law of this universe since the days of His eternity? Then, in the inexhaustible thinking of His wisdom, He prepared the heavens and the earth, and then, creating the light on the abysses of chaos, cradle of the universe also created by Him, He gave a beginning to motion and to the flight of time and of centuries, and called into being, into life and activity, all things according to their species and their kind, to the most imponderable atom. How rightly every intellect which contemplates and penetrates the heavens and weighs the stars and earth should exclaim, turning to God: *"Omnia in mensura et numero et pondere disposuisti*—You have disposed everything in measure and number and weight!"

The scientist almost feels the palpitation of this eternal wisdom, when his research reveals to him that the universe is formed as in one casting in the boundless foundry of time and space. Not only the starry heavens shine, composed of the same elements, but they even obey the same great and fundamental cosmic laws, always and wherever they appear, in their internal and external action. The same laws of gravitation and of the pressure of radiation determine the quantity of mass for the formation of the solar bodies in the immensity of the universe up to the farthest nebulous spirals; the same mysterious laws of the atomic nucleus regulate, through atomic composition and disintegration, the economy of the energy of all fixed stars.

This absolute unity of design and government which manifests itself in the inorganic world you find no less grandiose in the living organisms. What else does a simple look at the universal and common structure of the organisms and at the most recent discoveries and conclusions of anatomy and comparative physiology show you? Take the construction of a skeleton of a higher living being with analogous organs, and especially the disposition and function of sensitive organs—for instance, of the eye from the simplest forms to the very perfect visual organ of man; take, in the whole realm of living creatures, the fundamental laws of assimilation, metabolism, and generation. Does not all this indeed show a general and magnificent unified concept, realized and resplendent in various forms and in very many different ways? Is this not perhaps the closed and absolutely fixed unity of natural laws?

Divine Government of the Universe and Miracles

Yes; it is a unity closed with the key of that universal order of things against which, inasmuch as it depends on the first Cause of a Creative God, God Himself cannot act; because, if He should do so, He would operate against His own prescience or His will or His goodness; now, in Him "there is no change, nor the shadow of variation." But if this order is considered as dependent on secondary causes, God possesses its key and can leave it closed or open it and operate beyond it. Could it be that God, in creating the universe, made Himself subject to the order of secondary inferior causes? Is not this order, indeed, subject to Him, emanating from Him, not as a necessity of nature, but from arbitrary will? Hence He can act beyond the instituted order when He pleases; for instance, by working the effects of secondary causes without recourse to them, or producing other effects, to which they do not extend. What works then are these? They are works of which God alone holds the key in His secret and which He reserved for Himself in the passage of time amid the particular order of subordinated causes.

Before such works, extraordinary either because of the substance of the fact itself, or because of the person in which they manifest themselves, or because of the manner and order in which they are accomplished, people and scientists stand astonished. The miracle is born when the effects are manifest and the cause concealed. But the ignorance of the hidden cause, which astonishes the unbeliever, sharpens the eye of the faithful and of the learned, who, within certain limits, know and measure how far the work of nature, with its laws and forces, reaches; beyond that reach they see the work of a superior hidden and omnipotent hand, that hand which created the universal order of things, and in the process of the particular orders of cause and effect marked the moment and circumstances of its marvellous intervention.

This divine government of the universe certainly cannot but arouse a feeling of admiration and enthusiasm in the scientist, who in his research discovers and recognizes the traces of the wisdom of the Creator and supreme Legislator of Heaven and earth, Who with the hand of an invisible pilot guides all the creatures "to different ports—through the great sea of being—each one endowed with the instinct that carries it."

Yet, what are the tremendous laws of nature if not a shadow and mere idea of the depth and immensity of the divine design in the grandiose temple of the universe? Often—We have to confess Our human weakness—before the vision of the things and images of Our senses, that thought becomes dim and retreats; but if the thought of God enters the work of the scientist, he does not confuse it with the movements or images that he sees in or outside of himself; and that disposition of soul to search for and recognize God gives him, in his laborious study, the proper enthusiasm and copious compensation for all the labors endured in the interest of research and discovery, and, far from making him proud and conceited, teaches him humility and modesty.

Certainly, the more deeply the cultivator of knowledge and science pushes his research into the wonders of nature, the more he feels his insufficiency to penetrate and exhaust the wealth of the design of the divine construction and of the laws and norms which govern it. . . .

Further Progress of Science

Incessant is the progress of science. It is true that the successive states of its progress have not always followed the path which from first observations and discoveries leads directly to the hypothesis, from the hypothesis to the theory, and finally to the certain and unquestionable attainment of the truth. There are, instead, cases where the investigation follows a sort of curve; cases, namely, in which theories that seemed to have already conquered the world and reached the apex of undisputed doctrines, acceptance of which brought esteem in the realm of science, fall again to the level of hypotheses, to remain perhaps, later, completely abandoned.

Notwithstanding, however, the inevitable uncertainties and deviations that any human effort brings with it, the progress of science knows no pauses nor leaps.

Through new and broader avenues, humanity is advancing, but always like a pilgrim, toward deeper knowledge of the laws of the explored or unexplored universe, as it is spurred on by the natural thirst for truth; however, even after thousands of years human knowledge of the internal principles of the moving forces of the growth and processes of the world, and even more of the design and divine impulse which penetrates, moves, and directs everything, will be and will remain an imperfect and pale image of the divine conception. In the face of the prodigies of eternal wisdom which, in the sea of the living, govern everything with undeviating order and direct all things toward hidden harbors, the investigating thoughts of the scientist are blind and mute, and give way to that humble admiring adoration that sees before it the marvel of creation, in which the hand of man was not present and which it cannot imitate, but in which his eye can discern a sudden flash of the power of God. Before the many inscrutable enigmas of the order and concatenation of the laws of the immensely great and immensely small cosmos, the human mind must repeat the exclamation: *"O altitudo divitiarum sapientiae et scientiae Dei: quam incomprehensibilia sunt iudicia eius et investigabiles viae eius!*—O the depth of the riches of the wisdom and of the knowledge of God! How incomprehensible are His judgments, and how inscrutable His ways!" [1]

[1] Message, Inauguration of the Twelfth Year of the Pontifical Academy of Sciences, February 8, 1948

ON THE "NEW" WORLD ORDER

ON THE EVE of the first coming of Christ, when the Roman world seemed to embrace the entire globe, a new order was already expected, and Virgil sang of the great hope and the return of the virgin goddess of justice: *"Magnus ab integro saeculorum nascitur ordo; iam redit et Virgo*—Great and newly is born the order of the centuries; now returns the Virgin." Even today the entire world feels the need of a rebirth of order, in which each may work in his own way, in his rightful place, and according to his own ability. Look at the statesmen: what is and must be their mission? Is it not, certainly, to provide for the common good and temporal order, in harmony, obviously, with the exigencies of eternal and supernatural order? On the other hand, look at the Church. She has an even higher mission: to restore, promote, and extend, in the realm of human society, the Kingdom of God, outside of which there can never be consolidated that true, sincere, permanent, calm order, which is the correct definition of peace.[1]

Christian Moral Law a Prerequisite

The new order, which after the suffering and destruction of this past war all the peoples long to see realized, must be built upon the firm, immutable rock of moral law, manifested by the Creator Himself through the natural order, and engraved by Him, with indelible characters, in the hearts of men; moral law, whose observance must be inculcated and promoted by public opinion in all nations and all States with such unanimity of voice and force that no one can dare to put it in question or weaken its obliging bond.

Like a wonderful beacon, it must with the rays of its principles direct the course of the labors of men and nations, which must follow its admonishing, salutary, and profitable signals, if they do not want to condemn to storm and shipwreck every labor and effort to establish a new order. Summing up, therefore, and integrating what We expounded on other occasions, We still insist on certain essential prerequisites for an international order, which, while assuring a just and lasting peace to all peoples, will bring forth well-being and prosperity.

The Right to Neutrality

In the field of a new order founded on moral principles, there is no place for prejudice to the liberty, integrity, and security of other nations, whatever their territorial extension or capacity for defense. While it is inevitable that the great nations, because of their greater potential power, trace the path for the establishment of economic groups between themselves and the smaller, weaker nations, the right of these to have their liberty respected in the political field is no less incontestable than their right to effective protection of that neutrality in disputes among States which belongs to them according to natural as well as international law. Furthermore, the right to protection of their economic development, since only in this way can they adequately attain the common good, the material and spiritual well-being, of their own people.

The Right of Minorities

In the field of a new order founded on moral principles, there is no place for open or camouflaged oppression of the cultural and linguistic peculiarities of national minorities, for hindering or curtailing their economic capacity, for limiting or abolishing their natural fecundity. The more conscientiously the competent authorities of the State respect the rights of the minority, the more surely and effectively can it demand of its members that they carry out loyally the civic duties which are shared with other citizens.

Access to Basic Materials

In the field of a new order founded on moral principles, there is no place for narrow, egotistical calculations tending to corner sources of economic supply and basic materials to the exclusion of nations less favored by nature. In this connection, it is a great consolation to Us to see affirmed the necessity that all partake of the goods of the earth, even among those nations which in the realization of this principle would belong to the category of the givers and not of the receivers.

But it is a matter of equity to find a solution to this question—so decisive for world economics—which would proceed methodically and progressively with the necessary guarantees, and would take a lesson from the shortcomings and failures of the past. If, in the future peace, this point should not be faced squarely, it would remain in international relations as a germ capable of sprouting bitter contrasts and exasperating jealousies, leading in the end to new conflicts. It is necessary, however, to observe how a satisfactory solution of this problem is closely connected with another fundamental rule of the new order, of which We shall now speak.

Limitation of Armaments

In the field of a new order founded on moral principles, once the most dangerous igniters of an armed conflict are eliminated, there is no place for total war or an unchecked arms race. It must not be permitted that the tragedy of a world war, with its economic and social ruin and its moral aberrations and disturbances, should fall upon humanity for a third time. In order to stave off such a scourge, it is necessary to proceed seriously and honestly toward progressive and adequate limitation of armaments. The want of balance between the excessive armaments of the powerful States and the deficient armaments of the weak constitutes a threat to the preservation of the tranquillity and peace of the peoples, and calls for a firm proportionate limitation of the manufacture and possession of offensive weapons.

In keeping with the measure in which disarmament may take place, appropriate means, honorable and effective for all, must be established to give back to the principle "*pacta sunt servanda*—pacts must be observed," the vital and moral function which rightfully belongs to it in the juridical relations among States. This principle, which in the past has suffered alarming crises and undeniable infractions, now encounters an almost insuperable mistrust among the various peoples and their respective leaders. In order to restore reciprocal trust, institutions are called for which, after acquiring general respect, should dedicate themselves to the noble office of both guaranteeing the sincere implementation of treaties and promoting, according to the principles of right and equity, the desirable corrections or revisions.

We are not unaware of the quantity of difficulties to be surmounted, and the almost superhuman effort and good will needed on all sides in order to bring about a happy solution to the double undertaking outlined here. But this common labor is so essential for a lasting peace that nothing must deter responsible statesmen from undertaking it and co-operating with the forces of good will, which, looking toward the future good, will overcome the painful memories of attempts which failed in the past, and will not be deterred by the realization of the gigantic effort which such an undertaking entails.

Persecution of Religion

In the field of a new order founded on moral principles, there is no place for persecution of religion and of the Church. Living faith in a personal, transcending God releases a pure and enduring moral force which governs the whole course of life; because faith is not only a virtue, but also the divine entrance through which all virtues enter into the temple of the soul and form that strong and tenacious character which does not vacillate even in the severest tests of reason and justice. This is an eternally valid truth; but it is especially resplendent when, from the statesmen as from the least of citizens, the utmost in courage and moral energy are demanded in order to reconstruct a new Europe and a new world upon the ruins piled high by the violence, hatred, and schisms of world conflict.[2]

Propaganda of Hatred

Another indispensable prerequisite for such a new order is: victory over the hate which today divides the peoples; the renunciation, therefore, of systems and practices from which it constantly receives new nourishment. There is indeed in some countries at present an unrestrained propaganda which does not refrain from openly altering the truth and day by day, and almost hour by hour, presenting opposing nations in a false, outrageous light to public opinion. But whoever truly desires the well-being of the people, whoever longs to contribute to preserving the spiritual and moral foundation of future collaboration among peoples from incalculable damage, will consider it a sacred duty and lofty mission to prevent the loss, in the thoughts and feelings of men, of the natural ideals of truth, justice, courtesy, and co-operation for good, and, above all, of the sublime supernatural ideal of fraternal love brought by Christ into the world.

Absolute Autonomy of the State

The conception which assigns to the State unlimited authority is not only pernicious to the internal life of the nation, to its prosperity, and to the orderly increase of its well-being; it also damages relations between peoples, because it breaks the unity of international society, it rips out the foundations and the value of the rights of people, opens the way to the violation of the rights of others, and renders difficult understanding and peaceful coexistence.

In fact, although humanity, by disposition of the natural order established by God, divides itself into social groups, nations, or States, independent one from the other in the way they organize and direct their internal life, it is nonetheless linked by moral and juridical bonds into a huge community intended for the good of all peoples and regulated by special laws which safeguard its unity and promote its prosperity.

Now, it is evident to all that the so-called absolute autonomy of the State is in open contrast with that inherent natural law, that it actually radically denies it, leaving the stability of international relations at the mercy of the whim of the leaders and eliminating the possibility of a true union and a fruitful collaboration in the general interest.

Since for the existence of harmonious and lasting contacts and fruitful relations it is indispensable that peoples recognize and observe those principles of natural international law which regulate their normal development and function, such principles demand the respect of related rights to independence, life, and the possibility of progressive development in the ways of civilization; they further demand loyalty to the pacts, stipulated and sanctioned in keeping with the norms of international law.

International Law and Divine Law

There is no doubt that the indispensable condition of any peaceful coexistence between peoples is mutual good faith, anticipation and conviction of reciprocal faithfulness to the given word, the certainty that both sides are convinced that wisdom is better than weapons of war, and that they are prepared to discuss without relying on force or the threat of force in the case of delays, impediments, changes, and disputes, all of which can occur not from lack of good will but from changed circumstances or actual conflicting interests.

But, on the other hand, separating international law from the anchor of divine law and founding it on the autonomous will of States is to dethrone that very law and take away its most noble and valid titles, abandoning it to the inauspicious dynamics of private interest and collective egotism, all intent on promoting their own rights and ignoring those of others.

Revision of Treaties

It is also true that, with the passing of time and substantial change of circumstance, unforeseen and perhaps unforeseeable at the time of its stipulation, a treaty or some of its clauses may become or appear unjust or impractical, or too onerous for one of the parties; it is clear that, when this happens, one should immediately proceed with an honest discussion to modify or substitute the pact. But to consider pacts ephemeral, in principle, and tacitly to attribute to one's self the faculty to abrogate them unilaterally when they are no longer convenient, would destroy all reciprocal faith among States. Thus natural order would be upset and unbridgeable chasms would be dug to separate the various peoples and nations.

Today, all observe with fear the abyss to which the errors We have pointed out and their natural consequences have brought man. The proud illusions of infinite progress have collapsed and whoever should not yet be awake to this, the tragic present, will shake with the words of the prophet: "Listen, O you deaf, and look, O you blind." That which appeared to be external order was no more than invading confusion: derangement of the norms of moral life, which, divided from the majesty of divine law, had distorted all the fields of human endeavor.

Re-education of Mankind

But let us leave the past and turn our eyes toward that future which, according to the promises of the powerful in this world, once the bloody clashes are done, will consist of a new order founded on justice and prosperity. Will such a future be truly different; will it, above all, be better? Will the peace treaties, the new international order, be inspired by justice and equity toward all, by that spirit which frees and pacifies, or will there be a lamentable repetition of ancient and recent errors? To hope for a decisive change exclusively from the clash of war and its final outcome is vain, and experience demonstrates it to us. The hour of victory is an hour of external triumph for the side which succeeds in attaining it; but at the same time, it is the hour of temptation, in which the angel of justice struggles with the demon of violence; the heart of the victor is too easily hardened; moderation and farsighted wisdom appear to him to be weakness; the heat of popular passions, excited by the sacrifices and suffering endured, often veils the eyes even of responsible persons and causes them to ignore the admonishing voice of humanity and equity, overcome or silenced by inhumanity: Woe to the vanquished! Resolutions and decisions born under such conditions risk being no more than injustice in the guise of justice.

No, the salvation of peoples does not come by the external means of the sword, which can impose conditions of peace but does not create peace. The energies which must renew the face of the earth must proceed from the interior, the spirit. Once the bitterness and cruelty of the present struggle have cleared, the new world order of national and international life must no longer rest on the quicksands of changing, ephemeral regulations, left to the will of collective and individual egotism. Rather, they must rest on an unshakable foundation, the immovable rock of natural law and divine revelation. There the human legislator must draw that spirit of equilibrium, that acute sense of moral responsibility, without which it is easy to mistake the limits between legitimate use and abuse of power. Only in this way will his decisions have internal consistency, noble dignity, and religious sanction, and not be at the mercy of egotism and passion. Because, if it is true that the ills which beset present-day humanity are partly caused by economic imbalance and the struggle between interests for the equitable distribution of the goods which God has conceded to man to use for his sustenance and progress, it is no less true that their root is more profound and internal. It is found in religious faith and moral convictions, which have been perverted by the progressive detachment of peoples from the unity of doctrine and faith, and from customs and morals, once fostered by the unceasing, beneficent labor of the Church. The re-education of humanity, if it wishes to have any effect, must, above all, be spiritual and religious; and, therefore, it must arise from Christ as its indispensable foundation, be realized by justice, and be crowned by charity.

Among the laws which regulate the life of believing Christians and the postulates of genuine humanity there is no contrast, but common interest and mutual support. In the interest of a suffering humanity, materially and spiritually deeply shaken, We have no more ardent desire than this: that the present afflictions may open the eyes of many so that they may consider in their true light the Lord Jesus Christ and the mission of His Church on this earth, and that all those who exercise power resolve to leave to the Church a free path to work for the formation of the generations, according to the principles of justice and peace.

Unity of Religious Doctrine and Moral Code

If, on the one hand, the Church cannot renounce exercising this mission of hers, which has as its final goal the realization here on earth of the divine design to restore all things in Christ, whether they be celestial or terrestrial, on the other hand her work today appears to be more necessary than at any other time, since sad experience teaches that mere external means, human provisions, and political expedients do not bring about an efficacious mitigation of the ills which beset humanity.

Taking cognizance of the painful failure of human methods to calm the storms which threaten to engulf civilization, many turn their gaze with renewed hope to the Church, rock of truth and love, to this Chair of Peter, whence they feel may be given back to humanity that unity of religious doctrine and moral code which in other times gave consistency to peaceful relations among peoples.[3]

The Lessons of War

We preserve the hope that the nations which have passed through the school of suffering will retain its bitter lessons. In this hope We are comforted by the words of men who more than others have endured the suffering of war and with generous words have expressed, together with the affirmations of their own needs for security against all future aggression, their respect for the vital rights of other peoples and their aversion toward all usurpation of these same rights. It would be vain to expect that this wise judgment, dictated by the experience of history and lofty political sentiment, might be generally accepted by public opinion, or even a majority, as long as feelings run high. Among the peoples who have fought one another, hate and the incapacity for reciprocal understanding have given rise to a fog so dense that it cannot be hoped that the hour has already arrived in which a ray of light may rise to clear up the tragic darkness on both sides of the wall. But one thing We do know, and it is that the moment will come, perhaps earlier than people think, when both sides will recognize how, everything considered, there is only one way out of the entanglements in which struggle and hate have enveloped the world, namely, the return to a solidarity too long forgotten, solidarity not restricted to this or that people, but universal, founded on the intimate connection of their destinies and the rights belonging equally to them all.

At a time when peoples find themselves confronted with tasks which they may never have encountered before in their history, they feel stirring in their tormented hearts the impatient, somehow innate desire to take up the reins of their own destiny with greater autonomy than in the past, hoping that in this manner it will be easier for them to defend themselves against the periodic eruptions of the spirit of violence, which, like a torrent of flaming lava, spares nothing of what is dear and sacred to them.

By its very existence, the Church raises before the world a splendid beacon which constantly recalls this divine order. Her history clearly reflects her providential mission. The struggles which, forced by the abuse of power, she has had to sustain to defend the liberty which she received from God have been, at the same time, struggles for the liberty of man.

The Church has the mission to announce to the world, longing for better and more perfect forms of democracy, the highest and most necessary message there can possibly be: the dignity of man, the vocation to be children of God.[4]

[1] Address to Men of Catholic Action, September 20, 1942
[2] Radio Message to the World, December 24, 1941
[3] Encyclical *Summi Pontificatus,* October 20, 1939
[4] Radio Message to the World, December 24, 1944

THE LIMITS OF SCIENCE

IT IS ONLY a little more than a century and a half ago that, starting from purely rational premises, the first hypotheses were formulated about the discontinuous structure of matter and the existence of the elementary particles of matter, considered to be the final components of bodies. From that time onward, the molecules were counted, weighed, analyzed; then the atom, at first thought to be indivisible, was divided into its elements, examined, and its most intimate structures probed; the elementary electric charge, the mass of the proton were determined; the neutron, positron, and many other elementary particles were identified and their characteristics made known. A means was found to guide these particles, to accelerate them, and to bombard the atomic nuclei with them. But it was especially by utilizing neutrons that success was attained in producing artificial radioactivity, the fission of nuclei, the transformation of one element into other elements, and the release of enormous quantities of energy.

Ingenious theories and conceptions concerning the phenomena of the world were developed; new mathematical and geometrical systems were created. We cite only the special and the general theory of relativity, the quantum theory, wave mechanics, recent theories about the nature of nuclear forces, theories about the origin of cosmic rays, hypotheses about the source of stellar energy.

But the optimism aroused by such results soon meets with a setback: for anyone with a sense of responsibility who follows the course of events is filled with confusion and anguish. Anguish and confusion in the highest sense of the word, the sign of aspiration toward an ever more perfect organization of thought, an ever clearer view of the perspectives opening before us. The triumphs of science themselves call for two requirements to which We have already referred.

The question is, above all, to penetrate the innermost structure of material beings and examine the problems connected with the material foundation of their being and activity. Then the question arises: Can experimental science in itself solve these problems? Are they within its province, and do they fall within the field in which its methods of investigation can be applied? The answer must be no. Science starts out from sense perceptions, which are by their nature external; applying to them the workings of intelligence, it penetrates further and further into the secret recesses of things; but it has to stop short at a certain point, when questions arise which cannot be answered by the observation of the senses.

When the scientist interprets experimental data and applies himself to explaining phenomena that have their origin in material nature as such, he needs a light to show him the way in reverse, going from the absolute to the relative, from the necessary to the contingent, which can reveal to him the truth that science cannot reach by its own methods, because it completely eludes the senses. This light is philosophy, that is, the science of general laws, valid for every being, and therefore also for the sphere of natural sciences, beyond the laws that are known empirically.

The second requirement springs from the very nature of the human spirit, which desires a coherent and unified view of truth. If the different disciplines and their branches are merely juxtaposed like a kind of mosaic, the result obtained is an anatomical composition of knowledge, from which all life seems to have fled. Man, however, demands that a breath of living unity should quicken his knowledge: only thus does science become fruitful and culture breed an organic doctrine. Thence a second question arises: Can science accomplish, merely with its own characteristic means, this universal synthesis of thought? And in any case, since that knowledge is divided into innumerable particular disciplines, which one, among so many varieties, could achieve this synthesis? Here again We believe that science, by its very nature, is not able to provide such a universal synthesis.

This synthesis requires a solid and deeply rooted foundation, from which to draw its unity, and which may serve as a basis for the most general truths. The different parts of the construction, thus unified, must find in this foundation the elements which constitute their essential nature. A superior force is required here: unifying by its *universality,* clear in its *depth,* solid because of its *absolute character,* efficacious by its *necessity.* Once again, this force is philosophy.

Science and Philosophy

Alas! For some time now science and philosophy have been separated. It would be difficult to assess the causes and the responsibility of such a damaging fact. It is certain that the cause of this divorce is not to be sought in the nature itself of the two paths which lead to truth, but in historical contingencies and in people who did not always possess the good will and competence necessary.

Men of science believed, at a certain moment, that natural philosophy was a useless burden and refused to be directed by it. On the other hand, philosophers no longer followed the progress of science, and clung to formal positions that they should have abandoned. But when, as We have shown, the necessity of establishing a serious interpretation of the facts and of elaborating a comprehensive synthesis imposed itself, the scientists succumbed to the philosophies current at the moment. Many of them, perhaps, were not even fully aware that their scientific research was being guided by particular philosophical tendencies.

Hence, for example, mechanistic thought directed for a long time the scientific interpretation of phenomena observed. The defenders of this philosophical position believed that all natural phenomena could be reduced to a mass of physical, chemical, and mechanical forces, in which change and activity were the result merely of a different arrangement of the particles in space and of the forces or displacements to which each of them was subjected. It followed that, theoretically, any future effect whatever could be predicted with absolute certainty, provided that, at the outset, all the geometrical and mechanical data were known. According to this doctrine, the world is merely an enormous machine, composed of an innumerable series of other machines joined together.

Further progress in experimental research, however, demonstrated the inaccuracy of these hypotheses. Mechanics deduced from the facts of the macrocosm are unable to explain and interpret all the phenomena of the microcosm: other elements enter here which are beyond the scope of mechanistic interpretation.

The failure of mechanistic theory has led thinkers to entirely different hypotheses, distinguished rather by a kind of scientific idealism, in which consideration of the active observer plays the main part. For example, quantum mechanics and its fundamental principle of indeterminism, with the criticism of the principle of causality it presupposes, seem to be scientific hypotheses influenced by philosophical thought.

But because these hypotheses themselves do not satisfy completely the desire for total enlightenment, many noted thinkers are reduced to skepticism on the philosophical problems of science. They claim that we must be content to ascertain facts, and try to fit them into comprehensive and simple formulas, as prerequisites to calculating from the initial facts the possible developments of a physical system. This state of mind means renouncing conceptual introspection and losing the hope of establishing ingenious universal syntheses. We do not believe, however, that such pessimism is justified: We are rather of the opinion that the natural sciences, in permanent contact with a philosophy of critical realism, which was always that of the *philosophia perennis* in its most eminent representatives, may reach a general vision of the visible world capable of satisfying, to some extent, the search and the longing for truth.

But it is necessary to stress another point: if it is the duty of science to look for coherence and draw inspiration from sound philosophy, the latter may not arrogate to itself the claim to determine truths which belong exclusively to the sphere of experience and scientific method. For only experience, in the widest sense of the word, can indicate which, among the infinite variety of possible magnitudes and material laws, are those which the Creator really chose to realize.[1]

[1] Address to the Pontifical Academy of Sciences, April 24, 1955

RADIO AND TELEVISION

THE RADIO can be one of the most powerful means for spreading true civilization and culture. Today its services have become almost indispensable for educating men in the sense of solidarity, for the life of the State and the people; it is capable of creating a lively force of cohesion in peoples and between nations. It can bear witness before the whole world to the truth and glory of God, promote the victory of equity, bring light, consolation, hope, reconciliation, and love on this earth, and draw men and nations closer together. It can carry the voice of Christ, the truth of the Gospel, the spirit of the Gospel, and the charity of the Gospel to the ends of the earth. It gives also to Us, common Father of the faithful, the joy of being, at one and the same time, present to all Our children in the whole world, every time We send out Our messages and impart Our blessing.

All this the radio can do. But in the hands of blind or wicked men it can also lend itself to error and falsehood, base passions, sensuality, pride, covetousness, and hate; it can be turned into that open sepulcher full of malediction and bitterness of which St. Paul speaks and which swallows up the Christian virtues, sound civilization, peace, and human happiness. . . .

At the service of the dignity of life and Christian ethics: It should hold sacred the child's innocence, the youth's purity, the holy chastity of matrimony, and the happiness of a family life based on the fear and the love of God.

At the service of justice: It should hold sacred the inviolable human rights no less than the right of the authorities to exact from the individual and the community the duties necessary for the common good; the right of peoples to existence, in particular of the weaker members, and alike the right of the great family of nations to request the sacrifices necessary for the peace of the world; the right of the Church to bring, in the fullness of liberty, to all men and all peoples the wealth of the grace and the peace of Christ.

At the service of love: This is the duty of the present hour. At all costs it is necessary to overcome dissension and hate, of which the radio, too, has many times been made the instrument and agent. May it put its far-reaching powerful influence to the service of the noble ideal of Christian charity. . . .

Finally, We wish to draw attention to the understanding of the true needs of humanity and its spiritual nature, which the radio should serve by its musical transmissions. We have no intention of speaking now of those programs in which it would be very difficult to find any artistic merit, any educational value. . . . Rather, We refer to the recital of sacred music, as well as to the efforts to make accessible to the public the works, sacred and profane, of the great modern and ancient composers, whose masterpieces arouse in the mind and soul the lofty sentiments by which they were themselves animated.[1]

The responsibility of those people who make of the radio an instrument of intellectual or moral corruption presents no problem; it merely calls for the brand of infamy. That of the indifferent, the apathetic, the skeptical, very great by reason of the serious and often imperceptible consequences, calls for something else; it confronts us with the difficulty—a difficulty rather than a problem—of making him understand that he is doing wrong.

The problem arises when it is a question of presenting, with honest and often praiseworthy intentions, arguments, events, or questions legitimately interesting and useful from a literary, artistic, psychological, moral, or social point of view. And this is what then perplexes the mind: Should we hold our peace when it might be fitting or necessary to speak, or should we speak and run the risk of alarming certain ears, perturbing certain souls, but above all of contaminating the candid innocence of childish hearts? Adults have only themselves to blame for their indiscreet or unwise curiosity; but what about the children who, thoughtlessly and without serious malice, so easily evade on this point their parents' supervision? It is the duty of a speaker over the radio to use a language of such tact and reticence that he may be understood by adults without rousing the imagination or troubling the simplicity of the young.[2]

Who can praise sufficiently the tremendous services rendered by the radio in cases of urgent need and extreme danger? Who can tell the social usefulness of information in the mutual exchange of news by all the members of the great human family? Who can assess the contribution to culture in general made by the possibility of bringing to our ears lectures and lessons of the most varied nature and allowing us to enjoy the delight of fine diction and elevating music?

The Church, We said, takes an interest in all this. And is there reason to wonder? She stands above national diversities, she is universal. In the radio she sees a singularly valuable element for the fulfillment of her mission. It is true that listening to a Mass on the radio is not the same as taking part personally in the divine Sacrifice. The radio is not a complete substitute for personal contacts; but what an advantage it means for the Head of the Church and other shepherds of souls, allowing them to speak directly to their spiritual sons and daughters and to pray with them!

What intimate force and what religious stimulation can come from the microphone, which for many is the only comfort and the only support arriving from without! Think of the thousands of sick people confined to their beds; of the communities who have no church or priest. By means of the radio, they can at least still communicate with the sources of faith and grace.

Quite rightly, the radio may consider itself entrusted with an educational mission, provided, always, that it does not neglect the main object: being made in the image of God, man has the duty of perfecting this divine likeness in his way of thinking, wishing, and acting. Every form of education must tend to help him in this. The body of man, his temporal and material life, as We have often repeated, must be the object of respect and care. But his soul and his intellectual and spiritual life are incomparably more worthy of attention; they are, in reality, the final and supreme reason for all instruction and education. How, therefore, could the radio exclude religious teaching from the multifarious duties and aims it pursues? [3]

Television

The rapid advances which television has now made in many countries keep Our attention ever more alert to this marvellous gift of science and technology, at once precious and dangerous by reason of the profound reverberations which it is destined to provoke in the private and public life of nations.

We fully recognize the value of this brilliant conquest of science, which is a further manifestation of the wonderful splendors of God, Who "has given science to men that He may be honored in its marvels." Television too, therefore, imposes on all of us the duty of gratefulness which the Church tirelessly recommends to her children in the daily Holy Sacrifice of the Altar, with the admonition that "it is truly meet and just, right and salutary, always and everywhere, to give thanks" to God for His gifts.

In any case, it is not difficult to realize the innumerable advantages of television whenever it is placed at the service of man for his perfection.

In recent years, the movies and sports, to say nothing of the necessity of daily work, have tended to draw the members of the family increasingly away from home, upsetting the natural development of domestic life. How can We not rejoice to see television efficaciously contributing to the restoration of the balance, offering the whole family the chance of enjoying together pleasant recreation far from the dangers of unhealthy company and places?

Nor can We be indifferent to the beneficent influence which television is able to exercise from the social point of view in respect to culture, popular education, scholastic teaching, and the very life of peoples, who through that instrument will certainly be helped to know and understand one another better and to reach friendly concord and better mutual co-operation.

Such considerations, however, must not blind us to another aspect of this delicate and important question. Although, in fact, television properly controlled may constitute an effective means of wise and Christian education, it is equally true that it is not exempt from dangers which may be the result of abuses and profanation brought about by human weakness and malice—dangers all the more serious since the suggestive power of this instrument is greater and the public toward whom it is directed is wider and more indiscriminate. Unlike the theater and the movies, whose spectacles are limited to those who choose to enter, television is directed, above all, to family groups of every age and sex and of various cultural levels, bringing to them the daily news, sundry news items, and all kinds of spectacles. Like the radio, it can enter any house and go to any place, at any time, bringing with it not only sounds and words but also the concreteness and mobility of its images, which gives it greater emotional influence, particularly in respect to the young. To this must be added the fact that television programs are based, in great part, on films and plays, which, as experience has shown, all too frequently do not satisfy the requirements of natural and Christian ethics. Lastly, it should be pointed out that television finds its keenest and most attentive audience among children and adolescents, who, by reason of their age, can more easily fall prey to its fascination and, consciously or unconsciously, transmute into living reality the images they absorb from the animated picture on the screen. It is obvious, therefore, how intimately television affects the education of the young and the Christian spirit of family life.

If We consider the inestimable value of the family, which is the primary cell of society, and if We reflect that within the walls of the home not only the bodily but also the spiritual development of the child must begin and grow—precious hope of the Church and of its country—We cannot but proclaim to all those who share the responsibilities of television that the duties and responsibilities which rest on their shoulders are extremely serious before God and society.

Public authorities, above all, must take every precaution, so that the atmosphere of decency and restraint which should surround family life may not be offended or troubled.

Ever present in Our mind is the sad picture of the perturbing and evil power of the movies. But how can We help being horrified by the thought that through television the poisoned atmosphere of materialism, superficiality, and luxuriousness, which too often pervades the motion picture theaters, may penetrate the walls of the home? Truly, it would be impossible to imagine anything more fatal to the spiritual forces of a nation than that, before so many innocent souls, in the bosom of the family itself, there should be repeated those sensational revelations of pleasure-seeking, of passion, and of evil which can shake and ruin for all time a whole edifice of purity, goodness, and healthy individual and social education.

For these reasons, We deem it advisable to point out that the normal supervision which has to be exercised by the authorities responsible for public shows is not sufficient, in the case of television transmissions, to ensure satisfactory service from the moral point of view; there is need for a different criterion, as it is here a question of spectacles destined to reach into the family sanctuary. Thus we see, particularly in this field, that there is no foundation in the supposed right to indiscriminate liberty in art and in the plea that thought and the imparting of information are free; higher values are at stake, the violators of which would not be able to escape the heavy penalties threatened by the divine Savior, "Woe to the world because of scandals! . . . Woe to the man by whom the scandal cometh!"

We cherish a profound trust that the lofty sense of responsibility of those who preside over public life will prevail in the prevention of those sad possibilities which We have previously deplored. We are pleased to hope, rather, that as far as the programs are concerned, suitable instructions will be issued, so that television may serve for the healthy recreation of the citizens and likewise contribute in all circumstances to their education and moral elevation. But in order that such desirable measures may find their full application, a careful and active vigilance will have to be exercised by all.[4]

[1] Address to the Congress of the 50th Anniversary of the Convenzione Marconiane Radio, October 3, 1947

[2] Address to Radio Announcers, April 22, 1948

[3] Address to the Members of the International Radio Transmission Conference, May 5, 1950

[4] Apostolic Letter, January 1, 1954

THE THEATER

AN OLD AND RATHER WIDESPREAD PREJUDICE puts in opposition, almost as if reciprocally hostile, the Church and the dramatic profession. That erroneous conception is unfounded and unfair.

What, then, must the theater—or the movie theater—do to fulfill its mission of doing good? Theirs must be a work of art, but a work of art in the fullest and at the same time highest meaning of the word. . . .

The public, fascinated and forgetting that it has come to see and to hear, itself lives the scene of which it comes to be in a way the actor more than the witness; it lives, hears, thrills, shudders, with all the power of its faculties, in all the liveliness of its impressions. And this turmoil of all its being is moved and sustained by the authors, and by the actors and actresses of the theater and the movies. More often than not the impression is lasting, sometimes indelible. The spectator leaves the hall carrying with him and within him deep convictions or tenacious prejudices, lofty aspirations or abject cupidities.

If, in the evocation of the same facts, history, handled by different authors, may become tendentious and partial and serve for the propagation of opposite theses, what shall we say of the drama, which acts so directly on the soul of the spectator, and on his senses, imagination, and receptivity, even more than upon his reason and judgment?

This creates a formidable responsibility, but at the same time a noble and elevated one. How is it possible, then, that some take it lightly and without any scruples, and use their action and influence on the human spirit and heart, especially on the young and on adolescents, only to corrupt and degrade them?

For this fatal disorder We seem to see two main causes: The first is a lack of character and energy, which induces some to yield to the desires of a spoiled public, to flatter and even incite its passions and base instincts, and to beg of it in return applause and loud laughter and above all the large profits which it pays for such entertainments. Easy and big successes bring with them the inducement to offer continually new and similar ones; it requires so little talent to produce such spectacles and so little grace and ability to stage them. But, meanwhile, taste, already vulgar, becomes steadily coarser and requires increasingly potent poison, sinking thus to ever lower depths.

The other cause of the evil might seem less dangerous and harmful, so subtle is it and so human! There is a truly great temptation for an author to stress the acuity and depth of his psychological insight, carrying his analysis of characters, of their most delicate sentiments, their most impetuous passions, to the utmost limits and lavishing the riches of his palette on the representation of actions and customs. The temptation is equally strong for actors or actresses to force or attenuate their interpretation of the work of another according to their own personalities, often running close, if not surpassing, the limits of discretion in showing off their personal gifts and attractions, even the physical ones. In a novel, such moral anatomies, such realistic "exhibitionisms," such descriptions of luxury or misery, are liable to disturb the heart of the reader. What will happen, then, when, in the atmosphere and collective excitement of the hall, facts develop sensibly as in reality, but, as it were, condensed, compressed, rendered more intense by the surprising resources of the movies, or at the theater, in characters of flesh and blood, so easily identifiable with their parts that the thoughts, feelings, and passions which sway them really make their eyes sparkle, make them laugh and cry and their hearts throb?

It is therefore quite clear that every co-operator in a dramatic performance who surrenders to the whims of the public instead of dominating them, that is, who gives in to the inanities of vanity or allows himself to be conquered by the greed for profits which his conscience reproves, not only loses something of his own dignity, but also offends art—that art which he shows he does not love courageously enough to resist the caprices of bad taste nor with sufficient integrity to prefer it to the incentives of vainglory or money.

What a magnificent field of activity is offered, therefore, to dramatic authors, producers, and theatrical critics! It belongs to them to re-establish contact between the public and the beautiful and elevated creations of human genius, to work for the re-education of good taste and decent feelings. . . .

As to actors and actresses, the intense emotion of joy and pride that pervades the soul before a public all tense, eager, applauding, is very natural and easily understandable. Honor to those who, aware of their great responsibility, conscious of the nobility of their mission, see in their influence on souls only a means to elevate them above the earth and make them soar toward the ideal. Such are the actors and actresses who do not come upon the scene without having raised their thoughts and intentions to God, and it is no longer a surprise to see how sometimes Christ chooses from their ranks superior spirits that He illuminates and guides toward the mystic heights of a life of perfection.[1]

[1] Address to Catholic Theater Center, August 26, 1945

THE MISSION OF PUBLISHERS

THE FIRST MAN who, desirous of communicating his thought to other men in a more lasting form than the fleeting sound of words, carved, perhaps with a rough flint, on the walls of a cave, certain signs of which he determined and explained the interpretation, invented, at the same time, writing and the art of reading. Reading is to penetrate by means of more or less complicated graphic signs into the thoughts of others. Now, since "the thoughts of the just are justice, and the counsels of the wicked are impious," it follows that some books, like some words, are sources of light, strength, intellectual and moral freedom, while others bring only snares and temptations of sin; such is the teaching of the Holy Scriptures: *"Cogitationes iustorum iudicia, et consilia impiorum fraudulenta. Verba impiorum insidiantur sanguini; os iustorum liberabit eos*—The thoughts of the just are judgments; and the counsels of the wicked are deceitful. The words of the wicked lie in wait for blood: the mouth of the just shall deliver them." There are, therefore, good and bad things to read, just as there are good and bad words. . . .

Withdraw a moment within yourselves and ask yourselves sincerely whence comes the best that is in you. Why do you believe in God, in His Son become flesh for the redemption of the world, in His Mother Mary, whom He has made your Mother? Why do you obey His commandments, love your parents, your country, your neighbor? Why have you decided to found a family of which Jesus is the King, and in which you may transmit to your children the treasure of Christian virtues? Certainly because faith was infused into you in holy baptism; because your parents, your priest, your teachers, men and women, taught you by word of mouth and with their example to do good and to avoid evil. But delve further into your memories: among the best and the most decisive you will probably find that of some beneficial book; the catechism, sacred history, the Holy Gospel, the Roman Missal, the parish bulletin, *The Imitation of Christ,* the lives of the saints.

The Index

You know, however, that there are also bad books that are bad for everybody, like those poisons against which nobody can declare himself immune. As in every man the flesh is subject to weaknesses and the spirit is ready for rebellion, so such reading constitutes a danger for everybody. The Acts of the Apostles tells us that, during the preaching of St. Paul in Ephesus, many of those who had been addicted to vain and superstitious arts brought their books and publicly burned them; when the value of these writings on magic, thus reduced to cinders, was calculated, it was found to amount to over fifty thousand dinars. Afterwards, in the course of the centuries, the Roman Pontiffs took care to have a catalogue or *Index* published of books which the faithful are forbidden to read.

It is to be considered that many others, although not expressly enumerated, fall under the same condemnation and prohibition because they are harmful to faith and to morals. . . .

If We remind you of this, it is because of the extension of the evil, which is at present facilitated by the continuous growth of book production, and also by the freedom which many people attribute to themselves to read everything. Now, there cannot be freedom to read everything, just as there is not a freedom to eat and drink anything at hand, including perhaps even cocaine or prussic acid.

Certainly it is not forbidden you to enjoy the charm of stories of pure, wholesome human tenderness; the Holy Scriptures themselves offer similar scenes that have kept throughout the centuries their idyllic freshness: the meeting of Jacob and Rachel, and the engagement of young Tobias. And there have always been writers of great talent who have written good, morally sound novels.

But do not believe, young men and women, who allow yourselves to be at times led to reading, perhaps secretly, harmful books, do not believe that their poison will have no effect on you;

rather be afraid that this effect, if it is not immediate, will be all the more deadly.

The danger of bad literature is, indeed, under certain aspects, more fatal than that of bad company, because it can render itself more treacherously familiar. How many girls or young women, alone in their room, with the latest bestseller, allow themselves to be told by it the crude things they would not permit others to mention in their presence, or allow scenes to be described of which they would not want to be the victims or the actors for anything in the world! Alas! they are in this way preparing to become so tomorrow! Others, Christian men or women, who from their childhood have followed the straight and narrow path, also complain of the sudden increase of temptations which oppress them and of their growing weakness to resist them. Perhaps if they sincerely examined their consciences, they would have to admit that they had read a sensual novel, glanced through an immoral magazine, or let their eyes rest on indecent illustrations.[1]

Books in the Era of Movies and Television

We are living in the era of the motion picture and television. Without doubt both absorb a considerable part of the time which before used to belong to the printed word. Yet it happens that they are the very ones to increase the value of a good book. For, though we fully recognize the importance of the technique and art of the motion picture, yet the unilateral influence it exercises on man and especially on youth, with its almost purely visual action, carries with it such a danger of intellectual decay that it is already beginning to be considered as a danger for the people. It is all the more the duty of the good book, therefore, to educate the people to a deeper understanding of things, to make them think and ponder.[2]

[1] Address to Newlyweds, July 31, 1940

[2] Message to the International Meeting of Publishers of Books and Magazines, December 10, 1950

THE DUTY AND RESPONSIBILITY OF THE LITERARY CRITIC

THE SPECIAL JOY which We feel in receiving you to Our presence, dear Sons and book critics, is equal to the solicitude that belongs to Our duties as shepherd. Among other cares, We are much concerned with this matter, in order to bring to the children of Christ verdant pastures of the spirit, which today are found especially in reading.

We are grateful, therefore, for your gathering, because We see in each one of you a competent and faithful fellow laborer in Our pastoral ministry; collectively, you are a powerful barrier against the overflowing tide of useless literature. Such reading matter threatens to drag the great dignity of human nature into the mud of error and perversion. We need not point out here the necessity, the nobility, and the importance of right criticism. Your own firm persuasion of the great influence of reading on the habits and the lot of individuals and the community has inspired you to take up the difficult task, which is imposed on the critic by the vast literary production of our day. In a society like our own, so jealous to exercise the right of free press, the criticism of good people, based on a much more sacred right, is certainly one of the most proper means to prevent the spread of evil. This is all the more necessary, because such evil spreads under the appearance or pretext of good. In such matters, of the gravest danger to souls, the intervention of some higher authority is justified and necessary. Criticism, however, that is based on the norms of truth and morality is better adapted, perhaps, to the mentality of the modern man, who wishes to judge things for himself, though welcoming the assistance of a critic in whom he has confidence.

You do not confine your work, however, to the moral aspects of a book; but your criticism takes in the scientific, the literary, and the artistic qualities of a work. Thoroughgoing criticism, such as is expected by the public and by experts, is possible, though it involves much work. Such thoroughness in Catholic critics not only strengthens their authority with the public, but contributes a praiseworthy addition to culture, in line with the perennial tradition of the Church, always ready to assimilate the development of thought and expression. The heights or the depths reached by literature, especially that of the present day, depend largely on the clear judgment, the moral integrity, and the intellectual strength of the critics.

Recognizing this great responsibility resting on the critic, We deem it opportune to point out some fundamental principles to which his work must conform, if it is efficaciously to attain its end of guiding souls into secure paths.

The intention of guiding and advising others in the selection and evaluation of their reading is to no purpose unless we assume in the readers a disposition of spirit to accept the suggestions of others. Every effort of a critic is useless with people who of set purpose refuse to admit the critic's knowledge and competence, and who, consequently, have no confidence in him or in his judgment. There are readers with whom the critic has no success because, by nature or through faulty training, they rely on their own superior appraisal of their mental ability. Dominated by the suggestion of their own sufficiency, they expect from the critic only the confirmation of their own judgment, which they take to be certain and unchangeable. Rejection of objective criticism by such persons, often based on false ideological prejudices, must not discourage the critic. Such rejection only reflects the psychological deficiencies of such persons. With a public of good dispositions, the critic will work much more efficaciously if he knows how to gain their confidence. In fact, this is the starting point and the goal of all criticism, whether there is question of an individual critic or of magazines—and here all the more—that make criticism their collective aim. If the reader turns to a critic, it is because he believes in the critic's knowledge, integrity, and maturity, when expounding the contents of a book or passing a well-founded and unanswerable judgment. How is the critic to gain successfully the confidence of the reader? What is the function of the critic, and what can be rightly asked of the public?

The first requirement in the critic is the mental ability to read and properly understand the book in question. The mention of such a norm seems superfluous; it is not, however, a rare thing to meet reviewers who do not measure up to this first, elementary requisite. Evidently, a close reading, very often boring and fatiguing, must be free from prejudice; and the critic must be reading in subject matter that is sufficiently well known to him. Therefore, the critic must have a many-sided culture; the special knowledge required in a given subject; and a broad general culture that will enable him to place the book properly and to expound its principal contents.

Mere intellectual understanding, however, is not sufficient. The critic must be able to form a judgment which when stated shows his mental competency.

The critic must be able to judge and to evaluate; in other words, to apply wisely his general culture and specialized knowledge to the subject at hand. For this, he must have broad-mindedness, versatility; the ability to see and comprehend the relative bearings of a work, and to point out errors, shortcomings, and contradictions. From this impartial consideration of the good and the bad in a given work there will come limitation and distinction, the Yes and No in each case. Only then does the criticism reach its final form as ready for publication.

In applying the above-mentioned qualities of mind, the critic is influenced by the will, by the sensibility, and by character. This makes it necessary for the critic to have other characteristics. To prevent the will and emotions from negatively influencing his judgments, the critic must first of all be objective. He must show a liking for the author and confidence in him; unless, for positively grave and certain reasons, he is obliged to speak otherwise. A critic habitually subject to partiality should never attempt to write. Nobility of character and goodness of heart are always the best weapons of combat. This holds for the field of criticism, when ideas and opinions are in conflict. Nobility and kindness, however, are not to be confused with the ingenuity and credulity of a child, whose experience of life has not matured. A critic may have some of the qualities indicated, but they must always be joined to probity, integrity, and firmness of character. The critic must not write to please the author, or the publisher, or the public—often subject to strange sympathies or antipathies—or to follow his own inclination. Against his own better knowledge and conscience, against objective truth, a critic can make a false criticism. This false judgment may arise from a wrong interpretation of the meaning or of the questionable teaching of the author; or it may come by deliberately omitting important and relevant portions that should not be concealed. To each critic should apply the testimony given to our Redeemer by His enemies, hypocritically and yet truthfully: "Master, we know that Thou art truthful and that Thou teachest the way of God in truth and that Thou carest nought for any man; for Thou dost not regard the person of men" (Matthew 22, 16).

Firmness of character in a critic is shown especially when he writes with serenity and without fear of his own judgment; and when he defends his judgment, keeping always to strict justice. As a judge who lacks the courage to sustain the law should resign, so should a critic, if he loves an easy life more than the truth. Firmness, however, must always avoid arrogance; for this is an a priori presumption of the truth's being in favor of the critic and against the author. Both are subject to the same law in the service of truth; but the critic has the added duty of serving the truth with the maximum loyalty. In every case, the author and the critic should know that the truth is higher than either of them. An unjust criticism, as the word indicates, is not only an error of intellect but a real injury to the author. In such cases, the reputation of the author may greatly suffer; and, moreover, as is often the case, his rightful interests suffer loss. In such cases, the critic has a clear obligation of retraction. On the other hand, a justified criticism should not be withdrawn through fear of a powerful opponent. Such action would argue a deplorable lack of character and courage; it would also undermine the necessary confidence of the public, which rightly expects the critic to hold fast to his word, when it has been delivered according to the truth.[1]

[1] Address to Ecclesiastics Employed as Book Critics, February 13, 1956

ON MOVIES

THE EXTRAORDINARY INFLUENCE of the movies on present-day society is shown by the growing thirst which this society has for them, and which, reduced to numbers, constitute a quite new and remarkable phenomenon. What is the source of the fascination of this new art, which, sixty years after its first appearance, has arrived at the almost magical power of summoning into the darkness of its halls, and not without pay, crowds that are numbered by the billions? What is the secret of the spell which makes these same crowds its constant devotees? In the answer to such questions lie the fundamental causes which bring about the great importance and the wide popularity of the motion picture.

The first power of attraction of a film springs from its technical qualities, which perform the prodigy of transferring the spectator into an imaginary world, or, in a documentary film, of bringing reality, distant in space and time, right before his eyes. To the technical process, then, belongs the first place in the origin and development of the movies. It preceded the film, and first made it possible; it also makes it every day more attractive, adaptable, alive. The chief technical elements of a movie show were already in existence before the film was born; then gradually the film was taken under their control until at length it arrived at the point where it exacts from the technical process the invention of new methods to be placed at its service.

But to understand thoroughly the power of motion pictures, and to make a more exact evaluation of the movie, it is necessary to take note of the important part played in them by the laws of psychology, either in so far as they explain how the film influences the mind, or in so far as they are deliberately applied to produce a stronger impression on the viewer. With careful observation devotees of this science study the process of action and reaction produced by viewing the picture, applying the method of research and analysis, the fruits of experimental psychology, studying the hidden recesses of the subconscious and the unconscious. They investigate the film's influence not only as it is passively received by the viewer, but also by analyzing its related psychical "activation," according to immanent laws, that is, its power to grip the mind through the enchantment of the representation. If, through one or the other influence, the spectator remains truly a prisoner of the world unfolding before his eyes, he is forced to transfer somehow to the person of the actor his own ego, with its psychic tendencies, its personal experiences, its hidden and ill-defined desires. Through the duration of this sort of enchantment, owing in large part to the suggestion of the actor, the viewer moves in the actor's world as though it were his own, and even, to some degree, lives in his place, and almost within him, in perfect harmony

The Bishops of the World at the Pronouncement of the Marian Dogma, Nov. 1, 1950

At the Tomb of St. Peter, on the Eve of the Feast of Sts. Peter and Paul, June 28, 1955

of feeling, sometimes even being drawn by the action to suggest words and phrases. This procedure, which modern directors are well aware of and try to make use of, has been compared with the dream state, with this difference, that the visions and images of dreams come only from the intimate world of the one dreaming, whereas they come from the screen to the spectator, but in such a way that they arouse from the depths of his consciousness images that are more vivid and dearer to him. Often enough then it happens that the spectator, through pictures of persons and things, sees as real that which never actually happened, but which he has frequently pondered over deep within himself, and desired or feared. With cause, therefore, does the extraordinary power of the motion picture find its profoundest explanation in the internal structure of the psychic process, and the spectacle will be all the more gripping in proportion to the degree it stimulates these processes.

As a result, the director is constantly forced to sharpen his own psychological sensibility and his own insight by the efforts he must make to find the most effective form to give to a film the power described above, which may have a good or a bad moral effect. In fact, the internal dynamisms of the spectator's ego, in the depths of his nature, of his subconscious and unconscious, can lead him thus to the realm of light, of the noble and beautiful, just as they can bring him under the sway of darkness and depravation, at the mercy of powerful and uncontrolled instincts, depending on whether the picture plays up and arouses the qualities of one or the other camp, and focuses on it the attention, the desires and psychic impulses. Human nature's condition is such, in fact, that not always do the spectators possess or preserve the spiritual energy, the interior detachment, and frequently, too, the strength of will, to resist a captivating suggestion, and thus the capacity to control and direct themselves.

Along with these fundamental causes and reasons for the attractiveness and importance of motion pictures, another active psychic element has been amply brought to light. It is the free and personal interpretation of the viewer, and his anticipation of the action's subsequent development; it is this which obtains, in some degree, the delight proper to one who creates an event. From this element, too, the director draws profit, through apparently insignificant but skillful movements, as, for example, the gesture of a hand, a shrug of the shoulders, a half-open door.

Because of this inner power of the motion picture, and because of its wide influence on the masses of men and even on moral practices, it has drawn the attention not only of competent civil and ecclesiastical authority, but also of all groups possessed of calm judgment and a genuine sense of responsibility.

In truth, how could an instrument, in itself most noble, but so apt to uplift or degrade men, and so quick to produce good or spread evil, be left to its own devices, or made dependent on purely economic interests?

The watchfulness and response of public authorities, fully justified by law to defend the common civil and moral heritage, is made manifest in various ways: through the civil and ecclesiastical censure of pictures, and, if necessary, through banning them; through the listing of films by appropriate examining boards, which qualify them according to merit for the information of the public, and as a norm to be followed. It is indeed true that the spirit of our time, unreasonably intolerant of the intervention of public authority, would prefer censorship coming directly from the people.

It would indeed be desirable if good men would agree to ban corrupt movies wherever they are shown, and to combat them with the legal and moral weapons at their disposal; yet such action is not by itself enough. Private initiative and zeal can wane, and do in fact wane rather quickly, as experience shows. But not so the hostile and aggressive propaganda, which frequently draws rich profits from films, and which often finds a ready ally in the interior of man, that is, in his blind instinct and its allurements, or his brutal and base urges.

If, therefore, the civic and moral heritage of peoples and families is to be effectively safeguarded, it is most certainly right for public authority to exercise a due intervention in order to hinder or check the most dangerous influences.

The Ideal Film

The first quality which should mark the ideal film is respect for man. For there is indeed no reason whereby it can be exempted from the general norm which demands that he who deals with men should fully respect man.

However much differences of age, condition, and sex may suggest a difference in conduct and bearing, man is always man, with the dignity and nobility bestowed on him by the Creator, in Whose image and likeness he was made (Genesis 1, 26). In man there is a spiritual and immortal soul; there is the universe in miniature, with its multiplicity and variety of form, and the marvellous order of all its parts; there is thought and will, with a vast field in which to operate; there is emotional life, with its heights and depths; there is the world of the senses, with its numerous powers, perceptions, and feelings; there is the body, formed even to its minutest parts according to a teleology not yet fully grasped. Man has been made lord in this universe; freely he must direct his actions in accord with the laws of truth, goodness, and beauty, as they are manifested in nature, his social relations with his fellow men, and divine revelation.

Since the motion picture, as has been noted, can incline the soul of the viewer to good or to evil, We will call ideal only that film which not only does not offend what We have just described, but treats it respectfully. Even that is not enough! Rather We should say: that which strengthens and uplifts man in the consciousness of his dignity, that which increases his knowledge and love of the lofty natural position conferred on him by his Creator; that which tells him it is possible for him to increase the gifts of energy and virtue he disposes of within himself; that which strengthens his conviction that he can overcome obstacles and avoid erroneous solutions, that he can rise after every fall and return to the right path, that he can, in sum, progress from good to better through the use of his freedom and his faculties.

Such a motion picture would already contain the basic element of an ideal film; but more still can be attributed to it, if to respect for man is added a loving understanding of him. Recall the touching phrase of the Lord: "I have pity on this people."

The ideal motion picture must speak to the child in language suited to a child, to youth in a way fitted to it, to the adult as he expects to be spoken to, that is, using his own manner of seeing and understanding things.[1]

[1] Address to the Representatives of the Italian Movie Industry, June 21, 1955

SPORTS

EVERYTHING CONNECTED WITH PHYSICAL EXERCISE—with competition, emulation, sports—interests and attracts the youth of today. But young Christians also know that the race toward intellectual light, the advance into the mysterious and sometimes arduous terrain of revelation, the striving toward goodness and holiness, are proportionately more beautiful, noble, and stirring, as wisdom and virtue of the soul exceed and surpass muscular strength and the transient nimbleness and agility of the limbs.

The vigor of the body, which accompanies and embellishes the flowering of youth, is not diminished or lowered, but rather exalted and ennobled by the striving for religious culture and by the virtue which dominates the passions.[1]

He who reproaches the Church for not caring about the body and physical culture is just as far from the truth as he who would like to restrict her competence and her activity to "purely religious" things, "exclusively spiritual" matters. As if the body, God's creation just as much as is the soul to which it is united, should not have its share in the homage to be paid to the Creator! "Therefore, whether you eat or drink," wrote the Apostle of the Gentiles to the Corinthians, "or whatever else you do, do all to the glory of God." St. Paul speaks here of physical activity; sport comes under the words "whatever else you do." Actually, he often talks about this explicitly; he speaks about racing and wrestling, not with expressions of criticism or condemnation, but as an expert who elevates and ennobles them by a Christian approach.

For what, finally, are sports if not one of the forms of education of the body? Now this education is in strict relationship with morals. How then could the Church be indifferent to them?

Actually, she has always had a consideration and solicitude for the human body which materialism, in its idolatrous cult, has never shown. And that is natural, because it sees and knows in the body only the material flesh, whose vigor and beauty are born and bloom only to fade and die, like grass in the fields. Far different is the Christian conception. The human body is, in itself, the masterpiece of God in the order of visible creation. The Lord had destined it to bloom here below in order to unfold itself immortal in the glory of Heaven. He joined it to the spirit in the unity of human nature, so that the soul might enjoy the enchantment of God's works, to help it to behold in this mirror their common Creator, to get to know Him, worship Him, love Him! It was not God Who made the human body mortal, but sin; only because of sin must the body, taken from dust, one day return to dust. But the Lord will raise it again to recall it to life. Even when they are reduced to dust, the Church respects and honors bodies, dead only to rise again.

But the Apostle Paul leads us to an even higher vision: "Do you not know," he says, "that your body is a temple of the Holy Spirit Who is in you, Whom you have from God; and you are not your own? For you are bought with a great price. Glorify and bear God in your body."

What, then, is primarily the function and purpose of "sports," in a healthy, Christian sense, if not the cultivation of the dignity and the harmony of the human body, the development of health, vigor, agility, and gracefulness?

Nor should St. Paul be reproached for his energetic expression: "*Castigo corpus meum et in servitutem redigo*—I chastise my body and bring it into subjection," since in that same passage he draws an example from the fervid worshipers of sports. Sports, moderately and conscientiously practiced, strengthen the body, make it healthy, fresh, and vigorous. But to accomplish this task of education, the body is submitted to a rigorous and often harsh discipline which dominates it and keeps it truly in subjection: arduous training, resistance to pain, the habit of continence and strict temperance, all are indispensable conditions for whoever wants to reach for victory. Sports are an effective antidote against softness and easy living; they awaken the sense of order and train one to self-criticism and self-control, to hold danger in contempt, without bragging or cowardice. Thus they already go beyond mere physical robustness, to lead us on the way to moral strength and greatness. From the native country of sports, the proverbial "fair play" had its origin, that chivalrous and courteous emulation which elevates the spirits above the meanness of cheating, the tricks of a touchy and vindictive vanity, and preserves them from the excesses of a narrow, intransigent nationalism. Sports are a school of loyalty, courage, tolerance, resoluteness, universal brotherhood, all natural virtues, but which provide a solid basis for the supernatural virtues, and prepare one to support without flinching the weight of the gravest responsibilities.

To subject the body to healthy fatigue in order to rest the mind and get it ready for new labors, to sharpen the senses in order to acquire a greater intensity of penetration for the intellectual faculties, to exercise the muscles and become accustomed to effort in order to temper the character and to form a will as strong and as flexible as steel: such was the idea that the mountain-climbing priest had formed of sports.*

In this sense, sports are not an end, but a means; as such they must be and must remain subordinated to the end, which consists in the perfect, well-balanced formation and education of man as a whole, man whom sports help to carry out his duty readily and joyfully, both at work and in family life.

In the service of a healthy, robust, ardent life, in the service of a more fruitful activity in carrying out the duties of one's own state, sports can and must be also in the service of God. To this end, in fact, it encourages people to direct the physical strength and moral virtues which it develops; but whereas the pagan used to submit to the severe regimen of sport to obtain only a short-lived wreath, the Christian submits to it for a higher purpose, for an immortal prize.

For what would be the use of physical courage and energy of character if the Christian made use of them only for earthly ends, to win a "cup" or to parade as a superman? If he did not know, when necessary, how to cut down his sleep by a half hour or postpone a stadium appointment, rather than neglect assisting at Holy Mass on Sunday; if he did not succeed in overcoming respect of persons in the practice and defense of his religion; if he did not use his presence and his authority to stop or repress—by a look, a word, a gesture—a curse, foul language, an act of indecency; if he did not protect the youngest and the weakest against provocations and suspicious attentions; if he did not foster the habit of concluding his happy successes in sports with praise to God, the Creator and Lord of nature and of all its power? Keep always in mind that the highest honor and the holiest destiny of the body is to be the dwelling of a soul which is resplendent with moral purity and sanctified by divine grace.[2]

* This refers to Pope Pius XI. (*Translator's Note*)

[1] Address to Youth of Catholic Action, November 10, 1940

[2] Address to Youth of Catholic Action, May 20, 1945

CHURCH AND RELIGION

THE CHURCH

The Church Is the Mystical Body of Christ

WHEN ONE REFLECTS on the origin of this doctrine, there come to mind at once the words of the Apostle: "Where sin abounded, grace did more abound." All know that the father of the whole human race was constituted by God in so exalted a state that he was to hand on to his posterity, together with earthly existence, the heavenly life of divine grace. After the unhappy fall of Adam, the whole human race, infected by the hereditary stain, lost its participation in the divine nature, and we were all become "children of wrath." But the all-merciful God "so loved the world as to give His only-begotten Son"; and the Word of the Eternal Father with the same divine love assumed human nature from the race of Adam—but an innocent and spotless nature—so that He, as the new Adam, might be the source whence the grace of the Holy Spirit should flow unto all the children of the first parent. Through the sin of the first man they had been excluded from adoption as children of God; now, however, through the Word incarnate made brothers according to the flesh of the only-begotten Son of God, they receive also the power to become the sons of God. Through His death on the Cross, Christ Jesus not only satisfied the justice of the Eternal Father which had been violated, but He also won for us, His brethren, an ineffable flow of graces. It was possible for Him to impart these graces to mankind directly; but He willed to do so through a visible Church made up of men, so that through her all might co-operate with Him in dispensing the graces of Redemption. As the Word of God willed to make use of our nature, in order to redeem mankind, through His suffering and agony, in the same way throughout the centuries He makes use of the Church that the work begun may endure.

If we would define and describe this true Church of Jesus Christ

—which is the One, Holy, Catholic, Apostolic Roman Church—we shall find nothing more noble, more sublime, or more divine than the expression "the mystical body of Jesus Christ." This name springs from and flowers forth, as it were, in frequent teachings of the Sacred Scriptures and the holy Fathers.

The Church Is the Visible Body

That the Church is a body is frequently asserted in the Sacred Scriptures. "Christ," says the Apostle, "is the head of the body, the Church" (Colossians 1, 18). If the Church is a body, it must be an unbroken unity, according to the words of Paul: "Though many, we are one body in Christ" (Romans 12, 5). But it is not enough that the body of the Church should be an unbroken unity; it must also be something definite and perceptible to the senses as Our predecessor of happy memory, Leo XIII, in his Encyclical *Statis cognitum,* asserts: "The Church is visible because she is a body." Hence they err in a matter of divine truth who imagine the Church to be invisible, intangible, something merely "pneumatological," as they say, through which many Christian communities, though they differ from each other in their profession of faith, are united by an invisible bond.

But a body calls also for a multiplicity of members, which are linked together in such a way as to help one another. And as in the body, when one member suffers, all the other members share its pain, and the healthy members come to the assistance of the ailing, so in the Church the individual members do not live for themselves alone, but also help their fellows, and all work in mutual collaboration for the common comfort and for the more perfect building up of the whole body.

Again, as in nature a body is not formed by any haphazard grouping of members but must be constituted of organs, that is, of members that do not have the same function, and are arranged in due order; so for this reason above all the Church is called a body, because she is constituted by the organic structure of united parts, and consists of a variety of reciprocally dependent members. It is thus that the Apostle describes the Church when he writes: "As in one body we have many members, but all the members have not the same office: so we being many are one body in Christ, and every one members of one another" (Romans 12, 4, 5).

One must not think, however, that this ordered or "organic" structure of the body of the Church contains only hierarchical elements and with them is complete; or, as an opposite opinion holds, that it is composed only of those who enjoy charismatic gifts—though members gifted with miraculous powers will never be lacking in the Church. That those who exercise sacred authority in this body are its first and chief members, must be maintained uncompromisingly. It is through them, by commission of the Divine Redeemer Himself, that Christ's apostolate as Teacher, King, and Priest continues forever. At the same time, when the Fathers of the Church exalt this mystical body of Christ, with its ministries, its variety of ranks, its offices, its positions, its orders, its duties, they are thinking not only of those who have received Holy Orders, but of all those, too, who, following the evangelical counsels, spend their lives either actively among men or hidden in the silence of the cloister, or who aim at combining the active and contemplative life according to their rule; as also of those who, though living in the world, consecrate themselves wholeheartedly to spiritual or corporal works of mercy, and of those who live in the state of holy matrimony. Indeed, let this be clearly understood, especially in these our days: fathers and mothers of families, those who are godparents through Baptism, and in particular those members of the laity who collaborate with the ecclesiastical hierarchy in spreading the Kingdom of the Divine Redeemer, occupy an honorable, if often a lowly, place in the Christian community, and even they under the impulse of God and with His help can reach the heights of supreme holiness, which, as Jesus Christ has promised, will never be wanting to the Church.

The Holy Sacraments

Now we see that the human body is given the proper means to provide for its own life, health, and growth, and for that of all its members. Similarly the Savior of mankind out of His infinite goodness has provided in a wonderful way for His mystical body, endowing it with the Sacraments, so that, as though by an uninterrupted series of graces, its members should be sustained from birth to death, and that generous provision might be made for the social needs of the whole body. Through the waters of Baptism those who are born into this world dead in sin are not only born again and made members of the Church, but, being stamped with a spiritual seal, they become able and fit to receive the other Sacraments. By the chrism of Confirmation, the faithful are given added strength to protect and defend the Church, their Mother, and the faith she has given them. In the Sacrament of Penance, a saving medicine is offered for the members of the Church who have fallen into sin, not only to provide for their own health, but to remove from other members of the mystical body all dangers of contagion, or rather to afford them an incentive to virtue, and the example of a virtuous act.

Nor is that all; for in the Holy Eucharist the faithful are nourished and strengthened at the same banquet and by a divine, ineffable bond are united with each other and with the divine Head of the whole body. Finally, like a devoted mother, the Church is at the bedside of those who are sick unto death; and if it be not always God's will that by the holy anointing she restore health to this mortal body, nevertheless she administers spiritual medicine to the wounded soul and sends new citizens to Heaven, to be her new advocates, who will enjoy forever the happiness of God.

For the social needs of the Church Christ has provided in a particular way by the institution of two other Sacraments. Through Matrimony, in which the contracting parties are ministers of grace to each other, provision is made for the external and duly regulated increase of Christian society, and, what is of greater importance, for the correct religious education of the children, without which this mystical body would be in grave danger. Through Holy Orders men are set aside and consecrated to God, to offer the Sacrifice of the Eucharistic Victim, to nourish the flock of the faithful with the Bread of Angels and the food of doctrine, to guide them in the way of God's commandments and counsels, and to strengthen them with all other supernatural helps.

The Holy Spirit

Nor must one imagine that the body of the Church, just because it bears the name of Christ, is made up during the days of its earthly pilgrimage only of members conspicuous for their holiness, or that it consists only of those whom God has predestined to eternal happiness. It is owing to the Savior's infinite mercy that place is allowed in His mystical body here below for those whom, of old, He did not exclude from the banquet. For not every sin, however grave it may be, is such as of its own nature to sever a man from the body of the Church, as does schism or heresy or apostasy. Men may lose charity and divine grace through sin, thus becoming incapable of supernatural merit, and yet not be deprived of all life if they hold fast to faith and Christian hope, and if, illumined from above, they are spurred on by the interior promptings of the Holy Spirit to salutary fear and are moved to prayer and penance for their sins.

The Church which Christ founded by His blood, He strengthened on the day of Pentecost by a special power, given from Heaven. For, having solemnly installed in his exalted office him whom He had already nominated as His Vicar, He had ascended into Heaven; and sitting now at the right hand of the Father He wished to make known and proclaim His Spouse through the visible coming of the Holy Spirit with the sound of a mighty wind and tongues of fire. For just as He Himself when He began to preach was made known by His Eternal Father through the Holy Spirit descending and remaining upon Him in the form of a dove, so likewise, as the Apostles were about to enter upon their ministry of preaching, Christ our Lord sent the Holy Spirit down from Heaven, to touch them with tongues of fire and to point out, as by the finger of God, the supernatural mission and office of the Church.

Christ Is Head of the Body

That this mystical body which is the Church should be called Christ's is proved in the second place by the fact that He must be universally acknowledged as its actual Head. "He," as St. Paul says, "is the head of the body, the Church" (Colossians 1, 18). He is the head from whom the whole body, perfectly organized, "groweth and maketh increase unto the edifying of itself."

But our divine Savior governs and guides the society which He founded directly and personally also. For it is He Who reigns within the minds and hearts of men, and bends and subjects their wills to His good pleasure, even when they are rebellious. "The heart of the king is in the hand of the Lord; whithersoever he will he shall turn it" (Proverbs 21, 1). By this interior guidance He, the "Shepherd and Bishop of our souls," not only watches over individuals but exercises His Providence over the Universal Church, whether by enlightening and giving courage to the Church's rulers for the loyal and effective performance of their respective duties, or by singling out from the body of the Church—especially when times are grave—men and women of conspicuous holiness, who may point the way for the rest of Christendom to the perfecting of His mystical body. Moreover, from Heaven Christ never ceases to look down with especial love on His spotless Spouse so sorely tried in her earthly exile; and when He sees her in danger, saves her from the tempestuous sea either Himself or through the ministry of His angels, or through her whom we invoke as the Help of Christians, or through other heavenly advocates, and in calm and tranquil waters comforts her with the peace "which surpasseth all understanding."

The Pope Is the Visible Vicar of Christ

But we must not think that He rules only in a hidden or extraordinary manner. On the contrary, our Divine Redeemer also governs His mystical body in a visible and normal way through His Vicar on earth. You know, Venerable Brethren, that after He had ruled the "little flock" Himself during His pilgrimage on earth, Christ our Lord, when about to leave this world and return to the Father, entrusted to the Chief of the Apostles the visible government of the entire community He had founded. Since He was all wise He could not leave the body of the Church He had founded as a human society without a visible head. Nor against this may one argue that the primacy of jurisdiction established in the Church gives such a mystical body two heads. For Peter by virtue of his primacy is only Christ's Vicar; so that there is only one chief head of this body, namely Christ, Who never ceases Himself to guide the Church invisibly, though at the same time He rules it visibly, through him who is His representative on earth. After His glorious Ascension into Heaven this Church rested not on Him alone, but on Peter too, its visible foundation stone. That Christ and His Vicar constitute one head only is the solemn teaching of Our predecessor of immortal memory, Boniface VIII, in the Apostolic Letter *Unam Sanctam;* and his successors have never ceased to repeat the same.

They, therefore, walk in the path of dangerous error who believe that they can accept Christ as the head of the Church, while not adhering loyally to His Vicar on earth. They have taken away the visible head, broken the visible bonds of unity, and left the mystical body of the Redeemer so obscured and so maimed that those who are seeking the haven of eternal salvation can neither see it nor find it.

The Bishops

What We have thus far said of the Universal Church must be understood also of the individual Christian communities, the dioceses, whether Oriental or Latin, which go to make up the one Catholic Church. For they, too, are ruled by Jesus Christ through the voice of their respective Bishops.

The Church as Mystical Body of Christ

Now We come to that part of Our explanation in which We desire to make clear why the body of Christ, which is the Church, should be called mystical. This appellation, which is used by several early writers of the Church, has the sanction of numerous Pontifical documents. There are several reasons why it should be used; for by it we may distinguish the body of the Church, which is a society whose head and ruler is Christ, from His physical body, which, born of the Virgin Mother of God, now sits at the right hand of the Father and is hidden under the Eucharistic veils; and—something that is of greater importance in view of modern errors—this appellation enables us to distinguish it from any other body, whether in the physical or the moral order.

In a natural body the principle of unity unites the parts in such a manner that each lacks its own individual subsistence; conversely, in the mystical body the mutual union, though intrinsic, links the members by a bond which leaves to each the complete enjoyment of his own personality. Moreover, if we examine the relations existing between the several members and the whole body, in every physical, living body all the different members are ultimately destined to the good of the whole alone; while if we look to its ultimate usefulness, every moral association of men is in the end directed to the advancement of all in general and of each single member in particular; for they are persons. And thus—to return to Our theme—as the Son of the Eternal Father came down from Heaven for the salvation of us all, He likewise established the body of the Church and enriched it with the divine Spirit to ensure that immortal souls should attain eternal happiness according to the words of the Apostle: "All things are yours; and you are Christ's; and Christ is God's." For the Church exists both for the good of the faithful and for the glory of God and of Jesus Christ, Whom He sent.

But if we compare a mystical body with a moral body, it is to be noted that the difference between them is not slight; rather, it is very considerable and very important. In the moral body, the principle of union is nothing else than the common end, and the co-operation of all under the guidance of a social authority, for the attainment of that end; whereas in the mystical body of which We are speaking, this collaboration is supplemented by another internal principle, which exists effectively in the whole and in each of its parts, and whose excellence is such that of itself it is vastly superior to whatever bonds of union may be found in a physical or moral body. As We said above, this is something not of the natural but of the supernatural order; indeed, it is something in itself infinite, uncreated: the Spirit of God, Who, as St. Thomas, the Angelic Doctor, says, "numerically one and the same, fills and unifies the whole Church."

Hence, in its correct signification, the word "mystical" gives us to understand that the Church, a perfect society of its kind, is not made up of merely moral and juridical elements and principles. She is far superior to all other human societies; she surpasses them as grace surpasses nature, as things immortal are above all those that perish. Such human societies, and in the first place civil society, are by no means to be despised or belittled; but the Church in her entirety is not found within this natural order, any more than the whole of man is encompassed within the organism of our mortal body. Although the juridical principles, on which the Church rests and is established, derive from the divine constitution given to her by Christ and contribute to the attaining of her supernatural end, nevertheless that which lifts the society of Christians far above the whole natural order is the Spirit of our Redeemer Who penetrates and fills every part of the Church's being and is active within her until the end of time as the source of every grace and every gift and every miraculous power. Just as our composite mortal body, although it is a marvellous work of the Creator, falls far short of the eminent dignity of our soul, so the social structure of the Christian community, though it proclaims the wisdom of its divine Architect, still remains something inferior when compared to the spiritual gifts which give it beauty and life, and to the divine source whence they flow.

From what We have thus far written and explained, Venerable Brethren, it is clear, We think, how grievously they err who arbitrarily claim that the Church is something hidden and invisible, as also do those who look upon her as a mere human institution possessing a certain disciplinary code and external ritual, but not the power to communicate supernatural life.

For this reason We deplore and condemn the pernicious error of those who dream of a Church of their own imagination, a kind of society that finds its origin and growth in charity, to which, somewhat contemptuously, they oppose another, which they call juridical. But this distinction which they introduce is false: for they fail to understand that the reason which led our divine Redeemer to give to the community of men He founded the constitution of a society, perfect of its kind and containing all the juridical and social elements—namely, that He might perpetuate on earth the saving work of Redemption—was also the reason why He willed it to be enriched with the heavenly gifts of the Paraclete. The Eternal Father indeed willed it to be the "kingdom of the Son of His predilection"; but it was to be a real kingdom, in which all believers should make Him the entire offering of their intellect and will, and humbly and obediently model themselves on Him Who for our sake "was made obedient unto death" (Philippians 2, 8). There can, then, be no real opposition or conflict between the invisible mission of the Holy Spirit and the juridical commission of Ruler and Teacher received from Christ, since they mutually complement and perfect each other—as do the body and soul in man—and proceed from our one Redeemer Who not only said as He breathed on the Apostles, "Receive ye the Holy Spirit" (John 20, 22), but also clearly commanded,

"As the Father hath sent me, I also send you" (John 20, 21); and again, "He that heareth you heareth me" (Luke 10, 16).

Sin and Weakness Are Not Excluded

And if at times there appears in the Church something that indicates the weakness of our human nature, it should not be attributed to her juridical constitution, but rather to that regrettable inclination to evil found in each individual, which her divine Founder permits even at times in the most exalted members of His mystical body, for the purpose of testing the virtue of the shepherds no less than of the flocks, and that all may increase the merit of their Christian faith. For, as We said above, Christ did not wish to exclude sinners from His Church; hence if some of her members are suffering from spiritual maladies, that is no reason why we should lessen our love for the Church, but rather a reason why we should increase our devotion to her members. Certainly the loving Mother is spotless in the Sacraments, by which she gives birth to and nourishes her children; in the faith which she has always preserved inviolate; in her sacred laws imposed on all; in the evangelical counsels which she recommends; in those heavenly gifts and extraordinary graces though which, with inexhaustible fecundity, she generates hosts of martyrs, virgins, and confessors. But it cannot be laid to her charge if some members fall, weak or wounded. In their name she prays to God daily: "Forgive us our trespasses"; and with the brave heart of a mother she applies herself at once to the work of nursing them back to spiritual health.

When, therefore, we call the body of Jesus Christ "mystical," the very meaning of the word conveys a solemn warning. It is a warning that echoes in these words of St. Leo: "Recognize, O Christian, your dignity, and being made a sharer of the divine nature do not go back to your former worthlessness along the way of unseemly conduct. Keep in mind of what head and of what body you are a member." [1]

The Indestructibility of the Church

The Catholic Church, therefore, is the great visible mystery, because her head on earth, the Vicar of Christ, is visible, her ministers are visible, her life is visible, her worship is visible, her work and activity for the salvation and the perfection of men is visible. Visible, too, is her indestructibility, as it is proved historically, while her past is the token of her future. Hence a great historian, not a Catholic, of the last century, after recognizing, in spite of himself, that the Catholic Church has remained "full of life and of youthful vigor," remarked: "If we think of the tremendous storms it has survived, we find it difficult to conceive how it could perish." But if this indestructibility can be demonstrated by experience, it is, nevertheless, a mystery, because it cannot be explained naturally, but only by the fact, known to us by divine revelation, that Christ, Who founded the Church, is with her in every danger until the end of time.[2]

The Church, too, had and has her springtime; marvellous like herself. Do not the three great solemnities of Easter, Ascension, and Pentecost, in the season in which nature, awakening to new life, decks itself in greenery and blossom, and labors to produce the gifts of its harvests and fruits, constitute a spiritual spring, which makes nature's spring sweeter, lovelier, and dearer to us? They form, as it were, a sun in which shine three supreme truths, three overwhelming historical facts, three mysteries of unsurpassed splendor in the work of redemption; they are three fundamental and unshakable pillars of the gigantic edifice of the Holy Church. In their light, in their supernatural strength, these truths, equally present in every century of the history of the Church and equally obvious to all the generations of the faithful, illuminate with their historical reality the spring of Christianity, its budding, growth, and bloom even among winds and storms; because Christianity was born a giant, its forehead encircled with the rays of those three truths, which open up the period rightly called heroic: the three centuries from the foundation of the Church up to the peace with the Roman Empire in the year 312 in the time of Constantine.

These three fundamental mysteries, like brilliant rays from that light of the world that is Christ, guide and accompany the young Church, the Bride of Christ, on her way, watching over her first steps and encouraging her to rise, through the dark forest of paganism, and to reach the mountain of her predestined greatness. The first Christians, their minds, with tenacious constancy, absorbed in their faith in rebirth and their own resurrection, their eyes fixed longingly on the glorified figure seated on the right of the Father, and on the heavenly Jerusalem, the eternal, happy dwelling of those who remain faithful up to the end, their souls dominated by the certainty of the supporting presence of the Spirit, promised and sent by Jesus: thus we see them, towering above us with their lofty thought and vigorous action, vying with each other in courage and moral heroism, in the affirmation of the faith, in struggles and sufferings, leaving an example which had the power to win victory after victory throughout the centuries and up to the present time; even more so now when, to save and protect the honor and the name of Christian, it is necessary to sustain similar struggles and to face similar dangers. Before such heroes, on whose heads the laurel of the Christian warrior is often entwined with the palm of martyrdom, all uncertainty and hesitancy disappear. Is not the example of their heroic lives, calling us sharply to order, enough to drive darkness from our minds, breathe courage into our hearts, make us hold our heads high once more, reminding us, Christians of today, of our dignity, making us aspire to the lofty greatness, calling to mind the responsibilities which Christianity inspires in those who profess it?

This early Christianity, of whose beginning we are reminded by the approach of the solemnities of Ascension and Pentecost, is distinguished by four spiritual characteristics that are quite unmistakable:

1. Unshaken certainty of victory, based on profound faith.
2. Serene and unlimited readiness for sacrifice and sufferings.
3. Eucharistic ardor springing from the conviction of the social efficaciousness of a Eucharistic thought on all forms of social life.
4. Aspiration toward an ever closer and unbreakable unity of spirit and hierarchy.

This fourfold character of the early life of the Church presents in each of its dominant notes an appeal and at the same time a hope and a promise for Christianity in our days. But the real Christianity of today is not different from primitive Christianity. The youth of the Church is eternal, because the Church does not grow old, even though changing step according to the conditions of the time, in her journey toward eternity; the centuries she counts are but a day for her, and but a day are the centuries before her. Her youth in the times of the Caesars is the same that speaks to us.[3]

The Church Is Above Nationalism

The Catholic Church is by her very essence above nationalism. This has a double sense, one negative and one positive. The Church is a mother, *Sancta Mater Ecclesia,* a true mother, the mother of all the nations and all the peoples, no less than of all individual men, and just because she is a mother, she does not and cannot belong exclusively to this or that people, or even to one people more than to another, but to all equally. She is a mother, and therefore is not and cannot be a stranger in any place; she lives, or at least by her nature must live, among all peoples. In addition, while the mother, with her husband and children, forms a family, the Church, by virtue of an incomparably closer union, constitutes, more or better than a family, the mystical body of Christ. The Church, therefore, is above nationalism, because she is an invisible and all-embracing whole.

The Church unites all regions and all periods of redeemed humanity, without exceptions.

Securely established on such deep foundations, the Church, placed as she is in the midst of the history of mankind, among the confusion and the havoc of divergent energies and contradictory tendencies, although exposed to all assaults on her indivisible wholeness, is so far from being shaken by them that from her own life of wholeness and unity she irradiates and diffuses ever new healing and unifying powers among lacerated and divided humanity, powers of unifying divine grace, powers of the unifying Spirit, for which all are hungry, truths that prevail always and everywhere, ideals that throw light always and everywhere.

From this it is clear that it was and is a sacrilege against the *totus Christus,* Christ in His integrity, and at the same time a fatal blow against the unity of mankind, whenever an attempt has been or is being made to make the Church a prisoner and a slave of this or that particular people, to confine her to the narrow limits of a nation, as also to ban her from a nation. This laceration of the wholeness of the Church has reduced increasingly and continues to reduce the welfare, in the sense of true fullness of life, of the peoples that are victims of it.

But the national and State individualism of the last few centuries was not alone in trying to harm the interests of the Church, to weaken and impede her unified and unifying forces, which once took an essential part in the formation of the unity of Western Europe. An obsolete liberalism set out, without and against the Church, to create unity by means of lay culture and secularized humanism. Here and there, as the fruit of its dissolving action and at the same time as its enemy, totalitarianism supplanted it. In a word, after little more than a century, what was the result of all those efforts without and often against the Church? The decline of wholesome human liberty; compulsory organizations; a world that, for brutality and barbarity, for destruction and ruin, and above all for fatal disunion and lack of security, had never been equalled.

In confused times such as ours, the Church, for her own welfare and for that of humanity, must do her utmost to stress her indivisible and undivided wholeness. Today more than ever she must take up her stand above all nationalism. This spirit must penetrate and pervade her visible head, the Sacred College, all the action of the Holy See which, especially now, is faced with important duties regarding not only the present but even more so the future.

What is in question here is principally a matter of the spirit, of having the right sense of this supranationalism, and of not measuring or determining it according to mathematical proportions or on a rigorous statistical basis regarding the nationality of individual persons. In the long periods of time in which, by the will of Providence, the Italian nation, more than the others, has given the Church her head and many collaborators to the central government of the Holy See, the Church as a whole has always kept intact her supranational character.

Supranational because she embraces with the same love all nations and all peoples, she is also such, as We have already mentioned, because she is nowhere a stranger. She lives and thrives in every country in the world, and every country in the world contributes to her life and her development.

And so in the Church of today we see being accomplished more and more what St. Augustine magnified in his *City of God;* "The Church," he wrote, "calls her citizens from all parts, from all languages she gathers her pilgrim community on earth; she pays no heed to differences in customs, laws, institutions; she neither suppresses nor destroys any of these things, but rather preserves and follows. Even that which is different in the different nations, she directs toward the one and the same end of earthly peace, unless it prevents the veneration of the one supreme and true God."

Like a mighty lighthouse, the Church, in her all-embracing universality, casts her sheaf of light in these dark days through which we are passing.

For Our part, We are eager to make this same house more and more solid, more and more habitable for everyone, without exception. And so We do not want to omit anything that can express visibly that the Church has this supranational quality, the sign of her love for Christ, Whom she sees and serves with the richness of her members scattered throughout the whole world.[4]

The Church Is a Mother

The Church, who was sent by the divine Savior to all peoples to lead them to their eternal salvation, does not intend to intervene and to take sides in controversies about purely temporal matters.

She is a mother. Do not ask a mother to take sides for or against one or other of her children. Everybody must find and feel in her that clear-sighted and generous love, that intimate and unchangeable tenderness, that gives her faithful children the strength to walk with a firmer step in the royal road of truth and light, and inspires in those who have gone astray the desire to return to her maternal guidance.[5]

Any attentive observer who is able to examine and sum up present circumstances, in their concrete reality, necessarily remains struck by the sight of the severe obstacles that obstruct the apostolate of the Church. Like the flow of incandescent lava that yard by yard covers the slope of the volcano, so the devastating sea of the spirit of the times advances threateningly and spreads over all fields of life, all classes of society.

Its process and its rhythm, no less than its effects, vary according to the different countries, from a more or less conscious disavowal of the social influence of the Church to systematic mistrust, which in some forms of government takes on the character of open hostility and real persecution.[6]

But the Church cannot withdraw into inactivity in the secrecy of her temples and desert the mission given her by divine Providence to form the complete man, and to collaborate constantly in the constitution of a solid foundation for society. This mission is essential for her. Considered from this point of view, the Church can be called the society of those who, under the supernatural influence of grace, in the perfection of their personal dignity as sons of God and in the harmonious development of all human inclinations and energies, construct the powerful framework of human society.

Thus the principal significance of the Church's supranationalism is to give lasting figure and form to the foundations of human society, above all diversities, beyond the limits of time and space.[7]

[1] Encyclical *Mystici Corporis Christi,* June 29, 1943
[2] Address to Lenten Preachers, March 13, 1943
[3] Radio Broadcast, May 13, 1943
[4] Allocution to the Sacred College, December 24, 1945
[5] Allocution to the Sacred College, December 24, 1946
[6] Allocution to the Sacred College, December 23, 1950
[7] Allocution to the new Cardinals, February 20, 1946

THE PAPACY

CHRIST HAS CARRIED OUT His will to found one Church, indivisible and indestructible, in the promise to Peter, by the institution of the primacy, that is, of the Papacy. The Church, built on Peter and on his successors, and she alone, was to be the Church of Christ, unique and eternal unto the end of time through submission to a personal, visible head.

It was a disposition of divine Providence that Peter chose Rome as his episcopal seat. Here, in the Circus of Nero, as we know from incontestable archaeological evidence, he died as the confessor of Christ; under the central point of the gigantic cupola of St. Peter's was and is his burial place. His successors, the Popes, have continued his mission up to the present.

In the series of Roman Pontiffs there have been many who, like the Prince of Apostles, sealed with their blood their fidelity to Him Whose visible representatives they were. Many were great on account of their holiness, their genius, their learning, their authoritative personality. There have been some others whose purely human qualities were less adequate for the requirements of their supreme pastoral office. But the most violent storms that have raged from the time of the Apostle Peter up to our own days have not been able to shake the Church, nor to impair the divine mission of her heads. Every Pope receives it, at the very moment when he accepts his election, directly from Christ, with the powers and the privilege of infallibility granted him by God.

If ever one day (We say this as a mere hypothesis) material Rome were to crumble, if ever this very Vatican Basilica, the symbol of the one invincible Catholic Church, were to bury beneath its ruins the historical treasures, the sacred tombs it encloses, even then the Church would not crumble or crack, Christ's promise to Peter would always remain true, the Papacy, the one and indestructible Church founded on the Pope alive at that moment, would always endure.[1]

Peter's successors, they, too, mortal like all men, pass away. But the primacy of Peter will always exist, with the special assistance promised him, when Jesus charged him with the task of confirming his brothers in the faith. Whatever may be the name, the face, the human origins of any Pope, it is always Peter who lives in him; it is Peter who rules and governs; it is Peter, above all, who teaches and diffuses over the world the light of liberating truth. That caused a great holy orator to say that God has set up in Rome an everlasting Chair: "Peter will live in his successors; Peter will always speak from his Chair."[2]

As the Vicar of Him Who in a decisive hour, before the representative of the highest earthly authority of that time, spoke the great words, "For this was I born and for this came I into the world; that I should give testimony to the truth. Every one that is of the truth, heareth my voice," We feel that our primary duty to Our office, and also to Our times, is to give testimony, with apostolic firmness, to the truth: *"testimonium perhibere veritati."* This duty necessarily includes the exposure and refutation of human errors and faults, which must be known so that it may be possible to cure them and recover from them: you will know the truth and the truth will make you free. In the carrying out of this duty, We will not let

Ourselves be influenced by earthly considerations, nor will We hold back because of diffidence and opposition, refusals and incomprehension, nor for fear of being misunderstood and wrongly interpreted. But We will do so always animated by that spirit of paternal love which, while it suffers from the evils that torment the children, points out to them the remedy, that is, We will try to imitate the divine model of the shepherds, the Good Shepherd Jesus, Who is at the same time light and love.[3]

Schisms

This divine mandate, which from the first Peter through the long series of Roman Pontiffs has come down to Us, their unworthy successor, embraces, in the confused and torn world of today, an even greater aggregate of sacred responsibilities, and meets with obstacles and opposition which demand of the Church, in her visible head and her members, increased alacrity and vigilance.

Today, in fact, more than ever there is revealed to the eye of every clear-sighted and just observer the sad record of loss which the schisms from the Mother Church have inflicted on Christianity in the course of the centuries. In a stormy, tormented epoch like ours, when humanity is preparing to reap the consequences of a spiritual decadence which has precipitated it into the abyss; when in all the nations voices are raised demanding, for the gigantic work of post-war reorganization, in addition to exterior guarantees, also the indispensable juridical and moral foundations, it will be of essential importance to know what influence the current of ideas and rules of Christian life will be able to exercise on the contents and on the spirit of this future order and against the repeated predominance of false and fatal tendencies.

The Roman Catholic Mother Church, who has remained faithful to the constitution she received from her divine Founder, and who even today stands firm in the solidity of the rock on which His will constructed her, possesses in the primacy of Peter and his legitimate successors the certainty, guaranteed by the divine promises, of guarding and transmitting complete and inviolate, through centuries and millenniums, until the end of time, the whole sum of truth and grace that is contained in Christ's mission of redemption. And while the

Church, in the stimulating and comforting consciousness of this double possession, finds her strength able to conquer all the darkness of error and moral degradation, she pursues her task in the interests not only of Christianity but of the entire world, inspiring sentiments of conciliatory justice and genuine brotherly love in the great controversies, in which, often, blessing and calamity, plentiful harvests and crop failure, are to be found side by side.

But how much stronger and more efficacious the radiation of Christian thought and life would be on the moral foundations of the future plans for peace and social reconstruction if it were not for the vast division and dispersion of religious denominations which in the course of time have split away from the Mother Church! Who today would not recognize what constancy of faith, what a deep force of resistance against antireligious influences, have been lost by this division into numerous groups?

Rationalism

The story of rationalism and naturalism in the last two centuries is eloquent proof, among many others, of this grievous reality. Where the office entrusted to him who is invested with the primacy, *confirma fratres tuos*—strengthen thy brethren—is unable to exercise and carry on its protective and preserving action, the tare of rationalism has penetrated in a thousand different ways, with its swarms of harmful parasites, into the thoughts and minds of many who call themselves Christians, poisoning what had remained in them of the divine seed of revealed truth, causing above all darkness, schism, and increasing abandonment of faith in the divinity of Christ.

The Bond of Caesarea Philippi

From the day of the promise given at Caesarea Philippi, and of its fulfillment on Lake Tiberias, there exists a living bond between Christ and Peter, a bond which, though mysterious, is nonetheless real, a bond knotted in time but having its origin in the eternal counsels of the Almighty. The heavenly Father, Who revealed the mystery of the divinity of Christ to Simon, the son of Jona, and thus made him able to answer with an open and ready confession the

Redeemer's question, had from all eternity predestined the fisherman of Bethsaida for his unique office; and Christ Himself merely carried out the Father's will when in His promise and in the conferment of the primacy He used words which were to establish forever the uniqueness of the privileged position attributed to Peter.

Those, therefore, who—as was stated (or, rather, repeated) not so long ago by some representatives of religious denominations that profess to be Christians—declare that there is no Vicar of Christ on earth, because Christ Himself has promised to remain with His Church as her Head and Lord until the end of time, besides depriving every episcopal office of its foundation, completely misunderstand the profound meaning of the pontifical primacy, which is not negation, but fulfillment of that promise. For, if it is true that Christ in the fullness of His divine power disposes of the most varied forms of illumination and sanctification, in which He is really with those who confess Him, it is no less certain that He entrusted Peter and his successors with the guidance and the government of the Universal Church and the treasures of truth and grace of His work of redemption. The words of Christ to Peter leave no doubt as to their meaning: this was recognized and believed by both East and West, in times above suspicion, and with admirable harmony. To insist on creating an opposition between Christ as head of the Church and His Vicar, to see in the affirmation of the one the negation of the other, is to introduce confusion into the clearest and most luminous pages of the Gospel, to shut one's eyes to the most ancient and venerable testimony of tradition, and to deprive Christianity of that precious inheritance, a true knowledge and esteem of which may, at a time that is known only to God and by means of the light of grace which He alone can give, arouse in our separated brethren the longing for their ancestral home and the efficacious resolve to return to it.

The Vicar of Christ

When, every year, on the evening before the feast of the Prince of the Apostles, We visit Our Patriarchal Vatican Basilica, to implore, on the tomb of the first Peter, the strength to serve the flock entrusted to Us according to the designs and ends of the eternal High Priest, from the majestic vault of that lofty temple there shimmer before Our eyes in gleaming mosaics the mighty words with which Christ manifested His intention of building the Church on the rock of Peter, and they remind Us of Our imperious duty to preserve intact this incomparable heritage of the divine Redeemer. While We behold shining before Us the "glory" of Bernini, and above the Chair, held up by the gigantic figures of Ambrose and Augustine, of Athanasius and John Chrysostom, We see resplendent and dominating in a blaze of light the symbol of the Holy Ghost, We feel and experience the fullness of the sacred character, of the superhuman mission, that the will of the Lord with the assistance of the Spirit, promised and sent by Him, has conferred on this central point of the Church of the Living God, *columna et firmamentum veritatis*—pillar and support of truth.[4]

The imposing colonnade of Bernini opens wide its arms, in a symbolic gesture, as if to say to the travellers and pilgrims of every language and every nation that this vast temple is ready to receive them all in truth and in love.[5]

[1] Address to the Students of Rome, January 30, 1949
[2] Address to Newlyweds, January 17, 1940
[3] Encyclical *Summi Pontificatus,* December 24, 1939
[4] Allocution to the Sacred College, June 2, 1944
[5] Homily, First Anniversary of Pontificate, March 3, 1940

ON PRAYER

DEVOTION IS A GREAT VIRTUE that safeguards all the others. But its most beautiful and expressive act is prayer, which, for man, who is body and soul, represents the daily food of the soul just as material bread is the daily nourishment of the body.

Prayer is, first of all, collecting one's thoughts before the Lord. To seek out God, to find Him, it is enough to enter into yourselves, morning, night, or at any moment of the day. If you are joyfully in a state of grace, you will see in the intimacy of your soul with the eyes of faith God ever present as an immensely kind Father, ready to hear your requests and tell you also what He expects of you; you will find God present as a judge, merciful and ready to forgive; or, better still, as the Father of the prodigal son, Who will open to you His arms and heart, if you will only prostrate yourselves penitent, confessing: "Father, I have sinned against Heaven and against Thee." Oh, how many souls have been saved from obstinacy in sin, hardening, and eternal perdition with a brief examination of conscience every evening! How many owe their salvation to daily prayer!

Such an exercise of Christian devotion does not mean transforming the home into a church or oratory; it is a sacred impulse of souls which feel in themselves the strength and life of faith. Even in ancient pagan Rome, the family home used to have a sanctuary and an altar dedicated to the tutelary gods which, especially on festive days, were adorned with garlands of flowers and on which supplications and sacrifices were offered. It was a cult blemished by the error of polytheism; but at its recollection how many Christians should blush with shame, who, with the sign of Baptism on their brows, find neither the space in their rooms to place an image of the real God, nor the time, in the twenty-four hours of the day, to gather around Him the homage of the family!

Nothing furthers trusting prayer as much as the personal experience of efficacious prayers which loving Providence has answered, granting largely and fully that which was requested.

And yet for some, for many who do pray, the divine favors seem to be too slow in coming. What they ask seems to them good, useful, necessary, and beneficient not only for the body but also for their souls and for the souls of those dear to them; they pray with fervor for weeks and months, and yet have not received anything. The health necessary to care for her family has not yet been granted to the mother. The son and the daughter whose conduct endangers their eternal salvation have not yet mended their ways. Material difficulties that oppress parents who struggle to assure their children a piece of bread, instead of abating, become harsher and more menacing.

Under the weight of such thoughts, many look with surprise upon the sacred altars before which prayer is offered and perhaps remain scandalized and perplexed in hearing the Sacred Liturgy incessantly recall and proclaim the promises of the divine Savior: "Whatever you ask in prayer, believing, you will obtain. . . . Ask and it shall be given unto you. . . . He who asks, receives. . . . Whatever you will ask of My Father, in My name, I shall do. . . . In truth, in truth, I say unto you, that whatever you may ask of the Father in My name, He will give it unto you." Could the promises of the Savior have been more explicit, more clear, more solemn? Are not some, perhaps, tempted to see almost a derision in the silence of God to their petitions?

But God neither lies nor can lie; that which He has promised, He will keep; that which He has said, He will make good.[1]

Our Savior has nowhere promised to make us infallibly happy in this world; He has promised—as we read in the Gospels—to hear us as the father does the child, to whom he does not give, even if asked for it, a stone or a serpent or a scorpion for food, but bread, fish, and eggs, which nourish him and advance him in his living and growing. What Jesus, our Savior, has pledged to grant us infallibly as the fruit of our prayers are not those favors men often ask out of ignorance of what is really necessary for their health, but that "good spirit," that bread of supernatural gifts necessary or useful to our souls; that fish prepared by Him, which, as a future symbol, Christ reborn gave as food to the Apostles on the banks of Lake Tiberias; that egg, food for the little ones of piety and devotion, which men often do not distinguish from the stones most harmful to their spiritual health, offered to them by the tempter, Satan.

Prayer, therefore, should be a petitioning for that which is good for our souls, an incessant petitioning, but also a devout petitioning.

Devout prayer! What is it? It is not a prayer sounding mere words only, while mind and heart and eyes stray in all directions, but rather the prayer of meditation which, before God, is wholly animated by filial confidence, becomes illuminated with live faith, is imbued with love for God and for one's brethren; it is the prayer always unfolding in the grace of God, always meritorious of eternal life, always humble in its intimacy; it is the prayer which, when you kneel before the altars or the images of the Crucified and the Most Holy Virgin in your home, does not know the arrogance of the Pharisee, who vaunts himself better than other men, but, like the poor publican, makes you feel in your own hearts that whatever you may receive is coming to you by the mercy of God.

Prayer is a good which does not humiliate or lower, but rather exalts man and makes him great. The most excellent artists, the masters of visual psychology, have created nothing more soul-stirring than the representation of man in prayer. In the attitude of prayer man reveals his greatest nobility, hence it was strikingly affirmed that "man is great only when he is kneeling." [2]

[1] Address to Newlyweds, February 2, 1941, and April 12, 1942
[2] Address to General Audience, July 2, 1941

THE TEN COMMANDMENTS

CHRIST, AS HE SAID, did not come to undo and abolish the Law, but to fulfill it and lead it to perfection; and fulfilled by Him with His doctrine and His teachings are the Ten Commandments, which God proclaimed on Sinai for the people of Israel.

Of God's Commandments in General

The Ten Commandments are a law, given by God Himself, in which are also mirrored the vigor of human reason and of the intelligence of learned men; yet, what manifests itself to whoever examines the religious and moral conditions of the present hour, if not a painful contrast between the highest level of religious formation which today is offered to the people, on the one hand, and, on the other, the negligible profit drawn from it and the diminishing activating force carried into practical life? In earlier periods of Church history, general religious teaching was, as a rule, far simpler; but the entire process of human life was dominated and, through numerous sacred customs, imbued with the fear of God and the incontrovertible obligation to keep His Commandments.

From the middle of the last century, not only has Catholic science, with admirable daring, expanded more and more, but especially the ecclesiastical ministry itself has illuminated and expounded Catholic faith in its every aspect, amply and imposingly, and furnished moral norms for the most varying conditions of life,

The Pope and Bishop Sheen

The Pope with "Harlem Globe-Trotters" Basketball Team, July 17, 1953

The Pope Talking to U.S. Soldiers

both for the individual and for communities, striving in every way to bring the wealth of spiritual light to the souls of men. But when one asks whether among Catholic people the level of religious instruction and of moral conduct has equally risen, the answer, unfortunately, cannot be affirmative. In lamentable contrast with that high doctrinal development, the efficacy and the force of the religious impulse have been decreasing and waning.

We do not deny—in fact, it is clearly apparent—that there is no want of Catholics of exemplary faithfulness to God's Commandments, nor are Christian heroism and sanctity wanting. In this respect, our times do not yield to preceding periods and we do not fear to say that in some aspects they surpass them. But take a look at public life and you will find, alas, that it has become to a large extent de-Christianized, while contempt of and estrangement from the Christian way of life have become widely diffused. An overwhelming antireligious current is opposed to the believers who want to form their whole personal, family, and public life according to the law of God; they meet with grave difficulties and impediments in trying to make their convictions known and appreciated; hence, not a few succumb or become slack in the practice of religion. To breathe in the corrupt atmosphere of great modern cities and live a Christian life without absorbing their poison, one needs a profound spirit of faith and the strength and resistance of the martyrs.

The Guilt of Sin

A fact which always repeats itself in the history of the Church is that when faith and Christian morals clash with strong adverse currents of error or vitiated appetites, attempts are made to overcome the difficulties with some sort of easy compromise, or otherwise to side-step and elude them.

Even in what is due the Commandments of God an expedient is thought to have been found. In the field of morality, it has been said, there is enmity with God, loss of supernatural life, grave sin in an absolute sense, only when the act for which one has to answer was performed not only with the clear consciousness that it infringes the Commandment of God, but also with the express intention of thereby offending the Lord, of destroying union with

Him, of denying Him love. If this intention is lacking, that is, if man on his part did not want to sever friendship with God, the individual act—it is maintained—cannot harm him. To cite an example: the multiform deviations from the Sixth Commandment do not represent a grave fault for the believer if he otherwise wants to keep united with God and to remain His friend, nor do they involve mortal sin. Stupefying solution! Who does not see how in the clear knowledge that a determined human act is against the Commandment of God, it is implied that it cannot be directed to the end of union with Him, precisely because it contains the aversion, that is, the estrangement of the soul, from God and His will (*aversio a Deo fine ultimo*), an aversion which destroys union and friendship with Him, which is, precisely, the hallmark of grave sin? Is it, perhaps, not true what faith and theology teach: that each sin is an offense against God and aims to offend Him, because the intention inherent in grave sin is against the will of God as expressed in the Commandment of His which is violated? When man says "Yes" to the forbidden fruit, he says "No" to the prohibiting God; when he puts himself and his will before the law of God, he estranges himself from God and divine will; aversion to God and the intimate essence of grave sin consist in this.

The malice of any human act originates from its not conforming to its proper rule, which is twofold: one, the more proximate, is human reason itself; the other, supreme rule is the eternal law, which may be likened to the reason of God, whose light is reflected in the human conscience when it shows us how to distinguish between good and evil. The true believer does not ignore that the intention pointing to the object of mortal sin is not separable from the intention which violates divine will and law and severs all friendship with God, Who knows well how to recognize the good and bad intentions of human acts and to reward or punish them with His penetrating justice.

There Is Only One Way

There is but one way to achieve the love of God and to be in union and friendship with Him: the observance of His precepts. Words count little; what counts are deeds, and therefore the Redeemer used to say: "Not everyone that says to me, Lord, Lord, shall enter into the Kingdom of Heaven: but he who does the will of my Father, Who is in Heaven, he shall enter the Kingdom of Heaven."

Acknowledging God by fulfilling His holy will in all His Commandments and, better still, by unifying our will with His will—that, and that alone, is the way to Heaven. St. Paul proclaimed this axiom of moral life in energetic form: "Beware of erring: neither fornicators, nor idolators, nor adulterers, nor the effeminate, nor those who sin against nature, nor thieves, nor the avaricious, nor drunkards, nor evildoers, nor the rapacious, shall be heirs to the Kingdom of God."

The Apostle of the Gentiles had in mind not only the defection from God by the formal negation of faith or formal hate of Him, but also every grave lesion of moral virtue, and His word concerned not only the habit of sinning but also all the individual acts against morals and justice, which are mortal sins and bring with them eternal damnation. To give precisely to the religious man what amounts to a document of immunity from guilt in whatever he might do against the Commandments of God, can surely not be considered to be the redemption from moral misery, whose elimination is today the task of the Church.

Neo-Paganism

Today paganism seems reborn, and many have already exalted it in prose works and poems in opposition to Christianity; but the Church, from her appearance in the world, with the teachings of the Gospel and with the heroic virtue of her Apostles and her believers, took a stand against every sophism and every underhanded or open persecution by paganism. Her struggle always took the form of a frontal attack, opposing to pagan error the illuminated strength of Christian precepts and virtues. Not only the Epistles of St. Paul give a very clear testimony to the loftiness of the moral obligations imposed by the religion of Christ and to the struggle the faithful had to endure to observe them; but also, at the end of the apostolic period, the Letters of the Apocalypse to the seven churches are a no less manifest expression, with their continuous refrain: *"Vincenti . . . Qui vicerit."* "To the victor I shall give to eat of the tree of life, the hidden manna; and I will confess his name before my Father and before His Angels. The victor shall not be hurt by the second death."

The Moral Law

The fervor of the Christians in the first centuries made them inclined to profess their faith rather too openly than the opposite; so much so that at times their moral rigor surpassed the very limits of the reasonable measure demanded by the spirit of the Gospel. With great severity the Church Fathers did not hesitate to combat, because of the disorders they caused, the spectacles: gladiatorial contests, the theater, dances, feasts, and pastimes which seemed only natural amusements to pagan society. It is no wonder that faith should radically change and improve the habits of those who came in contact with it.

If, then, today the cry is so often raised: Return to early Christianity! a good beginning toward its realization is the amending and reform of morals; let that cry not be a vain noise but a serious and effective return, such as the exigencies of moral practice and life nowadays so urgently demand.

Christ did not find heroism in everyone; whoever showed but a trace of good will, to him He tendered His hand and inspired him with courage; at the same time, however, He did not refrain from making the highest demands: "If any man will come after Me, let him deny himself and take up his cross daily, and follow Me." "Be you therefore perfect, as also your heavenly Father is perfect." To lead man to such lofty goals, the Church aids everyone, always with the intention of bringing ever closer to the perfection of the heavenly Father all who believe in Christ and practice His teachings and commands.

The Church is on the mount, visible to all, "Mother of the Saints, image of the Supreme City," even if it is evident that the de-Christianization around her has gained and is gaining ground.

The Church stands firmly on her foundation, unshaken by the defections and the persecutions, because she is the force of God and of Christ. It has been said that, if there were no God, He would have to be invented: without a God Who traces for man the distinction and limits of good and evil, no moral law would light the way to reason on this earth. Wherever faith in a personal God is dominant, moral order, determined by the Ten Commandments, remains strong; otherwise, sooner or later, it crumbles miserably.

Of God's Commandments in Particular

If now we consider the Commandments of God individually, it may well be said that each one of them has become a cry of warning, pointing out grave moral perils. The past, too, has witnessed serious disorders: who could deny it? But several of the pillars which supported the ethical order, first among them faith in God, authority of the parents and of constituted public power, always remained solid and intact. Today, the whole edifice of morals is undermined, threatened, upset. A characteristic sign of such decadence is that, with the waning of belief in God and with the simultaneous exaggeration and abuse not infrequently exercised by public power, both the concrete forms and the very principle of authority are becoming "stumbling blocks" and being rejected.

We believe, nonetheless, that to improve and heal this state of affairs two remedies would be especially helpful. In the first place, let authority be returned to parents, with all its rights, even where they might have been restricted or absorbed, as, for example, in the fields of teaching and education. Then, let all those who have public authority, all the ruling classes, including the employers and the educators of youth, themselves set the example of righteous living, and let them exercise the moral authority inherent in their office in keeping with the tenets of justice and love. Before such a model of probity the world would be filled with admiration, seeing what prodigies of public tranquillity and trust might result.

In the field of reciprocal loyalty and veracity there reigns and expands a contaminated atmosphere in which persons of good faith find it difficult to breathe. Who would have thought that following the proud peak of civilization and culture which has been the boast of preceding generations, respect for law would encounter perils, trials, and violations such as only the darkest periods of history have known? But even in such matters the key to every solution is given by faith in a personal God, Who is fount of justice and has reserved to Himself the right over life and death. Nothing else but this faith can confer the moral force to observe the proper limits in the face of all insidious temptations to overstep them; keeping in mind that, excepting in cases of legitimate defense, of just war fought with just means, and of capital punishment inflicted by the public authority for well-determined and proven gravest crimes, human life is intangible.

On the Commandments called "of the first table," which concern God, We deem opportune two observations.

The first concerns the meaning itself of the worship to be rendered to God, a meaning which in the last hundred years has become obscured even among the faithful. If, in fact, it happens in every historical period that in the sanctuary of personal religious life men seek and try to advance their own interests, this is seen to be the case in boundless measure under the influence of the proud and vain culture which dominates the modern generations. They have wanted to reduce the relationship between God and man to the help of God in material and earthly needs; for the rest man wanted to help himself, as if he no longer needed divine support. The worship of God became a concept of usefulness. From the sphere of the spirit, religion fell to that of matter. Religious practice was reduced to seeking favors in Heaven for the needs on earth, almost keeping accounts with God: faith would waver if the help did not correspond to the desire. That religion and faith, above anything else, signify adoration and service of God; that there are Commandments of God which are always binding, in all places and in every circumstance; that, for the Christian, future life should dominate the one on earth; these concepts and these truths, which support and guide the intellect and the will of the believer, had become estranged from the thought and sentiments of the human spirit.

What remedy should one oppose to such failings? It is imperative that the great truths and the great concepts of faith be brought back, as life and reality, to all classes of people, to the upper classes even more than to those disinherited and tried by the want and misery in this world. This should at present be the foremost task of religious education; it is not only required but facilitated, since it is obvious that all the ills and misfortunes humanity now suffers through the decadence of morals and justice are the painful correction of the false concept of God and of religion, which have perverted religious practice.

It has been said that the prodigy of the present years are the millions of faithful who honor God and serve Him, subject to His Commandments, even though they have come to find themselves in indescribable want. Certainly there are such devout and fearless Christians, the glory of the Church.

The Sanctification of Feast Days

The worship of God, which in the course of human life should begin and end each day, imposes special duties for the sanctification of the feasts; and here applies Our second observation. One certainly cannot blame the Church with wanting to apply the Sunday precept with excessive harshness, she who determines and regulates it with that *benignitas et humanitas* of which her divine Founder gave her example. But against the profanation and the secularization of the day of the Lord, which with increasing speed is divested of its sacred character, and thereby estranges men from God, the Church, custodian of divine law, must oppose herself and react with holy firmness.

The Church must resist the absorption and distraction stemming from excessive sports, so that there is no longer time for prayer, for meditation, and for rest; the members of the family are necessarily separated one from the other; the children are alienated from their homes and away from the vigilance of their parents. Resist these pleasures without fear, since, like the immoral movies, they turn Sunday into a day of sin. Finally, man needs Sunday rest and recreation which, above everything else, is to the advantage of religious elevation, spiritual renewal, and the harmonious development of family life.

The Sixth Commandment

God, the name of God, and the worship of God constitute the "first table"; mankind, the duties and rights of human life, appear in the "second table," which, together with the first, forms the Decalogue almost in the way that love of God and love of neighbor unite to make a single love which from God flows to mankind. More numerous are the precepts contained in this "second table," and they call for many observations. But how could We omit recalling the words: *Non moechaberis*—Thou shalt not commit adultery? Is it saying too much if We regret that concerning this Commandment the very countries who boast a higher civilization present a spectacle of the most profound moral devastation? We know well how much economic and social reforms can contribute to the salvation of marriage and of the family; but such salvation, in the final analysis, remains a religious duty and a task whose curative process must start at the roots. The entire conception of the field of life which is contained in the Sixth Commandment is infected by what might be called "movie marriages," which are nothing else but an irreverent and shameless show of marriage conflicts and of conjugal unfaithfulness. The movies present marriage freed from any moral bond, as a setting and source of sensual pleasure only and not as the work of God, a holy institution, a natural office and candid bliss, in which the spiritual element always stands superior and dominates, a school and at the same time a triumph of a love faithful unto death, to the gates of eternity. Is it not, indeed, a duty of the care of souls to revive such a Christian vision of marriage among the faithful?

It is necessary that conjugal life should again be clothed and surrounded by that respect with which sane and incorrupt nature and revelation adorn it from the very beginning: respect for the forces which God has wondrously infused in nature to evoke new life, to build the family for the preservation of the human race. The education of youth to chastity of thought and affections, to continence before marriage, is not the final goal to which Christian pedagogy tends and aims, but it demonstrates the efficacy of its methods in preparing the spirit for the dangers which beset life. The youth who faces up to and victoriously engages in the struggle for purity will also observe the other Commandments of God and will be able to form a family according to the designs of the Creator. How, on the other hand, can chastity and conjugal faithfulness be expected or hoped for in a youth who could never dominate himself and rule his passions, hold bad invitations and bad examples in contempt, and who has permitted himself every moral disorder before marriage?

If the pastor of souls—as he has a sacred obligation before God and the Church—wants to obtain victory against the two cancers of the family, the abuse of marriage and the violation of conjugal fidelity, he must form and instruct with the light of faith a whole generation which from the early years has learned to think in a holy manner, to live in chastity, and to dominate itself.

To have holy thoughts, above all, about women. The "movie marriage" has here perhaps produced its most disastrous effects. It has deprived man of the respect for woman, and then deprived woman of self-respect. May education and the care of souls lead the minds and hearts back to the ancient and pure ideal of woman, pointing out to them the Immaculate Virgin and Mother of God, Mary, whose tender and trusting veneration has been at all times the preservation and salvation of feminine honor! [1]

[1] Allocution to Lenten Preachers, February 23, 1944

ERRONEOUS TRENDS IN MODERN THEOLOGY

FROM THE FIRST DAWN of rational speculation, since man began to reflect about the external universe and his inner world, the philosopher has never remained satisfied with observing the visible surface of things, which fall immediately under our experience, but has always tried to break through the outer shell, to penetrate to their soul, to seize the essence, to guess their nature and intimate constitution, until he is able to form an abstract conception of them from the contingent details, and thus give them a spiritual existence in his thought. In this way, philosophy, while spiritualizing and ennobling the real, at the same time discovers all the rational elements that are hidden in the real itself, unknown and inaccessible to the apprehension of the senses, in order to dwell on the object which is more proper to the mind, ready to embrace it in a wide, comprehensive vision.

And not only does it strip all things, so to speak, of their material concreteness, but it also floods them with the light of its universality. Just as the human mind is not satisfied with appearances, does not stop at phenomena, so it is not content with a fragmentary, disjointed contemplation of the parts of the universe, until it sees the connections, finds the causes and effects, and traces the principles that rule them, connect them up, subordinate and co-ordinate them into a complete picture of harmonious unity. No one dreams of questioning or doubting the value of analysis, to which modern progress owes so much. But is it not perhaps true that the necessity of the present time is synthesis? Is not the danger already felt that present-day science, in so far as it is and must be the generator and the guardian of civilization, may decline and become lost in particularism, restrictivism, and the absolute prevalence of specialization?

The restlessness, the anxiety of man can be distracted for only a moment by the sight and the study of learned, ingenious constructions; diversion of an instant, like a dream in restless sleep, if the construction, however skillful and apparently well balanced, is not founded on rock. Until he gets a final and satisfactory answer to the questions: What is the meaning of life, the meaning of pain, the meaning of death, he will continue to have the impression, which is unfortunately only too well founded, that he lacks solid ground under his feet. But what answer can philosophy give, if it itself is not based on the absolute, on a personal God, the beginning and the end of all things?

A purely deterministic and materialistic explanation of being and of history, irreconcilable with the most elementary truths of psychology, morality, and history, could not satisfy man nor give him happiness and peace.[1]

Exacting Truths

The dissensions and errors of man, in religion and morality, have always been the origin and the cause of great sorrow for all well-meaning people, and above all, for the sincere and faithful sons of the Church. This is especially the case today, when we see the very principles of Christian culture being violated on every side.

It is not really astonishing that, outside the fold of Christ, these disagreements and errors have always existed. In fact, although human reason, strictly speaking, with its own strength and natural light, can indeed arrive at the knowledge, real and certain, of one personal God, Who supports and rules the world with His Providence, and also at the knowledge of the natural law, imprinted by the Creator on our souls, yet there are many obstacles that prevent our reason from using this natural power efficaciously and fruitfully. For the truths that concern God and the relationship between men and God completely transcend the order of the things of the senses; and when they are put into practice in our lives, they call for sacrifice and abnegation.

In arriving at such truths, the human intellect meets with obstacles both because of the senses and of the imagination, and on account of evil passions due to original sin. And so it happens that men in these matters gladly persuade themselves that what they do not wish to be true is false, or at least doubtful. For these reasons it has to be said that divine revelation is morally necessary so that religious and moral truths which are not unattainable in themselves may be known by everybody, in the present conditions of mankind, with ease, absolute certainty, and without any error.

Monism, Dialectical Materialism, Existentialism

The human mind may even sometimes find difficulty in coming to an assured judgment of the credibility of the Catholic faith, although God has given so many astonishing outward signs by means of which the divine origin of the Christian religion can be proved with absolute certainty even with only the natural light of reason. For man, either because he is guided by prejudices or because instigated by passions and ill will, is not only capable of denying the obvious evidence of these outward signs, but also of resisting the inspirations that God sends to our souls.

Anyone observing the world of today, that is outside the fold of Christ, will easily be able to see the principal paths which the learned have taken. Some, in fact, without prudence and discernment, admit and set up as the origin of everything the evolutionist system, although it is not absolutely proved even in the field of natural sciences, and boldly adopt the monistic and pantheistic hypothesis of the universe being subject to continual evolution. The champions of Communism readily use this hypothesis in order to defend and propagate their dialectic materialism and banish from all minds every notion of God.

The false statements of this evolutionism, by which everything that is absolute, certain, and unchangeable is repudiated, have prepared the way for the aberrations of a new philosophy which, competing with idealism, immanentism, and pragmatism, has taken the name of existentialism, because, repudiating the immutable essence of things, it deals only with the "existence" of single individuals.

Added to this there is a false "historicism" which takes into account only events of human life and destroys the foundations of any absolute truth and law both in the field of philosophy and in that of Christian dogmas.

In such confusion of opinions, We are somewhat consoled to see those who had once been educated in rationalistic principles not infrequently return today to the sources of revealed truth, and recognize and profess the word of God, preserved in the Holy Scriptures, as the foundation of theology. At the same time, however, We regret the fact that not a few of these people, the more firmly they cling to the word of God, the more they debase the value of human reason, and the more they exalt the authority of God the Revealer, the more bitterly they despise the Magisterium of the Church, set up by Christ our Lord to guard and interpret the truths revealed by God. This contempt is not only in open contradiction with the Holy Scriptures, but is shown to be false even by experience itself. For frequently these same people complain publicly about the discord that reigns among them in the field of dogmas, and thus, unintentionally, they recognize the necessity of a living teaching authority.

Now these tendencies, which more or less stray from the straight and narrow path, cannot be ignored or overlooked by Catholic philosophers and theologians, whose duty it is to defend divine and human truths and to implant them in the minds of men. On the contrary, they must become familiar with these opinions, both because illnesses cannot be treated unless they are first well known, and because sometimes a grain of truth is hidden in the false statements, and, finally, because these errors stimulate our minds to examine with more diligence certain truths of both philosophy and theology.

Now, if our students of philosophy and theology sought only to gather the fruits We have mentioned from these doctrines, examining them with caution, there would be no reason for the teaching authority of the Church to intervene. But although We are aware that, in general, Catholic teachers and scholars avoid such errors, yet it is known that there exist even today, as in the times of the Apostles, people who, too keen on novelty and afraid of being considered ignorant of the discoveries made by science in this age of progress, try to elude the guidance of the sacred teaching authority and are therefore in danger of unconsciously departing from the revealed truths and leading others astray, too.

Another danger should be noted, which is all the more serious in that it is more hidden under an appearance of virtue. Many people, deploring the discord and confusion prevalent in human minds, are fired by imprudent zeal and stimulated by a strong desire to overthrow the barriers that divide the good and the honest among themselves; therefore they embrace a kind of "irenism"; and, overstepping the questions that divide men, not only do they try to drive back, with joined forces, the attacks of atheism, but also to reconcile opposite positions in the field of dogma itself. And, just as once there were those who wondered whether the traditional apologetics of the Church were more of a hindrance than a help in winning souls for Christ, so today we find those who dare to reach the point of asking in all seriousness whether theology and its methods, as they are in use in schools with the approval of ecclesiastical authority, should not only be improved, but also completely reformed, in order that the Kingdom of Christ may be propagated more efficaciously throughout the world, among men of any culture or of any religious opinions whatever.

If they had no other intention than that of making, with some innovations, ecclesiastical science and its method more adapted to present conditions and necessities, there would be little cause for fear; but some of them, carried away by an imprudent "irenism," seem to consider as an obstacle to the re-establishment of fraternal unity all that is founded on the very laws and principles given by Christ and on the institutions founded by Him, or what constitutes the defense and the support of the integrity of the faith. If these crumble, unity will, indeed, be reached, but only in common ruin.

These opinions, whether springing from a deplorable desire for novelty or from praiseworthy motives, are not always proposed with the same graduation, the same clarity, or in the same terms, and their supporters are not always in agreement among themselves; in fact, what is taught today more or less hiddenly and with restrictions and distinctions, tomorrow is proposed publicly by others, more audaciously and without any limitations, scandalizing many, especially the young clergy, and to the detriment of ecclesiastical authority. As greater prudence is observed in printed publications, these subjects are dealt with more freely in pamphlets distributed in private, in typed papers, and at meetings. These opinions are spread not only among the members of the secular and regular clergy, in seminaries and religious institutes, but also among laymen, especially among those engaged in bringing up and educating youth.

As for theology, some of them intend to reduce as much as possible the meaning of the dogmas; to free the dogma itself from the mode of expression the Church has used for so long, and from the philosophical concepts held by Catholic scholars, to return, in explaining the Catholic doctrine, to the expressions used by the Holy Scriptures and by the Holy Fathers. They hope in this way that the dogma, stripped of the elements that are extrinsic, as they say, to divine revelation, may be compared profitably with the dogmatic opinions of those who are separated from the Church, and that in this way it will be possible gradually to arrive at the assimilation of Catholic dogma with the opinions of the dissidents. In addition, by reducing the Catholic doctrine to such conditions, they think they are opening up the way to the possibility, thus satisfying present-day necessities, of expressing the dogmas with the categories of modern philosophy, whether it be immanentism, idealism, existentialism, or any other system. And therefore some of them, the more audacious, maintain that this can and must be done, because the mysteries of the faith, they affirm, can never be expressed with concepts that are absolutely true, but only with concepts that are approximate and continually changing, by which truth is manifested up to a certain point, but at the same time necessarily distorted. Therefore, they consider it not absurd, but absolutely necessary, for theology, as for the various philosophical systems, which in the course of time it uses as instruments, to substitute new concepts for the old; so that it may expound in a human way the same divine truths, using different approaches, that from certain points of view are also opposite, but—as they say—equivalent. They add, too, that the history of the dogmas consists in expounding the various forms which revealed truth has successively assumed, according to the different doctrines and the different opinions that have arisen in the course of the centuries.

Scholastic Concepts and the Teaching Authority of the Church

From what We have said, it is clear that these tendencies not only lead to relativism in dogma, but in fact already contain it; this relativism, furthermore, is much encouraged by the contempt for traditional doctrine and for the terms in which it is expressed. Everybody knows that the expressions of these concepts, used both in the schools and by the teaching authority of the Church, can be improved and perfected; it is, besides, well known that the Church has not always been constant in the use of those same words. It is also evident that the Church cannot be linked with any ephemeral philosophical system; but those ideas and those terms which, with general consent, were composed in the course of several centuries by Catholic scholars to arrive at some sort of knowledge and understanding of the dogma, certainly cannot be based upon such perishable foundations. No, they are based on principles and ideas deduced from a real knowledge of creation; and in deducing them, the human mind was illuminated by revealed truth, as by a star, through the Church. It is, therefore, not surprising if some of these ideas have not only been used in Ecumenical Councils but have also been so solemnly sanctioned that it is not permissible for us to depart from them.

For these reasons, it is extremely imprudent to neglect or reject or deprive of their value the concepts and expressions which people of no common intellect and sanctity, under the vigilance of the sacred teaching authority and not without illumination and guidance from the Holy Spirit, have found and perfected time and again throughout the centuries to express more and more accurately the truths of the faith, and to substitute for these the hypothetical notions and the fluctuating, vague expressions of the new philosophy, which, like the grass in the fields, are here today and withered tomorrow; this would be to make dogma itself like a reed shaken in the wind. Contempt for the words and ideas used by scholastic theologians, in itself, leads to the weakening of speculative theology, which some consider to be devoid of true certainty in so far as it is based on theological reasons.

Unfortunately, these lovers of novelty pass easily from contempt of scholastic theology to indifference and lack of esteem for the authority of the Church itself, which has given such noteworthy approval to that theology. This authority is made to appear by them as an obstacle to progress and a hindrance to science; it is considered by some non-Catholics as an unjust restraint, whereby learned theologians are prevented from giving new life to their science. And although for any theologian this sacred authority should in matters of faith and morals be the immediate and universal rule of truth (inasmuch as Christ our Lord entrusted to it the deposit of the faith—that is, Holy Scriptures and divine tradition—to be guarded, defended, and interpreted), yet sometimes no heed is taken, exactly as if it did not exist, of the duty incumbent on the faithful to avoid those errors which to a greater or lesser extent approach heresy, and therefore "to observe also the constitutions and decrees with which these false opinions are proscribed and prohibited by the Holy See." What is expounded in the Encyclicals of the Sovereign Pontiffs about the character and the constitution of the Church is intentionally and habitually overlooked by some people, with the aim of establishing a vague concept that they say comes from the ancient Fathers, especially Greek. The Pontiffs, in fact—they say —do not intend to pass judgment on questions that are the object of dispute among theologians; it is, therefore, necessary to go back to the primitive sources, and the constitutions and decrees of the teaching authority are to be explained with reference to the writings of the ancients.

When Does the Pope Teach "Ex Cathedra"?

These statements may appear very ingenious; yet they contain an error. It is indeed true that generally the Pontiffs leave theologians free in those questions which, in various ways, are a matter of discussion among the most well-known scholars; but history teaches that several questions which before were open to free discussion later could no longer be discussed.

Nor should it be thought that the teachings of the Encyclicals do not require, in themselves, full assent, on the pretext that the Pontiffs do not exercise here the power of their supreme authority. In fact, these teachings come from the ordinary authority, to which can also be applied the words: "He that heareth you, heareth me"; and what is more, anything that is proposed and inculcated in the Encyclicals is already, for other reasons, the patrimony of the Catholic doctrine. If, then, the Sovereign Pontiffs, especially in their decrees, pass a judgment on a matter which up till then was open to dispute, it is obvious to everyone that this question, according to the intention and the will of the Pontiffs themselves, can no longer be the object of free discussion among theologians.

It is also true that theologians must always go back to the sources of divine revelation; it is, in fact, their duty to indicate how the teachings of the living authority "are found either explicitly or implicitly" in the Holy Scriptures and in divine tradition. It should be added, also, that both these founts of the revelation contain such and so many treasures of truth as to be, in fact, inexhaustible. For this reason, the sacred sciences take on new youth with the study of the sacred sources; while, on the contrary, as we know from experience, speculation that neglects research into the sacred deposit becomes sterile. For this very reason, theology, even positive theology, cannot be likened to a mere historical science. For God has given His Church, together with these sacred founts, the living authority, also to illustrate and develop those truths which are contained only obscurely and, as it were, implicitly in the deposit of the faith. And the divine Redeemer did not entrust this deposit, for authentic interpretation, either to the individual believer or to the theologians themselves, but only to the authority of the Church. If, then, the Church exercises this office (as has often occurred in the course of the centuries), it is evident that the method which wants to explain things that are clear through things that are obscure is completely false; that, actually, it is necessary for everyone to follow the reverse order. Therefore, Our predecessor, Pius IX, while He taught that it is a noble task of theology to show how a doctrine defined by the Church is contained in the sources, not without serious reason added the following words: "in that same sense in which it has been defined by the Church."

The Interpretation of Holy Scriptures

Let us now return to the new theories about which We spoke before: some of them propose or instill into the mind various opinions that lower the divine authority of the Holy Scriptures. With audacity some of them pervert the meaning of the words of the Vatican Council, wherewith God is defined as the author of the Holy Scriptures; and they renew the opinion, already several times condemned, according to which the authority of Holy Scriptures extends only to those parts concerning God Himself or religion and morality. Actually, they falsely speak of a human meaning of the Bible, under which the divine meaning is hidden; and only the latter, they declare, is infallible. In the interpretation of the Holy Scriptures they refuse to take into account the analogy of faith and the tradition of the Church; so that the doctrine of the Holy Fathers and of the sacred teaching should be measured with that of the Holy Scriptures, explained, however, by the exegetes in a purely human way and not, rather, the Holy Scriptures explained according to the mind of the Church, which was made guardian and interpreter of the whole deposit of revealed truths by Christ our Lord.

Besides, the literal meaning of the Holy Scriptures and its explanation, worked out, under the vigilance of the Church, by competent exegetes, should, according to their false opinions, give way to a new exegesis, called symbolical and spiritual; and according to this exegesis, the books of the Old Testament, which today in the Church are a closed and hidden wellspring, would finally be open to everybody. In this way—they affirm—all the difficulties which are met by those who hold fast to the literal meaning of the Scriptures would disappear.

It should come as no surprise that such innovations in almost all parts of theology have produced their poisonous fruit. It is questioned whether human reason, without the help of divine revelation and grace, can demonstrate, with arguments taken from created things, the existence of a personal God; it is affirmed that the world had no beginning and that the creation of the world is necessary because it comes from the necessary liberality of divine love; and it is also affirmed that God does not have eternal and infallible foreknowledge of the free actions of man: all opinions contrary to the declarations of the Vatican Council.

The Character of the Mystical Body of Christ

Some others, again, question whether the angels are persons; and if there is an essential difference between matter and spirit. Still others distort the conception of the gratuitousness of the supernatural order, when they maintain that God cannot create intelligent beings without ordaining them and calling them to the vision of bliss. Nor is this enough; for, setting aside the definitions of the Council of Trent, they destroy the true concept of original sin, together with that of sin in general, as being an offense against God, as that also of the satisfaction made for us by Christ. And there are those who maintain that the doctrine of transubstantiation, inasmuch as it is founded on an antiquated conception of substance, must be corrected in order to reduce the real presence of Christ in the Eucharist to symbolism, so that the consecrated species would be no more than efficacious symbols of the spiritual presence of Christ and of His intimate union in the mystical body with the faithful.

Some do not consider themselves bound to the doctrine that We set forth in one of Our Encyclicals and which is based on the founts of revelation, according to which the mystical body of Christ and the Roman Catholic Church are one and the same thing. Some reduce to an empty formula the necessity of belonging to the true Church in order to obtain eternal salvation. Others, again, do not admit the rational character of the signs of credibility of the Christian faith.

It is well known that these errors, and others of the same kind, lurk among some of Our sons, all deceived by imprudent zeal or false science, and We are obliged to repeat, sorrowfully, to these sons very well-known truths and manifest errors, pointing out to them, anxiously, the dangers of error.

Human Reason in Church Doctrine

Everyone knows how highly the Church values human reason, which has the task of demonstrating with certainty the existence of a single personal God, of demonstrating invincibly by means of the divine signs the foundations of the Christian faith itself; and of showing in the proper light the law that the Creator has imprinted on the souls of men; and, finally, the task of arriving at a limited, but very useful, knowledge of mysteries.

But this task can be carried out properly and with ease only if reason has been duly cultivated; if, that is, it is nourished by that healthy philosophy which is, as it were, a patrimony inherited from preceding Christian ages and possesses a higher authority, since the authority of the Church herself has put alongside revealed truth its principles and main assertions, disclosed and established slowly throughout the ages by men of great genius. This philosophy, confirmed and commonly recognized by the Church, defends the real value of human knowledge, the unshakable principles of metaphysics—that is, of sufficient reason, of causality and finality; and, finally, maintains that it is possible to reach certain and unchangeable truth.

In this philosophy there are certainly several things that do not concern faith and morals, either directly or indirectly, and which, therefore, the Church leaves to be discussed freely by experts in the subject; but there is not the same liberty with regard to several others, especially with regard to the principles and principal assertions We have already spoken about. Even in these essential questions We can give philosophy more suitable, richer vestments; philosophy itself can be strengthened by the use of more efficacious expressions, by eliminating certain scholastic methods that are less suitable; it can also be enriched—but prudently—with the addition of certain elements that are the fruit of the progressive work of the human mind; but it must never be subverted or contaminated with false principles, nor regarded as an important monument, yes, but only archaeological. For truth and every philosophical manifestation of it cannot be subject to daily changes, especially when it is a question of the principles of human reason, well known in themselves, or of those assertions that are based both on the wisdom of centuries and also on the foundations of divine revelation. Whatever truth the human mind discovers, after sincere searching, cannot be in contradiction with already known truths; for God, supreme Truth, has created and supports the human intellect not in order that it may daily find new truths which contradict those already acquired, but that, when the errors which may have crept in have been eliminated, truth may be added to truth in the same order and with the same consistency with which we see the very nature of things constituted, on which truth draws. For this reason the Christian, whether he be a philosopher or a theologian, does not embrace hurriedly and lightly all the novelties that are daily excogitated, but examines them with the greatest care and weighs them attentively in order not to lose or corrupt the truth that has already been acquired, which would endanger and harm faith itself.

The Teachings of Thomas Aquinas

If what has been explained above is carefully considered, it will be easy to understand the reason why the Church insists on future priests' being instructed in the philosophical sciences "according to the method, the doctrine, and the principles of the Angelic Doctor," since, as the experience of several centuries has clearly shown, St. Thomas's method is remarkable for its outstanding superiority both in training pupils and in searching for the truth; then, too, his doctrine is in harmony with divine revelation and is very efficacious in protecting the foundations of the faith and also in gathering usefully and safely the fruits of wholesome progress.

It is, therefore, highly deplorable that today the philosophy confirmed and admitted by the Church should be the object of contempt by some people who imprudently declare it to be old-fashioned in form and rationalistic as regards the process of thought. They say that our philosophy erroneously defends the opinion that it is possible to present a metaphysics that is true absolutely; while, on the contrary, they maintain that truths, especially transcendental truths, cannot be more fittingly expressed than by means of diverse doctrines which complement one another, although they may in some respects be contradictory. And so scholastic philosophy, with its lucid exposition and solution of questions, with its careful determination of concepts and its clear distinctions, may be useful—they admit—as a preparation for the study of scholastic theology, which was so well suited to the mentality of medieval man; but it cannot give us—they add—a method and a philosophical orientation that correspond to the needs of our modern culture. They put forward, also, the objection that perennial philosophy is only the philosophy of immutable essences, while modern mentality is interested in the "existence of single individuals and of life that is always in the process of change." But while they despise this philosophy, they exalt the others, both ancient and modern, of Oriental and of Western peoples, so that they seem to be insinuating that all philosophies or opinions, with the addition, if necessary, of some corrections or some completion, can be reconciled with Catholic dogma. But no Catholic can doubt how false all that is, especially when it is a question of systems such as immanentism, idealism, materialism, both historical and dialectic, or even existentialism, when it professes atheism or when it denies the value of reasoning in the field of metaphysics.

Finally, they formulate this reproach to the philosophy of our schools: that in the process of thought it pays attention only to the intellect, and neglects the function of the will and of feeling. This is not true. For Christian philosophy has never denied the utility and the efficaciousness of the readiness of the soul to get to know and to embrace religious and moral truths; on the contrary, it has always taught that the lack of such readiness may be the cause whereby the intellect, under the influence of the passions and malice, may be obscured to the extent of not being able to see rightly. Moreover, the general doctor, St. Thomas, is of the opinion that the intellect may be able in some way to perceive the higher goods of the moral order, both natural and supernatural, in so far as it experiences within itself a certain "fellowship," whether natural or the fruit of grace, with these goods; it is clear of what help this knowledge, however obscure, may be to reason in its searchings. But it is one thing to recognize the power of the will and disposition of the soul to help reason to reach a more certain and stronger knowledge of moral truths, and it is another to maintain, as these innovators do, that the will and feeling have a certain intuitive power and that man, not being able to discern with certainty by his reason what he should embrace as being true, turns to his will which permits him to make a free resolution and choice among opposite opinions. This shows a confusion between knowledge and an act of will.

The Decisions of Leo XIII and Pius X

It is not astonishing that, with these new opinions, the two philosophical disciplines, which, by their nature, are closely linked with the teachings of the faith, that is, theodicy and ethics, are endangered. These people are of the opinion that the function of these two is not that of demonstrating with certainty some truth about God or any other transcendent being, but rather that of showing how perfectly coherent with the necessities of life are the truths that faith teaches about God, a personal Being, and about His precepts, and that, therefore, they must be accepted by everybody to avoid desperation and to obtain eternal salvation. All these affirmations and opinions are openly contrary to the decisions of Our predecessors Leo XIII and Pius X, and are irreconcilable with the decrees of the Vatican Council.

It would be unnecessary to deplore these aberrations if everyone, also in the philosophical field, were obedient, with due reverence, to the teaching authority of the Church, which, by divine institution, has the mission not only of guarding and interpreting the deposit of revelation, but also of watching over the philosophical sciences themselves in order that Catholic dogmas should not be harmed by false opinions.

Evolution and Genesis

We still have to speak about those questions which, although belonging to the positive sciences, are more or less connected with the truths of the Christian faith. Not a few people, in fact, urgently request that the Catholic religion should take those sciences into greater account. This is certainly a praiseworthy thing, when it is a question of facts that are really proved; but we must move with caution when it is, rather, a question of hypotheses, although with some scientific foundation, which concern the doctrine contained in the Holy Scriptures or also in tradition. If these hypotheses are, directly or indirectly, in contradiction with revealed doctrine, then they can in no way be admitted.

For these reasons the teaching authority of the Church does not forbid that, in conformity with the present state of science and theology, the doctrine of evolution should be examined and discussed by experts in both fields, in so far as it deals with research on the origin of the human body, which it states to come from pre-existent organic matter (the Catholic faith obliges us to believe that souls were created directly by God). But this must be done in such a way that the arguments of the two opinions, that is, the one favorable and the other contrary to evolution, should be weighed and judged with all necessary seriousness, moderation, and restraint, and on condition that they are all ready to submit to the judgment of the Church, to which Christ has entrusted the office of interpreting authentically the Holy Scriptures and of defending the dogmas of the faith. Some, however, overstep the limits of this freedom of discussion, acting as if it were already proved, beyond all doubt, that the human body originated in pre-existent organic matter, on the basis of initial data collected up to now, and of arguments based on these indications; that is, as if there were nothing in the sources of divine revelation that called for the greatest moderation and caution in this matter.

But as regards the other hypothesis, that is, so-called polygenism, the sons of the Church do not enjoy the same freedom. For the faithful cannot embrace this opinion which states that after Adam there existed here on earth real men who were not descended, by natural generation, from him, the forefather of all men; or else that Adam represents groups of many forefathers; now, these statements cannot be reconciled with what the founts of revelation and the decrees of the authority of the Church teach us about original sin, which comes from a sin really committed by Adam individually and personally, and which, transmitted to everyone through the generations, is an inherent property in each man.

As in the biological and anthropological sciences, so also in the historical sciences there are people who audaciously overstep the limits and the precautions set up by the Church. Particularly deplorable is a certain system of interpreting the historical books of the Old Testament too freely; the upholders of this system, to defend their ideas, wrongly refer to the letter that was sent not long ago to the Archbishop of Paris by the Pontifical Commission for Biblical Studies. This letter, in fact, points out that the first eleven chapters of Genesis, although they do not correspond to the historical method used by the best Greek and Latin authors or by experts of our own time, do, however, belong to the historical category in a real sense, which must be studied in more detail and determined by the exegetes; the same chapters—the letter further points out—with simple and metaphorical expressions, suited to the mentality of a barely civilized people, give an account of the principal truths that are fundamental for our salvation, and also a popular narration of the origin of humanity and of the elect people.

If the ancient authors of the Sacred Scriptures have taken something from popular accounts (which can be admitted), it must never be forgotten that they did so with the help of divine inspiration, which preserved them from all error in the choice and judgment of these documents. Therefore, the popular narrations inserted in the Holy Scriptures cannot be put on the same plane as mythology and the like, which are the fruit of lively imagination rather than of that love of truth and simplicity which are so outstanding in the Sacred Books, and also in the Old Testament, that we must affirm that our authors are obviously superior to the ancient profane writers.

The Obligation of Bishops

We know, indeed, that the majority of Catholic scholars, the fruit of whose studies is harvested by the universities, the seminaries, and the religious colleges, are far from those errors which, openly or secretly, are being spread today, either on account of the craze for novelty or also because of immoderate apostolic zeal. But We know, too, that these new opinions may take hold of imprudent persons; therefore, We prefer to prescribe a remedy at the outset, rather than wait to administer the medicine when the illness is already advanced. For this reason, after mature reflection and consideration before God, in order not to fail in Our sacred duty, We order Bishops and the Superiors General of religious Orders and Congregations to take every precaution to prevent such opinions from being voiced in schools or in meetings and lectures, or in writings of any kind, or from being taught, in any way, to clergymen or to the faithful.

Teachers of ecclesiastical institutes should know that they cannot, with a safe conscience, exercise the office of teaching that has been entrusted to them unless they accept religiously the rules We have set up, and observe them exactly in the teaching of their subjects. They should also infuse into the minds and souls of their students that dutiful reverence and obedience which they, in their assiduous work, must profess toward the teaching authority of the Church.

Let them try with all their strength and passion to contribute to the progess of the sciences they teach; but let them be careful not to overstep the boundary set by Us for the defense of the faith and Catholic doctrine. Let them examine scrupulously, but with all due prudence and caution, the new questions which modern culture and progress have brought to the foreground. Finally, let them not believe, through false "irenism," that it is possible to bring about the happy return into the bosom of the Church of dissidents and those in error, without teaching to everybody, sincerely, the whole truth in force in the Church, without any corruption or elimination.[2]

[1] Address to the Congress of Philosophy, November 29, 1946

[2] Encyclical *Humani generis,* August 12, 1950

ATHEISM

THE MODERN AGE, adding new mistakes to the doctrinal deviations of the past, has carried them to extremes, from which nothing but bewilderment and ruin could follow. And first of all, it is certain that the deep and ultimate root of the ills which we deplore in modern society is the denial and rejection of a universal norm of morality, both in individual and social life and in international relationships; that is, the disavowal, so widespread in our times, and the neglect of even the natural law which has its foundation in God, the almighty Creator and Father of all, supreme and absolute legislator, omniscient and just avenger of human actions. When God is denied, every foundation of morality is also shaken and there is a smothering, or at least a great weakening, of the voice of nature which teaches even the untaught, and peoples that have not yet reached civilization, what is good and what is bad, what is lawful and what is unlawful, and makes man feel responsible for his actions before a Supreme Judge.

Now, denial of the fundamental basis of morality had its first root in Europe in a departure from that doctrine of Christ of which the Chair of Peter is the depositary and the teacher; a doctrine that at one time had given spiritual cohesion to Europe, which, educated, ennobled, and refined by the Cross, had achieved such a degree of civil progress as to become the teacher of other peoples and other continents. Instead, detaching themselves from the infallible guardianship of the Church, not a few seceding brethren have gone so far as to subvert the central dogma of Christendom, the divinity of the Savior, thus quickening the process of spiritual dissolution.

Many perhaps, in departing from the doctrine of Christ, were not fully aware that they were being deceived by the mirage of glittering phrases that proclaimed such detachment to be a liberation from the bondage in which they were said to have been held before; nor did they foresee the bitter consequences of the sad barter between the truth that frees and the error that enslaves; nor did they think that, giving up the infinitely wise and fatherly law of God and the unifying and elevating doctrine of the love of Christ, they were giving themselves up to the will of pitiful, changeable human wisdom; they spoke of progress, when they were going backward; of elevation, when they were degrading themselves; of an ascent to maturity, when they were falling into bondage; they did not perceive the vanity of any human effort to substitute for the law of Christ some other thing that could equal it.

Faith in God and in Jesus Christ once weakened, and the light of moral principles once darkened in souls, there was discarded the only irreplaceable foundation of stability and tranquillity, of that internal and external order, private and public, which alone can generate and safeguard the prosperity of States.[1]

In the giddiness of material progress, in the victories of human ingenuity over the secrets of nature and over the forces of the elements of the earth, the seas, and the sky, in the anxious competition to surpass the summits reached by others, in the arenas of daring research, in the conquests and in the pride of science, of industry, of laboratories, of factories, in the greed for money and for pleasure, in the tense effort toward a supreme power more feared than contended for, more envied than equalled, in the turmoil of all this modern life, where can the naturally Christian soul of man find peace? Perhaps in finding contentment in itself? Perhaps in boasting to be king of the universe, enveloped by the fog of illusion which confuses matter with the spirit, the human with the divine, the momentary with the eternal? No; intoxicating dreams do not calm the storm in a soul and conscience put into turmoil by the impetus of the mind which stands above matter and, aware of its unrejectable immortal destiny, steps over toward the infinite and toward immense desires. Approach those souls and question them. They will answer you in the language of a child, not of a man. They did not have a mother who, when they were children, would speak of the Father in Heaven; they grew up between walls without a Cross, in homes where religion was not mentioned, in fields far away from an altar and from a steeple; they read books from which the names of God and Christ are absent; they heard priests and monks and nuns vituperated; they went from the countryside, from the city, from their homes, to the factory, to the shop, to the halls of knowledge, to every art and work, without entering a church, without knowing the parish priest, without a good thought put in their hearts.[2]

Too well known are the dangers and incentives, spiritual and moral, that now more than ever threaten the Christian principles of faith and life. . . .

Pulled into the giddy and impassioned whirl of happenings, too often the mind runs the risk of having its faculty and readiness to judge events according to the pure and unshakable rules of divine law dulled and weakened. And yet the Christian, strong in his faith, intrepid in his duty, if he must find himself prepared to participate in the events, the duties, and the sacrifices of the day, must be no less ready to reject the errors of his times; in such a manner that, the more he perceives the gathering of the darkness of unbelief and malice, the more brave and ready should he show himself in making resplendent the light of Christ, a guide to the erring, leading and escorting them home to the spiritual heritage which so many have forgotten or abandoned. Inaccessible to the blandishments of others, he will keep to the path without going astray in the night of earthly darkness. He will lift his eyes to the stars in the Heaven of eternity, the consoling goal and reward of his hope. The harder and heavier the sacrifices demanded of mankind, the more vigorous and active will be the force of the divine precept of love in his soul, and the longing and eagerness to make it the guide of his intentions and actions. And if the proud spirit of an atheistic materialism will ask him the question: *"Ubi est spes tua?*—Where is your hope?" then, fearing neither the present nor the future, he will answer with the righteous of the Old Covenant: "*Nolite ita loqui; quoniam filii sanctorum sumus, et vitam illam expectamus, quam Deus daturus est his, qui fidem suam nunquam mutant ab eo*—Speak not so: For we are the children of saints, and look for that life which God will give to those that never change their faith from Him." [3]

[1] Encyclical *Summi Pontificatus,* October 20, 1939
[2] Address to the Leaders of Catholic Action, May 3, 1951
[3] Address to the Sacred College, June 2, 1940

THE HOLY SCRIPTURES

The Present Status of Biblical Studies

THERE IS NO ONE who does not see that the conditions of Biblical studies and their subsidiary sciences have greatly changed within the last fifty years. When Our predecessor published the Encyclical *Providentissimus Deus,* only a few sites in Palestine had begun to be explored by excavations related to the Bible. Now, however, this kind of investigation is much more frequent and, since more precise methods and technical skill have been developed in the course of actual experience, it gives us information at once more abundant and more accurate. How much light has been derived from these explorations for the more correct and fuller understanding of the Holy Scriptures is known to all experts, as well as to all those who devote themselves to Biblical studies. The value of these excavations is enhanced by the repeated discovery of written documents, which considerably increase our knowledge of the languages, letters, events, customs, and forms of worship of most ancient times.

The Discovery of Papyri

Of no less importance is the discovery and investigation, so frequent in our times, of papyri which have contributed so much to the knowledge of letters and institutions, both public and private, especially of the time of Our Savior. Moreover, ancient codices of the

Holy Scriptures have been found, and edited with discerning thoroughness; the exegesis of the Fathers of the Church has been more widely and thoroughly examined; in sum, the manner of speaking, narrating, and writing in use among the ancients is illuminated by innumerable examples. All these advantages which, not without a special design of divine Providence, our age has acquired, are as it were an invitation and inducement to interpreters of the Holy Scriptures to make diligent use of this light, so abundantly given, to penetrate more deeply, explain more clearly, and expound more lucidly the Word of God.

Study of Biblical Languages

The Church Fathers, especially St. Augustine, had already recommended to the Catholic exegete, who undertook the investigation and explanation of the Sacred Scriptures, the study of the ancient languages and recourse to the original texts. However, such was the state of letters in those times that not many—and these few but imperfectly—knew the Hebrew language. In the Middle Ages, when scholastic theology was at the height of its vigor, the knowledge of even the Greek language had long since become so rare in the West that even the greatest Doctors of that time, in their exposition of the Holy Scriptures, had recourse only to the Latin version, known as the Vulgate. In this our time, however, not only is the Greek language, restored to new life since the Renaissance, familiar to almost all students of antiquity and letters, but the knowledge of Hebrew also and of other Oriental languages has spread far and wide among scholars. Moreover, there are now such abundant aids to the study of these languages that the Biblical scholar who by neglecting them would deprive himself of access to the original texts could not escape the stigma of levity and sloth.

Importance of Textual Criticism

The great importance which should be attached to textual criticism was aptly pointed out by Augustine, when, among the precepts for the study of the Holy Scriptures, he recommended above all work with a correct text. "The correction of the codices," says this enlightened Doctor of the Church, "should first of all engage the attention of those who wish to know the Sacred Scriptures so that the incorrect may give place to the correct." In the present day indeed this art, which is called textual criticism and which is used with great and praiseworthy results in the editions of profane writings, is also quite rightly employed in the case of the Holy Scriptures, because of that very reverence which is due to the Word of God. For its very purpose is to ensure that the sacred text be restored as perfectly as possible, be purified from the corruptions due to the carelessness of the copyists, and be freed, as far as possible, from interpolations and omissions, from the interchange and repetition of words, and from all other kinds of mistakes, which are wont to make their way gradually into writings handed down through many centuries. It is scarcely necessary to point out that this type of criticism—which some fifty years ago was applied by some quite arbitrarily and often in such a way that one might say that they tended to introduce into the sacred text their own preconceived ideas —today has rules so firmly established and secure that it has become a most valuable aid to the purer and more accurate editing of the sacred text and that any abuse can easily be discovered.

The "Literal" Meaning

Thoroughly prepared by the knowledge of the ancient languages and by the aids afforded by textual criticism, let the Catholic exegete undertake the greatest task of all those imposed on him, namely that of discovering and expounding the genuine meaning of the Sacred Books. In the performance of this task let the interpreters bear in mind that their foremost endeavor should be to discern and define clearly what has been called the "literal" sense of the Biblical words. Aided by the context and by comparison with similar passages, let them therefore, by means of their knowledge of languages, search out with all diligence the literal meaning of the words; all these aids, indeed, are also used in the study of profane writers, so that the mind of the author may be made abundantly clear. The commentators of the Holy Scriptures, mindful of the fact that here they deal with a divinely inspired text, the care and interpretation of which have been confided to the Church by God Himself, should no less carefully take into account the explanations and declarations of the teaching authority of the Church, as the interpretations given by the Holy Fathers, and also "the analogy of faith," as Leo XIII most wisely observed in the Encyclical *Providentissimus Deus*. With special zeal they should apply themselves not only to expounding exclusively those matters which belong to the historical, archaeological, philological, and other auxiliary sciences—as, to Our regret, is done in certain commentaries—but, having duly referred to these, in so far as they may aid the exegesis, they should set forth in particular the theological doctrine concerning faith and morals of the individual books or texts, so that their exposition may not only aid the professors of theology in their expositions and proofs of the dogmas of faith but also be of assistance to priests in their presentation of Christian doctrine to the people, and so finally may help all the faithful to lead a life that is holy and worthy of a Christian.

The Spiritual Meaning

An exposition of this kind, which is in the main theological, would serve to silence those who assert that they rarely if ever find anything in Biblical commentaries to raise their hearts to God, to nourish their souls, or to promote their interior life, and who recommend as only recourse a certain spiritual and, as they say, mystical interpretation. How little justified this assertion is appears from the experience of many who, assiduously considering and meditating the word of God, advanced in perfection and were moved to an intense love for God; and this same truth is clearly proved by the constant tradition of the Church and the precepts of the greatest Doctors. Doubtless not all spiritual sense is excluded from Sacred Scripture. For what was said and done in the Old Testament was ordained and disposed by God with such consummate wisdom that things past prefigured spiritually those that were to come under the new dispensation of grace. Wherefore the exegete, just as he must search out and expound the literal meaning of the words as they were intended and expressed by the sacred writer, so also must do for the spiritual sense, provided it is clearly intended by God. For God alone could have known this spiritual meaning and have revealed it to us. Now, our divine Savior Himself points out to us and teaches us this same sense in the Holy Gospel; the Apostles also, following the example of the Master, profess it in their spoken and written words; the unchanging tradition of the Church approves it; finally, the most ancient usage of the liturgy proclaims it, wherever the well-known principle may be rightly applied: "The rule of prayer is the rule of faith."

Let Catholic exegetes then disclose and expound this spiritual significance, intended and ordained by God, with that care which the dignity of the divine word demands; but let them scrupulously refrain from proposing as the genuine meaning of Sacred Scripture other figurative interpretations. It may indeed be useful, especially in preaching, to illustrate and present the matters of faith and morals by a broader use of the Sacred Text in the figurative sense, provided this be done with moderation and restraint; it should, however, never be forgotten that this use of the Sacred Scripture is, as it were, extrinsic to it and accidental, and that, especially in these days, it is not free from danger, since the faithful, in particular those who are well informed in the sciences sacred and profane, wish to know what God has told us in the Holy Scriptures rather than what an ingenious orator or writer may suggest by a clever use of the words of Scripture.

Interpretation of Sacred Scripture

We may rightly and deservedly hope that our times also will contribute something toward the deeper and more accurate interpretation of Sacred Scripture. For not a few things, especially in matters pertaining to history, were hardly touched upon or not fully explained by the commentators of past ages, since they lacked almost all the information required for a more explicit exposition. How difficult, and indeed well-nigh unintelligible, certain passages were even for the Church Fathers is shown, among other things, by the oft-repeated efforts of many of them to explain the first chapters of Genesis; likewise by the reiterated attempts of St. Jerome to translate the Psalms in such a manner that the literal sense, that which is expressed by the words themselves, might be clearly revealed. In other books or texts, one has only recently become aware of difficulties of interpretation, as a more profound knowledge of antiquity has given rise to new questions, which permit deeper insight into the points at issue. It is therefore quite wrong to pretend, as do some persons not fully informed of the status of Biblical studies, that nothing remains to be added by the Catholic exegete of our time to what Christian antiquity has produced; since, on the contrary, these our times have brought to light a great many things which call for fresh investigation and new examination, and which stimulate not a little the practical zeal of the present-day interpreter. . . .

The Use of the Bible in the Care of Souls

Whosoever considers the immense labors undertaken by Catholic exegetes during well-nigh two thousand years, so that the word of God, imparted to men through Holy Scripture, might daily be more deeply and fully understood and more intensely loved, will easily be convinced that it is the serious duty of the faithful, and especially of priests, to make free and holy use of this treasure, accumulated throughout so many centuries by the greatest intellects. For the Sacred Books were not given to men by God to satisfy their curiosity or to provide them with material for study and research, but, as the Apostle observes, in order that these Divine Words might "instruct in justice, by the faith which is in Christ Jesus," and "that the man of God may be perfect, equipped for every good work."

Let priests, therefore, who are bound by their office to care for the eternal salvation of the faithful, after they have themselves by diligent study perused the sacred pages and made them their own in prayer and meditation, assiduously distribute the heavenly treasures of the Divine Word in sermons, homilies, and exhortations; let them confirm Christian doctrine by sentences from the Sacred Books and illustrate it by outstanding examples from sacred history and in particular from the Gospel of Christ our Lord; and—avoiding with the greatest care those purely arbitrary and far-fetched adaptations which are not a use but rather an abuse of the Divine Word—let them set forth all this with such eloquence, lucidity, and clearness that the faithful may not only be moved and inspired to reform their lives, but may also conceive in their hearts the greatest veneration for Sacred Scripture. This veneration the Bishops should endeavor daily to increase and perfect among the faithful committed to their care, encouraging all those initiatives by which men, filled with apostolic zeal, laudably strive to excite and foster among Catholics a greater knowledge of and love for the Sacred Books. Let them favor, therefore, and lend help to those devout associations whose aim it is to distribute copies of the Sacred Scriptures, especially of the Gospels, among the faithful, and see to it that they are daily read in Christian families with piety and devotion.[1]

[1] Encyclical *Divino afflante spiritu,* September 30, 1943

TO PRIESTS

WE PRIESTS are ambassadors of Christ in the world, as it were, God exhorting men through our mouths. To this high conception of priesthood proposed to us by the Apostle of the Gentiles, let us raise up, beloved Sons, our eyes, our aspirations, and our purposes; and through our active zeal let us exalt and render venerable in the midst of the Christian people our noble rank of mediators and ambassadors of Christ. But in the sacred hierarchy, who else is nearer to the people than the parish priest, whose mission is characterized and defined by three words: apostle, father, shepherd?

Office and Obligation of the Parish Priest

In every parish priest there is an apostle; but, above all, he who carries on his work in a big city should feel within him the flame of the apostolic and missionary spirit and of the conquering zeal of a St. Paul. If you consider our modern times with their political and religious upheavals, with their variety of philosophic and scientific aberrations in instruction and education, you will soon see that the ancient spiritual conditions of society have changed to a point that not even here, in this our Rome, can one speak of a truly Catholic ground because, besides those who have remained firm in their faith—and they are splendid legions—there is no lack in every parish of a set of people who, grown indifferent to and estranged from the Church, constitute a missionary territory to be reconquered for Christ.

Pastoral Care

The parish priest is shepherd and father, shepherd of souls and spiritual father. We must always bear in mind, beloved Sons, that the action of the Church, turned entirely toward the Kingdom of God which is not of the world, if it is not to be sterile but rather vivifying, healthy, and effective, must be directed to the end that men may live and die in the grace of God. To instruct the faithful in Christian thought, to renew men in the following and imitation of Christ, to smooth the way, though always narrow, to the Kingdom of Heaven and render the city truly Christian; such is the mission of the priest, as teacher, father, and shepherd of his parish.

In the fulfillment of these duties, do not allow your zeal to be directed or fettered by your administrative work. Perhaps not a few of you are obliged to carry on a daily struggle, in order not to be weighed down by administrative worries and to find the means and time indispensable for the care of souls. Now, if organization and administration are without doubt valuable means of the apostolate, they must nevertheless be adapted and subordinated to the spiritual ministry and to the veritable and proper office of active pastorship.

By the divine counsel, also the priest, like every Bishop is "*ex hominibus assumptus, pro hominibus constituitur in iis quae sunt ad Deum, ut offerat dona et sacrificia pro peccatis*—taken from among men, ordained for men in the things that appertain to God, that he may offer up gifts and sacrifices for sins"; and so his sacred character as intermediary between God and men reveals itself, unfolds itself, rises and fully sublimates itself surrounded and enveloped by the supreme light of its mystery in the sacrifice of the Holy Mass and in the administration of the Sacraments. At the altar, at the baptismal font, in the tribunal of penance, at the Eucharistic table, at the marriage blessing, at the sickbed, in the agony of the dying, among children eager for the future and the road of life, in the families and the schools, in hospitals, in the pulpit and in assemblies, the priest is the servant, the most effectual instrument of the power, the love, the pardon, the redemption lavished by God upon fallen man. . . .

Take care, therefore, that your dignity always shine before your people, and that they know and understand with a lively faith the meaning and value of the Holy Sacrifice and the Sacraments which you administer, so that they may with lively and personal participation follow the sacred ceremonies and all the ineffable beauties of the holy liturgy.

Administering the Sacraments

After the Holy Sacrifice, your most serious and important act is the administering of the Sacrament of Penance, which has been called the plank of salvation after shipwreck. Be ready and generous in offering that plank to those sailing the tempestuous sea of life. Persist in this with special zeal and perfect self-devotion; sit in that divine tribunal of accusation, repentance, and pardon, as judges who nurture in their breasts the heart of a father, a friend, a physician, and a teacher. And if the essential aim of this Sacrament is to reconcile man with God, do not lose sight of the fact that, in the achievement of such a lofty purpose, a powerful aid is that spiritual direction which draws souls close to the paternal voice of the priest, to pour out to him their afflictions, their troubles, and their doubts, and makes them listen trustfully to his advice and admonishments. The Christian people feel an urgent need for confessors who, through virtue and theological and ascetic training, through maturity and calm judgment, are capable of giving enlightened and reliable rules for a good life, in a simple and clear manner and with tact and benevolence.

Preaching

What We have said up till now concerns particularly the devout and watchful minister of the parish. In addition to this, it is his strict duty to announce the word of God, essential duty of the apostle to whom is entrusted the *verbum reconciliationis*—the word of reconciliation. "*Vae enim mihi, si non evangelizavero*—For woe is unto me if I preach not the Gospel." Because "*Fides ex auditu, auditus autem per verbum Christi. . . . Quomodo credent ei, quem non audierunt? Quomodo autem audient sine praedicante?*—Faith then cometh by hearing; and hearing by the word of Christ. . . . How shall they believe him whom they have not heard? And how shall they hear, without a preacher?" As the intellect gives light to the will, so truth is the lamp of good action. The word is the vehicle of truth and unhappily also of error, which knocks at the door of the intellect and the will. You understand why the admonishments of the Apostle link faith and hearing, hearing and preacher, and why, to cure the blindness of the world by the knowledge of God, speaking from the shining wisdom of the universe, "*placuit Deo per stultitiam praedicationis salvos facere credentes*—it pleased God, by the foolishness of our preaching, to save them that believe." This is sublime folly: for the folly of God is wiser than men and the "shame of Golgotha" is the glory of Christ. Like the admonishments of the Apostle, these truths are also fitted to our times, in which religious ignorance is profound and fraught with dangers. . . .

With adults and those who are mature, be, in imitation of the Apostle Paul, Fathers and Doctors of perfection; with children and the young, make yourselves little, like mothers. Think not that with children and the ignorant you humiliate yourselves.

Catechizing

Equal in value to preaching is catechizing, the instruction of the young and the instruction of adults. In this office, the clergy of the parish can certainly count on the support of Catholic lay people; and to all those who collaborate in such a holy work, We are happy to send with fatherly feeling Our deep thanks and the Apostolic Blessing. Do not forget that the sacred canons regard this important mission as the first and natural care of him who has been given the cure of souls. The zeal of the priest and his ability will be a stimulus and example to his lay fellow workers; and the catechism hour will offer the parish priest a propitious occasion for meeting the younger generation of the parish. Whenever possible, do not neglect the opportunity of personally preparing the children for their first confession and communion; this is the first secret meeting of you and Christ, the divine Friend of children, with candid souls that approach you and the altar, and open up, like spring flowers in the first rays of the sun. They will keep this memory throughout the whole fluctuating course of their lives.

Lastly, We do not wish to pass over a characteristic feature of the picture of the Good Shepherd, Who was not only the true Light which illuminates every man coming into the world, He the truth, He the way, He the life. He also lavished His healing virtue on bodies and every human misery, *bene faciendo et sanando omnes*—doing good to all and healing all, and leaving to His Apostles and His Church the mandate of compassionate love for the poor, the suffering, the derelict, because life here below is a flux and reflux of good and evil, of tears and joy, of needs and assistance, of falls and risings, of struggles and victories. But the love for brothers all redeemed by Christ is the mysterious balm for every sorrow and misery.[1]

Rights and Duties of the Priest in Questions Regarding Public Life

It is the right and at the same time the essential duty of the Church, to instruct the faithful in word and writing, from the pulpit or in the other customary forms, in regard to everything that concerns faith and morals or is irreconcilable with her own doctrine and therefore inadmissible for Catholics, be it a question of philosophical or religious systems, or of the ends intended by their fosterers, or of their moral conceptions concerning the life of either individuals or the community.

The exercise of the right to vote is an act of serious moral responsibility, at least when it is a question of electing those who are called to give the country its constitution and laws, particularly those concerning, for example, the sanctification of holidays of obligation, matrimony, the family, the school, and settlement according to justice and equity of the multifarious social conditions. It is therefore for the Church to explain to the faithful the moral duties which derive from that electoral right.

The Catholic priest cannot simply be put on the same level as public officials or those invested with public authority or military or civil functions. Those are employees or representatives of the State, on which (without prejudice to the divine law) they are dependent and the legitimate interests of which they care for; the State, therefore, may issue orders pertaining to their conduct, even in political questions. The priest, on the other hand, is a minister of the Church and has a mission, which, as We have already pointed out, extends to the whole range of the religious and moral duties of the faithful. In the fulfillment of his mission he may therefore be obliged to give advice or instructions regarding public life also. Now it is evident that the possible abuses of such a mission cannot simply be left to the judgment of the civil power; otherwise, the shepherds of souls would be exposed to hindrance and vexations provoked by groups ill-disposed toward the Church, under the facile pretext of wanting to separate the clergy from politics. It must not be forgotten that, precisely under the pretext of wanting to oppose so-called "political Catholicism," National Socialism, which in reality only aimed at the destruction of the Church, moved against the latter all the apparatus of persecution, vexation, police espionage, against which Churchmen had to defend themselves and carry on a courageous struggle, even from the pulpit, with a heroism that today is admired throughout the world.[2]

[1] Address to Parish Priests and Lenten Preachers, September 6, 1940
[2] Allocution to the Sacred College, March 16, 1946

THE LAY APOSTOLATE

IT IS OFTEN SAID that the Church, in the last four centuries, has been exclusively "clerical" in order to react to the crisis which in the sixteenth century called for the abolition, pure and simple, of the hierarchy. And on such a premise it is insinuated that it is time she expand her cadres.

Such a judgment is far removed from reality, for it is precisely from the time of the Council of Trent that the laity has begun to organize itself and progress in apostolic activity. This is easily ascertainable; it is enough to recall, among many, two evident historical facts: the Marian Congregations of men actively exercising the lay apostolate in all the sectors of public life, and the progressive participation of women in the modern apostolate. And it is opportune to remember, in this connection, two great figures of Catholic history: that of Mary Ward, the incomparable woman whom Catholic England, in the darkest and bloodiest hours, gave to the Church; and St. Vincent de Paul, without doubt one of the greatest founders and promoters of the works of Catholic charity.

Nor should one fail to recognize the beneficial influence in the Catholic world, of the union which, up to the time of the French Revolution, linked in reciprocal relationship the two authorities established by God: Church and State. The closeness of their relationship on the common ground of public life created a general atmosphere of Christian spirit which, in large part, dispensed both priests and laymen from the onerous duty which they have to shoulder today in order to assure the defense and the practical realization of faith.

Development of the Separation of Church and State

At the end of the eighteenth century a new factor comes into play: on the one hand, the Constitution of the United States of America, which developed with extraordinary speed and where the Church was very soon to grow considerably in strength and vigor; on the other, the French Revolution, which, with its consequences in Europe and beyond the oceans, ended up in separating the Church from the State. Though not taking place everywhere at the same time and in the same way, this rupture had everywhere the logical result of compelling the Church to provide with her own means for the continuation of her activity, the fulfillment of her mandate, and the defense of her rights and her freedom. It was the origin of the so-called Catholic movements which, guided by priests and laymen, strong in their cohesion and sincere loyalty, led the great mass of believers to struggle and victory. Is this not, indeed, an initiation and an introduction of laymen into the apostolate?

The Mass of the Lukewarm

There is also, it is true, a mass of lukewarm, irresolute, and unstable persons, for whom religion may still be of some meaning, but a very vague one which has not the slightest influence on life. This amorphous mass, as experience teaches, can find itself suddenly, from one day to the next, faced with the need of making a decision.

As for the Church, she has a triple mission to accomplish for all: to make fervent believers adequate to the exigencies of these times; to introduce into the safe, healthy intimacy of the home those who are hesitating on the doorstep; to bring back to the fold those who have strayed from religion and who cannot be abandoned to their pitiful fate. A splendid task for the Church, but made extremely difficult by the fact that, even if on the whole she has greatly propagated herself, her clergy has not increased correspondingly. Now the clergy must dedicate itself, first of all, to the exercise of the ministry proper to the priest, wherein no one can substitute for him. The contribution of the laity to the apostolate is therefore an indispensable necessity.

All the faithful, without exception, are members of the mystical body of Jesus Christ. It follows that the law of nature, and even more strongly the law of Christ, obliges them to give a good example of a truly Christian life: "*Christi bonus odor sumus Deo in iis qui salvi fiunt et in iis qui pereunt*—For we are the good odor of Christ unto God, in them who are saved and in them who perish." All are therefore held, and today quite especially, to think, in prayer and sacrifice, not only of their own private needs, but also about the great intentions of the Kingdom of God in the world, according to the spirit of the "Our Father" taught to us by Jesus Christ Himself.

Not Everyone Is Called to the Apostolate

Can it be said that all are equally called to the apostolate in the strict sense of the word? God has not given everyone either the possibility or the aptitudes. One cannot demand that the bride dedicate herself to these works; or the mother who educates her children in the Christian manner and, in addition, must work to help her husband support the family. Not all, then, are called upon to be apostles.

It is certainly difficult to set the bounds of the field of action of the lay apostolate, properly called. Should one, for example, include the education given by a mother to her family, or by educators and teachers filled with holy zeal in the practice of their pedagogic profession; or the conduct of a reputable and firmly Catholic physician, whose conscience never compromises with natural and divine law, and who exerts all his efforts for the upholding of the Christian dignity of marriage and the protection of the sacred rights of the progeny; or even the action of a Catholic statesman in favor of a generous housing policy for the underprivileged?

Much would speak for a negative answer, if one considered all this as nothing but the simple fulfillment of professional duties, highly laudable, but in any case obligatory.

We know, however, that this simple fulfillment of a professional duty by millions and millions of conscientious and exemplary faithful is a powerful and irreplaceable factor in the salvation of souls.

Doubtless, the lay apostolate, in its true meaning, is mainly organized in Catholic Action and in other institutions of apostolic activity approved by the Church; but, besides these, there can be and there are lay apostles, men and women, who not only perceive the good to be accomplished, and the possibilities and means of doing it, but who do it out of a desire to bring other souls to truth and grace. We have in mind also a great many excellent laymen who, in the countries where the Church is persecuted as she was in the first centuries of Christianity, substitute to the best of their abilities for imprisoned priests, risking even their lives in order to impart the teachings of Christian doctrine, to instruct on religious living and the correct manner of Catholic thinking, to induce others to frequent the Sacraments, especially that of the Eucharist. All of these laymen you see at work; do not worry about asking to what organization they belong; admire, rather, and recognize gratefully the good they accomplish.

Far from Us any thought of undervaluing organizations or disesteeming their significance as a factor in the apostolate; We value them highly, above all in a world where the adversaries of the Church press upon her with the compact mass of their own organizations. But that must not lead us to a petty exclusivity, to what the Apostle used to call "*explorare libertatem*—to spy upon our liberty" (Galatians 2, 4).

Subordination and Interpretation

It is evident that the lay apostolate is subordinate to the ecclesiastical hierarchy, which is of divine institution; therefore it cannot be independent of it. To think differently would be to strike at the very foundation wall on which Christ Himself built His Church.

Hence, it would be erroneous to believe that, within the jurisdiction of the diocese, the lay apostolate is placed on a line parallel to the hierarchical apostolate, so that the Bishop himself cannot subordinate the parochial apostolate of the laity to the parish priest. He can indeed, and he can also establish as a general rule that the works of the lay apostolate intended for the parish itself should be placed under the authority of the parish priest. The Bishop has constituted him pastor of the entire parish, and, as such, he is responsible for the salvation of all his flock.

That there may be, on the other hand, extraparochial and even extradiocesan works for the lay apostolate—We prefer to say supraparochial and supradiocesan—according to where the good of the Church requires it, is also true and it is not necessary to repeat it.

If We compare the lay apostolate, or, more exactly, the militant Christian belonging to Catholic Action, to an instrument in the hands of the hierarchy, as is commonly done, We want to express that the ecclesiastical superiors must use him in the way the Creator and Lord makes use of rational beings as instruments, as secondary causes, "with a sweetness full of consideration." They should use their services, then, conscious of their own grave responsibility, encouraging them, suggesting initiatives, accepting gladly those that might be proposed, and, according to the opportuneness, approving them with broad vision. In decisive battles, the happiest initiatives come at times from the front. The history of the Church offers innumerable examples.

The basic requirement in apostolic work is the most cordial understanding between priests and laity. The apostolate of the one is not in competition with that of the other. In truth, We are not too pleased to hear here and there the expression "emancipation of the laity." It has a somewhat jarring note, and is also historically inexact. Were the great leaders, to whom We alluded in speaking of the Catholic movement of the last fifty years, children or minors who had to be emancipated? In the kingdom of grace all are considered adults. And that is what matters.

The appeal to the collaboration of the laity is not due to the weakness or failure of the clergy in the task of the present hour. That there are individual weaknesses belongs to the inevitable wretchedness of human nature, and one meets with them on both sides. But, generally speaking, the priest has eyes as good as those of the laymen to perceive the signs of the times, and he does not have a less sensitive ear to listen to the human heart. The layman is called to the apostolate as a collaborator of the priest, an often precious collaborator, and furthermore necessary because of the small numbers of the clergy, too scarce, We were saying, to be able to accomplish, alone, its proper mission.[1]

[1] Address to Lay Apostolate, October 14, 1951

CATHOLIC ACTION

"CATHOLIC ACTION"—the very word "action," exact and comprehensive at the same time, indicates the nature of the organization and distinguishes it from other Catholic associations. Not that these, too, do not exercise an action, but their action generally inclines toward a particular and determined object to be attained through an organized and permanent effort, whether they develop their activities in the religious and charitable sphere or in the social and economic sphere or in other fields of culture. Thus, these organizations generally take their name from the end they have in view.

"Catholic Action," however, is called by its name because, having a general rather than a particular or specific purpose, it is not a fixed axis around which gravitates the mechanism of any type of organization, but it is rather a meeting place where active Catholics join and organize.

Catholic Action—by a special title—is directly subordinated to the authority of the ecclesiastical hierarchy, whose collaborator it is in the apostolate. In Italian Catholic Action the presidency and the direction of the various diocesan and parochial groups belong to laymen, who, however, are seconded and guided by the ecclesiastical helpers; while in the Marian Congregations, which may also, rightfully, be called Catholic Action, the parish priest is the president. But in order that the assistance given to the women's associations may be really salutary and fruitful, the priests here act with greater reserve, leaving entirely to the care of wise, devout, religious women what the latter can—sometimes even better—do by themselves, restricting their own work to the priestly ministry.

These considerations regarding the organization of Catholic Action prompt Us to add a few general warnings suggested, among other things, by certain erroneous tendencies which have become evident in our times.

First of all, a word on the conception of the apostolate. It does not consist solely in the delivery of the good tidings of the Gospel, but also in leading men to the fount of salvation, though with full respect for their liberty, in converting them and educating the baptized, with serious effort, to become perfect Christians.

Laymen and the Hierarchical Apostolate

It would, moreover, be erroneous to see in Catholic Action—as some have recently asserted—something essentially new, a change in the structure of the Church, a new lay apostolate, working side by side with the Church and not subordinated to her. There has always been in the Church a collaboration of laymen with the hierarchical apostolate, in subordination to the Bishop and those to whom the Bishop has entrusted the responsibility of the care of souls under his authority. Catholic Action has wanted to give that collaboration only a new and timely form and organization for its improved and more efficacious operation.

Although Catholic Action, like the Church herself, is at first organized according to dioceses and parishes, nevertheless this does not prevent its further development beyond and above the restricted limits of the parish. As a matter of fact, it must be recognized that in spite of the great importance of the values and of the fundamental and irreplaceable endeavors of the parish, the rapidly increasing technical and spiritual complexity of modern life may urgently call for a wider extension of Catholic Action. But even so, Catholic Action must always remain a lay apostolate subordinated to the Bishop and his delegates.

The activity of Catholic Action extends to the whole religious and social sphere, that is, as far as the mission and work of the Church reaches. Now, we know very well that the normal growth and strengthening of religious life presupposes a certain measure of healthy economic and social conditions. It is heart-rending for everyone to see how economic distress and social ills make it more difficult to lead a Christian life according to the Commandments of God, and too often exact heroic sacrifices. But one cannot conclude from this that the Church must start by setting aside her religious mission and bring about, first of all, the healing of social distress. If, from the time of the Apostles, the Church has always been prompt in her defense and promotion of justice, in the face of the most serious social abuses, she has fulfilled her mission and, with the sanctification of souls and the conversion of the inward sentiments, she has sought to begin the correction also of social ills and injuries, convinced as she is that religious forces and Christian principles serve, more than any other means, to reach a cure.

The external and well-disciplined organization of Catholic Action does not exclude but, on the contrary, promotes personal perspicacity and the spirit of foresight and individual initiative—according to each person's qualities and capabilities—in permanent contact with the members of Catholic Action in the same locality and circle. Each one holds himself cordially ready whenever the need for some Catholic activity or campaign arises. Through his or her enthusiasm and devotion, each one contributes a disinterested assistance to other unions and associations, which may require co-operation so as to achieve their objectives more completely and surely.

In other words, the mentality of associates who would regard themselves as the inert wheels of a gigantic machine, incapable of moving until they were made to turn by the central force, would not be compatible with the true conception of Catholic Action. Nor would it be admissible to consider those in charge of Catholic Action as operators of an electric power station in front of the control panel, ready only to pull switches in order to regulate or direct the current in the vast system.

Above all, they must exercise a personal moral influence which will be the normal result of the esteem and sympathy which they may arouse and which will give prestige to their suggestions, to their advice, and to the authority of their experience every time there is a question of putting into motion the Catholic forces ready for action.

No Party Politics

There is no need for Us to stress that Catholic Action is not called upon to be a force in the field of party politics. Catholic citizens, as such, may well unite in an association of political activity; they have a perfect right to do so, no less as Christians than as citizens. The presence in its ranks, and the participation of members of Catholic Action—in the above sense and limits—is legitimate and may also be altogether desirable. On the other hand, it would not be permissible for Catholic Action to become an organization of party politics.

By reason of its nature, Catholic Action has not even the mission of being at the head of other associations and of exercising over them an office of quasi authoritative patronage. The fact that it is placed under the immediate direction of the ecclesiastical hierarchy does not bring with it any such consequence.

The specific purpose of Catholic Action consists, as We have said, in the fact that it is the meeting place of those active Catholics who are always ready to collaborate with the apostolate of the Church —apostolate through divine hierarchical institution—which finds its collaborators in the baptized and confirmed, who are supernaturally united to the Church. From this derives a consequence, which at the same time is a paternal warning, not for Catholic Action of any particular country but for Catholic Action of every country at all times. That is, its structure must be adapted in different territories to the particular circumstances of the place; but in one point all its members must be equal: "feel with the Church" in devotion to the cause of the Church, in obedience to those whom the Holy Spirit has appointed Bishops to rule the Church of God, in filial submission to the Supreme Shepherd, to Whose care Christ has entrusted His Church.[1]

Five Tasks of Catholic Action

What are today, for the men of Catholic Action, the most important tasks, the main spheres for their activity? We feel We should briefly indicate five especially:

Religious culture. A deep, firm knowledge of the Catholic faith, of its truths, of its mysteries, and of its divine forces. The expression "anemia of religious life" has been coined. It rings like a cry of alarm. That anemia must be attributed—in the first place and in all classes, among the educated as well as among the uneducated—to an often almost complete ignorance of religious matters. This ignorance must be fought, rooted out, and conquered.

Sanctification of feast days of obligation. Sunday must become once again the Lord's Day, the day of the adoration and glorification of God, of the Holy Sacrifice, of prayer, of rest, of recollection and reflection, of happy gatherings in the intimacy of the family. Painful experience has taught us that for not a few, even among those who work hard and honestly all through the week, Sunday has become the day of sin.

Truly, the outcome of this struggle between faith and disbelief will in great part depend on what one or the other of the two fronts will be able to make of Sunday; will it still carry engraved on its brow, clear and shining, the holy name of the Lord, or will this be completely obscured and neglected?

Salvation of the Christian family. The Christian mother must be preserved; Christian education of the young must be preserved, and therefore also the Christian school; it is necessary to preserve the Christian hearth, stronghold of the fear of God, of inviolate faithfulness, of sobriety, of love and peace, where rules that spirit which pervaded the house of Joseph in Nazareth.

To save the Christian family is precisely the principal mission of the Christian man. Do not forget: on his wishes, no less than on the woman herself, depends the destiny of the mother and of the family.

Social justice. For Catholics, the road to follow in the solution of the social question is clearly indicated by the doctrine of the Church.

A more equitable distribution of wealth is and remains a point in the program of Catholic social doctrine.

Without doubt, the result of the natural trend of things—and this is neither economically nor socially abnormal—is that the goods of the earth, within certain limits, are unequally divided. But the Church is against the accumulation of these goods in the hands of a relatively few extremely rich men, while vast sections of the people are condemned to pauperism and economic conditions unworthy of human beings.

In the same spirit, another moral sentiment must be revived: loyalty and veracity in human coexistence, consciousness of responsibility for the common good. It is disquieting to see to what extent loyalty and honesty have disappeared in economic and social life, as a consequence of the incredible disturbances of the war and post-war period. What is made manifest in this field is no longer just an external defect of character but reveals a serious internal malady, a spiritual poisoning which, to a large degree, is also the cause of that religious anemia.

The economic and financial chaos produced by every great cataclysm has stimulated and sharpened greed for gain which drives souls to ambiguous speculations and maneuvering to the detriment of the whole population. We have always blamed and condemned such maneuvering, no matter where it may have its origin, no less than every illicit business, every falsification, and all disobedience of just laws made by the State for the good of the civil community.

It is therefore for the men of Catholic Action to collaborate in the healing of this evil by word and work, above all by their own example, and then also through the most effective possible influence on public opinion.[2]

[1] Address to Leaders of Catholic Action, May 3, 1951
[2] Address to Union of Men of Catholic Action, September 7, 1947

SOCIETY AND POLITICS

INDIVIDUAL AND STATE

WHERE THE DEPENDENCY of human rights on divine rights is denied, where the highest appeal is to a vague concept of purely earthly authority, where an autonomy founded only on a utilitarian morality is claimed; there human rights themselves justly lose, in their most serious applications, the moral force which is the essential condition for their winning recognition and demanding sacrifices.

It is certainly true that power based on such weak, precarious foundations may sometimes achieve, because of contingent circumstances, material success which astonishes the superficial observer; but there comes a moment when there triumphs that inescapable law which strikes everything that is built on a hidden or open disproportion between the greatness of material and outward success and the weakness of inner values and their moral foundation. This disproportion always exists where public authority fails to recognize or repudiates the sovereignty of the supreme Legislator, Who, if He has given power to the rulers, has likewise determined and set its limits.

Civil sovereignty, in fact, was desired by the Creator in order that it might regulate social life according to the prescriptions of an order which is unchangeable in its universal principles, and that it might help the human being, in the temporal order, to attain physical, intellectual, and moral perfection and assist him in reaching his supernatural goal.

It is, therefore, the noble prerogative and mission of the State to control, help, and regulate the private and individual activities of national life, to make them converge harmoniously in the common good, which cannot be determined by arbitrary conceptions, nor draw its standards primarily from the material prosperity of society, but rather from the harmonious development and the natural perfection of man, for which society is destined, as a means, by the Creator.

To consider the State as an end, to which everything should be subordinated and directed, could only do harm to the true and lasting prosperity of nations. And that happens both when this unlimited authority is attributed to the State on behalf of the nation, the people, or even a social class, and when it is claimed by the State, as the absolute master, acting independently from any mandate.

For if the State attributes to itself and regulates private initiatives, these, governed as they are by delicate and complex internal laws, which guarantee and assure the attainment of the aim which they have in view, may suffer, with harm to the common good, by being dissociated from their natural sphere, that is, from responsible private activity.

Even the first and essential cell of society, the family, like its welfare and its growth, would then run the risk of being considered exclusively from the viewpoint of national power, and it would be forgotten that man and the family are by their nature prior to the State, and that the Creator gave them both strength and rights and assigned to them a mission, in keeping with unquestionable natural demands.

One-Sided Education of Youth

The education of the new generations would aim not at a balanced, harmonious development of physical forces and of all the intellectual and moral qualities, but at a unilateral formation of those civic virtues which are considered necessary for the achievement of political success; whereas those virtues which give society the sanction of generosity, humanity, and respect would be less stressed, as though they diminished the pride of the citizen.

We can see with painful clearness the dangers We fear will confront this generation and those to come as a result of the lack of recognition, of the diminution and gradual abolition of the rights of the family. Therefore, We proclaim Ourselves the determined defender of these rights, fully conscious of the duty Our apostolic ministry imposes upon Us.

The Right of Parents

The heavier the material sacrifices the State imposes on individuals and families, the more sacred and inviolate must be to it the rights of consciences. The State can lay claim to property and life, but never to the soul, redeemed by God. The mission assigned by God to parents, of providing for the material and spiritual welfare of their offspring and of giving them a harmonious formation, animated by a true religious spirit, cannot be taken away from them without a grave violation of their rights. This formation must of course also aim at preparing youth to carry out intelligently, conscientiously, and proudly those duties of a generous patriotism which gives to one's earthly fatherland its due measure of love, dedication, and collaboration. But, on the other hand, a formation that would omit or, worse still, purposely neglect to direct the eyes and heart of youth to their supernatural fatherland, would be a wrong done to youth, a wrong to the inalienable obligations and rights of the Christian family, an encroachment for which a remedy must be found also in the interest of the welfare of the people and the State. Such an education might seem to those responsible for it to be a source of additional strength and vigor; in reality it would be just the contrary, as the unhappy consequences would demonstrate. The crime of high treason against the King of kings and the Lord of rulers, perpetrated by an upbringing indifferent or hostile to the Christian spirit, the reversal of the "let the little children come unto Me," would bear the bitterest fruit.

On the other hand, that State which frees the torn, bleeding hearts of Christian fathers and mothers from their worries and re-establishes their rights is only promoting its own internal peace and setting the foundations of a happier future for the country. The souls of the children, given by God to the parents, consecrated in baptism with the regal seal of Christ, are a sacred trust, watched over by the jealous love of God. Christ Himself, Who uttered the "let the little children come unto Me," also threatened with terrible punishment, in spite of His goodness and mercy, those who outrage the favorites of His heart. And what greater and more lasting outrage is there than to bring youth up to follow a goal that takes it away from Christ, the way, the truth, and the life, and leads it to open or secret apostasy? This Christ, from Whom they want to alienate the young generations, present and future, is He who received from His eternal Father every power in Heaven and on earth. He holds the destiny of States, peoples, and nations in His almighty hand. It is in His power to cut short or to prolong life, growth, prosperity, and greatness. Of all that is on earth only the soul has everlasting life. An educational system that would not respect the sacred place of the Christian family which is under the protection of the holy Law of God, one that sapped its foundations, that barred from youth the way to Christ, to the Savior's springs of life and joy, and that considered apostasy from Christ and from the Church as a symbol of fidelity to the people or to a specific class, would be pronouncing its own condemnation and would in the course of time experience the inescapable truth of the prophet's words: "They that depart from Thee shall be written in sand." [1]

[1] Encyclical *Summi Pontificatus,* October 20, 1939

CHURCH AND STATE

The Essential Differences Between the Ecclesiastical and the Civil Judicial Establishments Considered in Their Origin and Their Nature

A RAPID SUPERFICIAL GLANCE at judicial laws and practice might lead one to believe that the ecclesiastical and civil procedures present only secondary differences, more or less like those noticeable in the administration of justice in two civilized States of the same juridical family. Even in their immediate objective they seem to coincide: actuation or enforcement, by means of a sentence, of the right established by the law that, in a particular case, is contested or infringed, that is, through a judgment emanating from the competent authority in conformity with the law. The several degrees of judicial instances are similarly to be found in both; in both, procedure shows the same principal elements: a request to bring the case to trial, summons, examination of witnesses, production of documents, questioning of plaintiff and defendant, conclusion of the trial, sentence, right of appeal.

Despite this, the great external and internal resemblance must not make one forget the great differences existing, firstly, in the origin and nature, secondly, in the object, thirdly, in the purpose.

Totalitarianism, Authoritarianism, Democracy

The judicial power is an essential part, and a necessary function, of the power of the two perfect societies, the ecclesiastical and the civil. For this reason, the question of the origin of judicial power becomes identified with that of the origin of power itself.

But precisely because of this, in addition to the resemblances already mentioned, some have tried to find other, even deeper ones. It is strange to see how some followers of the various modern conceptions concerning civil power have invoked, to confirm and support their opinions, presumed analogies with ecclesiastical power. This is no less true for the so-called "totalitarianism" and "authoritarianism" than for their opposite pole, the modern democracy. But, in reality, those deeper resemblances do not exist in any of the three cases, as will clearly be shown by a brief examination.

It is unquestionable that one of the vital needs of any human community and, therefore, that of the Church and State, is that unity in the diversity of its members should be durably ensured.

Now, "totalitarianism" can in no wise ever satisfy that need, for it gives to the civil power, in content and form, an undue scope in all fields of activity, and thus compresses everyone's own legitimate life —personal, communal, and professional—into a mechanical unit or plurality under the seal of nation, of race, or of class.

In Our Christmas Radio Broadcast of 1942, We particularly emphasized the sad consequences for judicial power of the conception and practice which abolishes the equality of all before the law and leaves judicial decisions at the mercy of a changeable collective instinct.

Furthermore, who could ever think that such erroneous interpretations infringing upon human rights can have determined the origin or influenced the action of the ecclesiastical tribunals? This never has been and never can be, because it is contrary to the very nature of the Church's social power, as we shall see presently.

But that fundamental need is also far from being satisfied by that other conception of civil power which can be indicated by the name of "authoritarianism" because it excludes citizens from any efficacious participation in, or influence on the formation of, the social will. It consequently splits the nations up into two categories, that of dominators and that of the dominated, whose reciprocal relations come to be purely mechanical, under the dominion of force, or, in other words, have a merely biological foundation.

The State: A Community for the Common Good

Who does not see how, in this way, the true nature of the authority of the State becomes profoundly subverted? Both of itself and through the exercise of its functions, this authority should tend to render the State a true community, closely united in its ultimate purpose, which is the common good. But in that system the notion of common good becomes so changing and so clearly shows itself to be, as it were, a deceitful cloak for the unilateral interest of the dominator, that an unbridled legislative "dynamism" precludes all juridical security and therefore suppresses a fundamental element of any true judicial order.

Never could such false dynamism submerge and take away the essential rights recognized as pertaining to individual physical persons and moral bodies in the Church. The nature of ecclesiastical power has nothing in common with that "authoritarianism," which has no point of reference with the hierarchical constitution of the Church.

Still to be examined is the democratic form of civil power, in which some would see a closer resemblance to the ecclesiastical power. Without doubt, where there is a true theoretical and practical democracy, it fulfills that vital requirement of every sound community to which We have referred. But this also happens, or may happen, in analogous conditions in other legitimate forms of government.

Differences Between Church and State

Ecclesiastical power is in fact essentially different from the civil power, and therefore also judicial power in the Church.

The origin of the Church, unlike that of the State, does not pertain to the natural law. The widest and most careful analysis of the human person offers no grounds for thinking that the Church, like civil society, would have had perforce to spring up and develop naturally.

She derives from a positive act of God, beyond and above the social disposition of man, though it is in perfect harmony therewith; therefore, ecclesiastical power—and hence also the corresponding judicial power—was born from the will and the act through which Christ founded His Church. But, once the Church had been constituted as a perfect society by the Redeemer, that did not prevent a good many features of resemblance to the structure of civil society from springing out of her very nature.

In one point, however, this fundamental difference appears with particular evidence. The foundation of the Church as a society was effected, unlike the origin of the State, not from the bottom up but from the top down, which means that Christ, Who in His Church achieved on earth the Kingdom of God by Him announced and intended for all men of all times, did not entrust to the community of the faithful the mission of Teacher, Priest, and Shepherd received from His Father for the salvation of the human race but communicated it to a college of Apostles, or messengers, chosen by Himself, so that through their preaching, their sacerdotal ministry, and through the social power of their office they might bring into the Church the multitude of the faithful, in order to sanctify and enlighten them and lead them to the full maturity of followers of Christ.

Consider the words with which He communicated His powers to them: the power to offer up the Sacrifice in memory of Him; the power to remit sins; the promise and giving of the supreme power of the keys to Peter and to his successors personally; and the communication of the power to bind and to loose to all the Apostles. Meditate finally on the words in which, before His ascension, He transmits to these same Apostles the universal mission received from His Father. Is there, perhaps, anything in all this that can give rise to doubts or equivocations? The whole history of the Church, from her beginning up to our own days, does not cease to re-echo those words and to render the same testimony with a clearness and precision which no subtlety could dull or mask. Now, all these words, all these testimonies, proclaim in unison that in the ecclesiastical power the essence, the central point according to the explicit will of Christ, and hence by divine right, is the mission given by Him to the ministers of effecting salvation in the community of the faithful and in all mankind.

Canon 109 of the Code of Canon Law has put this marvellous

edifice in a clear light: *"Qui in ecclesiasticam hierarchiam cooptantur, non ex populi vel potestatis saecularis consensu aut vocatione adleguntur; sed in gradibus potestatis ordinis constituuntur sacra ordinatione; in supremu pontificatu, ipsomet iure divino, adimpleta conditione legitimae electionis eiusdemque acceptationis; in reliquis gradibus iurisdictionis, canonica missione*—Admittance into the ecclesiastical hierarchy is not derived from the consent or approval of the people or of secular authorities; rather, the chosen ones enter the sacred hierarchy through consecration; the supreme pontificate is conferred directly by divine law, after fulfillment of the condition of a legal election and acceptance of this election; admittance into the other ranks of ecclesiastical government is achieved through canonical mission."

Responsibilities of the Members of the Ecclesiastical Hierarchy

"Non ex populi vel potestatis saecularis consensu aut vocatione—Not from the consensus or vocation of the people or secular authorities": in the course of the centuries the mass of the faithful or the secular power may often have participated in the designation of those on whom were to be conferred ecclesiastical offices—to which, as a matter of fact, including the office of Supreme Pontiff, can be elected the descendant of a noble lineage as well as the son of the humblest workingman's family. In reality, however, the members of the ecclesiastical hierarchy have received, and always do receive, their authority from on high and must answer for the exercise of their mandate solely either immediately to God, to Whom alone is subject the Roman Pontiff, or else, in the other degrees, to their hierarchical superiors, but they have no account to render either to the people or to the civil power, excepting, of course, the right of every one of the faithful to present in due form to competent ecclesiastical authority, or even directly to the supreme power of the Church, his petitions and his appeals, especially when the petitioner or appealer is prompted by motives affecting his personal responsibility for his own or other people's spiritual welfare.

From what We have said, there derive principally two conclusions:

1. In the Church, otherwise than in the State, the primordial subject of power, the supreme judge, the highest instance of appeal, is

never the community of the faithful. Therefore, there does not nor can there exist in the Church, as she was founded by Christ, a popular tribunal or a judicial power emanating from the people.

2. The question of the compass or the greatness of ecclesiastical power presents itself also in a way very different from that pertaining to the State. For the Church, what counts, in the first place, is the express will of Christ, in Whose power it was to give her, according to His wisdom and goodness, greater or smaller means and powers, excepting, of course, the minimum necessarily required by her nature and purpose. The power of the Church embraces the whole of man, the inner man and the outer man, in view of the attainment of the supernatural end, inasmuch as he is entirely subject to the law of Christ of which the Church was made custodian and fulfiller by her divine Founder, both in the outward sphere and in the inward sphere, or that of the conscience. Full and perfect power, therefore, though alien to that "totalitarianism" which neither admits nor acknowledges an honest reference to the clear and incontrovertible dictates of one's conscience and does violence to the laws of individual and social living written in the hearts of men. Indeed, the Church aims through her power not at the subjection of the human person but at ensuring its freedom and improvement, redeeming it from the weaknesses, the errors, and the deviations of the spirit and heart which, sooner or later, always end in dishonor and slavery.

The sacred character which ecclesiastical jurisdiction derives from its divine origin and from its belonging to the hierarchical power should inspire you, beloved Sons, with the highest esteem for your office and spur you on to fulfill its austere duties with lively faith, with unalterable rectitude, and with ever watchful zeal. But behind the veil of that austerity, what Splendor is not revealed to eyes that are able to see in the judicial power the majesty of justice, which in all its action tends to make the Church, Christ's Bride, appear "holy and immaculate" before her divine Spouse and before men! [1]

The Differences Between the Ecclesiastical and Civil Judicial Establishments, Considered in Their Object

What yesterday for many was the duty of the Church and was demanded of her sometimes even in a disorderly manner, that is, to resist the unjust impositions of totalitarian governments, oppressors of consciences, and to denounce and condemn them before the world (which she never failed to do, freely of her own accord and in fitting manner), is today, for those same men, risen to power, a crime and an illicit interference in the field belonging to civil authority. And those very arguments, which the tyrannical governments of yesterday used to bring against the Church in her struggle in defense of divine rights and the dignity and freedom rightly belonging to man, are now being used by the new dominators to fight her persevering action for the safeguarding of truth and justice. But the Church keeps straight on her road, always intent upon the end for which she was instituted by her divine Founder, namely, to lead men along the supernatural paths of virtue and goodness, to heavenly and eternal happiness: in which manner she also promotes at the same time peaceful and prosperous human coexistence.

This thought naturally brings Us again to speak of the essentially different purpose of the two societies. This difference founded on the purpose excludes, without any doubt, the forced submission and quasi insertion of the Church in the State, contrary to the nature of both, which every totalitarianism tends, at least in the beginning, to achieve. However, it certainly does not gainsay any union at all between the two societies, much less does it come to determine between them a cold and dissociating aura of agnosticism and indifference. If anyone should want to understand in this way the correct doctrine that Church and State are two distinct perfect societies, he would be wrong. He would not be able to explain the multifarious forms of union between the two powers that have been fruitful, though in different degree, in the past and present; above all, he would not take into account the fact that the Church and the State have their origin in the same source, God, and that both are entrusted with the care of the same man, of his personal, natural, and supernatural dignity. All this Our glorious predecessor Leo XIII could not, and did not wish to neglect, when, in his Encyclical *Immortale Dei* of November 1, 1885, he clearly delineated, on the basis of their different object, the boundaries of the two societies and pointed out that it more closely and chiefly belongs to the State to take care of the earthly interests of men and to the Church to procure for them heavenly and eternal blessings, inasmuch as man needs security and support both from the State for earthly things and from the Church for those that are eternal.

Do we not perhaps see in this, under certain aspects, some analogy with the relations between the body and the soul? The one and the other act jointly in such a way that the psychological character of a man feels at every moment the effects of his temperament and of his physiological conditions while, vice versa, moral impressions, excitement, and passion are reflected so powerfully on physical sensibility that the soul molds even the features of the face, on which it impresses, as it were, its own image.

Ecclesiastical Judicial Power

There exists, therefore, that difference of object, a difference which exercises a diverse and deep influence on the Church and the State, principally on the supreme power of both societies, and therefore also on their judicial power, which is only a part and a function thereof. Independently of the question whether or not individual ecclesiastical judges are or are not conscious of this, all their judicial activity is, and remains, included in the fullness of life of the Church with its high objective: *caelestia ac sempiterna bona comparare*—to be the mediator for celestial and eternal goods. This *finis operis* (end and purpose) of ecclesiastical judicial power gives it an objective mark and makes of it an institution of the Church as a supernatural society. And, as that mark derives from the ultraterrestrial objective of the Church, ecclesiastical judicial power will never fall into the rigidity and immobility to which purely earthly institutions are easily liable, on account of fear of responsibility, or indolence, or even of misguided efforts to safeguard what is, certainly, a great good: the safety of the law.

This does not mean, however, that in the ecclesiastical judicial establishment there is an area left entirely to the arbitrary discretion of the judge in the treatment of individual cases. These errors of a baneful "vitality" in the law are the sad products of our times in activities to which the Church is a stranger. Untouched by an anti-intellectualism rather widely diffused today, the Church remains firm in the principle: the judge decides in every single case according to the law; a principle which, without favoring excessive "juridical formalism," on the other hand rejects the "subjective discretion" which would come to place the judge no longer under, but above, the law. Clearly to understand the juridical provision according to the meaning of the legislator and rightly to examine individual cases in view of the provision to be applied, this intellectual work is an essential part of concrete judicial activity. Without such a procedure the judge's sentence would be a simple command, and not what the term "positive law" would express, namely, the bringing about, in individual and therefore concrete cases, of order in the world which, as a whole, was created by God's wisdom within an order and for order.

Is not this field of judicial activity indeed rich in life? There is more: ecclesiastical law has in view the common good of the ecclesiastical society and is therefore inseparably linked to the objective of the Church. When, therefore, the judge is applying the law to a particular case, he is co-operating in achieving the fullness of the end which lives in the Church. When, on the other hand, he is faced by doubtful cases, or when legislation leaves him freedom, the bond between the ecclesiastical judicial establishment and the objective of the Church will help him to find and motivate the right decision and to preserve his office from the stain of mere arbitrariness.

In any case, therefore, the relation of ecclesiastical judicial power to the end considered appears as the surest guarantee of the true vitality of its decisions, and while it sets up the ecclesiastical judge in an office willed by God, it inspires him with the high sense of responsibility which is, in the Church too, the indispensable safeguard, superior to any legal ordinance, of security under the law.

By this We do not mean in any way to ignore the practical difficulties which, notwithstanding everything, modern life entails for the ecclesiastical judicial power and which, from several aspects, are even more arduous than those in the civil sphere. Suffice it to consider only certain spiritual goods, in face of which the judicial power of the State feels itself less obligated, or even remains consciously indifferent. Typical are, in this sense, the cases of crimes against the faith or of apostasy, those concerning "liberty of conscience" and "religious tolerance," and also divorce. In these cases the Church, and therefore also the ecclesiastical judge, cannot assume the neutral attitude of States of mixed religious belief and still less that of a world fallen into unbelief and religious indifferentism, but they must let themselves be guided solely by the essential object assigned to the Church by God.

The Pope and Cardinal Stritch of Chicago

The Pope and Cardinal McIntyre of Los Angeles

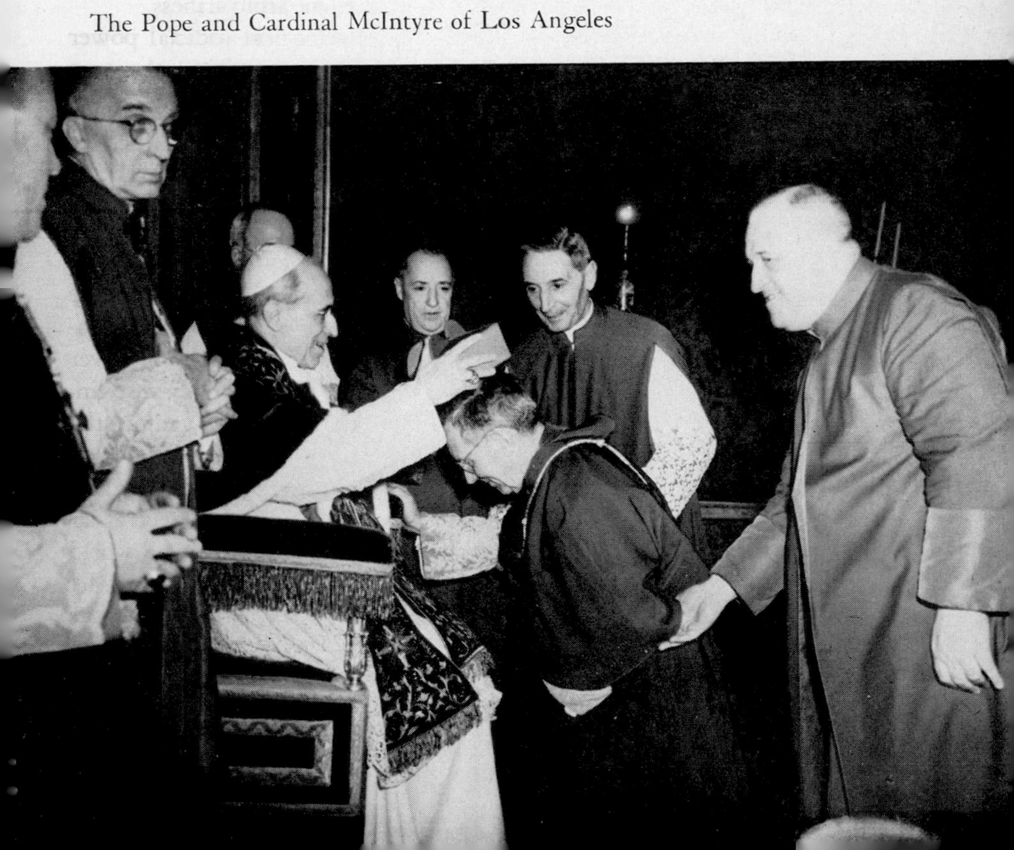

The Pope and Cardinal Mooney of Detroit

The Pope and Cardinal Spellman of New York

In this way we continually encounter again the profound difference to which the diversity of objective gives rise between the ecclesiastical and civil judicial power. Nothing, of course, prevents the one from availing itself of the results reached by the other, either in theoretical notions or in practical experience; it would nevertheless be a mistake to want to transfer mechanically the elements and norms of the one into the other, and, even more so, to want actually to make them equal. Ecclesiastical judicial power and the ecclesiastical judge do not have to look elsewhere for their ideal but must carry it in themselves; they must always keep before their mind's eye that the Church is a supernatural organism, in which is inherent a divine vital principle which must also move and direct the judicial power and the office of an ecclesiastical judge.

Judges of the Church are, in virtue of their office and by divine will, the Bishops of whom the Apostle says that "they have been constituted by the Holy Spirit to rule God's Church." But to "rule" includes to "judge" as a necessary function. Hence, according to the Apostle, the Holy Spirit calls the Bishops no less to the office of judge than to the government of the Church. From the Holy Spirit, therefore, derives the sacred nature of that office. The faithful of Christ's Church "purchased by Him through His Own blood" are those to whom the judicial activity refers. The law of Christ is fundamentally that according to which sentences are pronounced in the Church. The divine vital principle in the Church moves everyone, and all that which is in her, toward her own end, and hence also the judicial power and the judge: *"caelestia ac sempiterna bona comparare*—to provide celestial and eternal goods." [2]

[1] Allocution. Inauguration of the Juridical Year of the S. Romana Rota, October 2, 1945

[2] Allocution. Inauguration of the Juridical Year of the S. Romana Rota, October 29, 1947

THE SOCIAL ORDER

THE DIAL OF HISTORY today is registering a grave, decisive hour for the whole of humanity.

An ancient world lies shattered in ruins. To see a new world arise soon from those ruins, a world more sane, juridically better organized, and more in harmony with the exigencies of nature: that is the yearning of tortured peoples.

Will the painful, deadly errors of the past perhaps be followed by others no less deplorable, and will the world swing indefinitely from one extreme to the other? Or will the pendulum be arrested, thanks to the action of wise leaders, based on directions and solutions which do not contradict divine law and do not contrast with the human and the Christian conscience?

From the answer to this question depends the fate of Christian civilization in Europe and the world, a civilization which, far from casting prejudice upon the manifold forms peculiar to the characteristics of each people, inserts itself in them and revivifies their highest ethical principles: the moral law inscribed by the Creator in the hearts of men, the natural law deriving from God, the fundamental rights and the intangible dignity of the human person. And in order to bend the will of observing them more effectively, it infused into the individual men, into a whole people, and into the community of nations those superior energies which no human power is capable of conferring.

Christian Civilization, Its Fruits and Blessings

Thus it happens that Christian civilization, without suffocating or weakening the sane elements of the most varied native cultures, harmonizes them in essentials, creating in this manner a wide unity of sentiments and moral norms, most solid foundation of true peace, social justice, and brotherly love among all members of the great human family.

In one of those evolutions full of contradictions, the last century has witnessed, on the one hand, the systematic undermining of the very foundations of Christian civilization and, on the other, its constant spreading among all the peoples. Europe and the other continents still subsist, in different measure, from the vital forces and principles which the inheritance of Christian thought had transmitted to them as in a spiritual blood transfusion.

Some go so far as to forget this precious patrimony, to neglect it, even to repudiate it; but the fact of that hereditary succession remains all the same.

The clear-sightedness, devotion, courage, inventive genius, and the sentiment of fraternal charity of all upright and honest minds will determine in what measure and to what degree it will be given to Christian thought to maintain and support the gigantic task of restoring the social, economic, and international life on a plane which does not contrast with the moral and religious content of Christian civilization.

The Right to Private Property

In his Encyclical *Rerum Novarum* our glorious predecessor Leo XIII enunciated the principle that for every just economic and social order "the right of private property must be set as an unshakable foundation."

If it is true that the Church has always recognized "the natural right of property and the hereditary transmission of one's own belongings," it is, however, no less certain that this private property is in a special way the natural fruit of labor: the product of an intense activity of man, who acquires it thanks to his energetic determination to safeguard and develop, with his own strength, his own existence and that of his family, to create for himself and his own a sphere of just freedom, not only of an economic nature, but also political, cultural, and religious.

The Christian conscience cannot admit as just a social order which either denies, on principle, or renders practically impossible or vain the natural right of possession, both over consumer goods and over the means of production.

But it cannot likewise accept those systems which recognize the right of private property according to a wholly false concept, and are therefore in contrast with the genuine and sane social order.

Capitalism

Therefore, where, for example, "capitalism" is based on such erroneous conceptions and unduly claims for itself an unlimited right on property, without any subordination to the common good, the Church has reproved it as contrary to natural law.

We see, in fact, the ever increasing ranks of workers often faced with those excessive concentrations of economic goods which, frequently hidden under anonymous forms, succeed in evading their social obligations and place the worker in the near impossibility of creating property of his own.

We see medium and small property diminish and lose vigor in social life, compressed and restricted as it is to a defensive struggle ever more harsh and without hope of positive success.

We see, on the one hand, tremendous riches dominate private and public economy and often even civic affairs, and, on the other hand, the vast multitude of those who, deprived of any security, direct or indirect, in their life, lose all interest in the true and high values of the spirit, bar themselves against aspirations toward genuine liberty, cast themselves in the arms of any political party, slaves to whoever promises them, in one way or another, bread and tranquillity. And experience has shown of what tyranny humanity is capable in such conditions, even at the present time.

Private Property and Means of Production

Defending the principle of private property, then, the Church follows a lofty ethical-social aim. She does not intend purely and simply to sustain the present state of affairs, as if she saw therein the expression of divine will, nor to protect, as a matter of principle, the rich and the plutocrat against the poor and destitute. Quite the contrary! From her origins, she has been the guardian of the poor and oppressed against the tyranny of the powerful, and she has always championed the just protests of all classes of workers against every iniquity. But the Church aims rather to act so that the institution of private property may become what it should be, according to the designs of divine Wisdom and the dispositions of nature: an element of social order, a necessary prerequisite to private initiative, a stimulus to labor to the advantage of temporal and transcendental goals of life, and hence of the liberty and dignity of man, created in the image of God, Who from the very beginning assigned to him to use as he saw fit the mastery over material things.

Take away from the worker the hope of acquiring something in the way of personal property, and what other natural stimulus could you offer him to incite him to intense labor, saving, and sobriety, when today, not a few men and peoples, having lost everything, have nothing left but the ability to work? Or does one wish to perpetuate a wartime economy for which, in some countries, the public power keeps in hand all means of production, providing everything for everybody, but under the lash of a strong discipline? Or does one want the subjugation to the dictatorship of one political group, which, as the dominating class, will dispose of the means of production, but of bread also, and thereby of the will to work of the single individual?

The Right of the State to Expropriation

The social and economic policy of the future, the directive activity of the State, of the communities and professional institutions, cannot attain their lasting aim, which is the real fecundity of social life and the normal yield of the national economy, if not by respecting and safeguarding the vital function of private property in its personal and social value. When the distribution of property is an obstacle to this end—and this is not necessarily always originated by the extensiveness of private property—the State may, in the common interest, intervene to regulate its use, or even, if it is impossible to arrive at another solution, decree expropriation, giving a fair and equitable indemnity. For the same purpose, the small and medium-sized properties in agriculture, in the arts and trades, in commerce and industry, must be guaranteed and promoted; co-operative unions must assure to them the advantages of a large concern; where the large business concern today manifests itself to be more productive, the possibility must be offered to temper the labor agreement with a company-sharing contract.

Nor let it be said that technical progress is opposed to such a regime and pushes in its irresistible current all activity toward gigantic concerns and organizations, before which a social system founded on the private property of the single individual must perforce collapse. No; technical progress does not determine, as a fatal and necessary fact, economic life. Too often it has bowed docilely before the demands of egotistical calculations avid to increase capital indefinitely; why, then, should it not also bend to the need of maintaining and assuring the private property of all, the cornerstone of the social order? Even technical progress, as a social fact, must not prevail over the general good, but must instead be regulated by and subordinated to it.[1]

[1] Radio Message to the World, September 1, 1943

DICTATORSHIP AND DEMOCRACY

IN AN EVER INCREASING NUMBER of noble minds arises a thought, a constantly clearer and firmer will: a thorough reorganization of the world. Members of governments, the responsible representatives of nations, meet for talks and conferences, with a view to determining the basic rights and duties on which a community of States should be re-established, of tracing the path to a better, securer, worthier future for mankind.

Undoubtedly, the value, applicability, or efficacy of this or that proposal may be discussed; judgment on them may be suspended; but it is still true that the movement is in progress.

Furthermore—and this is perhaps the most important point—peoples have, as it were, reawakened from a long torpor. They have assumed a new, questioning, criticizing, suspicious attitude toward the State and those governing. Taught, as they are, by bitter experience, they oppose with greater impetuosity the monopolization of power by a dictatorial authority which is uncontrollable and intangible; and they ask for a system of government more consistent with the dignity and freedom of citizens.

These restless multitudes, in which the onslaught of war has left the deepest traces, are now filled with the persuasion—vague and confused, perhaps, at first, but now incontrovertible—that, if the possibility of controlling and correcting the action of those in power had not been lacking, the world would not have been dragged into the disastrous hurricane of war; and that, to prevent any such catastrophe in the future, efficacious guarantees must be vested in the people itself.

In view of this state of mind, is there any cause for wonder if the democratic tendency is pervading peoples and is widely obtaining the approval and assent of those who aspire to co-operate with greater efficacy in shaping the destiny of individuals and society?

The Church Reproves No Form of Government

It is scarcely necessary to recall that, according to the teaching of the Church, "it is not forbidden to prefer moderate governments of a popular form, without prejudice, however, to the Catholic doctrine concerning the origin and use of public power," and that the "Church reproves none of the different forms of government, provided they be in themselves suitable for securing the welfare of citizens."

If, therefore, We direct Our attention to the problem of democracy, in order to consider what are the canons according to which it must be regulated to deserve to be called a true and sound democracy, suitable to the present time, this plainly indicates that the care and concern of the Church is not so much directed to its structure and external organization—which depend upon each nation's individual aspirations—as to man, as such, who, far from being the object and a passive element of social life, truly is, and must be and remain, its subject, its basis, and its end.

Starting from the premise that democracy, taken in its wider meaning, admits of different forms and can find its realization in a monarchy as well as in a republic, two questions come up for our examination:

1. What features must distinguish men living in a democracy and under a democratic regime?

2. What features must distinguish the men holding public power in democracy?

The Citizen in a Democracy

To express his own opinion concerning the duties and sacrifices which are imposed upon him; not to be forced to obey without having been listened to: these are two of the citizen's rights, which have their expression in democracy, as its name itself indicates. From the solidity, the harmony, and the good fruits of this contact between the citizens and the government of a State, it can be seen whether a democracy is truly sound and balanced, and what is its force of life and development. As regards the measure and nature of the sacrifices asked of all the citizens—in our times when the activities of the State are so extensive and decisive—a democratic form of government appears to many people as a natural postulate imposed by reason itself. But when "more democracy and better democracy" is clamored for, the only meaning of such a demand would be to give the citizen increasingly the opportunities to form his own personal opinion, and to express it, and make it prevail in such ways as are consistent with the common good.

People and the "Masses"

From this flows a first necessary conclusion, with its practical consequence. The State does not contain in itself and does not mechanically gather within a given territory an amorphous agglomeration of individuals. The State is, and must be in reality, the organic and organizing unity of a true people.

People and amorphous multitude or, as one says, the "masses," are two different concepts. A people lives and moves by its own vitality; the mass is inert in itself, and can only be moved from without. A people lives by the fullness of the life of the men composing it, each one of whom—at his own post and in his own way—is a person conscious of his own responsibilities and his own convictions. The mass, on the contrary, waits for an impulsion from without, is an easy toy in the hands of whoever would exploit its instincts or emotionality, ready to follow in turn, today this, tomorrow that flag. Out of the vital exuberance of a true people, life flows out abundantly, richly, in the State and in all its organs, pouring into them, with unceasingly renewed vigor, the consciousness of their own responsibility, the true sense of the common good. The elementary force of the mass, skillfully handled and used, can also be employed by the State; in the ambitious hands of one or several individuals, joined artificially by their selfish tendencies, the State can, with the support of the mass reduced to a mere machine, impose its arbitrary will on the better part of the true people: the common interest is thereby affected grievously and for a long time, and the wound is often exceedingly difficult to heal.

Out of this there clearly flows another conclusion: the mass—such as We have now defined it—is the chief enemy of true democracy and of its ideals of freedom and equality.

In a people worthy of this name, the citizen feels in himself the consciousness of his personality, of his duties and rights, of his own freedom, coupled with respect for the freedom and dignity of others. In a people worthy of this name, all inequalities, issuing not from an arbitrary will but from the very nature of things, inequalities of education, possession, social status—without prejudice, let it be well understood, to justice and mutual charity—are no obstacle to the existence and prevalence of a genuine spirit of true brotherliness. On the contrary, far from affecting civil equality in any way, they confer upon it its legitimate meaning, that is to say that, before the State, each individual has the right honorably to live his own personal life, in the place and in the conditions which have been assigned to him by the designs and dispositions of Providence.

In contrast with this picture of the democratic ideal of liberty and equality in a people which is governed by honest and provident hands, what a spectacle is offered by a democratic State left to the arbitrariness of the mass! Freedom, as a moral duty of the person, is turned into a tyrannical pretension to give free vent to men's impulses and appetites to the detriment of other people. Equality degenerates into a mechanical levelling, into a drab uniformity: the sentiment of true honor, personal commitment, respect for tradition, dignity—in a word, all that gives life its true value—little by little sinks and disappears. And there remain only, on one hand, the deluded victims of an illusory outward show of democracy, naïvely mistaken for the very spirit of democracy and for freedom and equality; and, on the other, the more or less numerous profiteers who have been able, through financial or organizational manipulation, to secure for themselves a privileged condition and a position of power over others.

Qualities of Officeholders in a Democracy

The democratic State, whether monarchical or republican, must, like any other form of government, be vested with the power to command with real and effectual authority. The absolute order of beings and ends itself, which shows man as an autonomous person, that is to say, the subject of inviolable duties and rights, both origin and end of his social life, embraces also the State as a necessary society vested with authority, without which it could neither exist nor live. If men, availing themselves of personal freedom, should disown any subordination to a higher authority vested with the right of coercion, they would thereby undermine the foundation of their own dignity and freedom, that is to say, the absolute order of beings and ends.

Established on this same basis, the individual, the State, and the public power, with their respective rights, are bound together and connected in such a way that they either stand or fall together.

And inasmuch as the said absolute order, in the light of sound reason, and especially in the light of the Christian faith, can have no other origin than in a personal God, our Creator, it follows that man's dignity is the dignity of God's image, the dignity of the State is the dignity of the moral community willed by God, the dignity of the political authority is the dignity of its participation in God's authority.

No form of government can afford not to take into account this inner and indissoluble connection, democracy least of all. Therefore, if an individual holding office fails to see that connection or more or less neglects it, he shakes his own authority in its very basis. Similarly, if he fails to take such connection sufficiently into account, and does not see in his office the mission to realize the order willed by God, there will be the danger that the egoism born of power or selfish interests may prevail over the essential requirements of political and social ethics, and that the vain semblances of a democracy which is so only in form may serve, as often happens, as a mask for what is in reality least democratic.

Only a clear understanding of the ends assigned by God to every human society, coupled with a deep feeling for the sublime duties of social activity, can enable those in whom power is vested to fulfill their legislative, judicial, or executive obligations with the consciousness of their own responsibilities and with the objectivity, impartiality, loyalty, generosity, and incorruptibility without which it would be very difficult for a democratic government to succeed in securing the respect, confidence, and assent of the best part of the people.

The People's Representatives

A profound sense of the principles of a political and social order, sound and in harmony with the canons of law and justice, assumes particular importance in those who, in any form of democratic government, hold, wholly or in part, the legislative power, as the people's representatives, and inasmuch as the center of gravity of a properly constituted democracy lies in this popular representation, from which the political currents radiate into all fields of public life—for good as well as for evil—the question of the moral character, practical fitness, and intellectual capacity of members of Parliament is, for all peoples under a democratic regime, a question of life or death, of prosperity or decadence, of recovery or perpetual uneasiness. In order to be able to develop fruitful action and to gain esteem and confidence, any legislative body must—as indubitable experiences attest—gather within itself a choice selection of men who are intellectually outstanding and of firm character, and who look upon themselves as the representatives of the whole people and not, instead, as the agents of a group to whose particular interests the true needs and requirements of the common welfare are unfortunately too often sacrificed. A selection of men not restricted to any one profession or condition, but which can be the image of the manifold life of the whole people. A selection of men with solid Christian convictions, just and sure of judgment, of practical, well-balanced disposition, true to themselves in all circumstances; men of clear and sound philosophy, of steadfast and straightforward purposes; men capable, above all, by virtue of the authority emanating from their pure conscience and widely radiating around them, of being guides and leaders, especially at times when pressing necessities overexcite the impressionability of the people, and make it more liable to be misled and to go astray; men who, in transitional periods, which are generally tormented and torn by passion and by differences of opinion and conflicting programs, feel it doubly their duty to inject into the veins of the people and the State, consumed by the fire of a thousand fevers, the spiritual antidote of clear views, thoughtful kindliness, and justice equally favorable to all, together with a straining of wills toward national union and harmony in a spirit of genuine brotherhood.

Peoples whose spiritual and moral temperaments are sufficiently sound and fruitful find in themselves, and can give to the world, the heralds and instruments of democracy who live with such dispositions and know how to put them to practical use. Where, instead, such men are wanting, others come to take their post, to make of political activity the arena of their ambition, a race toward gains for themselves, their caste, or their class, while the pursuit of private interests causes the true commonweal to be lost sight of or endangered.

State Absolutism

A sound democracy, founded upon the unchanging principles of natural law and revealed truths, will be resolutely contrary to that corruption which attributes to State legislation an unbridled and unlimited power, and which renders the democratic regime itself, despite contrary but vain appearances, a system of absolutism, pure and simple.

State absolutism (not to be confused, as such, with an absolute monarchy, with which We are not now concerned) in fact does consist in the erroneous principle that the authority of the State is unlimited, and that, against it—even when it gives free vent to its despotic aims, overstepping the boundaries of good and evil—no appeal can be admitted to a higher and morally binding law.

A man imbued with right ideas concerning the State and the authority and power vested therein as the custodian of social order, will never think of offending the majesty of the positive law within the sphere of its natural jurisdiction. But this majesty of human positive law is without appeal only when it conforms—or at least is not contrary—to the absolute order, established by the Creator and put in a new light by the revelation of the Gospel. It cannot subsist except in so far as it respects the foundation on which rests the human person, no less than the State and public power. This is the basic criterion of any sound form of government, including democracy; and by this criterion the moral value of every particular law has to be judged.

It has been Our intention to point out the ways by which a democracy that corresponds to human dignity can, in harmony with natural law and God's designs made manifest through revelation, attain beneficial results. We do feel deeply, indeed, the supreme importance of this problem for the peaceful progress of the human family; but We are at the same time conscious of the high qualities which this form of government exacts from the moral maturity of individual citizens; a moral maturity which it would be vain to try to attain fully and surely if the light of the Stable of Bethlehem did not illuminate the dark path along which the peoples of this stormy present are marching toward a future which they hope will be more fortunate.[1]

[1] Radio Message to the World, December 24, 1944

ATHEISTIC DICTATORSHIPS

A WELL-KNOWN CHARACTERISTIC common to persecutors of all times is that, not content with physically crushing their victims, they want also to make them appear despicable and hateful to their country and to society.

Who does not remember the Roman martyrs immolated under Nero and made to appear as arsonists, abominable criminals, enemies of mankind? Modern persecutors show themselves to be the docile disciples of that inglorious school.

They copy their masters and models, if, indeed, they do not surpass them in cruelty, clever as they are in the art of employing the most recent progress in the technical sciences for the purpose of a domination and enslavement of the people which in the past would not have been conceivable.

The Church of Christ is following the road traced out for her by the divine Redeemer. She feels herself eternal; she knows that she cannot perish, that the most violent storms will not succeed in submerging her. She begs no favors; the threats and disfavor of earthly authorities do not intimidate her. She does not interfere in problems purely economic or political, nor does she occupy herself with debates on the usefulness or banefulness of one form of government or another. Always eager, in so far as she is able, to be at peace with all, she renders unto Caesar that which is Caesar's, but she cannot betray or abandon that which belongs to God.

Now, it is well known what the totalitarian and antireligious State requires and expects from the Church as the price for tolerance and its problematical recognition. To amplify, it would desire: a Church who remains silent, when she should speak out; a Church who weakens the law of God, adapting it to the taste of human desires, when she should loudly proclaim and defend it; a Church who detaches herself from the unwavering foundation upon which Christ built her, in order to repose comfortably on the shifting sands of the opinions of the day or to give herself up to the passing current; a Church who does not withstand the suppression of conscience and does not protect the legitimate rights and the just liberties of the people; a Church who with indecorous servility remains enclosed within the four walls of the temple, who forgets the divine mandate received from Christ: Go forth on the crossroads, teach all peoples.

Can the Pope Remain Silent?

The Pope has the divine promises; even in his human weakness, he is invincible and unshakable; messenger of truth and justice, the principle of the unity of the Church, his voice denounces errors, idolatry, superstition, it condemns iniquity, makes charity and virtue loved.

Can the Pope then remain silent when in a nation the churches which are united to the center of Christendom, to Rome, are snatched away through violence or cunning; when all the Greek-Catholic bishops are imprisoned because they refuse to apostatize from their faith; when priests and the faithful are persecuted and arrested because they refuse to leave their true Mother Church?

Can the Pope remain silent, when the right to educate their own children is taken away from parents by a minority regime which wants to alienate them from Christ?

Can the Pope remain silent when a State, surpassing the limits of its authority, arrogates to itself the power to abolish dioceses, to depose Bishops, to overturn the ecclesiastical organization, and to reduce it below the minimum requirements for the effectual cure of souls?

Can the Pope remain silent when things go so far that imprisonment is given as punishment to a priest guilty of refusing to violate the most sacred and inviolable of secrets, that of sacramental confession?

Is all this perhaps illegitimate interference in the political powers of the State? Who could honestly affirm anything of the kind? [1]

[1] Address to the People of Rome, February 2, 1949

ELECTIONS AND VOTING

IT IS A RIGHT AND A DUTY to draw the attention of the faithful to the extraordinary importance of elections and the moral responsibility which rests on everyone who has the right to vote. Without any doubt, the Church intends to remain outside and above political parties, but how can she remain indifferent to the composition of a Parliament, when the Constitution gives it power to pass laws which so directly affect the highest religious interests and even the condition of life of the Church herself? Then there are also other arduous questions, above all the problems and economic struggles which closely touch the well-being of the people. In so far as they are of a temporal order (though in reality they also affect the moral order) Churchmen leave to others the care of pondering and treating technically with them for the common welfare of the nation. From all this it follows that:

It is a strict duty for all who have the right, men or women, to take part in the elections. Whoever abstains, especially out of cowardice, commits a grave sin, a mortal fault.

Everyone has to vote according to the dictates of his own conscience. Now, it is evident that the voice of this conscience imposes upon every sincere Catholic the duty of giving his or her vote to those candidates, or those lists of candidates, who really offer sufficient assurances for safeguarding the rights of God and the souls of men, for the real good of individuals, families, and society, according to the law of God and moral Christian doctrine.[1]

[1] Address to the Delegates of the International Conference on Emigration, October 17, 1951

A WAGE which guarantees the existence of the family, making it possible for parents to fulfill their natural duty of rearing a progeny healthily fed and clothed; a dwelling fit for human beings; the possibility of providing children with sufficient instruction and a suitable education, the possibility of planning and making provision for bad times, sickness, and old age—these are social welfare conditions that must be achieved if we do not want society to be shaken in every season by ferments and dangerous quakings, but to grow quietly and advance in the peace and harmony of mutual love.

Conception of the Living Conditions Fit for Man

The Church, guardian and instructor of truth, in her assertion and bold defense of the rights of the working population, on various occasions opposing error, has had to put people on guard against letting themselves be deluded by the mirage of specious and fatuous theories and visions of future well-being or by the deceitful lures and urgings of false teachers of social prosperity who call bad good and good bad and who, claiming to be the friends of the people, do not permit the mutual agreements between capital and labor and between employers and employed that maintain and promote harmony for the progress and benefit of all.

But when have their words ever been answered by facts, or when have hopes smiled upon reality? Deception and disappointment were and are the only rewards of those who believed them and followed them down paths which, far from improving, only worsen and aggravate the conditions of life and of moral and material advancement. Such false shepherds would have people believe that salvation must proceed with a revolution which would change the social structure and assume a national character.

Social revolution boasts that it can raise the working classes to power: vain words and a mere semblance of impossible reality! The actual fact is that the working population is tied, yoked, and bound to the force of State capitalism, which restrains and subjugates everyone, the family no less than consciences, and transforms workers into a gigantic industrial machine. In a way not differing from other social orderings and systems, which it claims to oppose, it ties up, marshals, and compresses everything into one fearful instrument of war, which exacts not only the blood and health but also the goods and prosperity of the people. And if leaders become proud of this or that advantage or improvement realized in the field of labor, vaunting and boisterously proclaiming it to the four winds, such material profit never represents a worthy return for the sacrifices imposed on each one, which infringe upon personal rights, the liberty to manage one's home and to exercise a profession, upon citizenship and, particularly, upon freedom in the practice of religion and even in the life of the conscience.

No, salvation is not to be found in revolution. To aspire—with only one's own exclusive and material advantage in view, which seems, however, always uncertain—to a revolution which is to proceed from injustice and civil insubordination, and to render oneself responsible for shedding the blood of one's fellow countrymen and for the destruction of common wealth, is contrary to the genuine and sincere profession of Christianity. Woe to him who forgets that a genuine national society includes social justice and claims a fair and adequate participation of all in the wealth of the country.

Not in revolution but in harmonious evolution lies salvation and justice. The work of violence has always been to tear down, never to raise up; to inflame the passions, rather than appease them; to create hate and ruin, rather than to make brothers of the contenders; and it has flung men and parties into the bitter necessity of slowly rebuilding, after painful trial, upon the ruins of discord. Only a progressive and cautious evolution, courageous and in harmony with nature, enlightened and guided by the sacred Christian canons of right and justice, can lead to the realization of the honest desires and needs of the working man.

Not destruction, then, but construction and consolidation: not abolition of private ownership, the basis of family stability, but its promotion and spreading as the fruit of the conscientious efforts of every worker, male or female, so as to bring about the gradual reduction of that mass of bold and restless men who, sometimes through gloomy desperation and at other times through blind instincts, let themselves be carried away by every gust of false doctrine or by the subtle arts of agitators destitute of any moral sense. Not the dispersion of private capital, but the promotion of its prudently controlled marshalling as a means and buttress for the achievement and increase of the true material well-being of the whole population. We must not repress or give exclusive preference to industry but secure its harmonious co-ordination with artisanship and agriculture, which makes the national soil render up its multiform and necessary produce. In the exploitation of technical progress, we must not aim solely at the greatest possible profit, but also make use of the fruits which we obtain from it for the improvement of the living conditions of the worker, in order to lighten his labors and strengthen the bonds of his family with the land where he dwells and the work by which he lives. We must not aim at making the life of the individual depend entirely on the will of the State, but rather see to it that the State, whose duty it is to promote the common good, does by means of social institutions such as social security, health insurance, and social welfare integrate, assist, and complement the activity of labor associations, and particularly the endeavors of fathers and mothers who, by their work, secure their own living and that of their children.

Perhaps it will be said that this is but a visionary picture of a too beautiful reality—but how can it be realized and given life among the people? What is needed above all is great integrity of will and perfect loyalty of purpose and action in the conduct and government of public life, on the part of the citizens as much as on the part of the authorities. A spirit of true harmony and brotherhood must animate all, high and low, managers and workers, great and small, in brief, all the ranks of the people.[1]

Is Religion Opium for the People?

Man is the image of the one and triune God and therefore a person, brother of the God-man Jesus Christ, and with Him and by Him heir to an eternal life: this is his true dignity.

If there is any man in the world who should convince himself evermore of this truth and imbue himself with it, it is the worker. It was affirmed a long time ago, and it is still being affirmed, that religion renders the worker weak and slack in his daily life and in the defense of his public and private interests and that, like opium, it makes him drowsy, pacifying him entirely through the hope of a life to come. A manifest error! If the Church in her social doctrine always insists on the regard due to the innate dignity of man, if she requires in the labor contract a fair wage for the worker, if she claims for him effective assistance in his mental and spiritual needs, what is her reason if not that the worker is a human person, that his working capacity must not be considered and treated as "merchandise," and that his labors always represent a personal service?

It is precisely those reshapers of the world who arrogate to themselves the care of the interests of the workers almost as if it were their monopoly and who declare that theirs is the only truly "social" system, who do not defend the worker's individual dignity but make of his productive capacity a mere object of which the "society" disposes with absolute freedom and entirely at its own discretion.

The Church says that human liberty has its limits in the divine law and in the multiple duties which life brings with it; but at the same time, she strives, and will continue to strive until the end, in order that everyone, in the happiness of the home and in peaceful and decent conditions, may spend his days in harmony with God and men. The Church does not promise that complete equality which others proclaim, because she knows that the human community always and necessarily produces a scale of degrees and differences in physical and intellectual qualities, in inward dispositions and tendencies, in occupations and responsibilities. But at the same time, she does guarantee full equality in human dignity, as also in the heart of Him Who summons all those who are weary and burdened, calling on them to take up His yoke, so as to find peace and rest for their souls, because His yoke is sweet and His burden light.

In such manner, in order to safeguard liberty and human dignity and not to sponsor the special interests of this or that group, the Church rejects any kind of State totalitarianism, nor does she weaken with thoughts of a life to come the protection of the rights of the workers on this earth. Rather, those remodellers of the world we have mentioned, while they dazzle the eyes of the people with the mirage of a future of chimerical prosperity and unobtainable riches, sacrifice the dignity of the human person and domestic happiness—by setting up the superstition of technology and organization—to the idols of a misconceived earthly progress.

The Church, experienced educator of the human family and faithful to the mission which the divine Founder has entrusted to her, proclaims the truth of the only perfect bliss which is prepared for us in Heaven. But, precisely for this reason, she puts the faithful firmly, and with a strong footing, on the ground of the present reality. For the Supreme Judge, who awaits us at the end of our earthly life on the threshold of eternity, admonishes everyone, high and low, to make conscientious use of the gifts received from God, to avoid all injustice, and to seize every opportunity for doing works of love and kindness. Such is the only measure of every real progress, because then only is it genuine and not fictitious when it is also advancement toward God and to resemblance to Him. All purely worldly measures of progress are an illusion, We even feel inclined to say a mockery of man in a world which is under the law of original sin and its consequences, and which, therefore, being still imperfect, even with the divine light and grace, without that light and grace would fall into an abyss of wretchedness, injustice, and selfishness.

Moreover, only the religious idea of man can lead to a unified conception of his conditions of life. Where God is not the beginning and the end, where the order of His creation is not for all the guide and yardstick of liberty and action, unity between man and man cannot be achieved. The material conditions of life and work alone can never constitute the foundation of the unity of the working classes on the basis of an asserted uniformity of interests. Such an assumption would indeed do violence to nature and would simply create fresh oppression and division in the human family at a time when every honest worker aspires to a fair and peaceful order in private and public economy and social life as a whole.

Any legitimate power over men can have its origin and existence only from the authority of Him Who holds it by His nature in Heaven and on earth, without any limits of time or space: Jesus Christ, Who rules over the great ones of the earth, Who loves us and has redeemed us from sin with His blood, Whose glory and dominion is forever and ever.[2]

[1] Address to the Representatives of Italian Workers, January 13, 1943

[2] Address to Fiat Workers, October 31, 1948

CAPITAL AND LABOR

WITH BENEVOLENCE and warm interest, We see come to Us again and again workers and representatives of industrial organizations who, with deeply moving confidence, put their various troubles before Us.

We refer to the troubles of those who take part in industrial production. Erroneous and baneful in its consequences is the prejudice, unfortunately too widespread, which sees in them an irreducible opposition of conflicting interests. The opposition is only apparent. There are, in the economic field, activities and common interests which concern both management and labor. To want to disregard this mutual link and to attempt to break it is the result of the whim of blind and irrational despotism. Management and labor are not irreconcilable adversaries. They are co-operators in a mutual work. They eat, as it were, at the same table since, after all is said and done, they live by the net total profit of the national economy. Both have their own profit, and in this respect their reciprocal relations by no means make one side subject to the other.

Profit

To receive his own profit belongs to the personal dignity of every individual who, in one way or another, as a member of management or labor, contributes to the output of the national economy. In the budget of private industry the figure for wages may appear to be the expense of the employer. But in the economy of a nation there is only one kind of expenditure, that is, the natural wealth which is utilized for the national output, and which must therefore be continually renewed.

It follows that both sides must undertake to ensure that expenses are proportionate to the yield of the national output. If, therefore, the interest is mutual, why should it not be expressed in a common formula? Why should it not be right to assign the workers a fair share of responsibility in the formation and the development of the national economy?

Our unforgettable predecessor, Pius XI, had proposed a concrete and timely formula for this community of interests and responsibilities in the work of national economy when, in the Encyclical *Quadragesimo Anno,* he recommended "professional organization" in the various branches of production. To triumph over economic liberalism, nothing seemed to him in fact more suitable for the social economy than the adoption of a statute of public law founded on the mutual responsibility of all who are interested in production. This point of the Encyclical caused a great outcry: some saw in it a concession to modern political currents, and others a return to medieval times. It would have been much more reasonable to abandon inveterate and empty prejudices and in good faith to set to work for the realization of the thing itself and its numerous practical applications.

State Ownership

Today, however, this part of the Encyclical seems, unfortunately, to offer us an example of those propitious opportunities that are lost because they were not taken advantage of in time. Too late other forms of public political organization of social economies are devised, among them State ownership and the nationalization of industry, which today are in the foreground of discussion. Considered within just limits, the Church is not opposed to State ownership and holds that certain categories of wealth may legitimately be reserved to the public authorities, that is, possessions endowed with such power that they could not be transferred to individuals without endangering the common good. But to want to make of State ownership the general rule in the public organization of economies would mean subverting the order of things. The task of public rights is to serve, not to absorb, private rights. Economy, and, indeed, any other branch of human activity, is not by its nature a State institution but, on the contrary, the living product of the free enterprise of individuals and freely constituted groups.

It would be equally a mistake to affirm that any individual enterprise is by its nature a partnership where the relations between the partners are determined by the canons of distributive justice and where all, indiscriminately—whether owners or not of the means of production—have a right to their share of the property, or at least of the profits. A conception of this kind presupposes that every enterprise, by its nature, is in the sphere of public rights; but this supposition is incorrect: whether it be constituted in the form of a trust or association of all the workers as joint owners, or whether it be the private property of an individual who stipulates a working contract with all those employed by him, in either case the enterprise falls within the private juridical order of economic life.

The Formation of Capital and the Social Problem

What We have said applies to the juridical character of the enterprise as such, but for its members it may also entail a complex of individual relations and mutual responsibility, which must be taken into account. Whoever owns the means of production—either as an individual or as an association of workers or as a trust—must be the master of his own economic decisions, though always within the limits of the public economic law. It follows that his profit must be greater than that of his collaborators, but at the same time, the individual material well-being of all, which constitutes the object of social economy, must still further impose on him the duty of contributing through his savings to the increase of the national capital. Nor must it be forgotten that, just as it is extremely useful to a sound social economy that this increase of capital should come from the greatest possible number of sources, so is it most desirable that the workers also should contribute with the fruits of their savings to the formation of the national capital.[1]

In regard to property and the means of subsistence of mankind, the Encyclical *Rerum Novarum* expresses principles which, with the passage of time, have lost nothing of their original vigor and which today, fifty years later, still preserve their deep and vivifying force.

We Ourselves called the general attention to their basic premise in Our Encyclical *Sertum Laetitiæ,* addressed to the Bishops of the United States of America, a basic premise which, as We said, consists in the affirmation of the absolute need for "wealth created by God for all men to flow fairly to all according to the principles of justice and charity."

The Right to the Material Goods of the Earth

Every man, as a being endowed with reason, has from nature the basic right to use the material goods of the earth, it being, however, left to the human will and to the juridical forms of peoples to regulate more particularly its practical achievement. This individual right cannot in any way be suppressed, not even by other sure and unquestioned rights upon material goods. Without doubt, the natural order, derived from God, also requires that there should be private ownership and free reciprocal trading of goods with exchanges and gifts, as also the controlling function of public authority over both these institutions. All this, nevertheless, is subordinated to the natural purpose of material goods and could not make itself independent of the first and fundamental right which grants their use to all; rather, it should serve to make its achievement possible in accordance with its aim. In this way only can and must it be ensured that the ownership and use of material goods will bring to society fruitful peace and stability instead of precarious conditions engendering struggles and jealousy, and leaving society at the mercy of the implacable play between the strong and the weak.

The original right to the use of material goods, being closely connected with the dignity and other rights of the human person, offers him with the above-mentioned forms a sure material foundation of the utmost importance, as it enables him to rise to the fulfillment of his moral duties. The protection of this right will ensure the personal dignity of man and will help him to attend to and carry out freely the sum of those permanent obligations and resolutions for which he is directly responsible to the Creator. Indeed, man has the entirely personal duty of preserving and perfecting his material and spiritual life, in order to secure the religious and moral aim which God has assigned to all men and given them as a supreme law, binding always and in all cases, to be observed before all other duties.

To protect the inviolable sphere of human rights and facilitate the fulfillment of human duties is the essential business of all public authority. Does not, indeed, in this consist the genuine meaning of the common good that the State is called upon to promote? From this ensues that the care for that "common good" does not require so extensive a power over the members of the community that in virtue of it the public authority would be entitled to restrict the development of the individual activity described above, to decide directly on the beginning or (apart from the case of legitimate punishment) on the termination of human life, to determine at will the manner of its physical, spiritual, religious, and moral movement inconsistently with the personal duties and rights of man, and with such intent to abolish or deprive of efficacy the natural right to material goods. To deduce such extensive power from the care for the common good would mean inverting the sense of "common good" and falling into the error of affirming that the goal of man on earth is society, that society is an end in itself, that man has no other life awaiting him but that which ends here below.

So also national economy, as it is the fruit of the activity of men who work united in the community of the State, aims at nothing else but ensuring without interruption the material conditions in which the individual life of the citizens may be able to develop to the full. Where this is durably obtained, a people will in truth be economically rich because the general well-being, and consequently the personal right of all to the use of earthly goods, is in such manner achieved according to the Creator's purpose.

From this it will easily be perceived that the economic wealth of a people does not properly consist in the abundance of goods, measured according to a purely material calculation of their value, but rather in that which such abundance represents and effectively provides, namely, an adequate material foundation for the proper personal development of its members. If such a fair distribution of goods is not realized or is only imperfectly achieved, the genuine aim of national economy has not been reached; since, however great the abundance of available goods, the people not participating in them would not be economically rich, but poor. Instead, let such a fair distribution be actually effected in a durable manner, and you will see a people, even with a smaller quantity of goods at its disposal, become economically healthy.

It seems to Us particularly expedient to bring these fundamental concepts concerning the wealth and poverty of peoples under consideration today, when one is inclined to judge and measure such wealth and poverty with purely quantitative scales and criteria, as they are applied to space and bulk of goods. If, instead, the aim of national economy is rightly considered, it will enlighten the efforts of statesmen and peoples and illuminate them so that they may of their own accord set forth along a road that will not require continuous tributes of goods and blood but will give the fruits of peace and general welfare.

Labor

Connected with the use of material wealth is labor. The Encyclical *Rerum Novarum* teaches us that the properties of human labor are twofold: it is personal and it is necessary. It is personal because it is carried out through the exercise of the personal forces in man; it is necessary because, without it, it is not possible to procure that which is essential to life, the preservation of which is a natural and serious duty of each individual. To the personal duty of labor imposed by nature corresponds as its logical sequence the natural right of each individual to derive from labor the means of providing for his livelihood and that of his children: so highly is the order of nature ordained for the preservation of man.

But note that this duty and the corresponding right to work are imposed on and granted to the individual first and foremost by nature, and not by society, as though man were nothing more than a simple servant or functionary of the community. From this it follows that the duty and the right to organize the work of the people belong first of all to those immediately interested: employers and workers. But if they do not carry out their task or are unable to do so on account of special extraordinary contingencies, then it will be for the State to intervene in the sphere, division, and distribution of work, according to the form and measure required by the common good, properly understood.

In any case, any legitimate and beneficial State intervention in the field of work must be such as to preserve and respect its personal character, both in principle and, within the limits of possibility, as regards execution. And this will happen if the decrees of the State do not abolish or render impossible the exercise of other equally personal rights and duties, such as: the right to the true worship of God; to matrimony; the right of married people, of the father and the mother, to lead a conjugal and domestic life; the right to reasonable liberty in the choice of one's profession and the following of a true calling; this last being, more than any other, a personal right of the spirit of man, and a lofty one when there are added thereto the superior and immutable rights of God and of the Church, as in the choice and exercise of the priestly and religious vocations.

The Family

According to the doctrine of *Rerum Novarum,* nature itself has closely linked private ownership with the existence of human society and with its true civilization and, to an eminent degree, with the existence and development of the family. Such a link is more than openly apparent. Must not private ownership secure for the father of the family the healthy liberty which he needs to be able to fulfill the duties assigned to him by the Creator as regards the physical, spiritual, and religious well-being of the family?

In the family, the nation finds the natural and fruitful roots of its greatness and power. If private ownership is to lead to the good of the family, all public regulations, or rather all those of the State which govern the possession of it, must not only render possible and preserve such a function—a function which, in the natural order, is in certain respects superior to any other—but must bring it to ever greater perfection. The boast of civil progress would indeed be unnatural if—either through excessive levies or through too much immediate interference—it should empty private ownership of all meaning, practically depriving the family and its head of the liberty of pursuing the aim assigned by God to the improvement of family life.

Among all the goods which may be the object of private ownership, none conforms more closely to nature, according to the teaching of *Rerum Novarum,* than land, the homestead where the family lives and from whose fruits it derives, in whole or in part, its means of sustenance. And it is in the spirit of *Rerum Novarum* to affirm that, as a rule, only the stability which has its roots in a homestead makes of the family the most perfect and fruitful vital cell of society, marvellously uniting present and future generations through its progressive cohesion.[2]

[1] Address to the International *Union des Associations Patronales Catholiques,* April 27, 1941

[2] Encyclical *Rerum Novarum,* Commemorative Broadcast, June 1, 1941

THE DIGNITY OF LABOR

Too long, unfortunately, has the enemy of Christ sown tares among the people, and has not met at all points sufficient resistance from Catholics. Especially among the working class has he done and is still doing much to spread false ideas about man and the world, history, social and economic structures. Not infrequently the Catholic laborer, lacking a solid religious formation, is defenseless when such theories are advanced; he cannot give an answer and sometimes even is infected by the poison of error.

The religious training of Christians, and especially of workers, is one of the main duties of pastoral activity today. Just as the vital interests of the Church and of souls have forced the erection of Catholic schools for Catholic children, so too the well-grounded religious training of adults is of prime necessity. . . .

For these false principles are at work! How many times have We declared and explained the Church's love for the workers! Yet the monstrous lie is still spread about that "the Church is allied with capitalism against labor." She, mother and teacher of all men, is always concerned especially for her children who are in the more difficult circumstances, and in fact has made a great contribution to the equitable progress already obtained by certain categories of workers. We Ourselves said in Our Christmas Message of 1942: "Moved ever by religious motives, the Church condemned the various systems of Marxist socialism, and condemns them today, for it is her abiding duty and right to save men from trends and influences that jeopardize their eternal salvation. But the Church cannot be unaware of the fact that the laborer, in his effort to better his condition, strikes against a certain system which, far from being conformed to nature, is opposed to God's order and to the purpose He assigned to the goods of this world. However false, dangerous, and to be condemned are the methods followed, who, and particularly what priest or Christian, could remain deaf to the cry which is rising from the depths, and which, in the world of a just God, appeals to justice and the spirit of brotherhood?"

To enter into the world of social problems with its systems which do not derive from Him, whether they are called "lay humanism" or "socialism stripped of materialism," Jesus Christ does not wait for the door to be opened to Him. His divine kingdom of truth and justice is present even in regions where there is a constant threat of class warfare seizing the advantage. For that reason, the Church does not restrict itself to demanding a social order of greater justice, but sets out its fundamental principles, urging the rulers of nations, legislators, employers, and management to give them practical application.

But Our present Address is directed especially at the so-called "disillusioned" among Catholics. They are, indeed, not few in number, particularly among the youth, whose intentions remain of the best, but who would have looked for more action among the Catholic force in the public life of the country. . . .

We wish to call once again the attention of these "disillusioned" to the fact that neither new laws nor new institutions are adequate to give to each the security to exist, protected against every misused restriction, and to be able to develop with freedom in society. All will be in vain if the ordinary man lives in fear of coming under arbitrary rule, and does not succeed in freeing himself from the feeling that he is subject to the good and ill will of those who apply the laws, or of those who, as public officials, direct the institutions and organizations; if he perceives that, in daily life, all depends on connections which he—unlike others—perhaps does not have; if he suspects that behind the external show of what is called the State, there is hidden the manipulations of powerful organized groups.

The action of Christian forces in public life, then, certainly means that the promulgation of good laws and building up of institutions suited to the times is fostered; but it means, even more, that there is a setting aside of the rule of empty slogans and deceptive words, and that the ordinary man feels supported and sustained in his legitimate demands and expectations. It is essential to form a public opinion which, without hunting out scandal, points out with frankness and courage, persons and situations which do not conform to just laws and institutions, or which maliciously conceal truth. To give influence to the plain citizen, it is not enough to put the voting card or other similar devices into his hands. If he wants to be associated with the group of leaders, if he intends sometimes—for the common good—to put forward a remedy for the dearth of profitable ideas, and to stem the advance of egoism, he himself must possess the necessary personal energy and the ardent will to contribute to, and to pour into all public arrangements, a healthy morality.

There you have the basis of the hope which We have been expressing over the past ten years, and which We repeat today with redoubled confidence.

Dear working men and women of the whole world—let Us extend to you the tenderness of a father's affection, such as that with which Jesus drew to Himself the multitudes hungering after truth and justice; be assured that in every necessity you will have at your side a guide, a defender, a father.

Yes, beloved workers, the Pope and the Church cannot withdraw from the divine mission of guiding, protecting, and loving especially the suffering, who are all the more dear the more they are in need of defense and help, whether they be workers or other children of the people.

This duty and obligation We, the Vicar of Christ, desire to reaffirm clearly, with the intention that all may recognize the dignity of labor and that this dignity may be a motivation in forming the social order and the laws, founded on the equitable distribution of rights and duties.[1]

[1] Address on the Tenth Anniversary of the Christian Labor Unions of Italy, May 1, 1955

TO THE LABOR UNIONS

THE LABOR UNIONS and associations of Christian workers tend toward a common goal, which is that of raising the living standard of the worker.

What part will the Christian associations of workers play in the establishment of the new social order?

Socialization

The Christian associations agree to socialization only in those cases where it really seems called for by the common good, that is to say as the only truly efficacious means to remedy an abuse or to avoid the waste of a country's productive forces, and to assure the harnessing of these forces and their direction to the advantage of the economic interests of the nation, so that the national economy, in its regular and peaceful development, will open the way to the material prosperity of all the people, a prosperity such as to constitute at the same time a sound foundation for cultural and religious life, as well. In any case, furthermore, they recognize that socialization implies the obligation of a corresponding indemnity, that is to say, one calculated according to what under the actual circumstances is just and equitable for all the interested parties.

As for the democratization of the economy, it is threatened no less by monopoly, that is by the economic despotism of an anonymous conglomeration of private capital, than by the preponderance of organized masses, ready to use their power to the detriment of justice and the rights of others.

The time has now come to abandon empty phrases and to think, along with the *Quadragesimo Anno,* about a new organization of the productive forces of the people. Rising above the distinction between employers and employees, let all men be able to see and recognize that higher unity which binds to each other all those who collaborate in production. One has to see their bond and their solidarity in the obligations they share to provide together, in stability, for the common good and the needs of the whole community. May this solidarity extend to every branch of production, may it become the foundation of a better economic order, of a healthy and just autonomy, and may it open the way for the laboring classes to acquire honestly their share of responsibility in the conduct of national affairs.

May the Christian associations of workers promote the union and solidarity of men in the whole of economic life!

The most efficient agent—indeed, We might say the only efficient agent—for the creation of this sense of solidarity, sure guarantee of rectitude and social peace, lies in the spirit of the Gospel and flows from the heart of the God-Man, Savior of the world.[1]

[1] Address to the Christian Labor Associations of Italy, March 11, 1945

ON THE INTERNATIONALIZATION OF PRIVATE LAW

CAN ANYONE who has even briefly leafed through the history of civilization and reflected on the nature of law be surprised at the interest which the Church has unceasingly shown in it?

In a formula whose vigorous incisiveness bears the imprint of his genius, Plato sets down in the following terms the thought underlying the spirit of all antiquity: "In the first place, God is for us the just measure of all things, much more so than any man can be." This same idea is taught by the Church, but in all the fullness and profundity of truth, when, in declaring along with St. Paul that all paternity proceeds from God, it affirms as a consequence that, in order to regulate the reciprocal relations in the midst of the great human family, every law has its roots in God.

This is why the Church, in refuting the extremist juridical positivism which attributes to law a quasi-autonomous "sanctity" of its own, enfolds it in a more sublime and truer sanctity by obligating, in the last analysis, every man who is convinced of the existence and sovereignty of a personal God to be faithful to the law.

Furthermore, since the Church is a great social organism, a supranational community with solid foundations, could she subsist without a determined and precise body of law? Apart from this consideration, the logic of which is incontestable, though of a purely natural order, the Church knows that she was constituted by her divine Founder as a visible society provided with a juridical order; and the basis of this order, of this juridical statute, is none other than divine positive law. The final goal of all the life of the Church, her mission of leading men to God, to promote their union with God, is no doubt to be found in the sphere of the ultraterrestrial, in the supernatural; in short, it is something which takes place immediately and directly between God and man. Yes, but along the road on which this function is exercised and which leads to this end, each believer walks as a member of the ecclesiastical community, guided by the Church, among the particular and concrete conditions of existence. Now, community and the guidance of an authority are synonymous with the power of right and law.

A simple glance at the objective of private international law and

The Pope and Secretary of State John Foster Dulles, Oct. 24, 1955

The Pope and President Truman, Mrs. Truman, and Party, May 1956

The Cupola of St. Peter's Basilica

at its history suffices to show the difficulty of co-ordinating the various bodies of law.

Could past generations have thought possible, could they have even imagined, the technical progress in communications which in so short a time has brought all men closer together to the extent that the current expression "the world has become too small" is literally exact? The world is becoming so and will become increasingly so.

Furthermore, the Pan-European idea, the Council of Europe, and other movements are a manifestation of the general need to break with, or at least attenuate, the rigidity of the old conceptions of geographical boundaries, and to form large groups of community life and activity among the various countries. These practical considerations may not even be raised; but owing to the inevitable consequences of war and under the pressure of events, the overpopulation of some regions and the unemployment which results bring with them, through emigration and immigration, a real demographic mixture which, in the next half century, will probably greatly surpass in importance the migratory movements toward the two Americas during the course of the last one hundred and fifty years. How useful will the co-ordination of private law be then!

However, will it be possible to extend it to the fullest degree, to specific groups of States as well? Would a radical parity be truly advantageous everywhere? It is not easy to affirm this at the present time. In spite of everything, economic, social, and general cultural conditions could remain so different in some countries that a uniformity involving all countries and the whole body of private law would not fully respond to the needs of the common good.

However that may be, We recommend the following three points: first of all, an increasingly careful and efficient protection of all those who need it most, especially abandoned children and women left without support; toward these persons above all, the legislator should model his conduct on that of a parent. In the second place, a simplification of the juridical regime for all those who, for family motives, are forced to move frequently and periodically from one country to the other. Finally, recognition and direct and indirect application of the innate rights of man which, in so far as they are inherent in human nature, always conform to the common interest, and are furthermore those which must be taken as essential elements of the same common welfare; therefore the State has the duty of protecting them, fostering them, and assuring that in no case will they ever be sacrificed for an alleged reason of State.[1]

[1] Address to the First International Congress of Private Law, July 15, 1950

WAR AND PEACE

TERROR-STRICKEN, the people of the world have had to witness a new, immense improvement of the means and arts of destruction, and, at the same time, be spectators of an inner decay which, through the hardening and aberration of moral sensibility, precipitates the complete suppression of every sentiment of humanity and rushes toward such a darkening of reason and spirit as to verify the words of Wisdom: "All were tied by the same chain of darkness."

Only Christ can drive away the baneful spirits of error and sin, which have yoked humanity to a tyrannical and demeaning slavery, making it subservient to a dominating thought and will set in motion by insatiable greed.

Only Christ, Who rescued us from the sad bondage of guilt, can teach, and smooth the way to a noble and orderly freedom resting on, and sustained by, genuine righteousness and genuine moral consciousness.

Only Christ, "on Whose shoulders is the government," can, through His succoring omnipotence, elevate mankind, lift it out of the nameless afflictions that torment it in the course of this life, and set it on the road to happiness.

A Christian who is nourished by faith in Christ and lives in Him, in the certainty that He alone is the Way, the Truth, and the Life, takes his share of the sufferings and discomforts of this world to the crib of the Son of God, and in the presence of the newborn Babe finds consolation and support unknown to the world, which gives him the courage and strength to remain unshaken, neither faltering nor succumbing in the most tormenting and gravest ordeals.

It is sad and painful to think that innumerable men, though feeling in their search for a satisfying happiness in this life the bitterness of fallacious illusions and grievous delusions, have closed the way to all hope and, living as they do far from the Christian faith, do not know how to find the way again to that consolation which makes the heroes of the faith abound in joy in all their tribulations. They see shattered the edifice of beliefs in which they had humanly placed their faith and their ideal; but they never found that one true faith which would have been able to give them comfort and renew their souls. In this intellectual and moral faltering, they are seized by a depressing uncertainty of spirit and live in a state of inertia which oppresses their soul, and which only he can fully understand and fraternally pity who has the joy of living in the familiar, vivid splendor of a supernatural faith reaching beyond the turmoil of all temporal contingencies to become fixed in the eternal.

Among the host of such embittered and deluded persons it is not difficult to point to those who placed all their faith in the universal expansion of economic life, holding it to be alone fitted to unite all peoples in brotherhood, and awaiting from its grandiose organization, increasingly perfected and increasingly efficient, unique and unsuspected progress in the welfare of the human race.

With how much complacency and pride they contemplated the increase in international trade, the exchange, spanning all continents, of all the goods and all inventions and productions, and the triumphant march of this widespread modern engineering which knows no boundaries of space or time! Today, instead, what are they experiencing in reality? They see by now that this economy with its gigantic world relations and ties and with its intricate division and multiplication of labor has co-operated in a thousand ways to make the crisis of humanity general and more serious since, not corrected by any moral brake and without any ultraterrestrial light to enlighten it, it could not but end in an unworthy and humiliating exploitation of the human person and of nature, in a sad and fearful indigence on one side and in a haughty and provoking opulence on the other, in a tormented and implacable strife between the haves and the have-nots.

Those who awaited the salvation of society from the mechanism of world economy had been so deluded, because they had become not the lords and masters, but the slaves, of material riches which they had served, detaching them from the higher end of man and making them an end in themselves.

The disillusioned of the past thought and acted no differently in pinning their hopes for happiness and well-being exclusively on a certain kind of science and culture, unwilling to recognize the Creator of the universe; those pioneers and followers, not of true science, which is a marvellous reflection of God's light, but of a proud science which, giving no place at all to the work of a personal God subject to no limitations and superior to all that is of the earth, boasted of the ability to explain the happenings of this world through a rigid and deterministic concatenation of iron-clad natural laws.

But such a science cannot give happiness and well-being. Apostasy from the divine Word, by Whom all things were made, has led man to apostasy from the spirit, in such manner as to make it hard for him to pursue elevated intellectual and moral ideals and objectives. In this way, science, which had denied the spiritual life, while it vainly thought to have acquired full freedom and autonomy by disowning God, sees itself punished today through the most humiliating bondage, having become the slave and the practically automatic fulfiller of policies and orders that take into no account whatever the rights of truth and of the human person. What to that science seemed to be freedom was a chain of humiliation and ignominy; it will regain its original dignity only through a return to the eternal Word, fount of wisdom so foolishly abandoned and forgotten.[1]

The Spirit of Hatred

No people is immune to the danger of seeing some of its sons succumb to the call of passion and be sacrificed to the demon of hatred. What matters above all is the judgment which the public authority passes on such aberrations and degenerations of the fighting spirit, and the promptness in putting a stop to them.

Hence, it behooves the good name of that authority to see to it that, with the widening of the fields of war beyond their own boundaries, there be no weakening of the dignity of reason which dictates those supreme principles of promoting good and containing evil, which strengthen and lend honor to the dispositions of those in command, and make the subjects more willing and ready to submit their will and action to the common interest. And, therefore, the larger grow the territories which the conflict puts under foreign domination, the more urgent becomes the duty of putting the juridical system, which it is proposed to apply there, in harmony with the provisions of international law and, above all, with the requirements of humaneness and equity.[2]

On Military Occupation

To the occupying powers We say, without lacking in the respect owed to them: May your conscience and your honor guide you in the equitable, humane, and provident treatment of the population of occupied territories. Do not impose burdens upon them which you, in similar cases, have felt, or would feel to be, unjust.

New Weapons and Their Consequences

From the use of still more deadly instruments of strife We entreat belligerents to abstain until the last: every novelty in such means provokes an inevitable counterblow on the part of the adversary, the use of the same new weapon, but often rendered harsher and fiercer.[3]

It is well known to all how some rapid and far-reaching results of human achievements can actually create anxieties and fears in men, putting in grave danger their individual and social life. It is sufficient to consider what has recently taken place in the applications of nuclear energy.

Its use for peaceful purposes is the object of careful and continuous investigation, to which is given Our Blessing. Yet, all are aware that other uses have been sought, and found suitable, for producing, instead, destruction and death. And what a death! Every day is a melancholy step forward on this tragic road, is a hastening on to arrive alone, first, with greater advantage. And the human race almost loses hope of being able to stop this homicidal, this suicidal madness. To increase the alarm and terror, there have come modern radio-guided missiles, capable of traversing enormous distances, to carry thither, by means of atomic weapons, total destruction to men and things.[4]

In any case, there is a duty which is incumbent on all, a duty which tolerates no delay, no postponement, no hesitation, no shuffling: to do everything possible to proscribe and once for all banish a war of aggression as a legitimate solution of international differences and as an instrument of national aspirations. Many attempts have been made in the past toward that end. They have all failed. And they will continue to fail, until the healthier part of mankind demonstrates the firm will power, holily obstinate, as an obligation of conscience, to accomplish the mission which the past had undertaken without sufficient earnestness and determination.

War on War!

If ever a generation had to feel deep down in its conscience the cry "War on war!" it is certainly the present one. Gone, as it has, through an ocean of blood and tears, such as was perhaps never known in the past, it has lived war's unspeakable atrocities so intensely that the recollection of so many horrors cannot but remain impressed in its memory and in the depths of its soul, like the image of a hell upon which anyone who nourishes humane sentiments in his heart can have no more ardent wish than to close the door forever.

Without doubt the progress of human inventions, which was to mark the crystallization of greater welfare for the whole of humanity, has instead been directed to the destruction of what had been built up by the centuries. But this very thing has rendered more and more evident the immorality of wars of aggression. And if now to the recognition of this immorality there will be added the threat of a judicial intervention of the nations and of a punishment inflicted on the aggressor by the United Nations, so that war may always feel itself proscribed, always under the watchful guard of preventive action, then humanity, issuing from the dark night in which it has been submerged for so great a length of time, will be able to greet the dawn of a new and better era in its history.[5]

Nothing Is Lost with Peace

It is with the force of reason, not with that of armaments, that Justice makes its advances. And empires not founded on Justice are not blessed by God. A policy emancipated from morality betrays those themselves who want it so.

Nothing is lost with peace. Everything may be lost with war. Let men come again to understand one another. Negotiating with good will and with respect for their reciprocal rights, they will perceive that honorable success is never precluded to sincere and constructive negotiations.

And they will feel great—with true greatness—if, silencing the voice of passion, both collective and private, and leaving the dominance to reason, they shall have spared the blood of their brothers and spared their country ruins.

May it please the Almighty that the voice of this Father of the Christian family, of this Servant of servants who, unworthily indeed, but really, brings among men the person of Jesus Christ, His word and authority, may find a prompt and willing acceptance in minds and hearts.

Let the strong hear Us, so that they may not become weak in injustice. Let the powerful hear Us if they want their power to be, not destruction, but support for peoples and a safeguard in orderliness and work.

We entreat them through the blood of Christ, Whose conquering force in the world was meekness in life and death. And, entreating them, We know and feel that with Us are all the righteous of heart; all those who thirst and hunger for justice; all those who suffer already every pain on account of the afflictions of life. We have with Us the hearts of mothers, which beat in Ours; fathers, who would have to leave their families; the humble, who work and know not; the innocent, over whom hangs a tremendous menace; young men, gallant knights with the purest and noblest ideals. And with Us is all humanity, which awaits justice, bread, freedom, not the sword that kills and destroys. With Us is that Christ Who of brotherly love made His Commandment, fundamental, solemn; the substance of His religion, the promise of salvation for individuals and nations.[6]

War in Self-Defense

We, as head of the Church, have up to now avoided, just as We did in previous cases, calling Christendom to a crusade. We can, however, call for full understanding of the fact that, where religion is a vital living heritage, men do look upon the struggle unjustly forced on them by their enemy as a crusade.

If unpleasant realities force Us to set forth the terms of the struggle in clear language, no one can properly accuse Us of favoring the stiffening of opposing blocs, and still less of having in some fashion abandoned that mission of peace which flows from Our apostolic office. Rather, if We kept silence We would have to fear the judgment of God. We remain closely allied to the cause of peace, and God alone knows how much We yearn to be able to announce it in full and happy tones with the angels of Christmas.

We are convinced that today, too, in face of an enemy determined to impose on all peoples, in one way or another, a special and intolerable way of life, only the unanimous and courageous behavior of all who love the truth and the good can preserve peace, and will preserve it.

It would be a fatal error to repeat what, in similar circumstances, happened during the years preceding the Second World War, when all the threatened nations, and not merely the smallest, sought their safety at the expense of others, using them as shields, so to speak, and even seeking very questionable economic and political advantages from their neighbors' suffering. In the end all together were overwhelmed in the holocaust.

Hence a definite need of this period—a means of ensuring the whole world's peace and a fruitful share of its goods, a force which embraces, too, the peoples of Asia, Africa, the Near East, Palestine with its Holy Places—is the restoring of European solidarity. But this unity is not assured until all the associated nations realize that the political and economic defeats of one can nowhere, in the long run, result in true gains for the others.

A good course of action can never be had by mere sentiment; much less can a true political course for today be maintained with the sentiments of yesterday and the day before. Under such influence it would be impossible to judge correctly certain important questions, such as military service, weapons, war.

Present-day conditions, which find no counterparts in the past, should be clear to everyone. There is no longer room for doubt concerning the aims and methods which rely on tanks, when these latter noisily crash over borders, sowing death in order to force civilian peoples into a pattern of life they explicitly detest; when, destroying, as it were, the stages of possible negotiation and mediation, the threat is made of using atomic weapons to gain certain demands, be they justified or not.

It is clear that in the present circumstances a situation may arise in a nation wherein, after every effort to avoid war has been expended in vain, war—for effective self-defense and with the hope of a favorable outcome against unjust attack—could not be considered unlawful.

If, therefore, a body representative of the people and a government—both having been chosen by free elections—in a moment of extreme danger decide, by legitimate instruments of internal and external policy, on defensive precautions, and carry out the plans which they consider necessary, they do not act immorally; so that a Catholic citizen cannot invoke his own conscience in order to refuse to serve and fulfill those duties the law imposes. On this matter We feel that We are in perfect harmony with Our predecessors.

The United Nations

There are, then, occasions and times in the life of nations in which only recourse to higher principles can establish clearly the boundaries between right and wrong, between what is lawful and what is immoral, and bring peace to consciences faced with grave decisions. It is therefore consoling that in some countries, amid today's debates, men are talking about conscience and its demands.

Although the program which is at the foundation of the United Nations aims at the realization of absolute values in the coexistence of peoples, the recent past has shown that a false realism is making headway among not a few of its members, even where it is a question of restoring respect for those values of human society which are openly trampled upon.

The unilateral view, which tends to work in the various circumstances only according to personal interest and power, is succeeding in bringing about accusations of destroying the peace.

No one expects or demands the impossible, not even from the United Nations; but one should have a right to expect that their authority should have had its weight, at least through observers, in the places in which the basic values of man are in extreme danger.

Although the United Nations' condemnation of the grave violations of the rights of men and of entire nations is worthy of recognition, one may nevertheless wish that, in similar cases, the exercise of their rights, as members of this organization, be denied to States which refuse even the admission of observers—thus showing that their concept of State sovereignty threatens the very foundations of the United Nations.

This organization ought also to have the right and the power of forestalling all military intervention of one State in another, whatever the pretext under which it is effected, and also the right and power of assuming, by means of a sufficient police force, the safeguarding of order in the State which is threatened.

If We allude to these defects, it is because We desire to see the authority of the United Nations strengthened, especially for effecting general disarmament, which We have so much at heart. In fact, only in the ambit of an institution like the United Nations can the promise of individual nations to reduce armaments, especially to abandon production and use of certain weapons, be mutually exchanged under the strict obligation of international law.

Control of Armaments

Likewise only the United Nations is at present in a position to exact the observance of this obligation by assuming effective control of the armaments of all nations without exception.

Its exercise of aerial observation will assure certain and effective knowledge of the production and military preparedness for war with relative ease, while avoiding the disadvantages which the presence of foreign troops in a country can give rise to. Indeed, it approaches almost the miraculous, what technical science has been able to attain in this field.

The experiments conducted have given exceptionally important results, permitting one to produce concrete evidence of machines, individual persons, and objects existing on the ground, and, at least indirectly, in subterranean places.

Research thus far has shown how very difficult it would be to camouflage movements of troops or artillery, vast stores of arms, industrial centers important for war production. If these surveys could be permanent and systematic, it would be possible to ascertain the minutest details, and thus give a solid guarantee against eventual surprises.

Acceptance of the control: this is the point crucial for victory, where every nation will show its sincere desire for peace.

The desire for peace: free man's most valuable possession, this life's inestimable treasure, peace is the fruit of men's effort, but also a precious gift of God. The Christian knows it since he has understood it at the cradle of the newborn Son of God; on His truth and on His Commandments, the supreme absolute values, all order is founded and by them guarded and rendered fruitful in works of progress and civilization.[7]

[1] Broadcast to the World, December 24, 1943
[2] Allocution to the Sacred College, December 24, 1939
[3] Broadcast to the World, April 13, 1941
[4] Broadcast to the World, Easter, 1956
[5] Broadcast to the World, December 24, 1943
[6] Broadcast to the World, August 24, 1939
[7] Broadcast to the World, December 23, 1956

PEACE LETTER TO PRESIDENT TRUMAN

YOUR EXCELLENCY: We have just received from the hands of your personal representative, Mr. Myron Taylor, Your Excellency's letter of August 6, and We hasten to express Our satisfaction and thanks for this last testimony to the desire and determination of a great and free people to dedicate themselves, with their characteristic confidence and generosity, to the noble task of strengthening the foundations of that peace for which all peoples of the earth are longing. As their chosen leader, Your Excellency seeks to enlist and cement the co-operation of every force and power which can help to accomplish this task. No one more than We will hope for its success, and for the happy achievement of the goal We pledge Our resources and earnestly beg God's assistance.

What is proposed is to ensure the foundations of a lasting peace among nations. It were indeed futile to promise long life to any building erected on shifting sands or a cracked and crumbling base. The foundations, We know, of such a peace—the truth finds expression once again in Your Excellency's letter—can be secure only if they rest on bedrock faith in the one, true God, Creator of all men. The task, then, before the friends of peace is clear.

Is Your Excellency oversanguine in hoping to find men throughout the world ready to co-operate in such a worthy enterprise? We think not. Truth has lost none of its power to rally to its cause the most enlightened minds and noblest spirits. Their ardor is fed by the flame of righteous freedom struggling to break through injustice and lying. But those who possess the truth must be conscientious to define it clearly when its foes cleverly distort it, bold to defend it, and generous enough to set the course of their lives, both national and personal, by its dictates. This will require, moreover, correcting not a few aberrations. Social injustices, racial injustices, and religious animosities exist today among men and groups who boast of Christian civilization, and they are a very useful and often effective weapon in the hands of those who are bent on destroying all the good which that civilization has brought to man. It is for all sincere lovers of the great human family to unite in wresting those weapons from hostile hands. With that union will come hope that the enemies of God and free men will not prevail.

Certainly Your Excellency and all the defenders of the rights of the human person will find wholehearted co-operation from God's Church. Faithful custodian of eternal Truth and loving mother of all, from her foundation almost two thousand years ago, she has championed the individual against despotic rule, the laborer against oppression, religion against persecution. Her divinely given mission often brings her into conflict with the powers of evil, whose sole strength is in their physical force and brutalized spirit, and her leaders are sent into exile or cast into prison or die under torture. This is history of today. But the Church is unafraid. She cannot compromise with an avowed enemy of God. She must continue to teach the first and greatest commandment incumbent on every man: "Thou shalt love the Lord thy God with thy whole heart, with thy whole soul, with thy whole strength," and the second is like unto the first: "Thou shalt love thy neighbor as thyself." It is her changeless message, that man's first duty is to God, then to his fellow man; that that man serves his country best who serves his

God most faithfully; that the country that would shackle the word of God given to men through Jesus Christ helps not at all the lasting peace of the world. In striving with all the resources in her power to bring men and nations to a clear realization of their duty to God, the Church will go on, as she has always done, to offer the most effective contribution to the world's peace and man's eternal salvation.

We are pleased that Your Excellency's letter has given Us the opportunity of saying a word of encouragement for all those who are gravely intent on buttressing the fragile structure of peace until its foundation can be more firmly and wisely established. The munificent charity shown by the American people to the suffering and oppressed in every part of the world, truly worthy of the finest Christian traditions, is a fair token of their sincere desire for universal peace and prosperity. The vast majority of the peoples of the world, We feel sure, share that desire, even in countries where free expression is smothered. God grant that their forces may be united toward its realization. . . .

Let Us assure Your Excellency of Our cordial welcome to Mr. Taylor, your personal representative, on his return to Rome; and We are happy to renew the expression of Our good wishes for the people of the United States, for the members of their government, and in particular for its esteemed Chief Executive.[1]

[1] Letter to President Harry S. Truman, August 26, 1947

ATOMIC WEAPONS

HUMAN INVENTIVENESS, which was destined for quite other purposes, has developed and introduced today instruments of war so powerful as to awaken horror in the conscience of any person of good will, especially because they do not strike armies alone but often destroy private citizens, children, women, old people, the sick, and, along with them, sacred edifices and the most celebrated artistic monuments! Who is not horrified at the thought that new cemeteries will be added to those already numerous ones of the recent conflict, and that new, smoking ruins of suburbs and cities will pile up new, tragic remains? And who does not tremble at the thought that the destruction of new riches, inevitable consequence of war, may still further aggravate that economic crisis which grips almost all the peoples of the world, especially the more humble classes?

We, Who raise Our mind above the tides of human passion and Who feel paternally toward the people and nations of all races, desire the safety and tranquil security and daily increase of prosperity; each time We see the clear sky darken with threatening clouds and new dangers of conflict weigh upon humanity, We cannot refrain from raising Our voice to exhort all to put an end to disagreements, to make up differences, and to install that true peace which assures the rights of religion, of peoples, of individual citizens, publicly and sincerely recognized, as is necessary.

However, We know well that human means are inadequate to such a high purpose; what is needed, before all, is a renewal of conscience, a repression of passions, calming of hatreds, truly putting into practice the norms of justice, arriving at a more equitable distribution of wealth, stimulating reciprocal charity, urging all to virtue. To reach such a great objective, unquestionably, nothing can be more helpful than the Christian religion. Its divine doctrine teaches that men are brothers and make up one same family of which God is the Father, Christ is the Redeemer and Vivifier with His celestial grace, and whose immortal homeland is Heaven. If these divine teachings were truly practiced, then most certainly neither wars, discords, disorders, nor violations of civil and religious liberty would make public and private life sorrowful; rather, a tranquil serenity, founded on justice, would flood all hearts and the way would be open to the achievement of an always greater prosperity.

This is arduous, indeed, but necessary. And if it is necessary then there must be no delay and it must be put into practice immediately. And if it is arduous and above human strength, then it is necessary to turn with prayer and supplication to the Celestial Father, as in the course of the centuries, in every sort of difficulty, our ancestors always did, to their profit.[1]

Let there be punishment on an international scale for every war not called for by absolute necessity. The only constraint to wage war is defense against an injustice of the utmost gravity which strikes the entire community and which cannot be coped with by any other means—for otherwise one would give free course, in international relations, to brutal violence and irresponsibility. Defending oneself against any kind of injustice, however, is not sufficient reason to resort to war. When the losses that it brings are not comparable to those of the "injustice tolerated," one may have the obligation of "submitting to the injustice."

This is particularly applicable to the A.B.C. war (atomic, biological, chemical). It suffices now to ask ourselves if war may become necessary as a defense against an A.B.C. war. The answer will derive from the same principles which are decisive in determining the justification of war in general. In any case, another question poses itself first of all: Is it not possible, through international agreement, to outlaw and efficaciously avoid A.B.C. warfare?

After the horrors of the two world wars, We can only repeat that any kind of glorification of war must be condemned as an aberration of the intellect and the heart. Certainly, courage and devotion carried to point of giving one's life, when duty demands it, are great virtues; but to want to provoke war because it is the school of great virtues and an occasion to practice them, should be considered crime and folly.

What We have said indicates the right direction in which to find the answer to this other question: May the doctor place his science and activity in the service of A.B.C. war? He must never give support to an "injustice," even in the service of his own country; and when this type of war constitutes an injustice, the doctor cannot take part in it.[2]

[1] Encyclical *Mirabile Illud,* December 6, 1950
[2] Address to Military Doctors, October 19, 1953

TECHNOLOGY AND MATERIALISM

DOUBTLESS, technology leads contemporary man toward a peak never before achieved in the domination of the material world. The modern machine makes possible a method of production which substitutes and magnifies the energy of human labor, which frees itself entirely from the contribution of organic forces and assures a maximum of extensive and intensive potential and of precision at the same time. . . .

Technological Thinking

However, it seems undeniable that technology itself, having reached the peak of its splendor and achievement in our century, may, through outward circumstance, become transformed into a grave spiritual peril. To modern man, prone before its altar, it seems to communicate a sense of self-sufficiency and of satisfaction with his aspirations for boundless knowledge and power. With its multiple uses, with the absolute confidence it inspires, with the inexhaustible possibilities it promises, modern technology unfolds before contemporary man a vision so vast as to be confused by many with the infinite itself. As a consequence, one attributes to it an impossible autonomy, which in turn is transformed in the minds of some into an erroneous conception of life and of the world, designated as "technological thinking." But in what, precisely, does this consist? In this: that it is considered the highest value of man and of life to draw the greatest profit and power from the forces and elements of nature; that, in preference to all other human pursuits, one elects as the most coveted objective the development of technical processes for mechanical production, and that in them is seen the perfection of civilization and happiness on earth.

There is, first of all, a fundamental deception in this distorted vision of the world offered by "technological thinking." The panorama, at first sight endless, which technology spreads before the eyes of modern man, however vast it may be, remains nonetheless but a partial projection of life upon reality, expressing only reality's relationship to matter. A fascinating panorama, no doubt, which, however, in the end, encloses the man who too easily believes in the immensity and the omnipotence of technology, in a prison which is vast, it is true, but circumscribed, and therefore in the long run unbearable to man's genuine spirituality. His glance, far from reaching toward infinite reality, which is not material only, will feel mortified by the barriers which are necessarily raised before him. From this springs the hidden anxiety of contemporary man, become blind from having voluntarily surrounded himself with darkness.

Far more serious are the damages caused by "technological thinking," in the man who allows himself to become intoxicated by it, in the sphere of religious truth and in his relations with the supernatural. These, too, are the shadows to which the Evangelist St. John alludes, which the Incarnate Word of God has come to dissipate, and which impede the spiritual understanding of the mysteries of God.

Not that technology in itself, as a logical consequence, requires the renunciation of religious values—on the contrary, as We have said, it leads rather to their discovery—but that "technological thinking" places man in a condition detrimental to the searching, seeing, and accepting of supernatural truths and benefits. The mind which allows itself to be seduced by the conception of life mirrored in "technological thinking" remains insensible, unresponsive, and finally blind before those works of God, by their nature wholly different from technology, such as are the mysteries of the Christian faith. The remedy itself, which would consist in a redoubled effort to extend one's gaze beyond the barrier of darkness and stimulate in the soul the interest for supernatural realities, is rendered inefficacious from the start by the same technological approach, because it deprives man of a critical appraisal of the singular restlessness and superficiality of our times: a defect which even those who truly and sincerely approve technical progress must nonetheless recognize as one of its consequences. Men imbued with the technological spirit hardly ever find the calm, the serenity and interior life needed to be able to see the way which leads to the Son of God, become man.

They will even reach the point of defaming the Creator and His works, declaring human nature to be a defective instrument, if the active capacity of the brain and the other human organs, necessarily limited, impedes the realization of technological calculations and projects. Still less are they able to understand and esteem the lofty mysteries of divine life and economy, as, for example, the mystery of Christmas, in which the union of the Eternal Word with human nature achieves realities and greatness of a very different order from those considered by technology. Their thinking follows other ways and methods under the unilateral suggestion of that "technological thinking" which does not recognize and does not appreciate as reality anything except what can be expressed in figures and calculations.

In this way they believe they can break down reality into its elements, but their understanding remains on the surface and moves in only one direction. It is evident that he who adopts the technological method as the sole instrument of research for truth must renounce penetrating, for example, the profound realities of organic life, and still more those of spiritual life, the living realities of the individual and of human society, because these cannot be broken down into quantitative relations. How can one pretend to gain, from a mind so formed, assent and admiration before the imposing reality to which we have been elevated by Jesus Christ, through His incarnation, redemption, revelation, and grace?

Quite apart from the religious blindness which derives from "technological thinking," the man possessed by it becomes handicapped in his reasoning, precisely because he is the image of God. God is infinitely comprehensive intelligence, whereas "technological thinking" does everything possible to restrain in man the free expansion of his intellect. To the technologist, teacher or pupil, who wishes to save himself from this handicap, it is not enough to wish for an informed and profound education of the mind; what he needs, above all, is a religious formation which, contrary to what has been sometimes affirmed, is the most capable of protecting his thinking from unilateral influences. Then the narrowness of his knowledge will be shattered; then creation will appear illuminated to him in all its dimensions. Otherwise, the technological era will perform its monstrous masterpiece of transforming man into a giant of the physical world at the expense of his spirit, reduced to a pygmy of the supernatural and eternal world.

But the influence exerted by technological progress does not stop here, once it has been received in the consciousness as something autonomous and an end to itself. The danger of a "technological concept of life" escapes no one, that is, the danger of considering life exclusively for its technological values, as a technological element and factor. Its influence affects both the manner of living of modern men and their reciprocal relations.

Observe it for a moment, active in the people, among whom it is already spreading, and reflect particularly on how it has altered the human and Christian concept of labor, and what influence it exerts on legislation and administration. The people have received technical progress with favor, and rightly so, because it alleviates the burden of labor and increases productivity. But it must also be confessed that if this feeling is not contained within its just limits, the human and Christian concept of work is necessarily damaged. Equally, from a mistaken technical concept of life, and hence of labor, derives the considering of leisure as an end in itself, rather than regarding and using it as the necessary relief and rest, linked essentially to the rhythm of an ordered life, in which rest and labor alternate in a single texture, and integrate each other in a common harmony.

More visible is the influence of the "technological spirit" applied to labor, when Sunday is deprived of its singular dignity as the day of divine worship and of physical and spiritual rest for individuals and the family, and becomes instead only one of the free days in the course of the week, which can also be different for each member of the family, according to the greater returns that it is hoped to gain from such a technical distribution of material and human energy; or again, when professional labor becomes so conditioned and subjected to the "functioning" of the machine and other instruments, as rapidly to wear out the laborer, as if a year's practice of his profession had exhausted the strength of two or more years of his normal life.

We cannot omit drawing attention to the new form of materialism which the "technological spirit" introduces into life. It is enough to mention that this spirit empties life of its content, since technology is ordered to man and to the complex of material and spiritual values which are part of his nature and his personal dignity. Should the technological spirit reign autonomous, human society would be transformed into a colorless multitude, into something impersonal and mechanical, and therefore contrary to what nature and its Creator have demonstrably willed.

No doubt, a great part of humanity has not been touched yet by this "technological conception of life"; but it is to be feared that wherever technical progress enters without any controls, the danger of the aforementioned deformations will not delay in appearing. And We think with particular anxiety of the danger threatening the family, which in social life is the most solid principle of order, since it knows how to stimulate among its members innumerable personal tasks which are daily renewed, ties them with bonds of affection to house and home, and awakens in each of them love of family tradition in the production and preservation of common goods. On the other hand, where the technological concept of life penetrates, the family loses the personal tie of its unity, loses its warmth and stability.

The "technological concept of life" is therefore nothing else but a particular form of materialism, in that it offers as a final answer to the question of existence a mathematical formula and a utilitarian calculation. For this reason, modern technological development, as if aware of being enveloped by darkness, manifests uncertainties and anxiety, especially noticeable in the measures taken by those who busy themselves in the feverish research for continually more complicated and more risky systems. A world so guided cannot consider itself illumined by that light, nor animated by that life, which the Word, splendor of the glory of God, become man, has come to communicate to all men.

Religion and Life

In the dawning of the history of the Church, during the reign of Trajan, St. Ignatius of Antioch set down a thought fascinating to modern souls as well, as the discovery of a treasure of experience from two thousand years ago: "In times in which it is an object of hate, Christianity is not a matter of persuasive words, but of greatness."

Truly, in the religious crisis of our times—the gravest, perhaps, that humanity has passed through since the origins of Christianity—the reasoned and scientific exposition of the truths of faith, however efficacious it may be and is in reality, is not enough. Nor suffices the often skimpy measure of a Christian life nourished merely from conventional habits. What is necessary today is the greatness of a Christianity lived in its fullness with persevering constancy; what is necessary is the vigorous and valorous host of Christian men and women who, living in the midst of the world, are ready at every instant to fight for their faith, for the law of God, for Christ, their eyes fixed on Him as a model to imitate, as a leader to follow in their apostolic work.

Quite recently, Christianity has been advised—if it intends to maintain a certain importance, and if it wishes to overcome its static period—to adapt itself to modern life and thought, to scientific discoveries, and to the extraordinary power of technological resources in the face of which historical forms and their old dogmas are merely dimming lights of the past on the verge of going out.

What an error this is, and how it lays bare the vain illusions of superficial minds! They seem to want the Church to enter into the narrow forms of purely human organizations. As if the new configuration of the world, as if the present domain of science and technology, occupied the entire field and no longer left any space free for supernatural life, which flows out from every side! Those marvellous discoveries (which the Church favors and promotes) do not suffice to abolish and absorb her; on the contrary, they bring to light, with greater force and effect than before, the "eternal power of God."

But modern thought and life must be led back and won over to Christ again. Christ, His truth, His grace, are no less necessary to the humanity of our times than to that of yesterday and the day before, and of all the centuries past and future. He is the only source of salvation.

The desire to draw a clear line of distinction between religion and life, between the supernatural and the natural, between the Church and the world, as if these had nothing whatsoever to do with each other, as if the rights of God did not have value in all the multiform reality of daily human and social life, is completely alien to Catholic thought, is openly anti-Christian. Therefore, so long as dark powers increase their pressure, so long as they make every attempt to banish the Church and religion from the world and from life, it is all the more necessary on the part of the Church herself to conduct a tenacious and persevering action in order to reconquer and submit all the fields of human life to the gentle reign of Christ, so that His spirit may breathe more fully in it, His law reign more sovereignly, His love triumph more victoriously. This is what must be understood by the Reign of Christ.

This office of the Church is most arduous; but it is only the disillusioned deserters without conscience who, in homage to a misunderstood supernaturalism, would like to reduce the Church to a "purely religious" sphere, as they say, while by doing so they only favor the hand of their adversaries.[1]

[1] Allocution to the Sacred College, December 24, 1953

ON THE ESTABLISHMENT OF THE HIERARCHY IN THE UNITED STATES

IN OUR DESIRE to enrich the crown of your holy joy We cross in spirit the vast spaces of the seas and find Ourselves in your midst as you celebrate the one hundred and fiftieth anniversary of the establishment of the ecclesiastical hierarchy in the United States of America. And this We do with great gladness, because an occasion is thus afforded Us, as gratifying as it is solemn, of giving public testimony of Our esteem and Our affection for the youthfully vigorous and illustrious American people.

When Pope Pius VI gave you your first Bishop in the person of the American, John Carroll, and set him over the See of Baltimore, small and of slight importance was the Catholic population of your land. At that time, too, the condition of the United States was so perilous that its structure and its very political unity were threatened by grave crisis. Because of the long and exhausting war the public treasury was burdened with debt, industry languished, and the citizenry, wearied by misfortunes, was split into contending parties. This ruinous and critical state of affairs was put to rights by George Washington, famed for his courage and keen intelligence. He was a close friend of the Bishop of Baltimore. Thus the Father of His Country and the pioneer pastor of the Church in that land so dear to Us, bound together by the ties of friendship and clasping, so to speak, each the other's hand, form a picture for their descendants, a lesson to all future generations, and a proof that reverence for the Faith of Christ is a holy and established principle of the American people, seeing that it is the foundation of morality and decency, consequently the source of prosperity and progress.

We cannot refrain from a public expression of praise for those missionary enterprises proper to your own nation which devote themselves with zeal and energy to the wider diffusion of the Catholic Faith. . . .

We confess that We feel a special paternal affection, which is certainly inspired by Heaven, for the Negro people dwelling among you; for in the field of religion and education We know they need special care and comfort and are very deserving of it. We therefore invoke an abundance of heavenly blessing, and We pray fruitful success for those whose generous zeal is devoted to their welfare.

You well know where it is necessary that you exercise a more discerning vigilance and what program of action should be marked out for priests and faithful in order that the religion of Christ may overcome the obstacles in its path and be a luminous guide to the minds of men, govern their morals, and, for the sole purpose of salvation, permeate the marrow and the arteries of human society. The progress of exterior and material possessions, even though it is to be considered of no little account, because of the manifold and appreciable utility which it gives to life is nonetheless not enough for man, who is born for higher and brighter destinies. . . .

Social Relations

We desire to touch upon another question of weighty importance, the social question, which, remaining unsolved, has been agitating States for a long time and sowing among the classes the seeds of hatred and mutual hostility. You know full well what aspect it assumes in America, what acrimonies, what disorders it produces. It is not necessary therefore that We dwell on these points. The fundamental point of the social question is this, that the goods created by God for all men should in the same way reach all, justice guiding and charity helping. The history of every age teaches that there were always rich and poor; that it will always be so we may gather from the unchanging tenor of human destinies. Worthy of honor are the poor who fear God because theirs is the Kingdom of Heaven and because they readily abound in spiritual graces. But the rich, if they are upright and honest, are God's dispensers and providers of this world's goods; as ministers of divine Providence they assist the indigent through whom they often receive gifts for the soul and whose hand—so they may hope—will lead them into the eternal tabernacles.

God, Who provides for all with counsels of supreme bounty, has ordained that for the exercise of virtues and for the testing of one's worth there be in the world rich and poor; but He does not wish that some have exaggerated riches while others are in such straits that they lack the bare necessities of life.

Now if the rich and the prosperous are obliged out of ordinary motives of pity to act generously toward the poor their obligation is all the greater to do them justice. The salaries of the workers, as is just, are to be such that they are sufficient to maintain them and their families. Solemn are the words of Our predecessor, Pius XI, on this question: "Every effort must therefore be made that fathers of families receive a wage sufficient to meet adequately normal domestic needs. If under present circumstances this is not always feasible, social justice demands that reforms be introduced without delay which will guarantee such a wage to every adult workingman. In this connection We praise those who have most prudently and usefully attempted various methods by which an increased wage is paid in view of increased family burdens and special provision made for special needs" (Encyclical *Quadragesimo Anno*).

Because a social relation is one of man's natural requirements and since it is legitimate to promote by common effort decent livelihood, it is not possible without injustice to deny or to limit either to the producers or to the laboring and farming classes the free faculty of uniting in associations by means of which they may defend their proper rights and secure the betterment of the goods of soul and of body, as well as the honest comforts of life.

But let the unions in question draw their vital force from principles of wholesome liberty; let them take their form from the lofty rules of justice and of honesty, and, conforming themselves to those norms, let them act in such a manner that in their care for the interests of their class they violate no one's rights; let them continue to strive for harmony and respect the common weal of civil society.

What a proud vaunt it will be for the American people, by nature inclined to grandiose undertakings and to liberality, if they untie the knotty and difficult social question by following the sure paths illuminated by the light of the Gospel and thus lay the basis of a happier age! [1]

[1] Encyclical *Sertum Laetitiae,* Feast of All Saints, 1939

TO THE CHRISTIANS IN RUSSIA

WHEN THE LAST TERRIBLE CONFLICT broke out, We did everything within Our possibilities, by word, exhortation, and action, to contribute toward the end of dissensions with an equitable and just peace, and that all peoples, regardless of differences of race, might unite in friendship and brotherly love and collaborate with one another to reach greater prosperity. Never, in those times, did We utter one word that might seem unjust or harsh to any group among the belligerents. We did, of course, as is Our duty, censure any iniquity and any violation of law; but We did this in such a way as to avoid scrupulously anything that would add to the afflictions of the oppressed peoples. And when from some sides pressure was brought to bear upon Us to induce Us to approve, in any way, by voice or in writing, the war waged against Russia in 1941, We never consented to do this, as We stated openly on February 25, 1946, in the allocution addressed to the Sacred College and all diplomatic representatives to the Holy See.

When there is question of defending the cause of religion, truth, justice, and Christian civilization, We certainly cannot be silent; but Our thoughts and Our intentions have always this aim in view: that not by force of arms, but by the majesty of law, should all peoples be governed; and that each of them, in possession of civil and religious freedom within the boundaries of their own country, should be led toward concord and peace. . . . Our words and Our exhortations did and do concern all the nations, and therefore you too, who are always present in Our heart, and whose pressing needs and calamities We desire to alleviate as much as is within Our power. Those who love truth and not falsehood know that throughout the course of the recent conflict We showed Ourselves impartial toward all the belligerents, and We often gave proof of this with words and deeds; and in Our ardent charity We have embraced all nations, even those whose rulers profess to be enemies of the Apostolic See, and those, too, in which the enemies of God are fiercely opposed to Christianity or divinity, and seek to blot it out from the minds of the citizens. For by Christ's mandate, which entrusted the whole flock of Christian people to St. Peter, the Prince of Apostles —whose unworthy successor We are—We love all peoples intensely and desire to procure for all of them prosperity on earth, and eternal salvation. All of them, therefore, whether in armed warfare with one another or separated by grave dissensions, are considered by Us as so many beloved children; and We desire nothing else, We pray to God for nothing else for them, than mutual concord, just and real peace, and ever greater prosperity.

What is more, if some of them, led astray by lies and calumnies, openly declare their hostility to Us, We feel for them a greater commiseration and a more ardent affection.

We have, it is true, condemned and rejected, as the duty of Our office demands, the errors that the upholders of atheistic Communism teach and try to spread, to the great detriment of nations; but, far from rejecting the erring, We want them to return to truth and to be led back on the right road. We have also unmasked and condemned those lies that were often presented in the false guise of truth, precisely because We cherish paternal affection for you and seek your welfare. For We are firmly convinced that nothing but great harm will come to you from these errors, and that they not only deprive your souls of that supernatural light and those supreme comforts that piety and worship of God bestow, but also strip you of human dignity and of that just freedom which is every citizen's birthright.

We are aware that many of you cling to the Christian faith in the sanctuary of your conscience, that in no way do you allow yourselves to be induced to favor the enemies of religion, but that, on the contrary, it is your ardent desire to profess the precepts of Christianity, the only sure foundation of civil life, not only in private but, if it were possible, as it should be for all free people, also openly. And We know, too—and this gives Us hope and great comfort—that you love and honor with eager affection the Virgin Mary, Mother of God, and that you venerate Her sacred images. We know that in the Kremlin itself a temple was built—today, unfortunately, no longer used for divine worship—dedicated to the Most Holy Mary Assumed into Heaven; and this is evident proof of the love your ancestors and you bear the Great Mother of God.

Russia and the Mother of God

Now, We know that where people turn with sincere and ardent piety toward the Most Holy Mother of God, there is always hope of salvation. In fact, though men, however impious and powerful, seek to uproot from the hearts of the citizens holy religion and Christian virtue, though Satan himself strive to foster with every means this sacrilegious struggle, in accordance with the saying of the Apostle of the peoples: "For our wrestling is not against flesh and blood, but against the principalities and the powers, against the world rulers of this darkness, against the spiritual forces of wickedness on high . . . ," yet, if Mary intervenes with her support, the gates of Hell will not prevail. For She is the benign and powerful Mother of God and of all of us, and never has it happened in the world that anyone has turned to Her in supplication without experiencing Her all-powerful intercession. Go on, then, as is your wont, venerating Her with fervent piety, loving Her ardently, and invoking Her with these words, which are familiar to you: "To thee alone it has been granted, most holy and pure Mother of God, never to be refused."

We, too, together with you raise to Her Our supplicant invocations, that the Christian truth, the adornment and support of human society, may flourish and gain vigor among the peoples of Russia, and that all the deceptions of the enemies of religion, all their errors and deceitful tricks, may be rejected by you; that public and private conduct may once more conform to evangelical standards; that those especially among you who profess the Catholic faith, although deprived of their shepherds, may intrepidly resist the assaults of impiety, if it is necessary, even unto death, so that just freedom which is the heritage of the human being, of citizens and of Christians, may be restored to all, as is their due, and in the first place to the Church, who has the divine mandate of bringing up mankind in religious truths and in virtue; and, last of all, that true peace may shine upon the whole of humanity, and that this peace, founded on justice and fed on charity, may successfully guide all the nations toward that general prosperity of citizens and peoples which springs from mutual concord.

May our loving Mother deign to look with benign eyes also at those who are organizing the forces of militant atheists and encouraging their initiatives in every way. May She illuminate their minds with the light that comes from above, and direct with divine grace their hearts to salvation.

And We humbly beg the most merciful Mother to assist each one of you in the present calamities, and to obtain from Her divine

Son that light that comes from Heaven for your minds, and to stamp upon your souls that virtue and that strength which will enable you, supported by divine grace, victoriously to overcome impiety and error.[1]

[1] Apostolic Letter *Sacro Vergente Anno,* July 7, 1952

THE CHURCH SUFFERING PERSECUTION IN CENTRAL AND EASTERN EUROPE

WHILE WITH HEAVY HEART We consider the grave trials the Catholic Church is suffering in many lands at the hands of atheistic materialism in control there, Our thoughts turn to the situation prevailing in Central Europe five centuries ago, which occasioned the Apostolic Letter *Cum his superioribus annis* of Our predecessor of immortal memory, Callistus III, on June 29, 1456.

A grave danger threatened, where it had not already befallen, the Christian peoples dwelling in the fruitful regions washed by the Danube River, and the surrounding lands, a danger to their lives, their property, their very faith. This was especially the case of Hungary and the lands today called Albania, Bulgaria, Czechoslovakia, Yugoslavia, Rumania; threatened, too, were those who lived in more distant regions, especially the Germans and Poles. Taking account of that crisis, the tireless Pontiff Callistus III saw it as his duty to exhort paternally the Catholic shepherds and flocks to repent and expiate their own sins, to reform their customs in accord with Christian moral principles, to invoke God's powerful aid through fervent prayer. Moreover, the Pontiff labored with tireless energy to remove by every possible means the danger threatening the Church's children; he attributed to divine help the victory finally won by those who—under the inspiration of St. John Capistrano and the military leadership of John Hunyady—so strenuously defended the fortress of Belgrade. To commemorate this event in the Liturgy, and to give due thanks to God, the feast of the Transfiguration of our Lord Jesus Christ was instituted, to be celebrated throughout the world on August 6th (cf. Apostolic Letter, *Inter divinæ dispositionis,* August 6, 1457).

Today, also, alas, you who dwell in those countries We have mentioned suffer grievous conditions, along with many other Catholics of the Eastern as well as of the Latin rite, whose boundaries are east of your own, or north, along the Baltic coast. More than ten years have passed, as you know by experience, since Christ's Church was stripped of her rights, though not in the same way everywhere. Pious associations and religious groups were dissolved and scattered, and shepherds, either hindered from exercising their office or forced from their sees, have been sent into exile, or jailed. The Catholic dioceses of the Eastern Rite also have been recklessly suppressed, and their clergy and faithful urged by every ruse to schism. We know, moreover, that many have been bitterly persecuted for their fearless, sincere, and courageous efforts to profess and defend their faith. Our greatest grief springs from the realization that the minds of children and youth are being steeped in false and perverse doctrines, so they may be separated from God and His divine precepts to their great loss here below and to the danger of their eternal salvation.

We, Who by divine Providence sit upon the throne of Peter, contemplate this sad, sad vision, which We have already commented on in previous Apostolic Letters; and We cannot in conscience remain silent today. For We must obey that grave, yet sweet, command Christ our Lord gave to the Prince of the Apostles and to his successors: "Strengthen thy brethren" (Luke, 22, 32). We, too, must be faithful in fulfilling it; hence again and again do We wish to strengthen your holy determination and show you Our affection, you who, in your loyalty to and love for Christ, bear so many sorrows and trials, and such anguish.

Our eyes and heart turn to Our Venerable Brothers in the episcopacy, who are distinguished for their active fidelity to the Apostolic See; to the priests also, both secular, as they say, and religious, and to the phalanx of all those men and women consecrated to the divine service, and finally to all the other beloved sons and daughters who under so many and such great difficulties are defending and advancing as far as they can the peaceful and peace-bringing Kingdom of Jesus Christ. In Our solicitude for you who have for the cause of Christ endured suffering, sacrifice, and loss, We offer daily prayer and supplication to Almighty God that in His merciful kindness He will sustain and strengthen your faith, that He will alleviate your sorrow, that He will console you with heavenly blessings, that He will heal perfectly the afflicted and ailing members of the mystical body of Christ, and that finally, when this present storm has passed, He will command to shine forth among you, among all peoples, a true and serene peace which will be fostered by truth, justice, and charity.

Never, as you know so well, does our Redeemer forget His Church. Never does He abandon it. Rather the more the Bark of Peter is tossed by the raging waves, the more the Divine Pilot is vigilant, although at times He seems to sleep (cf. Matthew 8, 24; Luke 8, 23). Meditate daily on His promise which pours certain hope and solace into the souls of Christians when they are especially harassed: "I am with you all days even unto the consummation of the world" (Matthew 28, 20); and, "if God is for us who is against us?" (Romans 8, 31). Christ, therefore, is with you. He will never deny His help to you if you ask it. And yet He demands from all that they obey diligently and perfectly the precepts of the Catholic Church, and that they preserve with magnanimous heart their faith. You know what is at stake: it is your eternal salvation and the salvation of your children and neighbors, which today, owing to the ever growing course of atheism, is placed in the gravest peril.

But in this spiritual struggle if each and every one shows strength and loyalty in the fight—as We trust they will—they may be glorious victims but never conquered. Thus from unjust persecution and the sufferings of martyrs will be born new triumphs of the Church, to be inscribed in her annals in letters of gold. And far from us the thought that the disciples of Jesus Christ are leaving the field of battle broken in spirit, that they are concealing or belittling the profession of their faith, that they have thrown away their arms, cowards, or are asleep while the enemy is striving to overthrow the Kingdom of God. Even if this were partly the case—which God forbid—irreparable harm and calamity would befall not only the deserters but also the Christian world.

We realize—and it is consoling to Us—that there are very many among you who with noble determination are ready to sacrifice all, even liberty and life, rather than jeopardize the integrity of the Catholic religion. We also realize that not a few of Christ's shepherds have already given to others in this an example of unconquerable fortitude. You especially, beloved Sons, Cardinals of the Holy Roman Church, have been made a spectacle to the world, to angels, and to men (cf. I Corinthians 4, 9). However, We also realize with regret that human frailty and uncertainty totters especially when these sufferings and persecutions last for a long time. For then some lose heart and their courage slackens. And, what is worse, they think that the doctrine of Christ must be mitigated and adapted, as they say, to the times and circumstances of things and places. They say it is necessary to mitigate and change the principles of the Catholic religion so that there may be a certain false union between it and the errors of the advancing age.

If some there are who, weak and bewildered, cause others to be likewise, let the pastors of the Church remind them of that solemn promise of the divine Redeemer: "Heaven and earth will pass but My words will never pass" (Matthew 24, 35). Likewise it is their duty to encourage them to put their trust and confidence in Him Whose Providence does not err in act and Who will not deprive of His assistance those whom He has confirmed in His love (cf. Missale Romanum).

Never will He permit the faithful and brave children of His Church to be lacking divine grace and fortitude, and thus miserably yield to the enemy in this struggle for salvation, be unhappily drawn from the side of Christ, and helpless, contemplate the spiritual and pitiful ruin of their people.

You, however, beloved Sons, priest and lay, be always united to those whom the Holy Spirit has chosen to rule the Church of God; even though these are at the present time restrained and cannot strengthen you by their word, still religiously and faithfully reflect in mind and soul upon the exhortations which they gave you in the past. Still, though the greatest difficulties impede you, may you, compelled by apostolic zeal, generously and industriously perform all your religious duties, and above all preserve the faith intact. What is more, in so far as it lies within your power, strive earnestly that the light of Christ shall illumine all others, and above all do this through the example of constancy in your Christian life after the manner of Christians of old when the wave of persecutions broke upon the Church.

Let those who are slipping, who waver, who are weak, learn from you to fortify their spirit, to profess the faith candidly and openly, to attend to their religious duties, and to dedicate themselves entirely to Christ. The upright and vigorous forces of your soul and effective Christian piety, of which illustrious testimony has often been reported to Us, affords Us no little solace and bids Us hope that you may be able to transmit intact to future generations the most precious treasure of Christian faith and of your loyalty to the Church and the Apostolic See and establish it as a sacred heritage.

Be convinced that the entire Christian family looks with reverential awe at what you bear so long in silence, in tribulation, and in all dire straits; and turn your supplications to the most merciful God that you succumb not to the sharp blows of impiety nor to the insidious fallacies of error, but that with the strenuous fortitude of the holy martyrs you give testimony before all of your faith so that even your persecutors—the command of Christian charity extends also to them—may obtain pardon from Him Who expects to embrace lovingly all His prodigal sons.[1]

[1] Apostolic Letter to the Archbishops and Bishops of Central and Eastern Europe, June 29, 1956

THE EASTERN CHURCHES

ALL THE EASTERN CHURCHES—as history teaches—have always been loved with the tenderest affection by the Roman Pontiffs, and therefore they, hardly able to bear the separation of the East from the original fold, and driven, not indeed by human interest, but only by divine charity and by the desire for common salvation, by repeated entreaties invited these separated brothers to return as early as possible to that unity from which they had so unhappily broken away. Indeed, the same Supreme Pontiffs know well from experience the fruitful abundance which will derive from this happily reintegrated union for all Christian society, and in particular for the Eastern Churches themselves. In fact, from the full and perfect unity of all Christians there cannot but come a great increase to the mystical body of Jesus Christ and to all its individual members.

No Abandonment of Rites and Usages

In this connection it must be noted that the Eastern Churches need have no fear of being constrained, upon their return to unity of faith and government, to abandon their legitimate rites and usages; this fact Our predecessors declared openly more than once. "There is no reason to doubt, therefore, that We or Our successors will take away anything from your law, your patriarchal privileges, or from the rituals in use in each of your churches."

And although the happy day has not yet arrived in which it will be given to Us to embrace with paternal affection all the peoples of the East, once more returned to the true fold, nevertheless We note with joy that not a few children of these regions, who have recognized the Chair of the Blessed Peter as the bulwark of Catholic unity, persevere tenaciously in the defense and strengthening of this unity.[1]

The Eastern Churches, in more recent times, and also in Our own, have always been the particular object of Our solicitude, as everyone knows. In fact, as soon as We were elevated, without any personal merit of Ours, by the mysterious design of God, to the Chair of the Prince of Apostles, We turned Our mind and Our heart to those who "are outside the Catholic Church" and whom We ardently wish to see return as soon as possible to the fold of Our common Father, home of their ancestors. We have given other proofs of Our paternal benevolence during the course of Our Pontificate. But at present, unfortunately, additional considerations call for Our care and Our solicitude. In fact, in many regions where the Eastern rite is in general use, a new tempest has been unleashed which seeks to upset, devastate, and utterly destroy flourishing Christian communities. If, in the past centuries, some particular dogma of Catholic doctrine was attacked, today they rashly go far beyond; and they seek to eradicate from civilized society, from the family, from universities, schools, and from the life of the people everything divine or pertaining to divinity, as if these were absurd or nefarious things, and they trample upon rights, institutions, and sacred laws. We know that there are many Christians of the Eastern rite who weep bitterly at seeing their Bishops murdered or banished, or so hindered as not to be able to talk freely to their flocks or to exercise over them, as it should be, their proper authority; at seeing many of their temples put to profane uses or left in a state of the most squalid neglect; at knowing that now those who pray can no longer raise to Heaven from these temples their voices, beautifully intoned according to your liturgy, to call down the dew of heavenly grace for the elevation of minds, the consolation of hearts, and the remedy of such a great burden of afflictions.

We know that many are relegated to prisons or concentration camps, or, if they live in their own homes, they cannot exercise those sacrosanct rights which are theirs: that is, not only the right to profess their faith in the sanctuary of their conscience, but also to be able to teach it openly, to defend it and propagate it in the family circle, for the necessary education of the children, and in school for the upright formation of the pupil's character.

We know also, however, that the sons of the Eastern Churches, united in brotherhood with the faithful of the Latin rite, together endure with fortitude the bereavements of these persecutions, and both participate equally in the martyrdom, the triumph, and the glory which derive from it. In fact, they persevere in their faith with heroic spirit; resist the enemies of Christianity with the same indomitable strength with which their forefathers once resisted; raise their supplications to Heaven, if not publicly, at least in private; remain faithfully attached to the Roman Pontiff and to their pastors; and also venerate especially the Blessed Virgin Mary, most loving and most powerful Queen of Heaven and earth, to Whose Immaculate Heart We have consecrated them all. All this is without doubt a pledge of certain victory in the future—of that victory, however, which does not spring from the blood of men in conflict with one another, which is not nourished by an unbridled desire for earthly power, but which is based upon proper and legitimate freedom; upon justice, not practiced with words alone, but also with deeds, toward citizens, peoples, and nations; upon peace and Christian charity which unite all in the bonds of friendship; upon religion, above all, which regulates conduct according to what is right, tempers private ambitions, placing them in the service of the public welfare, raises the minds to Heaven, and, finally, safeguards civilized society and concord among all.

Slander and Persecution

This constitutes the object of Our fondest hopes. Meanwhile, however, the news which comes to Us is such as to deepen the bitterness of Our grief. Day and night, with paternal solcitude, We turn Our mind and heart to those who had been entrusted to Us by divine mandate and whom We know to be treated, in some places, in such an unseemly manner as to be made the objects of slander because of their firm attachment to the Catholic faith, and to be deprived of their legitimate rights, sometimes not excluding even those so innate in human nature that, if they are violated by force, fear, or any other means, the very dignity of man is degraded.

All this is such a bitter cause of grief to Us that We cannot withhold Our tears when We pray to the most merciful God and Father of compassion that He may benevolently enlighten those responsible for so sad a situation and put an end to these many evils.

But, in the midst of so many and such great calamities which sadden Our soul and yours, We can find some reason for comfort in the news which has come to Us. In fact, it is known to Us that those who are in such deplorable and desperate circumstances remain firm in their faith with such intrepid constancy as to awaken Our admiration and that of all decent people. To all of them, therefore, goes Our paternal praise; may their strength increase, may they be firmly convinced that We, as a common Father whom the care for all the Churches moves and "the charity of Christ presses," raise fervent prayers every day that the Kingdom of Jesus Christ, herald of peace for individual souls, peoples, and nations, may triumph everywhere.

Before the unhappy spectacle of such evils, which have struck not only Our sons among the laity but above all those invested with sacerdotal dignity, precisely so that what is written in the Sacred Scripture: "They will smite the shepherd and the sheep of the flock shall be scattered," may come to pass, We cannot fail to call the attention of all to the fact that, in the course of centuries, not only among civilized peoples but also among barbarians, priests, as intermediaries between God and man, have always been regarded with proper veneration. And when the divine Redeemer, having dispelled the darkness of error, taught us the heavenly truths, and out of His great benevolence wished to make us sharers in His eternal priesthood, this veneration increased even more so that Bishops and priests were considered as most loving fathers, desirous of nothing else but the common welfare of the flock entrusted to their care.

Nevertheless the divine Redeemer Himself had said: "No disciple is above his teacher"; "If they have persecuted Me, they will persecute you also"; "Blessed are you when men reproach you and persecute you and, speaking falsely, say all manner of evil against you for My sake. Rejoice and exult, for your reward is great in Heaven."

There is, therefore, no reason to wonder if in our day, and perhaps more than in past centuries, the Church of Jesus Christ and especially His ministers are stricken with persecutions, falsehoods, calumnies, and all sorts of affliction; but rather let us place our trust in Him Who, if He predicted future calamities, also admonished us with these words: "In the world you will have affliction. But take courage, for I have overcome the world."

If, for those innumerable legions of people who, in those regions, suffer infirmities, grief, and anguish, or are in prison, We cannot put into practice the words of Jesus: "[I was] sick, and you visited Me, I was in prison, and you came to Me," we can at least do something for them; with our prayers and works of penance we can implore our most merciful Lord to send His consoling angels to these our suffering brothers and sons, and shower upon them ample heavenly gifts which will console and strengthen their spirits, and lift them up to heavenly things.

And We wish especially that all priests, who can offer up the Holy Eucharist every day, shall remember those Bishops and priests who, far from their churches and their faithful, do not have the opportunity of approaching the altar to celebrate the divine Sacrifice and nourish themselves and their faithful with that divine Food from which our souls draw a sweetness which surpasses all desire and receive that strength which leads to victory. Drawn together in close brotherly union, let the faithful also do this, as they participate in the same offering and in the same sacrifice: to the end that in every part of the earth and in all rites which constitute the ornament of the Church, there will go up to God and to His heavenly

Mother the unanimous voices of those who pray to obtain divine mercy in behalf of these afflicted communities of Christians.[2]

[1] Encyclical *Orientales omnes Ecclesias,* December 23, 1945
[2] Encyclical *Orientales Ecclesias,* December 15, 1952

THE TASK OF THE CHRISTIAN PRESS

THE PRESS must be undeviatingly loyal to the truth, lest its tremendous influence be exercised amiss. The truth of which We speak is the truth in vision, whereby you see events really as they happen, and the truth in presentation, whereby you report faithfully events as you have seen them, and interpret them by no other standards than those of justice and of charity.

Now truth is dispassionate, not partisan; factual, not fanciful. Truth is not venal; it does not fear to be known, but it asks only to be presented in the clear, white light of objectivity, not in any spectral tint of prejudice or conjecture. Truth, too, is discreet and knows that reality must at times be circumscribed by reserve, that evil is not to be garnished while the good is slurred over. Truth is modest and aware that death may enter the soul through the windows of the eyes. Alas, does not experience teach that incalculable harm may come to domestic and civil society through an unethical press that would lose sight of the demands of truth? [1]

The Catholic Journalist

Modern man likes to appear free and independent. But very often this is only a façade, behind which hide paltry, empty beings, without the spiritual strength to unmask falsehood, without the energy to resist the violence of those who are capable of putting into effect all the discoveries of modern technology, all the refined arts of persuasion, to deprive them of freedom of thought and reduce them to the state of "reeds shaken by the wind."

Could one affirm, without hesitancy, that the majority of men are capable of judging and understanding facts and currents at their true value, in a way that shows that their opinion is guided by reason? . . .

Numerous are those whose vision does not transcend their own limited specialization or purely technical capacity. The education of public opinion in everyday life certainly cannot be expected from such men, nor firmness on their part in the face of clever propaganda which unduly claims the privilege of molding opinion just as it wishes. In this respect, men of Christian spirit, straightforward, upright, and clear, even though often without much formal education, are far superior.

Thus the men to whom the task of enlightening and guiding public opinion should be entrusted are often found to be in a highly unfavorable condition freely and successfully to carry out their task, some because of ill will or incapacity, others because they are being obstructed and impeded. This unfavorable situation damages above all the Catholic press in its action at the service of public opinion.

In this situation, the evils most to be feared for the Catholic journalist are faintheartedness and discouragement. Look at the Church: for almost two thousand years, through the most varied tribulations, contradictions, lack of understanding, and persecutions, both hidden and open, she has never been dejected and has never allowed herself to become disheartened. Take her as your example. Consider, in the deplorable shortcomings We have pointed out, the double picture of what should not be and what should be the Catholic press.

In every aspect of its being and its activity it should oppose an insurmountable obstacle to the growing retrogression and disappearance of the basic conditions for a healthy public opinion, and consolidate and reinforce that which still survives. Let it renounce with pleasure the fleeting advantages of vulgar interests or cheap popularity; let it know how to resist with energetic and proud dignity all direct and indirect attempts at corruption. Let it have the courage—even at the cost of pecuniary sacrifices—to banish from its columns every advertisement or publicity item which is offensive to faith or morals. By so doing, it will gain in intrinsic value and succeed in winning esteem, then confidence; it will justify the oft-repeated injunction: "A Catholic newspaper in every Catholic home."

Educating the Public

But, even under the best internal and external conditions in which to develop and propagate, public opinion is not infallible or always absolutely spontaneous. The complexity or the novelty of events and situations can exercise a notable influence on its formation, without taking into account that it cannot easily free itself from preconceived judgments and prevailing currents in the field of ideas, even when the reaction is objectively justifiable or frankly imposes itself. It is in this case that the press has an outstanding job to do in forming opinion, not by dominating or governing it, but by serving it usefully.

This delicate mission presupposes, in those who concern themselves with the Catholic press, competence, general culture, above all philosophical and theological, writing talent, and psychological tact. But the foremost prerequisite is character. That is to say, a profound love and unalterable respect for the divine order which embraces and pervades every aspect of life: a love and respect which the Catholic journalist should not feel and nourish only in the intimacy of his own heart, but should cultivate in the hearts of his readers. Sometimes the flame burning in this way is enough to relight or revive the almost extinguished spark of conviction and feeling stifled in the depths of conscience. In other cases, broadness of viewpoint and judgment may open their eyes, too timidly fixed upon time-worn prejudices.

We believe that this Catholic conception of public opinion, of its function and the service rendered it by the press, is both adapted to and necessary for pointing out to mankind, according to your ideal, the path of truth, justice, and peace.

This Catholic conception of public opinion and of the service rendered to it by the press is also a solid guarantee of peace. Peace is served by a true freedom of thought and by man's right to his own judgment, always, that is, in the light of divine law.

Where public opinion ceases to express itself freely, peace is in danger.

We wish to add yet another word concerning public opinion within the sphere of the Church herself, regarding those questions open to free discussion. This will astonish only those who do not know the Church or who have a wrong impression of her. Since she is a living body, something would be lacking in her life if she were deficient in public opinion and if this lack were attributable to her pastors and faithful. But here, also, the Catholic press can perform a very useful service. However, it is extremely important that in this service the journalist must possess, above all, the character of which We have spoken, consisting of an unalterable respect and a profound love for the divine order, that is, in the present case, for the Church who not only forms part of the eternal designs but also of the earthly life here below, in space and in time; divine, yes, but formed of human members and organs.

If he possesses this character, the Catholic journalist will know how to guard himself against mute servility as well as uncontrolled criticism. He will join, with acute discernment, in the formation of a Catholic opinion within the Church, especially in a situation such as exists today in which this opinion wavers between the equally dangerous poles of an unreal and illusory spiritualism and a defeatist and materialistic realism. Keeping equally distant from these two extremes, the Catholic press should exercise its influence on public opinion within the Church, in the midst of the faithful. Only thus can be avoided false ideas on the mission and possibilities of the Church in temporal matters, and, especially today, on the social question and the problem of peace.[2]

[1] Address to U.S.A. Press Representatives, April 27, 1946 (in English)

[2] Address to the International Congress of the Catholic Press, February 1, 1950

THE EUROPEAN UNION

WHEN, AFTER THE LAST WAR, the leaders of several nations decided to bring international institutions into being which would be charged with the task of organizing peace, the cruel experience of the past half century weighed upon their debates and continually reminded them that to obtain a chance of success a generous idea is not enough. In particular, the practical realization of a European Union, the urgency of which was felt by everybody, and toward which everybody almost instinctively oriented himself, encountered two principal obstacles: one inherent in the structure of the State, the other psychological and moral. The first involves a series of economic, social, military, and political problems. The nations desirous of forming an association find themselves on different planes, from the viewpoint of natural resources and industrial development and of social progress. They cannot proceed to a life in common without first providing for the means necessary to maintain a general equilibrium. But much more important appears the need for the so-called European spirit, the consciousness of internal unity, founded not upon the satisfaction of economic necessity but rather on the perception of common spiritual values, a perception so clear as to justify and keep alive the steadfast will to live united.

It is easy to recognize that of all the backers of a united Europe serious concessions are required. The transfer of industries, re-adaptation of labor, local fluctuations and difficulties in certain sectors of production—here are some of the matters which governments and peoples will have to face. They may be temporary difficulties, but also of long duration, which will surely not always be compensated for by short-term economic advantages, as within a single nation when the poorer regions get to enjoy an equal standard of life only by virtue of the contribution of the richer regions. It is necessary, therefore, to cause public opinion in each nation to accept sacrifices, perhaps of a permanent nature, to explain their necessity and inspire the desire to remain, notwithstanding these sacrifices, united with the other nations and to continue to help them.

It is easy to imagine the natural reaction of the egoisms, almost instinctively ready to shut themselves off from the others, a dangerous weapon in the hands of the opponents and of all those whose discreditable purpose is to profit by the sufferings of others. It is necessary, then, right from the beginning, to realize that a prospect of material advantages will not be enough to foster the will for sacrifices indispensable to final success. Sooner or later these advantages will be seen to be illusory or fallacious. The interests of common defense will also be offered as a reason; without doubt fear easily awakens a violent reaction, but usually very brief and without constructive force, incapable of directing and co-ordinating the various energies toward a common goal.

If solid guarantees are sought for co-operation among peoples, as indeed in every form of human co-operation, in the private or public sphere, in circumscribed sectors as well as on an international plane, only values of a spiritual order turn out to be effective. They alone bring about a triumph over the vicissitudes which fortuitous circumstances or, more often, human wickedness are not slow in provoking. Both among nations and among individuals nothing lasts without a true friendship.[1]

Our grave apprehensions with regard to Europe are motivated by the incessant disillusionments which for many years have wrecked the sincere desire for peace and relaxation of tension cherished by the European peoples, largely because of a materialistic approach to the problem of peace. We are thinking especially of those who consider the question of peace as being of a technical nature and view the life of individuals and of nations under a combined technical-economic aspect. This materialistic concept of life threatens to become the rule of conduct of the busy agents of peace and the recipe of their pacifist policy. They believe that the secret of the solution would be to give material prosperity to all peoples through constant increase in the productivity of labor and the standard of living, just as, a hundred years ago, another similar formula won the absolute confidence of statesmen: Free trade means eternal peace.

But no sort of materialism has ever been a satisfactory means for the establishment of peace, since peace is above all an attitude of the spirit and only on a secondary level is it a harmonious equilibrium of external forces. It is, then, an error in principle to entrust peace to modern materialism, which corrupts man at the roots and suffocates his personal and spiritual life. Besides, experience leads to the same state of mistrust in that it demonstrates that, even in our time, when the costly potential of technical and economic forces is distributed more or less equally between both sides, it imposes a reciprocal fear. The resultant peace therefore would be one based solely on fear, not the peace which means certainty of the future. It is necessary to repeat this untiringly and to persuade those among the people who allow themselves to be easily deceived by the mirage that peace consists in an abundance of wealth, whereas a stable peace is above all a problem of spiritual unity and moral inclinations.[2]

[1] Address to the Representatives of the "European College," 1953
[2] Allocution to the Sacred College, December 24, 1953

THE CHURCH AND HISTORY

ALTHOUGH HISTORY is an ancient science, it was only during the last few centuries and with the development of historical criticism that it reached its present perfection. Thanks to the scrupulousness of its methods and the indefatigable zeal of its specialists, historians can congratulate themselves on being able to know the past in greater detail and to judge it more accurately than any of their predecessors.

History is one of the sciences which have a close relationship to the Catholic Church. The Catholic Church is herself a historical fact; like a mighty range of mountains, she is present throughout the history of the last two thousand years; whatever the attitude taken toward her, it is, therefore, impossible to avoid her. The judgments passed on her are extremely varied; they range from total acceptance to the most determined rejection. But whatever the final verdict of the historian may be, whose task it is to see and to expound—as far as possible just as they happened—facts, events, and circumstances, the Church expects him in any case to be aware of the historical consciousness she has of herself, that is, of the way in which she considers herself as a historical fact and in which she considers her relationship to human history.

We should like to say a word about this consciousness the Church has of herself, mentioning facts, circumstances, and conceptions which seem to Us to take on a more fundamental significance.

God as Lord of History

To begin with, We should like to refute an objection which arises, as it were, at once. Christianity, it used to be and still is said, necessarily takes up a hostile position in relation to history because it sees in it a manifestation of evil and sin; Catholicism and historicism are antithetical concepts. Let us first of all notice that the objection thus formulated considers history and historicism as equivalent concepts. In this, it is wrong. The term "historicism" designates a philosophical system, one which sees in all spiritual reality, in knowledge of the truth, in religion, morality, and law, nothing but change and evolution, and consequently rejects all that is permanent, eternally valid, and absolute. Such a system is certainly irreconcilable with the Catholic conception of the world and, in general, with any religion which recognizes a personal God.

The Catholic Church knows that all events occur according to the will or the permission of divine Providence and that God reaches His objectives in history. As the great St. Augustine said with classical brevity: what God intends "*hoc fit, hoc agitur; etsi paulatim peragitur, indesinenter agitur*—that happens, that is done; and though it is done only step by step, it still is being done incessantly." God is really the Lord of history.

This statement in itself already answers the objections mentioned. Between Christianity and history there is no opposition in the sense that history is only an emanation or manifestation of evil. The Catholic Church has never taught such a doctrine. From the days of the early Christians, from the Patristic period, but especially at the time of the spiritual conflict with Protestantism and Jansenism, she has always ranged herself on the side of nature; she says of the latter that it has not been corrupted by sin, that it has remained inwardly intact, even in fallen man, that pre-Christian man and the non-Christian could and can perform good, virtuous actions, not to mention the fact that the whole of humanity, including pre-Christian humanity, is under the influence of Christ's grace.

The Church readily recognizes the good and the great in the pre-Christian era as well as outside Christianity. . . .

The Church as Historical Fact

Let Us now speak about the Church herself as a historical fact: at the same time as she fully affirms her divine origin and her supernatural character, the Church is conscious of having entered humanity as a historical fact. Her divine Founder, Jesus Christ, is a historical personality. His life, death, and resurrection are historical facts. It sometimes happens that even those who deny Christ's divinity admit His resurrection, because it is, in their opinion, too well vouched for historically; anybody wanting to deny it would have to annul the whole of ancient history, for none of its facts is better proved than that of the resurrection of Christ. The mission and the development of the Church are historical facts.

The Excavations under St. Peter's Basilica

Here in Rome, St. Peter and St. Paul can be cited: Paul belongs, even from a purely historical point of view, to the most remarkable figures in humanity. As for the Apostle Peter and his position in the Church of Christ, although proof of his stay and death in Rome is not of essential importance for the Catholic faith, We nevertheless caused the well-known excavations to be carried out under the Basilica. The method is approved by critics; the result —the discovery of Peter's tomb under the dome, exactly under the present papal altar—was recognized by the great majority of critics, and even the most extreme skeptics were impressed by what the excavations revealed.

The Mission of the Church

The origins of Christianity and of the Catholic Church are historical facts, proved and determined in time and place. Of that the Church is quite conscious. She knows, too, that her mission, although belonging by its nature and aims to the religious and moral domain, situated in the beyond and in eternity, nevertheless penetrates right into the heart of human history. Always and everywhere, constantly adapting herself to the circumstances of time and place, she tries to form, according to Christ's law, persons, the single individual and, as far as possible, all individuals, thus reaching, also, the moral foundations of life in society. The aim of the Church is the naturally good man, penetrated, ennobled, and strengthened by truth and Christ's grace.

The Church wants to make men "firm in their inviolate integrity as images of God; men proud of their personal dignity and wholesome liberty; men rightly jealous of equality with their fellow men in all that concerns the very heart of human dignity; men solidly attached to their country and their traditions." That is the intention of the Church as We formulated it in Our address of February 20, 1946, on the occasion of the investment of the new Cardinals. We add: in the present century as in that which has passed, in which the problems of the family, society, the State, and the social order have acquired an ever-increasing and even capital importance, the Church has done everything possible to contribute to the solution of these questions and, let Us hope, with some success. The Church is convinced, however, that she cannot work more efficaciously than by continuing to form men in the way We have described.

To attain these aims, the Church does not act only as an ideological system. No doubt she is also defined as such, when the expression "Catholicism" is used, which is a term not fully adequate. She is much more than a mere ideological system; she is a reality, like visible nature, like the people, or the State. She is a living organism with her own finality and vital principle. Unchangeable in the constitution and structure which the divine Founder Himself gave to her, she has accepted and accepts the elements which she needs or considers useful for her development and her action: men and human institutions, philosophical and cultural inspirations, political forces and social ideas or institutions, principles and activities. Therefore, the Church, spreading throughout the whole world, underwent various changes in the course of the centuries; in her essence, however, she always remained identical, because the multitude of elements she received from the beginning were subjected to the same basic faith. The Church could be astoundingly broad and at the same time inflexibly severe. If we consider the whole of her history, we see that she was both, with an unfailing instinct as to what suited different peoples and the whole of humanity. Hence she has rejected all movements which are too naturalistic, contaminated to some extent by the spirit of moral license, but also gnostic tendencies, falsely spiritualistic and puritan. The history of canon law, up to the code which is now in force, gives a large number of significant proofs. Take, for example, the ecclesiastical legislation on marriage and the recent pontifical declarations about questions of conjugal partnership and the family in all their aspects: you will find there an example, among many others, of the way in which the Church thinks and works.

Church and State

By virtue of a similar principle, she has regularly intervened in the field of public life, to guarantee a fair balance between duty and obligation on the one hand, and right and freedom on the other. Political authority has never disposed of a more trustworthy advocate than the Catholic Church; for the Church founds the authority of the State on the will of the Creator, on God's commandment. Certainly, because she attributes a religious value to public authority, the Church has opposed arbitrariness in the State, and tyranny in all its forms.

And now We come to two problems which deserve special attention: the relations between Church and State, between Church and culture.

In the pre-Christian period, the public authority, the State, was competent both in profane matters and in the field of religion. The Catholic Church is conscious that her divine Founder transmitted to her the field of religion, the religious and moral guidance of men in its entirety, independently of the power of the State. Since then, there exists a history of relations between the Church and the State, and this history has greatly interested inquirers.

Leo XIII has summed up, as it were, in a formula, the very nature of these relations, in the luminous presentation of his Encyclicals *Diuturnum illud, Immortale Dei* (1881) and *Sapientiae christianae* (1890): the two powers, Church as well as State, are both sovereign. Their nature, like the ends they pursue, fixes the limits within which they rule "*iure proprio*—in their own right." Like the State, the Church, too, possesses sovereign rights over everything she needs to achieve her aim, even over material means. "*Quidquid igitur est in rebus humanis quoquo modo sacrum, quidquid ad salutem animarum cultumve Dei pertinet, sive tale illud sit natura sua, sive rursus tale intelligatur propter causam ad quam refertur, id est omne in potestate arbitrioque Ecclesiae*—

Everything, therefore, which in human things is in any way sacred, anything pertaining to the salvation of souls and the worship of God, be it such by its nature or be it understood as such for the connection with its end—all this falls within the power and authority of the Church." The State and the Church are independent powers, but they must not therefore ignore each other, still less combat each other; it conforms far more with nature and the divine will that they should collaborate in mutual understanding, since their activity is applied to the same subject—the Catholic citizen. Of course, cases of conflict are possible: when State laws attack divine law, the Church is morally obliged to oppose them.

It can be said that, with the exception of a very few centuries—for the first millennium as well as for the last four centuries—the formula of Leo XIII reflects more or less explicitly the consciousness of the Church; and even during the intermediate period, there were representatives of the doctrine of the Church, perhaps even a majority, who shared the same opinion.

If Church and State knew hours or years of struggle, there were, from Constantine the Great up to contemporary and even recent times, periods of quiet, often long ones, during which the two powers collaborated in complete harmony in the education of men. The Church does not hide the fact that on principle she considers this collaboration as normal, and that she takes as her ideal the unity of the people in the true religion and unanimity of action between herself and the State. But it is known, too, that for some time now events have been moving rather in the opposite direction, that is, toward multiplicity of religious denominations and conceptions of life within the same national community—in which Catholics make up a more or less strong minority. It may be interesting and even surprising for the historian to meet in the United States of America an example, among others, of the way in which the Church succeeds in taking root and flourishing in the most disparate situations.

In the history of relations between Church and State, the Concordats play, as is known, an important part. What We said in this connection in a discourse on December 6, 1953, holds true for historical appreciation. In the Concordats, We said, the Church seeks juridical security and the independence necessary for her mission. "It is possible," We added, "that Church and State may proclaim in a Concordat their common religious conviction; but it can also happen that the Concordat has the aim, among others, of preventing quarrels about questions of principle, and of eliminating, from the outset, possible occasions for conflict. When the Church has put her signature to a Concordat, it is valid in all its contents. But the underlying meaning may involve fine distinctions of which both contracting parties are aware; it may signify express approval, but it may mean also mere tolerance, according to principles which serve as standards for the coexistence of the Church and her faithful with powers and men of another faith."

The Church and culture: the Catholic Church has exercised a powerful, even decisive, influence on the cultural development of the last two thousand years. But she is convinced that the source of this influence lies in the spiritual element which characterizes herself, her religious and moral life, to the extent that if she were to weaken, her cultural sway, too, for example in the field of order and social peace, would suffer.

The Church and the Western World

Several historians, or perhaps more exactly, historical philosophers, maintain that the place of Christianity, and therefore of the Catholic Church, is in the Western world. . . . The Church is conscious of having received her mission and task for all time to come and for all men, and consequently of being tied to no determined culture. St. Augustine, in the past, was deeply moved when the conquest of Rome by Alaric shook the Roman Empire with the first blow that presaged its ruin; but he had not thought that it would last forever. In the *City of God* he drew a clear distinction between the existence of the Church and the destiny of the Roman Empire. In this his thought was Catholic.

What is called the West or the Western world has undergone profound modifications since the Middle Ages: the religious schism of the sixteenth century, rationalism and liberalism leading to the nineteenth-century State, to its policy of force and its secularized civilization. It was, therefore, inevitable that the relations of the Catholic Church with the West should undergo a change. But the culture of the Middle Ages itself cannot be characterized as

Catholic culture; it, too, although intimately linked to the Church, drew its elements from different sources. Even the religious unity characteristic of the Middle Ages is not specific to it; it was already a typical note of Christian antiquity in the Eastern and Western Roman Empire, from Constantine the Great to Charlemagne.

The Catholic Church does not identify herself with any culture; her essence prevents this. She is, however, ready to maintain contacts with all cultures. She recognizes and leaves untouched what, in them, is not contrary to nature. But into each of them, she introduces the truth and grace of Jesus Christ and thus confers a deep similarity to them all. This, in fact, is her most efficacious contribution to universal peace.

The whole world today is still undergoing the action of another element, which it is predicted will cause the history of humanity (in its profane aspect) considerable upheaval: modern science and technology, which Europe, or, rather, the Western countries, have created during these last centuries; however, people who assimilate them must also consent to the dangers they entail *"für das Menschsein*—for human existence," as the philosopher Jaspers says. In fact, science and technology are in process of becoming the common good of humanity. What causes anxiety are not only the dangers with which they threaten the human way of life, but the realization that they prove incapable of damming the spiritual alienation which separates races and continents; in fact, the latter seems to be increasing. If we desire to avoid catastrophe, it will, therefore, be necessary to set up, at the same time, on a higher plane, powerful religious and moral forces of unification and thus ensure the common welfare of humanity. The Catholic Church is conscious of possessing these forces and believes she is no longer obliged to provide historical proof. Moreover, she does not take up a position of hostility toward modern science and technology, but acts rather as a counterweight and a factor of equilibrium. Therefore, in a period in which science and technology are triumphant, she will be able to fulfill her task just as well as she did during the past centuries.[1]

[1] Address to the International Congress of Historical Sciences, September 7, 1955

GLOSSARY

Agnosticism	Philosophical doctrine that considers the existence and the nature of God as unknowable
Allocution	Solemn address delivered by the Pope, dealing with matters of faith or grave immediate problems
Charismatic gifts	Supernatural gifts, as, for instance, the healing of the sick
Encyclical	Circular letter issued by the Pope
Eugenics	Science dealing with methods for influencing hereditary strains
Electron	A particle of the atom spinning around the nucleus of the atom
Genetics	The study of the biological development of living organisms, with special emphasis on hereditary factors
Hedonism	Philosophical teaching which considers pleasure the foremost goal of man
Hierarchy	The authority given by Christ to the Apostles for governing the Church; also, the organized body of the clergy in its successive orders and grades
Jansenism	A theological system laid down by Bishop Cornelius Jansen (1585–1638) and involving the doctrine of grace. Jansen's teachings were repudiated by the Church.
Macrocosm and Microcosm	Macrocosm designates the great world as universe; microcosm designates man as "the small world" which reflects the large world
Manichaeism	Heresy named for its founder, the Persian Mani; he envisaged two conflicting worlds as the origin of things, one of light and one of darkness, from the mingling of which the creation of the world originated

Monism	Derived from the Greek, *monos,* "single, unique," monism is the name for those theories that deny any principle of duality, as, for instance, body and soul, spirit and matter, etc.
Neutron	A particle of the atom of nearly the same mass as the proton, but not electrically charged
Paleontology	The study of extinct animals and plants known to us through fossilized specimens
Phylogenesis	The evolution of a race or of a related group of organisms as contrasted to the development of individual organisms
Positivism	A system of philosophy that admits only positive facts and phenomena observable by the senses
Proton	A unit particle of matter belonging to the atom
Rationalism	A system of philosophy that sets intellect and reason above feeling and will

INDEX

Photo Sources

Frontispiece, Karsh, Ottawa; facing pages 28, 29 bottom, 95, 127 top, 222, 223, 286, 287, 318 Felici, Rome; 29 top, 126 top, 127 bottom, 190, 191 Foto Attualità Giordani, Rome; 94 Mondadori Press, Milano; 319 Herbert Kiesler, Rome; 126 bottom Associated Press

D1034606

Robert Louis Stevenson, Aet. 43.
From a photograph by Falk, of Sydney.

LETTERS AND MISCELLANIES OF ROBERT LOUIS STEVENSON

LETTERS TO HIS FAMILY AND FRIENDS ❦

SELECTED AND EDITED WITH NOTES AND INTRODUCTION BY SIDNEY COLVIN ❦ ❦ ❦ ❦

II

PUBLISHED IN ❦
NEW YORK BY
CHARLES SCRIBNER'S
SONS . ❦ ❦ 1909 ❦

THE SCRIBNER PRESS
CS

CONTENTS

VIII

LIFE AT BOURNEMOUTH (*Continued*)

IX

THE UNITED STATES AGAIN

WINTER IN THE ADIRONDACKS

CONTENTS

X

PACIFIC VOYAGES

XI

LIFE IN SAMOA

XII

LIFE IN SAMOA (*Continued*)

CONTENTS

LIST OF ILLUSTRATIONS

VIII

LIFE AT BOURNEMOUTH

Continued

(January, 1886–July, 1887)

VIII

LIFE AT BOURNEMOUTH

Continued

(JANUARY, 1886–JULY, 1887)

THE following section gives the pith of the writer's correspondence from the date of the publication of *Jekyll and Hyde* in January, 1886, down to that of his father's death in May, 1887. The period was one of trying ill-health and of meagre production, but at the same time of fast-growing literary reputation and popularity. *Jekyll and Hyde*, after threatening for the first week or two to fall flat, in no long time caught the attention of all classes of readers, was quoted from a hundred pulpits, and made the writer's name familiar to multitudes both in England and America whom it had never reached before. A success scarcely inferior, though of another kind, was made a few months afterwards by *Kidnapped*, which Stevenson finished in the spring, and which was published in the early summer. After completing this task in March, he was able to do little work during the remainder of the year, except in preparing materials for the *Life of Fleeming Jenkin*, and in writing occasional verses which helped to make up the collection published in the following year under the title *Underwoods.*

For some weeks of April he was much taken up with a scheme which had nothing to do with literature, and which the few friends to whom he confided it regarded as wildly Quixotic and unwise. In these years he had, as we have seen, taken deeply to heart both what he thought the guilty remissness of Government action in the matter of the Soudan garrisons and of Gordon, and the tameness of acquiescence with which the national conscience appeared to take the results. He had been not less disturbed at the failure, hitherto, of successive administrations to assert the reign of law in Ireland. He was no blind partisan of the English cause in that country, and had even written of the hereditary hatred of Irish for English as a sentiment justified by the facts of history. But he held strongly that private warfare, the use of dynamite and the knife, with the whole system of agrarian vengeances and the persecution of the weak, were means which no end could justify; and that redress of grievances, whatever form it might ultimately take, must be preceded by the re-establishment of law. In *More New Arabian Nights*, published the year before, he had endeavoured "to make dynamite ridiculous if he could not make it horrible," and to the old elements of fantastic invention, and humorously solemn realism in the unreal, had added the new element of a witty and scornful criminal psychology. A case that now appealed to him with especial force was that of the cruel persecution kept up against the widow and daughters of the murdered man Curtin. He determined that if no one else would take up the duty of resisting such persecution without regard to consequences, he would take it up himself, in the hope of more effectually rousing the public conscience to the evils of the time. His plan was to go with his family, occupy and live upon the derelict farm, and let happen what would. This, as the letters referring to the matter plainly show, was no irresponsible dream or whim, but a purpose conceived in absolute and sober earnest. His wife and household were prepared to follow, though under protest, had he persisted; as it seemed for some weeks that he certainly would, until at last the arguments of his friends persuaded him to give up his purpose. The one consideration, I believe, which in the end prevailed with him was that of his father's declining health. But to the last, I think, he was never well satisfied that in giving way he had not been a coward, preferring fireside ease and comfort to the calls of a public duty. In the early autumn of the same year, 1886, he took a longer and more successful excursion from home than usual, staying without break-down for two or three weeks at the Monument, as he always called my house at the British Museum, and seeing something of kindred spirits among his elders, such as Mr. Robert Browning, Mr. J. R. Lowell, the painters Burne-Jones and W. B. Richmond, and others who had hitherto delighted in his work and now learned to delight no less in his society.

Thence he went with Mr. Henley for a short trip to Paris, chiefly in order to see the sculptor Rodin and his old friends Mr. and Mrs. W. H. Low. From this trip he returned none the worse, but during all the later autumn and winter at Bournemouth was again hampered in his work by renewed and prolonged attacks of illness. A further cause of trouble was the distressing failure of his father's health and spirits, attended by symptoms which plainly indicated the beginning of the end. After spending a part of the winter at Bournemouth and a part at Torquay, both parents returned to Edinburgh in April, 1887; and within a few weeks after their arrival Stevenson was summoned north to his father's death-bed.

To Mrs. de Mattos

1886
ÆT. 36

With this cousin the writer had always been on terms of close affection, and he now dedicated to her *The Strange Case of Dr. Jekyll and Mr. Hyde.* In the dedication as published only the second verse stands.

[Skerryvore, Bournemouth], *January 1st, 1886.*

DEAREST KATHARINE,—Here, on a very little book and accompanied with lame verses, I have put your name. Our kindness is now getting well on in years; it must be nearly of age; and it gets more valuable to me with every time I see you. It is not possible to express any sentiment, and it is not necessary to try, at least between us. You know very well that I love you dearly, and that I always will. I only wish the verses were better, but at least you like the story; and it is sent to you by the one that loves you—Jekyll, and not Hyde. R. L. S.

Ave!

Bells upon the city are ringing in the night;
High above the gardens are the houses full of light;
On the heathy Pentlands is the curlew flying free;
And the broom is blowing bonnie in the north countrie.

We cannae break the bonds that God decreed to bind,
Still we'll be the children of the heather and the wind;
Far away from home, O, it's still for you and me
That the broom is blowing bonnie in the north countrie!

R. L. S.

To Alison Cunningham

[Skerryvore, Bournemouth], *Jan. 1st, 1886.*

MY DEAR KINNICUM,—I am a very bad dog, but not for the first time. Your book, which is very interesting, came duly; and I immediately got a very bad cold indeed, and have been fit for nothing whatever. I am a bit better now, and aye on the mend; so I write to tell you, I thought of you on New Year's Day; though, I own, it would have been more decent if I had thought in time for you to get my letter then. Well, what can't be cured must be endured, Mr. Lawrie; and you must be content with what I give. If I wrote all the letters I ought to write, and at the proper time, I should be very good and very happy; but I doubt if I should do anything else.

I suppose you will be in town for the New Year; and I hope your health is pretty good. What you want

1886 ÆT. 36

is diet; but it is as much use to tell you that as it is to tell my father. And I quite admit a diet is a beastly thing. I doubt, however. if it be as bad as not being allowed to speak, which I have tried fully, and do not like. When, at the same time, I was not allowed to read, it passed a joke. But these are troubles of the past, and on this day, at least, it is proper to suppose they won't return. But we are not put here to enjoy ourselves: it was not God's purpose; and I am prepared to argue, it is not our sincere wish. As for our deserts, the less said of them the better, for somebody might hear, and nobody cares to be laughed at. A good man is a very noble thing to see. but not to himself; what he seems to God is, fortunately, not our business; that is the domain of faith; and whether on the first of January or the thirty-first of December, faith is a good word to end on.

My dear Cummy. many happy returns to you and my best love.—The worst correspondent in the world,

ROBERT LOUIS STEVENSON.

TO MR. AND MRS. THOMAS STEVENSON

[SKERRYVORE, BOURNEMOUTH], *January 1st, 1886.*

MY DEAR PEOPLE,—Many happy returns of the day to you all; I am fairly well and in good spirits; and much and hopefully occupied with dear Jenkin's life. The inquiry in every detail, every letter that I read, makes me think of him more nobly. I cannot imagine how I got his friendship; I did not deserve it. I believe the notice will be interesting and useful.

My father's last letter, owing to the use of a quill pen

and the neglect of blotting-paper, was hopelessly illegible. Every one tried, and every one failed to decipher an important word on which the interest of one whole clause (and the letter consisted of two) depended.

I find I can make little more of this; but I'll spare the blots.—Dear people, ever your loving son, R. L. S.

I will try again, being a giant refreshed by the house being empty. The presence of people is the great obstacle to letter-writing. I deny that letters should contain news (I mean mine; those of other people should). But mine should contain appropriate sentiments and humorous nonsense, or nonsense without the humour. When the house is empty, the mind is seized with a desire—no, that is too strong—a willingness to pour forth unmitigated rot, which constitutes (in me) the true spirit of correspondence. When I have no remarks to offer (and nobody to offer them to), my pen flies, and you see the remarkable consequence of a page literally covered with words and genuinely devoid of sense. I can always do that, if quite alone, and I like doing it; but I have yet to learn that it is beloved by correspondents. The deuce of it is, that there is no end possible but the end of the paper; and as there is very little left of that—if I cannot stop writing—suppose you give up reading. It would all come to the same thing; and I think we should all be happier. . . .

To W. H. Low

In the following letter R. L. S. accepts the dedication of Mr. Low's illustrated edition of Keats's *Lamia*, and sends him in return the newly

1886
ÆT. 36

published *Jekyll and Hyde*, and a set of verses afterwards printed in the *Century Magazine* and *Underwoods*, and engraved by Mr. St. Gaudens on his medallion portrait of the author. The terms of the *Lamia* dedication are as follows: "In testimony of loyal friendship and of a common faith in doubtful tales from Faery-Land, I dedicate to Robert Louis Stevenson my work in this book." The Latin legend inscribed above the design runs: "Neque est ullum certius amicitiæ vinculum quam consensus et societas consiliorum et voluntatum."

[SKERRYVORE, BOURNEMOUTH], *Jan. 2nd, 1886.*

MY DEAR LOW,—*Lamia* has come, and I do not know how to thank you, not only for the beautiful art of the designs, but for the handsome and apt words of the dedication. My favourite is "Bathes unseen," which is a masterpiece; and the next, "Into the green recessed woods," is perhaps more remarkable, though it does not take my fancy so imperiously. The night scene at Corinth pleases me also. The second part offers fewer opportunities. I own I should like to see both *Isabella* and the *Eve* thus illustrated; and then there 's *Hyperion* —O, yes, and *Endymion!* I should like to see the lot: beautiful pictures dance before me by hundreds: I believe *Endymion* would suit you best. It also is in faery-land; and I see a hundred opportunities, cloudy and flowery glories, things as delicate as the cobweb in the bush; actions, not in themselves of any mighty purport, but made for the pencil: the feast of Pan, Peona's isle, the "slabbed margin of a well," the chase of the butterfly, the nymph, Glaucus, Cybele, Sleep on his couch, a farrago of unconnected beauties. But I divagate; and all this sits in the bosom of the publisher.

What is more important, I accept the terms of the

dedication with a frank heart, and the terms of your Latin legend fairly. The sight of your pictures has once more awakened me to my right mind; something may come of it; yet one more bold push to get free of this prisonyard of the abominably ugly, where I take my daily exercise with my contemporaries. I do not know, I have a feeling in my bones, a sentiment which may take on the forms of imagination, or may not. If it does, I shall owe it to you; and the thing will thus descend from Keats even if on the wrong side of the blanket. If it can be done in prose — that is the puzzle — I divagate again. Thank you again: you can draw and yet you do not love the ugly: what are you doing in this age? Flee, while it is yet time; they will have your four limbs pinned upon a stable door to scare witches. The ugly, my unhappy friend, is *de rigueur:* it is the only wear! What a chance you threw away with the serpent! Why had Apollonius no pimples? Heavens, my dear Low, you do not know your business. . . .

I send you herewith a Gothic gnome for your Greek nymph; but the gnome is interesting, I think, and he came out of a deep mine, where he guards the fountain of tears. It is not always the time to rejoice.—Yours ever,
R. L. S.

The gnome's name is *Jekyll & Hyde;* I believe you will find he is likewise quite willing to answer to the name of Low or Stevenson.

Same day.— I have copied out on the other sheet some bad verses, which somehow your picture sug-

1886 ÆT. 36

gested; as a kind of image of things that I pursue and cannot reach, and that you seem — no, not to have reached — but to have come a thought nearer to than I. This is the life we have chosen: well, the choice was mad, but I should make it again.

What occurs to me is this: perhaps they might be printed in (say) the *Century* for the sake of my name; and if that were possible, they might advertise your book. It might be headed as sent in acknowledgment of your *Lamia*. Or perhaps it might be introduced by the phrases I have marked above. I dare say they would stick it in: I want no payment, being well paid by *Lamia*. If they are not, keep them to yourself.

To Will H. Low

Damned bad lines in return for a beautiful book.

Youth now flees on feathered foot.
Faint and fainter sounds the flute ;
Rarer songs of Gods.
And still,
Somewhere on the sunny hill,
Or along the winding stream,
Through the willows, flits a dream;
Flits, but shows a smiling face,
Flees, but with so quaint a grace,
None can choose to stay at home,
All must follow — all must roam.

This is unborn beauty: she
Now in air floats high and free,

Takes the sun, and breaks the blue;—
Late, with stooping pinion flew
Raking hedgerow trees, and wet
Her wing in silver streams, and set
Shining foot on temple roof.
Now again she flies aloof,
Coasting mountain clouds, and kissed
By the evening's amethyst.

In wet wood and miry lane
Still we pound and pant in vain;
Still with earthy foot we chase
Waning pinion, fainting face;
Still, with grey hair, we stumble on
Till—behold!—the vision gone!

Where has fleeting beauty led?
To the doorway of the dead!
qy. omit? [Life is gone, but life was gay:
We have come the primrose way!][1]

R. L. S.

To Edmund Gosse

SKERRYVORE, BOURNEMOUTH, *Jan. 2nd, 1886.*

MY DEAR GOSSE,—Thank you for your letter, so interesting to my vanity. There is a review in the *St. James's*, which, as it seems to hold somewhat of your opinions, and is besides written with a pen and not a poker, we think may possibly be yours. The *Prince*[2]

[1] In *Underwoods* the lines thus queried stand with the change:
"Life is over; life was gay."

[2] *Prince Otto.*

1886
ÆT. 36

has done fairly well in spite of the reviews, which have been bad: he was, as you doubtless saw, well slated in the *Saturday;* one paper received it as a child's story; another (picture my agony) described it as a "Gilbert comedy." It was amusing to see the race between me and Justin M'Carthy: the Milesian has won by a length.

That is the hard part of literature. You aim high, and you take longer over your work, and it will not be so successful as if you had aimed low and rushed it. What the public likes is work (of any kind) a little loosely executed; so long as it is a little wordy, a little slack, a little dim and knotless, the dear public likes it; it should (if possible) be a little dull into the bargain. I know that good work sometimes hits; but, with my hand on my heart, I think it is by an accident. And I know also that good work must succeed at last; but that is not the doing of the public; they are only shamed into silence or affectation. I do not write for the public; I do write for money, a nobler deity; and most of all for myself, not perhaps any more noble, but both more intelligent and nearer home.

Let us tell each other sad stories of the bestiality of the beast whom we feed. What he likes is the newspaper; and to me the press is the mouth of a sewer, where lying is professed as from an university chair, and everything prurient, and ignoble, and essentially dull, finds its abode and pulpit. I do not like mankind; but men, and not all of these — and fewer women. As for respecting the race, and, above all, that fatuous rabble of burgesses called "the public," God save me from such irreligion! — that way lies disgrace and dishonour.

There must be something wrong in me, or I would not be popular.

This is perhaps a trifle stronger than my sedate and permanent opinion. Not much, I think. As for the art that we practise, I have never been able to see why its professors should be respected. They chose the primrose path; when they found it was not all primroses, but some of it brambly, and much of it uphill, they began to think and to speak of themselves as holy martyrs. But a man is never martyred in any honest sense in the pursuit of his pleasure; and *delirium tremens* has more of the honour of the cross. We were full of the pride of life, and chose, like prostitutes, to live by a pleasure. We should be paid if we give the pleasure we pretend to give; but why should we be honoured?

I hope some day you and Mrs. Gosse will come for a Sunday; but we must wait till I am able to see people. I am very full of Jenkin's life; it is painful, yet very pleasant, to dig into the past of a dead friend, and find him, at every spadeful, shine brighter. I own, as I read, I wonder more and more why he should have taken me to be a friend. He had many and obvious faults upon the face of him; the heart was pure gold. I feel it little pain to have lost him, for it is a loss in which I cannot believe; I take it, against reason, for an absence; if not to-day, then to-morrow, I still fancy I shall see him in the door; and then, now when I know him better, how glad a meeting! Yes, if I could believe in the immortality business, the world would indeed be too good to be true; but we were put here to do what service we can, for honour and not for hire: the sods

1886
ÆT. 36

cover us, and the worm that never dies, the conscience, sleeps well at last; these are the wages, besides what we receive so lavishly day by day; and they are enough for a man who knows his own frailty and sees all things in the proportion of reality. The soul of piety was killed long ago by that idea of reward. Nor is happiness, whether eternal or temporal, the reward that mankind seeks. Happinesses are but his wayside campings; his soul is in the journey; he was born for the struggle, and only tastes his life in effort and on the condition that he is opposed. How, then, is such a creature, so fiery, so pugnacious, so made up of discontent and aspiration, and such noble and uneasy passions—how can he be rewarded but by rest? I would not say it aloud; for man's cherished belief is that he loves that happiness which he continually spurns and passes by; and this belief in some ulterior happiness exactly fits him. He does not require to stop and taste it; he can be about the rugged and bitter business where his heart lies; and yet he can tell himself this fairy tale of an eternal tea-party, and enjoy the notion that he is both himself and something else; and that his friends will yet meet him, all ironed out and emasculate, and still be lovable,—as if love did not live in the faults of the beloved only, and draw its breath in an unbroken round of forgiveness! But the truth is, we must fight until we die; and when we die there can be no quiet for mankind but complete resumption into—what?—God, let us say—when all these desperate tricks will lie spellbound at last.

Here came my dinner and cut this sermon short—*excusez*.

R. L. S.

SKERRYVORE.

To James Payn

The late Mrs. Buckle, a daughter of Mr. James Payn married to the editor of the *Times*, had laughingly remonstrated, through her father, on recognising some features of her own house in Queen Square, Bloomsbury, in the description of that tenanted by the fair Cuban in the section of Stevenson's *Dynamiter* which tells the story of the Brown Box.

Skerryvore, Bournemouth, *Jan. 2nd, 1886.*

DEAR JAMES PAYN,—Your very kind letter came very welcome; and still more welcome the news that you see ——'s tale. I will now tell you (and it was very good and very wise of me not to tell it before) that he is one of the most unlucky men I know, having put all his money into a pharmacy at Hyères, when the cholera (certainly not his fault) swept away his customers in a body. Thus you can imagine the pleasure I have to announce to him a spark of hope, for he sits to-day in his pharmacy, doing nothing and taking nothing, and watching his debts inexorably mount up.

To pass to other matters: your hand, you are perhaps aware, is not one of those that can be read running; and the name of your daughter remains for me undecipherable. I call her, then, your daughter—and a very good name too—and I beg to explain how it came about that I took her house. The hospital was a point in my tale; but there is a house on each side. Now the true house is the one before the hospital: is that No. 11? If not, what do you complain of? If it is, how can I help what is true? Everything in *The Dynamiter* is not true; but the story of the Brown Box is, in almost every particular; I lay my hand on my heart and swear

1886 ÆT. 36

to it. It took place in that house in 1884; and if your daughter was in that house at the time, all I can say is she must have kept very bad society.

But I see you coming. Perhaps your daughter's house has not a balcony at the back? I cannot answer for that; I only know that side of Queen Square from the pavement and the back windows of Brunswick Row. Thence I saw plenty of balconies (terraces rather); and if there is none to the particular house in question, it must have been so arranged to spite me.

I now come to the conclusion of this matter. I address three questions to your daughter:—

1st. Has her house the proper terrace?
2nd. Is it on the proper side of the hospital?
3rd. Was she there in the summer of 1884?

You see, I begin to fear that Mrs. Desborough may have deceived me on some trifling points, for she is not a lady of peddling exactitude. If this should prove to be so, I will give your daughter a proper certificate, and her house property will return to its original value.

Can man say more?—Yours very truly,

ROBERT LOUIS STEVENSON.

I saw the other day that the Eternal had plagiarised from *Lost Sir Massingberd:* good again, sir! I wish he would plagiarise the death of Zero.

To W. H. Low

The late Sir Percy and Lady Shelley had in these days attached themselves warmly to R. L. S., and saw in his ways and character a living image of those of the poet, Sir Percy's father, as they imagined him.

SKERRYVORE, BOURNEMOUTH,
Jan. Somethingorother-th, 1886.

MY DEAR LOW,—I send you two photographs: they are both done by Sir Percy Shelley, the poet's son, which may interest. The sitting down one is, I think, the best; but if they choose that, see that the little reflected light on the nose does not give me a turn-up; that would be tragic. Don't forget "Baronet" to Sir Percy's name.

We all think a heap of your book; and I am well pleased with my dedication.—Yours ever,

R. L. STEVENSON.

P. S.—Apropos of the odd controversy about Shelley's nose: I have before me four photographs of myself, done by Shelley's son: my nose is hooked, not like the eagle, indeed, but like the accipitrine family in man: well, out of these four, only one marks the bend, one makes it straight, and one suggests a turn-up. This throws a flood of light on calumnious man—and the scandal-mongering sun. For personally I cling to my curve. To continue the Shelley controversy: I have a look of him, all his sisters had noses like mine; Sir Percy has a marked hook; all the family had high cheek-bones like mine; what doubt, then, but that this turn-up (of which Jeaffreson accuses the poet, along with much other *fatras*) is the result of some accident similar to what has happened in my photographs by his son?

R. L. S.

TO THOMAS STEVENSON

[SKERRYVORE, BOURNEMOUTH, *January 25, 1886.*]

MY DEAR FATHER,—Many thanks for a letter quite like yourself. I quite agree with you, and had already planned

1886
ÆT. 36

a scene of religion in *Balfour;* the Society for the Propagation of Christian Knowledge furnishes me with a catechist whom I shall try to make the man. I have another catechist, the blind, pistol-carrying highway robber, whom I have transferred from the Long Island to Mull. I find it a most picturesque period, and wonder Scott let it escape. The *Covenant* is lost on one of the Tarrans, and David is cast on Earraid, where (being from inland) he is nearly starved before he finds out the island is tidal; then he crosses Mull to Toronsay, meeting the blind catechist by the way; then crosses Morven from Kinlochaline to Kingairloch, where he stays the night with the good catechist; that is where I am; next day he is to be put ashore in Appin, and be present at Colin Campbell's death. To-day I rest, being a little run down. Strange how liable we are to brain fag in this scooty family! But as far as I have got, all but the last chapter, I think David is on his feet, and (to my mind) a far better story and far sounder at heart than *Treasure Island.*

I have no earthly news, living entirely in my story, and only coming out of it to play patience. The Shelleys are gone; the Taylors kinder than can be imagined. The other day, Lady Taylor drove over and called on me; she is a delightful old lady, and great fun. I mentioned a story about the Duchess of Wellington which I had heard Sir Henry tell; and though he was very tired, he looked it up and copied it out for me in his own hand.—Your most affectionate son,

ROBERT LOUIS STEVENSON.

To C. W. Stoddard

Skerryvore, Bournemouth, *Feb. 13th, 1886.*

MY DEAR STODDARD,—I am a dreadful character; but, you see, I have at last taken pen in hand; how long I may hold it, God knows. This is already my sixth letter to-day, and I have many more waiting; and my wrist gives me a jog on the subject of scrivener's cramp, which is not encouraging.

I gather you were a little down in the jaw when you wrote your last. I am as usual pretty cheerful, but not very strong. I stay in the house all winter, which is base; but, as you continue to see, the pen goes from time to time, though neither fast enough nor constantly enough to please me.

My wife is at Bath with my father and mother, and the interval of widowery explains my writing. Another person writing for you when you have done work is a great enemy to correspondence. To-day I feel out of health, and sha'n't work; and hence this so much overdue reply.

I was re-reading some of your *South Sea Idyls* the other day: some of the chapters are very good indeed; some pages as good as they can be.

How does your class get along? If you like to touch on *Otto*, any day in a by-hour, you may tell them—as the author's last dying confession—that it is a strange example of the difficulty of being ideal in an age of realism; that the unpleasant giddy-mindedness, which spoils the book and often gives it a wanton air of unreality and juggling with air-bells, comes from unsteadiness of key; from the too great realism of some chapters and passages—some of which I have now spotted, others

I dare say I shall never spot — which disprepares the imagination for the cast of the remainder.

Any story can be made *true* in its own key; any story can be made *false* by the choice of a wrong key of detail or style: Otto is made to reel like a drunken — I was going to say man, but let us substitute cipher — by the variations of the key. Have you observed that the famous problem of realism and idealism is one purely of detail? Have you seen my "Note on Realism" in Cassell's *Magazine of Art;* and "Elements of Style" in the *Contemporary;* and "Romance" and "Humble Apology" in *Longmans'?* They are all in your line of business; let me know what you have not seen and I'll send 'em.

I am glad I brought the old house up to you. It was a pleasant old spot, and I remember you there, though still more dearly in your own strange den upon a hill in San Francisco; and one of the most San Francisco-y parts of San Francisco.

Good-bye, my dear fellow, and believe me your friend, ROBERT LOUIS STEVENSON.

TO J. A. SYMONDS

SKERRYVORE, BOURNEMOUTH [*Spring, 1886*].

MY DEAR SYMONDS, — If we have lost touch, it is (I think) only in a material sense; a question of letters, not hearts. You will find a warm welcome at Skerryvore from both the lightkeepers; and, indeed, we never tell ourselves one of our financial fairy tales, but a run to Davos is a prime feature. I am not changeable in friendship; and I think I can promise you you have a pair of trusty well-wishers and friends in Bournemouth:

whether they write or not is but a small thing; the flag may not be waved, but it is there.

Jekyll is a dreadful thing, I own; but the only thing I feel dreadful about is that damned old business of the war in the members. This time it came out; I hope it will stay in, in future.

Raskolnikoff[1] is easily the greatest book I have read in ten years; I am glad you took to it. Many find it dull: Henry James could not finish it: all I can say is, it nearly finished me. It was like having an illness. James did not care for it because the character of Raskolnikoff was not objective; and at that I divined a great gulf between us, and, on further reflection, the existence of a certain impotence in many minds of to-day, which prevents them from living *in* a book or a character, and keeps them standing afar off, spectators of a puppet show. To such I suppose the book may seem empty in the centre; to the others it is a room, a house of life, into which they themselves enter, and are tortured and purified. The Juge d'Instruction I thought a wonderful, weird, touching, ingenious creation: the drunken father, and Sonia, and the student friend, and the uncircumscribed, protoplasmic humanity of Raskolnikoff, all upon a level that filled me with wonder: the execution also, superb in places. Another has been translated — *Humiliés et Offensés.* It is even more incoherent than *Le Crime et le Châtiment*, but breathes much of the same lovely goodness, and has passages of power. Dostoieffsky is a devil of a swell, to be sure. Have you heard that he became a stout, imperialist conservative? It is interesting to know. To some-

[1] The name of the hero in Dostoieffsky's *Le Crime et le Châtiment.*

thing of that side, the balance leans with me also in view of the incoherency and incapacity of all. The old boyish idea of the march on Paradise being now out of season, and all plans and ideas that I hear debated being built on a superb indifference to the first principles of human character, a helpless desire to acquiesce in anything of which I know the worst assails me. Fundamental errors in human nature of two sorts stand on the skyline of all this modern world of aspirations. First, that it is happiness that men want; and second, that happiness consists of anything but an internal harmony. Men do not want, and I do not think they would accept, happiness; what they live for is rivalry, effort, success — the elements our friends wish to eliminate. And, on the other hand, happiness is a question of morality — or of immorality, there is no difference — and conviction. Gordon was happy in Khartoum, in his worst hours of danger and fatigue; Marat was happy, I suppose, in his ugliest frenzy; Marcus Aurelius was happy in the detested camp; Pepys was pretty happy, and I am pretty happy on the whole, because we both somewhat crowingly accepted a *via media*, both liked to attend to our affairs, and both had some success in managing the same. It is quite an open question whether Pepys and I ought to be happy; on the other hand, there is no doubt that Marat had better be unhappy. He was right (if he said it) that he was *la misère humaine*, cureless misery — unless perhaps by the gallows. Death is a great and gentle solvent; it has never had justice done it, no, not by Whitman. As for those crockery chimney-piece ornaments, the bourgeois (*quorum pars*), and their cowardly dislike of dying and killing, it is merely one symptom of a thousand how utterly they have got out of touch of life. Their dislike of capital punishment and their treatment of their domestic servants are for me the two flaunting emblems of their hollowness.

God knows where I am driving to. But here comes my lunch.

Which interruption, happily for you, seems to have stayed the issue. I have now nothing to say, that had formerly such a pressure of twaddle. Pray don't fail to come this summer. It will be a great disappointment, now it has been spoken of, if you do.—Yours ever,

ROBERT LOUIS STEVENSON.

To W. H. Low

The following letter relates to a suggestion which Mr. Gilder, as editor of the *Century Magazine*, had already made in the Hyères time nearly three years previously, and had now lately revived, that Stevenson and his friend Mr. W. H. Low should make a joint excursion down the Rhone, the result to be a book written by R. L. S. and illustrated by Mr. Low. Considerations of health caused the plan to be promptly abandoned for the second time.

[SKERRYVORE, BOURNEMOUTH, *March*, *1886*.]

MY DEAR LOW,—This is the most enchanting picture. Now understand my state: I am really an invalid, but of a mysterious order. I might be a *malade imaginaire*, but for one too tangible symptom, my tendency to bleed from the lungs. If we could go, (*1st*) We must have money enough to travel with *leisure and comfort*—especially the first. (*2nd*) You must be prepared for a comrade who would go to bed some part of every day

1886
ÆT. 36

and often stay silent. (*3rd*) You would have to play the part of a thoughtful courier, sparing me fatigue, looking out that my bed was warmed, etc. (*4th*) If you are very nervous, you must recollect a bad hæmorrhage is always on the cards, with its concomitants of anxiety and horror for those who are beside me.

Do you blench? If so, let us say no more about it.

If you are still unafraid, and the money were forthcoming, I believe the trip might do me good, and I feel sure that, working together, we might produce a fine book. The Rhone is the river of Angels. I adore it: have adored it since I was twelve, and first saw it from the train.

Lastly, it would depend on how I keep from now on. I have stood the winter hitherto with some credit, but the dreadful weather still continues, and I cannot holloa till I am through the wood.

Subject to these numerous and gloomy provisos, I embrace the prospect with glorious feelings.

I write this from bed, snow pouring without, and no circumstance of pleasure except your letter. That, however, counts for much. I am glad you liked the doggerel: I have already had a liberal cheque, over which I licked my fingers with a sound conscience. I had not meant to make money by these stumbling feet, but if it comes, it is only too welcome in my handsome but impecunious house.

Let me know soon what is to be expected — as far as it does not hang by that inconstant quantity, my want of health. Remember me to Madam with the best thanks and wishes; and believe me your friend,

ROBERT LOUIS STEVENSON.

To Mrs. Fleeming Jenkin

[Skerryvore, Bournemouth, *April, 1886.*]

MY DEAR MRS. JENKIN,—I try to tell myself it is good nature, but I know it is vanity that makes me write.

I have drafted the first part of Chapter VI., Fleeming and his friends, his influence on me, his views on religion and literature, his part at the Savile; it should boil down to about ten pages, and I really do think it admirably good. It has so much evoked Fleeming for myself that I found my conscience stirred just as it used to be after a serious talk with him: surely that means it is good? I had to write and tell you, being alone.

I have excellent news of Fanny, who is much better for the change. My father is still very yellow, and very old, and very weak, but yesterday he seemed happier, and smiled, and followed what was said; even laughed, I think. When he came away, he said to me, "Take care of yourself, my dearie," which had a strange sound of childish days, and will not leave my mind.

You must get Litolf's *Gavottes Célèbres:* I have made another trover there: a musette of Lully's. The second part of it I have not yet got the hang of; but the first—only a few bars! The gavotte is beautiful and pretty hard, I think, and very much of the period; and at the end of it, this musette enters with the most really thrilling effect of simple beauty. O—it 's first-rate. I am quite mad over it. If you find other books containing Lully, Rameau, Martini, please let me know; also you might tell me, you who know Bach, where the easiest

1886
ÆT. 36

is to be found. I write all morning, come down, and never leave the piano till about five; write letters, dine, get down again about eight, and never leave the piano till I go to bed. This is a fine life.—Yours most sincerely,

R. L. S.

If you get the musette (Lully's), please tell me if I am right, and it was probably written for strings. Anyway, it is as neat as—as neat as Bach—on the piano; or seems so to my ignorance.

I play much of the Rigadoon; but it 's strange, it don't come off *quite* so well with me!

There is the first part of the musette copied (from memory, so I hope there 's nothing wrong). Is it not angelic? But it ought, of course, to have the gavotte before. The gavotte is in G, and ends on the keynote thus (if I remember):—

staccato, I think. Then you sail into the musette.

N. B.—Where I have put an "A," is that a dominant

eleventh, or what? or just a seventh on the D? and if the latter, is that allowed? It sounds very funny. Never mind all my questions; if I begin about music (which is my leading ignorance and curiosity), I have always to babble questions: all my friends know me now, and take no notice whatever. The whole piece is marked allegro; but surely could easily be played too fast? The dignity must not be lost; the periwig feeling.

To Thomas Stevenson

Want of health preventing the author at this time from carrying the adventures of David Balfour, as narrated in *Kidnapped*, through to their issue as originally designed, it was resolved to wind them up for the present with the discomfiture of the wicked uncle, leaving open the possibility of a sequel, which was supplied six years later in *Catriona*.

[Skerryvore, Bournemouth, *March, 1886.*]

My dear Father,—The David problem has to-day been decided. I am to leave the door open for a sequel if the public take to it, and this will save me from butchering a lot of good material to no purpose. Your letter from Carlisle was pretty like yourself, sir, as I was pleased to see; the hand of Jekyll, not the hand of Hyde. I am for action quite unfit, and even a letter is beyond me; so pray take these scraps at a vast deal more than their intrinsic worth. I am in great spirits about David, Colvin agreeing with Henley, Fanny, and myself in thinking it far the most human of my labours hitherto. As to whether the long-eared British public may take to it, all think it more than doubtful; I wish they would, for I could do a second volume with ease

1886
ÆT. 36

and pleasure, and Colvin thinks it sin and folly to throw away David and Alan Breck upon so small a field as this one.—Ever your affectionate son, R. L. S.

To Mrs. Fleeming Jenkin

The following sets forth the *pros* and *cons* which were balancing each other in his mind in regard to his scheme of going to make a stand in his own person against agrarian outrage in Ireland.

[Skerryvore, Bournemouth],
April 15 or 16 (the hour not being known), 1886.

MY DEAR MRS. JENKIN,—It is I know not what hour of the night; but I cannot sleep, have lit the gas, and here goes.

First, all your packet arrived: I have dipped into the Schumann already with great pleasure. Surely, in what concerns us there is a sweet little chirrup; the *Good Words* arrived in the morning just when I needed it, and the famous notes that I had lost were recovered also in the nick of time.

And now I am going to bother you with my affairs: premising, first, that this is *private;* second, that whatever I do the *Life* shall be done first, and I am getting on with it well; and third, that I do not quite know why I consult you, but something tells me you will hear with fairness.

Here is my problem. The Curtin women are still miserable prisoners; no one dare buy their farm of them, all the manhood of England and the world stands aghast before a threat of murder. (1) Now, my work can be done anywhere; hence I can take up without loss a backgoing Irish farm, and live on, though not (as I had originally written) in it: First Reason. (2) If I should be killed, there are a good many who would feel it: writers are so much in the public eye, that a writer being murdered would attract attention, throw a bull's-eye light upon this cowardly business: Second Reason. (3) I am not unknown in the States, from which the funds come that pay for these brutalities: to some faint extent, my death (if I should be killed) would tell there: Third Reason. (4) *Nobody else is taking up this obvious and crying duty:* Fourth Reason. (5) I have a crazy health and may die at any moment, my life is of no purchase in an insurance office, it is the less account to husband it, and the business of husbanding a life is dreary and demoralising: Fifth Reason.

I state these in no order, but as they occur to me. And I shall do the like with the objections.

First Objection: It will do no good; you have seen Gordon die, and nobody minded; nobody will mind if you die. This is plainly of the devil. Second Objection: You will not even be murdered, the climate will miserably kill you, you will strangle out in a rotten damp heat, in congestion, etc. Well, what then? It changes nothing: the purpose is to brave crime; let me brave it, for such time and to such an extent as God allows. Third Objection: The Curtin women are probably highly uninteresting females. I have n't a doubt of it. But the Government cannot, men will not, protect them. If I am the only one to see this public duty, it is to the public and the Right I should perform it — not to Mesdames Curtin. Fourth Objection: I am

1886
ÆT. 36

married. "I have married a wife!" I seem to have heard it before. It smells ancient! what was the context? Fifth Objection: My wife has had a mean life (1), loves me (2), could not bear to lose me (3). (1) I admit: I am sorry. (2) But what does she love me for? and (3) she must lose me soon or late. And after all, because we run this risk, it does not follow we should fail. Sixth Objection: My wife would n't like it. No, she would n't. Who would? But the Curtins don't like it. And all those who are to suffer if this goes on, won't like it. And if there is a great wrong, somebody must suffer. Seventh Objection: I won't like it. No, I will not; I have thought it through, and I will not. But what of that? And both she and I may like it more than we suppose. We shall lose friends, all comforts, all society: so has everybody who has ever done anything; but we shall have some excitement, and that 's a fine thing; and we shall be trying to do the right, and that 's not to be despised. Eighth Objection: I am an author with my work before me. See Second Reason. Ninth Objection: But am I not taken with the hope of excitement? I was at first. I am not much now. I see what a dreary, friendless, miserable, God-forgotten business it will be. And anyway, is not excitement the proper reward of doing anything both right and a little dangerous? Tenth Objection: But am I not taken with a notion of glory? I dare say I am. Yet I see quite clearly how all points to nothing coming, to a quite inglorious death by disease and from the lack of attendance; or even if I should be knocked on the head, as these poor Irish promise, how little any one will care. It will be a smile at a thousand breakfast-tables. I am nearly forty now; I have not many illusions. And if I had? I do not love this health-tending, housekeeping life of mine. I have a taste for danger, which is human, like the fear of it. Here is a fair cause; a just cause; no knight ever set lance in rest for a juster. Yet it needs not the strength I have not, only the passive courage that I hope I could muster, and the watchfulness that I am sure I could learn.

Here is a long midnight dissertation; with myself; with you. Please let me hear. But I charge you this: if you see in this idea of mine the finger of duty, do not dissuade me. I am nearing forty, I begin to love my ease and my home and my habits, I never knew how much till this arose; do not falsely counsel me to put my head under the bed-clothes. And I will say this to you: my wife, who hates the idea, does not refuse. "It is nonsense," says she, "but if you go, I will go." Poor girl, and her home and her garden that she was so proud of! I feel her garden most of all, because it is a pleasure (I suppose) that I do not feel myself to share.

1. Here is a great wrong.
2. " a growing wrong.
3. " a wrong founded on crime.
4. " crime that the Government cannot prevent.
5. " crime that it occurs to no man to defy.
6. But it has occurred to me.
7. Being a known person, some will notice my defiance.
8. Being a writer, I can *make* people notice it.
9. And, I think, *make* people imitate me.

1886
ÆT. 36

10. Which would destroy in time this whole scaffolding of oppression.

11. And if I fail, however ignominiously, that is not my concern. It is, with an odd mixture of reverence and humorous remembrances of Dickens, be it said—it is A-nother's.

And here, at I cannot think what hour of the morning, I shall dry up, and remain,—Yours, really in want of a little help, R. L. S.

Sleepless at midnight's dewy hour.
" " witching "
" " maudlin "
etc.

Next morning.—Eleventh Objection: I have a father and mother. And who has not? Macduff's was a rare case; if we must wait for a Macduff. Besides, my father will not perhaps be long here. Twelfth Objection: The cause of England in Ireland is not worth supporting. *A qui le dites vous?* And I am not supporting that. Home Rule, if you like. Cause of decency, the idea that populations should not be taught to gain public ends by private crime, the idea that for all men to bow before a threat of crime is to loosen and degrade beyond redemption the whole fabric of man's decency.

To Mrs. Fleeming Jenkin

The first paragraph of the following refers to the *Life of Fleeming Jenkin;* the second, to a remark of his correspondent that a task such as he had proposed to himself in Ireland should be undertaken by a society rather than an individual.

[SKERRYVORE, BOURNEMOUTH, *April, 1886.*]

MY DEAR MRS. JENKIN, — The Book — It is all drafted: I hope soon to send you for comments Chapters III., IV., and V. Chapter VII. is roughly but satisfactorily drafted: a very little work should put that to rights. But Chapter VI. is no joke; it is a *mare magnum:* I swim and drown and come up again; and it is all broken ends and mystification: moreover, I perceive I am in want of more matter. I must have, first of all, a little letter from Mr. Ewing about the phonograph work: *If* you think he would understand it is quite a matter of chance whether I use a word or a fact out of it. If you think he would not: I will go without. Also, could I have a look at Ewing's *précis?* And lastly, I perceive I must interview you again about a few points; they are very few, and might come to little; and I propose to go on getting things as well together as I can in the meanwhile, and rather have a final time when all is ready and only to be criticised. I do still think it will be good. I wonder if Trélat would let me cut? But no, I think I would n't after all; 't is so quaint and pretty and clever and simple and French, and gives such a good sight of Fleeming: the plum of the book, I think.

You misunderstood me in one point: I always hoped to found such a society; that was the outside of my dream, and would mean entire success. *But* — I cannot play Peter the Hermit. In these days of the Fleet Street journalist, I cannot send out better men than myself, with wives or mothers just as good as mine, and sisters (I may at least say) better, to a danger and a long-drawn dreariness that I do not share. My wife

1886 ÆT. 36

says it 's cowardice; what brave men are the leader-writers! Call it cowardice; it is mine. Mind you, I may end by trying to do it by the pen only: I shall not love myself if I do; and is it ever a good thing to do a thing for which you despise yourself?—even in the doing? And if the thing you do is to call upon others to do the thing you neglect? I have never dared to say what I feel about men's lives, because my own was in the wrong: shall I dare to send them to death? The physician must heal himself; he must honestly *try* the path he recommends: if he does not even try, should he not be silent?

I thank you very heartily for your letter, and for the seriousness you brought to it. You know, I think when a serious thing is your own, you keep a saner man by laughing at it and yourself as you go. So I do not write possibly with all the really somewhat sickened gravity I feel. And indeed, what with the book, and this business to which I referred, and Ireland, I am scarcely in an enviable state. Well, I ought to be glad, after ten years of the worst training on earth—valetudinarianism—that I can still be troubled by a duty. You shall hear more in time; so far, I am at least decided: I will go and see Balfour when I get to London.

We have all had a great pleasure: a Mrs. Rawlinson came and brought with her a nineteen-year-old daughter, simple, human, as beautiful as—herself; I never admired a girl before, you know it was my weakness: we are all three dead in love with her. How nice to be able to do so much good to harassed people by—yourself!—Ever yours, R. L. S.

To Miss Rawlinson

Here follows a compliment in verse to the young lady last mentioned, whose Christian name was May.

[Skerryvore, Bournemouth, *April, 1886.*]

Of the many flowers you brought me,
  Only some were meant to stay,
And the flower I thought the sweetest
  Was the flower that went away.

Of the many flowers you brought me,
  All were fair and fresh and gay,
But the flower I thought the sweetest
  Was the blossom of the May.

Robert Louis Stevenson.

To Miss Monroe

The next is in answer to criticisms on *Prince Otto* received from a lady correspondent in Chicago.

Skerryvore, Bournemouth, *May 25th, 1886.*

Dear Miss Monroe,—(I hope I have this rightly) I must lose no time in thanking you for a letter singularly pleasant to receive. It may interest you to know that I read to the signature without suspecting my correspondent was a woman; though in one point (a reference to the Countess) I might have found a hint of the truth. You are not pleased with Otto; since I judge you do not like weakness; and no more do I. And yet I have more than tolerance for Otto, whose faults

1886 ÆT. 36

are the faults of weakness, but never of ignoble weakness, and who seeks before all to be both kind and just. Seeks, not succeeds. But what is man? So much of cynicism to recognise that nobody does right is the best equipment for those who do not wish to be cynics in good earnest. Think better of Otto, if my plea can influence you; and this I mean for your own sake—not his, poor fellow, as he will never learn your opinion; but for yours, because, as men go in this world (and women too), you will not go far wrong if you light upon so fine a fellow; and to light upon one and not perceive his merits is a calamity. In the flesh, of course, I mean; in the book the fault, of course, is with my stumbling pen. Seraphina made a mistake about her Otto; it begins to swim before me dimly that you may have some traits of Seraphina?

With true ingratitude you see me pitch upon your exception; but it is easier to defend oneself gracefully than to acknowledge praise. I am truly glad that you should like my books; for I think I see from what you write that you are a reader worth convincing. Your name, if I have properly deciphered it, suggests that you may be also something of my countrywoman; for it is hard to see where Monroe came from, if not from Scotland. I seem to have here a double claim on your good nature: being myself pure Scotch and having appreciated your letter, make up two undeniable merits which, perhaps, if it should be quite without trouble, you might reward with your photograph.—Yours truly, ROBERT LOUIS STEVENSON.

To Miss Monroe

[Skerryvore, Bournemouth, *June, 1886.*]

MY DEAR MISS MONROE,—I am ill in bed and stupid, incoherently stupid; yet I have to answer your letter, and if the answer is incomprehensible you must forgive me. You say my letter caused you pleasure; I am sure, as it fell out, not near so much as yours has brought to me. The interest taken in an author is fragile: his next book, or your next year of culture, might see the interest frosted or outgrown; and himself, in spite of all, you might probably find the most distasteful person upon earth. My case is different. I have bad health, am often condemned to silence for days together—was so once for six weeks, so that my voice was awful to hear when I first used it, like the whisper of a shadow—have outlived all my chief pleasures, which were active and adventurous, and ran in the open air: and being a person who prefers life to art, and who knows it is a far finer thing to be in love, or to risk a danger, than to paint the finest picture or write the noblest book, I begin to regard what remains to me of my life as very shadowy. From a variety of reasons, I am ashamed to confess I was much in this humour when your letter came. I had a good many troubles; was regretting a high average of sins; had been recently reminded that I had outlived some friends, and wondering if I had not outlived some friendships; and had just, while boasting of better health, been struck down again by my haunting enemy, an enemy who was exciting at first, but has now, by the iteration of his strokes, become merely annoying and inex-

1886 ÆT. 36

pressibly irksome. Can you fancy that to a person drawing towards the elderly this sort of conjunction of circumstances brings a rather aching sense of the past and the future? Well, it was just then that your letter and your photograph were brought to me in bed; and there came to me at once the most agreeable sense of triumph. My books were still young; my words had their good health and could go about the world and make themselves welcome; and even (in a shadowy and distant sense) make something in the nature of friends for the sheer hulk that stays at home and bites his pen over the manuscripts. It amused me very much to remember that I had been in Chicago, not so many years ago, in my proper person; where I had failed to awaken much remark, except from the ticket collector; and to think how much more gallant and persuasive were the fellows that I now send instead of me, and how these are welcome in that quarter to the sitter of Herr Platz, while their author was not very welcome even in the villainous restaurant where he tried to eat a meal and rather failed.

And this leads me directly to a confession. The photograph which shall accompany this is not chosen as the most like, but the best-looking. Put yourself in my place, and you will call this pardonable. Even as it is, even putting forth a flattered presentment, I am a little pained; and very glad it is a photograph and not myself that has to go; for in this case, if it please you, you can tell yourself it is my image—and if it displease you, you can lay the blame on the photographer; but in that, there were no help, and the poor author might belie his labours.

Kidnapped should soon appear; I am afraid you may not like it, as it is very unlike *Prince Otto* in every way; but I am myself a great admirer of the two chief characters, Alan and David. *Virginibus Puerisque* has never been issued in the States. I do not think it is a book that has much charm for publishers in any land; but I am to bring out a new edition in England shortly, a copy of which I must try to remember to send you. I say try to remember, because I have some superficial acquaintance with myself: and I have determined, after a galling discipline, to promise nothing more until the day of my death: at least, in this way, I shall no more break my word, and I must now try being churlish instead of being false.

I do not believe you to be the least like Seraphina. Your photograph has no trace of her, which somewhat relieves me, as I am a good deal afraid of Seraphinas — they do not always go into the woods and see the sunrise, and some are so well mailed that even that experience would leave them unaffected and unsoftened. The "hair and eyes of several complexions" was a trait taken from myself; and I do not bind myself to the opinions of Sir John. In this case, perhaps — but no, if the peculiarity is shared by two such pleasant persons as you and I (as you and me — the grammatical nut is hard), it must be a very good thing indeed, and Sir John must be an ass.

The *Book Reader* notice was a strange jumble of fact and fancy. I wish you could have seen my father's old assistant and present partner when he heard my father described as an "inspector of lighthouses," for we are all very proud of the family achievements, and

1886
ÆT. 36

the name of my house here in Bournemouth is stolen from one of the sea-towns of the Hebrides which are our pyramids and monuments. I was never at Cambridge, again; but neglected a considerable succession of classes at Edinburgh. But to correct that friendly blunderer were to write an autobiography.—And so now, with many thanks, believe me yours sincerely,

ROBERT LOUIS STEVENSON.

To R. A. M. STEVENSON

During these months, as already indicated, Stevenson was very much taken up, in by-hours, with trying to learn something of the theory and practice of music, and spent much of his time "pickling," as he called it, in an elementary manner on the piano. He even tried his hand in an experimental way at composition, and had sent one of his attempts for criticism to his cousin, Mr. R. A. M. Stevenson, who was better versed in the art.

SKERRYVORE, BOURNEMOUTH, *July, 1886.*

SIR,—Your foolish letter was unduly received. There may be hidden fifths, and if there are, it shows how dam spontaneous the thing was. I could tinker and tic-tac-toe on a piece of paper, but scorned the act with a Threnody, which was poured forth like blood and water on the groaning organ. If your heart (which was what I addressed) remained unmoved, let us refer to the affair no more: crystallised emotion, the statement and the reconciliation of the sorrows of the race and the individual, is obviously no more to you than supping sawdust. Well, well. If ever I write another Threnody! My next op. will probably be a Passepied and fugue in G (or D).

The mind is in my case shrunk to the size and sp. gr. of an aged Spanish filbert. O, I am so jolly silly. I now pickle with some freedom (1) the refrain of Martini's *Moutons;* (2) *Sul margine d'un rio,* arranged for the infant school by the Aged Statesman; (3) the first phrase of Bach's musette (Sweet Englishwoman, No. *3*),[1] the rest of the musette being one prolonged cropper, which I take daily for the benefit of my health. All my other works (of which there are many) are either arranged (by R. L. Stevenson) for the manly and melodious forefinger, or else prolonged and melancholy croppers. . . . I find one can get a notion of music very nicely. I have been pickling deeply in the Magic Flute; and have arranged *La dove prende,* almost to the end, for two melodious forefingers. I am next going to score the really nobler *Colomba o tortorella* for the same instruments.

This day is published
The works of Ludwig van Beethoven
arranged
and wiederdurchgearbeiteted
for two melodious forefingers
by,
Sir,—Your obedient servant,
PIMPERLY STIPPLE.

That 's a good idea? There 's a person called Lenz who actually does it—beware his den; I lost eighteen-pennies on him, and found the bleeding corpses of pieces of music divorced from their keys, despoiled of their graces, and even changed in time; I do not wish

1 *Suite anglaise.*

1886
ÆT. 36

to regard music (nor to be regarded) through that bony Lenz. You say you are "a spumfed idiot"; but how about Lenz? And how about me, sir, me?

I yesterday sent Lloyd by parcel post, at great expense, an empty matchbox and empty cigarette-paper book, a bell from a cat's collar, an iron kitchen spoon, and a piece of coal more than half the superficies of this sheet of paper. They are now (appropriately enough) speeding towards the Silly Isles; I hope he will find them useful. By that, and my telegram with prepaid answer to yourself, you may judge of my spiritual state. The finances have much brightened; and if *Kidnapped* keeps on as it has begun, I may be solvent. —Yours, THRENODIÆ AVCTOR

(The authour of ane Threnodie).

Op. 2: Scherzo (in G Major) expressive of the Sense of favours to come.

To R. A. M. STEVENSON

SKERRYVORE [BOURNEMOUTH, *July, 1886*].

DEAR BOB,—Herewith another shy; more melancholy than before, but I think not so abjectly idiotic. The musical terms seem to be as good as in Beethoven, and that, after all, is the great affair. Bar the dam bareness of the bass, it looks like a piece of real music from a distance. I am proud to say it was not made one hand at a time; the bass was of synchronous birth with the treble; they are of the same age, sir, and may God have mercy on their souls!—Yours, THE MAESTRO.

1886
ÆT. 36

To Mr. and Mrs. Thomas Stevenson

Mr. and Mrs. Thomas Stevenson had been thinking of trying a winter at Bournemouth for the sake of being near their son, a plan which was eventually carried out. The health of the former was now fast and painfully breaking. Mr. J. W. Alexander, the well-known American artist, had been down at Skerryvore with an introduction from Mr. Gosse, and had made a drawing of Stevenson's head.

[Skerryvore, Bournemouth], *July 7th, 1886.*

MY DEAR PEOPLE,—It is probably my fault, and not yours, that I did not understand. I think it would be well worth trying the winter in Bournemouth; but I would only take the house by the month—this after mature discussion. My leakage still pursues its course; if I were only well, I have a notion to go north and get in (if I could) at the inn at Kirkmichael, which has always smiled upon me much. If I did well there, we might then meet and do what should most smile at the time.

Meanwhile, of course, I must not move, and am in a rancid box here, feeling the heat a great deal, and pretty tired of things. Alexander did a good thing of me at last; it looks like a mixture of an Aztec idol, a lion, an Indian Rajah, and a woman; and certainly represents a mighty comic figure. F. and Lloyd both think it is the best thing that has been done of me up to now.

You should hear Lloyd on the penny whistle, and me on the piano! Dear powers, what a concerto! I now live entirely for the piano, he for the whistle; the neigh-

1886 ÆT. 36 bours, in a radius of a furlong and a half, are packing up in quest of brighter climes.—Ever yours,

R. L. S.

P. S.—Please say if you can afford to let us have money for this trip, and if so, how much. I can see the year through without help, I believe, and supposing my health to keep up; but can scarce make this change on my own metal. R. L. S.

To Charles Baxter

[Skerryvore, Bournemouth, *July, 1886.*]

DEAR CHARLES,—Doubtless, if all goes well, towards the 1st of August we shall be begging at your door. Thanks for a sight of the papers, which I return (you see) at once, fearing further responsibility.

Glad you like Dauvit; but eh, man, yon 's terrible strange conduc' o' thon man Rankeillor. Ca' him a legal adviser! It would make a bonny law-shuit, the Shaws case; and yon paper they signed, I 'm thinking, wouldnae be muckle thought o' by Puggy Deas.—Yours ever, R. L. S.

To Thomas Stevenson

"Coolin," mentioned below, had been a favourite Skye terrier of Heriot Row days.

[Skerryvore, Bournemouth], *July 28, 1886.*

MY DEAR FATHER,—We have decided not to come to Scotland, but just to do as Dobell wished, and take an outing. I believe this is wiser in all ways; but I own it is a disappointment. I am weary of England; like Alan,

"I weary for the heather," if not for the deer. Lloyd has gone to Scilly with Katharine and C., where and with whom he should have a good time. David seems really to be going to succeed, which is a pleasant prospect on all sides. I am, I believe, floated financially; a book that sells will be a pleasant novelty. I enclose another review; mighty complimentary, and calculated to sell the book too.

Coolin's tombstone has been got out, honest man! and it is to be polished, for it has got scratched, and have a touch of gilding in the letters, and be sunk in the front of the house. Worthy man, he, too, will maybe weary for the heather, and the bents of Gullane, where (as I dare say you remember) he gaed clean gyte, and jumped on to his crown from a gig, in hot and hopeless chase of many thousand rabbits. I can still hear the little cries of the honest fellow as he disappeared; and my mother will correct me, but I believe it was two days before he turned up again at North Berwick: to judge by his belly, he had caught not one out of these thousands, but he had had some exercise.

I keep well.—Ever your affectionate son,

R. L. S.

To Mrs. Thomas Stevenson

Having given up going to Scotland for a summer change, Stevenson had started on the "outing" which he mentions in the last letter. It took the shape of a ten days' visit to my house at the British Museum, followed by another made in the company of Mr. Henley to Paris, chiefly for the sake of seeing the W. H. Low's and the sculptor Rodin.

British Museum [*August 10th, 1886*].

My dear Mother,—We are having a capital holiday, and I am much better, and enjoying myself to the nines.

1886
ÆT. 36

Richmond is painting my portrait. To-day I lunch with him, and meet Burne-Jones; to-night Browning dines with us. That sounds rather lofty work, does it not? His path was paved with celebrities. To-morrow we leave for Paris, and next week, I suppose, or the week after, come home. Address here, as we may not reach Paris. I am really very well.—Ever your affectionate son,

R. L. S.

To T. Watts-Dunton

Skerryvore, Bournemouth [*September, 1886*].

Dear Mr. Watts,—The sight of the last *Athenæum* reminds me of you, and of my debt, now too long due. I wish to thank you for your notice of *Kidnapped;* and that not because it was kind, though for that also I valued it, but in the same sense as I have thanked you before now for a hundred articles on a hundred different writers. A critic like you is one who fights the good fight, contending with stupidity, and I would fain hope not all in vain; in my own case, for instance, surely not in vain.

What you say of the two parts in *Kidnapped* was felt by no one more painfully than by myself. I began it partly as a lark, partly as a pot-boiler; and suddenly it moved, David and Alan stepped out from the canvas, and I found I was in another world. But there was the cursed beginning, and a cursed end must be appended; and our old friend Byles the butcher was plainly audible tapping at the back door. So it had to go into the world, one part (as it does seem to me) alive, one part merely galvanised: no work, only an essay. For a man of tentative method, and weak health, and a scarcity of private means, and not too much of that frugality which is the artist's proper virtue, the days of sinecures and patrons look very golden: the days of professional literature very hard. Yet I do not so far deceive myself as to think I should change my character by changing my epoch; the sum of virtue in our books is in a relation of equality to the sum of virtues in ourselves; and my *Kidnapped* was doomed, while still in the womb and while I was yet in the cradle, to be the thing it is.

And now to the more genial business of defence. You attack my fight on board the *Covenant:* I think it literal. David and Alan had every advantage on their side—position, arms, training, a good conscience; a handful of merchant sailors, not well led in the first attack, not led at all in the second, could only by an accident have taken the round-house by attack; and since the defenders had firearms and food, it is even doubtful if they could have been starved out. The only doubtful point with me is whether the seamen would have ever ventured on the second onslaught; I half believed they would not; still the illusion of numbers and the authority of Hoseason would perhaps stretch far enough to justify the extremity.—I am, dear Mr. Watts, your very sincere admirer,

ROBERT LOUIS STEVENSON.

TO FREDERICK LOCKER-LAMPSON

Mr. Locker-Lampson, better known as Frederick Locker, the friend of Tennyson and most accomplished writer of *vers de société* in his

1886 ÆT. 36

time, had asked Stevenson, through their common friend Mr. Andrew Lang, for a set of verses, and he had sent the following — hitherto only printed, I believe, at the head of a very scarce volume: — "Rowfant Rhymes, by Frederick Locker, with an introduction by Austin Dobson. Cleveland, The Rowfant Club, 1895. 127 copies only printed."

SKERRYVORE, *September 4, 1886.*

Not roses to the rose, I trow,
The thistle sends, nor to the bee
Do wasps bring honey. Wherefore now
Should Locker ask a verse from me?

Martial, perchance, — but he is dead,
And Herrick now must rhyme no more;
Still burning with the muse, they tread
(And arm in arm) the shadowy shore.

They, if they lived, with dainty hand,
To music as of mountain brooks,
Might bring you worthy words to stand
Unshamed, dear Locker, in your books.

But tho' these fathers of your race
Be gone before, yourself a sire,
To-day you see before your face
Your stalwart youngsters touch the lyre.

On these — on Lang, or Dobson — call,
Long leaders of the songful feast.
They lend a verse your laughing fall —
A verse they owe you at the least.

To Frederick Locker-Lampson

To Mr. Locker's acknowledgment of these verses Stevenson replied as follows, asking his correspondent's interest on behalf of a friend who had been kind to him at Hyères, in procuring a nomination for her son to the Blue-Coat School.

[Skerryvore], Bournemouth, *September, 1886.*

Dear Locker,—You take my verses too kindly, but you will admit, for such a bluebottle of a versifier to enter the house of Gertrude, where her necklace hangs, was not a little brave. Your kind invitation, I fear, must remain unaccepted; and yet—if I am very well—perhaps next spring—(for I mean to be very well)—my wife might. . . . But all that is in the clouds with my better health. And now look here: you are a rich man and know many people, therefore perhaps some of the Governors of Christ's Hospital. If you do, I know a most deserving case, in which I would (if I could) do anything. To approach you, in this way, is not decent; and you may therefore judge by my doing it, how near this matter lies to my heart. I enclose you a list of the Governors, which I beg you to return, whether or not you shall be able to do anything to help me.

The boy's name is ——; he and his mother are very poor. It may interest you in her cause if I tell you this: that when I was dangerously ill at Hyères, this brave lady, who had then a sick husband of her own (since dead) and a house to keep and a family of four to cook for, all with her own hands, for they could afford no servant, yet took watch-about with my wife,

1886 ÆT. 36

and contributed not only to my comfort, but to my recovery in a degree that I am not able to limit. You can conceive how much I suffer from my impotence to help her, and indeed I have already shown myself a thankless friend. Let not my cry go up before you in vain!—Yours in hope, ROBERT LOUIS STEVENSON.

TO FREDERICK LOCKER-LAMPSON

Mr. Locker, apparently misunderstanding the application, had replied with a cheque.

SKERRYVORE, BOURNEMOUTH, *September, 1886.*

MY DEAR LOCKER,—That I should call myself a man of letters, and land myself in such unfathomable ambiguities! No, my dear Locker, I did not want a cheque; and in my ignorance of business, which is greater even than my ignorance of literature, I have taken the liberty of drawing a pen through the document and returning it; should this be against the laws of God or man, forgive me. All that I meant by my excessively disgusting reference to your material well-being was the vague notion that a man who is well off was sure to know a Governor of Christ's Hospital; though how I quite arrived at this conclusion I do not see. A man with a cold in the head does not necessarily know a ratcatcher; and the connection is equally close—as it now appears to my awakened and somewhat humbled spirit. For all that, let me thank you in the warmest manner for your friendly readiness to contribute. You say you have hopes of becoming a miser: I wish I had; but indeed I believe you deceive yourself, and are as far from it as ever. I wish I had any excuse to keep your cheque, for it is much more elegant to receive than to return; but I have my way of making it up to you, and I do sincerely beg you to write to the two Governors. This extraordinary outpouring of correspondence would (if you knew my habits) convince you of my great eagerness in this matter. I would promise gratitude; but I have made a promise to myself to make no more promises to anybody else, having broken such a host already, and come near breaking my heart in consequence; and as for gratitude, I am by nature a thankless dog, and was spoiled from a child up. But if you can help this lady in the matter of the Hospital, you will have helped the worthy. Let me continue to hope that I shall make out my visit in the spring, and believe me, yours very truly, ROBERT LOUIS STEVENSON.

It may amuse you to know that a very long while ago, I broke my heart to try to imitate your verses, and failed hopelessly. I saw some of the evidences the other day among my papers, and blushed to the heels.

R. L. S.

I give up finding out your name in the meantime, and keep to that by which you will be known — Frederick Locker.

TO FREDERICK LOCKER-LAMPSON

[SKERRYVORE, BOURNEMOUTH],
24th September, 1886.

MY DEAR LOCKER,—You are simply an angel of light, and your two letters have gone to the post; I trust they will reach the hearts of the recipients—at least, that

1886 ÆT. 36

could not be more handsomely expressed. About the cheque: well now, I am going to keep it; but I assure you Mrs. —— has never asked me for money, and I would not dare to offer any till she did. For all that I shall stick to the cheque now, and act to that amount as your almoner. In this way I reward myself for the ambiguity of my epistolary style.

I suppose, if you please, you may say your verses are thin (would you so describe an arrow, by the way, and one that struck the gold? It scarce strikes me as exhaustively descriptive), and, thin or not, they are (and I have found them) inimitably elegant. I thank you again very sincerely for the generous trouble you have taken in this matter which was so near my heart, and you may be very certain it will be the fault of my health and not my inclination, if I do not see you before very long; for all that has passed has made me in more than the official sense sincerely yours,

ROBERT LOUIS STEVENSON.

TO SIDNEY COLVIN

The following refers first, if I remember right, to some steps that were being taken to obtain recognition in the form of a knighthood for the elder Stevenson's public services; next, to the writer's own work at the time in hand; and lastly to my volume on Keats then in preparation for Mr. Morley's series.

SKERRYVORE, *Dec. 14, 1886.*

MY DEAR COLVIN,—This is first-rate of you, the Lord love you for it! I am truly much obliged. He—my father—is very changeable; at times, he seems only a slow quiet edition of himself; again, he will be very heavy and blank; but never so violent as last spring; and therefore, to my mind, better on the whole.

1887
ÆT. 37

I am splendid. I have been writing much verse—quite the bard, in fact; and also a dam tale to order, which will be what it will be: I don't love it, but some of it is passable in its mouldy way, *The Misadventures of John Nicholson.* All my bardly exercises are in Scotch; I have struck my somewhat ponderous guitar in that tongue to no small extent: with what success, I know not, but I think it 's better than my English verse; more marrow and fatness, and more ruggedness.

How goes *Keats?* Pray remark, if he (Keats) hung back from Shelley, it was not to be wondered at, *when so many of his friends were Shelley's pensioners.* I forget if you have made this point; it has been borne in upon me reading Dowden and the *Shelley Papers;* and it will do no harm if you have made it. I finished a poem to-day, and writ 3000 words of a story, *tant bien que mal;* and have a right to be sleepy, and (what is far nobler and rarer) am so.—My dear Colvin, ever yours,

THE REAL MACKAY.

TO FREDERICK LOCKER-LAMPSON

Stevenson suffered more even than usual after the turn of the year and during the spring of 1887, and for several months his correspondence almost entirely fails. This is in reply to an invitation to Rowfant for Easter.

SKERRYVORE, BOURNEMOUTH, *February 5th, 1887.*

MY DEAR LOCKER,—Here I am in my bed as usual, and it is indeed a long while since I went out to dinner.

1887
ÆT. 37

You do not know what a crazy fellow this is. My winter has not so far been luckily passed, and all hope of paying visits at Easter has vanished for twelve calendar months. But because I am a beastly and indurated invalid, I am not dead to human feelings; and I neither have forgotten you nor will forget you. Some day the wind may round to the right quarter and we may meet; till then I am still truly yours,

ROBERT LOUIS STEVENSON.

TO HENRY JAMES

[SKERRYVORE, BOURNEMOUTH, *February, 1887.*]

MY DEAR JAMES,—My health has played me it in once more in the absurdest fashion, and the creature who now addresses you is but a stringy and white-faced *bouilli* out of the pot of fever, with the devil to pay in every corner of his economy. I suppose (to judge by your letter) I need not send you these sheets, which came during my collapse by the rush. I am on the start with three volumes, that one of tales,[1] a second one of essays,[2] and one of—ahem—verse.[3] This is a great order, is it not? After that I shall have empty lockers. All new work stands still; I was getting on well with Jenkin when this blessed malady unhorsed me, and sent me back to the dung-collecting trade of the republisher. I shall reissue *Virg. Puer.* as Vol. I. of *Essays*, and the new vol. as Vol. II. of ditto; to be sold, however, separately. This is but a dry maundering; however, I am quite unfit—"I am for action quite unfit Either of exercise or wit." My father is in a variable

[1] *The Merry Men.* [2] *Memories and Portraits.* [3] *Underwoods.*

state; many sorrows and perplexities environ the house of Stevenson; my mother shoots north at this hour on business of a distinctly rancid character; my father (under my wife's tutorage) proceeds to-morrow to Salisbury; I remain here in my bed and whistle; in no quarter of heaven is anything encouraging apparent, except that the good Colvin comes to the hotel here on a visit. This dreary view of life is somewhat blackened by the fact that my head aches, which I always regard as a liberty on the part of the powers that be. This is also my first letter since my recovery. God speed your laudatory pen!

My wife joins in all warm messages.—Yours,

R. L. S.

To W. H. Low

Mr. Low and his wife, who were at this time leaving Paris for good, had been meditating a visit to the Stevensons at Bournemouth on their way home to the United States.

[*April, 1887.*]

MY DEAR LOW,—The fares to London may be found in any continental Bradshaw or sich; from London to Bournemouth impoverished parties who can stoop to the third class get their ticket for the matter of 10*s.*, or, as my wife loves to phrase it, "a half a pound." You will also be involved in a 3*s.* fare to get to Skerryvore; but this, I dare say, friends could help you in on your arrival; so that you may reserve your energies for the two tickets—costing the matter of a pound—and the usual gratuities to porters. This does not seem to me much: considering the intellectual pleasures that await

1887 ÆT. 37 you here, I call it dirt cheap. I *believe* the third class from Paris to London (*viâ* Dover) is *about* forty francs, but I cannot swear. Suppose it to be fifty.

	frcs.
50 × 2 = 100	100
The expense of spirit or spontaneous lapse of coin on the journey, at 5 frcs. a head, 5 × 2 = 10	10
Victuals on ditto, at 5 frcs. a head, 5 × 2 = 10	10
Gratuity to stewardess, in case of severe prostration, at 3 francs	3
One night in London, on a modest footing, say 20	20
Two tickets to Bournemouth at 12.50, 12.50 × 2 = 25	25
Porters and general devilment, say 5 . .	5
Cabs in London, say 2 shillings, and in Bournemouth, 3 shillings = 5 shillings, 6 frcs. 25	6.25
frcs. .	179.25

Or, the same in pounds, *£7 3s. 6½d.*
Or, the same in dollars, $35.45,

if there be any arithmetical virtue in me. I have left out dinner in London in case you want to blow out, which would come extry, and with the aid of *vangs fangs* might easily double the whole amount—above all if you have a few friends to meet you.

In making this valuable project, or budget, I discovered for the first time a reason (frequently overlooked) for the singular costliness of travelling with your wife.

Anybody would count the tickets double; but how few would have remembered — or indeed has any one ever remembered? — to count the spontaneous lapse of coin double also? Yet there are two of you, each must do his daily leakage, and it must be done out of your travelling fund. You will tell me, perhaps, that you carry the coin yourself: my dear sir, do you think you can fool your Maker? Your wife has to lose her quota; and by God she will — if you kept the coin in a belt. One thing I have omitted: you will lose a certain amount on the exchange, but this even I cannot foresee, as it is one of the few things that vary with the way a man has.—I am, dear sir, yours financially,

SAMUEL BUDGETT.

To ALISON CUNNINGHAM

SKERRYVORE, *April 16th, 1887.*

MY DEAREST CUMMY,—As usual, I have been a dreary bad fellow and not written for ages; but you must just try to forgive me, to believe (what is the truth) that the number of my letters is no measure of the number of times I think of you, and to remember how much writing I have to do. The weather is bright, but still cold; and my father, I 'm afraid, feels it sharply. He has had — still has, rather — a most obstinate jaundice, which has reduced him cruelly in strength, and really upset him altogether. I hope, or think, he is perhaps a little better; but he suffers much, cannot sleep at night, and gives John and my mother a severe life of it to wait upon him. My wife is, I think, a little

1887 ÆT. 37

better, but no great shakes. I keep mightily respectable myself.

Coolin's tombstone is now built into the front wall of Skerryvore, and poor Bogie's (with a Latin inscription also) is set just above it. Poor, unhappy wee man, he died, as you must have heard, in fight, which was what he would have chosen; for military glory was more in his line than the domestic virtues. I believe this is about all my news, except that, as I write, there is a blackbird singing in our garden trees, as it were at Swanston. I would like fine to go up the burnside a bit, and sit by the pool and be young again — or no, be what I am still, only there instead of here, for just a little. Did you see that I had written about John Todd? In this month's *Longman* it was; if you have not seen it, I will try and send it you. Some day climb as high as Halkerside for me (I am never likely to do it for myself), and sprinkle some of the well-water on the turf. I am afraid it is a pagan rite, but quite harmless, and *ye can sain it wi' a bit prayer.* Tell the Peewies that I mind their forebears well. My heart is sometimes heavy, and sometimes glad to mind it all. But for what we have received, the Lord make us truly thankful. Don't forget to sprinkle the water, and do it in my name; I feel a childish eagerness in this.

Remember me most kindly to James, and with all sorts of love to yourself, believe me, your laddie,

ROBERT LOUIS STEVENSON.

P. S.—I suppose Mrs. Todd ought to see the paper about her man; judge of that, and if you think she would not dislike it, buy her one from me, and let me know. The article is called "Pastoral," in *Longman's Magazine* for April. I will send you the money; I would to-day, but it 's the Sabbie day, and I cannae.

R. L. S.

Remembrances from all here.

To Sidney Colvin

Within a fortnight after the date of the above Stevenson went himself, and for the last time, to Scotland; not, indeed, to visit his old haunts among the Pentlands, but to be present, too late for recognition, at the death of his father (May 8, 1887). Business detained him for some weeks, and the following was written just before his return to Bournemouth.

[Edinburgh, *June, 1887.*]

MY DEAR S. C.,—At last I can write a word to you. Your little note in the *P. M. G.* was charming. I have written four pages in the *Contemporary*, which Bunting found room for: they are not very good, but I shall do more for his memory in time.

About the death, I have long hesitated, I was long before I could tell my mind; and now I know it, and can but say that I am glad. If we could have had my father, that would have been a different thing. But to keep that changeling — suffering changeling — any longer, could better none and nothing. Now he rests; it is more significant, it is more like himself. He will begin to return to us in the course of time, as he was and as we loved him.

My favourite words in literature, my favourite scene — "O let him pass," Kent and Lear — was played for me here in the first moment of my return. I believe

1887
ÆT. 37

Shakespeare saw it with his own father. I had no words ; but it was shocking to see. He died on his feet, you know; was on his feet the last day, knowing nobody — still he would be up. This was his constant wish; also that he might smoke a pipe on his last day. The funeral would have pleased him; it was the largest private funeral in man's memory here.

We have no plans, and it is possible we may go home without going through town. I do not know; I have no views yet whatever; nor can have any at this stage of my cold and my business.— Ever yours, R. L. S.

IX

THE UNITED STATES AGAIN:

WINTER IN THE ADIRONDACKS

(August, 1887–October, 1888)

IX

THE UNITED STATES AGAIN:

WINTER IN THE ADIRONDACKS

(August, 1887–October, 1888)

DURING the two years and nine months of Stevenson's residence at Bournemouth, preceding the date of his father's death, he had made no apparent progress towards recovery. Every period of respite had been quickly followed by a relapse, and all his work, brilliant and varied as it was, had been done under conditions which would have reduced almost any other man to inactivity. The close and frequently recurring struggles against the danger of death from hæmorrhage and exhaustion, which he had been used, when they first occurred, to find exciting, grew in the long run merely irksome; and even his persistent high courage and gaiety, sustained as they were by the devoted affection of his wife and many friends, began occasionally, for the first time, to fail him. Accordingly, when in May, 1887, the death of his father severed the strongest of the ties which bound him to the old country, he was very ready to listen to the advice of his physicians, who were unanimous in thinking his case not hopeless, but urged him to try some complete change of climate, surroundings, and mode of life. His wife's connections pointing to the West, he thought of the mountain health-resorts of Colorado, and of their growing reputation for the cure of lung patients. Having let his house at Bournemouth, he accordingly took passage on board the ss. *Ludgate Hill*, sailing for New York from London on August 21st, 1887, with his whole party, consisting of his wife, his widowed mother, whom they had persuaded to join them, his young stepson, and a trusted servant, Valentine Roch.

It was the moment when his reputation had first reached its height in the United States, owing to the popularity first of *Treasure Island* and then of *Kidnapped*, and more especially to the immense impression made by *The Strange Case of Dr. Jekyll and Mr. Hyde.* He experienced consequently for the first time the pleasures, such as they were, of celebrity, and also its inconveniences; found the most hospitable of refuges in the house of his kind friends, Mr. and Mrs. Charles Fairchild, at Newport; and quickly made many other friends, including Mr. C. Scribner and Mr. E. L. Burlingame, the owner and the editor of *Scribner's Magazine*, from whom he immediately received and accepted very advantageous offers of work. Having been dissuaded from braving for the present the fatigue of the long journey to Colorado and the extreme rigour of its winter climate, he determined to try instead a season at Saranac Lake in the Adirondack Mountains, New York State, which had lately been coming into reputation as a place of cure. There, under the care of the well-known resident physician, Dr. Trudeau, he spent nearly seven months, from the end of September, 1887, to the end of April, 1888, with results on the whole favourable to his own health, though not to that of his wife, who was never well at these high altitudes. His work during the winter consisted of the twelve papers published in the course of 1888 in *Scribner's Magazine*, including perhaps the most striking of all his essays, *A Chapter on Dreams, Pulvis et Umbra, Beggars, The Lantern Bearers, Random Memories,* etc.; as well as the greater part of *The Master of Ballantrae* and *The Wrong Box* — the last originally conceived and drafted by Mr. Lloyd Osbourne.

The following letters are selected from those which tell of his preparations to leave his Bournemouth home in the summer of 1887, of his voyage to New York and reception there at this date, and of his winter's life and work at Saranac.

To W. E. Henley

1887
ÆT. 37

During the two months following his father's death Stevenson had suffered much both from his old complaints and from depression of mind. His only work had been in preparing for press the verse collection *Underwoods*, the *Life of Fleeming Jenkin*, and the volume of essays called *Memories and Portraits.*

[Skerryvore, Bournemouth], *August, 1887.*

Dear Lad, — I write to inform you that Mr. Stevenson's well-known work, *Virginibus Puerisque*, is about to be reprinted. At the same time a second volume called *Memories and Portraits* will issue from the roar-

1887 ÆT. 37

ing loom. Its interest will be largely autobiographical, Mr. S. having sketched there the lineaments of many departed friends, and dwelt fondly, and with a m'istened eye, upon bygone pleasures. The two will be issued under the common title of *Familiar Essays;* but the volumes will be vended separately to those who are mean enough not to hawk at both.

The blood is at last stopped: only yesterday. I began to think I should not get away. However, I hope — I hope — remark the word — no boasting — I hope I may luff up a bit now. Dobell, whom I saw, gave as usual a good account of my lungs, and expressed himself, like his neighbours, hopefully about the trip. He says, my uncle says, Scott says, Brown says — they all say — You ought not to be in such a state of health; you should recover. Well, then, I mean to. My spirits are rising again after three months of black depression: I almost begin to feel as if I should care to live: I would, by God! And so I believe I shall.—Yours,

BULLETIN M'GURDER.

How has the Deacon gone?

To W. H. Low

[SKERRYVORE, BOURNEMOUTH], *August 6th, 1887.*

MY DEAR LOW,— We — my mother, my wife, my stepson, my maidservant, and myself, five souls — leave, if all is well, Aug. 20th, per Wilson line ss. *Ludgate Hill.* Shall probably evade N. Y. at first, cutting straight to a watering-place: Newport, I believe, its name. Afterwards we shall steal incognito into *la bonne ville,* and see no one but you and the Scribners, if it may be so managed. You must understand I have been very seedy indeed, quite a dead body; and unless the voyage does miracles, I shall have to draw it dam fine. Alas, "The Canoe Speaks" is now out of date; it will figure in my volume of verses now imminent. However, I may find some inspiration some day.—Till very soon, yours ever, R. L. S.

1887
ÆT. 37

To Miss Adelaide Boodle

The lady to whom the following (and much correspondence yet to come) is addressed had been an attached friend of the Skerryvore household. She had given R. L. S. a paper-cutter by way of farewell token at his starting.

Bournemouth, *August 19th, 1887.*

My dear Miss Boodle,—I promise you the paper-knife shall go to sea with me; and if it were in my disposal, I should promise it should return with me too. All that you say, I thank you for very much; I thank you for all the pleasantness that you have brought about our house; and I hope the day may come when I shall see you again in poor old Skerryvore, now left to the natives of Canada, or to worse barbarians, if such exist. I am afraid my attempt to jest is rather *à contre-cœur.* Good-bye—*au revoir*—and do not forget your friend,

Robert Louis Stevenson.

To Messrs. Chatto and Windus

The titles and proofs mentioned in the text are presumably those of *Underwoods* and *Memories and Portraits.*

Bournemouth [*August, 1887*].

Dear Sirs,—I here enclose the two titles. Had you not better send me the bargains to sign? I shall be

1887 ÆT. 37 here till Saturday; and shall have an address in London (which I shall send you) till Monday, when I shall sail. Even if the proofs do not reach you till Monday morning, you could send a clerk from Fenchurch Street Station at 10.23 A. M. for Galleons Station, and he would find me embarking on board the *Ludgate Hill*, Island Berth, Royal Albert Dock. Pray keep this in case it should be necessary to catch this last chance. I am most anxious to have the proofs with me on the voyage.—Yours very truly, ROBERT LOUIS STEVENSON.

To Sidney Colvin

A succession of Stevenson's friends had visited and spent part of the day or evening with him at Armfield's hotel on Sunday, August 20th, each bringing some farewell gift or another (as related by Mr. Gosse in his volume *Critical Kitcats*, p. 297). Among these, Mr. Henry James's gift had been a case of champagne for consumption during the journey. On the morning of the 21st I accompanied him to the docks, saw him and his party embarked on board the steamer *Ludgate Hill*, a vessel sailing from the port of London and carrying animals and freight as well as passengers. They had chosen to go by this route for the sake alike of economy and amusement, rather than by one of the sumptuous liners sailing from Liverpool or Southampton. Leaving the ship's side as she weighed anchor, and waving farewell to the party from the boat which landed me, I little knew what was the truth, that I was looking on the face of my friend for the last time. The letters next following were written during or immediately after his passage across the Atlantic. "The Commodore" is of course R. L. S.

H. M. S. "VULGARIUM," OFF HAVRE DE GRACE,
this 22nd day of August [*1887*].

SIR,—The weather has been hitherto inimitable. The berths are excellent, the pasture swallowable, the champagne of H. James (to recur to my favourite adjective) inimitable. As for the Commodore, he slept awhile in the evening, tossed off a cup of Henry James with his plain meal, walked the deck till eight, among sands and floating lights and buoys and wrecked brigantines, came down (to his regret) a minute too soon to see Margate lit up, turned in about nine, slept, with some interruptions, but on the whole sweetly, until six, and has already walked a mile or so of deck, among a fleet of other steamers waiting for the tide, within view of Havre, and pleasantly entertained by passing fishing-boats, hovering sea-gulls, and Vulgarians pairing on deck with endearments of primitive simplicity. There, sir, can be viewed the sham quarrel, the sham desire for information, and every device of these two poor ancient sexes (who might, you might think, have learned in the course of the ages something new) down to the exchange of head-gear.

I am, sir, yours,

BOLD BOB BOLTSPRIT.

B. B. B. (*alias* the Commodore) will now turn to his proofs. Havre de Grace is a city of some show. It is for-ti-fied; and, so far as I can see, is a place of some trade. It is situ-ated in France, a country of Europe. You always complain there are no facts in my letters.

R. L. S.

TO SIDNEY COLVIN

NEWPORT, R. I., U. S. A. [*September, 1887*].

MY DEAR COLVIN,—So long it went excellent well, and I had a time I am glad to have had; really enjoying my life. There is nothing like being at sea, after all. And O, why have I allowed myself to rot so long on land? But on the Banks I caught a cold, and I have not yet got over it. My reception here was idiotic to the last degree. . . . It is very silly, and not pleasant, except where humour enters; and I confess the poor interviewer lads pleased me. They are too good for their trade; avoided anything I asked them to avoid, and were no more vulgar in their reports than they could help. I liked the lads.

O, it was lovely on our stable-ship, chock full of stallions. She rolled heartily, rolled some of the fittings out of our state-room, and I think a more dangerous cruise (except that it was summer) it would be hard to imagine. But we enjoyed it to the masthead, all but Fanny; and even she perhaps a little. When we got in, we had run out of beer, stout, cocoa, soda-water, water, fresh meat, and (almost) of biscuit. But it was a thousandfold pleasanter than a great big Birmingham liner like a new hotel; and we liked the officers, and made friends with the quartermasters, and I (at least) made a friend of a baboon (for we carried a cargo of apes), whose embraces have pretty near cost me a coat. The passengers improved, and were a very good specimen lot, with no drunkard, no gambling that I saw, and less grumbling and backbiting than one would have asked of poor human nature. Apes, stallions, cows, matches, hay, and poor men-folk, all, or almost all, came successfully to land.—Yours ever, R. L. S.

To Henry James

[Newport, U. S. A., *September, 1887.*]

MY DEAR JAMES,—Here we are at Newport in the house of the good Fairchilds; and a sad burthen we have laid upon their shoulders. I have been in bed practically ever since I came. I caught a cold on the Banks after having had the finest time conceivable, and enjoyed myself more than I could have hoped on board our strange floating menagerie: stallions and monkeys and matches made our cargo; and the vast continent of these incongruities rolled the while like a haystack; and the stallions stood hypnotised by the motion, looking through the ports at our dinner-table, and winked when the crockery was broken; and the little monkeys stared at each other in their cages, and were thrown overboard like little bluish babies; and the big monkey, Jacko, scoured about the ship and rested willingly in my arms, to the ruin of my clothing; and the man of the stallions made a bower of the black tarpaulin, and sat therein at the feet of a raddled divinity, like a picture on a box of chocolates; and the other passengers, when they were not sick, looked on and laughed. Take all this picture, and make it roll till the bell shall sound unexpected notes and the fittings shall break loose in our state-room, and you have the voyage of the

1887 ÆT. 37

Ludgate Hill. She arrived in the port of New York, without beer, porter, soda-water, curaçoa, fresh meat, or fresh water; and yet we lived, and we regret her.

My wife is a good deal run down, and I am no great shakes.

America is, as I remarked, a fine place to eat in, and a great place for kindness; but, Lord, what a silly thing is popularity! I envy the cool obscurity of Skerryvore. If it even paid, said Meanness! and was abashed at himself.—Yours most sincerely, R. L. S.

To Sidney Colvin

[New York: *end of September, 1887.*]

MY DEAR S. C.,—Your delightful letter has just come, and finds me in a New York hotel, waiting the arrival of a sculptor (St. Gaudens) who is making a medallion of yours truly and who is (to boot) one of the handsomest and nicest fellows I have seen. I caught a cold on the Banks; fog is not for me; nearly died of interviewers and visitors, during twenty-four hours in New York; cut for Newport with Lloyd and Valentine, a journey like fairy-land for the most engaging beauties, one little rocky and pine-shaded cove after another, each with a house and a boat at anchor, so that I left my heart in each and marvelled why American authors had been so unjust to their country; caught another cold on the train; arrived at Newport to go to bed and to grow worse, and to stay in bed until I left again; the Fairchilds proving during this time kindness itself; Mr. Fairchild simply one of the most engaging men in the world, and one of the children, Blair, *æt.* ten, a great joy and amusement in his solemn adoring attitude to the author of *Treasure Island.*

Here I was interrupted by the arrival of my sculptor. I have begged him to make a medallion of himself and give me a copy. I will not take up the sentence in which I was wandering so long, but begin fresh. I was ten or twelve days at Newport; then came back convalescent to New York. Fanny and Lloyd are off to the Adirondacks to see if that will suit; and the rest of us leave Monday (this is Saturday) to follow them up. I hope we may manage to stay there all winter. I have a splendid appetite and have on the whole recovered well after a mighty sharp attack. I am now on a salary of £500 a year for twelve articles in *Scribner's Magazine* on what I like; it is more than £500, but I cannot calculate more precisely. You have no idea how much is made of me here; I was offered £2000 for a weekly article — eh heh! how is that? but I refused that lucrative job. The success of *Underwoods* is gratifying. You see, the verses are sane; that is their strong point, and it seems it is strong enough to carry them.

A thousand thanks for your grand letter. —Ever yours,

R. L. S.

To W. E. Henley

The verses herein alluded to were addressed to Dr. Gordon Hake in return for some received from him. They are those beginning "In the beloved hour that ushers day," and printed as No. xix. in *Songs of Travel.*

New York [*September, 1887*].

MY DEAR LAD, — Herewith verses for Dr. Hake, which please communicate. I did my best with the inter-

1887 ÆT. 37 And to think there are parties with yachts who would make the exchange! I know a little about fame now; it is no good compared to a yacht; and anyway there is more fame in a yacht, more genuine fame; to cross the Atlantic and come to anchor in Newport (say) with the Union Jack, and go ashore for your letters and hang about the pier, among the holiday yachtsmen — that 's fame, that 's glory, and nobody can take it away; they can't say your book is bad; you *have* crossed the Atlantic. I should do it south by the West Indies, to avoid the damned Banks; and probably come home by steamer, and leave the skipper to bring the yacht home.

Well, if all goes well, we shall maybe sail out of Southampton water some of these days and take a run to Havre, and try the Baltic, or somewhere.

Love to you all.— Ever your afft.,

ROBERT LOUIS STEVENSON.

TO EDMUND GOSSE

The following refers to a review by Mr. Gosse of Stevenson's volume of verse called *Underwoods*. The book had been published a few weeks previously, and is dedicated, as readers will remember, to a number of physicians who had attended him at sundry times and places.

SARANAC LAKE, *Oct. 8th, 1887.*

MY DEAR GOSSE,— I have just read your article twice, with cheers of approving laughter. I do not believe you ever wrote anything so funny: Tyndall's "shell," the passage on the Davos press and its invaluable issues, and that on V. Hugo and Swinburne, are exquisite; so,

I say it more ruefully, is the touch about the doctors. For the rest, I am very glad you like my verses so well; and the qualities you ascribe to them seem to me well found and well named. I own to that kind of candour you attribute to me: when I am frankly interested, I suppose I fancy the public will be so too; and when I am moved, I am sure of it. It has been my luck hitherto to meet with no staggering disillusion. "Before" and "After" may be two; and yet I believe the habit is now too thoroughly ingrained to be altered. About the doctors, you were right, that dedication has been the subject of some pleasantries that made me grind, and of your happily touched reproof which made me blush. And to miscarry in a dedication is an abominable form of book-wreck; I am a good captain, I would rather lose the tent and save my dedication.

I am at Saranac Lake in the Adirondacks, I suppose for the winter: it seems a first-rate place; we have a house in the eye of many winds, with a view of a piece of running water — Highland, all but the dear hue of peat — and of many hills — Highland also, but for the lack of heather. Soon the snow will close on us; we are here some twenty miles — twenty-seven, they say, but this I profoundly disbelieve — in the woods; communication by letter is slow and (let me be consistent) aleatory; by telegram is as near as may be impossible.

I had some experience of American appreciation; I liked a little of it, but there is too much; a little of that would go a long way to spoil a man; and I like myself better in the woods. I am so damned candid and ingenuous (for a cynic), and so much of a "cweatu' of im-

1887 ÆT. 37

pulse — aw" (if you remember that admirable Leech), that I begin to shirk any more taffy; I think I begin to like it too well. But let us trust the Gods; they have a rod in pickle; reverently I doff my trousers, and with screwed eyes await the *amari aliquid* of the great God Busby.

I thank you for the article in all ways, and remain yours affectionately, R. L. S.

To W. H. Low

[SARANAC LAKE, *October, 1887*.]

SIR, — I have to trouble you with the following *paroles bien senties*. We are here at a first-rate place. "Baker's" is the name of our house, but we don't address there; we prefer the tender care of the Post-Office, as more aristocratic (it is no use to telegraph even to the care of the Post-Office, who does not give a single damn[1]). Baker's has a prophet's chamber, which the hypercritical might describe as a garret with a hole in the floor: in that garret, sir, I have to trouble you and your wife to come and slumber. Not now, however: with manly hospitality, I choke off any sudden impulse. Because, first, my wife and my mother are gone (a note for the latter, strongly suspected to be in the hand of your talented wife, now sits silent on the mantel shelf), one to Niagara and t' other to Indianapolis. Because, second, we are not yet installed. And because, third, I won't have you till I have a buffalo robe and leggings,

1 "But he was more than usual calm;
He did not give a single damn." — *Marjorie Fleming.*

THE COTTAGE AT SARANAC LAKE OCCUPIED BY ROBERT LOUIS STEVENSON.

lest you should want to paint me as a plain man, which I am not, but a rank Saranacker and wild man of the woods.—Yours, ROBERT LOUIS STEVENSON.

TO WILLIAM ARCHER

The Wondrous Tale referred to in the following is Stevenson's *Black Arrow*, which had been through Mr. Archer's hands in proof.

SARANAC LAKE, *October, 1887*.

DEAR ARCHER,—Many thanks for the Wondrous Tale. It is scarcely a work of genius, as I believe you felt. Thanks also for your pencillings; though I defend "shrew," or at least many of the shrews.

We are here (I suppose) for the winter in the Adirondacks, a hill and forest country on the Canadian border of New York State, very unsettled and primitive and cold, and healthful, or we are the more bitterly deceived. I believe it will do well for me; but must not boast.

My wife is away to Indiana to see her family; my mother, Lloyd, and I remain here in the cold, which has been exceeding sharp, and the hill air, which is inimitably fine. We all eat bravely, and sleep well, and make great fires, and get along like one o'clock.

I am now a salaried party; I am a *bourgeois* now; I am to write a weekly paper for *Scribner's*, at a scale of payment which makes my teeth ache for shame and diffidence. The editor is, I believe, to apply to you; for we were talking over likely men, and when I instanced you, he said he had had his eye upon you from the first. It is worth while, perhaps, to get in tow with the Scribners; they are such thorough gentlefolk

1887 ÆT. 37

in all ways that it is always a pleasure to deal with them. I am like to be a millionaire if this goes on, and be publicly hanged at the social revolution: well, I would prefer that to dying in my bed; and it would be a godsend to my biographer, if ever I have one. What are you about? I hope you are all well and in good case and spirits, as I am now, after a most nefast experience of despondency before I left; but indeed I was quite run down. Remember me to Mrs. Archer, and give my respects to Tom.—Yours very truly,

ROBERT LOUIS STEVENSON.

To Henry James

The "dear Alexander" mentioned below is Mr. J. W. Alexander, the well-known American artist, who had been a welcome visitor to Stevenson at Bournemouth, and had drawn his portrait there. The humorous romance proceeding from Mr. Osbourne's typewriter was the first draft of *The Wrong Box*; or, as it was originally called, *The Finsbury Tontine*, or *A Game of Bluff*. The article by Mr. Henry James referred to in the last paragraph is one on R. L. S. which had appeared in the *Century Magazine* for October, and was reprinted in *Partial Portraits*.

[SARANAC LAKE, *October, 1887*.] I know not the day; but the month it is the drear October by the ghoul-haunted woodland of Weir.

MY DEAR HENRY JAMES,—This is to say, *First*, the voyage was a huge success. We all enjoyed it (bar my wife) to the ground: sixteen days at sea with a cargo of hay, matches, stallions, and monkeys, and in a ship with no style on, and plenty of sailors to talk to, and the endless pleasures of the sea — the romance of it, the sport of the scratch dinner and the smashing crockery, the pleasure — an endless pleasure — of balancing to the swell: well, it 's over.

1887
ÆT. 37

Second, I had a fine time, rather a troubled one, at Newport and New York; saw much of and liked hugely the Fairchilds, St. Gaudens the sculptor, Gilder of the *Century* — just saw the dear Alexander — saw a lot of my old and admirable friend Will Low, whom I wish you knew and appreciated — was medallioned by St. Gaudens, and at last escaped to

Third, Saranac Lake, where we now are, and which I believe we mean to like and pass the winter at. Our house — emphatically "Baker's" — is on a hill, and has a sight of a stream turning a corner in the valley — bless the face of running water! — and sees some hills too, and the paganly prosaic roofs of Saranac itself; the Lake it does not see, nor do I regret that; I like water (fresh water I mean) either running swiftly among stones, or else largely qualified with whisky. As I write, the sun (which has been long a stranger) shines in at my shoulder; from the next room, the bell of Lloyd's typewriter makes an agreeable music as it patters off (at a rate which astonishes this experienced novelist) the early chapters of a humorous romance; from still further off — the walls of Baker's are neither ancient nor massive — rumours of Valentine about the kitchen stove come to my ears; of my mother and Fanny I hear nothing, for the excellent reason that they have gone sparking off, one to Niagara, one to Indian-

1887
ÆT. 37

apolis. People complain that I never give news in my letters. I have wiped out that reproach.

But now, *Fourth*, I have seen the article; and it may be from natural partiality, I think it the best you have written. O—I remember the Gautier, which was an excellent performance; and the Balzac, which was good; and the Daudet, over which I licked my chops; but the R. L. S. is better yet. It is so humorous, and it hits my little frailties with so neat (and so friendly) a touch; and Alan is the occasion for so much happy talk, and the quarrel is so generously praised. I read it twice, though it was only some hours in my possession; and Low, who got it for me from the *Century*, sat up to finish it ere he returned it; and, sir, we were all delighted. Here is the paper out, nor will anything, not even friendship, not even gratitude for the article, induce me to begin a second sheet; so here with the kindest remembrances and the warmest good wishes, I remain, yours affectionately, R. L. S.

To Charles Baxter

[Saranac Lake], *18th November, 1887.*

MY DEAR CHARLES,—No likely I 'm going to waste a sheet of paper. . . . I am offered £1600 ($8000) for the American serial rights on my next story! As you say, times are changed since the Lothian Road. Well, the Lothian Road was grand fun too; I could take an afternoon of it with great delight. But I 'm awfu' grand noo, and long may it last!

Remember me to any of the faithful—if there are

any left. I wish I could have a crack with you.—
—Yours ever affectionately, R. L. S.

I find I have forgotten more than I remembered of business. . . . Please let us know (if you know) for how much Skerryvore is let; you will here detect the female mind; I let it for what I could get; nor shall the possession of this knowledge (which I am happy to have forgot) increase the amount by so much as the shadow of a sixpenny piece; but my females are agog.
—Yours ever, R. L. S.

To Charles Scribner

Shortly after the date of the present correspondence Stevenson, to his great advantage, put all his publishing arrangements (as he had already put his private business) into the hands of his friend, Mr. Baxter. Meantime he was managing them himself; and an occasional lapse of memory or attention betrayed him once or twice into misunderstandings, and once at least into conflicting agreements with two different publishers, both his friends. He was the first to denounce the error when he became aware of it, and suffered sharply from the sense of his own unintentional fault. The next two letters, and some allusions in those which follow, relate to this affair.

[Saranac Lake, *November 20 or 21, 1887.*]

My dear Mr. Scribner,— Heaven help me, I am under a curse just now. I have played fast and loose with what I said to you; and that, I beg you to believe, in the purest innocence of mind. I told you you should have the power over all my work in this country; and about a fortnight ago, when M'Clure was here, I calmly signed a bargain for the serial publication of a story. You will scarce believe that I did this in mere oblivion; but I

1887 ÆT. 37

did; and all that I can say is that I will do so no more, and ask you to forgive me. Please write to me soon as to this.

Will you oblige me by paying in for three articles, as already sent, to my account with John Paton & Co., 52 William Street. This will be most convenient for us.

The fourth article is nearly done; and I am the more deceived, or it is *A Buster*.

Now as to the first thing in this letter, I do wish to hear from you soon; and I am prepared to hear any reproach, or (what is harder to hear) any forgiveness; for I have deserved the worst.—Yours sincerely,

ROBERT LOUIS STEVENSON.

TO E. L. BURLINGAME

[SARANAC LAKE, *November, 1887*.]

DEAR MR. BURLINGAME,—I enclose corrected proof of *Beggars*, which seems good. I mean to make a second sermon, which, if it is about the same length as *Pulvis et Umbra*, might go in along with it as two sermons, in which case I should call the first "The Whole Creation," and the second "Any Good." We shall see; but you might say how you like the notion.

One word: if you have heard from Mr. Scribner of my unhappy oversight in the matter of a story, you will make me ashamed to write to you, and yet I wish to beg you to help me into quieter waters. The oversight committed—and I do think it was not so bad as Mr. Scribner seems to think it—and discovered, I was in a miserable position. I need not tell you that my first impulse was to offer to share or to surrender the price agreed upon when it should fall due; and it is almost to my credit that I arranged to refrain. It is one of these positions from which there is no escape; I cannot undo what I have done. And I wish to beg you—should Mr. Scribner speak to you in the matter—to try to get him to see this neglect of mine for no worse than it is: unpardonable enough, because a breach of an agreement; but still pardonable, because a piece of sheer carelessness and want of memory, done, God knows, without design and since most sincerely regretted. I have no memory. You have seen how I omitted to reserve the American rights in *Jekyll:* last winter I wrote and demanded, as an increase, a less sum than had already been agreed upon for a story that I gave to *Cassell's.* For once that my forgetfulness has, by a cursed fortune, seemed to gain, instead of lose, me money, it is painful indeed that I should produce so poor an impression on the mind of Mr. Scribner. But I beg you to believe, and if possible to make him believe, that I am in no degree or sense a *faiseur,* and that in matters of business my design, at least, is honest. Nor (bating bad memory and self-deception) am I untruthful in such affairs.

If Mr. Scribner shall have said nothing to you in the matter, please regard the above as unwritten, and believe me, yours very truly,

ROBERT LOUIS STEVENSON.

To E. L. BURLINGAME

[SARANAC LAKE, *November, 1887.*]

DEAR MR. BURLINGAME,—The revise seemed all right, so I did not trouble you with it; indeed, my demand

1887 ÆT. 37

for one was theatrical, to impress that obdurate dog, your reader. Herewith a third paper: it has been a cruel long time upon the road, but here it is, and not bad at last, I fondly hope. I was glad you liked *The Lantern Bearers;* I did, too. I thought it was a good paper, really contained some excellent sense, and was ingeniously put together. I have not often had more trouble than I have with these papers; thirty or forty pages of foul copy, twenty is the very least I have had. Well, you pay high; it is fit that I should have to work hard, it somewhat quiets my conscience.—Yours very truly, ROBERT LOUIS STEVENSON.

TO J. A. SYMONDS

SARANAC LAKE, ADIRONDACK MOUNTAINS,
NEW YORK, U. S. A., *November 21, 1887.*

MY DEAR SYMONDS,—I think we have both meant and wanted to write to you any time these months; but we have been much tossed about, among new faces and old, and new scenes and old, and scenes (like this of Saranac) which are neither one nor other. To give you some clue to our affairs, I had best begin pretty well back. We sailed from the Thames in a vast bucket of iron that took seventeen days from shore to shore. I cannot describe how I enjoyed the voyage, nor what good it did me; but on the Banks I caught friend catarrh. In New York and then in Newport I was pretty ill; but on my return to New York, lying in bed most of the time, with St. Gaudens the sculptor sculping me, and my old friend Low around, I began to pick up once more. Now here we are in a kind of wilderness of hills and firwoods and boulders and snow and wooden houses. So far as we have gone the climate is grey and harsh, but hungry and somnolent; and although not charming like that of Davos, essentially bracing and briskening. The country is a kind of insane mixture of Scotland and a touch of Switzerland and a dash of America, and a thought of the British Channel in the skies. We have a decent house —

December 6th.

— A decent house, as I was saying, sir, on a hill-top, with a look down a Scottish river in front, and on one hand a Perthshire hill; on the other, the beginnings and skirts of the village play hide-and-seek among other hills. We have been below zero, I know not how far (·10 at 8 A. M. once), and when it is cold it is delightful; but hitherto the cold has not held, and we have chopped in and out from frost to thaw, from snow to rain, from quiet air to the most disastrous north-westerly curdlers of the blood. After a week of practical thaw, the ice still bears in favoured places. So there is hope.

I wonder if you saw my book of verses? It went into a second edition, because of my name, I suppose, and its *prose* merits. I do not set up to be a poet. Only an all-round literary man: a man who talks, not one who sings. But I believe the very fact that it was only speech served the book with the public. Horace is much a speaker, and see how popular! most of Martial is only speech, and I cannot conceive a person who does not love his Martial; most of Burns, also, such as *The Louse, The Toothache, The Haggis,* and lots more

1887 ÆT. 37

of his best. Excuse this little apology for my house; but I don't like to come before people who have a note of song, and let it be supposed I do not know the difference.

To return to the more important — news. My wife again suffers in high and cold places; I again profit. She is off to-day to New York for a change, as heretofore to Berne, but I am glad to say in better case than then. Still it is undeniable she suffers, and you must excuse her (at least) if we both prove bad correspondents. I am decidedly better, but I have been terribly cut up with business complications: one disagreeable, as threatening loss; one, of the most intolerable complexion, as involving me in dishonour. The burthen of consistent carelessness: I have lost much by it in the past; and for once (to my damnation) I have gained. I am sure you will sympathise. It is hard work to sleep; it is hard to be told you are a liar, and have to hold your peace, and think, "Yes, by God, and a thief too!" You remember my lectures on Ajax, or the Unintentional Sin? Well, I know all about that now. Nothing seems so unjust to the sufferer: or is more just in essence. *Laissez passer la justice de Dieu.*

Lloyd has learned to use the typewriter, and has most gallantly completed upon that the draft of a tale, which seems to me not without merit and promise, it is so silly, so gay, so absurd, in spots (to my partial eyes) so genuinely humorous. It is true, he would not have written it but for *The New Arabian Nights;* but it is strange to find a young writer funny. Heavens, but I was depressing when I took the pen in hand! And now I doubt if I am sadder than my neighbours. Will this beginner move in the inverse direction?

Let me have your news, and believe me, my dear Symonds, with genuine affection, yours,

ROBERT LOUIS STEVENSON.

To W. E. HENLEY

The following refers to a volume on the elder Dumas, which Mr. Henley was at this time preparing to write, and which he proposed to dedicate to his friend.

SARANAC LAKE [*December, 1887*].

MY DEAR LAD, — I was indeed overjoyed to hear of the Dumas. In the matter of the dedication, are not cross-dedications a little awkward? Lang and Rider Haggard did it, to be sure. Perpend. And if you should conclude against a dedication, there is a passage in *Memories and Portraits* written *at* you, when I was most desperate (to stir you up a bit), which might be quoted: something about Dumas still waiting hls biographer. I have a decent time when the weather is fine; when it is grey, or windy, or wet (as it too often is), I am merely degraded to the dirt. I get some work done every day with a devil of a heave; not extra good ever; and I regret my engagement. Whiles I have had the most deplorable business annoyances too; have been threatened with having to refund money; got over that; and found myself in the worse scrape of being a kind of unintentional swindler. These have worried me a great deal; also old age with his stealing steps seems to have clawed me in his clutch to some tune.

Do you play All Fours? We are trying it; it is still

1887 ÆT. 37 all haze to me. Can the elder hand *beg* more than once? The Port Admiral is at Boston mingling with millionaires. I am but a weed on Lethe wharf. The wife is only so-so. The Lord lead us all: if I can only get off the stage with clean hands, I shall sing Hosanna. "Put" is described quite differently from your version in a book I have; what are your rules? The Port Admiral is using a game of put in a tale of his, the first copy of which was gloriously finished about a fortnight ago, and the revise gallantly begun: *The Finsbury Tontine* it is named, and might fill two volumes, and is quite incredibly silly, and in parts (it seems to me) pretty humorous.—Love to all from

AN OLD, OLD MAN.

I say, Taine's *Origines de la France Contemporaine* is no end; it would turn the dead body of Charles Fox into a living Tory.

TO MRS. FLEEMING JENKIN

[SARANAC LAKE, *December, 1887.*]

MY DEAR MRS. JENKIN,—The Opal is very well; it is fed with glycerine when it seems hungry. I am very well, and get about much more than I could have hoped. My wife is not very well; there is no doubt the high level does not agree with her, and she is on the move for a holiday to New York. Lloyd is at Boston on a visit, and I hope has a good time. My mother is really first-rate; she and I, despairing of other games for two, now play All Fours out of a gamebook, and have not yet discovered its niceties, if any.

You will have heard, I dare say, that they made a great row over me here. They also offered me much money, a great deal more than my works are worth: I took some of it, and was greedy and hasty, and am now very sorry. I have done with big prices from now out. Wealth and self-respect seem, in my case, to be strangers.

1887
ÆT. 37

We were talking the other day of how well Fleeming managed to grow rich. Ah, that is a rare art; something more intellectual than a virtue. The book has not yet made its appearance here; the life alone, with a little preface, is to appear in the States; and the Scribners are to send you half the royalties. I should like it to do well, for Fleeming's sake.

Will you please send me the Greek water-carrier's song? I have a particular use for it.

Have I any more news, I wonder?—and echo wonders along with me. I am strangely disquieted on all political matters; and I do not know if it is "the signs of the times" or the sign of my own time of life. But to me the sky seems black both in France and England, and only partly clear in America. I have not seen it so dark in my time; of that I am sure.

Please let us have some news; and excuse me, for the sake of my well-known idleness; and pardon Fanny, who is really not very well, for this long silence.—Very sincerely your friend,

ROBERT LOUIS STEVENSON.

TO MISS ADELAIDE BOODLE

The lady at Bournemouth (the giver of the paper-knife) to whom the following letter is addressed had been trusted to keep an eye on

Stevenson's interests in connection with his house (which had been let) and other matters, and to report thereon from time to time. In their correspondence Stevenson is generally referred to as the Squire, and the lady as the Gamekeeper.

[SARANAC LAKE, *December, 1887.*]

MY DEAR MISS BOODLE,—I am so much afraid, our gamekeeper may weary of unacknowledged reports! Hence, in the midst of a perfect horror of detestable weathers of a quite incongruous strain, and with less desire for correspondence than—well, than—well, with no desire for correspondence, behold me dash into the breach. Do keep up your letters. They are most delightful to this exiled backwoods family; and in your next, we shall hope somehow or other to hear better news of you and yours — that in the first place — and to hear more news of our beasts and birds and kindly fruits of earth and those human tenants who are (truly) too much with us.

I am very well; better than for years: that is for good. But then my wife is no great shakes; the place does not suit her — it is my private opinion that no place does — and she is now away down to New York for a change, which (as Lloyd is in Boston) leaves my mother and me and Valentine alone in our wind-beleaguered hilltop hatbox of a house. You should hear the cows butt against the walls in the early morning while they feed; you should also see our back log when the thermometer goes (as it does go) away — away below zero, till it can be seen no more by the eye of man — not the thermometer, which is still perfectly visible, but the mercury, which curls up into the bulb like a hibernating bear; you should also see the lad who "does chores" for us, with his red stockings and his thirteen-year-old face, and his highly manly tramp into the room; and his two alternative answers to all questions about the weather: either "Cold," or with a really lyrical movement of the voice, "*Lovely*—raining!"

Will you take this miserable scrap for what it is worth? Will you also understand that I am the man to blame, and my wife is really almost too much out of health to write, or at least does n't write?—And believe me, with kind remembrances to Mrs. Boodle and your sisters, very sincerely yours,

ROBERT LOUIS STEVENSON.

TO CHARLES BAXTER

[SARANAC LAKE], *12th December, '87.*

Give us news of all your folk. A Merry Christmas from all of us.

MY DEAR CHARLES,—Will you please send £20 to —— for a Christmas gift from ——? Moreover, I cannot remember what I told you to send to ——; but as God has dealt so providentially with me this year, I now propose to make it £20.

I beg of you also to consider my strange position. I jined a club which it was said was to defend the Union; and I had a letter from the secretary, which his name I believe was Lord Warmingpan (or words to that effect), to say I am elected, and had better pay up a certain sum of money, I forget what. Now I cannae verra weel draw a blank cheque and send to—

LORD WARMINGPAN (or words to that effect),
London, England.

1887
ÆT. 37

And, man, if it was possible, I would be dooms glad to be out o' this bit scrapie. Mebbe the club was ca'd "The Union," but I wouldnae like to sweir; and mebbe it wasnae, or mebbe only words to that effec'—but I wouldnae care just exac'ly about sweirin'. Do ye no think Henley, or Pollick, or some o' they London fellies, micht mebbe perhaps find out for me? and just what the soom was? And that you would aiblins pay for me? For I thocht I was sae dam patriotic jinin', and it would be a kind o' a come-doun to be turned out again. Mebbe Lang would ken; or mebbe Rider Haggyard: they 're kind o' Union folks. But it 's my belief his name was Warmingpan whatever.—Yours,

THOMSON,
alias ROBERT LOUIS STEVENSON.

Could it be Warminster?[1]

TO MISS MONROE

The play of *Deacon Brodie* was at this time being performed at Chicago, with Mr. E. J. Henley in the title-part.

SARANAC LAKE, NEW YORK [*December 19, 1887*].

DEAR MISS MONROE,—Many thanks for your letter and your good wishes. It was much my desire to get to Chicago: had I done—or if I yet do—so, I shall hope to see the original of my photograph, which is one of my show possessions; but the fates are rather contrary. My wife is far from well; I myself dread worse than almost any other imaginable peril, that miraculous and

[1] The secretary was really, I believe, Lord Pollington.

My dear Henry James

It may please you to know how our family has been employed. In the silence of the snow, the afternoon lamp has lighted an eager fireside group; my mother reading, Fanny, Lloyd and I devoted listeners; and the work was really one of the best works I ever heard; and its author is to be praised and honoured; and what do you suppose is the name of it? and have you ever read it yourself. and (I am bound I will get to the bottom of the page before I blow the gaff, if I have to fight it out on this line all summer; for if you have not to turn a leaf, there can be no suspense, the conspectary eye being swift to pick out proper names; and without suspense, there can be little pleasure in this world, to my mind at least) and in short the name of it is

Roderick Hudson. if you please. My dear James, it is very spirited, and very sound, and very noble too. Hudson, Mrs Hudson, Rowland. O, all first rate. Rowland a very fine fellow. Hudson as good as he can stick (did you know Hudson? I suspect you did) Mrs H his real born mother, a thing rarely managed in fiction.

We are all keeping pretty fit and pretty hearty; but this letter is not from me to you, it is from a reader of R. H to the author of the same, and it says nothing, and has nothing to say, but thank you.

We are going to re-read Casamassima as a proper pendant. Sir, I think these two are your best; and care not who knows it.

May I beg you, the next time Roderick is printed off, to go over the sheets of the last few chapters, and strike out "immense" and "tremendous"? You have simply dropped them there like your pocket-handkerchief; and all you have to do is to pick them up and pouch them, and your room — what do I say? — your cathedral! — will be swept and garnished.

I am, dear Sir.

Your delighted reader

Robert Louis Stevenson

P.S. Perhaps it is a pang of causeless honesty, perhaps I hope it will set a value on my praise of Roderick, perhaps it's a burst of the diabolic, but I must break out with the news that I can't bear the Portrait of a Lady. I read it all, and I wept too; but I can't stand your having written it; and I beg you will write no more of the like. Infra, sir; Below you: I can't help it — it may be your favourite work, but in my eyes it's BELOW YOU to write and me to read. I thought Roderick was going to be another such at the beginning; and I cannot describe my pleasure as I found it taking bones and blood, and looking out at me with a moved and human countenance, whose lineaments are written in my memory until my last of days.

R. L. S.

My wife begs your forgiveness. I believe for her silence.

really insane invention the American Railroad Car. Heaven help the man — may I add the woman — that sets foot in one! Ah, if it were only an ocean to cross, it would be a matter of small thought to me — and great pleasure. But the railroad car — every man has his weak point; and I fear the railroad car as abjectly as I do an earwig, and, on the whole, on better grounds. You do not know how bitter it is to have to make such a confession; for you have not the pretension nor the weakness of a man. If I do get to Chicago, you will hear of me: so much can be said. And do you never come east?

I was pleased to recognise a word of my poor old Deacon in your letter. It would interest me very much to hear how it went and what you thought of piece and actors; and my collaborator, who knows and respects the photograph, would be pleased too.—Still in the hope of seeing you, I am, yours very truly,

ROBERT LOUIS STEVENSON.

To Henry James

SARANAC LAKE [*Winter, 1887-8*].

MY DEAR HENRY JAMES,— It may please you to know how our family has been employed. In the silence of the snow the afternoon lamp has lighted an eager fireside group: my mother reading, Fanny, Lloyd, and I devoted listeners; and the work was really one of the best works I ever heard; and its author is to be praised and honoured; and what do you suppose is the name of it? and have you ever read it yourself? and (I am

1887
ÆT. 37

bound I will get to the bottom of the page before I blow the gaff, if I have to fight it out on this line all summer; for if you have not to turn a leaf, there can be no suspense, the conspectory eye being swift to pick out proper names; and without suspense, there can be little pleasure in this world, to my mind at least)—and, in short, the name of it is *Roderick Hudson*, if you please. My dear James, it is very spirited, and very sound, and very noble too. Hudson, Mrs. Hudson, Rowland, O, all first-rate: Rowland a very fine fellow; Hudson as good as he can stick (did you know Hudson? I suspect you did), Mrs. H. his real born mother, a thing rarely managed in fiction.

We are all keeping pretty fit and pretty hearty; but this letter is not from me to you, it is from a reader of *R. H.* to the author of the same, and it says nothing, and has nothing to say, but thank you.

We are going to re-read *Casamassima* as a proper pendant. Sir, I think these two are your best, and care not who knows it.

May I beg you, the next time *Roderick* is printed off, to go over the sheets of the last few chapters, and strike out "immense" and "tremendous"? You have simply dropped them there like your pocket-handkerchief; all you have to do is to pick them up and pouch them, and your room—what do I say?—your cathedral!—will be swept and garnished.—I am, dear sir, your delighted reader, ROBERT LOUIS STEVENSON.

P. S.—Perhaps it is a pang of causeless honesty, perhaps I hope it will set a value on my praise of *Roderick*, perhaps it 's a burst of the diabolic, but I must break out with the news that I can't bear the *Portrait of a Lady*. I read it all, and I wept too; but I can't stand your having written it; and I beg you will write no more of the like. *Infra*, sir; Below you: I can't help it — it may be your favourite work, but in my eyes it 's BELOW YOU to write and me to read. I thought *Roderick* was going to be another such at the beginning; and I cannot describe my pleasure as I found it taking bones and blood, and looking out at me with a moved and human countenance, whose lineaments are written in my memory until my last of days. R. L. S.

My wife begs your forgiveness; I believe for her silence.

To Sidney Colvin

SARANAC LAKE [*December, 1887*].

MY DEAR COLVIN, — This goes to say that we are all fit, and the place is very bleak and wintry, and up to now has shown no such charms of climate as Davos, but is a place where men eat and where the cattarh, catarrh (cattarrh, or cattarrhh) appears to be unknown. I walk in my verandy in the snaw, sir, looking down over one of those dabbled wintry landscapes that are (to be frank) so chilly to the human bosom, and up at a grey, English — nay, *mehercle*, Scottish — heaven; and I think it pretty bleak; and the wind swoops at me round the corner, like a lion, and fluffs the snow in my face; and I could aspire to be elsewhere; but yet I do not catch cold, and yet, when I come in, I eat. So that hitherto Saranac, if not deliriously delectable, has not

1887
ÆT. 37

(4) Clementina, *engaged to the first, married to the second.*

(5) Ephraim Mackellar, *land steward at Durrisdeer and narrator of the most of the book.*

(6) Francis Burke, Chevalier de St. Louis, *one of Prince Charlie's Irishmen and narrator of the rest.*

Besides these, many instant figures, most of them dumb or nearly so: Jessie Brown the whore, Captain Crail, Captain MacCombie, our old friend Alan Breck, our old friend Riach (both only for an instant), Teach the pirate (vulgarly Blackbeard), John Paul and Macconochie, servants at Durrisdeer. The date is from 1745 to '65 (about). The scene, near Kirkcudbright, in the States, and for a little moment in the French East Indies. I have done most of the big work, the quarrel, duel between the brothers, and announcement of the death to Clementina and my Lord — Clementina, Henry, and Mackellar (nicknamed Squaretoes) are really very fine fellows; the Master is all I know of the devil. I have known hints of him, in the world, but always cowards; he is as bold as a lion, but with the same deadly, causeless duplicity I have watched with so much surprise in my two cowards. 'T is true, I saw a hint of the same nature in another man who was not a coward; but he had other things to attend to; the Master has nothing else but his devilry. Here come my visitors — and have now gone, or the first relay of them; and I hope no more may come. For mark you, sir, this is our 'day'— Saturday, as ever was; and here we sit, my mother and I, before a large wood fire and await the enemy with the most steadfast courage; and without snow and greyness: and the woman Fanny in New York for her health, which is far from good; and the lad Lloyd at the inn in the village because he has a cold; and the handmaid Valentine abroad in a sleigh upon her messages; and to-morrow Christmas and no mistake. Such is human life: *la carrière humaine.* I will enclose, if I remember, the required autograph.

I will do better, put it on the back of this page. Love to all, and mostly, my very dear Colvin, to yourself. For whatever I say or do, or don't say or do, you may be very sure I am,—Yours always affectionately,

R. L. S.

To Miss Adelaide Boodle

Saranac Lake, Adirondacks,
N. Y., U. S. A., *Christmas, 1887.*

MY DEAR MISS BOODLE,—And a very good Christmas to you all; and better fortune; and if worse, the more courage to support it—which I think is the kinder wish in all human affairs. Somewhile—I fear a good while—after this, you should receive our Christmas gift; we have no tact and no taste, only a welcome and (often) tonic brutality; and I dare say the present, even after my friend Baxter has acted on and reviewed my hints, may prove a White Elephant. That is why I dread presents. And therefore pray understand if any element of that hamper prove unwelcome, *it is to be exchanged.* I will not sit down under the name of a giver of White Elephants. I never had any elephant

1888
ÆT. 38

To E. L. Burlingame

[Saranac Lake, *Winter, 1887-8.*]

Dear Mr. Burlingame,—I am keeping the sermon to see if I can't add another. Meanwhile, I will send you very soon a different paper which may take its place. Possibly some of these days soon I may get together a talk on things current, which should go in (if possible) earlier than either. I am now less nervous about these papers; I believe I can do the trick without great strain, though the terror that breathed on my back in the beginning is not yet forgotten.

The Master of Ballantrae I have had to leave aside, as I was quite worked out. But in about a week I hope to try back and send you the first four numbers: these are all drafted, it is only the revision that has broken me down, as it is often the hardest work. These four I propose you should set up for me at once, and we 'll copyright 'em in a pamphlet. I will tell you the names of the *bona fide* purchasers in England.

The numbers will run from twenty to thirty pages of my manuscript. You can give me that much, can you not? It is a howling good tale—at least these first four numbers are; the end is a trifle more fantastic, but 't is all picturesque.

Don't trouble about any more French books; I am on another scent, you see, just now. Only the *French in Hindustan* I await with impatience, as that is for *Ballantrae.* The scene of that romance is Scotland—the States—Scotland—India—Scotland—and the States again; so it jumps like a flea. I have enough about the States now, and very much obliged I am; yet if Drake's *Tragedies of the Wilderness* is (as I gather) a collection of originals, I should like to purchase it. If it is a picturesque vulgarisation, I do not wish to look it in the face. Purchase, I say; for I think it would be well to have some such collection by me with a view to fresh works.—Yours very sincerely,

ROBERT LOUIS STEVENSON.

P.S.—If you think of having *The Master* illustrated, I suggest that Hole would be very well up to the Scottish, which is the larger, part. If you have it done here, tell your artist to look at the hall of Craigievar in Billing's *Baronial and Ecclesiastical Antiquities*, and he will get a broad hint for the hall at Durrisdeer: it is, I think, the chimney of Craigievar and the roof of Pinkie, and perhaps a little more of Pinkie altogether; but I should have to see the book myself to be sure. Hole would be invaluable for this. I dare say if you had it illustrated, you could let me have one or two for the English edition. R. L. S.

TO WILLIAM ARCHER

The following refers to Mr. Bernard Shaw's novel *Cashel Byron's Profession*, which had been sent Stevenson to read by their common friend Mr. Archer.

[SARANAC LAKE, *Winter, 1887-88.*]

MY DEAR ARCHER,—What am I to say? I have read your friend's book with singular relish. If he has

1888
ÆT. 38

written any other, I beg you will let me see it; and if he has not, I beg him to lose no time in supplying the deficiency. It is full of promise; but I should like to know his age. There are things in it that are very clever, to which I attach small importance; it is the shape of the age. And there are passages, particularly the rally in presence of the Zulu king, that show genuine and remarkable narrative talent — a talent that few will have the wit to understand, a talent of strength, spirit, capacity, sufficient vision, and sufficient self-sacrifice, which last is the chief point in a narrator.

As a whole, it is (of course) a fever dream of the most feverish. Over Bashville the footman I howled with derision and delight; I dote on Bashville — I could read of him for ever; *de Bashville je suis le fervent* — there is only one Bashville, and I am his devoted slave; *Bashville est magnifique, mais il n'est guère possible.* He is the note of the book. It is all mad, mad and deliriously delightful; the author has a taste in chivalry like Walter Scott's or Dumas', and then he daubs in little bits of socialism; he soars away on the wings of the romantic griffon — even the griffon, as he cleaves air, shouting with laughter at the nature of the quest — and I believe in his heart he thinks he is labouring in a quarry of solid granite realism.

It is this that makes me — the most hardened adviser now extant — stand back and hold my peace. If Mr. Shaw is below five-and-twenty, let him go his path; if he is thirty, he had best be told that he is a romantic, and pursue romance with his eyes open; — or perhaps he knows it; — God knows! — my brain is softened.

It is HORRID FUN. All I ask is more of it. Thank you

for the pleasure you gave us, and tell me more of the inimitable author.

(I say, Archer, my God, what women!) — Yours very truly, ROBERT LOUIS STEVENSON.

To WILLIAM ARCHER

[SARANAC LAKE, *February, 1888.*]

MY DEAR ARCHER,— Pretty sick in bed; but necessary to protest and continue your education.

Why was Jenkin an amateur in my eyes? You think because not amusing (I think he often was amusing). The reason is this: I never, or almost never, saw two pages of his work that I could not have put in one without the smallest loss of material. That is the only test I know of writing. If there is anywhere a thing said in two sentences that could have been as clearly and as engagingly and as forcibly said in one, then it 's amateur work. Then you will bring me up with old Dumas. Nay, the object of a story is to be long, to fill up hours; the story-teller's art of writing is to water out by continual invention, historical and technical, and yet not seem to water; seem on the other hand to practise that same wit of conspicuous and declaratory condensation which is the proper art of writing. That is one thing in which my stories fail: I am always cutting the flesh off their bones.

I would rise from the dead to preach!

Hope all well. I think my wife better, but she 's not allowed to write; and this (only wrung from me by

1888 ÆT. 38 desire to Boss and Parsonise and Dominate, strong in sickness) is my first letter for days, and will likely be my last for many more. Not blame my wife for her silence: doctor's orders. All much interested by your last, and fragment from brother, and anecdotes of Tomarcher.—The sick but still Moral R. L. S.

Tell Shaw to hurry up: I want another.

To William Archer

In early days in Paris, Stevenson's chivalrous feelings were once shocked by the scene in the *Demi-Monde* of Dumas *fils* where Suzanne d'Auge is trapped by Olivier de Jalin. His correspondent had asked to know exactly what was the sequel.

[Saranac Lake, *Spring, 1888?*]

MY DEAR ARCHER,—It happened thus. I came forth from that performance in a breathing heat of indignation. (Mind, at this distance of time and with my increased knowledge, I admit there is a problem in the piece; but I saw none then, except a problem in brutality; and I still consider the problem in that case not established.) On my way down the *Français* stairs, I trod on an old gentleman's toes, whereupon, with that suavity that so well becomes me, I turned about to apologise, and on the instant, repenting me of that intention, stopped the apology midway, and added something in French to this effect: No, you are one of the *lâches* who have been applauding that piece. I retract my apology. Said the old Frenchman, laying his hand on my arm, and with a smile that was truly heavenly in temperance, irony, good nature, and knowledge of the world, "Ah, monsieur, vous êtes bien jeune!"—Yours very truly, ROBERT LOUIS STEVENSON.

1888
ÆT. 38

To E. L. BURLINGAME

[SARANAC, *February, 1888*].

DEAR MR. BURLINGAME,—Will you send me (from the library) some of the works of my dear old G. P. R. James? With the following especially I desire to make or to renew acquaintance: *The Songster, The Gipsy, The Convict, The Stepmother, The Gentleman of the Old School, The Robber.*

Excusez du peu.

This sudden return to an ancient favourite hangs upon an accident. The "Franklin County Library" contains two works of his, *The Cavalier* and *Morley Ernstein.* I read the first with indescribable amusement—it was worse than I had feared, and yet somehow engaging; the second (to my surprise) was better than I had dared to hope: a good, honest, dull, interesting tale, with a genuine old-fashioned talent in the invention when not strained; and a genuine old-fashioned feeling for the English language. This experience awoke appetite, and you see I have taken steps to stay it. R. L. S.

To E. L. BURLINGAME

[SARANAC LAKE, *February, 1888.*]

DEAR MR. BURLINGAME,—1. Of course then don't use it. Dear Man, I write these to please you, not myself,

1888
ÆT. 38

and you know a main sight better than I do what is good. In that case, however, I enclose another paper, and return the corrected proof of *Pulvis et Umbra*, so that we may be afloat.

2. I want to say a word as to *The Master*. (*The Master of Ballantrae* shall be the name by all means.) If you like and want it, I leave it to you to make an offer. You may remember I thought the offer you made when I was still in England too small; by which I did not at all mean, I thought it less than it was worth, but too little to tempt me to undergo the disagreeables of serial publication. This tale (if you want it) you are to have; for it is the least I can do for you; and you are to observe that the sum you pay me for my articles going far to meet my wants, I am quite open to be satisfied with less than formerly. I tell you I do dislike this battle of the dollars. I feel sure you all pay too much here in America; and I beg you not to spoil me any more. For I am getting spoiled: I do not want wealth, and I feel these big sums demoralise me.

My wife came here pretty ill; she had a dreadful bad night; to-day she is better. But now Valentine is ill; and Lloyd and I have got breakfast, and my hand somewhat shakes after washing dishes.—Yours very sincerely, ROBERT LOUIS STEVENSON.

P. S.—Please order me the *Evening Post* for two months. My subscription is run out. *The Mutiny* and *Edwardes* to hand.

To Sidney Colvin

[Saranac Lake, *March, 1888.*]

MY DEAR COLVIN,—Fanny has been very unwell. She is not long home, has been ill again since her return, but is now better again to a degree. You must not blame her for not writing, as she is not allowed to write at all, not even a letter. To add to our misfortunes, Valentine is quite ill and in bed. Lloyd and I get breakfast; I have now, 10.15, just got the dishes washed and the kitchen all clear, and sit down to give you as much news as I have spirit for, after such an engagement. Glass is a thing that really breaks my spirit: I do not like to fail, and with glass I cannot reach the work of my high calling—the artist's.

I am, as you may gather from this, wonderfully better: this harsh, grey, glum, doleful climate has done me good. You cannot fancy how sad a climate it is. When the thermometer stays all day below 10°, it is really cold; and when the wind blows, O commend me to the result. Pleasure in life is all delete; there is no red spot left, fires do not radiate, you burn your hands all the time on what seem to be cold stones. It is odd, zero is like summer heat to us now; and we like, when the thermometer outside is really low, a room at about 48°: 60° we find oppressive. Yet the natives keep their holes at 90° or even 100°.

This was interrupted days ago by household labours. Since then I have had and (I tremble to write it, but it does seem as if I had) beaten off an influenza. The cold is exquisite. Valentine still in bed. The proofs of the

1888 ÆT. 38

first part of *The Master of Ballantrae* begin to come in; soon you shall have it in the pamphlet form; and I hope you will like it. The second part will not be near so good; but there — we can but do as it 'll do with us. I have every reason to believe this winter has done me real good, so far as it has gone; and if I carry out my scheme for next winter, and succeeding years, I should end by being a tower of strength. I want you to save a good holiday for next winter; I hope we shall be able to help you to some larks. Is there any Greek Isle you would like to explore? or any creek in Asia Minor? — Yours ever affectionately, R. L. S.

TO THE REV. DR. CHARTERIS

The Rev. Dr. Charteris, of Edinburgh, had been one of the most intimate and trusted friends of Stevenson's father, and R. L. S. turns to him accordingly for memories and impressions.

[SARANAC LAKE, *Winter, 1887–1888.*]

MY DEAR DR. CHARTERIS, — I have asked Douglas and Foulis to send you my last volume, so that you may possess my little paper on my father in a permanent shape; not for what that is worth, but as a tribute of respect to one whom my father regarded with such love, esteem, and affection. Besides, as you will see, I have brought you under contribution, and I have still to thank you for your letter to my mother; so more than kind; in much, so just. It is my hope, when time and health permit, to do something more definite for my father's memory. You are one of the very few who can (if you will) help me. Pray believe that I lay on you no obligation; I know too well, you may believe me, how difficult it is to put even two sincere lines upon paper, where all, too, is to order. But if the spirit should ever move you, and you should recall something memorable of your friend, his son will heartily thank you for a note of it.—With much respect, believe me, yours sincerely, ROBERT LOUIS STEVENSON.

TO HENRY JAMES

[SARANAC LAKE, *March, 1888.*]

MY DEAR DELIGHTFUL JAMES,—To quote your heading to my wife, I think no man writes so elegant a letter, I am sure none so kind, unless it be Colvin, and there is more of the stern parent about him. I was vexed at your account of my admired Meredith: I wish I could go and see him; as it is, I will try to write. I read with indescribable admiration your *Emerson*. I begin to long for the day when these portraits of yours shall be collected: do put me in. But Emerson is a higher flight. Have you a *Tourgueneff?* You have told me many interesting things of him, and I seem to see them written, and forming a graceful and *bildend* sketch. My novel is a tragedy; four parts out of six or seven are written, and gone to Burlingame. Five parts of it are sound, human tragedy; the last one or two, I regret to say, not so soundly designed; I almost hesitate to write them; they are very picturesque, but they are fantastic; they shame, perhaps degrade, the beginning. I wish I

1888
ÆT. 38

knew; that was how the tale came to me, however. I got the situation; it was an old taste of mine: The older brother goes out in the '45, the younger stays; the younger, of course, gets title and estate and marries the bride designate of the elder — a family match, but he (the younger) had always loved her, and she had really loved the elder. Do you see the situation? Then the devil and Saranac suggested this *dénouement*, and I joined the two ends in a day or two of constant feverish thought, and began to write. And now — I wonder if I have not gone too far with the fantastic. The elder brother is an INCUBUS: supposed to be killed at Culloden, he turns up again and bleeds the family of money; on that stopping he comes and lives with them, whence flows the real tragedy, the nocturnal duel of the brothers (very naturally, and indeed, I think, inevitably arising), and second supposed death of the elder. Husband and wife now really make up, and then the cloven hoof appears. For the third supposed death and the manner of the third reappearance is steep; steep, sir. It is even very steep, and I fear it shames the honest stuff so far; but then it is highly pictorial, and it leads up to the death of the elder brother at the hands of the younger in a perfectly cold-blooded murder, of which I wish (and mean) the reader to approve. You see how daring is the design. There are really but six characters, and one of these episodic, and yet it covers eighteen years, and will be, I imagine, the longest of my works.—Yours ever, R. L. S.

Read Gosse's Raleigh. First-rate.—Yours ever,
R. L. S.

TO THE REV. DR. CHARTERIS

SARANAC LAKE, ADIRONDACKS,
NEW YORK, U. S. A., *Spring, 1888.*

MY DEAR DR. CHARTERIS,—The funeral letter, your notes, and many other things, are reserved for a book, *Memorials of a Scottish Family,* if ever I can find time and opportunity. I wish I could throw off all else and sit down to it to-day. Yes, my father was a "distinctly religious man," but not a pious. The distinction painfully and pleasurably recalls old conflicts; it used to be my great gun — and you, who suffered for the whole Church, know how needful it was to have some reserve artillery! His sentiments were tragic; he was a tragic thinker. Now, granted that life is tragic to the marrow, it seems the proper function of religion to make us accept and serve in that tragedy, as officers in that other and comparable one of war. Service is the word, active service, in the military sense; and the religious man — I beg pardon, the pious man — is he who has a military joy in duty — not he who weeps over the wounded. We can do no more than try to do our best. Really, I am the grandson of the manse — I preach you a kind of sermon. Box the brat's ears!

My mother — to pass to matters more within my competence — finely enjoys herself. The new country, some new friends we have made, the interesting experiment of this climate — which (at least) is tragic — all have done her good. I have myself passed a better winter than for years, and now that it is nearly over have some diffident hopes of doing well in the summer and "eating a little more air" than usual.

I thank you for the trouble you are taking, and my mother joins with me in kindest regards to yourself and Mrs. Charteris.—Yours very truly,

ROBERT LOUIS STEVENSON.

To S. R. CROCKETT

[SARANAC LAKE, *Spring, 1888.*]

DEAR MINISTER OF THE FREE KIRK AT PENICUIK,—For O, man, I cannae read your name!—That I have been so long in answering your delightful letter sits on my conscience badly. The fact is I let my correspondence accumulate until I am going to leave a place; and then I pitch in, overhaul the pile, and my cries of penitence might be heard a mile about. Yesterday I despatched thirty-five belated letters: conceive the state of my conscience, above all as the Sins of Omission (see boyhood's guide, the Shorter Catechism) are in my view the only serious ones; I call it my view, but it cannot have escaped you that it was also Christ's. However, all that is not to the purpose, which is to thank you for the sincere pleasure afforded by your charming letter. I get a good few such; how few that please me at all, you would be surprised to learn—or have a singularly just idea of the dulness of our race; how few that please me as yours did, I can tell you in one word—*None.* I am no great kirkgoer, for many reasons—and the sermon 's one of them, and the first prayer another, but the chief and effectual reason is the stuffiness.

I am no great kirkgoer, says I, but when I read you letter of yours, I thought I would like to sit under ye. And then I saw ye were to send me a bit buik, and says I, I 'll wait for the bit buik, and then I 'll mebbe can read the man's name, and anyway I can kill twa birds wi' ae stane. And, man! the buik was ne'er heard tell o'!

That fact is an adminicle of excuse for my delay.

And now, dear minister of the illegible name, thanks to you, and greeting to your wife, and may you have good guidance in your difficult labours, and a blessing on your life. ROBERT LOUIS STEVENSON.

(No just so young sae young 's he was, though —
I 'm awfae near forty, man.)

ADDRESS c/o CHARLES SCRIBNER'S SONS,
743 BROADWAY, NEW YORK.

Don't put "N. B." in your paper: put *Scotland*, and be done with it. Alas, that I should be thus stabbed in the home of my friends! The name of my native land is not *North Britain*, whatever may be the name of yours. R. L. S.

TO MISS FERRIER

[SARANAC LAKE, *April, 1888.*]

MY DEAREST COGGIE,—I wish I could find the letter I began to you some time ago when I was ill; but I can't, and I don't believe there was much in it anyway. We have all behaved like pigs and beasts and barn-door poultry to you; but I have been sunk in work,

1888 ÆT. 38

you shall read, rather than to that when I am writing) a very pretty boy, and (to my European views) startlingly self-possessed. My time of observation was so limited that you must pardon me if I can say no more: what else I marked, what restlessness of foot and hand, what graceful clumsiness, what experimental designs upon the furniture, was but the common inheritance of human youth. But you may perhaps like to know that the lean flushed man in bed, who interested you so little, was in a state of mind extremely mingled and unpleasant: harassed with work which he thought he was not doing well, troubled with difficulties to which you will in time succeed, and yet looking forward to no less a matter than a voyage to the South Seas and the visitation of savage and desert islands.—Your father's friend, ROBERT LOUIS STEVENSON.

TO HENRY JAMES

MANASQUAN (ahem!), NEW JERSEY,
May 28th, 1888.

MY DEAR JAMES,—With what a torrent it has come at last! Up to now, what I like best is the first number of *A London Life*. You have never done anything better, and I don't know if perhaps you have ever done anything so good as the girl's outburst: tip-top. I have been preaching your later works in your native land. I had to present the Beltraffio volume to Low, and it has brought him to his knees; he was *amazed* at the first part of Georgina's Reasons, although (like me) not so well satisfied with Part II. It is annoying to find the American public as stupid as the English, but they will waken up in time: I wonder what they will think of *Two Nations?* . . .

This, dear James, is a valedictory. On June 15th the schooner yacht *Casco* will (weather and a jealous providence permitting) steam through the Golden Gates for Honolulu, Tahiti, the Galapagos, Guayaquil, and—I hope *not* the bottom of the Pacific. It will contain your obedient 'umble servant and party. It seems too good to be true, and is a very good way of getting through the green-sickness of maturity, which, with all its accompanying ills, is now declaring itself in my mind and life. They tell me it is not so severe as that of youth; if I (and the *Casco*) are spared, I shall tell you more exactly, as I am one of the few people in the world who do not forget their own lives.

Good-bye, then, my dear fellow, and please write us a word; we expect to have three mails in the next two months: Honolulu, Tahiti, and Guayaquil. But letters will be forwarded from Scribner's, if you hear nothing more definite directly. In 3 (three) days I leave for San Francisco.—Ever yours most cordially, R. L. S.

X

PACIFIC VOYAGES

(JUNE, 1888–NOVEMBER, 1890)

X
PACIFIC VOYAGES

(JUNE, 1888–NOVEMBER, 1890)

IT was on the 28th of June, 1888, that Stevenson started from the harbour of San Francisco on what was only intended to be a health and pleasure excursion of a few months' duration, but turned into a voluntary exile prolonged until the hour of his death. His company consisted, besides himself, of his wife, his mother, his stepson Mr. Lloyd Osbourne, and the servant Valentine Roch. They sailed on board the schooner yacht *Casco*, Captain Otis, and made straight for the Marquesas, dropping anchor on the 28th of July in Anaho Bay, the harbour of the island of Nukahiva. The magic effect of this first island landfall on his mind he has described in the opening chapter of his book *The South Seas.*

After spending six weeks in this group they sailed southeastwards, visiting (a somewhat perilous piece of navigation) several of the coral atolls of the Paumotus or Low Archipelago. Thence they arrived in the first week of October at the Tahitian group or "Society Islands." In these their longest stay was not at the

Thence he returned in October to take up his abode for good on his Samoan property, where the work of clearing and planting had been going on busily during his absence. The letters in the following section are selected from those which reached his correspondents in England and the United States at intervals, necessarily somewhat rare, during these voyages.

To Sidney Colvin

Yacht "Casco," Anaho Bay, Nukahiva,
Marquesas Islands [*July, 1888*].

1888
Æt. 38

MY DEAR COLVIN,—From this somewhat (ahem!) out of the way place, I write to say how d' ye do. It is all a swindle: I chose these isles as having the most beastly population, and they are far better and far more civilised than we. I know one old chief Ko-o-amua, a great cannibal in his day, who ate his enemies even as he walked home from killing 'em, and he is a perfect gentleman and exceedingly amiable and simple-minded: no fool, though.

The climate is delightful; and the harbour where we lie one of the loveliest spots imaginable. Yesterday evening we had near a score of natives on board; lovely parties. We have a native god; very rare now. Very rare and equally absurd to view.

This sort of work is not favorable to correspondence: it takes me all the little strength I have to go about and see, and then come home and note, the strangeness around us. I should n't wonder if there came trouble here some day, all the same. I could name a nation that is not beloved in certain islands — and it does not know it![1] Strange: like ourselves, perhaps, in India! Love to all and much to yourself. R. L. S.

To Charles Baxter

YACHT "CASCO," AT SEA, NEAR THE PAUMOTUS,
7 A. M., *September 6th, 1888, with a dreadful pen.*

MY DEAR CHARLES,—Last night as I lay under my blanket in the cockpit, courting sleep, I had a comic seizure. There was nothing visible but the southern stars, and the steersman there out by the binnacle lamp; we were all looking forward to a most deplorable landfall on the morrow, praying God we should fetch a tuft of palms which are to indicate the Dangerous Archipelago; the night was as warm as milk, and all of a sudden I had a vision of—Drummond Street. It came on me like a flash of lightning: I simply returned thither, and into the past. And when I remember all I hoped and feared as I pickled about Rutherford's in the rain and the east wind; how I feared I should make a mere shipwreck, and yet timidly hoped not; how I feared I should never have a friend, far less a wife, and yet passionately hoped I might; how I hoped (if I did not take to drink) I should possibly write one little book, etc. etc. And then now—what a change! I feel somehow as if I should like the incident set upon a brass plate at the corner of that dreary thoroughfare for all students to read, poor devils, when their hearts are down. And

[1] The French; the Marquesas, Paumotus, and Tahiti being all dependencies of France.

1888
ÆT. 38

To Charles Baxter

Taiti, as ever was, *6th October, 1888.*

My dear Charles,— . . . You will receive a lot of mostly very bad proofs of photographs: the paper was so bad. Please keep them very private, as they are for the book. We send them, having learned so dread a fear of the sea, that we wish to put our eggs in different baskets. We have been thrice within an ace of being ashore: we were lost (!) for about twelve hours in the Low Archipelago, but by God's blessing had quiet weather all the time; and once, in a squall, we cam' so near gaun heels ower hurdies, that I really dinnae ken why we didnae athegither. Hence, as I say, a great desire to put our eggs in different baskets, particularly on the Pacific (aw-haw-haw!) Pacific Ocean.

You can have no idea what a mean time we have had, owing to incidental beastlinesses, nor what a glorious, owing to the intrinsic interest of these isles. I hope the book will be a good one; nor do I really very much doubt that — the stuff is so curious; what I wonder is, if the public will rise to it. A copy of my journal, or as much of it as is made, shall go to you also; it is, of course, quite imperfect, much being to be added and corrected; but O, for the eggs in the different baskets.

All the rest are well enough, and all have enjoyed the cruise so far, in spite of its drawbacks. We have had an awfae time in some ways, Mr. Baxter; and if I wasnae sic a verra patient man (when I ken that I *have* to be) there wad hae been a braw row; and ance if I hadnae happened to be on deck about three in the marnin', I *think* there would have been *murder* done. The American Mairchant Marine is a kent service; ye 'll have heard its praise, I 'm thinkin'; an' if ye never did, ye can get *Twa Years Before the Mast*, by Dana, whaur forbye a great deal o' pleisure, ye 'll get a' the need-cessary information. Love to your father and all the family.—Ever your affectionate friend,

ROBERT LOUIS STEVENSON.

TO MISS ADELAIDE BOODLE

This lady, as we have seen, had made Mr. Stevenson a present of a paper-cutter when he left Bournemouth; and it is in the character of the paper-cutter that he now writes.

TAITI, *October 10th, 1888.*

DEAR GIVER,—I am at a loss to conceive your object in giving me to a person so locomotory as my proprietor. The number of thousand miles that I have travelled, the strange bed-fellows with which I have been made acquainted, I lack the requisite literary talent to make clear to your imagination. I speak of bed-fellows; pocket-fellows would be a more exact expression, for the place of my abode is in my master's right-hand trouser-pocket; and there, as he waded on the resounding beaches of Nukahiva, or in the shallow tepid water on the reef of Fakarava, I have been overwhelmed by and buried among all manner of abominable South Sea shells, beautiful enough in their way, I make no doubt, but singular company for any

1888
ÆT. 38

you sight an island, and drop anchor in a new world. Much trouble has attended this trip, but I must confess more pleasure. Nor should I ever complain, as in the last few weeks, with the curing of my illness indeed, as if that were the bursting of an abscess, the cloud has risen from my spirits and to some degree from my temper. Do you know what they call the *Casco* at Fakarava? The *Silver Ship*. Is that not pretty? Pray tell Mrs. Jenkin, *die silberne Frau*, as I only learned it since I wrote her. I think of calling the book by that name: *The Cruise of the Silver Ship*—so there will be one poetic page at least—the title. At the Sandwiches we shall say farewell to the *S. S.* with mingled feelings. She is a lovely creature: the most beautiful thing at this moment in Taiti.

Well, I will take another sheet, though I know I have nothing to say. You would think I was bursting: but the voyage is all stored up for the book, which is to pay for it, we fondly hope; and the troubles of the time are not worth telling; and our news is little.

Here I conclude (Oct. 24th, I think), for we are now stored, and the Blue Peter metaphorically flies.

R. L. S.

To William and Thomas Archer

Stevenson addresses part of this letter, as he does the whole of another later on, to a young son of Mr. Archer's, but rather to amuse himself than his nominal correspondent, who was then aged three.

Taiti, *October 17th, 1888.*

DEAR ARCHER,—Though quite unable to write letters, I nobly send you a line signifying nothing. The voyage has agreed well with all; it has had its pains, and its extraordinary pleasures; nothing in the world can equal the excitement of the first time you cast anchor in some bay of a tropical island, and the boats begin to surround you, and the tattooed people swarm aboard. Tell Tomarcher, with my respex, that hide-and-seek is not equal to it; no, nor hidee-in-the-dark; which, for the matter of that, is a game for the unskilful: the artist prefers daylight, a good-sized garden, some shrubbery, an open paddock, and — come on, Macduff.

TOMARCHER, I am now a distinguished litterytour, but that was not the real bent of my genius. I was the best player of hide-and-seek going; not a good runner, I was up to every shift and dodge, I could jink very well, I could crawl without any noise through leaves, I could hide under a carrot plant, it used to be my favourite boast that I always *walked* into the den. You may care to hear, Tomarcher, about the children in these parts; their parents obey them, they do not obey their parents; and I am sorry to tell you (for I dare say you are already thinking the idea a good one) that it does not pay one halfpenny. There are three sorts of civilisation, Tomarcher: the real old-fashioned one, in which children either had to find out how to please their dear papas, or their dear papas cut their heads off. This style did very well, but is now out of fashion. Then the modern European style: in which children have to behave reasonably well, and go to school and say their prayers, or their dear papas *will know the reason why*. This does fairly well. Then there is the South Sea Island plan, which does not do one bit. The children beat their parents here; it

1888
ÆT. 38

does not make their parents any better; so do not try it.

Dear Tomarcher, I have forgotten the address of your new house, but will send this to one of your papa's publishers. Remember us all to all of you, and believe me, yours respectably,

ROBERT LOUIS STEVENSON.

TO CHARLES BAXTER

The stanzas which end this letter have already been printed, with one additional, in *Songs of Travel*, but gain effect, I think, from being given here in their place.

TAUTIRA (THE GARDEN OF THE WORLD), OTHERWISE CALLED HANS-CHRISTIAN-ANDERSEN-VILLE
[*November, 1888*].

MY DEAR CHARLES,—Whether I have a penny left in the wide world, I know not, nor shall know, till I get to Honolulu, where I anticipate a devil of an awakening. It will be from a mighty pleasant dream at least: Tautira being mere Heaven. But suppose, for the sake of argument, any money to be left in the hands of my painful doer, what is to be done with it? Save us from exile would be the wise man's choice, I suppose; for the exile threatens to be eternal. But yet I am of opinion—in case there should be *some* dibs in the hand of the P. D., *i.e.* painful doer; because if there be none, I shall take to my flageolet on the high-road, and work home the best way I can, having previously made away with my family—I am of opinion that if —— and his are in the customary state, and you are thinking of an offering, and there should be still some funds over, you would be a real good P. D. to put some in with yours and tak' the credit o't, like a wee man! I know it 's a beastly thing to ask; but it, after all, does no earthly harm, only that much good. And besides, like enough there 's nothing in the till, and there is an end. Yet I live here in the full lustre of millions; it is thought I am the richest son of man that has yet been to Tautira: I!—and I am secretly eaten with the fear of lying in pawn, perhaps for the remainder of my days, in San Francisco. As usual, my colds have much hashed my finances.

Do tell Henley I write this just after having dismissed Ori the sub-chief, in whose house I live, Mrs. Ori, and Pairai, their adopted child, from the evening hour of music: during which I Publickly (with a *k*) Blow on the Flageolet. These are words of truth. Yesterday I told Ori about W. E. H., counterfeited his playing on the piano and the pipe, and succeeded in sending the six feet four there is of that sub-chief somewhat sadly to his bed; feeling that his was not the genuine article after all. Ori is exactly like a colonel in the Guards.—I am, dear Charles, ever yours affectionately,

R. L. S.

TAUTIRA, *10th November*, '88.

MY DEAR CHARLES,—Our mainmast is dry-rotten, and we are all to the devil; I shall lie in a debtor's jail. Never mind, Tautira is first chop. I am so besotted that I shall put on the back of this my attempt at words to *Wandering Willie;* if you can conceive at all the difficulty, you will also conceive the vanity with which

1888
ÆT. 38

I regard any kind of result; and whatever mine is like, it has some sense, and Burns's has none.

Home no more home to me, whither must I wander?
  Hunger my driver, I go where I must.
Cold blows the winter wind over hill and heather;
  Thick drives the rain, and my roof is in the dust.
Loved of wise men was the shade of my roof-tree,
  The true word of welcome was spoken in the door—
Dear days of old, with the faces in the firelight,
  Kind folks of old, you come again no more.

Home was home then, my dear, full of kindly faces,
  Home was home then, my dear, happy for the child.
Fire and the windows bright glittered on the moorland;
  Song, tuneful song, built a palace in the wild.
Now, when day dawns on the brow of the moorland,
  Lone stands the house, and the chimney-stone is cold.
Lone let it stand, now the friends are all departed,
  The kind hearts, the true hearts, that loved the place
    of old.
R. L. S.

To J. A. Symonds

The following is the draft of a proposed dedication to the South Sea travel-book which was to be the fruit of the present voyages, as is explained in a note at the end.

November 11th, 1888.

One November night, in the village of Tautira, we sat at the high table in the hall of assembly, hearing the natives sing. It was dark in the hall, and very warm; though at times the land wind blew a little shrewdly through the chinks, and at times, through the larger openings, we could see the moonlight on the lawn. As the songs arose in the rattling Tahitian chorus, the chief translated here and there a verse. Farther on in the volume you shall read the songs themselves; and I am in hopes that not you only, but all who can find a savour in the ancient poetry of places, will read them with some pleasure. You are to conceive us, therefore, in strange circumstances and very pleasing; in a strange land and climate, the most beautiful on earth; surrounded by a foreign race that all travellers have agreed to be the most engaging; and taking a double interest in two foreign arts.

We came forth again at last, in a cloudy moonlight, on the forest lawn which is the street of Tautira. The Pacific roared outside upon the reef. Here and there one of the scattered palm-built lodges shone out under the shadow of the wood, the lamplight bursting through the crannies of the wall. We went homeward slowly, Ori a Ori carrying behind us the lantern and the chairs, properties with which we had just been enacting our part of the distinguished visitor. It was one of those moments in which minds not altogether churlish recall the names and deplore the absence of congenial friends; and it was your name that first rose upon our lips. "How Symonds would have enjoyed this evening!" said one, and then another. The word caught in my mind; I went to bed, and it was still there. The glittering, frosty solitudes in which your days are cast, arose before me: I seemed to see you walking there in the late night, under the pine-trees and the stars; and I received the image with something like remorse.

1888
ÆT. 38

There is a modern attitude towards fortune; in this place I will not use a graver name. Staunchly to withstand her buffets and to enjoy with equanimity her favours was the code of the virtuous of old. Our fathers, it should seem, wondered and doubted how they had merited their misfortunes: we, rather how we have deserved our happiness. And we stand often abashed, and sometimes revolted, at those partialities of fate by which we profit most. It was so with me on that November night: I felt that our positions should be changed. It was you, dear Symonds, who should have gone upon that voyage and written this account. With your rich stores of knowledge, you could have remarked and understood a thousand things of interest and beauty that escaped my ignorance; and the brilliant colours of your style would have carried into a thousand sickrooms the sea air and the strong sun of tropic islands. It was otherwise decreed. But suffer me at least to connect you, if only in name and only in the fondness of imagination, with the voyage of the "Silver Ship."

ROBERT LOUIS STEVENSON.

DEAR SYMONDS,—I send you this (November 11th), the morning of its completion. If I ever write an account of this voyage, may I place this letter at the beginning? It represents—I need not tell you, for you too are an artist—a most genuine feeling, which kept me long awake last night; and though perhaps a little elaborate, I think it a good piece of writing. We are *in heaven here*. Do not forget R. L. S.

Please keep this: I have no perfect copy.
Tautira, on the peninsula of Tahiti.

To Thomas Archer

Tautira, Island of Tahiti [*November, 1888*].

DEAR TOMARCHER,—This is a pretty state of things! seven o'clock and no word of breakfast! And I was awake a good deal last night, for it was full moon, and they had made a great fire of cocoanut husks down by the sea, and as we have no blinds or shutters, this kept my room very bright. And then the rats had a wedding or a school-feast under my bed. And then I woke early, and I have nothing to read except Virgil's *Æneid*, which is not good fun on an empty stomach, and a Latin dictionary, which is good for naught, and by some humorous accident, your dear papa's article on Skerryvore. And I read the whole of that, and very impudent it is, but you must not tell your dear papa I said so, or it might come to a battle in which you might lose either a dear papa or a valued correspondent, or both, which would be prodigal. And still no breakfast; so I said "Let 's write to Tomarcher."

This is a much better place for children than any I have hitherto seen in these seas. The girls (and sometimes the boys) play a very elaborate kind of hopscotch. The boys play horses exactly as we do in Europe; and have very good fun on stilts, trying to knock each other down, in which they do not often succeed. The children of all ages go to church and are allowed to do what they please, running about the aisles, rolling balls, stealing mamma's bonnet and publicly sitting on it, and at last going to sleep in the middle of the floor. I forgot to say that the whips to play horses, and the balls to roll about the church — at least I never saw them used elsewhere — grow ready-made on trees; which is rough on toy-shops. The whips are so good that I wanted to play horses myself; but no such luck! my hair is grey, and I am a great, big, ugly man. The balls are rather hard, but very light and quite round. When you grow up and become offensively rich, you can charter a ship in the port of London, and have it come back to you entirely loaded with these balls; when you could satisfy your mind as to their character, and give them away when done with to your uncles and aunts. But what I really wanted to tell you was this: besides the tree-top toys (Hush-a-by, toy-shop, on the tree-top!), I have seen some real *made* toys, the first hitherto observed in the South Seas.

This was how. You are to imagine a four-wheeled gig; one horse; in the front seat two Tahiti natives, in their Sunday clothes, blue coat, white shirt, kilt (a little longer than the Scotch) of a blue stuff with big white or yellow flowers, legs and feet bare; in the back seat me and my wife, who is a friend of yours; under our feet, plenty of lunch and things: among us a great deal of fun in broken Tahitian, one of the natives, the sub-chief of the village, being a great ally of mine. Indeed we have exchanged names; so that he is now called Rui, the nearest they can come to Louis, for they have no *l* and no *s* in their language. Rui is six feet three in his stockings, and a magnificent man. We all have straw hats, for the sun is strong. We drive between the sea, which makes a great noise, and the mountains; the road is cut through a forest mostly of fruit trees, the very creepers, which take the place of our ivy, heavy with a great and delicious fruit, bigger than your head and far nicer, called Barbedine. Presently we came to a house in a pretty garden, quite by itself, very nicely kept, the doors and windows open, no one about, and no noise but that of the sea. It looked like a house in a fairy tale, and just beyond we must ford a river, and there we saw the inhabitants. Just in the mouth of the river, where it met the sea waves, they were ducking and bathing and screaming together like a covey of birds: seven or eight little naked brown boys and girls as happy as the day was long; and on the banks of the stream beside them, real toys—toy ships, full rigged, and with their sails set, though they were lying in the dust on their beam ends. And then I knew for sure they were all children in a fairy story, living alone together in that lonely house with the only toys in all the island; and that I had myself driven, in my four-wheeled gig, into a corner of the fairy story, and the question was, should I get out again? But it was all right; I guess only one of the wheels of the gig had got into the fairy story; and the next jolt the whole thing vanished, and we drove on in our sea-side forest as before, and I have the honour to be Tomarcher's valued correspondent, TERIITERA, which he was previously known as

ROBERT LOUIS STEVENSON.

TO SIDNEY COLVIN

YACHT "CASCO," AT SEA, *14th January, 1889.*

MY DEAR COLVIN,—Twenty days out from Papeete. Yes, sir, all that, and only (for a guess) in 4° north or

1889 ÆT. 39

at the best 4° 30′, though already the wind seems to smell a little of the North Pole. My handwriting you must take as you get, for we are speeding along through a nasty swell, and I can only keep my place at the table by means of a foot against the divan, the unoccupied hand meanwhile gripping the ink-bottle. As we begin (so very slowly) to draw near to seven months of correspondence, we are all in some fear; and I want to have letters written before I shall be plunged into that boiling pot of disagreeables which I constantly expect at Honolulu. What is needful can be added there.

We were kept two months at Tautira in the house of my dear old friend, Ori a Ori, till both the masts of this invaluable yacht had been repaired. It was all for the best: Tautira being the most beautiful spot, and its people the most amiable, I have ever found. Besides which, the climate suited me to the ground; I actually went sea-bathing almost every day, and in our feasts (we are all huge eaters in Taiarapu) have been known to apply four times for pig. And then again I got wonderful materials for my book, collected songs and legends on the spot; songs still sung in chorus by perhaps a hundred persons, not two of whom can agree on their translation; legends, on which I have seen half a dozen seniors sitting in conclave and debating what came next. Once I went a day's journey to the other side of the island to Tati, the high chief of the Tevas—*my* chief that is, for I am now a Teva and Teriitera, at your service—to collect more and correct what I had already. In the meanwhile I got on with my work, almost finished *The Master of Ballantrae*, which contains more human work than anything of mine but *Kidnapped*, and wrote the half of another ballad, *The Song of Rahéro*, on a Taiarapu legend of my own clan, sir—not so much fire as *The Feast of Famine*, but promising to be more even and correct. But the best fortune of our stay at Tautira was my knowledge of Ori himself, one of the finest creatures extant. The day of our parting was a sad one. We deduced from it a rule for travellers: not to stay two months in one place—which is to cultivate regrets.

At last our contemptible ship was ready; to sea we went, bound for Honolulu and the letter-bag, on Christmas Day; and from then to now have experienced every sort of minor misfortune, squalls, calms, contrary winds and seas, pertinacious rains, declining stores, till we came almost to regard ourselves as in the case of Vanderdecken. Three days ago our luck seemed to improve, we struck a leading breeze, got creditably through the doldrums, and just as we looked to have the N. E. trades and a straight run, the rains and squalls and calms began again about midnight, and this morning, though there is breeze enough to send us along, we are beaten back by an obnoxious swell out of the north. Here is a page of complaint, when a verse of thanksgiving had perhaps been more in place. For all this time we must have been skirting past dangerous weather, in the tail and circumference of hurricanes, and getting only annoyance where we should have had peril, and ill-humour instead of fear.

I wonder if I have managed to give you any news this time, or whether the usual damn hangs over my letter? "The midwife whispered, Be thou dull!" or at

1889
ÆT. 39

least inexplicit. Anyway I have tried my best, am exhausted with the effort, and fall back into the land of generalities. I cannot tell you how often we have planned our arrival at the Monument: two nights ago, the 12th January, we had it all planned out, arrived in the lights and whirl of Waterloo, hailed a hansom, span up Waterloo Road, over the bridge, etc. etc., and hailed the Monument gate in triumph and with indescribable delight. My dear Custodian, I always think we are too sparing of assurances: Cordelia is only to be excused by Regan and Goneril in the same nursery; I wish to tell you that the longer I live, the more dear do you become to me; nor does my heart own any stronger sentiment. If the bloody schooner did n't send me flying in every sort of direction at the same time, I would say better what I feel so much; but really, if you were here, you would not be writing letters, I believe; and even I, though of a more marine constitution, am much perturbed by this bobbery and wish—O ye Gods, how I wish!—that it was done, and we had arrived, and I had Pandora's Box (my mail bag) in hand, and was in the lively hope of something eatable for dinner instead of salt horse, tinned mutton, duff without any plums, and pie fruit, which now make up our whole repertory. O Pandora's Box! I wonder what you will contain. As like as not you will contain but little money: if that be so, we shall have to retire to 'Frisco in the *Casco*, and thence by sea *via* Panama to Southampton, where we should arrive in April. I would like fine to see you on the tug: ten years older both of us than the last time you came to welcome Fanny and me to England. If we have money, however, we shall do a little differently: send the *Casco* away from Honolulu empty of its high-born lessees, for that voyage to 'Frisco is one long dead beat in foul and at last in cold weather; stay awhile behind, follow by steamer, cross the States by train, stay awhile in New York on business, and arrive probably by the German Line in Southampton. But all this is a question of money. We shall have to lie very dark awhile to recruit our finances: what comes from the book of the cruise, I do not want to touch until the capital is repaid. R. L. S.

To E. L. Burlingame

Honolulu [*January, 1889*].

MY DEAR BURLINGAME,—Here at last I have arrived. We could not get away from Tahiti till Christmas Day, and then had thirty days of calms and squalls, a deplorable passage. This has thrown me all out of gear in every way. I plunge into business.

1. *The Master:* Herewith go three more parts. You see he grows in bulk; this making ten already, and I am not yet sure if I can finish it in an eleventh; which shall go to you *quam primum*—I hope by next mail.

2. *Illustrations to M.* I totally forgot to try to write to Hole. It was just as well, for I find it impossible to forecast with sufficient precision. You had better throw off all this and let him have it at once. *Please do: all, and at once: see further;* and I should hope he would still be in time for the later numbers. The three pictures I have received are so truly good that I should bitterly regret having the volume imperfectly

1889 ÆT. 39

equipped. They are the best illustrations I have seen since I don't know when.

3. Money. To-morrow the mail comes in, and I hope it will bring me money either from you or home, but I will add a word on that point.

4. My address will be Honolulu — no longer Yacht *Casco*, which I am packing off — till probably April.

5. As soon as I am through with *The Master*, I shall finish the *Game of Bluff* — now rechristened *The Wrong Box*. This I wish to sell, cash down. It is of course copyright in the States; and I offer it to you for five thousand dollars. Please reply on this by return. Also please tell the typewriter who was so good as to be amused by our follies that I am filled with admiration for his piece of work.

6. *Master* again. Please see that I have n't the name of the Governor of New York wrong (1764 is the date) in part ten. I have no book of reference to put me right. Observe you now have up to August inclusive in hand, so you should begin to feel happy.

Is this all? I wonder, and fear not. Henry the Trader has not yet turned up: I hope he may to-morrow, when we expect a mail. Not one word of business have I received either from the States or England, nor anything in the shape of coin; which leaves me in a fine uncertainty and quite penniless on these islands. H. M.[1] (who is a gentleman of a courtly order and much tinctured with letters) is very polite; I may possibly ask for the position of palace doorkeeper. My voyage has been a singular mixture of good and ill fortune. As far as regards interest and material, the

[1] King Kalakaua.

fortune has been admirable; as far as regards time, money, and impediments of all kinds, from squalls and calms to rotten masts and sprung spars, simply detestable. I hope you will be interested to hear of two volumes on the wing. The cruise itself, you are to know, will make a big volume with appendices; some of it will first appear as (what they call) letters in some of M'Clure's papers. I believe the book when ready will have a fair measure of serious interest: I have had great fortune in finding old songs and ballads and stories, for instance, and have many singular instances of life in the last few years among these islands.

The second volume is of ballads. You know *Ticonderoga*. I have written another: *The Feast of Famine*, a Marquesan story. A third is half done: *The Song of Rahéro*, a genuine Tahitian legend. A fourth dances before me. A Hawaiian fellow this, *The Priest's Drought*, or some such name. If, as I half suspect, I get enough subjects out of the islands, *Ticonderoga* shall be suppressed, and we 'll call the volume *South Sea Ballads*. In health, spirits, renewed interest in life, and, I do believe, refreshed capacity for work, the cruise has proved a wise folly. Still we 're not home, and (although the friend of a crowned head) are penniless upon these (as one of my correspondents used to call them) "lovely but *fatil* islands." By the way, who wrote *The Lion of the Nile?* My dear sir, that is Something Like. Overdone in bits, it has a true thought and a true ring of language. Beg the anonymous from me, to delete (when he shall republish) the two last verses, and end on "the lion of the Nile." One Lampman has a good sonnet on a "Winter Evening" in, I think, the same number: he seems ill named, but I am tempted to hope a man is not always answerable for his name.[1] For instance, you would think you knew mine. No such matter. It is—at your service and Mr. Scribner's and that of all of the faithful—Teriitera (pray pronounce Tayree-Tayra) or (*gallicé*) Téri-téra.

R. L. S.

More when the mail shall come.

I am an idiot. I want to be clear on one point. Some of Hole's drawings must of course be too late; and yet they seem to me so excellent I would fain have the lot complete. It is one thing for you to pay for drawings which are to appear in that soul-swallowing machine, your magazine: quite another if they are only to illustrate a volume. I wish you to take a brisk (even a fiery) decision on the point; and let Hole know. To resume my desultory song, I desire you would carry the same fire (hereinbefore suggested) into your decision on *The Wrong Box;* for in my present state of benighted ignorance as to my affairs for the last seven months—I know not even whether my house or my mother's house have been let—I desire to see something definite in front of me—outside the lot of palace doorkeeper. I believe the said *Wrong Box* is a real lark; in which, of course, I may be grievously deceived; but the typewriter is with me. I may also be deceived as to the numbers of *The Master* now going and already gone; but to me they seem First Chop, sir, First Chop. I hope I shall pull off that damned ending; but it still

[1] This is the Canadian poet Mr. Archibald Lampman, the news of whose death reaches England as these sheets are preparing for the press.

depresses me: this is your doing, Mr. Burlingame: you would have it there and then, and I fear it—I fear that ending. R. L. S.

1889
ÆT. 39

To Charles Baxter

Honolulu, *February 8th, 1889.*

MY DEAR CHARLES,—Here we are at Honolulu, and have dismissed the yacht, and lie here till April anyway, in a fine state of haze, which I am yet in hopes some letter of yours (still on the way) may dissipate. No money, and not one word as to money! However, I have got the yacht paid off in triumph, I think; and though we stay here impignorate, it should not be for long, even if you bring us no extra help from home. The cruise has been a great success, both as to matter, fun, and health; and yet, Lord, man! we 're pleased to be ashore! Yon was a very fine voyage from Tahiti up here, but—the dry land 's a fine place too, and we don't mind squalls any longer, and eh, man, that 's a great thing. Blow, blow, thou wintry wind, thou hast done me no appreciable harm beyond a few grey hairs! Altogether, this foolhardy venture is achieved; and if I have but nine months of life and any kind of health, I shall have both eaten my cake and got it back again with usury. But, man, there have been days when I felt guilty, and thought I was in no position for the head of a house.

Your letter and accounts are doubtless at S. F., and will reach me in course. My wife is no great shakes; she is the one who has suffered most. My mother has had a Huge Old Time; Lloyd is first chop; I so well

1889
ÆT. 39

that I do not know myself—sea-bathing, if you please, and what is far more dangerous, entertaining and being entertained by His Majesty here, who is a very fine intelligent fellow, but O, Charles! what a crop for the drink! He carries it too like a mountain with a sparrow on its shoulders. We calculated five bottles of champagne in three hours and a half (afternoon), and the sovereign quite presentable, although perceptibly more dignified at the end. . . .

The extraordinary health I enjoy and variety of interests I find among these islands would tempt me to remain here; only for Lloyd, who is not well placed in such countries for a permanency; and a little for Colvin, to whom I feel I owe a sort of filial duty. And these two considerations will no doubt bring me back — to go to bed again—in England.—Yours ever affectionately,

R. L. S.

To R. A. M. Stevenson

Honolulu, Hawaiian Islands, *February, 1889.*

MY DEAR BOB, — My extremely foolhardy venture is practically over. How foolhardy it was I don't think I realised. We had a very small schooner, and, like most yachts, over-rigged and over-sparred, and like many American yachts on a very dangerous sail plan. The waters we sailed in are, of course, entirely unlighted, and very badly charted; in the Dangerous Archipelago, through which we were fools enough to go, we were perfectly in ignorance of where we were for a whole night and half the next day, and this in the midst of invisible islands and rapid and variable currents; and we were lucky when we found our whereabouts at last. We have twice had all we wanted in the way of squalls: once, as I came on deck, I found the green sea over the cockpit coamings and running down the companion like a brook to meet me; at that same moment the foresail sheet jammed and the captain had no knife; this was the only occasion on the cruise that ever I set a hand to a rope, but I worked like a Trojan, judging the possibility of hæmorrhage better than the certainty of drowning. Another time I saw a rather singular thing: our whole ship's company as pale as paper from the captain to the cook; we had a black squall astern on the port side and a white squall ahead to starboard; the complication passed off innocuous, the black squall only fetching us with its tail, and the white one slewing off somewhere else. Twice we were a long while (days) in the close vicinity of hurricane weather, but again luck prevailed, and we saw none of it. These are dangers incident to these seas and small craft. What was an amazement, and at the same time a powerful stroke of luck, both our masts were rotten, and we found it out —I was going to say in time, but it was stranger and luckier than that. The head of the mainmast hung over so that hands were afraid to go to the helm; and less than three weeks before—I am not sure it was more than a fortnight—we had been nearly twelve hours beating off the lee shore of Eimeo (or Moorea, next island to Tahiti) in half a gale of wind with a violent head sea: she would neither tack nor wear once, and had to be boxed off with the mainsail—you can imagine what an ungodly show of kites we carried—

1889
ÆT. 39

and yet the mast stood. The very day after that, in the southern bight of Tahiti, we had a near squeak, the wind suddenly coming calm; the reefs were close in with, my eye! what a surf! The pilot thought we were gone, and the captain had a boat cleared, when a lucky squall came to our rescue. My wife, hearing the order given about the boats, remarked to my mother, "Is n't that nice? We shall soon be ashore!" Thus does the female mind unconsciously skirt along the verge of eternity. Our voyage up here was most disastrous—calms, squalls, head sea, waterspouts of rain, hurricane weather all about, and we in the midst of the hurricane season, when even the hopeful builder and owner of the yacht had pronounced these seas unfit for her. We ran out of food, and were quite given up for lost in Honolulu: people had ceased to speak to Belle[1] about the *Casco*, as a deadly subject.

But the perils of the deep were part of the programme; and though I am very glad to be done with them for a while and comfortably ashore, where a squall does not matter a snuff to any one, I feel pretty sure I shall want to get to sea again ere long. The dreadful risk I took was financial, and double-headed. First, I had to sink a lot of money in the cruise, and if I did n't get health, how was I to get it back? I have got health to a wonderful extent; and as I have the most interesting matter for my book, bar accidents, I ought to get all I have laid out and a profit. But, second (what I own I never consider till too late), there

[1] Stevenson's stepdaughter, Mrs. Strong, who was at this time living at Honolulu, and joined his party and family for good when they continued their voyage from thence in the following June.

was the danger of collisions, of damages and heavy repairs, of disablement, towing, and salvage; indeed, the cruise might have turned round and cost me double. Nor will this danger be quite over till I hear the yacht is in San Francisco; for though I have shaken the dust of her deck from my feet, I fear (as a point of law) she is still mine till she gets there.

From my point of view, up to now the cruise has been a wonderful success. I never knew the world was so amusing. On the last voyage we had grown so used to sea-life that no one wearied, though it lasted a full month, except Fanny, who is always ill. All the time our visits to the islands have been more like dreams than realities: the people, the life, the beach-combers, the old stories and songs I have picked up, so interesting; the climate, the scenery, and (in some places) the women, so beautiful. The women are handsomest in Tahiti, the men in the Marquesas; both as fine types as can be imagined. Lloyd reminds me, I have not told you one characteristic incident of the cruise from a semi-naval point of view. One night we were going ashore in Anaho Bay; the most awful noise on deck; the breakers distinctly audible in the cabin; and there I had to sit below, entertaining in my best style a negroid native chieftain, much the worse for rum! You can imagine the evening's pleasure.

This naval report on cruising in the South Seas would be incomplete without one other trait. On our voyage up here I came one day into the dining-room, the hatch in the floor was open, the ship's boy was below with a baler, and two of the hands were carry-

1889 ÆT. 39

ing buckets as for a fire; this meant that the pumps had ceased working.

One stirring day was that in which we sighted Hawaii It blew fair, but very strong; we carried jib, foresail, and mainsail, all single-reefed, and she carried her lee rail under water and flew. The swell, the heaviest I have ever been out in — I tried in vain to estimate the height, *at least* fifteen feet — came tearing after us about a point and a half off the wind. We had the best hand — old Louis — at the wheel; and, really, he did nobly, and had noble luck, for it never caught us once. At times it seemed we must have it; Louis would look over his shoulder with the queerest look and dive down his neck into his shoulders; and then it missed us somehow, and only sprays came over our quarter, turning the little outside lane of deck into a mill race as deep as to the cockpit coamings. I never remember anything more delightful and exciting. Pretty soon after we were lying absolutely becalmed under the lee of Hawaii, of which we had been warned; and the captain never confessed he had done it on purpose, but when accused, he smiled. Really, I suppose he did quite right, for we stood committed to a dangerous race, and to bring her to the wind would have been rather a heart-sickening manœuvre.

R. L. S.

To Marcel Schwob

At Honolulu, Stevenson found awaiting him, among the accumulations of the mail-bag, two letters of friendly homage—the first, I think, he had received from any foreign *confrère*—addressed to him by a distinguished young French scholar and man of letters, M. Marcel Schwob.

HONOLULU, SANDWICH ISLANDS,
February 8th, 1889.

DEAR SIR,—I thank you—from the midst of such a flurry as you can imagine, with seven months' accumulated correspondence on my table—for your two friendly and clever letters. Pray write me again. I shall be home in May or June, and not improbably shall come to Paris in the summer. Then we can talk; or in the interval I may be able to write, which is to-day out of the question. Pray take a word from a man of crushing occupations, and count it as a volume. Your little *conte* is delightful. Ah yes, you are right, I love the eighteenth century; and so do you, and have not listened to its voice in vain.—The Hunted One, ROBERT LOUIS STEVENSON.

TO CHARLES BAXTER

HONOLULU, *8th March, 1889.*

MY DEAR CHARLES,—At last I have the accounts: the Doer has done excellently, and in the words of——, "I reciprocate every step of your behaviour." . . . I send a letter for Bob in your care, as I don't know his Liverpool address, by which (for he is to show you part of it) you will see we have got out of this adventure—or hope to have—with wonderful fortune. I have the retrospective horrors on me when I think of the liabilities I incurred; but, thank God, I think I 'm in port again, and I have found one climate in which I can enjoy life. Even Honolulu is too cold for me; but

1889 ÆT. 39

I have had from my chief friend in this part of the world: go and see her, and get a hearing of it; it will do you good; it is a better method of correspondence than even Henry James's.[1] I jest, but seriously it is a strange thing for a tough, sick middle-aged scrivener like R. L. S. to receive a letter so conceived from a man fifty years old, a leading politician, a crack orator, and the great wit of his village: boldly say, "the highly popular M. P. of Tautira." My nineteenth century strikes here, and lies alongside of something beautiful and ancient. I think the receipt of such a letter might humble, shall I say even ——? and for me, I would rather have received it than written *Redgauntlet* or the *Sixth Æneid*. All told, if my books have enabled or helped me to make this voyage, to know Rui, and to have received such a letter, they have (in the old pref-

[1] The following is the letter in question: —

"I make you to know my great affection. At the hour when you left us, I was filled with tears; my wife, Rui Telime, also, and all of my household. When you embarked I felt a great sorrow. It is for this that I went upon the road, and you looked from that ship, and I looked at you on the ship with great grief until you had raised the anchor and hoisted the sails. When the ship started I ran along the beach to see you still; and when you were on the open sea I cried out to you, 'Farewell, Louis'; and when I was coming back to my house I seemed to hear your voice crying, 'Rui, farewell.' Afterwards I watched the ship as long as I could until the night fell; and when it was dark I said to myself, 'If I had wings I should fly to the ship to meet you, and to sleep amongst you, so that I might be able to come back to shore and to tell Rui Telime, "I have slept upon the ship of Teriitera."' After that we passed that night in the impatience of grief. Towards eight o'clock I seemed to hear your voice, 'Teriitera — Rui — here is the hour for *putter* and *tiro*' [cheese and syrup]. I did not sleep that night, thinking continually of you, my very dear friend, until the

atorial expression) not been writ in vain. It would seem from this that I have been not so much humbled as puffed up; but, I assure you, I have in fact been both. A little of what that letter says is my own earning; not all, but yet a little; and the little makes me proud, and all the rest ashamed; and in the contrast, how much more beautiful altogether is the ancient man than him of to-day!

Well, well, Henry James is pretty good, though he *is* of the nineteenth century, and that glaringly. And to curry favour with him, I wish I could be more explicit; but, indeed, I am still of necessity extremely vague, and cannot tell what I am to do, nor where I am to go for some while yet. As soon as I am sure, you shall hear. All are fairly well—the wife, your countrywoman, least of all; troubles are not entirely wanting; but on the whole we prosper, and we are all affectionately yours,

ROBERT LOUIS STEVENSON.

morning; being then still awake, I went to see Tapina Tutu on her bed, and alas, she was not there. Afterwards I looked into your rooms; they did not please me as they used to do. I did not hear your voice saying, 'Hail Rui'; I thought then that you had gone, and that you had left me. Rising up, I went to the beach to see your ship, and I could not see it. I wept, then, until the night, telling myself continually, 'Teriitera returns into his own country and leaves his dear Rui in grief, so that I suffer for him, and weep for him.' I will not forget you in my memory. Here is the thought: I desire to meet you again. It is my dear Teriitera makes the only riches I desire in this world. It is your eyes that I desire to see again. It must be that your body and my body shall eat together at one table: there is what would make my heart content. But now we are separated. May God be with you all. May His word and His mercy go with you, so that you may be well and we also, according to the words of Paul.

"ORI A ORI, that is to say, RUI."

1889 ÆT. 39 highest form of gambling; and yet I love the sea as much as I hate gambling. Fine, clean emotions; a world all and always beautiful; air better than wine; interest unflagging: there is upon the whole no better life.—Yours ever, R. L. S.

To E. L. Burlingame

Honolulu [*April, 1889*].

MY DEAR BURLINGAME,—This is to announce the most prodigious change of programme. I have seen so much of the South Seas that I desire to see more, and I get so much health here that I dread a return to our vile climates. I have applied accordingly to the missionary folk to let me go round in the *Morning Star;* and if the Boston Board should refuse, I shall get somehow to Fiji, hire a trading schooner, and see the Fijis and Friendlies and Samoa. He would be a South Seayer, Mr. Burlingame. Of course, if I go in the *Morning Star*, I see all the eastern (or western?) islands.

Before I sail, I shall make out to let you have the last of *The Master:* though I tell you it sticks!—and I hope to have had some proofs forbye, of the verses anyway. And now to business.

I want (if you can find them) in the British sixpenny edition, if not, in some equally compact and portable shape—Seaside Library, for instance—the Waverley Novels entire, or as entire as you can get 'em, and the following of Marryat: *Phantom Ship, Peter Simple, Percival Keene, Privateersman, Children of the New Forest, Frank Mildmay, Newton Forster, Dog Fiend* (*Snarleyow*). Also *Midshipman Easy, Kingsburn*, Carlyle's *French Revolution,* Motley's *Dutch Republic,* Lang's *Letters on Literature,* a complete set of my works, *Jenkin,* in duplicate; also *Familiar Studies,* ditto.

I have to thank you for the accounts, which are satisfactory indeed, and for the cheque for $1000. Another account will have come and gone before I see you. I hope it will be equally roseate in colour. I am quite worked out, and this cursed end of *The Master* hangs over me like the arm of the gallows; but it is always darkest before dawn, and no doubt the clouds will soon rise; but it is a difficult thing to write, above all in Mackellarese; and I cannot yet see my way clear. If I pull this off, *The Master* will be a pretty good novel or I am the more deceived; and even if I don't pull it off, it 'll still have some stuff in it.

We shall remain here until the middle of June anyway; but my mother leaves for Europe early in May. Hence our mail should continue to come here; but not hers. I will let you know my next address, which will probably be Sydney. If we get on the *Morning Star,* I propose at present to get marooned on Ponape, and take my chance of getting a passage to Australia. It will leave times and seasons mighty vague, and the cruise is risky; but I shall know something of the South Seas when it is done, or else the South Seas will contain all there is of me. It should give me a fine book of travels, anyway.

Low will probably come and ask some dollars of you. Pray let him have them, they are for outfit. O, another complete set of my books should go to Captain A. H. Otis, care of Dr. Merritt, Yacht *Casco,* Oakland, Cal. —In haste, R. L. S.

1889 ÆT. 39

space. You will see there no sign of the Squire, however; and being a person of a humane disposition, you will only glance in over the balcony railing at the merry-makers in the summer parlour, and proceed further afield after the Exile. You look round, there is beautiful green turf, many trees of an outlandish sort that drop thorns — look out if your feet are bare; but I beg your pardon, you have not been long enough in the South Seas — and many oleanders in full flower. The next group of buildings is ramshackle, and quite dark; you make out a coach-house door, and look in — only some cocoanuts; you try round to the left and come to the sea front, where Venus and the moon are making luminous tracks on the water, and a great swell rolls and shines on the outer reef; and here is another door — all these places open from the outside — and you go in, and find photography, tubs of water, negatives steeping, a tap, and a chair and an inkbottle, where my wife is supposed to write; round a little further, a third door, entering which you find a picture upon the easel and a table sticky with paints; a fourth door admits you to a sort of court, where there is a hen sitting — I believe on a fallacious egg. No sign of the Squire in all this. But right opposite the studio door you have observed a third little house, from whose open door lamplight streams and makes hay of the strong moonlight shadows. You had supposed it made no part of the grounds, for a fence runs round it lined with oleander; but as the Squire is nowhere else, is it not just possible he may be here? It is a grim little wooden shanty; cobwebs bedeck it; friendly mice inhabit its recesses; the mailed cockroach walks upon the wall; so also, I regret to say, the scorpion. Herein are two pallet beds, two mosquito curtains, strung to the pitch-boards of the roof, two tables laden with books and manuscripts, three chairs, and, in one of the beds, the Squire busy writing to yourself, as it chances, and just at this moment somewhat bitten by mosquitoes. He has just set fire to the insect powder, and will be all right in no time; but just now he contemplates large white blisters, and would like to scratch them, but knows better. The house is not bare; it has been inhabited by Kanakas, and — you know what children are! — the bare wood walls are pasted over with pages from the *Graphic*, *Harper's Weekly*, etc. The floor is matted, and I am bound to say the matting is filthy. There are two windows and two doors, one of which is condemned; on the panels of that last a sheet of paper is pinned up, and covered with writing. I cull a few plums:—

"A duck-hammock for each person.
A patent organ like the commandant's at Taiohae.
Cheap and bad cigars for presents.
Revolvers.
Permanganate of potass.
Liniment for the head and sulphur.
Fine-tooth comb."

What do you think this is? Simply life in the South Seas foreshortened. These are a few of our desiderata for the next trip, which we jot down as they occur.

There, I have really done my best and tried to send something like a letter — one letter in return for all your dozens. Pray remember us all to yourself, Mrs. Boodle, and the rest of your house. I do hope your mother will be better when this comes. I shall write and give you a

1889 ÆT. 39 new address when I have made up my mind as to the most probable, and I do beg you will continue to write from time to time and give us airs from home. To-morrow — think of it — I must be off by a quarter to eight to drive into the palace and breakfast with his Hawaiian Majesty at 8.30: I shall be dead indeed. Please give my news to Scott, I trust he is better; give him my warm regards. To you we all send all kinds of things, and I am the absentee Squire,

ROBERT LOUIS STEVENSON.

To Charles Baxter

HONOLULU, *April, 1889.*

MY DEAR CHARLES,— As usual, your letter is as good as a cordial, and I thank you for it, and all your care, kindness, and generous and thoughtful friendship, from my heart. I was truly glad to hear a word of Colvin, whose long silence has terrified me; and glad to hear that you condoned the notion of my staying longer in the South Seas, for I have decided in that sense. The first idea was to go in the *Morning Star*, missionary ship; but now I have found a trading schooner, the *Equator*, which is to call for me here early in June and carry us through the Gilberts. What will happen then, the Lord knows. My mother does not accompany us: she leaves here for home early in May, and you will hear of us from her; but not, I imagine, anything more definite. We shall get dumped on Butaritari, and whether we manage to go on to the Marshalls and Carolines, or whether we fall back on Samoa, Heaven must decide; but I mean to fetch back into the course of the *Richmond*— (to think you don't know what the *Richmond* is! — *the* steamer of the Eastern South Seas, joining New Zealand, Tongatabu, the Samoas, Taheite, and Raratonga, and carrying by last advices sheep in the saloon!) — into the course of the *Richmond* and make Taheite again on the home track. Would I like to see the *Scots Observer?* Would n't I not? But whaur? I 'm direckit at space. They have nae post-offishes at the Gilberts, and as for the Car'lines! Ye see, Mr. Baxter, we 're no just in the punkshewal *centre* o' civ'lisation. But pile them up for me, and when I 've decided on an address, I 'll let you ken, and ye 'll can send them stavin' after me.— Ever your affectionate R. L. S.

To Charles Baxter

The reference in the first paragraph is to the publication in the press, which Mr. Baxter had permitted, of one of Stevenson's letters written during the earlier part of his voyage. R. L. S. had remonstrated, always greatly disliking the publication of private letters during the writer's lifetime; and now writes to soften the effect of his remonstrance.

Honolulu, *10th May, 1889.*

MY DEAR CHARLES,—I am appalled to gather from your last just to hand that you have felt so much concern about the letter. Pray dismiss it from your mind. But I think you scarce appreciate how disagreeable it is to have your private affairs and private unguarded expressions getting into print. It would soon sicken any one of writing letters. I have no doubt that letter was very

1889
ÆT. 39

wisely selected, but it just shows how things crop up. There was a raging jealousy between the two yachts; our captain was nearly in a fight over it. However, no more; and whatever you think, my dear fellow, do not suppose me angry with you or ——; although I was *annoyed at the circumstance*—a very different thing. But it is difficult to conduct life by letter, and I continually feel I may be drifting into some matter of offence, in which my heart takes no part.

I must now turn to a point of business. This new cruise of ours is somewhat venturesome; and I think it needful to warn you not to be in a hurry to suppose us dead. In these ill-charted seas, it is quite on the cards we might be cast on some unvisited, or very rarely visited, island; that there we might lie for a long time, even years, unheard of; and yet turn up smiling at the hinder end. So do not let me be "rowpit" till you get some certainty we have gone to Davie Jones in a squall, or graced the feast of some barbarian in the character of Long Pig.

I have just been a week away alone on the lee coast of Hawaii, the only white creature in many miles, riding five and a half hours one day, living with a native, seeing four lepers shipped off to Molokai, hearing native causes, and giving my opinion as *amicus curiæ* as to the interpretation of a statute in English; a lovely week among God's best—at least God's sweetest works—Polynesians. It has bettered me greatly. If I could only stay there the time that remains, I could get my work done and be happy; but the care of my family keeps me in vile Honolulu, where I am always out of sorts, amidst heat and cold and cesspools and beastly *haoles.*[1] What is a haole? You are one; and so, I am sorry to say, am I. After so long a dose of whites, it was a blessing to get among Polynesians again even for a week.

Well, Charles, there are waur haoles than yoursel', I 'll say that for ye; and trust before I sail I shall get another letter with more about yourself.—Ever your affectionate friend, R. L. S.

To W. H. Low

The allusions in the latter half of this letter are to the departure for Europe of the young Hawaiian princess Kaiulani (see the poem beginning "When from her land to mine she goes," in *Songs of Travel*, and to the circumstances of the great hurricane at Apia on March 15th, 1889.

HONOLULU, (*about*) *20th May, '89.*

MY DEAR LOW,— . . . The goods have come; many daughters have done virtuously, but thou excellest them all.—I have at length finished *The Master;* it has been a sore cross to me; but now he is buried, his body's under hatches,—his soul, if there is any hell to go to, gone to hell; and I forgive him: it is harder to forgive Burlingame for having induced me to begin the publication, or myself for suffering the induction.— Yes, I think Hole has done finely; it will be one of the most adequately illustrated books of our generation; he gets the note, he tells the story—*my* story: I know only one failure — the Master standing on the beach.— You must have a letter for me at Sydney — till further

[1] The Hawaiian name for white men.

1889 ÆT. 39

notice. Remember me to Mrs. Will H., the godlike sculptor, and any of the faithful. If you want to cease to be a republican, see my little Kaiulani, as she goes through — but she is gone already. You will die a red: I wear the colours of that little royal maiden, *Nous allons chanter à la ronde, si vous voulez!* only she is not blonde by several chalks, though she is but a half-blood, and the wrong half Edinburgh Scots like mysel'. But, O Low, I love the Polynesian: this civilisation of ours is a dingy, ungentlemanly business; it drops out too much of man, and too much of that the very beauty of the poor beast: who has his beauties in spite of Zola and Co. As usual, here is a whole letter with no news: I am a bloodless, inhuman dog; and no doubt Zola is a better correspondent.— Long live your fine old English admiral — yours, I mean — the U. S. A. one at Samoa; I wept tears and loved myself and mankind when I read of him: he is not too much civilised. And there was Gordon, too; and there are others, beyond question. But if you could live, the only white folk, in a Polynesian village; and drink that warm, light *vin du pays* of human affection, and enjoy that simple dignity of all about you — I will not gush, for I am now in my fortieth year, which seems highly unjust, but there it is, Mr. Low, and the Lord enlighten your affectionate

R. L. S.

To Mrs. R. L. Stevenson

The following two letters were written during and immediately after Stevenson's trip to the noted leper settlement, the scene of Father Damien's labours, at Molokai.

KALAWAO, MOLOKAI [*May, 1889*].

1889
ÆT. 39

DEAR FANNY,—I had a lovely sail up. Captain Cameron and Mr. Gilfillan, both born in the States, yet the first still with a strong Highland, and the second still with a strong Lowland accent, were good company; the night was warm, the victuals plain but good. Mr. Gilfillan gave me his berth, and I slept well, though I heard the sisters sick in the next state-room, poor souls. Heavy rolling woke me in the morning; I turned in all standing, so went right on the upper deck. The da¸ was on the peep out of a low morning bank, and we were wallowing along under stupendous cliffs. As the lights brightened, we could see certain abutments and buttresses on their front where wood clustered and grass grew brightly. But the whole brow seemed quite impassable, and my heart sank at the sight. Two thousand feet of rock making 19° (the Captain guesses) seemed quite beyond my powers. However, I had come so far; and, to tell you the truth, I was so cowed with fear and disgust that I dared not go back on the adventure in the interests of my own self-respect. Presently we came up with the leper promontory: lowland, quite bare and bleak and harsh, a little town of wooden houses, two churches, a landing-stair, all unsightly, sour, northerly, lying athwart the sunrise, with the great wall of the pali cutting the world out on the south. Our lepers were sent on the first boat, about a dozen, one poor child very horrid, one white man, leaving a large grown family behind him in Honolulu, and then into the second stepped the sisters and myself. I do not know how it would have been with me had the sisters not been there. My horror of the horri-

1889 ÆT. 39

ble is about my weakest point; but the moral loveliness at my elbow blotted all else out; and when I found that one of them was crying, poor soul, quietly under her veil, I cried a little myself; then I felt as right as a trivet, only a little crushed to be there so uselessly. I thought it was a sin and a shame she should feel unhappy; I turned round to her, and said something like this: "Ladies, God Himself is here to give you welcome. I 'm sure it is good for me to be beside you; I hope it will be blessed to me; I thank you for myself and the good you do me." It seemed to cheer her up; but indeed I had scarce said it when we were at the landing-stairs, and there was a great crowd, hundreds of (God save us!) pantomime masks in poor human flesh, waiting to receive the sisters and the new patients.

Every hand was offered: I had gloves, but I had made up my mind on the boat's voyage *not* to give my hand, that seemed less offensive than the gloves. So the sisters and I went up among that crew, and presently I got aside (for I felt I had no business there) and set off on foot across the promontory, carrying my wrap and the camera. All horror was quite gone from me: to see these dread creatures smile and look happy was beautiful. On my way through Kalaupapa I was exchanging cheerful *alohas* with the patients coming galloping over on their horses; I was stopping to gossip at house-doors; I was happy, only ashamed of myself that I was here for no good. One woman was pretty, and spoke good English, and was infinitely engaging and (in the old phrase) towardly; she thought I was the new white patient; and when she found I was only a visitor, a curious change came in her face and voice—the only sad thing—morally sad, I mean—that I met that morning. But for all that, they tell me none want to leave. Beyond Kalaupapa the houses became rare; dry stone dykes, grassy, stony land, one sick pandanus; a dreary country; from overhead in the little clinging wood shogs of the pali chirruping of birds fell; the low sun was right in my face; the trade blew pure and cool and delicious; I felt as right as ninepence, and stopped and chatted with the patients whom I still met on their horses, with not the least disgust. About half-way over, I met the superintendent (a leper) with a horse for me, and O, was n't I glad! But the horse was one of those curious, dogged, cranky brutes that always dully want to go somewhere else, and my traffic with him completed my crushing fatigue. I got to the guest-house, an empty house with several rooms, kitchen, bath, etc. There was no one there, and I let the horse go loose in the garden, lay down on the bed, and fell asleep.

Dr. Swift woke me and gave me breakfast, then I came back and slept again while he was at the dispensary, and he woke me for dinner; and I came back and slept again, and he woke me about six for supper; and then in about an hour I felt tired again, and came up to my solitary guest-house, played the flageolet, and am now writing to you. As yet, you see, I have seen nothing of the settlement, and my crushing fatigue (though I believe that was moral and a measure of my cowardice) and the doctor's opinion make me think the pali hopeless. "You don't look a strong man," said the doctor; "but are you sound?" I told him the truth; then he said it was out of the question, and

1889 ÆT. 39

if I were to get up at all, I must be carried up. But, as it seems, men as well as horses continually fall on this ascent: the doctor goes up with a change of clothes—it is plain that to be carried would in itself be very fatiguing to both mind and body; and I should then be at the beginning of thirteen miles of mountain road to be ridden against time. How should I come through? I hope you will think me right in my decision: I mean to stay, and shall not be back in Honolulu till Saturday, June first. You must all do the best you can to make ready.

Dr. Swift has a wife and an infant son, beginning to toddle and run, and they live here as composed as brick and mortar—at least the wife does, a Kentucky German, a fine enough creature, I believe, who was quite amazed at the sisters shedding tears! How strange is mankind! Gilfillan too, a good fellow I think, and far from a stupid, kept up his hard Lowland Scottish talk in the boat while the sister was covering her face; but I believe he knew, and did it (partly) in embarrassment, and part perhaps in mistaken kindness. And that was one reason, too, why I made my speech to them. Partly, too, I did it, because I was ashamed to do so, and remembered one of my golden rules, "When you are ashamed to speak, speak up at once." But, mind you, that rule is only golden with strangers; with your own folks, there are other considerations. This is a strange place to be in. A bell has been sounded at intervals while I wrote, now all is still but a musical humming of the sea, not unlike the sound of telegraph wires; the night is quite cool and pitch dark, with a small fine rain; one light over in the leper settlement, one cricket whistling in the garden, my lamp here by my bedside, and my pen cheeping between my inky fingers.

Next day, lovely morning, slept all night, 80° in the shade, strong, sweet Anaho trade-wind. LOUIS.

TO SIDNEY COLVIN

[HONOLULU, *May or June, 1889.*]

MY DEAR COLVIN,—I am just home after twelve days' journey to Molokai, seven of them at the leper settlement, where I can only say that the sight of so much courage, cheerfulness, and devotion strung me too high to mind the infinite pity and horror of the sights. I used to ride over from Kalawao to Kalaupapa (about three miles across the promontory, the cliff-wall, ivied with forest and yet inaccessible from steepness, on my left), go to the Sisters' home, which is a miracle of neatness, play a game of croquet with seven leper girls (90° in the shade), get a little old-maid meal served me by the Sisters, and ride home again, tired enough, but not too tired. The girls have all dolls, and love dressing them. You who know so many ladies delicately clad, and they who know so many dressmakers, please make it known it would be an acceptable gift to send scraps for doll dressmaking to the Reverend Sister Maryanne, Bishop Home, Kalaupapa, Molokai, Hawaiian Islands.

I have seen sights that cannot be told, and heard stories that cannot be repeated: yet I never admired my poor race so much, nor (strange as it may seem) loved life more than in the settlement. A horror of moral beauty broods over the place: that 's like bad Victor Hugo, but it is the only way I can express the sense that lived with me all these days. And this even though it was in great part Catholic, and my sympathies flew never with so much difficulty as towards Catholic virtues. The pass-book kept with heaven stirs me to anger and laughter. One of the sisters calls the place "the ticket office to heaven." Well, what is the odds? They do their darg, and do it with kindness and efficiency incredible; and we must take folk's virtues as we find them, and love the better part. Of old Damien, whose weaknesses and worse perhaps I heard fully, I think only the more. It was a European peasant: dirty, bigotted, untruthful, unwise, tricky, but superb with generosity, residual candour and fundamental good-humour: convince him he had done wrong (it might take hours of insult) and he would undo what he had done and like his corrector better. A man, with all the grime and paltriness of mankind, but a saint and hero all the more for that. The place as regards scenery is grand, gloomy, and bleak. Mighty mountain walls descending sheer along the whole face of the island into a sea unusually deep; the front of the mountain ivied and furred with clinging forest, one viridescent cliff: about half-way from east to west, the low, bare, stony promontory edged in between the cliff and the ocean; the two little towns (Kalawao and Kalaupapa) seated on either side of it, as bare almost as bathing machines upon a beach; and the population — gorgons and chimæras dire. All this tear of the nerves I bore admirably; and the day after I got away, rode twenty miles along the opposite coast and up into the mountains: they call it twenty, I am doubtful of the figures: I should guess it nearer twelve; but let me take credit for what residents allege; and I was riding again the day after, so I need say no more about health. Honolulu does not agree with me at all: I am always out of sorts there, with slight headache, blood to the head, etc. I had a good deal of work to do and did it with miserable difficulty; and yet all the time I have been gaining strength, as you see, which is highly encouraging. By the time I am done with this cruise I shall have the material for a very singular book of travels: names of strange stories and characters, cannibals, pirates, ancient legends, old Polynesian poetry,— never was so generous a farrago. I am going down now to get the story of a shipwrecked family, who were fifteen months on an island with a murderer: there is a specimen. The Pacific is a strange place; the nineteenth century only exists there in spots: all round, it is a no man's land of the ages, a stir-about of epochs and races, barbarisms and civilisations, virtues and crimes.

It is good of you to let me stay longer, but if I had known how ill you were, I should be now on my way home. I had chartered my schooner and made all arrangements before (at last) we got definite news. I feel highly guilty; I should be back to insult and worry you a little. Our address till further notice is to be c/o R Towns and Co., Sydney. That is final: I only got the arrangement made yesterday; but you may now publish it abroad.—Yours ever, R. L. S.

1889
ÆT. 39

To James Payn

The following was written to his old friend of *Cornhill Magazine* days, Mr. James Payn, on receiving in Hawaii news of that gentleman's ill-health and gathering deafness.

Honolulu, H. I., *June 13th, 1889.*

MY DEAR JAMES PAYN,—I get sad news of you here at my offsetting for further voyages: I wish I could say what I feel. Sure there was never any man less deserved this calamity; for I have heard you speak time and again, and I remember nothing that was unkind, nothing that was untrue, nothing that was not helpful, from your lips. It is the ill-talkers that should hear no more. God knows, I know no word of consolation; but I do feel your trouble. You are the more open to letters now; let me talk to you for two pages. I have nothing but happiness to tell; and you may bless God you are a man so sound-hearted that (even in the freshness of your calamity) I can come to you with my own good fortune unashamed and secure of sympathy. It is a good thing to be a good man, whether deaf or whether dumb; and of all our fellow craftsmen (whom yet they count a jealous race), I never knew one but gave you the name of honesty and kindness: come to think of it gravely, this is better than the finest hearing. We are all on the march to deafness, blindness, and all conceivable and fatal disabilities; we shall not all get there with a report so good. My good news is a health astonishingly reinstated. This climate; these voyagings; these landfalls at dawn; new islands peaking from the morning bank; new forested harbours; new passing alarms of squalls and surf; new interests of gentle natives,—the whole tale of my life is better to me than any poem.

I am fresh just now from the leper settlement of Molokai, playing croquet with seven leper girls, sitting and yarning with old, blind, leper beachcombers in the hospital, sickened with the spectacle of abhorrent suffering and deformation amongst the patients, touched to the heart by the sight of lovely and effective virtues in their helpers: no stranger time have I ever had, nor any so moving. I do not think it a little thing to be deaf, God knows, and God defend me from the same!—but to be a leper, or one of the self-condemned, how much more awful! and yet there 's a way there also. "There are Molokais everywhere," said Mr. Dutton, Father Damien's dresser; you are but new landed in yours; and my dear and kind adviser, I wish you, with all my soul, that patience and courage which you will require. Think of me meanwhile on a trading schooner, bound for the Gilbert Islands, thereafter for the Marshalls, with a diet of fish and cocoanut before me; bound on a cruise of—well, of investigation to what islands we can reach, and to get (some day or other) to Sydney, where a letter addressed to the care of R. Towns & Co. will find me sooner or later; and if it contain any good news, whether of your welfare or the courage with which you bear the contrary, will do me good.—Yours affectionately (although so near a stranger),

ROBERT LOUIS STEVENSON.

1889
ÆT. 39

To Sidney Colvin

Stevenson and his party sailed accordingly on the trading schooner *Equator*, "on a certain bright June day in 1889," for the Gilbert Islands, a scattered group of atolls in the Western Pacific. Their expectation was to come back into civilisation again by way of the Carolines, Manila, and the China ports; but instead of this, circumstances which occurred to change the trader's course took them southwards to Samoa, where they arrived in December of the same year. Their second voyage was thus of six months' duration; in the course of it they spent two periods of about six weeks each on land, first at one and then at another of the two island capitals, Butaritari and Apemama. The following letter is the first which reached Stevenson's friends from this part of his voyage, and was written in two instalments, the first from on board the *Equator* in the lagoon of the island of Apaiang; the second, six weeks later, from the settlement on shore at Apemama, which the king, his friend Tembinoka, allowed him and his party to occupy during their stay. The account of this stay at Apemama and of the character of the king, Tembinoka, is far the most interesting and attractive part of the volume called *The South Seas* (Vol. XIX of the Thistle edition), which was the literary result — and on the whole, despite the high hopes he had built on it, an unsuccessful result — of these voyages.

SCHOONER "EQUATOR," APAIANG LAGOON,
August 22nd, 1889.

MY DEAR COLVIN,—The missionary ship is outside the reef trying (vainly) to get in; so I may have a chance to get a line off. I am glad to say I shall be home by June next for the summer, or we shall know the reason why. For God's sake be well and jolly for the meeting. I shall be, I believe, a different character from what you have seen this long while. This cruise is up to now a huge success, being interesting, pleasant, and profitable. The beachcomber is perhaps the most interesting character here; the natives are very different, on the whole, from Polynesians: they are moral, standoffish (for good reasons), and protected by a dark tongue. It is delightful to meet the few Hawaiians (mostly missionaries) that are dotted about, with their Italian *brio* and their ready friendliness. The whites are a strange lot, many of them good, kind, pleasant fellows; others quite the lowest I have ever seen even in the slums of cities. I wish I had time to narrate to you the doings and character of three white murderers (more or less proven) I have met. One, the only undoubted assassin of the lot, quite gained my affection in his big home out of a wreck, with his New Hebrides wife in her savage turban of hair and yet a perfect lady, and his three adorable little girls in Rob Roy Macgregor dresses, dancing to the hand organ, performing circus on the floor with startling effects of nudity, and curling up together on a mat to sleep, three sizes, three attitudes, three Rob Roy dresses, and six little clenched fists: the murderer meanwhile brooding and gloating over his chicks, till your whole heart went out to him; and yet his crime on the face of it was dark: disembowelling, in his own house, an old man of seventy, and him drunk.

It is lunch-time, I see, and I must close up with my warmest love to you. I wish you were here to sit upon me when required. Ah! if you were but a good sailor! I will never leave the sea, I think; it is only there that a Briton lives: my poor grandfather, it is from him I inherit the taste, I fancy, and he was round many islands in his day; but I, please God, shall beat him at that before the recall is sounded. Would you

1889
ÆT. 39

be surprised to learn that I contemplate becoming a shipowner? I do, but it is a secret. Life is far better fun than people dream who fall asleep among the chimney stacks and telegraph wires.

Love to Henry James and others near.—Ever yours, my dear fellow, ROBERT LOUIS STEVENSON.

EQUATOR TOWN, APEMAMA, *October, 1889.*

No *Morning Star* came, however; and so now I try to send this to you by the schooner *J. L. Tiernan.* We have been about a month ashore, camping out in a kind of town the king set up for us: on the idea that I was really a "big chief" in England. He dines with us sometimes, and sends up a cook for a share of our meals when he does not come himself. This sounds like high living! alas, undeceive yourself. Salt junk is the mainstay; a low island, except for cocoanuts, is just the same as a ship at sea: brackish water, no supplies, and very little shelter. The king is a great character—a thorough tyrant, very much of a gentleman, a poet, a musician, a historian, or perhaps rather more a genealogist—it is strange to see him lying in his house among a lot of wives (nominal wives) writing the History of Apemama in an account-book; his description of one of his own songs, which he sang to me himself, as "about sweethearts, and trees, and the sea—and no true, all-the-same lie," seems about as compendious a definition of lyric poetry as a man could ask. Tembinoka is here the great attraction: all the rest is heat and tedium and villainous dazzle, and yet more villainous mosquitoes. We are like to be here, however, many a long week before we get away, and then whither? A strange trade this voyaging: so vague, so bound-down, so helpless. Fanny has been planting some vegetables, and we have actually onions and radishes coming up: ah, onion-despiser, were you but awhile in a low island, how your heart would leap at sight of a coster's barrow! I think I could shed tears over a dish of turnips. No doubt we shall all be glad to say farewell to low islands — I had near said for ever. They are very tame; and I begin to read up the directory, and pine for an island with a profile, a running brook, or were it only a well among the rocks. The thought of a mango came to me early this morning and set my greed on edge; but you do not know what a mango is, so ——.

1889
ÆT. 39

I have been thinking a great deal of you and the Monument of late, and even tried to get my thoughts into a poem, hitherto without success. God knows how you are: I begin to weary dreadfully to see you — well, in nine months, I hope; but that seems a long time. I wonder what has befallen me too, that flimsy part of me that lives (or dwindles) in the public mind; and what has befallen *The Master*, and what kind of a Box the Merry Box has been found. It is odd to know nothing of all this. We had an old woman to do devil-work for you about a month ago, in a Chinaman's house on Apaiang (August 23rd or 24th). You should have seen the crone with a noble masculine face, like that of an old crone [*sic*], a body like a man's (naked all but the feathery female girdle), knotting cocoanut leaves and muttering spells: Fanny and I, and the good captain of the *Equator*, and the Chinaman and his native wife and sister-in-law, all squatting on

1889 ÆT. 39

the floor about the sibyl; and a crowd of dark faces watching from behind her shoulder (she sat right in the doorway) and tittering aloud with strange, appalled, embarrassed laughter at each fresh adjuration. She informed us you were in England, not travelling and now no longer sick; she promised us a fair wind the next day, and we had it, so I cherish the hope she was as right about Sidney Colvin. The shipownering has rather petered out since I last wrote, and a good many other plans beside.

Health? Fanny very so-so; I pretty right upon the whole, and getting through plenty work: I know not quite how, but it seems to me not bad and in places funny.

South Sea Yarns:

1. *The Wrecker*		R. L. S.
2. *The Pearl Fisher*	by	and
3. *The Beachcombers*		Lloyd O.

The Pearl Fisher, part done, lies in Sydney. It is *The Wrecker* we are now engaged upon: strange ways of life, I think, they set forth: things that I can scarce touch upon, or even not at all, in my travel book; and the yarns are good, I do believe. *The Pearl Fisher* is for the *New York Ledger:* the yarn is a kind of Monte Cristo one. *The Wrecker* is the least good as a story, I think; but the characters seem to me good. *The Beachcombers* is more sentimental. These three scarce touch the outskirts of the life we have been viewing; a hot-bed of strange characters and incidents: Lord, how different from Europe or the Pallid States! Farewell. Heaven knows when this will get to you. I burn to be in Sydney and have news. R. L. S.

To Sidney Colvin

The following, written in the last days of the sail southwards from the Gilberts to Samoa, contains the full plan of the *South Seas* book as it had now been conceived. The verses at the end have already been printed (*Songs of Travel*, p. 58); but I give them here with the context, as in similar instances above. The allusion to the two colossal images from the Easter Islands, which used to stand under the portico to the right hand of the visitor entering the Museum, has partly lost its point since they have been moved.

SCHOONER "EQUATOR," AT SEA. 190 MILES OFF SAMOA.
Monday, December 2nd, 1889.

MY DEAR COLVIN,—We are just nearing the end of our long cruise. Rain, calms, squalls, bang—there 's the foretopmast gone; rain, calm, squalls, away with the staysail; more rain, more calm, more squalls; a prodigious heavy sea all the time, and the *Equator* staggering and hovering like a swallow in a storm; and the cabin, a great square, crowded with wet human beings, and the rain avalanching on the deck, and the leaks dripping everywhere: Fanny, in the midst of fifteen males, bearing up wonderfully. But such voyages are at the best a trial. We had one particularity: coming down on Winslow Reef, p. d. (position doubtful): two positions in the directory, a third (if you cared to count that) on the chart; heavy sea running, and the night due. The boats were cleared, bread put on board, and we made up our packets for a boat voyage of four or five hundred miles, and turned in, expectant of a crash. Needless to say it did not come, and no doubt we were far to leeward. If we only had twopenceworth of wind, we might be at dinner in Apia to-morrow evening; but no

1889
ÆT. 39

such luck: here we roll, dead before a light air—and that is no point of sailing at all for a fore and aft schooner—the sun blazing overhead, thermometer 88°, four degrees above what I have learned to call South Sea temperature; but for all that, land so near, and so much grief being happily astern, we are all pretty gay on board, and have been photographing and draught-playing and sky-larking like anything. I am minded to stay not very long in Samoa and confine my studies there (as far as any one can forecast) to the history of the late war. My book is now practically modelled: if I can execute what is designed, there are few better books now extant on this globe, bar the epics, and the big tragedies, and histories, and the choice lyric poetics and a novel or so—none. But it is not executed yet; and let not him that putteth on his armour, vaunt himself. At least, nobody has had such stuff; such wild stories, such beautiful scenes, such singular intimacies, such manners and traditions, so incredible a mixture of the beautiful and horrible, the savage and civilised. I will give you here some idea of the table of contents, which ought to make your mouth water. I propose to call the book *The South Seas:* it is rather a large title, but not many people have seen more of them than I, perhaps no one—certainly no one capable of using the material.

Part I. General. "Of schooners, islands, and maroons."

CHAPTER I. Marine.
" II. Contraband (smuggling, barratry, labour traffic).
" III. The Beachcomber.

CHAPTER IV. Beachcomber stories. i. The Murder of the Chinaman. ii. Death of a Beachcomber. iii. A Character. iv. The Apia Blacksmith.

Part II. The Marquesas.

" V. Anaho. i. Arrival. ii. Death. iii. The Tapu. iv. Morals. v. Hoka.

" VI. Tai-o-hae. i. Arrival. ii. The French. iii. The Royal Family. iv. Chiefless Folk. v. The Catholics. vi. Hawaiian Missionaries.

" VII. Observations of a Long Pig. i. Cannibalism. ii. Hatiheu. iii. Frère Michel. iv. Toa-hauka and Atuona. v. The Vale of Atuona. vi. Moipu. vii. Captain Hati.

Part III. The Dangerous Archipelago.

" VIII. The Group.

" IX. A House to let in a Low Island.

" X. A Paumotuan Funeral. i. The Funeral. ii. Tales of the Dead.

Part IV. Tahiti.

" XI. Tautira.

" XII. Village Government in Tahiti.

" XIII. A Journey in Quest of Legends.

" XIV. Legends and Songs.

" XV. Life in Eden.

" XVI. Note on the French Regimen.

Part V. The Eight Islands.

" XVII. A Note on Missions.

" XVIII. The Kona Coast of Hawaii. i. Hookena.

1889
ÆT. 39

CHAPTER XVIII. ii. A Ride in the Forest. iii. A Law Case. iv. The City of Refuge. v. The Lepers.
" XIX. Molokai. i. A Week in the Precinct. ii. History of the Leper Settlement. iii. The Mokolii. iv. The Free Island.

Part VI. The Gilberts.

" XX. The Group. ii. Position of Woman. iii. The Missions. iv. Devil-work. v. Republics.
" XXI. Rule and Misrule on Makin. i. Butaritari, its King and Court. ii. History of Three Kings. iii. The Drink Question.
" XXII. A Butaritarian Festival.
" XXIII. The King of Apemama. i. First Impressions. ii. Equator Town and the Palace. iii. The Three Corselets.

Part VII. Samoa.

which I have not yet reached.

Even as so sketched it makes sixty chapters, not less than 300 *Cornhill* pages; and I suspect not much under 500. Samoa has yet to be accounted for: I think it will be all history, and I shall work in observations on Samoan manners, under the similar heads in other Polynesian islands. It is still possible, though unlikely, that I may add a passing visit to Fiji or Tonga, or even both; but I am growing impatient to see yourself, and I do not want to be later than June of coming to England. Anyway, you see it will be a large work, and as it will be copiously illustrated, the Lord knows what it will cost. We shall return, God willing, by Sydney, Ceylon, Suez and, I guess, Marseilles the many-masted (copyright epithet). I shall likely pause a day or two in Paris, but all that is too far ahead — although now it begins to look near — so near, and I can hear the rattle of the hansom up Endell Street, and see the gates swing back, and feel myself jump out upon the Monument steps — Hosanna! — home again. My dear fellow, now that my father is done with his troubles, and 17 Heriot Row no more than a mere shell, you and that gaunt old Monument in Bloomsbury are all that I have in view when I use the word home; some passing thoughts there may be of the rooms at Skerryvore, and the blackbirds in the chine on a May morning; but the essence is S. C. and the Museum. Suppose, by some damned accident, you were no more: well, I should return just the same, because of my mother and Lloyd, whom I now think to send to Cambridge; but all the spring would have gone out of me, and ninety per cent. of the attraction lost. I will copy for you here a copy of verses made in Apemama.

I heard the pulse of the besieging sea
Throb far away all night. I heard the wind
Fly crying, and convulse tumultuous palms.
I rose and strolled. The isle was all bright sand,
And flailing fans and shadows of the palm:
The heaven all moon, and wind, and the blind vault—
The keenest planet slain, for Venus slept.
The King, my neighbour, with his host of wives,
Slept in the precinct of the palisade:

1889
ÆT. 39

Where single, in the wind, under the moon,
Among the slumbering cabins, blazed a fire,
Sole street-lamp and the only sentinel.
To other lands and nights my fancy turned,
To London first, and chiefly to your house,
The many-pillared and the well-beloved.
There yearning fancy lighted; there again
In the upper room I lay and heard far off
The unsleeping city murmur like a shell;
The muffled tramp of the Museum guard
Once more went by me; I beheld again
Lamps vainly brighten the dispeopled street;
Again I longed for the returning morn,
The awaking traffic, the bestirring birds,
The consentaneous trill of tiny song
That weaves round monumental cornices
A passing charm of beauty: most of all,
For your light foot I wearied, and your knock
That was the glad reveillé of my day.
Lo, now, when to your task in the great house
At morning through the portico you pass,
One moment glance where, by the pillared wall,
Far-voyaging island gods, begrimed with smoke,
Sit now unworshipped, the rude monument
Of faiths forgot and races undivined;
Sit now disconsolate, remembering well
The priest, the victim, and the songful crowd,
The blaze of the blue noon, and that huge voice
Incessant, of the breakers on the shore.
As far as these from their ancestral shrine,
So far, so foreign, your divided friends
Wander, estranged in body, not in mind. R. L. S.

To E. L. Burlingame

SCHOONER "EQUATOR," AT SEA,
Wednesday, 4th December, 1889.

MY DEAR BURLINGAME,—We are now about to rise, like whales, from this long dive, and I make ready a communication which is to go to you by the first mail from Samoa. How long we shall stay in that group I cannot forecast; but it will be best still to address at Sydney, where I trust, when I shall arrive, perhaps in one month from now, more probably in two or three, to find all news.

Business.—Will you be likely to have a space in the Magazine for a serial story, which should be ready, I believe, by April, at latest by autumn? It is called *The Wrecker;* and in book form will appear as number 1 of *South Sea Yarns* by R. L. S. and Lloyd Osbourne. Here is the table as far as fully conceived, and indeed executed.[1] . . .

The story is founded on fact, the mystery I really believe to be insoluble; the purchase of a wreck has never been handled before, no more has San Francisco. These seem all elements of success. There is, besides, a character, Jim Pinkerton, of the advertising American, on whom we build a good deal; and some sketches of the American merchant marine, opium smuggling in Honolulu, etc. It should run to (about) three hundred pages of my MS. I would like to know if this tale smiles upon you, if you will have a vacancy, and what

[1] Table of chapter headings follows

1889 ÆT. 39

you will be willing to pay. It will of course be copyright in both the States and England. I am a little anxious to have it tried serially, as it tests the interest of the mystery.

Pleasure.—We have had a fine time in the Gilbert group, though four months on low islands, which involves low diet, is a largish order; and my wife is rather down. I am myself, up to now, a pillar of health, though our long and vile voyage of calms, squalls, cataracts of rain, sails carried away, foretopmast lost, boats cleared and packets made on the approach of a p. d. reef, etc., has cured me of salt brine, and filled me with a longing for beefsteak and mangoes not to be depicted. The interest has been immense. Old King Tembinoka of Apemama, the Napoleon of the group, poet, tyrant, altogether a man of mark, gave me the woven corselets of his grandfather, his father and his uncle, and what pleased me more, told me their singular story, then all manner of strange tales, facts and experiences for my South Sea book, which should be a Tearer, Mr. Burlingame: no one at least has had such stuff.

We are now engaged in the hell of a dead calm, the heat is cruel—it is the only time when I suffer from heat: I have nothing on but a pair of serge trousers, and a singlet without sleeves of Oxford gauze—O, yes, and a red sash about my waist; and yet as I sit here in the cabin, sweat streams from me. The rest are on deck under a bit of awning; we are not much above a hundred miles from port, and we might as well be in Kamchatka. However, I should be honest: this is the first calm I have endured without the added bane of a heavy swell, and the intoxicated blue-bottle wallowings and knockings of the helpless ship.

I wonder how you liked the end of *The Master;* that was the hardest job I ever had to do; did I do it?

My wife begs to be remembered to yourself and Mrs. Burlingame. Remember all of us to all friends, particularly Low, in case I don't get a word through for him.—I am, yours very sincerely,

ROBERT LOUIS STEVENSON.

TO CHARLES BAXTER

The following was written soon after the termination of the voyage of the *Equator* and Stevenson's first landing in Samoa, where he was engaged in collecting materials for the account (then intended to be the concluding part of his great projected South Sea book) of the war and hurricane of the previous year.

SAMOA [*December, 1889*].

MY DEAR BAXTER,— . . . I cannot return until I have seen either Tonga or Fiji or both: and I must not leave here till I have finished my collections on the war—a very interesting bit of history, the truth often very hard to come at, and the search (for me) much complicated by the German tongue, from the use of which I have desisted (I suppose) these fifteen years. The last two days I have been mugging with a dictionary from five to six hours a day; besides this, I have to call upon, keep sweet, and judiciously interview all sorts of persons—English, American, German, and Samoan. It makes a hard life; above all, as after every interview I have to come and get my notes straight on the nail. I

1889 ÆT. 39

have a boy, Henry, who interprets and copies for me, and is a great nuisance. He said he wished to come to me in order to learn "long explessions." Henry goes up along with us; and as I am not fond of him, he may before the trip is over hear some "stlong explessions." I am writing this on the back balcony at Moors', palms and a hill like the hill of Kinnoull looking in at me; myself lying on the floor, and (like the parties in Handel's song) "clad in robes of virgin white"; the ink is dreadful, the heat delicious, a fine going breeze in the palms, and from the other side of the house the sudden angry splash and roar of the Pacific on the reef, where the warships are still piled from last year's hurricane, some under water, one high and dry upon her side, the strangest figure of a ship was ever witnessed; the narrow bay there is full of ships; the men-of-war covered with sail after the rains, and (especially the German ship, which is fearfully and awfully top heavy) rolling almost yards in, in what appears to be calm water.

Samoa, Apia at least, is far less beautiful than the Marquesas or Tahiti: a more gentle scene, gentler acclivities, a tamer face of nature; and this much aided, for the wanderer, by the great German plantations with their countless regular avenues of palms. The island has beautiful rivers, of about the bigness of our waters in the Lothians, with pleasant pools and waterfalls and overhanging verdure, and often a great volume of sound, so that once I thought I was passing near a mill, and it was only the voice of the river. I am not specially attracted by the people; but they are courteous; the women very attractive, and dress lovely; the men purposelike, well set up, tall, lean, and dignified. As I write, the breeze is brisking up, doors are beginning to slam, and shutters; a strong draught sweeps round the balcony; it looks doubtful for to-morrow. Here I shut up.—Ever your affectionate

1890
ÆT. 40

R. L. STEVENSON.

TO DR. SCOTT

This gentleman is the physician to whose assiduous care and kindness, as recorded in the dedication to *Underwoods*, Stevenson owed so much during his invalid years at Bournemouth.

APIA, SAMOA, *January 20th, 1890.*

MY DEAR SCOTT,—Shameful indeed that you should not have heard from me before! I have now been some twenty months in the South Seas, and am (up to date) a person whom you would scarce know. I think nothing of long walks and rides: I was four hours and a half gone the other day, partly riding, partly climbing up a steep ravine. I have stood a six months' voyage on a copra schooner with about three months ashore on coral atolls, which means (except for cocoanuts to drink) no change whatever from ship's food. My wife suffered badly—it was too rough a business altogether—Lloyd suffered—and, in short, I was the only one of the party who "kept my end up."

I am so pleased with this climate that I have decided to settle; have even purchased a piece of land from three to four hundred acres, I know not which till the survey is completed, and shall only return next summer to wind up my affairs in England; thenceforth I mean to be a subject of the High Commissioner.

1890
ÆT. 40

Now you would have gone longer yet without news of your truant patient, but that I have a medical discovery to communicate. I find I can (almost immediately) fight off a cold with liquid extract of coca; two or (if obstinate) three teaspoonfuls in the day for a variable period of from one to five days sees the cold generally to the door. I find it at once produces a glow, stops rigour, and though it makes one very uncomfortable, prevents the advance of the disease. Hearing of this influenza, it occurred to me that this might prove remedial; and perhaps a stronger exhibition—injections of cocaine, for instance—still better.

If on my return I find myself let in for this epidemic, which seems highly calculated to nip me in the bud, I shall feel very much inclined to make the experiment. See what a gulf you may save me from if you shall have previously made it on *anima vili*, on some less important sufferer, and shall have found it worse than useless.

How is Miss Boodle and her family? Greeting to your brother and all friends in Bournemouth.—Yours very sincerely, ROBERT LOUIS STEVENSON.

TO CHARLES BAXTER

After a stay of four or five weeks at Apia, during which he had fallen more and more in love with Samoa and the Samoans, and bought the property on which he afterwards settled, Stevenson took steamer again, this time for Sydney, where he had ordered his letters to await him. This and the two following letters were written during the passage. I again print in their original place a set of verses which have already appeared in *Songs of Travel*.

Februar den Zen, 1890.

1890
ÆT. 40

DAMPFER "LÜBECK" ZWISCHEN APIA UND SYDNEY.

MY DEAR CHARLES,—I have got one delightful letter from you, and heard from my mother of your kindness in going to see her. Thank you for that: you can in no way more touch and serve me. . . . Ay, ay, it is sad to sell 17; sad and fine were the old days: when I was away in Apemama, I wrote two copies of verse about Edinburgh and the past, so ink black, so golden bright. I will send them, if I can find them, for they will say something to you, and indeed one is more than half addressed to you. This is it—

TO MY OLD COMRADES

Do you remember—can we e'er forget?—
How, in the coiled perplexities of youth,
In our wild climate, in our scowling town,
We gloomed and shivered, sorrowed, sobbed, and
feared?
The belching winter wind, the missile rain,
The rare and welcome silence of the snows,
The laggard morn, the haggard day, the night,
The grimy spell of the nocturnal town,
Do you remember?—Ah, could one forget!
As when the fevered sick that all night long
Listed the wind intone, and hear at last
The ever-welcome voice of the chanticleer
Sing in the bitter hour before the dawn,—
With sudden ardour, these desire the day:

(Here a squall sends all flying.)

1890
ÆT. 40

T.'s flag, which my wife designed for him: in a word, what I can do best for you. It will be thus a foretaste of my book of travels. I shall ask you to let me have, if I wish it, the use of the plates made, and to make up a little tract of the verses and illustrations, of which you might send six copies to H. M. Tembinoka, King of Apemama, *via* Butaritari, Gilbert Islands. It might be best to send it by Crawford and Co., S. F. There is no postal service; and schooners must take it, how they may and when. Perhaps some such note as this might be prefixed:

At my departure from the island of Apemama, for which you will look in vain in most atlases, the king and I agreed, since we both set up to be in the poetical way, that we should celebrate our separation in verse. Whether or not his Majesty has been true to his bargain, the laggard posts of the Pacific may perhaps inform me in six months, perhaps not before a year. The following lines represent my part of the contract, and it is hoped, by their pictures of strange manners, they may entertain a civilised audience. Nothing throughout has been invented or exaggerated; the lady herein referred to as the author's Muse, has confined herself to stringing into rhyme facts and legends that I saw or heard during two months' residence upon the island.

R. L. S.

You will have received from me a letter about *The Wrecker*. No doubt it is a new experiment for me, being disguised so much as a study of manners, and the interest turning on a mystery of the detective sort. I think there need be no hesitation about beginning it in the fall of the year. Lloyd has nearly finished his part, and I shall hope to send you very soon the MS. of about the first four-sevenths. At the same time, I have been employing myself in Samoa, collecting facts about the recent war; and I propose to write almost at once and to publish shortly a small volume, called I know not what —the War in Samoa, the Samoa Trouble, an Island War, the War of the Three Consuls, I know not—perhaps you can suggest. It was meant to be a part of my travel book; but material has accumulated on my hands until I see myself forced into volume form, and I hope it may be of use, if it come soon. I have a few photographs of the war, which will do for illustrations. It is conceivable you might wish to handle this in the Magazine, although I am inclined to think you won't, and to agree with you. But if you think otherwise, there it is. The travel letters (fifty of them) are already contracted for in papers; these I was quite bound to let M'Clure handle, as the idea was of his suggestion, and I always felt a little sore as to one trick I played him in the matter of the end-papers. The war volume will contain some very interesting and picturesque details: more I can't promise for it. Of course the fifty newspaper letters will be simply patches chosen from the travel volume (or volumes) as it gets written.

But you see I have in hand:—

Say half done.	1. *The Wrecker.*
Lloyd's copy half done, mine not touched.	2. *The Pearl Fisher* (a novel promised to the *Ledger*, and which will form, when it comes in book

	form, No. 2 of our *South Sea Yarns*).
Not begun, but all material ready.	3. *The War Volume.*
Ditto.	4. *The Big Travel Book,* which includes the letters.
You know how they stand.	5. *The Ballads.*

Excusez du peu! And you see what madness it would be to make any fresh engagement. At the same time, you have *The Wrecker* and the *War Volume,* if you like either—or both—to keep my name in the Magazine.

It begins to look as if I should not be able to get any more ballads done this somewhile. I know the book would sell better if it were all ballads; and yet I am growing half tempted to fill up with some other verses. A good few are connected with my voyage, such as the *Home of Tembinoka* sent herewith, and would have a sort of slight affinity to the *South Sea Ballads.* You might tell me how that strikes a stranger.

In all this, my real interest is with the travel volume, which ought to be of a really extraordinary interest.

I am sending you *Tembinoka* as he stands; but there are parts of him that I hope to better, particularly in stanzas III. and II. I scarce feel intelligent enough to try just now; and I thought at any rate you had better see it, set it up if you think well, and let me have a proof; so, at least, we shall get the bulk of it straight. I have spared you Teñkoruti, Tenbaitcke, Tembinatake, and other barbarous names, because I thought the dentists in the States had work enough without my assistance; but my chief's name is TEMBINOKA, pronounced, according to the present quite modern habit in the Gilberts, Tembinok'. Compare in the margin Tengkorootch; a singular new trick, setting at defiance all South Sea analogy, for nowhere else do they show even the ability, far less the will, to end a word upon a consonant. Loia is Lloyd's name, ship becomes shipé, teapot, tipoté, etc. Our admirable friend Herman Melville, of whom, since I could judge, I have thought more than ever, had no ear for languages whatever: his Hapar tribe should be Hapaa, etc.

But this is of no interest to you: suffice it, you see how I am as usual up to the neck in projects, and really all likely bairns this time. When will this activity cease? Too soon for me, I dare to say. R. L. S.

TO JAMES PAYN

February 4th, 1890, SS. "LÜBECK."

MY DEAR JAMES PAYN,—In virtue of confessions in your last, you would at the present moment, if you were along of me, be sick; and I will ask you to receive that as an excuse for my hand of write. Excuse a plain seaman if he regards with scorn the likes of you pore landlubbers ashore now. (Reference to nautical ditty.) Which I may however be allowed to add that when eight months' mail was laid by my side one evening in Apia, and my wife and I sat up the most of the night to peruse the same—(precious indisposed we were

1890
ÆT. 40

next day in consequence) — no letter, out of so many, more appealed to our hearts than one from the pore, stick-in-the-mud, land-lubbering, common (or garden) Londoner, James Payn. Thank you for it; my wife says, "Can't I see him when we get back to London?" I have told her the thing appeared to me within the spear of practical politix. (Why can't I spell and write like an honest, sober, God-fearing litry gent? I think it 's the motion of the ship.) Here I was interrupted to play chess with the chief engineer; as I grow old, I prefer the "athletic sport of cribbage," of which (I am sure I misquote) I have just been reading in your delightful *Literary Recollections.* How you skim along, you and Andrew Lang (different as you are), and yet the only two who can keep a fellow smiling every page, and ever and again laughing out loud. I joke wi' deeficulty, I believe; I am not funny; and when I am, Mrs. Oliphant says I 'm vulgar, and somebody else says (in Latin) that I 'm a whore, which seems harsh and even uncalled for: I shall stick to weepers; a 5*s.* weeper, 2*s.* 6*d.* laugher, 1*s.* shocker.

My dear sir, I grow more and more idiotic; I cannot even feign sanity. Sometime in the month of June a stalwart weather-beaten man, evidently of seafaring antecedents, shall be observed wending his way between the Athenæum Club and Waterloo Place. Arrived off No. 17. he shall be observed to bring his head sharply to the wind, and tack into the outer haven. "Captain Payn in the harbour?"—"Ay, ay, sir. What ship?" —"Barquentine R. L. S., nine hundred and odd days out from the port of Bournemouth, homeward bound, with yarns and curiosities."

Who was it said, "For God's sake, don't speak of it!" about Scott and his tears? He knew what he was saying. The fear of that hour is the skeleton in all our cupboards; that hour when the pastime and the livelihood go together; and—I am getting hard of hearing myself; a pore young child of forty, but new come frae my Mammy, O!

Excuse these follies, and accept the expression of all my regards.—Yours affectionately,

R. L. STEVENSON.

TO CHARLES BAXTER

Stevenson had not been long at Sydney—just long enough to write and print the famous *Letter to Dr. Hyde* in defence of Father Damien—when, to his heavy disappointment, he fell ill again with one of his old bad attacks of fever and hæmorrhage from the lungs. It was this experience which finally determined him to settle for good on his new island property in Samoa, which at first he had thought of rather as an occasional refuge and resting-place in the intervals between future projected yachting voyages.

UNION CLUB, SYDNEY, *March 7th, 1890.*

MY DEAR CHARLES,—I did not send off the enclosed before from laziness; having gone quite sick, and being a blooming prisoner here in the club, and indeed in my bedroom. I was in receipt of your letters and your ornamental photo, and was delighted to see how well you looked, and how reasonably well I stood. . . . I am sure I shall never come back home except to die; I may do it, but shall always think of the move as suicidal, unless a great change comes over me, of which as

1890
ÆT. 40

yet I see no symptom. This visit to Sydney has smashed me handsomely; and yet I made myself a prisoner here in the club upon my first arrival. This is not encouraging for further ventures; Sydney winter — or, I might almost say, Sydney spring, for I came when the worst was over — is so small an affair, comparable to our June depression at home in Scotland. . . . The pipe is right again; it was the springs that had rusted, and ought to have been oiled. Its voice is now that of an angel; but, Lord! here in the club I dare not wake it! Conceive my impatience to be in my own backwoods and raise the sound of minstrelsy. What pleasures are to be compared with those of the Unvirtuous Virtuoso? — Yours ever affectionately, the Unvirtuous Virtuoso, ROBERT LOUIS STEVENSON.

TO SIDNEY COLVIN

To try and recover from the effects of his illness at Sydney, Stevenson determined to take another voyage; and started accordingly in April with his party on a trading steamer, the *Janet Nicoll*, which took him by a long and devious course among many groups of islands that he had not yet visited, returning to Sydney in August by way of New Caledonia. On the first night out of Auckland harbour the voyage nearly came to a premature end through the blowing up of some trade fireworks, or materials for fireworks, which had been packed in the stateroom.

SS. "JANET NICOLL," OFF UPOLU [*Spring, 1890*].

MY DEAREST COLVIN, — I was sharply ill at Sydney, cut off, right out of bed, in this steamer on a fresh island cruise, and have already reaped the benefit. We are excellently found this time, on a spacious vessel, with an excellent table; the captain, supercargo, our one fellow passenger, etc., very nice; and the charterer, Mr. Henderson, the very man I could have chosen. The truth is, I fear, this life is the only one that suits me; so long as I cruise in the South Seas, I shall be well and happy — alas, no, I do not mean that, and *absit omen!*— I mean that, so soon as I cease from cruising, the nerves are strained, the decline commences, and I steer slowly but surely back to bedward. We left Sydney, had a cruel rough passage to Auckland, for the *Janet* is the worst roller I was ever aboard of. I was confined to my cabin, ports closed, self shied out of the berth, stomach (pampered till the day I left on a diet of perpetual egg-nog) revolted at ship's food and ship eating, in a frowsy bunk, clinging with one hand to the plate, with the other to the glass, and using the knife and fork (except at intervals) with the eyelid. No matter: I picked up hand over hand. After a day in Auckland, we set sail again; were blown up in the main cabin with calcium fires, as we left the bay. Let no man say I am unscientific: when I ran, on the alert, out of my state-room, and found the main cabin incarnadined with the glow of the last scene of a pantomime, I stopped dead: "What is this?" said I. "This ship is on fire, I see that; but why a pantomime?" And I stood and reasoned the point, until my head was so muddled with the fumes that I could not find the companion. A few seconds later, the captain had to enter crawling on his beily, and took days to recover (if he has recovered) from the fumes. By singular good fortune, we got the hose down in time and saved the ship, but Lloyd lost most of his clothes and a great part of our photographs

1890
ÆT. 40

was destroyed. Fanny saw the native sailors tossing overboard a blazing trunk; she stopped them in time, and behold, it contained my manuscripts. Thereafter we had three (or two) days fine weather: then got into a gale of wind, with rain and a vexatious sea. As we drew into our anchorage in a bight of Savage Island, a man ashore told me afterwards the sight of the *Janet Nicoll* made him sick; and indeed it was rough play, though nothing to the night before. All through this gale I worked four to six hours per diem, spearing the ink-bottle like a flying fish, and holding my papers together as I might. For of all things, what I was at was history — the Samoan business — and I had to turn from one to another of these piles of manuscript notes, and from one page to another in each, until I should have found employment for the hands of Briareus. All the same, this history is a godsend for a voyage; I can put in time getting events co-ordinated and the narrative distributed, when my much-heaving numskull would be incapable of finish or fine style. At Savage we met the missionary barque *John Williams*. I tell you it was a great day for Savage Island: the path up the cliffs was crowded with gay islandresses (I like that feminine plural) who wrapped me in their embraces, and picked my pockets of all my tobacco, with a manner something between a whore and a child, which a touch would have made revolting, but as it was, was simply charming like the Golden Age. One pretty, little, stalwart minx, with a red flower behind her ear, had searched me with extraordinary zeal; and when, soon after, I missed my matches, I accused her (she still following us) of being the thief. After some delay, and with a subtle smile, she produced the box, gave me *one match*, and put the rest away again. Too tired to add more.—Your most affectionate R. L. S.

To E. L. Burlingame

SS. "Janet Nicoll," off Peru Island,
Kingsmills Group, *July 13th, '90.*

MY DEAR BURLINGAME,—I am moved to write to you in the matter of the end papers. I am somewhat tempted to begin them again. Follow the reasons *pro* and *con*:—

1st. I must say I feel as if something in the nature of the end paper were a desirable finish to the number, and that the substitutes of occasional essays by occasional contributors somehow fail to fill the bill. Should you differ with me on this point, no more is to be said. And what follows must be regarded as lost words.

2nd. I am rather taken with the idea of continuing the work. For instance, should you have no distaste for papers of the class called *Random Memories*, I should enjoy continuing them (of course at intervals), and when they were done I have an idea they might make a readable book. On the other hand, I believe a greater freedom of choice might be taken, the subjects more varied and more briefly treated, in somewhat approaching the manner of Andrew Lang in the *Sign of the Ship*; it being well understood that the broken sticks[1] method is one not very suitable (as Colonel Burke would say) to my genius, and not very likely to be pushed far in

[1] French *bâtons rompus*: disconnected thoughts or studies.

1890 ÆT. 40

my practice. Upon this point I wish you to condense your massive brain. In the last lot I was promised, and I fondly expected to receive, a vast amount of assistance from intelligent and genial correspondents. I assure you, I never had a scratch of a pen from any one above the level of a village idiot, except once, when a lady sowed my head full of grey hairs by announcing that she was going to direct her life in future by my counsels. Will the correspondents be more copious and less irrelevant in the future? Suppose that to be the case, will they be of any use to me in my place of exile? Is it possible for a man in Samoa to be in touch with the great heart of the People? And is it not perhaps a mere folly to attempt, from so hopeless a distance, anything so delicate as a series of papers? Upon these points, perpend, and give me the results of your perpensions.

3rd. The emolument would be agreeable to your humble servant.

I have now stated all the *pros*, and the most of the *cons* are come in by the way. There follows, however, one immense Con (with a capital "C"), which I beg you to consider particularly. I fear that, to be of any use for your magazine, these papers should begin with the beginning of a volume. Even supposing my hands were free, this would be now impossible for next year. You have to consider whether, supposing you have no other objection, it would be worth while to begin the series in the middle of a volume, or desirable to delay the whole matter until the beginning of another year.

Now supposing that the *cons* have it, and you refuse

my offer, let me make another proposal, which you will be very inclined to refuse at the first off-go, but which I really believe might in time come to something. You know how the penny papers have their answers to correspondents. Why not do something of the same kind for the "culchawed"? Why not get men like Stimson, Brownell, Professor James, Goldwin Smith, and others who will occur to you more readily than to me, to put and to answer a series of questions of intellectual and general interest, until at last you should have established a certain standard of matter to be discussed in this part of the Magazine?

I want you to get me bound volumes of the Magazine from its start. The Lord knows I have had enough copies; where they are I know not. A wandering author gathers no magazines.

The Wrecker is in no forrader state than in last reports. I have indeed got to a period when I cannot well go on until I can refresh myself on the proofs of the beginning. My respected collaborator, who handles the machine which is now addressing you, has indeed carried his labours farther, but not, I am led to understand, with what we used to call a blessing; at least, I have been refused a sight of his latest labours. However, there is plenty of time ahead, and I feel no anxiety about the tale, except that it may meet with your approval.

All this voyage I have been busy over my *Travels*, which, given a very high temperature and the saloon of a steamer usually going before the wind, and with the cabins in front of the engines, has come very near to prostrating me altogether. You will therefore un-

1890
ÆT. 40

derstand that there are no more poems. I wonder whether there are already enough, and whether you think that such a volume would be worth the publishing? I shall hope to find in Sydney some expression of your opinion on this point. Living as I do among—not the most cultured of mankind ("splendidly educated and perfect gentlemen when sober")—I attach a growing importance to friendly criticisms from yourself.

I believe that this is the most of our business. As for my health, I got over my cold in a fine style, but have not been very well of late. To my unaffected annoyance, the blood-spitting has started again. I find the heat of a steamer decidedly wearing and trying in these latitudes, and I am inclined to think the superior expedition rather dearly paid for. Still, the fact that one does not even remark the coming of a squall, nor feel relief on its departure, is a mercy not to be acknowledged without gratitude. The rest of the family seem to be doing fairly well; both seem less run down than they were on the *Equator*, and Mrs. Stevenson very much less so. We have now been three months away, have visited about thirty-five islands, many of which were novel to us, and some extremely entertaining; some also were old acquaintances, and pleasant to revisit. In the meantime, we have really a capital time aboard ship, in the most pleasant and interesting society, and with (considering the length and nature of the voyage) an excellent table. Please remember us all to Mr. Scribner, the young chieftain of the house, and the lady, whose health I trust is better. To Mrs. Burlingame we all desire to be remembered, and I hope you will give our news to Low, St. Gaudens, Faxon, and others of the faithful in the city. I shall probably return to Samoa direct, having given up all idea of returning to civilisation in the meanwhile. There, on my ancestral acres, which I purchased six months ago from a blind Scots blacksmith, you will please address me until further notice. The name of the ancestral acres is going to be Vailima; but as at the present moment nobody else knows the name, except myself and the co-patentees, it will be safer, if less ambitious, to address R. L. S., Apia, Samoa. The ancestral acres run to upwards of three hundred; they enjoy the ministrations of five streams, whence the name. They are all at the present moment under a trackless covering of magnificent forest, which would be worth a great deal if it grew beside a railway terminus. To me, as it stands, it represents a handsome deficit. Obliging natives from the Cannibal Islands are now cutting it down at my expense. You would be able to run your magazine to much greater advantage if the terms of authors were on the same scale with those of my cannibals. We have also a house about the size of a manufacturer's lodge. 'T is but the egg of the future palace, over the details of which on paper Mrs. Stevenson and I have already shed real tears; what it will be when it comes to paying for it, I leave you to imagine. But if it can only be built as now intended, it will be with genuine satisfaction and a growunded pride that I shall welcome you at the steps of my Old Colonial Home, when you land from the steamer on a long-merited holiday. I speak much at my ease; yet I do not know, I may be now an outlaw, a bankrupt, the abhorred of all

1890
ÆT. 40

good men. I do not know, you probably do. Has Hyde[1] turned upon me? Have I fallen, like Danvers Carew?

It is suggested to me that you might like to know what will be my future society. Three consuls, all at loggerheads with one another, or at the best in a clique of two against one; three different sets of missionaries, not upon the best of terms; and the Catholics and Protestants in a condition of unhealable ill-feeling as to whether a wooden drum ought or ought not to be beaten to announce the time of school — the pertinacity of this dispute and the importance attached to it by the Catholics is something not to be conceived. The native population, very genteel, very songful, very agreeable, very good-looking, chronically spoiling for a fight (a circumstance not to be entirely neglected in the design of the palace). As for the white population of (technically, "The Beach"), I don't suppose it is possible for any person not thoroughly conversant with the South Seas to form the smallest conception of such a society, with its grog-shops, its apparently unemployed hangers-on, its merchants of all degrees of respectability and the reverse. The paper, of which I must really send you a copy — if yours were really a live magazine, you would have an exchange with the editor: I assure you, it has of late contained a great deal of matter about one of your contributors — rejoices in the name of *Samoa Times and South Sea Advertiser*. The advertisements in the *Advertiser* are permanent, being simply subsidies for its existence. A dashing warfare of newspaper

[1] The Rev. Dr. Hyde, of Honolulu: in reference to Stevenson's letter on Father Damien.

correspondence goes on between the various residents, who are rather fond of recurring to one another's antecedents. But when all is said, there are a lot of very nice, pleasant people, and I don't know that Apia is very much worse than half a hundred towns that I could name. ROBERT LOUIS STEVENSON.

TO CHARLES BAXTER

As above indicated, on the way between Samoa and Sydney Stevenson left the *Janet Nicoll* for a week's stay in New Caledonia, during which he was hospitably received by the French officials.

HOTEL SEBASTOPOL, NOUMEA, *August, 1890.*

MY DEAR CHARLES, — I have stayed here a week while Lloyd and my wife continue to voyage in the *Janet Nicoll;* this I did, partly to see the convict system, partly to shorten my stay in the extreme cold — hear me with my extreme! *moi qui suis originaire d'Edimbourg* — of Sydney at this season. I am feeling very seedy, utterly fatigued, and overborne with sleep. I have a fine old gentleman of a doctor, who attends and cheers and entertains, if he does not cure me; but even with his ministrations I am almost incapable of the exertion sufficient for this letter; and I am really, as I write, falling down with sleep. What is necessary to say, I must try to say shortly. Lloyd goes to clear out our establishments: pray keep him in funds, if I have any; if I have not, pray try to raise them. Here is the idea: to install ourselves, at the risk of bankruptcy, in Samoa. It is not the least likely it will pay (although it may); but it is almost certain it will support life, with

1890 ÆT. 40

very few external expenses. If I die, it will be an endowment for the survivors, at least for my wife and Lloyd; and my mother, who might prefer to go home, has her own. Hence I believe I shall do well to hurry my installation. The letters are already in part done; in part done is a novel for Scribner; in the course of the next twelve months I should receive a considerable amount of money. I am aware I had intended to pay back to my capital some of this. I am now of opinion I should act foolishly. Better to build the house and have a roof and farm of my own; and thereafter, with a livelihood assured, save and repay. . . . There is my livelihood, all but books and wine, ready in a nutshell; and it ought to be more easy to save and to repay afterwards. Excellent, say you, but will you save and will you repay? I do not know, said the Bell of Old Bow. . . . It seems clear to me. . . . The deuce of the affair is that I do not know when I shall see you and Colvin. I guess you will have to come and see me: many a time already we have arranged the details of your visit in the yet unbuilt house on the mountain. I shall be able to get decent wine from Noumea. We shall be able to give you a decent welcome, and talk of old days. *Apropos* of old days, do you remember still the phrase we heard in Waterloo Place? I believe you made a piece for the piano on that phrase. Pray, if you remember it, send it me in your next. If you find it impossible to write correctly, send it me *à la recitative*, and indicate the accents. Do you feel (you must) how strangely heavy and stupid I am? I must at last give up and go sleep; I am simply a rag.

The morrow: I feel better, but still dim and groggy. To-night I go to the governor's; such a lark — no dress clothes — twenty-four hours' notice — able-bodied Polish tailor — suit made for a man with the figure of a puncheon — same hastily altered for self with the figure of a bodkin — sight inconceivable. Never mind; dress clothes, "which nobody can deny"; and the officials have been all so civil that I liked neither to refuse nor to appear in mufti. Bad dress clothes only prove you are a grisly ass; no dress clothes, even when explained, indicate a want of respect. I wish you were here with me to help me dress in this wild raiment, and to accompany me to M. Noel-Pardon's. I cannot say what I would give if there came a knock now at the door and you came in. I guess Noel-Pardon would go begging, and we might burn the fr. 200 dress clothes in the back garden for a bonfire; or what would be yet more expensive and more humorous, get them once more expanded to fit you, and when that was done, a second time cut down for my gossamer dimensions.

I hope you never forget to remember me to your father who has always a place in my heart, as I hope I have a little in his. His kindness helped me infinitely when you and I were young; I recall it with gratitude and affection in this town of convicts at the world's end. There are very few things, my dear Charles, worth mention: on a retrospect of life, the day's flash and colour, one day with another, flames, dazzles, and puts to sleep; and when the days are gone, like a fast-flying thaumatrope, they make but a single pattern. Only a few things stand out; and among these — most

1890 ÆT. 40

plainly to me—Rutland Square.—Ever, my dear Charles, your affectionate friend,

ROBERT LOUIS STEVENSON.

P. S.—Just returned from trying on the dress clo'. Lord, you should see the coat! It stands out at the waist like a bustle, the flaps cross in front, the sleeves are like bags.

To E. L. BURLINGAME

The next letter is in acknowledgment of proofs received from Messrs. Scribner of a proposed volume of verse to contain, besides *Ticonderoga* and the two ballads on Marquesan and Tahitian legends, a number of the other miscellaneous verses which he had written in the course of his travels. In the end, the ballads only stood for publication at this time; the other verses were reserved, and have been posthumously published under the title *Songs of Travel*.

UNION CLUB, SYDNEY [*August, 1890*].

MY DEAR BURLINGAME,—

Ballads.

The deuce is in this volume. It has cost me more botheration and dubiety than any other I ever took in hand. On one thing my mind is made up: the verses at the end have no business there, and throw them down. Many of them are bad, many of the rest want nine years' keeping, and the remainder are not relevant—throw them down; some I never want to hear of more, others will grow in time towards decent items in a second *Underwoods*—and in the meanwhile, down with them! At the same time, I have a sneaking idea the ballads are not altogether without merit—I don't know if they 're poetry, but they're good narrative, or I 'm deceived. (You 've never said one word about them, from which I astutely gather you are dead set against: "he was a diplomatic man"—extract from epitaph of E. L. B.—"and remained on good terms with Minor Poets.") You will have to judge: one of the Gladstonian trinity of paths must be chosen. (1st) Either publish the five ballads, such as they are, in a volume called *Ballads;* in which case pray send sheets at once to Chatto and Windus. Or (2nd) write and tell me you think the book too small, and I 'll try and get into the mood to do some more. Or (3rd) write and tell me the whole thing is a blooming illusion; in which case draw off some twenty copies for my private entertainment, and charge me with the expense of the whole dream.

In the matter of rhyme no man can judge himself; I am at the world's end, have no one to consult, and my publisher holds his tongue. I call it unfair and almost unmanly. I do indeed begin to be filled with animosity; Lord, wait till you see the continuation of *The Wrecker,* when I introduce some New York publishers. . . . It 's a good scene; the quantities you drink and the really hideous language you are represented as employing may perhaps cause you one tithe of the pain you have inflicted by your silence on, sir, The Poetaster,

R. L. S.

Lloyd is off home; my wife and I dwell sundered: she in lodgings, preparing for the move; I here in the

1890 ÆT. 40

club, and at my old trade—bedridden. Naturally, the visit home is given up; we only wait our opportunity to get to Samoa, where, please, address me.

Have I yet asked you to despatch the books and papers left in your care to me at Apia, Samoa? I wish you would, *quam primum*. R. L. S.

To Henry James

Proceeding from New Caledonia to Sydney, Stevenson again made a stay there of about a month, before going to settle in his new island home and superintend the operations of planning and building.

Union Club, Sydney, *August, 1890.*

MY DEAR HENRY JAMES,—Kipling is too clever to live. The *Bête Humaine* I had already perused in Noumea, listening the while to the strains of the convict band. He is a Beast; but not human, and, to be frank, not very interesting. "Nervous maladies: the homicidal ward," would be the better name: O, this game gets very tedious.

Your two long and kind letters have helped to entertain the old familiar sickbed. So has a book called *The Bondman*, by Hall Caine; I wish you would look at it. I am not half-way through yet. Read the book, and communicate your views. Hall Caine, by the way, appears to take Hugo's view of History and Chronology. (*Later;* the book does n't keep up; it gets very wild.)

I must tell you plainly—I can't tell Colvin—I do not think I shall come to England more than once, and then it 'll be to die. Health I enjoy in the tropics; even here, which they call sub- or semi-tropical, I come only to catch cold. I have not been out since my arrival; live here in a nice bedroom by the fireside, and read books and letters from Henry James, and send out to get his *Tragic Muse*, only to be told they can't be had as yet in Sydney; and have altogether a placid time. But I can't go out! The thermometer was nearly down to 50° the other day—no temperature for me, Mr. James: how should I do in England? I fear not at all. Am I very sorry? I am sorry about some seven or eight people in England, and one or two in the States. And outside of that, I simply prefer Samoa. These are the words of honesty and soberness. (I am fasting from all but sin, coughing, *The Bondman*, a couple of eggs and a cup of tea.) I was never fond of towns, houses, society, or (it seems) civilisation. Nor yet it seems was I ever very fond of (what is technically called) God's green earth. The sea, islands, the islanders, the island life and climate, make and keep me truly happier. These last two years I have been much at sea, and I have *never wearied;* sometimes I have indeed grown impatient for some destination; more often I was sorry that the voyage drew so early to an end; and never once did I lose my fidelity to blue water and a ship. It is plain, then, that for me my exile to the place of schooners and islands can be in no sense regarded as a calamity.

Good-bye just now: I must take a turn at my proofs.

N. B.—Even my wife has weakened about the sea. She wearied, the last time we were ashore, to get afloat again.—Yours ever, R. L. S.

1890
ÆT. 40

To Marcel Schwob

Union Club, Sydney, *August 19th, 1890.*

MY DEAR MR. SCHWOB,—*Mais, alors, vous avez tous les bonheurs, vous!* More about Villon; it seems incredible: when it is put in order, pray send it me.

You wish to translate the *Black Arrow:* dear sir, you are hereby authorised; but I warn you, I do not like the work. Ah, if you, who know so well both tongues, and have taste and instruction—if you would but take a fancy to translate a book of mine that I myself admired—for we sometimes admire our own—or I do—with what satisfaction would the authority be granted! But these things are too much to expect. *Vous ne détestez pas alors mes bonnes femmes? moi, je les déteste.* I have never pleased myself with any women of mine save two character parts, one of only a few lines—the Countess of Rosen, and Madame Desprez in *The Treasure of Franchard.*

I had indeed one moment of pride about my poor *Black Arrow:* Dickon Crookback I did, and I do, think is a spirited and possible figure. Shakespeare's—O, if we can call that cocoon Shakespeare!—Shakespeare's is spirited—one likes to see the untaught athlete butting against the adamantine ramparts of human nature, head down, breach up; it reminds us how trivial we are to-day, and what safety resides in our triviality. For spirited it may be, but O, sure not possible! I love Dumas and I love Shakespeare: you will not mistake me when I say that the Richard of the one reminds me of the Porthos of the other; and if by any sacrifice of my own literary baggage I could clear the *Vicomte de Bragelonne* of Porthos, *Jekyll* might go, and *The Master*, and the *Black Arrow*, you may be sure, and I should think my life not lost for mankind if half a dozen more of my volumes must be thrown in.

The tone of your pleasant letters makes me egotistical; you make me take myself too gravely. Comprehend how I have lived much of my time in France, and loved your country, and many of its people, and all the time was learning that which your country has to teach—breathing in rather that atmosphere of art which can only there be breathed; and all the time knew—and raged to know—that I might write with the pen of angels or of heroes, and no Frenchman be the least the wiser! And now steps in M. Marcel Schwob, writes me the most kind encouragement, and reads and understands, and is kind enough to like my work.

I am just now overloaded with work. I have two huge novels on hand—*The Wrecker* and *The Pearl Fisher*, in collaboration with my stepson: the latter, *The Pearl Fisher*, I think highly of, for a black, ugly, trampling, violent story, full of strange scenes and striking characters. And then I am about waist-deep in my big book on the South Seas: *the* big book on the South Seas it ought to be, and shall. And besides, I have some verses in the press, which, however, I hesitate to publish. For I am no judge of my own verse; self-deception is there so facile. All this and the cares of an impending settlement in Samoa keep me very busy, and a cold (as usual) keeps me in bed.

Alas, I shall not have the pleasure to see you yet

awhile, if ever. You must be content to take me as a wandering voice, and in the form of occasional letters from recondite islands; and address me, if you will be good enough to write, to Apia, Samoa. My stepson, Mr. Osbourne, goes home meanwhile to arrange some affairs; it is not unlikely he may go to Paris to arrange about the illustrations to my *South Seas;* in which case I shall ask him to call upon you, and give you some word of our outlandish destinies. You will find him intelligent, I think; and I am sure, if (*par hasard*) you should take any interest in the islands, he will have much to tell you.—Herewith I conclude, and am your obliged and interested correspondent,

ROBERT LOUIS STEVENSON.

P. S.—The story you refer to has got lost in the post.

TO ANDREW LANG

UNION CLUB, SYDNEY [*August, 1890*].

MY DEAR LANG,—I observed with a great deal of surprise and interest that a controversy in which you have been taking sides at home, in yellow London, hinges in part at least on the Gilbert Islanders and their customs in burial. Nearly six months of my life has been passed in the group: I have revisited it but the other day; and I make haste to tell you what I know. The upright stones—I enclose you a photograph of one on Apemama—are certainly connected with religion; I do not think they are adored. They stand usually on the windward shore of the islands, that is to say, apart from habitation (on *enclosed islands,* where the people live on the sea side, I do not know how it is, never having lived on one). I gathered from Tembinoka, Rex Apemamæ, that the pillars were supposed to fortify the island from invasion: spiritual martellos. I think he indicated they were connected with the cult of Tenti — pronounce almost as chintz in English, the *t* being explosive; but you must take this with a grain of salt, for I know no word of Gilbert Island; and the King's English, although creditable, is rather vigorous than exact. Now, here follows the point of interest to you: such pillars, or standing stones, have no connection with graves. The most elaborate grave that I have ever seen in the group — to be certain — is in the form of a *raised border* of gravel, usually strewn with broken glass. One — of which I cannot be sure that it was a grave, for I was told by one that it was, and by another that it was not — consisted of a mound about breast-high in an excavated taro swamp, on the top of which was a child's house, or rather *maniapa* — that is to say, shed, or open house, such as is used in the group for social or political gatherings — so small that only a child could creep under its eaves. I have heard of another great tomb on Apemama, which I did not see; but here again, by all accounts, no sign of a standing stone. My report would be — no connection between standing stones and sepulture. I shall, however, send on the terms of the problem to a highly intelligent resident trader, who knows more than perhaps any one living, white or native, of the Gilbert group; and you shall have the result. In Samoa, whither I return for

1890 ÆT. 40

good, I shall myself make inquiries; up to now, I have neither seen nor heard of any standing stones in that group.—Yours, R. L. STEVENSON.

TO MRS. CHARLES FAIRCHILD

UNION CLUB, SYDNEY [*September, 1890*].

MY DEAR MRS. FAIRCHILD,—I began a letter to you on board the *Janet Nicoll* on my last cruise, wrote, I believe, two sheets, and ruthlessly destroyed the flippant trash. Your last has given me great pleasure and some pain, for it increased the consciousness of my neglect. Now, this must go to you, whatever it is like.

. . . You are quite right; our civilisation is a hollow fraud, all the fun of life is lost by it; all it gains is that a larger number of persons can continue to be contemporaneously unhappy on the surface of the globe. O, unhappy! — there is a big word and a false — continue to be not nearly — by about twenty per cent. — so happy as they might be: that would be nearer the mark.

When — observe that word, which I will write again and larger — WHEN you come to see us in Samoa, you will see for yourself a healthy and happy people.

You see, you are one of the very few of our friends rich enough to come and see us; and when my house is built, and the road is made, and we have enough fruit planted and poultry and pigs raised, it is undeniable that you must come — must is the word; that is the way in which I speak to ladies. You and Fairchild. anyway — perhaps my friend Blair — we 'll arrange details in good time. It will be the salvation of your souls, and make you willing to die.

Let me tell you this: In '74 or 5 there came to stay with my father and mother a certain Mr. Seed, a prime minister or something of New Zealand. He spotted what my complaint was; told me that I had no business to stay in Europe; that I should find all I cared for, and all that was good for me, in the Navigator Islands; sat up till four in the morning persuading me, demolishing my scruples. And I resisted: I refused to go so far from my father and mother. O, it was virtuous, and O, was n't it silly! But my father, who was always my dearest, got to his grave without that pang; and now in 1890, I (or what is left of me) go at last to the Navigator Islands. God go with us. It is but a Pisgah sight when all is said; I go there only to grow old and die; but when you come, you will see it is a fair place for the purpose.

Flaubert[1] has not turned up; I hope he will soon; I knew of him only through Maxime Descamps.—With kindest messages to yourself and all of yours, I remain,

ROBERT LOUIS STEVENSON.

[1] His letters.

XI

LIFE IN SAMOA

(NOVEMBER, 1890–DECEMBER, 1892)

XI

LIFE IN SAMOA

(NOVEMBER, 1890–DECEMBER, 1892)

FROM November, 1890, until his death four years later, Stevenson lived in his island home on the mountain-side above Apia, without change except for two or three excursions to Sydney and Auckland, and one, in 1893, to Honolulu. His life there was brimful of interest and occupation. With all the zest and energy of his nature he played a threefold part: as planter, settler, and leading white resident; as unofficial politician and political critic; and as man of letters. In the first of these characters he had to superintend the building of the handsome new house which in course of time was made ready for his occupation, with the clearing of the jungle and planting and management of the land; but these latter cares devolved after a while almost entirely upon his wife, who has a special gift in such matters, and on his step son and daughter. He ruled in a spirit of affectionate kindness, tempered with firm justice, a kind of feudal clan of servants and retainers whom he by degrees gathered about him; while among both white residents and visitors from a distance he exercised a social influence and hospitality which increased with every year. The name the natives knew him by was Tusitala, "teller of tales," and he was supposed by them to be the master of an inexhaustible store of wealth, perhaps even to be the holder of the magic bottle of his own story, the *Bottle Imp*. In matters political, he was drawn into interference by the evils which he saw arising from the fact that these small and remote islands had in recent years become the scene of political intrigue and rivalry carried on by three great world powers against each other, with scant regard to the wishes and welfare of the native population. His action embroiled him for a while more or less seriously with most of the white officials in the island, and at one period of the struggle he was threatened with deportation. Impartial witnesses agree that his criticisms of official action were thoroughly justified, and that his efforts were all in the direction of peace and concord. He certainly lacked neither anxious goodwill, nor shrewd insight into character, both white and native. Had he been tested he would have shown, as I imagine (and as the late Sir George Grey declared), the true instincts of a ruler; and the course of recent events has tended strongly to confirm his judgment and testify to his foresight. In the third field, his own special life's work of literature, his activity in these days was more strenuous than ever. His habit was to begin work at six in the morning or earlier, continuing with scarce an interruption till the midday meal, and often resuming again until four or five in the afternoon. In addition to the various forms of historical or contemporary romance and tale which constituted his main work and source of income, he was busy with a record of his Pacific experiences; with a history of the local troubles; and with the annals of his own Scottish forebears. He had come by this time to suffer a good deal from scrivener's cramp; and both in literary work and correspondence his labours were greatly lightened by the affectionate services as amanuensis of his stepdaughter, Mrs. Strong, who had joined the family in 1889. Both stepchildren were indeed to him of the greatest help and comfort. Mr. Lloyd Osbourne, having at Stevenson's own request refused offers both of official employment as secretary to the Samoan Land Commission and of an opening with a publishing firm in the United States, remained at his side to the end, and filled faithfully in all points of duty and devotion the place of an adopted son. His domestic content was completed by the presence, during the greater part of his time in Samoa, of his mother, whose love for her son and natural adaptability enabled her to share with delight the new conditions and new interests of his life, and by that of a cousin, Mr. Graham Balfour, who was for two long periods his inmate, and became one of his most trusted friends.

From the date of his final settlement at Samoa, Stevenson made a habit of setting down his everyday doings and feelings in journal-letters which he made up and sent off monthly to myself. Such parts of this correspondence as seemed likely to be of general interest have already been published separately.[1] The letters which now follow are selected from those which he addressed in the same years to other correspondents, old and new: some to intimates of earlier days with whom he desired to keep in touch; some to strangers whose acquaintance he sought to make from his place of exile, or who wrote thither doing him homage, and begging to make his; some to editors and publishers on literary affairs and projects. Scarce any writer

[1] *Vailima Letters*, Methuen, 1895.

has had so loyal or so devoted a following among the men of letters of a generation younger than his own, and of these several are among the most frequent of his new correspondents. Speaking generally, these miscellaneous letters from Samoa are much less full than the "Vailima Letters" addressed to myself of the island politics and purely local interests which in these years claimed so much of his attention; they give a larger place to literature and home thoughts, to chance moods and speculations, and to personal and general interests outside the islands. The writer has lost, he will be found averring, our European perspective. Signs that this was indeed to some extent the case may perhaps be noticed here and there; but it will be seen also that he has lost none of the vividness and variety of his interests, and none of his old attaching power of giving utterance to the warmth of heart and feeling that is in him.

I have divided these letters from Samoa into two periods: one of just over two years, November, 1890, to December, 1892, and a second of two years all but one month, from January, 1893, to December, 1894. The first of these was the happiest part of his life at Vailima, alike as to health, productive power, and inward satisfaction. After the renewed attack of illness which had brought him down at Sydney in the spring of 1890, he had for almost two years no relapse, and found himself able to live a life of comparative freedom and activity in the open air, to ride, bathe, and boat with freedom, and to work harder than most men are accustomed to work in full health. Within the period covered by this first division of these Samoan letters he had been able to write the greater part of *The Wrecker*, and nearly the whole of the South Sea book (the latter a heavy strain for a disappointing result); to compose his *Foot-note to History* — an appeal to the European powers, and especially to Germany, for a wiser handling of Samoan difficulties, but an appeal which for the time being failed of its effect — and at the same time to produce a masterly piece of Polynesian fiction in *The Beach of Falesá*, and all but the best of his Scottish romances in *Catriona.*

To E. L. Burlingame

The opening sentences of the following refer, of course, to *The Wrecker.*

1890
ÆT. 40

VAILIMA, APIA, SAMOA, *Nov. 7, 1890.*

I WISH you to add to the words at the end of the prologue; they run, I think, thus, "And this is the yarn of Loudon Dodd"; add, "not as he told, but as he wrote it afterwards for his diversion." This becomes the more needful, because, when all is done, I shall probably revert to Tai-o-hae, and give final details about the characters in the way of a conversation between Dodd and Havers. These little snippets of information and *faits-divers* have always a disjointed, broken-backed appearance; yet, readers like them. In this book we have introduced so many characters, that this kind of epilogue will be looked for; and I rather hope, looking far ahead, that I can lighten it in dialogue.

We are well past the middle now. How does it strike you? and can you guess my mystery? It will make a fattish volume!

I say, have you ever read *The Highland Widow?* I never had till yesterday: I am half inclined, bar a trip

1890 ÆT. 40

or two, to think it Scott's masterpiece; and it has the name of a failure! Strange things are readers.

I expect proofs and revises in duplicate.

We have now got into a small barrack at our place. We see the sea six hundred feet below filling the end of two vales of forest. On one hand the mountain runs above us some thousand feet higher; great trees stand round us in our clearing; there is an endless voice of birds; I have never lived in such a heaven; just now, I have fever, which mitigates but not destroys my gusto in my circumstances.—You may envy

ROBERT LOUIS STEVENSON.

. . . O, I don't know if I mentioned that having seen your new tail to the magazine, I cried off interference, at least for this trip. Did I ask you to send me my books and papers, and all the bound volumes of the mag.? *quorum pars.* I might add that were there a good book or so—new—I don't believe there is—such would be welcome.

I desire—I positively begin to awake—to be remembered to Scribner, Low, St. Gaudens, Russell Sullivan. Well, well, you fellows have the feast of reason and the flow of soul; I have a better-looking place and climate: you should hear the birds on the hill now! The day has just wound up with a shower; it is still light without, though I write within here at the cheek of a lamp; my wife and an invaluable German are wrestling about bread on the back verandah; and how the birds and the frogs are rattling, and piping, and hailing from the woods! Here and there a throaty chuckle; here and there, cries like those of jolly children who have lost

FIRST HOUSE AT VAILIMA, WITH VAEA MOUNTAIN IN THE BACKGROUND.

their way; here and there, the ringing sleigh-bell of the tree frog. Out and away down below me on the sea it is still raining; it will be wet under foot on schooners, and the house will leak; how well I know that! Here the showers only patter on the iron roof, and sometimes roar; and within, the lamp burns steady on the tafa-covered walls, with their dusky tartan patterns, and the book-shelves with their thin array of books; and no squall can rout my house or bring my heart into my mouth.— The well-pleased South Sea Islander,

R. L. S.

To E. L. Burlingame

The intention here announced was only carried out to the extent of finishing one paper, "My First Book," and beginning a few others— "Genesis of the Master of Ballantrae," "Rosa Quo Locorum," etc. (see Thistle edition, *Miscellanies*, vol. xx.). The "long experience of gambling places" is a phrase which must not be misunderstood. Stevenson loved risk, but hated gambling for money, and had known the tables only as a looker-on during holiday or invalid travels as a boy and young man. "Tamate" is the native (Raratongan) word for trader, used especially as a name for the famous missionary pioneer, the Rev. James Chalmers.

[Vailima, *December, 1890.*]

My dear Burlingame,— By some diabolical accident, I have mislaid your last. What was in it? I know not, and here I am caught unexpectedly by the American mail, a week earlier than by computation. The computation, not the mail, is supposed to be in error. The vols. of *Scribner's* have arrived, and present a noble appearance in my house, which is not a noble structure at present. But by autumn we hope to be sprawling in our verandah, twelve feet, sir, by eighty-eight in front, and seventy-two on the flank; view of the sea and mountains, sunrise, moonrise, and the German fleet at anchor three miles away in Apia harbour. I hope some day to offer you a bowl of kava there, or a slice of a pineapple, or some lemonade from my own hedge. "I know a hedge where the lemons grow"—*Shakespeare.* My house at this moment smells of them strong; and the rain, which a while ago roared there, now rings in minute drops upon the iron roof. I have no *Wrecker* for you this mail, other things having engaged me. I was on the whole rather relieved you did not vote for regular papers, as I feared the traces. It is my design from time to time to write a paper of a reminiscential (beastly word) description; some of them I could scarce publish from different considerations; but some of them—for instance, my long experience of gambling places—Homburg, Wiesbaden, Baden-Baden, old Monaco, and new Monte Carlo—would make good magazine padding, if I got the stuff handled the right way. I never could fathom why verse was put in magazines; it has something to do with the making-up, has it not? I am scribbling a lot just now; if you are taken badly that way, apply to the South Seas. I could send you some, I believe, anyway, only none of it is thoroughly ripe. If you have kept back the volume of ballads, I 'll soon make it of a respectable size if this fit continue. By the next mail you may expect some more *Wrecker*, or I shall be displeased. Probably no more than a chapter, however, for it is a hard one, and I am denuded of my proofs, my collaborator having walked away with them to England; hence some trouble in catching the just note.

I am a mere farmer: my talk, which would scarce interest you on Broadway, is all of fuafua and tuitui, and black boys, and planting and weeding, and axes and cutlasses; my hands are covered with blisters and full of thorns; letters are, doubtless, a fine thing, so are beer and skittles, but give me farmering in the tropics for real interest. Life goes in enchantment; I come home to find I am late for dinner; and when I go to bed at night, I could cry for the weariness of my loins and thighs. Do not speak to me of vexation, the life brims with it, but with living interest fairly.

Christmas I go to Auckland, to meet Tamate, the New Guinea missionary, a man I love. The rest of my life is a prospect of much rain, much weeding and making of paths, a little letters, and devilish little to eat.—I am, my dear Burlingame, with messages to all whom it may concern, very sincerely yours,

ROBERT LOUIS STEVENSON.

TO HENRY JAMES

Mr. La Farge, mentioned below, is of course the distinguished painter and decorator in stained glass, whose collection of drawings made in Samoa was exhibited in Paris in 1895. Mr. Henry Adams is the historian. The pinch in the matter of eatables only lasted for a little while, until Mrs. Stevenson had taken her bearings and made her arrangements in the matter of marketing, etc.

VAILIMA, APIA, SAMOA, *December 29th, 1890.*

MY DEAR HENRY JAMES,—It is terrible how little everybody writes, and how much of that little disappears in the capacious maw of the Post Office. Many letters, both from and to me, I now know to have been lost in transit: my eye is on the Sydney Post Office, a large ungainly structure with a tower, as being not a hundred miles from the scene of disappearance; but then I have no proof. The *Tragic Muse* you announced to me as coming; I had already ordered it from a Sydney bookseller: about two months ago he advised me that his copy was in the post; and I am still tragically museless.

News, news, news. What do we know of yours? What do you care for ours? We are in the midst of the rainy season, and dwell among alarms of hurricanes, in a very unsafe little two-storied wooden box 650 feet above and about three miles from the sea-beach. Behind us, till the other slope of the island, desert forest, peaks, and loud torrents; in front green slopes to the sea, some fifty miles of which we dominate. We see the ships as they go out and in to the dangerous roadstead of Apia; and if they lie far out, we can even see their topmasts while they are at anchor. Of sounds of men, beyond those of our own labourers, there reach us, at very long intervals, salutes from the warships in harbour, the bell of the cathedral church, and the low of the conch-shell calling the labour boys on the German plantations. Yesterday, which was Sunday— the *quantième* is most likely erroneous; you can now correct it — we had a visitor — Baker of Tonga. Heard you ever of him? He is a great man here: he is accused of theft, rape, judicial murder, private poisoning, abortion, misappropriation of public moneys — oddly enough, not forgery, nor arson: you would be amused if you knew how thick the accusations fly in this South

Sea world. I make no doubt my own character is something illustrious; or if not yet, there is a good time coming.

But all our resources have not of late been Pacific. We have had enlightened society: La Farge the painter, and your friend Henry Adams: a great privilege—would it might endure. I would go oftener to see them, but the place is awkward to reach on horseback. I had to swim my horse the last time I went to dinner; and as I have not yet returned the clothes I had to borrow, I dare not return in the same plight: it seems inevitable—as soon as the wash comes in, I plump straight into the American consul's shirt or trousers! They, I believe, would come oftener to see me but for the horrid doubt that weighs upon our commissariat department; we have *often* almost nothing to eat; a guest would simply break the bank; my wife and I have dined on one avocado pear; I have several times dined on hard bread and onions. What would you do with a guest at such narrow seasons?—eat him? or serve up a labour boy fricasseed?

Work? work is now arrested, but I have written, I should think, about thirty chapters of the South Sea book; they will all want rehandling, I dare say. Gracious, what a strain is a long book! The time it took me to design this volume, before I could dream of putting pen to paper, was excessive; and then think of writing a book of travels on the spot, when I am continually extending my information, revising my opinions, and seeing the most finely finished portions of my work come part by part in pieces. Very soon I shall have no opinions left. And without an opinion,

1890
ÆT. 40

how to string artistically vast accumulations of fact? Darwin said no one could observe without a theory; I suppose he was right; 't is a fine point of metaphysic; but I will take my oath, no man can write without one—at least the way he would like to—and my theories melt, melt, melt, and as they melt the thaw-waters wash down my writing, and leave unideal tracts—wastes instead of cultivated farms.

Kipling is by far the most promising young man who has appeared since—ahem—I appeared. He amazes me by his precocity and various endowment. But he alarms me by his copiousness and haste. He should shield his fire with both hands "and draw up all his strength and sweetness in one ball." ("Draw all his strength and all His sweetness up into one ball"? I cannot remember Marvell's words.) So the critics have been saying to me; but I was never capable of—and surely never guilty of—such a debauch of production. At this rate his works will soon fill the habitable globe; and surely he was armed for better conflicts than these succinct sketches and flying leaves of verse? I look on, I admire, I rejoice for myself; but in a kind of ambition we all have for our tongue and literature I am wounded. If I had this man's fertility and courage, it seems to me I could heave a pyramid.

Well, we begin to be the old fogies now; and it was high time *something* rose to take our places. Certainly Kipling has the gifts; the fairy godmothers were all tipsy at his christening: what will he do with them?

Good-bye, my dear James; find an hour to write to us, and register your letter.—Yours affectionately,

R. L. S.

To Rudyard Kipling

In 1890, on first becoming acquainted with Mr. Kipling's *Soldiers Three*, Stevenson had written off his congratulations red-hot. "Well and indeed, Mr. Mulvaney," so ran the first sentences of his note, "but it 's as good as meat to meet in with you, sir. They tell me it was a man of the name of Kipling made ye; but indeed and they can't fool me; it was the Lord God Almighty that made you." Taking the cue thus offered, Mr. Kipling had written back in the character of his own Irishman, Thomas Mulvaney, addressing Stevenson's Highlander, Alan Breck Stewart. In the following letter, which belongs to an uncertain date in 1891, Alan Breck is made to reply. "The gentleman I now serve with" means, of course, R. L. S. himself.

[VAILIMA, *1891*.]

SIR,—I cannot call to mind having written you, but I am so throng with occupation this may have fallen aside. I never heard tell I had any friends in Ireland, and I am led to understand you are come of no considerable family. The gentleman I now serve with assures me, however, you are a very pretty fellow and your letter deserves to be remarked. It 's true he is himself a man of a very low descent upon the one side; though upon the other he counts cousinship with a gentleman, my very good friend, the late Mr. Balfour of the Shaws, in the Lothian; which I should be wanting in good fellowship to forget. He tells me besides you are a man of your hands; I am not informed of your weapon; but if all be true it sticks in my mind I would be ready to make exception in your favour, and meet you like one gentleman with another. I suppose this 'll be your purpose in your favour, which I could very ill make out; it 's one I would be sweir to baulk you of. It seems, Mr. McIlvaine, which I take to be your name, you are in the household of a gentleman of the name of Coupling: for whom my friend is very much engaged. The distances being very uncommodious, I think it will be maybe better if we leave it to these two to settle all that 's necessary to honour. I would have you to take heed it 's a very unusual condescension on my part, that bear a King's name; and for the matter of that I think shame to be mingled with a person of the name of Coupling, which is doubtless a very good house but one I never heard tell of, any more than Stevenson. But your purpose being laudable, I would be sorry (as the word goes) to cut off my nose to spite my face.—I am, sir, your humble servant,

A. STEWART,
Chevalier de St. Louis.

TO MARCEL SCHWOB

SYDNEY, *January 19th, 1891.*

MY DEAR SIR,—*Sapristi, comme vous y allez! Richard III.* and Dumas, with all my heart; but not *Hamlet. Hamlet* is great literature; *Richard III.* a big, black, gross, sprawling melodrama, writ with infinite spirit but with no refinement or philosophy by a man who had the world, himself, mankind, and his trade still to learn. I prefer the *Vicomte de Brage-*

lonne to *Richard III.;* it is better done of its kind: I simply do not mention the *Vicomte* in the same part of the building with *Hamlet,* or *Lear,* or *Othello,* or any of those masterpieces that Shakespeare survived to give us.

Also, *comme vous y allez* in my commendation! I fear my *solide éducation classique* had best be described, like Shakespeare's, as "little Latin and no Greek," and I was educated, let me inform you, for an engineer. I shall tell my bookseller to send you a copy of *Memories and Portraits,* where you will see something of my descent and education, as it was, and hear me at length on my dear Vicomte. I give you permission gladly to take your choice out of my works, and translate what you shall prefer, too much honoured that so clever a young man should think it worth the pains. My own choice would lie between *Kidnapped* and *The Master of Ballantrae.* Should you choose the latter, pray do not let Mrs. Henry thrust the sword up to the hilt in the frozen ground—one of my inconceivable blunders, an exaggeration to stagger Hugo. Say "she sought to thrust it in the ground." In both these works you should be prepared for Scotticisms used deliberately.

I fear my stepson will not have found time to get to Paris; he was overwhelmed with occupation, and is already on his voyage back. We live here in a beautiful land, amid a beautiful and interesting people. The life is still very hard: my wife and I live in a two-roomed cottage, about three miles and six hundred and fifty feet above the sea;

1891 ÆT. 41

we have had to make the road to it; our supplies are very imperfect; in the wild weather of this (the hurricane) season we have much discomfort: one night the wind blew in our house so outrageously that we must sit in the dark; and as the sound of the rain on the roof made speech inaudible, you may imagine we found the evening long. All these things, however, are pleasant to me. You say *l'artiste inconscient* set off to travel: you do not divide me right. 0.6 of me is artist; 0.4, adventurer. First, I suppose, come letters; then adventure; and since I have indulged the second part, I think the formula begins to change: 0.55 of an artist, 0.45 of the adventurer were nearer true. And if it had not been for my small strength, I might have been a different man in all things.

Whatever you do, do not neglect to send me what you publish on Villon: I look forward to that with lively interest. I have no photograph at hand, but I will send one when I can. It would be kind if you would do the like, for I do not see much chance of our meeting in the flesh: and a name, and a handwriting, and an address, and even a style? I know about as much of Tacitus, and more of Horace; it is not enough between contemporaries, such as we still are. I have just remembered another of my books, which I re-read the other day, and thought in places good—*Prince Otto.* It is not as good as either of the others; but it has one recommendation—it has female parts, so it might perhaps please better in France.

I will ask Chatto to send you, then—*Prince Otto,*

Memories and Portraits, *Underwoods*, and *Ballads*, none of which you seem to have seen. They will be too late for the New Year: let them be an Easter present.

1891
ÆT. 41

You must translate me soon; you will soon have better to do than to transvase the work of others.—Yours very truly,

ROBERT LOUIS STEVENSON,
With the worst pen in the South Pacific.

TO CHARLES BAXTER

SS. "LÜBECK," AT SEA [*on the return voyage from Sydney, March, 1891*].

MY DEAR CHARLES,—Perhaps in my old days I do grow irascible; "the old man virulent" has long been my pet name for myself. Well, the temper is at least all gone now; time is good at lowering these distemperatures; far better is a sharp sickness, and I am just (and scarce) afoot again after a smoking hot little malady at Sydney. And the temper being gone, I still think the same. . . . We have not our parents for ever; we are never very good to them; when they go and we have lost our front-file man, we begin to feel all our neglects mighty sensibly. I propose a proposal. My mother is here on board with me; to-day for once I mean to make her as happy as I am able, and to do that which

1891 ÆT. 41 I know she likes. You, on the other hand, go and see your father, and do ditto, and give him a real good hour or two. We shall both be glad hereafter.—Yours ever.

R. L. S.

To H. B. Baildon

Mr. H. Bellyse Baildon, at present Lecturer on English Literature at the University of Vienna, had been an old schoolmate and fellow aspirant in literature with Stevenson at Edinburgh. "Chalmers," of course, is the Rev. James Chalmers of Raratonga and New Guinea already referred to above, the admirable missionary, explorer, and administrator, whom Stevenson sometimes expressed a desire to survive, for the sake only of writing his life.

Vailima, Upolu [*Undated, but written in 1891*].

MY DEAR BAILDON,—This is a real disappointment. It was so long since we had met, I was anxious to see where time had carried and stranded us. Last time we saw each other—it must have been all ten years ago, as we were new to the thirties—it was only for a moment, and now we 're in the forties, and before very long we shall be in our graves. Sick and well, I have had a splendid life of it, grudge nothing, regret very little—and then only some little corners of misconduct for which I deserve hanging, and must infallibly be damned—and, take it all over, damnation and all, would hardly change with any man of my time, unless perhaps it were Gordon or our friend Chalmers: a man I admire for his virtues, love for his faults, and envy for the really A 1 life he has, with everything heart—my heart, I mean—could wish. It is curious to think you will read this in the grey metropolis; go the first grey, east-windy day into the Caledonian Station, if it looks at all as it did of yore: I met Satan there. And then go and stand by the cross, and remember the other one—him that went down—my brother, Robert Fergusson. It is a pity you had not made me out, and seen me as patriarch and planter. I shall look forward to some record of your time with Chalmers: you can't weary me of that fellow, he is as big as a house and far bigger than any church, where no man warms his hands. Do you know anything of Thomson? Of A——, B——, C——, D——, E——, F——, at all? As I write C's name mustard rises to my nose; I have never forgiven that weak, amiable boy a little trick he played me when I could ill afford it: I mean that whenever I think of it, some of the old wrath kindles, not that I would hurt the poor soul, if I got the world with it. And Old X——? Is he still afloat? Harmless barque! I gather you ain't married yet, since your sister, to whom I ask to be remembered, goes with you. Did you see a silly tale, *John Nicholson's Predicament*,[1] or some such name, in which I made free with your home at Murrayfield? There is precious little sense in it, but it might amuse. Cassell's published it in a thing called *Yule-Tide* years ago, and nobody that ever I heard of read or has ever seen *Yule-Tide*. It is addressed to a class we never met — readers of Cassell's series and that class of conscientious chaff, and my tale was dull, though I don't recall that it was

[1] *The Misadventures of John Nicholson.*

1891 ÆT. 41

conscientious. Only, there 's the house at Murrayfield and a dead body in it. Glad the *Ballads* amused you. They failed to entertain a coy public, at which I wondered, not that I set much account by my verses, which are the verses of Prosator; but I do know how to tell a yarn, and two of the yarns are great. *Rahéro* is for its length a perfect folk-tale: savage and yet fine, full of tailforemost morality, ancient as the granite rocks; if the historian, not to say the politician, could get that yarn into his head, he would have learned some of his A B C. But the average man at home cannot understand antiquity; he is sunk over the ears in Roman civilisation; and a tale like that of *Rahéro* falls on his ears inarticulate. The *Spectator* said there was no psychology in it; that interested me much: my grandmother (as I used to call that able paper, and an able paper it is, and a fair one) cannot so much as observe the existence of savage psychology when it is put before it. I am at bottom a psychologist and ashamed of it; the tale seized me one-third because of its picturesque features, two-thirds because of its astonishing psychology, and the *Spectator* says there 's none. I am going on with a lot of island work, exulting in the knowledge of a new world, "a new created world" and new men; and I am sure my income will DECLINE and FALL off; for the effort of comprehension is death to the intelligent public, and sickness to the dull.

I do not know why I pester you with all this trash, above all as you deserve nothing. I give you my warm *talofa* ("my love to you," Samoan salutation). Write me again when the spirit moves you. And some day, if I still live, make out the trip again and let us hob-a-nob with our grey pows on my verandah.—Yours sincerely,

ROBERT LOUIS STEVENSON.

To W. CRAIBE ANGUS

Mr. Craibe Angus of Glasgow was one of the chief organizers of the Burns Exhibition in that city, and had proposed to send out to Samoa a precious copy of the *Jolly Beggars* to receive the autograph of R. L. S. and be returned for the purposes of that Exhibition. The line quoted, "But still our hearts are true," etc., should, it appears, run, "But still the blood is strong, the heart is Highland." The author of the *Canadian Boat Song* which opens thus was Hugh, twelfth Earl of Eglinton. The first quotation is, of course, from Burns.

VAILIMA, SAMOA, *April, 1891.*

DEAR MR. ANGUS,—Surely I remember you! It was W. C. Murray who made us acquainted, and we had a pleasant crack. I see your poet is not yet dead. I remember even our talk—or you would not think of trusting that invaluable *Jolly Beggars* to the treacherous posts, and the perils of the sea, and the carelessness of authors. I love the idea, but I could not bear the risk. However—

"Hale be your heart, hale be your fiddle—"

it was kindly thought upon.

My interest in Burns is, as you suppose, perennial. I would I could be present at the exhibition, with the purpose of which I heartily sympathise; but the *Nancy* has not waited in vain for me, I have followed my chest, the anchor is weighed long ago, I have said my last farewell to the hills and the heather and the lynns: like Leyden, I have gone into far lands to die, not stayed like Burns to mingle in the end with Scottish soil. I shall not even return like Scott for the last scene. Burns Exhibitions are all over. 'T is a far cry to Lochow from tropical Vailima.

"But still our hearts are true, our hearts are Highland,
And we in dreams behold the Hebrides."

When your hand is in, will you remember our poor Edinburgh Robin? Burns alone has been just to his promise; follow Burns, he knew best, he knew whence he drew fire — from the poor, white-faced, drunken, vicious boy that raved himself to death in the Edinburgh madhouse. Surely there is more to be gleaned about Fergusson, and surely it is high time the task was set about. I may tell you (because your poet is not dead) something of how I feel: we are three Robins who have touched the Scots lyre this last century. Well, the one is the world's, he did it, he came off, he is for ever; but I and the other — ! what bonds we have — born in the same city; both sickly; both pestered, one nearly to madness, one to the madhouse, with a damnatory creed; both seeing the stars and the dawn, and wearing shoe-leather on the same ancient stones, under the same pends, down the same closes, where our common ancestors clashed in their armour, rusty or bright. And the old Robin, who was before Burns and the flood, died in his acute, painful youth, and left the models of the great things that were to come; and the new, who came after, outlived his greensickness, and has faintly tried to parody the finished work. If you will collect the strays of Robin Fergusson, fish for material, collect any last re-echoing of gossip, command me to do what you prefer—to write the preface—to write the whole if you prefer: anything, so that another monument (after Burns's) be set up to my unhappy predecessor on the causey of Auld Reekie. You will never know, nor will any man, how deep this feeling is: I believe Fergusson lives in me. I do, but tell it not in Gath; every man has these fanciful superstitions, coming, going, but yet enduring; only most men are so wise (or the poet in them so dead) that they keep their follies for themselves.—I am, yours very truly, ROBERT LOUIS STEVENSON.

TO EDMUND GOSSE

VAILIMA, *April, 1891.*

MY DEAR GOSSE,—I have to thank you and Mrs. Gosse for many mementos, chiefly for your *Life* of your father. There is a very delicate task, very delicately done. I noted one or two carelessnesses, which I meant to point out to you for another edition; but I find I lack the time, and you will remark them for yourself against a new edition. There were two, or perhaps three, flabbinesses of style which (in your work) amazed me. Am I right in thinking you were a shade bored over the last chapters? or was it my own fault that made me think them susceptible of a more athletic compression? (The flabbinesses were not there, I think, but in the more admirable part, where they showed the bigger.) Take it all together, the book struck me as if you had been hurried at the last, but particularly hurried over the proofs, and could still

1891 ÆT. 41

spend a very profitable fortnight in earnest revision and (towards the end) heroic compression. The book, in design, subject, and general execution, is well worth the extra trouble. And even if I were wrong in thinking it specially wanted, it will not be lost; for do we not know, in Flaubert's dread confession, that "prose is never done"? What a medium to work in, for a man tired, perplexed among different aims and subjects, and spurred by the immediate need of "siller"! However, it's mine for what it's worth; and it's one of yours, the devil take it; and you know, as well as Flaubert, and as well as me, that it is *never done;* in other words, it is a torment of the pit, usually neglected by the bards who (lucky beggars!) approached the Styx in measure. I speak bitterly at the moment, having just detected in myself the last fatal symptom, three blank verses in succession—and I believe, God help me, a hemistich at the tail of them; hence I have deposed the labourer, come out of hell by my private trap, and now write to you from my little place in purgatory. But I prefer hell: would I could always dig in those red coals—or else be at sea in a schooner, bound for isles unvisited: to be on shore and not to work is emptiness—suicidal vacancy.

I was the more interested in your *Life* of your father, because I meditate one of mine, or rather of my family. I have no such materials as you, and (our objections already made) your attack fills me with despair; it is direct and elegant, and your style is always admirable to me—lenity, lucidity, usually a high strain of breeding, an elegance that has a pleasant air of the accidental. But beware of purple passages. I wonder if you think as well of your purple passages as I do of mine? I wonder if you think as ill of mine as I do of yours? I wonder; I can tell you at least what is wrong with yours—they are treated in the spirit of verse. The spirit—I don't mean the measure, I don't mean you fall into bastard cadences; what I mean is that they seem vacant and smoothed out, ironed, if you like. And in a style which (like yours) aims more and more successfully at the academic, one purple word is already much; three—a whole phrase—is inadmissible. Wed yourself to a clean austerity: that is your force. Wear a linen ephod, splendidly candid. Arrange its folds, but do not fasten it with any brooch. I swear to you, in your talking robes, there should be no patch of adornment; and where the subject forces, let it force you no further than it must; and be ready with a twinkle of your pleasantry. Yours is a fine tool, and I see so well how to hold it; I wonder if you see how to hold mine? But then I am to the neck in prose, and just now in the "dark *interstylar* cave," all methods and effects wooing me, myself in the midst impotent to follow any. I look for dawn presently, and a full flowing river of expression, running whither it wills. But these useless seasons, above all, when a man *must* continue to spoil paper, are infinitely weary.

We are in our house after a fashion; without furniture, 't is true, camping there, like the family after a sale. But the bailiff has not yet appeared; he will probably come after. The place is beautiful beyond dreams; some fifty miles of the Pacific spread in front;

1891
ÆT. 41

deep woods all round; a mountain making in the sky a profile of huge trees upon our left; about us, the little island of our clearing, studded with brave old gentlemen (or ladies, or "the twa o' them") whom we have spared. It is a good place to be in; night and morning, we have Theodore Rousseaus (always a new one) hung to amuse us on the walls of the world; and the moon — this is our good season, we have a moon just now — makes the night a piece of heaven. It amazes me how people can live on in the dirty north; yet if you saw our rainy season (which is really a caulker for wind, wet, and darkness — howling showers, roaring winds, pit-blackness at noon) you might marvel how we could endure that. And we can't. But there 's a winter everywhere; only ours is in the summer. Mark my words: there will be a winter in heaven — and in hell. *Cela rentre dans les procédés du bon Dieu; et vous verrez!* There 's another very good thing about Vailima, I am away from the little bubble of the literary life. It is not all beer and skittles, is it? By the by, my *Ballads* seem to have been dam bad; all the crickets sing so in their crickety papers; and I have no ghost of an idea on the point myself: verse is always to me the unknowable. You might tell me how it strikes a professional bard: not that it really matters, for, of course, good or bad, I don't think I shall get into *that* galley any more. But I should like to know if you join the shrill chorus of the crickets. The crickets are the devil in all to you: 't is a strange thing, they seem to rejoice like a strong man in their injustice. I trust you got my letter about your Browning book. In case it missed, I wish to say again that your publication of Browning's kind letter, as an illustration of *his* character, was modest, proper, and in radiant good taste.—In Witness whereof, etc., etc.,

ROBERT LOUIS STEVENSON.

TO MISS RAWLINSON

The next is written to a young friend and visitor of Bournemouth days on the news of her engagement.

VAILIMA, APIA, SAMOA, *April, 1891.*

MY DEAR MAY,—I never think of you by any more ceremonial name, so I will not pretend. There is not much chance that I shall forget you until the time comes for me to forget all this little turmoil in a corner (though indeed I have been in several corners) of an inconsiderable planet. You remain in my mind for a good reason, having given me (in so short a time) the most delightful pleasure. I shall remember, and you must still be beautiful. The truth is, you must grow more so, or you will soon be less. It is not so easy to be a flower, even when you bear a flower's name. And if I admired you so much, and still remember you, it is not because of your face, but because you were then worthy of it, as you must still continue.

Will you give my heartiest congratulations to Mr. S.? He has my admiration; he is a brave man; when I was young, I should have run away from the sight of you, pierced with the sense of my unfitness. He is more wise and manly. What a good husband he will have to be! And you—what a good wife! Carry your love tenderly. I will never forgive him—or you—it

1891
ÆT. 41

because you keep a promise to your fellow man, your helper and creditor in life, by just so much as I was tempted to think the less of you (O not much, or I would never have been angry) when I thought you were the swallower of a (tinfoil) formula.

I must say I was uneasy about my letter, not because it was too strong as an expression of my unregenerate sentiments, but because I knew full well it should be followed by something kinder. And the mischief has been in my health. I fell sharply sick in Sydney, was put aboard the *Lübeck* pretty bad, got to Vailima, hung on a month there, and did n't pick up as well as my work needed; set off on a journey, gained a great deal, lost it again; and am back at Vailima, still no good at my necessary work. I tell you this for my imperfect excuse that I should not have written you again sooner to remove the bad taste of my last.

A road has been called Adelaide Road; it leads from the back of our house to the bridge, and thence to the garden, and by a bifurcation to the pig pen. It is thus much traversed, particularly by Fanny. An oleander, the only one of your seeds that prospered in this climate, grows there; and the name is now some week or ten days applied and published. ADELAIDE ROAD leads also into the bush, to the banana patch, and by a second bifurcation over the left branch of the stream to the plateau and the right hand of the gorges. In short, it leads to all sorts of good, and is besides, in itself, a pretty winding path, bound downhill among big woods to the margin of the stream.

What a strange idea, to think me a Jew-hater! Isaiah and David and Heine are good enough for me; and I leave more unsaid. Were I of Jew blood, I do not think I could ever forgive the Christians; the ghettos would get in my nostrils like mustard or lit gunpowder. Just so you as being a child of the Presbytery, I retain —I need not dwell on that. The ascendant hand is what I feel most strongly; I am bound in and in with my forebears; were he one of mine, I should not be struck at all by Mr. Moss of Bevis Marks, I should still see behind him Moses of the Mount and the Tables and the shining face. We are all nobly born; fortunate those who know it; blessed those who remember.

I am, my dear Adelaide, most genuinely yours,

ROBERT LOUIS STEVENSON.

Write by return to say you are better, and I will try to do the same.

TO CHARLES BAXTER

The following refers to a literary project which had occupied the writer's mind for years, but which never got executed, beyond, that is, a few unrevised opening chapters composed at Bournemouth.

[VAILIMA], *Tuesday, 19th May, '91.*

MY DEAR CHARLES,—I don't know what you think of me, not having written to you at all during your illness. I find two sheets begun with your name, but that is no excuse. . . . I am keeping bravely; getting about better every day, and hope soon to be in my usual fettle. My books begin to come; and I fell once more on the Old Bailey session papers. I have 1778, 1784, and 1786. Should you be able to lay hands on any other volumes, above all a little later, I should be

1891
ÆT. 41

very glad you should buy them for me. I particularly want *one* or *two* during the course of the Peninsular War. Come to think, I ought rather to have communicated this want to Bain. Would it bore you to communicate to that effect with the great man? The sooner I have them, the better for me. 'T is for Henry Shovel. But Henry Shovel has now turned into a work called "The Shovels of Newton French: Including Memoirs of Henry Shovel, a Private in the Peninsular War," which work is to begin in 1664 with the marriage of Skipper, afterwards Alderman Shovel of Bristol, Henry's great-great-grandfather, and end about 1832 with his own second marriage to the daughter of his runaway aunt. Will the public ever stand such an opus? Gude kens, but it tickles me. Two or three historical personages will just appear: Judge Jeffreys, Wellington, Colquhoun, Grant, and I think Townsend the runner. I know the public won't like it; let 'em lump it then; I mean to make it good; it will be more like a saga.—Adieu, yours ever affectionately, R. L. STEVENSON.

TO E. L. BURLINGAME

For the result of the suggestion made in the following, see *Scribner's Magazine* for October, 1893, p. 494.

VAILIMA [*Summer, 1891*].

MY DEAR BURLINGAME,—I find among my grandfather's papers his own reminiscences of his voyage round the north with Sir Walter, eighty years ago, *labuntur anni!* They are not remarkably good, but he was not a bad observer, and several touches seem to me speaking. It has occurred to me you might like them to appear in the Magazine. If you would, kindly let me know, and tell me how you would like it handled. My granddad's MS. runs to between six and seven thousand words, which I could abbreviate of anecdotes that scarce touch Sir W. Would you like this done? Would you like me to introduce the old gentleman? I had something of the sort in my mind, and could fill a few columns rather *apropos*. I give you the first offer of this, according to your request; for though it may forestall one of the interests of my biography, the thing seems to me particularly suited for prior appearance in a magazine.

I see the first number of *The Wrecker;* I thought it went lively enough; and by a singular accident, the picture is not unlike Tai-o-hae!

Thus we see the age of miracles, etc.—Yours very sincerely,
R. L. S.

Proofs for next mail.

To W. Craibe Angus

[*Summer, 1891.*]

DEAR MR. ANGUS,—You can use my letter as you will. The parcel has not come; pray Heaven the next post bring it safe. Is it possible for me to write a preface here? I will try if you like, if you think I must: though surely there are Rivers in Assyria. Of course you will send me sheets of the catalogue; I suppose it (the preface) need not be long: perhaps it should be rather very short? Be sure you give me your views upon these points. Also tell me what names to mention among those of your helpers, and do remember to register everything, else it is not safe.

The true place (in my view) for a monument to Fergusson were the churchyard of Haddington. But as that would perhaps not carry many votes, I should say one of the two following sites:—First, either as near the site of the old Bedlam as we could get, or, second, beside the Cross, the heart of his city. Upon this I would have a fluttering butterfly, and, I suggest, the citation,

Poor butterfly, thy case I mourn.

For the case of Fergusson is not one to pretend about. A more miserable tragedy the sun never shone upon, or (in consideration of our climate) I should rather say refused to brighten.—Yours truly,

ROBERT LOUIS STEVENSON.

Where Burns goes will not matter. He is no local poet, like your Robin the First; he is general as the casing air. Glasgow, as the chief city of Scottish men, would do well; but for God's sake, don't let it be like the Glasgow memorial to Knox: I remember, when I first saw this, laughing for an hour by Shrewsbury clock.

R. L. S.

TO H. C. IDE

The following is written to the American Land Commissioner (later Chief Justice for a term) in Samoa, whose younger daughter, then at home in the States, had been born on a Christmas Day, and consequently regarded herself as defrauded of her natural rights to a private anniversary of her own.

[VAILIMA, *June 19, 1891.*]

DEAR MR. IDE,—Herewith please find the DOCUMENT, which I trust will prove sufficient in law. It seems to me very attractive in its eclecticism; Scots, English, and Roman law phrases are all indifferently introduced, and a quotation from the works of Haynes Bailey can hardly fail to attract the indulgence of the Bench.—Yours very truly, ROBERT LOUIS STEVENSON.

I, Robert Louis Stevenson, Advocate of the Scots Bar, author of *The Master of Ballantrae* and *Moral Emblems*, stuck civil engineer, sole owner and patentee of the Palace and Plantation known as Vailima in the island of Upolu, Samoa, a British Subject, being in sound mind, and pretty well, I thank you, in body:

In consideration that Miss Annie H. Ide, daughter of H. C. Ide, in the town of Saint Johnsbury, in the county of Caledonia, in the state of Vermont, United States of America, was born, out of all reason, upon Christmas Day, and is therefore out of all justice denied the consolation and profit of a proper birthday;

And considering that I, the said Robert Louis Stevenson, have attained an age when O, we never mention it, and that I have now no further use for a birthday of any description;

And in consideration that I have met H. C. Ide, the father of the said Annie H. Ide, and found him about as white a land commissioner as I require:

Have transferred, and *do hereby transfer*, to the said Annie H. Ide, *all and whole* my rights and privileges in the thirteenth day of November, formerly my birthday, now, hereby, and henceforth, the birthday of the

1891
ÆT. 41

No person now alive has beaten Adela: I adore Adela and her Maker. Sic subscrib.

ROBERT LOUIS STEVENSON.

A Sublime Poem to follow.

Adela, Adela, Adela Chart,
What have you done to my elderly heart?
Of all the ladies of paper and ink
I count you the paragon, call you the pink.
The word of your brother depicts you in part:
"You raving maniac!" Adela Chart;
But in all the asylums that cumber the ground,
So delightful a maniac was ne'er to be found.

I pore on you, dote on you, clasp you to heart,
I laud, love, and laugh at you, Adela Chart,
And thank my dear maker the while I admire
That I can be neither your husband nor sire.

Your husband's, your sire's were a difficult part;
You 're a byway to suicide, Adela Chart;
But to read of, depicted by exquisite James,
O, sure you're the flower and quintessence of dames.

R. L. S.

Eructavit cor meum.

My heart was inditing a goodly matter about Adela Chart.

Though oft I 've been touched by the volatile dart,
To none have I grovelled but Adela Chart.
There are passable ladies, no question, in art—

But where is the marrow of Adela Chart?
I dreamed that to Tyburn I passed in the cart—
I dreamed I was married to Adela Chart:
From the first I awoke with a palpable start,
The second dumfoundered me, Adela Chart!

Another verse bursts from me, you see; no end to the violence of the Muse.

To E. L. Burlingame

October 8th, 1891.

MY DEAR BURLINGAME,—All right, you shall have the *Tales of my Grandfather* soon, but I guess we'll try and finish off *The Wrecker* first. *Apropos* of whom, please send some advanced sheets to Cassell's—away ahead of you—so that they may get a dummy out.

Do you wish to illustrate *My Grandfather?* He mentions as excellent a portrait of Scott by Basil Hall's brother. I don't think I ever saw this engraved; would it not, if you could get track of it, prove a taking embellishment? I suggest this for your consideration and inquiry. A new portrait of Scott strikes me as good. There is a hard, tough, constipated old portrait of my grandfather hanging in my aunt's house, Mrs. Alan Stevenson, 16 St. Leonard's Terrace, Chelsea, which has never been engraved—the better portrait, Joseph's bust, has been reproduced, I believe, twice—and which, I am sure, my aunt would let you have a copy of. The plate could be of use for the book when we get so far, and thus to place it in the Magazine might be an actual saving.

1891
ÆT. 41

To W. Craibe Angus

Vailima, Samoa, *November, 1891.*

MY DEAR MR. ANGUS,— Herewith the invaluable sheets. They came months after your letter, and I trembled; but here they are, and I have scrawled my vile name on them, and "thocht shame" as I did it. I am expecting the sheets of your catalogue, so that I may attack the preface. Please give me all the time you can. The sooner the better; you might even send me early proofs as they are sent out, to give me more incubation. I used to write as slow as judgment; now I write rather fast; but I am still "a slow study," and sit a long while silent on my eggs. Unconscious thought, there is the only method: macerate your subject, let it boil slow, then take the lid off and look in — and there your stuff is, good or bad. But the journalist's method is the way to manufacture lies; it is will-worship — if you know the luminous Quaker phrase; and the will is only to be brought in the field for study, and again for revision. The essential part of work is not an act, it is a state.

I do not know why I write you this trash.

Many thanks for your handsome dedication. I have not yet had time to do more than glance at Mrs. Begg; it looks interesting.— Yours very truly,

Robert Louis Stevenson.

To Miss Annie H. Ide

Vailima, Samoa [*November, 1891*].

MY DEAR LOUISA,—Your picture of the church, the photograph of yourself and your sister, and your very witty and pleasing letter, came all in a bundle, and made me feel I had my money's worth for that birthday. I am now, I must be, one of your nearest relatives; exactly what we are to each other, I do not know, I doubt if the case has ever happened before—your papa ought to know, and I don't believe he does; but I think I ought to call you in the meanwhile, and until we get the advice of counsel learned in the law, my name-daughter. Well, I was extremely pleased to see by the church that my name-daughter could draw; by the letter, that she was no fool; and by the photograph, that she was a pretty girl, which hurts nothing. See how virtues are rewarded! My first idea of adopting you was entirely charitable; and here I find that I am quite proud of it, and of you, and that I chose just the kind of name-daughter I wanted. For I can draw too, or rather I mean to say I could before I forgot how; and I am very far from being a fool myself, however much I may look it; and I am as beautiful as the day, or at least I once hoped that perhaps I might be going to be. And so I might. So that you see we are well met, and peers on these important points. I am very glad also that you are older than your sister. So should I have been, if I had had one. So that the number of points and virtues which you have inherited from your name-father is already quite surprising.

I wish you would tell your father — not that I like to encourage my rival — that we have had a wonderful time here of late, and that they are having a cold day on Mulinuu, and the consuls are writing reports, and I am writing to the *Times*, and if we don't get rid of our friends this time I shall begin to despair of everything but my name-daughter.

You are quite wrong as to the effect of the birthday on your age. From the moment the deed was registered (as it was in the public press with every solemnity), the 13th of November became your own *and only* birthday, and you ceased to have been born on Christmas Day. Ask your father: I am sure he will tell you this is sound law. You are thus become a month and twelve days younger than you were, but will go on growing older for the future in the regular and human manner from one 13th November to the next. The effect on me is more doubtful; I may, as you suggest, live for ever; I might, on the other hand, come to pieces like the one-horse shay at a moment's notice; doubtless the step was risky, but I do not the least regret that which enables me to sign myself your revered and delighted name-father, ROBERT LOUIS STEVENSON.

TO NED ORR

The following is in answer to an application for an autograph from a young gentleman in the United States.

VAILIMA, UPOLU, SAMOA, *November 28th, 1891.*

DEAR SIR, — Your obliging communication is to hand. I am glad to find that you have read some of my books, and to see that you spell my name right. This is a point (for some reason) of great difficulty; and I believe that a gentleman who can spell Stevenson with a *v* at sixteen should have a show for the Presidency before fifty. By that time

"I, nearer to the wayside inn,"

predict that you will have outgrown your taste for autographs, but perhaps your son may have inherited the collection, and on the morning of the great day will recall my prophecy to your mind. And in the papers of 1921 (say) this letter may arouse a smile.

Whatever you do, read something else besides novels and newspapers; the first are good enough when they are good; the second, at their best, are worth nothing. Read great books of literature and history; try to understand the Roman Empire and the Middle Ages; be sure you do not understand when you dislike them; condemnation is non-comprehension. And if you know something of these two periods, you will know a little more about to-day, and may be a good President.

I send you my best wishes, and am yours,

ROBERT LOUIS STEVENSON,
Author of a vast quantity of little books.

TO E. L. BURLINGAME

The next letter announces to his New York publishers the beginning of his volume on the troubles of Samoa, *A Foot-note to History.*

[VAILIMA, *December, 1891.*]

MY DEAR BURLINGAME,—The end of *The Wrecker* having but just come in, you will, I dare say, be appalled to

1891
ÆT. 41

receive three (possibly four) chapters of a new book of the least attractive sort: a history of nowhere in a corner, for no time to mention, running to a volume! Well, it may very likely be an illusion; it is very likely no one could possibly wish to read it, but I wish to publish it. If you don't cotton to the idea, kindly set it up at my expense, and let me know your terms for publishing. The great affair to me is to have per return (if it might be) four or five — better say half a dozen — sets of the roughest proofs that can be drawn. There are a good many men here whom I want to read the blessed thing, and not one would have the energy to read MS. At the same time, if you care to glance at it, and have the time, I should be very glad of your opinion as to whether I have made any step at all towards possibly inducing folk at home to read matter so extraneous and outlandish. I become heavy and owlish; years sit upon me; it begins to seem to me to be a man's business to leave off his damnable faces and say his say. Else I could have made it pungent and light and lively. In considering, kindly forget that I am R. L. S.; think of the four chapters as a book you are reading, by an inhabitant of our "lovely but fatil" islands; and see if it could possibly amuse the hebetated public. I have to publish anyway, you understand; I have a purpose beyond; I am concerned for some of the parties to this quarrel. What I want to hear is from curiosity; what I want you to judge of is what we are to do with the book in a business sense. To me it is not business at all; I had meant originally to lay all the profits to the credit of Samoa; when it comes to the pinch of writing, I judge this unfair — I give too much — and I mean to keep (if there be any profit at all) one-half for the artizan; the rest I shall hold over to give to the Samoans *for that which I choose and against work done.* I think I have never heard of greater insolence than to attempt such a subject; yet the tale is so strange and mixed, and the people so oddly charactered — above all, the whites — and the high note of the hurricane and the warships is so well prepared to take popular interest, and the latter part is so directly in the day's movement, that I am not without hope but some may read it; and if they don't, a murrain on them! Here is, for the first time, a tale of Greeks — Homeric Greeks — mingled with moderns, and all true; Odysseus alongside of Rajah Brooke, *proportion gardée;* and all true. Here is for the first time since the Greeks (that I remember) the history of a handful of men, where all know each other in the eyes, and live close in a few acres, narrated at length, and with the seriousness of history. Talk of the modern novel; here is a modern history. And if I had the misfortune to found a school, the legitimate historian might lie down and die, for he could never overtake his material. Here is a little tale that has not "caret"-ed its "vates"; "sacer" is another point.

R. L. S.

To Henry James

Mr. Henry James was in the habit of sending out for Stevenson's reading books that seemed likely to interest him, and among the last had been M. Paul Bourget's *Sensations d'Italie.*

December 7th, 1891.

MY DEAR HENRY JAMES,—Thanks for yours; your former letter was lost; so it appears was my long and

1892
ÆT. 42

bless you for the gift of him. I have really enjoyed this book as I—almost as I—used to enjoy books when I was going twenty—twenty-three; and these are the years for reading! R. L. S.

To E. L. Burlingame

[Vailima], *Jan. 2nd, '92.*

MY DEAR BURLINGAME,—Overjoyed you were pleased with *Wrecker*, and shall consider your protests. There is perhaps more art than you think for in the peccant chapter, where I have succeeded in packing into one a dedication, an explanation, and a termination. Surely you had not recognised the phrase about boodle? It was a quotation from Jim Pinkerton, and seemed to me agreeably skittish. However, all shall be prayerfully considered.

To come to a more painful subject. Herewith go three more chapters of the wretched *History;* as you see, I approach the climax. I expect the book to be some 70,000 words, of which you have now 45. Can I finish it for next mail? I am going to try! 'T is a long piece of journalism, and full of difficulties here and there, of this kind and that, and will make me a power of friends to be sure. There is one Becker who will probably put up a window to me in the church where he was baptised; and I expect a testimonial from Captain Hand.

Sorry to let the mail go without the Scott; this has been a bad month with me, and I have been below myself. I shall find a way to have it come by next, or know the reason why. The mail after, anyway.

A bit of a sketch map appears to me necessary for my *History;* perhaps two. If I do not have any, 't is impossible any one should follow; and I, even when not at all interested, demand that I shall be able to follow; even a tourist book without a map is a cross to me; and there must be others of my way of thinking. I enclose the very artless one that I think needful. Vailima, in case you are curious, is about as far again behind Tanugamanono as that is from the sea.

M'Clure is publishing a short story of mine, some 50,000 words, I think, *The Beach of Falesá;* when he 's done with it, I want you and Cassell to bring it out in a little volume; I shall send you a dedication for it; I believe it good; indeed, to be honest, very good. Good gear that pleases the merchant.

The other map that I half threaten is a chart for the hurricane. Get me Kimberley's report of the hurricane: not to be found here. It is of most importance; I *must* have it with my proofs of that part, if I cannot have it earlier, which now seems impossible.—Yours in hot haste,
R. L. STEVENSON.

TO J. M. BARRIE

The following is the first of several letters to Mr. J. M. Barrie, for whose work Stevenson had a warm admiration, and with whom he soon established by correspondence a cordial friendship.

VAILIMA, SAMOA, *February, 1892.*

DEAR MR. BARRIE,—This is at least the third letter I have written you, but my correspondence has a bad habit of not getting so far as the post. That which I that you have illustrated so nobly, is yet alive. She has her rights and laws, and is our mother, our queen, and our instrument. Now in that living tongue *where* has one sense, *whereas* another. In the *Heathslayings Story*, p. 241, line 13, it bears one of its ordinary senses. Elsewhere and usually through the two volumes, which is all that has yet reached me of this entrancing publication, *whereas* is made to figure for *where.*

For the love of God, my dear and honoured Morris, use *where,* and let us know *whereas* we are, wherefore our gratitude shall grow, whereby you shall be the more honoured wherever men love clear language, whereas now, although we honour, we are troubled.

Whereunder, please find inscribed to this very impudent but yet very anxious document, the name of one of the most distant but not the youngest or the coldest of those who honour you.

ROBERT LOUIS STEVENSON.

TO MRS. CHARLES FAIRCHILD

The projected visit of Mr. Kipling, with his wife and brother-in-law, to Samoa, which is mentioned towards the close of this letter, never took place, much to the regret of both authors.

[VAILIMA, *March, 1892.*]

MY DEAR MRS. FAIRCHILD,—I am guilty in your sight, but my affairs besiege me. The chief-justiceship of a family of nineteen persons is in itself no sinecure, and sometimes occupies me for days: two weeks ago for four days almost entirely, and for two days entirely. Besides which, I have in the last few months written all but one chapter of a *History of Samoa* for the last eight or nine years; and while I was unavoidably delayed in the writing of this, awaiting material, put in one-half of *David Balfour*, the sequel to *Kidnapped*. Add the ordinary impediments of life, and admire my busyness. I am now an old, but healthy skeleton, and degenerate much towards the machine. By six at work: stopped at half-past ten to give a history lesson to a step-grandson; eleven, lunch; after lunch we have a musical performance till two; then to work again; bath, 4.40; dinner, five; cards in the evening till eight; and then to bed — only I have no bed, only a chest with a mat and blankets — and read myself to sleep. This is the routine, but often sadly interrupted. Then you may see me sitting on the floor of my verandah haranguing and being harangued by squatting chiefs on a question of a road; or more privately holding an inquiry into some dispute among our familiars, myself on my bed, the boys on the floor — for when it comes to the judicial I play dignity — or else going down to Apia on some more or less unsatisfactory errand. Altogether it is a life that suits me, but it absorbs me like an ocean. That is what I have always envied and admired in Scott; with all that immensity of work and study, his mind kept flexible, glancing to all points of natural interest. But the lean hot spirits, such as mine, become hypnotised with their bit occupations — if I may use Scotch to you — it is so far more scornful than any English idiom. Well, I can't help being a skeleton, and you are to take this devious passage for an apology.

1892
ÆT. 42

I thought *Aladdin* capital fun; but why, in fortune,

1892
ÆT. 42

best of his race) is a really serious chief with a good "name." Tina is the name; it is not in the Almanach de Gotha, it must have got dropped at press. The odd thing is, we rather share the prejudice. I have almost always — though not quite always — found the higher the chief the better the man through all the islands; or, at least, that the best man came always from a highish rank. I hope Helen will continue to prove a bright exception.

With love to Fairchild and the Huge Schoolboy, I am, my dear Mrs. Fairchild, yours very sincerely,

ROBERT LOUIS STEVENSON.

To E. L. Burlingame

The first sentences of the following refer to the *Foot-note to History*, Chapter x. of which, relating to the hurricane of 1889, was first published in the *Scots Observer*, edited by Mr. Henley.

[VAILIMA, *March, 1892.*]

MY DEAR BURLINGAME,—Herewith Chapters IX. and X., and I am left face to face with the horrors and dilemmas of the present regimen: pray for those that go down to the sea in ships. I have promised Henley shall have a chance to publish the hurricane chapter if he like, so please let the slips be sent *quam primum* to C. Baxter, W. S., 11 S. Charlotte Street, Edinburgh. I got on mighty quick with that chapter — about five days of the toughest kind of work. God forbid I should ever have such another pirn to wind. When I invent a language, there shall be a direct and an indirect pronoun differently declined — then writing would be some fun.

DIRECT	INDIRECT
He	Tu
Him	Tum
His	Tus

Ex.: *He* seized *tum* by *tus* throat; but *tu* at the same moment caught *him* by *his* hair. A fellow could write hurricanes with an inflection like that! Yet there would be difficulties too.

Do what you please about *The Beach;* and I give you *carte blanche* to write in the matter to Baxter—or telegraph if the time press—to delay the English contingent. Herewith the two last slips of *The Wrecker.* I cannot go beyond. By the way, pray compliment the printers on the proofs of the Samoa racket, but hint to them that it is most unbusiness-like and unscholarly to clip the edges of the galleys; these proofs should really have been sent me on large paper; and I and my friends here are all put to a great deal of trouble and confusion by the mistake. For, as you must conceive, in a matter so contested and complicated, the number of corrections and the length of explanations is considerable.

Please add to my former orders—

Le Chevalier des Touches } by Barbey d'Aurévilly.
Les Diaboliques . . }

Correspondance de Henri Beyle (Stendhal).

Yours sincerely,

R. L. STEVENSON.

To T. W. Dover

Stevenson's correspondent in this case is an artizan, who had been struck by the truth of a remark in his essay on "Beggars," that it is

1892 ÆT. 42

All seems to flourish with you; I also prosper; none the less for being quit of that abhorred task, Samoa. I could give a supper party here were there any one to sup. Never was such a disagreeable task, but the thing had to be told. . . .

There, I trust I am done with this cursed chapter of my career, bar the rotten eggs and broken bottles that may follow, of course. Pray remember, speed is now all that can be asked, hoped, or wished. I give up all hope of proofs, revises, proof of the map, or sic like; and you on your side will try to get it out as reasonably seemly as may be.

Whole Samoa book herewith. Glory be to God.—Yours very sincerely, ROBERT LOUIS STEVENSON.

TO CHARLES BAXTER

VAILIMA PLANTATION, UPOLU, SAMOAN ISLANDS,
18th July, 1892.

MY DEAR CHARLES,—. . . I have been now for some time contending with powers and principalities, and I have never once seen one of my own letters to the *Times.* So when you see something in the papers that you think might interest the exiles of Upolu, do not think twice, out with your saxpence, and send it flying to Vailima. Of what you say of the past, eh, man, it was a queer time, and awful miserable, but there 's no sense in denying it was awful fun. Do you mind the youth in Highland garb and the tableful of coppers? Do you mind the SIGNAL of Waterloo Place?—Hey, how the blood stands to the heart at such a memory!—Hae ye the notes o't? Gie 's them.—Gude's sake, man, gie 's the notes o't; I mind ye made a tüne o't an' played it on your pinanny; gie 's the notes. Dear Lord, that past.

Glad to hear Henley's prospects are fair: his new volume is the work of a real poet. He is one of those who can make a noise of his own with words, and in whom experience strikes an individual note. There is perhaps no more genuine poet living, bar the Big Guns. In case I cannot overtake an acknowledgment to himself by this mail, please let him hear of my pleasure and admiration. How poorly —— compares! He is all smart journalism and cleverness: it is all bright and shallow and limpid, like a business paper—a good one, *s'entend;* but there is no blot of heart's blood and the Old Night: there are no harmonics, there is scarce harmony to his music; and in Henley—all of these; a touch, a sense within sense, a sound outside the sound, the shadow of the inscrutable, eloquent beyond all definition. The First London Voluntary knocked me wholly.—Ever yours affectionately, my dear Charles,

ROBERT LOUIS STEVENSON.

Kind memories to your father and all friends.

TO W. E. HENLEY

VAILIMA PLANTATION, UPOLU, SAMOA,
August 1st, 1892.

MY DEAR HENLEY,—It is impossible to let your new volume pass in silence. I have not received the same thrill of poetry since G. M.'s *Joy of Earth* volume and

1892 ÆT. 42 *Love in a Valley;* and I do not know that even that was so intimate and deep. Again and again I take the book down, and read, and my blood is fired as it used to be in youth. *Andante con moto* in the *Voluntaries*, and the thing about the trees at night (No. XXIV. I think) are up to date my favourites. I did not guess you were so great a magician; these are new tunes, this is an undertone of the true Apollo; these are not verse, they are poetry — inventions, creations, in language. I thank you for the joy you have given me, and remain your old friend and present huge admirer,

ROBERT LOUIS STEVENSON.

The hand is really the hand of Esau, but under a course of threatened scrivener's cramp.

For the next edition of the Book of Verses, pray accept an emendation. Last three lines of Echoes No. XLIV. read —

"But life in act? How should the grave
Be victor over these,
Mother, a mother of men?"

The two vocatives scatter the effect of this inimitable close. If you insist on the longer line, equip "grave" with an epithet. R. L. S.

TO E. L. BURLINGAME

VAILIMA, UPOLU, *August 1st, '92.*

MY DEAR BURLINGAME, — Herewith *My Grandfather.* I have had rather a bad time suppressing the old gentleman, who was really in a very garrulous stage; as for getting him *in order*, I could do but little towards that; however, there are one or two points of interest which may justify us in printing. The swinging of his stick and not knowing the sailor of Coruiskin, in particular and the account of how he wrote the lives in the Bell Book particularly please me. I hope my own little introduction is not egoistic; or rather I do not care if it is. It was that old gentleman's blood that brought me to Samoa.

By the by, vols. vii., viii., and ix. of Adams's *History* have never come to hand; no more have the dictionaries.

Please send me *Stonehenge on the Horse*, *Stories and Interludes* by Barry Pain, and *Edinburgh Sketches and Memoirs* by David Masson. *The Wrecker* has turned up. So far as I have seen it is very satisfactory, but on pp. 548, 549, there has been a devil of a miscarriage, the two Latin quotations instead of following each other being separated (doubtless for printing considerations) by a line of prose. My compliments to the printers; there is doubtless such a thing as good printing, but there is such a thing as good sense.

The sequel to *Kidnapped*, *David Balfour* by name, is about three-quarters done and gone to press for serial publication. By what I can find out it ought to be through hand with that and ready for volume form early next spring.—Yours very sincerely, R. L. S.

To Andrew Lang

Mr. Andrew Lang had been supplying Stevenson with some books and historical references for his proposed novel of *The Young Chevalier*.

1892
ÆT. 42

August 14, 1745.

TO MISS AMELIA BALFOUR—MY DEAR COUSIN,—We are going an expedition to leeward on Tuesday morning. If a lady were perhaps to be encountered on horseback—say, towards the Gasi-gasi river—about six A. M., I think we should have an episode somewhat after the style of the '45. What a misfortune, my dear cousin, that you should have arrived while your cousin Graham was occupying my only guest-chamber—for Osterley Park is not so large in Samoa as it was at home—but happily our friend Haggard has found a corner for you!

The King over the Water—the Gasi-gasi water—will be pleased to see the clan of Balfour mustering so thick around his standard.

I have (one serious word) been so lucky as to get a really secret interpreter, so all is for the best in our little adventure into the *Waverley Novels.*—I am your affectionate cousin, ROBERT LOUIS STEVENSON.

Observe the stealth with which I have blotted my signature, but we must be political *à outrance.*

TO THE COUNTESS OF JERSEY

MY DEAR COUSIN,—I send for your information a copy of my last letter to the gentleman in question. 'T is thought more wise, in consideration of the difficulty and peril of the enterprise, that we should leave the town in the afternoon, and by several detachments. If you would start for a ride with the Master of Haggard and Captain Lockhart of Lee, say at three o'clock of the afternoon, you would make some rencounters by the wayside which might be agreeable to your political opinions. All present will be staunch.

The Master of Haggard might extend his ride a little, and return through the marsh and by the nuns' house (I trust that has the proper flavour), so as a little to diminish the effect of separation.—I remain, your affectionate cousin to command, O TUSITALA.

P. S.—It is to be thought this present year of grace will be historical.

TO MRS. CHARLES FAIRCHILD

[VAILIMA, *August, 1892.*]

MY DEAR MRS. FAIRCHILD,—Thank you a thousand times for your letter. You are the Angel of (the sort of) Information (that I care about); I appoint you successor to the newspaper press; and I beg of you, whenever you wish to gird at the age, or think the bugs out of proportion to the roses, or despair, or enjoy any cosmic or epochal emotion, to sit down again and write to the Hermit of Samoa. What do I think of it all? Well, I love the romantic solemnity of youth; and even in this form, although not without laughter, I have to love it still. They are such ducks! But what are they made of? We were just as solemn as that about atheism and the stars and humanity; but we were all for belief anyway — we held atheism and sociology (of which none of us, nor indeed anybody, knew anything) for a gospel and an iron rule of life; and it

1892
ÆT. 42

there were finer touches still; as when Belle and Lady Jersey came out to brush their teeth in front of the rebel King's palace, and the night guard squatted opposite on the grass and watched the process; or when I and my interpreter, and the King with his secretary, mysteriously disappeared to conspire.—Ever yours sincerely,

R. L. STEVENSON.

TO GORDON BROWNE

VAILIMA, SAMOA, *Autumn, 1892.*

To the Artist who did the illustrations to "Uma."

DEAR SIR,—I only know you under the initials G. B., but you have done some exceedingly spirited and satisfactory illustrations to my story *The Beach of Falesá*, and I wish to write and thank you expressly for the care and talent shown. Such numbers of people can do good black and whites! So few can illustrate a story, or apparently read it. You have shown that you can do both, and your creation of Wiltshire is a real illumination of the text. It was exactly so that Wiltshire dressed and looked, and you have the line of his nose to a nicety. His nose is an inspiration. Nor should I forget to thank you for Case, particularly in his last appearance. It is a singular fact—which seems to point still more directly to inspiration in your case—that your missionary actually resembles the flesh-and-blood person from whom Mr. Tarleton was drawn. The general effect of the islands is all that could be wished; indeed, I have but one criticism to make, that in the background of Case taking the dollar from Mr. Tarleton's head — head — not hand, as the fools have printed it — the natives have a little too much the look of Africans.

But the great affair is that you have been to the pains to illustrate my story instead of making conscientious black and whites of people sitting talking. I doubt if you have left unrepresented a single pictorial incident. I am writing by this mail to the editor in the hopes that I may buy from him the originals, and I am, dear sir, your very much obliged

ROBERT LOUIS STEVENSON.

TO MISS MORSE

The next is an answer to an acknowledgment from a lady in the United States, one of many similar which he from time to time received, of help and encouragement derived from his writings.

VAILIMA, SAMOAN ISLANDS, *October 7th, 1892.*

DEAR MADAM,— I have a great diffidence in answering your valued letter. It would be difficult for me to express the feelings with which I read it—and am now trying to re-read it as I dictate this.

You ask me to forgive what you say "must seem a liberty," and I find that I cannot thank you sufficiently or even find a word with which to qualify your letter. Dear Madam, such a communication even the vainest man would think a sufficient reward for a lifetime of labour. That I should have been able to give so much help and pleasure to your sister is the subject of my grateful wonder.

1892
ÆT. 42

That she, being dead, and speaking with your pen, should be able to repay the debt with such a liberal interest, is one of those things that reconcile us with the world and make us take hope again. I do not know what I have done to deserve so beautiful and touching a compliment; and I feel there is but one thing fit for me to say here, that I will try with renewed courage to go on in the same path, and to deserve, if not to receive, a similar return from others.

You apologise for speaking so much about yourselves. Dear Madam, I thought you did so too little. I should have wished to have known more of those who were so sympathetic as to find a consolation in my work, and so graceful and so tactful as to acknowledge it in such a letter as was yours.

Will you offer to your mother the expression of a sympathy which (coming from a stranger) must seem very airy, but which yet is genuine; and accept for yourself my gratitude for the thought which inspired you to write to me and the words which you found to express it. ROBERT LOUIS STEVENSON.

TO E. L. BURLINGAME

VAILIMA PLANTATION, SAMOAN ISLANDS,
Oct. 10th, 1892.

MY DEAR BURLINGAME,—It is now, as you see, the 10th of October, and there has not reached the Island of Upolu one single copy, or rag of a copy, of the Samoa book. I lie; there has come one, and that in the pocket of a missionary man who is at daggers drawn with me, who lends it to all my enemies, conceals it from all my friends, and is bringing a lawsuit against me on the strength of expressions in the same which I have forgotten, and now cannot see. This is pretty tragic, I think you will allow; and I was inclined to fancy it was the fault of the Post-Office. But I hear from my sister-in-law Mrs. Sanchez that she is in the same case, and has received no "Foot-note." I have also to consider that I had no letter from you last mail, although you ought to have received by that time "My Grandfather and Scott," and "Me and my Grandfather." Taking one consideration with another, therefore, I prefer to conceive that No. 743 Broadway has fallen upon gentle and continuous slumber, and is become an enchanted palace among publishing houses. If it be not so, if the "Foot-notes" were really sent, I hope you will fall upon the Post-Office with all the vigour you possess. How does *The Wrecker* go in the States? It seems to be doing exceptionally well in England.—Yours sincerely,

ROBERT LOUIS STEVENSON.

TO J. M. BARRIE

VAILIMA PLANTATION, SAMOAN ISLANDS,
November 1st, 1892.

DEAR MR. BARRIE,—I can scarce thank you sufficiently for your extremely amusing letter. No, the *Auld Licht Idylls* never reached me—I wish it had, and I wonder extremely whether it would not be good for me to have a pennyworth of the Auld Licht pulpit. It is a singular thing that I should live here in the South

1892
ÆT. 42

Seas under conditions so new and so striking, and yet my imagination so continually inhabit that cold old huddle of grey hills from which we come. I have just finished *David Balfour;* I have another book on the stocks, *The Young Chevalier*, which is to be part in France and part in Scotland, and to deal with Prince Charlie about the year 1749; and now what have I done but begun a third which is to be all moorland together, and is to have for a centrepiece a figure that I think you will appreciate—that of the immortal Braxfield—Braxfield himself is my *grand premier*, or since you are so much involved in the British drama, let me say my heavy lead. . . .

Your descriptions of your dealings with Lord Rintoul are frightfully unconscientious. You should never write about anybody until you persuade yourself at least for the moment that you love him, above all anybody on whom your plot revolves. It will always make a hole in the book; and if he has anything to do with the mechanism, prove a stick in your machinery. But you know all this better than I do, and it is one of your most promising traits that you do not take your powers too seriously. *The Little Minister* ought to have ended badly; we all know it did; and we are infinitely grateful to you for the grace and good feeling with which you lied about it. If you had told the truth, I for one could never have forgiven you. As you had conceived and written the earlier parts, the truth about the end, though indisputably true to fact, would have been a lie, or what is worse, a discord in art. If you are going to make a book end badly, it must end badly from the beginning. Now your book began to end well. You let yourself fall in love with, and fondle, and smile at your puppets. Once you had done that your honour was committed—at the cost of truth to life you were bound to save them. It is the blot on *Richard Feverel*, for instance, that it begins to end well; and then tricks you and ends ill. But in that case there is worse behind, for the ill-ending does not inherently issue from the plot—the story *had*, in fact, *ended well* after the great last interview between Richard and Lucy—and the blind, illogical bullet which smashes all has no more to do between the boards than a fly has to do with the room into whose open window it comes buzzing. It *might* have so happened; it needed not; and unless needs must, we have no right to pain our readers. I have had a heavy case of conscience of the same kind about my Braxfield story. Braxfield—only his name is Hermiston—has a son who is condemned to death; plainly, there is a fine tempting fitness about this; and I meant he was to hang. But now on considering my minor characters, I saw there were five people who would—in a sense who must—break prison and attempt his rescue. They were capable, hardy folks, too, who might very well succeed. Why should they not then? Why should not young Hermiston escape clear out of the country? and be happy, if he could, with his—— But soft! I will not betray my secret or my heroine. Suffice it to breathe in your ear that she was what Hardy calls (and others in their plain way don't) a Pure Woman. Much virtue in a capital letter, such as yours was.

Write to me again in my infinite distance. Tell me about your new book. No harm in telling *me;* I am too far off to be indiscreet; there are too few near me who would care to hear. I am rushes by the riverside, and the stream is in Babylon: breathe your secrets to me fearlessly; and if the Trade Wind caught and carried them away, there are none to catch them nearer than Australia, unless it were the Tropic Birds. In the unavoidable absence of my amanuensis, who is buying eels for dinner, I have thus concluded my despatch, like St. Paul, with my own hand.

And in the inimitable words of Lord Kames, Faur ye weel, ye bitch.—Yours very truly,

ROBERT LOUIS STEVENSON.

TO E. L. BURLINGAME

VAILIMA PLANTATION, *Nov. 2nd, 1892.*

MY DEAR BURLINGAME,—In the first place, I have to acknowledge receipt of your munificent cheque for three hundred and fifty dollars. Glad you liked the Scott voyage; rather more than I did upon the whole. As the proofs have not turned up at all there can be no question of returning them, and I am therefore very much pleased to think you have arranged not to wait. The volumes of Adams arrived along with yours of October 6th. One of the dictionaries has also blundered home, apparently from the Colonies, the other is still to seek. I note and sympathise with your bewilderment as to *Falesá*. My own direct correspondence with Mr. Baxter is now about three months in abeyance. Altogether you see how well it would be if you could do anything to wake up the Post-Office. Not a single copy of the "Foot-note" has yet reacnea Samoa, but I hear of one having come to its address in Hawaii. Glad to hear good news of Stoddard.— Yours sincerely,

R. L. STEVENSON.

P. S.— Since the above was written an aftermath of post matter came in, among which were the proofs of *My Grandfather*. I shall correct and return them, but as I have lost all confidence in the Post-Office, I shall mention here: first galley, 4th line from the bottom, for "AS" read "OR."

Should you ever again have to use my work without waiting for proofs, bear in mind this golden principle. From a congenital defect, I must suppose, I am unable to write the word OR—wherever I write it the printer unerringly puts AS—and those who read for me had better, wherever it is possible, substitute OR for AS. This the more so since many writers have a habit of using AS, which is death to my temper and confusion to my face.

R. L. S.

TO LIEUTENANT EELES

The following is addressed to one of Stevenson's best friends among the officers of H. M. S. the *Curaçoa*, which had been for some time on the South Pacific station.

VAILIMA PLANTATION, UPOLU, SAMOAN ISLANDS,
November 15th, 1892.

DEAR EELES,—In the first place, excuse me writing to you by another hand, as that is the way in which alone all my correspondence gets effected. Before I took to

1892 ÆT. 42

this method, or rather before I found a victim, it simply did n't get effected.

Thank you again and again, first for your kind thought of writing to me, and second for your extremely amusing and interesting letter. You can have no guess how immediately interesting it was to our family. First of all, the poor soul at Nukufetau is an old friend of ours, and we have actually treated him ourselves on a former visit to the island. I don't know if Hoskin would approve of our treatment; it consisted, I believe, mostly in a present of stout and a recommendation to put nails in his water-tank. We also (as you seem to have done) recommended him to leave the island; and I remember very well how wise and kind we thought his answer. He had half-caste children (he said) who would suffer and perhaps be despised if he carried them elsewhere; if he left them there alone, they would almost certainly miscarry; and the best thing was that he should stay and die with them. But the cream of the fun was your meeting with Buckland. We not only know him, but (as the French say) we don't know anybody else; he is our intimate and adored original; and — prepare your mind — he was, is, and ever will be, TOMMY HADDON![1] As I don't believe you to be inspired, I suspect you to have suspected this. At least it was a mighty happy suspicion. You are quite right: Tommy is really "a good chap," though about as comic as they make them.

I was extremely interested in your Fiji legend, and perhaps even more so in your capital account of the *Curaçoa's* misadventure. Alas, we have nothing

[1] A character in *The Wrecker*.

so thrilling to relate. All hangs and fools on in this isle of misgovernment, without change, though not without novelty, but wholly without hope, unless perhaps you should consider it hopeful that I am still more immediately threatened with arrest. The confounded thing is, that if it comes off, I shall be sent away in the *Ringarooma* instead of the *Curaçoa*. The former ship burst upon by the run — she had been sent off by despatch and without orders — and to make me a little more easy in my mind she brought newspapers clamouring for my incarceration. Since then I have had a conversation with the German Consul. He said he had read a review of my Samoa book, and if the review were fair, must regard it as an insult, and one that would have to be resented. At the same time, I learn that letters addressed to the German squadron lie for them here in the Post-Office. Reports are current of other English ships being on the way — I hope to goodness yours will be among the number. And I gather from one thing and another that there must be a holy row going on between the powers at home, and that the issue (like all else connected with Samoa) is on the knees of the gods. One thing, however, is pretty sure — if that issue prove to be a German Protectorate, I shall have to tramp. Can you give us any advice as to a fresh field of energy? We have been searching the atlas, and it seems difficult to fill the bill. How would Raratonga do? I forget if you have been there. The best of it is that my new house is going up like winking, and I am dictating this letter to the accompaniment of saws and hammers. A hundred black boys and about a score draught-oxen perished, or at least barely

Also, in case Pitcairn does not come down late enough, I wish as full a report as possible of a Scotch murder trial between 1790–1820. Understand, *the fullest possible.*

Is there any book which would guide me as to the following facts?

The Justice-Clerk tries some people capitally on circuit. Certain evidence cropping up, the charge is transferred to the J.-C.'s own son. Of course, in the next trial the J.-C. is excluded, and the case is called before the Lord-Justice General.

Where would this trial have to be? I fear in Edinburgh, which would not suit my view. Could it be again at the circuit town?

ROBERT LOUIS STEVENSON.

TO MRS. FLEEMING JENKIN

December 5th, 1892.

MY DEAR MRS. JENKIN,—. . . So much said, I come with guilty speed to what more immediately concerns myself. Spare us a month or two for old sake's sake, and make my wife and me happy and proud. We are only fourteen days from San Francisco, just about a month from Liverpool; we have our new house almost finished. The thing *can* be done; I believe we can make you almost comfortable. It is the loveliest climate in the world, our political troubles seem near an end. It can be done, *it must!* Do, please, make a virtuous effort, come and take a glimpse of a new world I am sure you do not dream of, and some old friends who do often dream of your arrival.

Alas, I was just beginning to get eloquent, and there goes the lunch bell, and after lunch I must make up the mail.

Do come. You must not come in February or March — bad months. From April on it is delightful.—Your sincere friend, ROBERT LOUIS STEVENSON.

TO HENRY JAMES

December 5th, 1892.

MY DEAR JAMES,—How comes it so great a silence has fallen? The still small voice of self-approval whispers me it is not from me. I have looked up my register, and find I have neither written to you nor heard from you since June 22nd, on which day of grace that invaluable work began. This is not as it should be. How to get back? I remember acknowledging with rapture *The Lesson of the Master*, and I remember receiving *Marbot*: was that our last relation?

Hey, well! anyway, as you may have probably gathered from the papers, I have been in devilish hot water, and (what may be new to you) devilish hard at work. In twelve calendar months I finished *The Wrecker*, wrote all of *Falesá* but the first chapter (well, much of), the *History of Samoa*, did something here and there to my *Life of my Grandfather*, and began And Finished *David Balfour*. What do you think of it for a year? Since then I may say I have done nothing beyond draft three chapters of another novel, *The Justice-Clerk*, which

and re-read the Edinburgh Eleven, and had a great mind to write a parody and give you all your sauce back again, and see how you would like it yourself. And then I read (for the first time—I know not how) the *Window in Thrums;* I don't say that it is better than *The Minister;* it 's less of a tale—and there is a beauty, a material beauty, of the tale *ipse,* which clever critics nowadays long and love to forget; it has more real flaws; but somehow it is—well, I read it last anyway, and it 's by Barrie. And he 's the man for my money. The glove is a great page; it is startlingly original, and as true as death and judgment. Tibbie Birse in the Bur'al is great, but I think it was a journalist that got in the word "official." The same character plainly had a word to say to Thomas Haggard. Thomas affects me as a lie—I beg your pardon; doubtless he was somebody you knew, that leads people so far astray. The actual is not the true.

I am proud to think you are a Scotchman—though to be sure I know nothing of that country, being only an English tourist, quo' Gavin Ogilvy. I commend the hard case of Mr. Gavin Ogilvy to J. M. Barrie, whose work is to me a source of living pleasure and heartfelt national pride. There are two of us now that the Shirra might have patted on the head. And please do not think when I thus seem to bracket myself with you, that I am wholly blinded with vanity. Jess is beyond my frontier line; I could not touch her skirt; I have no such glamour of twilight on my pen. I am a capable artist; but it begins to look to me as if you were a man of genius. Take care of yourself for my sake. It 's a devilish hard thing for a man who writes so many novels as I do, that I should get so few to read. And I can read yours, and I love them.

A pity for you that my amanuensis is not on stock to-day, and my own hand perceptibly worse than usual.—Yours, ROBERT LOUIS STEVENSON.

December 5th, 1892.

P. S.—We have, for a wonder of wonders, visitors here. They tell me your health is not strong. Man, come out here and try the Prophet's chamber. There 's only one bad point to us—we do rise early. The Amanuensis states that you are a lover of silence—and that ours is a noisy house—and she is a chatterbox. I am not answerable for these statements, though I do think there is a touch of garrulity about my premises. We have so little to talk about, you see. The house is three miles from town, in the midst of great silent forests. There is a burn close by, and when we are not talking you can hear the burn, and the birds, and the sea breaking on the coast three miles away and six hundred feet below us, and about three times a month a bell—I don't know where the bell is, nor who rings it; it may be the bell in Hans Andersen's story for all I know. It is never hot here—86 in the shade is about our hottest—and it is never cold except just in the early mornings. Take it for all in all, I suppose this island climate to be by far the healthiest in the world—even the influenza entirely lost its sting. Only two patients died, and one was a man nearly eighty, and the other a child below four months. I won't tell you if it is beautiful, for I want you to come here and see for yourself. Everybody on the premises except my wife has some Scotch blood in

1892
ÆT. 42

their veins — I beg your pardon — except the natives — and then my wife is a Dutchwoman — and the natives are the next thing conceivable to Highlanders before the forty-five. We would have some grand cracks!

R. L. S.

COME, it will broaden your mind, and be the making of me.

XII

LIFE IN SAMOA

Continued

(January, 1893 – December, 1894)

XII

LIFE IN SAMOA

Continued

(JANUARY, 1893–DECEMBER, 1894)

FROM about the date of the last letter, that is, from the end of 1892, things began to go less fortunately for the exile of Vailima. The influenza did not pass away without leaving its usual weakening and depressing consequences. From a trip which the family took for the sake of change to Sydney, in February, 1893, they returned with health unimproved; and in April of the same year the illness of Mrs. Stevenson caused her husband some weeks of the gravest anxiety. In August he had the chagrin of witnessing the outbreak of war in the island, which he had vainly striven to prevent, and the defeat and banishment of Mataafa, in whom he believed as the one man of governing capacity among the native chiefs, and whom, in the interest alike of whites and natives, he had desired to see the Powers not crush, but conciliate. Later in the autumn of the same year he took a trip to Honolulu, where he had a renewed attack of influenza, and again underwent some weeks of fever and prostration. The only work he was able to finish during the year was *The Ebb Tide*, and that on a plan much abridged from his original intention; it remains an episode of ocean adventure and villainy, set forth indeed with extraordinary vividness and force, but lapsing, as its author was painfully aware, into that sin of ugliness which he himself most of all condemned in the art of his age. For the rest, he felt his power of work to be flagging. With *St. Ives* and his own family history he made indeed fair progress, but both of these he regarded as in a manner holiday tasks, not calling for any very serious exercise of his powers. He fell into arrears in regard to one or two magazine stories for which he had contracted, and with none of his more ambitious schemes of historical romance, *Sophia Scarlet, The Young Chevalier, Heathercat*, and *Weir of Hermiston*, did he feel himself well able to cope.

This state of things lasted through the spring and summer of 1894, and brought with it a considerable degree of inward strain and anxiety. He had not yet put by any provision for his wife and step-family (the income from the moderate fortune left by his father naturally going to his mother during her life). His gains from literature had since 1887 been considerable, at the rate of between £4000 and £5000 a year; but his hospitable, though in no sense extravagant, mode of life at Vailima, together with his habitual generosity, which scarce knew check or limit, towards the less fortunate among his friends and acquaintances in various parts of the world, made his expenditure about equal to his income. What if his power of earning were now to cease? The thought haunted him much during the last two years of his life, and its importunity was no doubt increased by some physical premonition that his vital powers, so frail from the cradle, and always with so cheerful a courage overtaxed, were near exhaustion. In the end, as all his readers know, they revived for one crowning effort upon *Weir of Hermiston;* and in that effort he fell. Some of the letters which follow give glimpses of the fits of depression and life-weariness which now at times assailed him. But it was only in writing, and then but rarely, that he let such signs appear. At the end of this book, as at the beginning, the reader must be warned, if he would form a faithful picture of the man, that at the touch of direct human intercourse the cast of gravity, nay, sadness, which was part of his character, and which will be found overshadowing his spirits in some of these letters, was at once and almost invariably dispersed. To those about him, whether visitors or inmates, he remained the impersonation of life and spirit, maintaining to the last the same charming gaiety as ever, the same happy eagerness in all pursuits and interests; and fulfilling without failure the words of his own prayer, "Give us to awake with smiles, give us to labour smiling. . . . As the sun lightens the world, so let our loving-kindness make bright this house of our habitation."

To Charles Baxter

1893
ÆT. 43

Of the books mentioned below, *Dr. Syntax's Tour* and Rowlandson's *Dance of Death* had been for use in furnishing customs and manners in the English part of *St. Ives;* "Pitcairn" is *Pitcairn's Criminal*

Trials of Scotland from 1488 to 1624. As to the name of Stevenson and its adoption by some members of the proscribed clan of Macgregor, Stevenson had been greatly interested by the facts laid before him by his correspondent here mentioned, Mr. Macgregor Stevenson of New York, and had at first delightedly welcomed the idea that his own ancestors might have been fellow clansmen of Rob Roy. But further correspondence on the subject of his own descent held with a trained genealogist, his namesake Mr. J. Horne Stevenson of Edinburgh, convinced him that the notion must be abandoned.

[*April, 1893.*]

. . . About *The Justice-Clerk*, I long to go at it, but will first try to get a short story done. Since January I have had two severe illnesses, my boy, and some heartbreaking anxiety over Fanny; and am only now convalescing. I came down to dinner last night for the first time, and that only because the service had broken down, and to relieve an inexperienced servant. Nearly four months now I have rested my brains; and if it be true that rest is good for brains, I ought to be able to pitch in like a giant refreshed. Before the autumn, I hope to send you some *Justice-Clerk*, or *Weir of Hermiston*, as Colvin seems to prefer; I own to indecision. Received *Syntax*, *Dance of Death*, and *Pitcairn*, which last I have read from end to end since its arrival, with vast improvement. What a pity it stops so soon! I wonder is there nothing that seems to prolong the series? Why does n't some young man take it up? How about my old friend Fountainhall's *Decisions?* I remember as a boy that there was some good reading there. Perhaps you could borrow me that, and send it on loan; and perhaps Laing's *Memorials* therewith; and a work I 'm ashamed to say I have never read, *Balfour's Letters*. . . . I have come by accident, through a correspondent, on one very curious and interesting fact—namely, that Stevenson was one of the names adopted by the Macgregors at the proscription. The details supplied by my correspondent are both convincing and amusing; but it would be highly interesting to find out more of this. R. L. S.

1893
ÆT. 43

TO A. CONAN DOYLE

The reference in the postscript here is, I believe, to the Journals of the Society for Psychical Research.

VAILIMA, APIA, SAMOA, *April 5th, 1893.*

DEAR SIR,—You have taken many occasions to make yourself very agreeable to me, for which I might in decency have thanked you earlier. It is now my turn; and I hope you will allow me to offer you my compliments on your very ingenious and very interesting adventures of Sherlock Holmes. That is the class of literature that I like when I have the toothache. As a matter of fact, it was a pleurisy I was enjoying when I took the volume up; and it will interest you as a medical man to know that the cure was for the moment effectual. Only the one thing troubles me: can this be my old friend Joe Bell?—I am, yours very truly,

ROBERT LOUIS STEVENSON.

P. S.—And lo, here is your address supplied me here in Samoa! But do not take mine, O frolic fellow Spookist, from the same source; mine is wrong.

R. L. S.

1893
ÆT. 43

To S. R. Crockett

Glencorse Church in the Pentlands, mentioned by Stevenson with so much emotion in the course of this letter, served him for the scene of Chapter VI. in *Weir of Hermiston*, where his old associations and feelings in connection with the place have so admirably inspired him.

Vailima, Samoa, *May 17th, 1893.*

DEAR MR. CROCKETT,—I do not owe you two letters, nor yet nearly one, sir! The last time I heard of you, you wrote about an accident, and I sent you a letter to my lawyer, Charles Baxter, which does not seem to have been presented, as I see nothing of it in his accounts. Query, was that lost? I should not like you to think I had been so unmannerly and so inhuman. If you have written since, your letter also has miscarried, as is much the rule in this part of the world, unless you register.

Your book is not yet to hand, but will probably follow next month. I detected you early in the *Bookman*, which I usually see, and noted you in particular as displaying a monstrous ingratitude about the foot-note. Well, mankind is ungrateful; "Man's ingratitude to man makes countless thousands mourn," quo' Rab—or words to that effect. By the way, an anecdote of a cautious sailor: "Bill, Bill," says I to him, "*or words to that effect.*"

I shall never take that walk by the Fisher's Tryst and Glencorse. I shall never see Auld Reekie. I shall never set my foot again upon the heather. Here I am until I die, and here will I be buried. The word is out and the doom written. Or, if I do come, it will be a voyage to a further goal, and in fact a suicide; which, however, if I could get my family all fixed up in the money way, I might, perhaps, perform, or attempt. But there is a plaguey risk of breaking down by the way; and I believe I shall stay here until the end comes like a good boy, as I am. If I did it, I should put upon my trunks: "Passenger to — Hades."

How strangely wrong your information is! In the first place, I should never carry a novel to Sydney; I should post it from here. In the second place, *Weir of Hermiston* is as yet scarce begun. It 's going to be excellent, no doubt; but it consists of about twenty pages. I have a tale, a shortish tale in length, but it has proved long to do, *The Ebb Tide*, some part of which goes home this mail. It is by me and Mr. Osbourne, and is really a singular work. There are only four characters, and three of them are bandits — well, two of them are, and the third is their comrade and accomplice. It sounds cheering, does n't it? Barratry, and drunkenness, and vitriol, and I cannot tell you all what, are the beams of the roof. And yet — I don't know — I sort of think there 's something in it. You 'll see (which is more than I ever can) whether Davis and Attwater come off or not.

Weir of Hermiston is a much greater undertaking, and the plot is not good, I fear; but Lord Justice Clerk Hermiston ought to be a plum. Of other schemes, more or less executed, it skills not to speak.

I am glad to hear so good an account of your activity and interests, and shall always hear from you with pleasure; though I am, and must continue, a mere sprite of the inkbottle, unseen in the flesh. Please

1893
ÆT. 43

remember me to your wife and to the four-year-old sweetheart, if she be not too engrossed with higher matters. Do you know where the road crosses the burn under Glencorse Church? Go there, and say a prayer for me: *moriturus salutat.* See that it 's a sunny day; I would like it to be a Sunday, but that 's not possible in the premises; and stand on the right-hand bank just where the road goes down into the water, and shut your eyes, and if I don't appear to you! well, it can't be helped, and will be extremely funny.

I have no concern here but to work and to keep an eye on this distracted people. I live just now wholly alone in an upper room of my house, because the whole family are down with influenza, bar my wife and myself. I get my horse up sometimes in the afternoon and have a ride in the woods; and I sit here and smoke and write, and rewrite, and destroy, and rage at my own impotence, from six in the morning till eight at night, with trifling and not always agreeable intervals for meals.

I am sure you chose wisely to keep your country charge. There a minister can be something, not in a town. In a town, the most of them are empty houses — and public speakers. Why should you suppose your book will be slated because you have no friends? A new writer, if he is any good, will be acclaimed generally with more noise than he deserves. But by this time you will know for certain.—I am, yours sincerely,

ROBERT LOUIS STEVENSON.

P. S.—Be it known to this fluent generation that I,

R. L. S., in the forty-third of my age and the twentieth of my professional life, wrote twenty-four pages in twenty-one days, working from six to eleven, and again in the afternoon from two to four or so, without fail or interruption. Such are the gifts the gods have endowed us withal: such was the facility of this prolific writer! R. L. S.

To Augustus St. Gaudens

Vailima, Samoa, *May 29th, 1893.*

MY DEAR GOD-LIKE SCULPTOR,—I wish in the most delicate manner in the world to insinuate a few commissions:—

No. 1. Is for a couple of copies of my medallion, as gilt-edged and high-toned as it is possible to make them. One is for our house here, and should be addressed as above. The other is for my friend Sidney Colvin, and should be addressed—Sidney Colvin, Esq., Keeper of the Print Room, British Museum, London.

No. 2. This is a rather large order, and demands some explanation. Our house is lined with varnished wood of a dark ruddy colour, very beautiful to see; at the same time, it calls very much for gold; there is a limit to picture frames, and really you know there has to be a limit to the pictures you put inside of them. Accordingly, we have had an idea of a certain kind of decoration, which, I think, you might help us to make practical. What we want is an alphabet of gilt letters (very much such as people play with), and all mounted on spikes like drawing-pins; say two spikes to each letter, one at top, and one at bottom. Say that they were this height, I and that you chose a model of some really exquisitely fine, clear type from some Roman monument, and that they were made either of metal or some composition gilt—the point is, could not you, in your land of wooden houses, get a manufacturer to take the idea and manufacture them at a venture, so that I could get two or three hundred pieces or so at a moderate figure? You see, suppose you entertain an honoured guest, when he goes he leaves his name in gilt letters on your walls; an infinity of fun and decoration can be got out of hospitable and festive mottoes; and the doors of every room can be beautified by the legend of their names. I really think there is something in the idea, and you might be able to push it with the brutal and licentious manufacturer, using my name if necessary, though I should think the name of the godlike sculptor would be more germane. In case you should get it started, I should tell you that we should require commas in order to write the Samoan language, which is full of words written thus: la'u, ti'e ti'e. As the Samoan language uses but a very small proportion of the consonants, we should require a double or treble stock of all vowels and of F, G, L, U, N, P, S, T, and V.

The other day in Sydney, I think you might be interested to hear, I was sculpt a second time by a man called ——, as well as I can remember and read. I must n't criticise a present, and he had very little time to do it in. It is thought by my family to be an excellent likeness of Mark Twain. This poor fellow, by the by, met with the devil of an accident. A model of a statue which he had just finished with a desperate effort was smashed to smithereens on its way to exhibition.

Please be sure and let me know if anything is likely to come of this letter business, and the exact cost of each letter, so that I may count the cost before ordering.—Yours sincerely,

ROBERT LOUIS STEVENSON.

TO EDMUND GOSSE

"My Grandfather" in the following means not the *Scribner* paper already several times referred to, but the chapters on Robert Stevenson in the projected book of family memoirs, variously called *Northern Lights*, *History of the Stevensons*, and finally *History of a Family of Engineers*.

June 10th, 1893.

MY DEAR GOSSE,—My mother tells me you never received the very long and careful letter that I sent you more than a year ago; or is it two years?

I was indeed so much surprised at your silence that I wrote to Henry James and begged him to inquire if you had received it; his reply was an (if possible) higher power of the same silence; whereupon I bowed my head and acquiesced. But there is no doubt the letter was written and sent; and I am sorry it was lost, for it contained, among other things, an irrecoverable criticism of your father's *Life*, with a number of suggestions for another edition, which struck me at the time as excellent.

1893
ÆT. 43

But that is an old story, ever new with me. Taine gone, and Renan, and Symonds, and Tennyson, and Browning; the suns go swiftly out, and I see no suns to follow, nothing but a universal twilight of the demi-divinities, with parties like you and me and Lang beating on toy drums and playing on penny whistles about glow-worms. But Zola is big anyway; he has plenty in his belly; too much, that is all; he wrote the *Débâcle* and he wrote *La Bête Humaine*, perhaps the most excruciatingly silly book that I ever read to an end. And why did I read it to an end, W. E. G.? Because the animal in me was interested in the lewdness. Not sincerely, of course, my mind refusing to partake in it; but the flesh was slightly pleased. And when it was done, I cast it from me with a peal of laughter, and forgot it, as I would forget a Montépin. Taine is to me perhaps the chief of these losses; I did luxuriate in his *Origines;* it was something beyond literature, not quite so good, if you please, but so much more systematic, and the pages that had to be "written" always so adequate. Robespierre, Napoleon, were both excellent good.

June 18th, '93.

Well, I have left fiction wholly, and gone to my *Grandfather*, and on the whole found peace. By next month my *Grandfather* will begin to be quite grown up. I have already three chapters about as good as done; by which, of course, as you know, I mean till further notice or the next discovery. I like biography far better than fiction myself: fiction is too free. In biography you have your little handful of facts, little bits of a puzzle, and you sit and think, and fit 'em together this way and that, and get up and throw 'em down, and say damn, and go out for a walk. And it 's real soothing; and when done, gives an idea of finish to the writer that is very peaceful. Of course, it 's not really so finished as quite a rotten novel; it always has and always must have the incurable illogicalities of life about it, the fathoms of slack and the miles of tedium. Still, that 's where the fun comes in; and when you have at last managed to shut up the castle spectre (dulness), the very outside of his door looks beautiful by contrast. There are pages in these books that may seem nothing to the reader; but you *remember what they were, you know what they might have been,* and they seem to you witty beyond comparison. In my *Grandfather* I 've had (for instance) to give up the temporal order almost entirely; doubtless the temporal order is the great foe of the biographer; it is so tempting, so easy, and lo! there you are in the bog!—Ever yours,

R. L. STEVENSON.

With all kind messages from self and wife to you and yours. My wife is very much better, having been the early part of this year alarmingly ill. She is now all right, only complaining of trifles, annoying to her, but happily not interesting to her friends. I am in a hideous state, having stopped drink and smoking; yes, both. No wine, no tobacco; and the dreadful part of it is that—looking forward—I have—what shall I say?—nauseating intimations that it ought to be for ever.

1893
ÆT. 43

To Henry James

Vailima Plantation, Samoan Islands,
June 17th, 1893.

MY DEAR HENRY JAMES,—I believe I have neglected a mail in answering yours. You will be very sorry to hear that my wife was exceedingly ill, and very glad to hear that she is better. I cannot say that I feel any more anxiety about her. We shall send you a photograph of her taken in Sydney in her customary island habit as she walks and gardens and shrilly drills her brown assistants. She was very ill when she sat for it, which may a little explain the appearance of the photograph. It reminds me of a friend of my grandmother's who used to say when talking to younger women, "Aweel, when I was young, I wasnae just exactly what ye wad call *bonny*, but I was pale, penetratin', and interestin'." I would not venture to hint that Fanny is "no bonny," but there is no doubt but that in this presentment she is "pale, penetratin', and interestin'."

As you are aware, I have been wading deep waters and contending with the great ones of the earth, not wholly without success. It is, you may be interested to hear, a dreary and infuriating business. If you can get the fools to admit one thing, they will always save their face by denying another. If you can induce them to take a step to the right hand, they generally indemnify themselves by cutting a caper to the left. I always held (upon no evidence whatever, from a mere sentiment or intuition) that politics was the dirtiest, the most foolish, and the most random of human employments. I always held, but now I know it! Fortunately, you have nothing to do with anything of the kind, and I may spare you the horror of further details.

I received from you a book by a man by the name of Anatole France. Why should I disguise it? I have no use for Anatole. He writes very prettily, and then afterwards? Baron Marbot was a different pair of shoes. So likewise is the Baron de Vitrolles, whom I am now perusing with delight. His escape in 1814 is one of the best pages I remember anywhere to have read. But Marbot and Vitrolles are dead, and what has become of the living? It seems as if literature were coming to a stand. I am sure it is with me; and I am sure everybody will say so when they have the privilege of reading *The Ebb Tide.* My dear man, the grimness of that story is not to be depicted in words. There are only four characters, to be sure, but they are such a troop of swine! And their behaviour is really so deeply beneath any possible standard, that on a retrospect I wonder I have been able to endure them myself until the yarn was finished. Well, there is always one thing; it will serve as a touchstone. If the admirers of Zola admire him for his pertinent ugliness and pessimism, I think they should admire this; but if, as I have long suspected, they neither admire nor understand the man's art, and only wallow in his rancidness like a hound in offal, then they will certainly be disappointed in *The Ebb Tide.* Alas! poor little tale, it is not *even* rancid.

By way of an antidote or febrifuge, I am going on at

a great rate with my *History of the Stevensons,* which I hope may prove rather amusing in some parts at least. The excess of materials weighs upon me. My grandfather is a delightful comedy part; and I have to treat him besides as a serious and (in his way) a heroic figure, and at times I lose my way, and I fear in the end will blur the effect. However, *à la grâce de Dieu!* I 'll make a spoon or spoil a horn. You see, I have to do the Building of the Bell Rock by cutting down and packing my grandsire's book, which I rather hope I have done, but do not know. And it makes a huge chunk of a very different style and quality between Chapters II. and IV. And it can't be helped! It is just a delightful and exasperating necessity. You know, the stuff is really excellent narrative: only, perhaps there 's too much of it! There is the rub. Well, well, it will be plain to you that my mind is affected; it might be with less. *The Ebb Tide* and *Northern Lights* are a full meal for any plain man.

I have written and ordered your last book, *The Real Thing,* so be sure and don't send it. What else are you doing or thinking of doing? News I have none, and don't want any. I have had to stop all strong drink and all tobacco, and am now in a transition state between the two, which seems to be near madness. You never smoked, I think, so you can never taste the joys of stopping it. But at least you have drunk, and you can enter perhaps into my annoyance when I suddenly find a glass of claret or a brandy-and-water give me a splitting headache the next morning. No mistake about it; drink anything, and there 's your headache. Tobacco just as bad for me. If I live through this breach of habit, I shall be a white-livered puppy indeed. Actually I am so made, or so twisted, that I do not like to think of a life without the red wine on the table and the tobacco with its lovely little coal of fire. It does n't amuse me from a distance. I may find it the Garden of Eden when I go in, but I don't like the colour of the gate-posts. Suppose somebody said to you, you are to leave your home, and your books, and your clubs, and go out and camp in mid-Africa, and command an expedition, you would howl, and kick, and flee. I think the same of a life without wine and tobacco; and if this goes on, I 've got to go and do it, sir, in the living flesh!

I thought Bourget was a friend of yours? And I thought the French were a polite race? He has taken my dedication with a stately silence that has surprised me into apoplexy. Did I go and dedicate my book[1] to the nasty alien, and the 'norrid Frenchman, and the Bloody Furrineer? Well, I would n't do it again; and unless his case is susceptible of explanation, you might perhaps tell him so over the walnuts and the wine, by way of speeding the gay hours. Sincerely, I thought my dedication worth a letter.

If anything be worth anything here below! Do you know the story of the man who found a button in his hash, and called the waiter? "What do you call that?" says he. "Well," said the waiter, "what d' you expect? Expect to find a gold watch and chain?" Heavenly apologue, is it not? I expected (rather) to find a gold watch and chain; I expected to be able to smoke to excess and drink to comfort all the

[1] *Across the Plains.*

1893 ÆT. 43 days of my life; and I am still indignantly staring on this button! It 's not even a button; it 's a teetotal badge!—Ever yours, ROBERT LOUIS STEVENSON.

To Henry James

APIA, *July, 1893.*

MY DEAR HENRY JAMES,—Yes. *Les Trophées*[1] is, on the whole, a book. It is excellent; but is it a life's work? I always suspect *you* of a volume of sonnets up your sleeve; when is it coming down? I am in one of my moods of wholesale impatience with all fiction and all verging on it, reading instead, with rapture, *Fountainhall's Decisions.* You never read it: well, it has n't much form, and is inexpressibly dreary, I should suppose, to others—and even to me for pages. It 's like walking in a mine underground, and with a damned bad lantern, and picking out pieces of ore. This, and war, will be my excuse for not having read your (doubtless) charming work of fiction. The revolving year will bring me round to it; and I know, when fiction shall begin to feel a little *solid* to me again, that I shall love it, because it 's James. Do you know, when I am in this mood, I would rather try to read a bad book? It 's not so disappointing, anyway. And *Fountainhall* is prime, two big folio volumes, and all dreary, and all true, and all as terse as an obituary; and about one interesting fact on an average in twenty pages, and ten of them unintelligible for technicalities. There 's literature, if you like! It feeds; it falls about you genuine

[1] Volume of sonnets by Joseph-Marie de Hérédia.

like rain. Rain: nobody has done justice to rain in literature yet: surely a subject for a Scot. But then you can't do rain in that ledger-book style that I am trying for—or between a ledger-book and an old ballad. How to get over, how to escape from, the besotting *particularity* of fiction. "Roland approached the house; it had green doors and window blinds; and there was a scraper on the upper step." To hell with Roland and the scraper!—Yours ever, R. L. S.

To A. Conan Doyle

Vailima, *July 12, 1893.*

MY DEAR DR. CONAN DOYLE,—*The White Company* has not yet turned up; but when it does—which I suppose will be next mail—you shall hear news of me. I have a great talent for compliment, accompanied by a hateful, even a diabolic frankness.

Delighted to hear I have a chance of seeing you and Mrs. Doyle; Mrs. Stevenson bids me say (what is too true) that our rations are often spare. Are you Great Eaters? Please reply.

As to ways and means, here is what you will have to do. Leave San Francisco by the down mail, get off at Samoa, and twelve days or a fortnight later you can continue your journey to Auckland per Upolu, which will give you a look at Tonga and possibly Fiji by the way. Make this a *first part of your plans.*

We are in the midst of war here; rather a nasty business, with the head-taking; and there seem signs of other trouble. But I believe you need make no

1893
ÆT. 43

change in your design to visit us. All should be well over; and if it were not, why! you need not leave the steamer.—Yours very truly,

ROBERT LOUIS STEVENSON.

To Charles Baxter

19th July, '93.

. . . We are in the thick of war—see *Illustrated London News*—we have only two outside boys left to us. Nothing is doing, and *per contra* little paying. . . . My life here is dear; but I can live within my income for a time at least—so long as my prices keep up—and it seems a clear duty to waste none of it on gadding about. . . . My life of my family fills up intervals, and should be an excellent book when it is done, but big, damnably big.

My dear old man, I perceive by a thousand signs that we grow old, and are soon to pass away; I hope with dignity; if not, with courage at least. I am myself very ready; or would be—will be—when I have made a little money for my folks. The blows that have fallen upon you are truly terrifying; I wish you strength to bear them. It is strange, I must seem to you to blaze in a Birmingham prosperity and happiness; and to myself I seem a failure. The truth is, I have never got over the last influenza yet, and am miserably out of heart and out of kilter. Lungs pretty right, stomach nowhere, spirits a good deal overshadowed; but we'll come through it yet, and cock our bonnets. (I confess with sorrow that I am not yet quite sure about the *in-*

tellects; but I hope it is only one of my usual periods of non-work. They are more unbearable now, because I cannot rest. *No rest but the grave for Sir Walter!* O, the words ring in a man's head.) R. L. S.

To A. Conan Doyle

Vailima, *August 23rd, 1893.*

MY DEAR DR. CONAN DOYLE,—I am reposing after a somewhat severe experience upon which I think it my duty to report to you. Immediately after dinner this evening it occurred to me to re-narrate to my native overseer Simalè your story of *The Engineer's Thumb.* And, sir, I have done it. It was necessary, I need hardly say, to go somewhat farther afield than you have done. To explain (for instance) what a railway is, what a steam hammer, what a coach and horse, what coining, what a criminal, and what the police. I pass over other and no less necessary explanations. But I did actually succeed; and if you could have seen the drawn, anxious features and the bright, feverish eyes of Simalè, you would have (for the moment at least) tasted glory. You might perhaps think that, were you to come to Samoa, you might be introduced as the Author of *The Engineer's Thumb.* Disabuse yourself. They do not know what it is to make up a story. *The Engineer's Thumb* (God forgive me) was narrated as a piece of actual and factual history. Nay, and more, I who write to you have had the indiscretion to perpetuate a trifling piece of fiction entitled *The Bottle Imp.* Parties who come up to visit my unpretentious mansion, after having admired the ceilings by Vanderputty and the tapestry by Gobbling, manifest towards the end a certain uneasiness which proves them to be fellows of an infinite delicacy. They may be seen to shrug a brown shoulder, to roll up a speaking eye, and at last the secret bursts from them: "Where is the bottle?" Alas, my friends (I feel tempted to say), you will find it by the Engineer's Thumb! Talofa-soifuia.

Oaie, O lau no moni, O Tusitala.

More commonly known as R. L. STEVENSON.

Have read *The Refugees;* Condé and old P. Murat very good; Louis XIV. and Louvois with the letter-bag very rich. You have reached a trifle wide perhaps; too *many* celebrities? Though I was delighted to re-encounter my old friend Du Chaylu. Old Murat is perhaps your high-water mark; 't is excellently human, cheerful, and real. Do it again. Madame de Maintenon struck me as quite good. Have you any document for the decapitation? It sounds steepish. The devil of all that first part is that you see old Dumas; yet your Louis XIV. is *distinctly good.* I am much interested with this book, which fulfils a good deal, and promises more. Question: how far a Historical Novel should be wholly episodic? I incline to that view, with trembling. I shake hands with you on old Murat. R. L. S.

To George Meredith

September 5th, 1893,
VAILIMA PLANTATION, UPOLU, SAMOA.

MY DEAR MEREDITH,—I have again and again taken up the pen to write to you, and many beginnings have gone into the waste paper basket (I have one now—for the second time in my life—and feel a big man on the strength of it). And no doubt it requires some decision to break so long a silence. My health is vastly restored, and I am now living patriarchally in this place six hundred feet above the sea on the shoulder of a mountain of 1500. Behind me, the unbroken bush slopes up to the backbone of the island (3 to 4000) without a house, with no inhabitants save a few runaway black boys, wild pigs and cattle, and wild doves and flying foxes, and many parti-coloured birds, and many black, and many white: a very eerie, dim, strange place and hard to travel. I am the head of a household of five whites, and of twelve Samoans, to all of whom I am the chief and father: my cook comes to me and asks leave to marry—and his mother, a fine old chief woman, who has never lived here, does the same. You may be sure I granted the petition. It is a life of great interest, complicated by the Tower of Babel, that old enemy. And I have all the time on my hands for literary work. My house is a great place; we have a hall fifty feet long with a great red-wood stair ascending from it, where we dine in state—myself usually dressed in a singlet and a pair of trousers—and attended on by servants in a single garment, a kind of kilt — also flowers and leaves — and their hair often powdered with lime. The European who came upon it suddenly would think it was a dream. We have prayers on Sunday night — I am a perfect pariah in the island not to have them oftener, but the spirit is unwilling and the flesh proud, and I cannot go it more. It is strange to see the long line of the brown folk crouched along the wall with lanterns at intervals before them in the big shadowy hall, with an oak cabinet at one end of it and a group of Rodin's (which native taste regards as *prodigieusement leste*) presiding over all from the top — and to hear the long rambling Samoan hymn rolling up (God bless me, what style! But I am off business to-day, and this is not meant to be literature).

I have asked Colvin to send you a copy of *Catriona*, which I am sometimes tempted to think is about my best work. I hear word occasionally of the *Amazing Marriage*. It will be a brave day for me when I get hold of it. Gower Woodsere is now an ancient, lean, grim, exiled Scot, living and labouring as for a wager in the tropics; still active, still with lots of fire in him, but the youth — ah, the youth, where is it? For years after I came here, the critics (those genial gentlemen) used to deplore the relaxation of my fibre and the idleness to which I had succumbed. I hear less of this now; the next thing is they will tell me I am writing myself out! and that my unconscientious conduct is bringing their grey hairs with sorrow to the dust. I do not know — I mean I do know one thing. For fourteen years I have not had a day's real health; I have wakened sick and gone to bed weary; and I have done my work unflinchingly. I have written in bed, and written out of it, written in hemorrhages, written in sickness, written torn by coughing, written when my head swam for weakness; and for so long, it seems to me I have won my wager and recovered my glove. I am better now; have been, rightly speaking, since first I came to the Pacific; and still, few are the days when I am not in some physical distress. And the battle goes on — ill or well, is a trifle; so as it goes. I was made for a contest, and the Powers have so willed that my battle-field should be this dingy, inglorious one of the bed and the physic bottle. At least I have not failed, but I would have preferred a place of trumpetings, and the open air over my head.

This is a devilish egotistical yarn. Will you try to imitate me in that if the spirit ever moves you to reply? And meantime be sure that way in the midst of the Pacific there is a house on a wooded island where the name of George Meredith is very dear, and his memory (since it must be no more) is continually honoured.—Ever your friend,

ROBERT LOUIS STEVENSON.

Remember me to Mariette, if you please; and my wife sends her most kind remembrances to yourself.

R. L. S.

To Augustus St. Gaudens

Mr. St. Gaudens's large medallion portrait in bronze, executed from sittings given in 1887, had at last found its way to Apia, but not yet to Vailima.

Vailima, *September, 1893.*

MY DEAR ST. GAUDENS,—I had determined not to write to you till I had seen the medallion, but it looks as if that might mean the Greek Kalends or the day after to-morrow. Reassure yourself, your part is done, it is ours that halts—the consideration of conveyance over our sweet little road on boys' backs, for we cannot very well apply the horses to this work; there is only one; you cannot put it in a panier; to put it on the horse's back we have not the heart. Beneath the beauty of R. L. S., to say nothing of his verses, which the publishers find heavy enough, and the genius of the god-like sculptor, the spine would snap and the well-knit limbs of the (ahem) cart-horse would be loosed by death. So you are to conceive me, sitting in my house, dubitative, and the medallion chuckling in the warehouse of the German firm, for some days longer; and hear me meanwhile on the golden letters.

Alas, they are all my fancy painted, but the price is prohibitive. I cannot do it. It is another day-dream burst. Another gable of Abbotsford has gone down, fortunately before it was builded, so there 's nobody injured—except me. I had a strong conviction that I was a great hand at writing inscriptions, and meant to exhibit and test my genius on the walls of my house; and now I see I can't. It is generally thus. The Battle of the Golden Letters will never be delivered. On making preparation to open the campaign, the King found himself face to face with invincible difficulties, in which the rapacity of a mercenary soldiery and the complaints of an impoverished treasury played an equal part.—Ever yours,

ROBERT LOUIS STEVENSON.

I enclose a bill for the medallion; have been trying to find your letter, quite in vain, and therefore must request you to pay for the bronze letters yourself and let me know the damage. R. L. S.

TO J. HORNE STEVENSON

The following refers to the introduction to the history of his own family which Stevenson was then preparing under the title "A Family of Engineers," and which remained in a fragmentary condition at his death. I give this letter as a sample of many which passed between the two namesakes on this subject; omitting the remainder as too technical to be of general interest.

VAILIMA, SAMOA, *November 5th, 1893.*

MY DEAR STEVENSON,—A thousand thanks for your voluminous and delightful collections. Baxter—so soon as it is ready—will let you see a proof of my introduction, which is only sent out as a sprat to catch whales. And you will find I have a good deal

1893 ÆT. 43

of what you have, only mine in a perfectly desultory manner, as is necessary to an exile. My uncle's pedigree is wrong; there was never a Stevenson of Caldwell, of course, but they were tenants of the Muirs; the farm held by them is in my introduction; and I have already written to Charles Baxter to have a search made in the Register House. I hope he will have had the inspiration to put it under your surveillance. Your information as to your own family is intensely interesting, and I should not wonder but what you and we and old John Stevenson, "land labourer in the parish of Dailly," came all of the same stock. Ayrshire — and probably Cunningham — seems to be the home of the race — our part of it. From the distribution of the name — which your collections have so much extended without essentially changing my knowledge of — we seem rather pointed to a British origin. What you say of the Engineers is fresh to me, and must be well thrashed out. This introduction of it will take a long while to walk about! — as perhaps I may be tempted to let it become long; after all, I am writing *this* for my own pleasure solely. Greetings to you and other Speculatives of our date, long bygone, alas! — Yours very sincerely,

ROBERT LOUIS STEVENSON.

P. S. — I have a different version of my grandfather's arms — or my father had if I could find it. R. L. S.

To John P——n

The next two numbers are in answer to letters of appreciation received from two small boys in England, whose mother desires that they should remain nameless.

Vailima, Samoa, *December 3rd, 1893.*

DEAR JOHNNIE,—Well, I must say you seem to be a tremendous fellow! Before I was eight I used to write stories—or dictate them at least—and I had produced an excellent history of Moses, for which I got £1 from an uncle; but I had never gone the length of a play, so you have beaten me fairly on my own ground. I hope you may continue to do so, and thanking you heartily for your nice letter, I shall beg you to believe me yours truly,

Robert Louis Stevenson.

To Russell P——n

Vailima, Samoa, *December 3rd, 1893.*

DEAR RUSSELL,—I have to thank you very much for your capital letter, which came to hand here in Samoa along with your mother's. When you "grow up and write stories like me," you will be able to understand that there is scarce anything more painful than for an author to hold a pen; he has to do it so

1893 ÆT. 43

MY DEAR CHARLES,—The above is my story, and I wonder if any light can be thrown on it. I prefer the girl's father dead; and the question is, How in that case could Lieutenant George Murray get his order to "apprehend" and his power to "sell" her in marriage?

Or—might Lieutenant G. be her tutor, and she fugitive to the Pringles, and on the discovery of her whereabouts hastily married?

A good legal note on these points is very ardently desired by me; it will be the corner-stone of my novel.

This is for—I am quite wrong to tell you—for you will tell others—and nothing will teach you that all my schemes are in the air, and vanish and reappear again like shapes in the clouds—it is for *Heathercat:* whereof the first volume will be called *The Killing Time,* and I believe I have authorities ample for that. But the second volume is to be called (I believe) *Darien,* and for that I want, I fear, a good deal of truck:—

Darien Papers,
Carstairs Papers,
Marchmont Papers,
Jerviswoode Correspondence,

I hope may do me. Some sort of general history of the Darien affair (if there is a decent one, which I misdoubt), it would also be well to have—the one with most details, if possible. It is singular how obscure to me this decade of Scots history remains, 1690–1700—a deuce of a want of light and grouping to it! However, I believe I shall be mostly out of Scotland in my tale; first in Carolina, next in Darien. I want also—I am the daughter of the horse-leech truly — "Black's new large map of Scotland," sheets 3, 4, and 5, a 7*s.* 6*d.* touch. I believe, if you can get the

Caldwell Papers,

they had better come also; and if there be any reasonable work — but no, I must call a halt. . . .

I fear the song looks doubtful, but I 'll consider of it, and I can promise you some reminiscences which it will amuse me to write, whether or not it will amuse the public to read of them. But it 's an unco business to supply deid-heid coapy.

To J. M. Barrie

VAILIMA, SAMOA, *December 7th, 1893.*

MY DEAR BARRIE,— I have received duly the *magnum opus*, and it really is a *magnum opus.*[1] It is a beautiful specimen of Clark's printing, paper sufficient, and the illustrations all my fancy painted. But the particular flower of the flock to whom I have hopelessly lost my heart is Tibby Birse. I must have known Tibby Birse when she was a servant's mantua-maker in Edinburgh and answered to the name of Miss *Broddie.* She used to come and sew with my nurse, sitting with her legs crossed in a masculine manner; and swinging her foot emphatically, she used to pour forth a perfectly un-

[1] *A Window in Thrums*, with illustrations by W. Hole, R. S. A. (Hodder & Stoughton, 1892).

1893
ÆT. 43

broken stream of gossip. I did n't hear it, I was immersed in far more important business with a box of bricks, but the recollection of that thin, perpetual, shrill sound of a voice has echoed in my ears sinsyne. I am bound to say she was younger than Tibbie, but there is no mistaking that and the indescribable and eminently Scottish expression.

I have been very much prevented of late, having carried out thoroughly to my own satisfaction two considerable illnesses, had a birthday, and visited Honolulu, where politics are (if possible) a shade more exasperating than they are with us. I am told that it was just when I was on the point of leaving that I received your superlative epistle about the cricket eleven. In that case it is impossible I should have answered it, which is inconsistent with my own recollection of the fact. What *I* remember is that I sat down under your immediate inspiration and wrote an answer in every way worthy. If I did n't, as it seems proved that I could n't, it will never be done now. However, I did the next best thing, I equipped my cousin Graham Balfour with a letter of introduction, and from him, if you know how — for he is rather of the Scottish character — you may elicit all the information you can possibly wish to have as to us and ours. Do not be bluffed off by the somewhat stern and monumental first impression that he may make upon you. He is one of the best fellows in the world, and the same sort of fool that we are, only better-looking, with all the faults of Vailimans and some of his own — I say nothing about virtues.

I have lately been returning to my wallowing in the mire. When I was a child, and indeed until I was nearly a man, I consistently read Covenanting books. Now that I am a greybeard — or would be, if I could raise the beard — I have returned, and for weeks back have read little else but Wodrow, Walker, Shields, etc. Of course this is with an idea of a novel, but in the course of it I made a very curious discovery. I have been accustomed to hear refined and intelligent critics — those who know so much better what we are than we do ourselves, those who tell us it is time to stop working in I and to work it B.C. — trace down my literary descent from all sorts of people, including Addison, of whom I could never read a word. Well, laigh i' your lug, sir — the clue was found. My style is from the Covenanting writers. Take a particular case — the fondness for rhymes. I don't know of any English prose-writer who rhymes except by accident, and then a stone had better be tied around his neck and himself cast into the sea. But my Covenanting buckies rhyme all the time — a beautiful example of the unconscious rhyme above referred to.

Do you know, and have you really tasted, these delightful works? If not, it should be remedied; there is enough of the Auld Licht in you to be ravished.

I suppose you know that success has so far attended my banners — my political banners I mean, and not my literary. In conjunction with the Three Great Powers I have succeeded in getting rid of My President and My Chief-Justice. They 've gone home, the one to Germany, the other to Souwegia. I hear little echoes of footfalls of their departing footsteps through the medium of the newspapers. . . .

Whereupon I make you my salute with the firm remark that it is time to be done with trifling and give us a great book, and my ladies fall into line with me to pay you a most respectful courtesy, and we all join in the cry, "Come to Vailima!"

My dear sir, your soul's health is in it—you will never do the great book, you will never cease to work in L., etc., till you come to Vailima.

ROBERT LOUIS STEVENSON.

TO RICHARD LE GALLIENNE

VAILIMA, SAMOA, *December 28th, 1893.*

DEAR MR. LE GALLIENNE,—I have received some time ago, through our friend Miss Taylor, a book of yours. But that was by no means my first introduction to your name. The same book had stood already on my shelves; I had read articles of yours in the *Academy;* and by a piece of constructive criticism (which I trust was sound) had arrived at the conclusion that you were Log-roller. Since then I have seen your beautiful verses to your wife. You are to conceive me, then, as only too ready to make the acquaintance of a man who loved good literature and could make it. I had to thank you, besides, for a triumphant exposure of a paradox of my own: the literary-prostitute disappeared from view at a phrase of yours—"The essence is not in the pleasure but the sale." True: you are right, I was wrong; the author is not the whore, but the libertine; and yet I shall let the passage stand. It is an error, but it illustrated the truth for which I was contending, that literature — painting — all art, are no other than pleasures, which we turn into trades.

And more than all this, I had and I have to thank you for the intimate loyalty you have shown to myself; for the eager welcome you give to what is good — for the courtly tenderness with which you touch on my defects. I begin to grow old; I have given my top note, I fancy;— and I have written too many books. The world begins to be weary of the old booth; and if not weary, familiar with the familiarity that breeds contempt. I do not know that I am sensitive to criticism, if it be hostile; I am sensitive indeed, when it is friendly; and when I read such criticism as yours, I am emboldened to go on and praise God.

You are still young, and you may live to do much. The little, artificial popularity of style in England tends, I think, to die out; the British pig returns to his true love, the love of the styleless, of the shapeless, of the slapdash and the disorderly. There is trouble coming, I think; and you may have to hold the fort for us in evil days.

Lastly, let me apologise for the crucifixion that I am inflicting on you (*bien à contrecœur*) by my bad writing. I was once the best of writers; landladies, puzzled as to my "trade," used to have their honest bosoms set at rest by a sight of a page of manuscript. — "Ah," they would say, "no wonder they pay you for that"; — and when I sent it in to the printers, it was given to the boys! I was about thirty-nine, I think, when I had a turn of scrivener's palsy; my hand got worse; and for the first time, I received clean proofs. But it has gone beyond that now, I know I

1894 ÆT. 44

How exquisite is your character of the critic in *Essays in London!* I doubt if you have done any single thing so satisfying as a piece of style and of insight.—Yours ever, R. L. S.

To Charles Baxter

Mr. Baxter, after much preliminary consideration and inquiry, had matured and submitted to Stevenson the scheme of the Edinburgh edition, to which this letter is his reply. The paper on *Treasure Island* appeared in the *Idler* for August, 1889, and was afterwards reprinted in the miscellany, *My First Book* (Chatto and Windus, 1894). (See Edinburgh edition, *Miscellanies*, vol. iv., p. 285.)

1st January, '94.

MY DEAR CHARLES,—I am delighted with your idea, and first, I will here give an amended plan and afterwards give you a note of some of the difficulties.

[Plan of the Edinburgh edition — 14 vols.]

. . . It may be a question whether my *Times* letters might not be appended to the *Foot-note* with a note of the dates of discharge of Cedercrantz and Pilsach.

I am particularly pleased with this idea of yours, because I am come to a dead stop. I never can remember how bad I have been before, but at any rate I am bad enough just now, I mean as to literature; in health I am well and strong. I take it I shall be six months before I'm heard of again, and this time I could put in to some advantage in revising the text and (if it were thought desirable) writing prefaces. I do not know how many of them might be thought desirable. I have written a paper on *Treasure Island*, which is to appear shortly. *Master of Ballantrae*—I have one drafted. *The Wrecker* is quite sufficiently done already with the last chapter, but I suppose an historic introduction to *David Balfour* is quite unavoidable. *Prince Otto* I don't think I could say anything about, and *Black Arrow* don't want to. But it is probable I could say something to the volume of *Travels*. In the verse business I can do just what I like better than anything else, and extend *Underwoods* with a lot of unpublished stuff. *Apropos*, if I were to get printed off a very few poems which are somewhat too intimate for the public, could you get them run up in some luxurious manner, so that fools might be induced to buy them in just a sufficient quantity to pay expenses and the thing remain still in a manner private? We could supply photographs of the illustrations—and the poems are of Vailima and the family—I should much like to get this done as a surprise for Fanny. R. L. S.

To H. B. Baildon

Vailima, *January 15th, 1894.*

My dear Baildon,—Last mail brought your book and its Dedication. "Frederick Street and the gardens, and the short-lived Jack o' Lantern," are again with me—and the note of the east wind, and Freebel's voice, and the smell of soup in Thomson's stair. Truly, you had no need to put yourself under the protection of any other saint, were that saint our Tamate himself! Yourself were enough, and yourself coming with so rich a sheaf.

word; it is a small age, and I am of it. I could have wished to be otherwise busy in this world. I ought to have been able to build lighthouses and write *David Balfours* too. *Hinc illæ lacrymæ.* I take my own case as most handy, but it is as illustrative of my quarrel with the age. We take all these pains, and we don't do as well as Michael Angelo or Leonardo, or even Fielding, who was an active magistrate, or Richardson, who was a busy bookseller. *J'ai honte pour nous;* my ears burn.

I am amazed at the effect which this Chicago exhibition has produced upon you and others. It set Mrs. Fairchild literally mad — to judge by her letters. And I wish I had seen anything so influential. I suppose there was an aura, a halo, some sort of effulgency about the place; for here I find you louder than the rest. Well, it may be there is a time coming; and I wonder, when it comes, whether it will be a time of little, exclusive, one-eyed rascals like you and me, or parties of the old stamp who can paint and fight, and write and keep books of double entry, and sculp, and scalp. It might be. You have a lot of stuff in the kettle, and a great deal of it Celtic. I have changed my mind progressively about England: practically the whole of Scotland is Celtic, and the western half of England, and all Ireland, and the Celtic blood makes a rare blend for art. If it is stiffened up with Latin blood, you get the French. We were less lucky: we had only Scandinavians, themselves decidedly artistic, and the low German lot. However, that is a good starting-point, and with all the other elements in your crucible, it may come to something great very easily. I wish you would hurry up and let me see it. Here is a long while I have been waiting for something *good* in art; and what have I seen? Zola's *Débâcle* and a few of Kipling's tales. Are you a reader of Barbey d'Aurévilly? He is a never-failing source of pleasure to me, for my sins, I suppose. What a work is the *Rideau Cramoisi!* and *L'Ensorcelée!* and *Le Chevalier des Touches!*

1894
ÆT. 44

This is degenerating into mere twaddle. So please remember us all most kindly to Mrs. Low, and believe me ever yours, ROBERT LOUIS STEVENSON.

P. S.— Were all your privateers voiceless in the war of 1812? Did *no one* of them write memoirs? I shall have to do my privateer from chic, if you can't help me.[1] My application to Scribner has been quite in vain. See if you can get hold of some historic sharp in the club, and tap him; they must some of them have written memoirs or notes of some sort; perhaps still unprinted; if that be so, get them copied for me.

R. L. S.

To H. B. Baildon

VAILIMA, *January 30th, 1894.*

MY DEAR BAILDON,— "Call not blessed."— Yes, if I could die just now, or say in half a year, I should have had a splendid time of it on the whole. But it gets a little stale, and my work will begin to senesce; and

[1] This question is with a view to the adventures of the hero in *St. Ives*, who, according to Stevenson's original plan, was to have been picked up from his foundered balloon by an American privateer.

1894 ÆT. 44

parties to shy bricks at me; and now it begins to look as if I should survive to see myself impotent and forgotten. It 's a pity suicide is not thought the ticket in the best circles.

But your letter goes on to congratulate me on having done the one thing I am a little sorry for; a little — not much — for my father himself lived to think that I had been wiser than he. But the cream of the jest is that I have lived to change my mind; and think that he was wiser than I. Had I been an engineer, and literature my amusement, it would have been better perhaps. I pulled it off, of course, I won the wager, and it is pleasant while it lasts; but how long will it last? I don't know, say the Bells of Old Bow.

All of which goes to show that nobody is quite sane in judging himself. Truly, had I given way and gone in for engineering, I should be dead by now. Well, the gods know best.

. . . I hope you got my letter about the rescue.— Adieu,
R. L. S.

True for you about the benefit: except by kisses, jests, song, *et hoc genus omne*, man *cannot* convey benefit to another. The universal benefactor has been there before him.

To J. H. Bates

The next is to a correspondent in Cincinnati, who had been the founder of an R. L. S. Society in that city, "originally," he writes me, under date April 7, 1895, "the outcome of a boyish fancy, but it has now grown into something more substantial."

VAILIMA, SAMOA, *March 25th, 1894*.

MY DEAR MR. JOE H. BATES,—I shall have the greatest pleasure in acceding to your complimentary request. I shall think it an honour to be associated with your chapter, and I need not remind you (for you have said it yourself) how much depends upon your own exertions, whether to make it to me a real honour or only a derision. This is to let you know that I accept the position that you have seriously offered to me in a quite serious spirit. I need scarce tell you that I shall always be pleased to receive reports of your proceedings; and if I do not always acknowledge them, you are to remember that I am a man very much occupied otherwise, and not at all to suppose that I have lost interest in my chapter.

In this world, which (as you justly say) is so full of sorrow and suffering, it will always please me to remember that my name is connected with some efforts after alleviation, nor less so with purposes of innocent recreation which, after all, are the only certain means at our disposal for bettering human life.

With kind regards, to yourself, to Mr. L. C. Congdon, to E. M. G. Bates, and to Mr. Edward Hugh Higlee Bates, and the heartiest wishes for the future success of the chapter, believe me, yours cordially,

ROBERT LOUIS STEVENSON.

TO WILLIAM ARCHER

VAILIMA, SAMOA, *March 27th, 1894*.

MY DEAR ARCHER,—Many thanks for your *Theatrical World*. Do you know, it strikes me as being really

1894 ÆT. 44

very good? I have not yet read much of it, but so far as I have looked, there is not a dull and not an empty page in it. Hazlitt, whom you must often have thought of, would have been pleased. Come to think of it, I shall put this book upon the Hazlitt shelf. You have acquired a manner that I can only call august; otherwise, I should have to call it such amazing impudence. The *Bauble Shop* and *Becket* are examples of what I mean. But it "sets you weel."

Marjorie Fleming I have known, as you surmise, for long. She was possibly—no, I take back possibly—she was one of the greatest works of God. Your note about the resemblance of her verses to mine gave me great joy, though it only proved me a plagiarist. By the by, was it not over the *Child's Garden of Verses* that we first scraped acquaintance? I am sorry indeed to hear that my esteemed correspondent Tomarcher has such poor taste in literature.[1] I fear he cannot have inherited this trait from his dear papa. Indeed, I may say I know it, for I remember the energy of papa's disapproval when the work passed through his hands on its way to a second birth, which none regrets more than myself. It is an odd fact, or perhaps a very natural one: I find few greater pleasures than reading my own works, but I never, O I never read *The Black Arrow*. In that country Tomarcher reigns supreme. Well, and after all, if Tomarcher likes it, it has not been written in vain.

We have just now a curious breath from Europe. A young fellow just beginning letters, and no fool, turned up here with a letter of introduction in the well-known

[1] As to admire *The Black Arrow*.

blue ink and decorative hieroglyphs of George Meredith. His name may be known to you. It is Sidney Lysaght. He is staying with us but a day or two, and it is strange to me and not unpleasant to hear all the names, old and new, come up again. But oddly the new are so much more in number. If I revisited the glimpses of the moon on your side of the ocean, I should know comparatively few of them.

My amanuensis deserts me—I should have said you, for yours is the loss, my script having lost all bond with humanity. One touch of nature makes the whole world kin: that nobody can read my hand. It is a humiliating circumstance that thus evens us with printers!

You must sometimes think it strange—or perhaps it is only I that should so think it—to be following the old round, in the gas lamps and the crowded theatres, when I am away here in the tropical forest and the vast silences!

My dear Archer, my wife joins me in the best wishes to yourself and Mrs. Archer, not forgetting Tom; and I am yours very cordially,

ROBERT LOUIS STEVENSON.

TO W. B. YEATS

VAILIMA, SAMOA, *April 14, 1894.*

DEAR SIR,—Long since when I was a boy I remember the emotions with which I repeated Swinburne's poems and ballads. Some ten years ago, a similar spell was cast upon me by Meredith's *Love in a Val-*

1894 ÆT. 44

ley; the stanzas beginning "When her mother tends her" haunted me and made me drunk like wine; and I remember waking with them all the echoes of the hills about Hyères. It may interest you to hear that I have a third time fallen in slavery: this is to your poem called the *Lake Isle of Innisfrae.* It is so quaint and airy, simple, artful, and eloquent to the heart—but I seek words in vain. Enough that "always night and day I hear lake water lapping with low sounds on the shore," and am, yours gratefully,

ROBERT LOUIS STEVENSON.

TO GEORGE MEREDITH

The young lady referred to in the following is Mr. Meredith's daughter, now Mrs. H. Sturgis; the bearer of the introduction, Mr. Sidney Lysaght, author of *The Marplot* and *One of the Grenvilles.* It is only in the first few chapters of Mr. Meredith's *Amazing Marriage* that the character of Gower Woodsere has been allowed to retain any likeness to that of R. L. S.

VAILIMA, SAMOA, *April 17th, 1894.*

MY DEAR MEREDITH,—Many good things have the gods sent to me of late. First of all there was a letter from you by the kind hand of Mariette, if she is not too great a lady to be remembered in such a style; and then there came one Lysaght with a charming note of introduction in the well-known hand itself. We had but a few days of him, and liked him well. There was a sort of geniality and inward fire about him at which I warmed my hands. It is long since I have seen a young man who has left in me such a favourable impression; and I find myself telling myself, "O, I must tell this to Lysaght," or, "This will interest him," in a manner very unusual after so brief an acquaintance. The whole of my family shared in this favourable impression, and my halls have re-echoed ever since, I am sure he will be amused to know, with *Widdicombe Fair*.

He will have told you doubtless more of my news than I could tell you myself; he has your European perspective, a thing long lost to me. I heard with a great deal of interest the news of Box Hill. And so I understand it is to be enclosed! Allow me to remark, that seems a far more barbaric trait of manners than the most barbarous of ours. We content ourselves with cutting off an occasional head.

I hear we may soon expect the *Amazing Marriage*. You know how long, and with how much curiosity, I have looked forward to the book. Now, in so far as you have adhered to your intention, Gower Woodsere will be a family portrait, age twenty-five, of the highly respectable and slightly influential and fairly aged *Tusitala*. You have not known that gentleman; console yourself, he is not worth knowing. At the same time, my dear Meredith, he is very sincerely yours—for what he is worth, for the memories of old times, and in the expectation of many pleasures still to come. I suppose we shall never see each other again; flitting youths of the Lysaght species may occasionally cover these unconscionable leagues and bear greetings to and fro. But we ourselves must be content to converse on an occasional sheet of notepaper, and I shall never see whether you have grown older, and you shall never deplore that Gower Woodsere should have declined into the pantaloon *Tusitala*. It is perhaps better so. Let us continue to see each other as we were, and accept, my dear Meredith, my love and respect.

ROBERT LOUIS STEVENSON.

P. S.—My wife joins me in the kindest messages to yourself and Mariette.

TO CHARLES BAXTER

[VAILIMA], *April 17, '94*.

MY DEAR CHARLES,—*St. Ives* is now well on its way into the second volume. There remains no mortal doubt that it will reach the three volume standard.

I am very anxious that you should send me—

1st. *Tom and Jerry*, a cheap edition.

2nd. The book by Ashton—the *Dawn of the Century*, I think it was called—which Colvin sent me, and which has miscarried, and

3rd. If it is possible, a file of the *Edinburgh Courant* for the years 1811, 1812, 1813, or 1814. I should not care for a whole year. If it were possible to find me three months, winter months by preference, it would do my business not only for *St. Ives*, but for *The Justice-Clerk* as well. Suppose this to be impossible, perhaps I could get the loan of it from somebody; or perhaps it would be possible to have some one read a file for me and make notes. This would be extremely bad, as unhappily one man's food is another man's poison, and the reader would probably leave out everything I should choose. But if you are reduced to that, you might mention to the man who is to read for me that balloon ascensions are in the order of the day.

4th. It might be as well to get a book on balloon ascension, particularly in the early part of the century.

. . . .

III. At last this book has come from Scribner, and, alas! I have the first six or seven chapters of *St. Ives* to recast entirely. Who could foresee that they clothed the French prisoners in yellow? But that one fatal fact—and also that they shaved them twice a week—damns the whole beginning. If it had been sent in time, it would have saved me a deal of trouble. . . .

I have had a long letter from Dr. Scott Dalgleish, 25 Mayfield Terrace, asking me to put my name down to the Ballantine Memorial Committee. I have sent him a pretty sharp answer in favour of cutting down the memorial and giving more to the widow and children. If there is to be any foolery in the way of statues or other trash, please send them a guinea; but if they are going to take my advice and put up a simple tablet with a few heartfelt words, and really devote the bulk of the subscriptions to the wife and family, I will go to the length of twenty pounds, if you will allow me (and if the case of the family be at all urgent), and at least I direct you to send ten pounds. I suppose you had better see Scott Dalgleish himself on the matter. I take the opportunity here to warn you that my head is simply spinning with a multitude of affairs, and I shall probably forget a half of my business at last.

R. L. S.

TO MRS. SITWELL

VAILIMA, *April, 1894.*

MY DEAR FRIEND,—I have at last got some photographs, and hasten to send you, as you asked, a portrait of Tusitala. He is a strange person; not so lean, say experts, but infinitely battered; mighty active again on the whole; going up and down our break-neck road at all hours of the day and night on horseback; holding meetings with all manner of chiefs; quite a political personage—God save the mark!—in a small way, but at heart very conscious of the inevitable flat failure that awaits every one. I shall never do a better book than *Catriona,* that is my high-water mark, and the trouble of production increases on me at a great rate—and mighty anxious about how I am to leave my family: an elderly man, with elderly preoccupations, whom I should be ashamed to show you for your old friend; but not a hope of my dying soon and cleanly, and "winning off the stage." Rather I am daily better in physical health. I shall have to see this business out, after all; and I think, in that case, they should have—they might have—spared me all my ill-health this decade past, if it were not to unbar the doors. I have no taste for old age, and my nose is to be rubbed in it in spite of my face. I was meant to die young, and the gods do not love me.

This is very like an epitaph, bar the handwriting, which is anything but monumental, and I dare say I had better stop. Fanny is down at her own cottage planting or deplanting or replanting, I know not which, and she will not be home till dinner, by which time the mail will be all closed, else she would join me in all good messages and remembrances of love. I hope you will congratulate Burne-Jones from me on his baronetcy. I cannot make out to be anything but raspingly, harrowingly sad; so I will close, and not affect levity which I cannot feel. Do not altogether forget me; keep a corner of your memory for the exile LOUIS.

TO CHARLES BAXTER

[VAILIMA, *May, 1894.*]

MY DEAR CHARLES,—My dear fellow, I wish to assure you of the greatness of the pleasure that this Edinburgh Edition gives me. I suppose it was your idea to give it that name. No other would have affected me in the same manner. Do you remember, how many years ago—I would be afraid to hazard a guess—one night when I communicated to you certain intimations of early death and aspirations after fame? I was particularly maudlin; and my remorse the next morning on a review of my folly has written the matter very deeply in my mind; from yours it may easily have fled. If any one at that moment could have shown me the Edinburgh Edition, I suppose I should have died. It is with gratitude and wonder that I consider "the way in which I have been led." Could a more preposterous idea have occurred to us in those days when we used to search our pockets for coppers, too often in vain, and combine forces to produce the threepence necessary for two glasses of beer, or wander down the Lothian Road without any, than that I should be strong and well at the age of forty-three in the island of Upolu, and that you should be at home bringing out the Edinburgh Edition? If it had been possible, I should almost have preferred the Lothian Road Edition, say, with a picture of the old Dutch smuggler on the covers. I have now something heavy on my mind. I had always a great sense of kinship with poor Robert Fergusson—so clever a boy, so wild, of such a mixed strain, so unfortunate, born in the same town with me, and, as I always felt, rather by express intimation than from evidence, so like myself. Now the injustice with which the one Robert is rewarded and the other left out in the cold sits heavy on me, and I wish you could think of some way in which I could do honour to my unfortunate namesake. Do you think it would look like affectation to dedicate the whole edition to his memory? I think it would. The sentiment which would dictate it to me is too abstruse; and besides, I think my wife is the proper person to receive the dedication of my life's work. At the same time, it is very odd—it really looks like the transmigration of souls—I feel that I must do something for Fergusson; Burns has been before me with the gravestone. It occurs to me you might take a walk down the Canongate and see in what condition the stone is. If it be at all uncared for, we might repair it, and perhaps add a few words of inscription.

I must tell you, what I just remembered in a flash as I was walking about dictating this letter—there was in the original plan of *The Master of Ballantrae* a sort of introduction describing my arrival in Edinburgh on a visit to yourself and your placing in my hands the papers of the story. I actually wrote it, and then condemned the idea as being a little too like Scott, I suppose. Now I must really find the MS. and try to finish it for the E. E. It will give you, what I should so much like you to have, another corner of your own in that lofty monument.

Suppose we do what I have proposed about Fergusson's monument, I wonder if an inscription like this would look arrogant—

> This stone originally erected
> by Robert Burns has been
> repaired at the
> charges of Robert Louis Stevenson,
> and is by him rededicated to
> the memory of Robert Fergusson,
> as the gift of one Edinburgh
> lad to another.

In spacing this inscription I would detach the names of Fergusson and Burns, but leave mine in the text.

Or would that look like sham modesty, and is it better to bring out the three Roberts?

1894
ÆT. 44

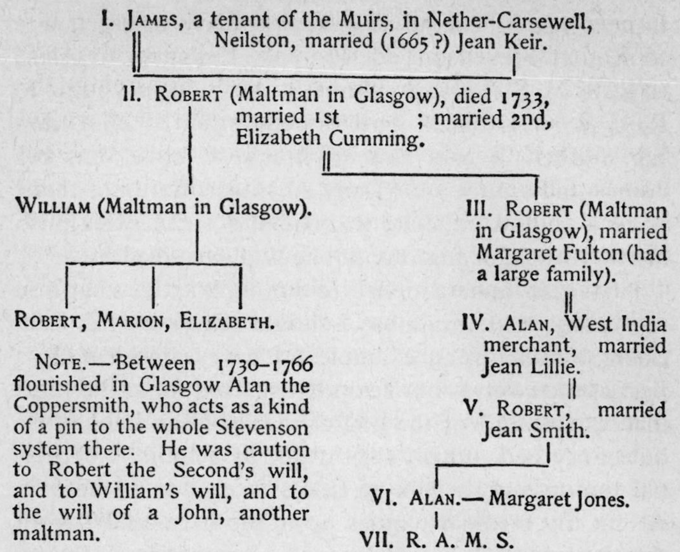

Enough genealogy. I do not know if you will be able to read my hand. Unhappily, Belle, who is my amanuensis, is out of the way on other affairs, and I have to make the unwelcome effort. (O, this is beautiful, I am quite pleased with myself.) Graham has just arrived last night (my mother is coming by the other steamer in three days), and has told me of your meeting, and he said you looked a little older than I did; so that I suppose we keep step fairly on the downward side of the hill. He thought you looked harassed, and I could imagine that too. I sometimes feel harassed. I have a great family here about me, a great anxiety. The loss (to use my grandfather's expression), the "loss" of our family is that we are disbelievers in the morrow — perhaps I should say, rather, in next year. The future is *always* black to us; it was to Robert Stevenson; to Thomas; I suspect to Alan; to R. A. M. S. it was so almost to his ruin in youth; to R. L. S., who had a hard hopeful strain in him from his mother, it was not so much so once, but becomes daily more so. Daily so much more so, that I have a painful difficulty in believing I can ever finish another book, or that the public will ever read it.

I have so huge a desire to know exactly what you are doing, that I suppose I should tell you what I am doing by way of an example. I have a room now, a part of the twelve-foot verandah sparred in, at the most inaccessible end of the house. Daily I see the sunrise out of my bed, which I still value as a tonic, a perpetual tuning-fork, a look of God's face once in the day. At six my breakfast comes up to me here, and I work till eleven. If I am quite well, I sometimes go out and bathe in the river before lunch, twelve. In the afternoon I generally work again, now alone drafting, now with Belle dictating. Dinner is at six, and I am often in bed by eight. This is supposing me to stay at home. But I must often be away, sometimes all day long, sometimes till twelve, one, or two at night, when you might see me coming home to the sleeping house, sometimes in a trackless darkness, sometimes with a glorious tropic moon, everything drenched with dew—unsaddling and creeping to bed; and you would no longer be surprised that I live out in this country, and not in Bournemouth—in bed.

My great recent interruptions have (as you know) come from politics; not much in my line, you will say. But it is impossible to live here and not feel very sorely

1894 ÆT. 44

the consequences of the horrid white mismanagement. I tried standing by and looking on, and it became too much for me. They are such illogical fools; a logical fool in an office, with a lot of red tape, is conceivable. Furthermore, he is as much as we have any reason to expect of officials — a thoroughly commonplace, unintellectual lot. But these people are wholly on wires; laying their ears down, skimming away, pausing as though shot, and presto! full spread on the other tack. I observe in the official class mostly an insane jealousy of the smallest kind, as compared to which the artist's is of a grave, modest character — the actor's, even; a desire to extend his little authority, and to relish it like a glass of wine, that is *impayable*. Sometimes, when I see one of these little kings strutting over one of his victories — wholly illegal, perhaps, and certain to be reversed to his shame if his superiors ever heard of it — I could weep. The strange thing is that they *have nothing else*. I auscultate them in vain; no real sense of duty, no real comprehension, no real attempt to comprehend, no wish for information — you cannot offend one of them more bitterly than by offering information, though it is certain that you have *more*, and obvious that you have *other*, information than they have; and talking of policy, they could not play a better stroke than by listening to you, and it need by no means influence their action. *Tenez*, you know what a French post-office or railway official is? That is the diplomatic card to the life. Dickens is not in it; caricature fails.

All this keeps me from my work, and gives me the unpleasant side of the world. When your letters are disbelieved it makes you angry, and that is rot; and I wish I could keep out of it with all my soul. But I have just got into it again, and farewell peace!

My work goes along but slowly. I have got to a crossing-place, I suppose; the present book, *Saint Ives*, is nothing; it is in no style in particular, a tissue of adventures, the central character not very well done, no philosophic pith under the yarn; and, in short, if people will read it, that 's all I ask; and if they won't, damn them! I like doing it, though; and if you ask me, why!—After that I am on *Weir of Hermiston* and *Heathercat*, two Scotch stories, which will either be something different, or I shall have failed. The first is generally designed, and is a private story of two or three characters in a very grim vein. The second—alas! the thought—is an attempt at a real historical novel, to present a whole field of time; the race—our own race—the west land and Clydesdale bluebonnets, under the influence of their last trial, when they got to a pitch of organisation in madness that no other peasantry has ever made an offer at. I was going to call it *The Killing Time*, but this man Crockett has forestalled me in that. Well, it 'll be a big smash if I fail in it; but a gallant attempt. All my weary reading as a boy, which you remember well enough, will come to bear on it; and if my mind will keep up to the point it was in a while back, perhaps I can pull it through.

For two months past, Fanny, Belle, Austin (her child), and I have been alone; but yesterday, as I mentioned, Graham Balfour arrived, and on Wednesday my mother and Lloyd will make up the party to its full strength. I wish you could drop in for a month or a week, or two hours. That is my chief want. On the whole, it is an unexpectedly pleasant corner I have dropped into for an end of it, which I could scarcely have foreseen from Wilson's shop, or the Princes Street Gardens, or the Portobello Road. Still, I would like to hear what my *alter ego* thought of it; and I would sometimes like to have my old *maître ès arts* express an opinion on what I do. I put this very tamely, being on the whole a quiet elderly man; but it is a strong passion with me, though intermittent. Now, try to follow my example and tell me something about yourself, Louisa, the Bab, and your work; and kindly send me some specimens of what you 're about. I have only seen one thing by you, about Notre Dame in the *Westminster* on St. James, since I left England, now I suppose six years ago.

I have looked this trash over, and it is not at all the letter I wanted to write—not truck about officials, ancestors, and the like rancidness—but you have to let your pen go in its own broken-down gait, like an old butcher's pony, stop when it pleases, and go on again as it will.—Ever, my dear Bob, your affectionate cousin,
R. L. STEVENSON.

TO HENRY JAMES

VAILIMA, *July 7, 1894.*

DEAR HENRY JAMES,—I am going to try and dictate to you a letter or a note, and begin the same without any spark of hope, my mind being entirely in abeyance. This malady is very bitter on the literary man. I have had it now coming on for a month, and it seems to get worse instead of better. If it should prove to be softening of the brain, a melancholy interest will attach to the present document. I heard a great deal about you from my mother and Graham Balfour; the latter declares that you could take a First in any Samoan subject. If that be so, I should like to hear you on the theory of the constitution. Also to consult you on the force of the particles *o lo' o* and *ua*, which are the subject of a dispute among local pundits. You might, if you ever answer this, give me your opinion on the origin of the Samoan race, just to complete the favour.

They both say that you are looking well, and I suppose I may conclude from that that you are feeling passably. I wish I was. Do not suppose from this that I am ill in body; it is the numskull that I complain of. And when that is wrong, as you must be very keenly aware, you begin every day with a smarting disappointment, which is not good for the temper. I am in one of the humours when a man wonders how any one can be such an ass as to embrace the profession of letters, and not get apprenticed to a barber or keep a baked-potato stall. But I have no doubt in the course of a week, or perhaps to-morrow, things will look better.

We have at present in port the model warship of Great Britain. She is called the *Curaçoa*, and has the nicest set of officers and men conceivable. They, the officers, are all very intimate with us, and the front verandah is known as the Curaçoa Club, and the road up to Vailima is known as the Curaçoa Track. It was rather a surprise to me; many naval officers have I known, and somehow had not learned to think entirely well of them, and perhaps sometimes ask myself a little uneasily how that kind of men could do great actions?

And now, if you are not sick of the *Curaçoa* and Manu'a, I am at least on paper. And I decline any longer to give you examples of how not to write.

By the by, you sent me long ago a work by Anatole France, which I confess I did not *taste*. Since then I have made the acquaintance of the *Abbé Coignard*, and have become a faithful adorer. I don't think a better book was ever written.

And I have no idea what I have said, and I have no idea what I ought to have said, and I am a total ass, but my heart is in the right place, and I am, my dear Henry James, yours, R. L. S.

To Marcel Schwob

Vailima, Upolu, Samoa, *July 7, 1894*.

DEAR MR. MARCEL SCHWOB,—Thank you for having remembered me in my exile. I have read *Mimes* twice as a whole; and now, as I write, I am reading it again as it were by accident and a piece at a time, my eye catching a word and travelling obediently on through the whole number. It is a graceful book, essentially graceful, with its haunting, agreeable melancholy, its pleasing savour of antiquity. At the same time, by its merits, it shows itself rather as the promise of something else to come, than a thing final in itself. You have yet to give us — and I am expecting it with impatience — something of a larger gait; something daylit, not twilit; something with the colours of life, not the flat tints of a temple illumination; something that shall be *said* with all the clearnesses and the trivialities of speech, not *sung* like a semi-articulate lullaby. It will not please yourself as well, when you come to give it us, but it will please others better. It will be more of a whole, more worldly, more nourished, more commonplace — and not so pretty, perhaps not even so beautiful. No man knows better than I, that, as we go on in life, we must part from prettiness and the graces. We but attain qualities to lose them; life is a series of farewells, even in art; even our proficiencies are deciduous and evanescent. So here with these exquisite pieces, the XVIIth, XVIIIth, and IVth, of the present collection. You will perhaps never excel them; I should think the "Hermes" never. Well, you will do something else, and of that I am in expectation.—Yours cordially,

ROBERT LOUIS STEVENSON.

TO AUGUSTUS ST. GAUDENS

VAILIMA, SAMOA, *July 8, 1894.*

MY DEAR ST. GAUDENS,—This is to tell you that the medallion has been at last triumphantly transported up the hill and placed over my smoking-room mantelpiece. It is considered by everybody a first-rate but flattering portrait. We have it in a very good light, which brings out the artistic merits of the god-like sculptor to great advantage. As for my own opinion, I believe it to be a speaking likeness, and not flattered at all; possibly a little the reverse. The verses (curse the rhyme) look remarkably well.

Please do not longer delay, but send me an account for the expense of the gilt letters. I was sorry indeed that they proved beyond the means of a small farmer.—Yours very sincerely, ROBERT LOUIS STEVENSON.

To Miss Adelaide Boodle

VAILIMA, *July 14, 1894.*

MY DEAR ADELAIDE,—. . . So, at last, you are going into mission work? where I think your heart always was. You will like it in a way, but remember it is dreary long. Do you know the story of the American tramp who was offered meals and a day's wage to chop with the back of an axe on a fallen trunk. "Damned if I can go on chopping when I can't see the chips fly!" You will never see the chips fly in mission work, never; and be sure you know it beforehand. The work is one long dull disappointment, varied by acute revulsions; and those who are by nature courageous and cheerful, and have grown old in experience, learn to rub their hands over infinitesimal successes. However, as I really believe there is some good done in the long run—*gutta cavat lapidem non vi* in this business—it is a useful and honourable career in which no one should be ashamed to embark. Always remember the fable of the sun, the storm, and the traveller's cloak. Forget wholly and for ever all small pruderies, and remember that *you cannot change ancestral feelings of right and wrong without what is practically soul-murder.* Barbarous as the customs may seem, always hear them with patience, always judge them with gentleness, always find in them some seed of good; see that you always develop them; remember that all you can do is to civilise the man in the line of his own civilisation, such as it is. And never expect, never believe in, thaumaturgic conversions. They may do very well for St. Paul; in the case of an Andaman islander they mean less than nothing. In fact, what you have to do is to teach the parents in the interests of their great-grandchildren.

Now, my dear Adelaide, dismiss from your mind the least idea of fault upon your side; nothing is further from the fact. I cannot forgive you, for I do not know your fault. My own is plain enough, and the name of it is cold-hearted neglect; and you may busy yourself more usefully in trying to forgive me. But ugly as my fault is, you must not suppose it to mean more than it does; it does not mean that we have at all forgotten you, that we have become at all indifferent to the thought of you. See, in my life of Jenkin, a remark of his, very well expressed, on the friendships of men who do not write to each other. I can honestly say that I have not changed to you in any way; though I have behaved thus ill, thus cruelly. Evil is done by want of—well, principally by want of industry. You can imagine what I would say (in a novel) of any one who had behaved as I have done. *Deteriora sequor.* And you must somehow manage to forgive your old friend; and if you will be so very good, continue to give us news of you, and let us share the knowledge of your adventures, sure that it will be always followed with interest—even if it is answered with the silence of ingratitude. For I am not a fool; I know my faults, I know they are ineluctable, I know they are growing on me. I know I may offend again, and I warn you of it. But the next time I offend, tell me so plainly and frankly like a lady, and don't lacerate my heart and bludgeon my vanity with imaginary faults of your own

1894
ÆT. 44

and purely gratuitous penitence. I might suspect you of irony!

We are all fairly well, though I have been off work and off — as you know very well — letter-writing. Yet I have sometimes more than twenty letters, and sometimes more than thirty, going out each mail. And Fanny has had a most distressing bronchitis for some time, which she is only now beginning to get over. I have just been to see her; she is lying — though she had breakfast an hour ago, about seven — in her big, cool, mosquito-proof room, ingloriously asleep. As for me, you see that a doom has come upon me: I cannot make marks with a pen — witness "ingloriously" above; and my amanuensis not appearing so early in the day, for she is then immersed in household affairs, and I can hear her "steering the boys" up and down the verandahs — you must decipher this unhappy letter for yourself and, I fully admit, with everything against you. A letter should be always well written; how much more a letter of apology! Legibility is the politeness of men of letters, as punctuality of kings and beggars. By the punctuality of my replies, and the beauty of my handwriting, judge what a fine conscience I must have!

Now, my dear gamekeeper, I must really draw to a close. For I have much else to write before the mail goes out three days hence. Fanny being asleep, it would not be conscientious to invent a message from her, so you must just imagine her sentiments. I find I have not the heart to speak of your recent loss. You remember, perhaps, when my father died, you told me those ugly images of sickness, decline, and impaired reason, which then haunted me day and night, would pass away and be succeeded by things more happily characteristic. I have found it so. He now haunts me, strangely enough, in two guises; as a man of fifty, lying on a hillside and carving mottoes on a stick, strong and well; and as a younger man, running down the sands into the sea near North Berwick, myself—*ætat.* 11—somewhat horrified at finding him so beautiful when stripped! I hand on your own advice to you in case you have forgotten it, as I know one is apt to do in seasons of bereavement.—Ever yours, with much love and sympathy,

ROBERT LOUIS STEVENSON.

To Mrs. Baker

This refers again to the printing of some of his books in Braille type for the blind.

VAILIMA, SAMOA, *July 16, 1894.*

DEAR MRS. BAKER,—I am very much obliged to you for your letter and the enclosure from Mr. Skinner. Mr. Skinner says he "thinks Mr. Stevenson must be a very kind man"; he little knows me. But I am very sure of one thing, that you are a very kind woman. I envy you—my amanuensis being called away, I continue in my own hand, or what is left of it—unusually legible, I am thankful to see—I envy you your beautiful choice of an employment. There must be no regrets at least for a day so spent; and when the night falls you need ask no blessing on your work.

"Inasmuch as ye have done it unto one of these."—Yours truly, ROBERT LOUIS STEVENSON.

1894
ÆT. 44

To J. M. Barrie

This journal-letter to Mr. Barrie covers a period of a month. In the interval between two of its parts (August 6th and August 12th) the news of Mr. Barrie's engagement and marriage, which took place soon after his recovery from a dangerous illness, had reached Samoa.

VAILIMA, *July 13, 1894.*

MY DEAR BARRIE,—This is the last effort of an ulcerated conscience. I have been so long owing you a letter, I have heard so much of you, fresh from the press, from my mother and Graham Balfour, that I have to write a letter no later than to-day, or perish in my shame. But the deuce of it is, my dear fellow, that you write such a very good letter that I am ashamed to exhibit myself before my junior (which you are, after all) in the light of the dreary idiot I feel. Understand that there will be nothing funny in the following pages. If I can manage to be rationally coherent, I shall be more than satisfied.

In the first place, I have had the extreme satisfaction to be shown that photograph of your mother. It bears evident traces of the hand of an amateur. How is it that amateurs invariably take better photographs than professionals? I must qualify invariably. My own negatives have always represented a province of chaos and old night in which you might dimly perceive fleecy spots of twilight, representing nothing; so that, if I am right in supposing the portrait of your mother to be yours, I must salute you as my superior. Is that your mother's breakfast? Or is it only afternoon tea? If the first, do let me recommend to Mrs. Barrie to add an egg to her ordinary. Which, if you please, I will ask her to eat to the honour of her son, and I am sure she will live much longer for it, to enjoy his fresh successes. I never in my life saw anything more deliciously characteristic. I declare I can hear her speak. I wonder my mother could resist the temptation of your proposed visit to Kirriemuir, which it was like your kindness to propose. By the way, I was twice in Kirriemuir, I believe in the year '71, when I was going on a visit to Glenogil. It was Kirriemuir, was it not? I have a distinct recollection of an inn at the end—I think the upper end—of an irregular open place or square, in which I always see your characters evolve. But, indeed, I did not pay much attention; being all bent upon my visit to a shooting-box, where I should fish a real trout-stream, and I believe preserved. I did, too, and it was a charming stream, clear as crystal, without a trace of peat—a strange thing in Scotland—and alive with trout; the name of it I cannot remember, it was something like the Queen's River, and in some hazy way connected with memories of Mary Queen of Scots. It formed an epoch in my life, being the end of all my trout-fishing. I had always been accustomed to pause and very laboriously to kill every fish as I took it. But in the Queen's River I took so good a basket that I forgot these niceties; and when I sat down, in a hard rain shower, under a bank, to take my sandwiches and sherry, lo! and behold, there was the basketful of trouts still kicking in their agony. I had a very unpleasant conversation with my conscience. All that afternoon I persevered in fishing, brought home my basket in triumph, and sometime that night, "in

1894 ÆT. 44

the wee sma' hours ayont the twal," I finally forswore the gentle craft of fishing. I dare say your local knowledge may identify this historic river; I wish it could go farther and identify also that particular Free kirk in which I sat and groaned on Sunday. While my hand is in I must tell you a story. At that antique epoch you must not fall into the vulgar error that I was myself ancient. I was, on the contrary, very young, very green, and (what you will appreciate, Mr. Barrie) very shy. There came one day to lunch at the house two very formidable old ladies—or one very formidable, and the other what you please—answering to the honoured and historic name of the Miss C—— A——'s of Balnamoon. At table I was exceedingly funny, and entertained the company with tales of geese and bubbly-jocks. I was great in the expression of my terror for these bipeds, and suddenly this horrid, severe, and eminently matronly old lady put up a pair of gold eyeglasses, looked at me awhile in silence, and pronounced in a clangorous voice her verdict. "You give me very much the effect of a coward, Mr. Stevenson!" I had very nearly left two vices behind me at Glenogil—fishing and jesting at table. And of one thing you may be very sure, my lips were no more opened at that meal.

July 29th.

No, Barrie, 't is in vain they try to alarm me with their bulletins. No doubt, you 're ill, and unco ill, I believe; but I have been so often in the same case that I know pleurisy and pneumonia are in vain against Scotsmen who can write. (I once could.) You cannot imagine probably how near me this common calamity brings you. *Ce que j'ai toussé dans ma vie!* How often and how long have I been on the rack at night and learned to appreciate that noble passage in the Psalms when somebody or other is said to be more set on something than they "who dig for hid treasures—yea, than those who long for the morning"—for all the world, as you have been racked and you have longed. Keep your heart up, and you 'll do. Tell that to your mother, if you are still in any danger or suffering. And by the way, if you are at all like me—and I tell myself you are very like me—be sure there is only one thing good for you, and that is the sea in hot climates. Mount, sir, into "a little frigot" of 5000 tons or so, and steer peremptorily for the tropics; and what if the ancient mariner, who guides your frigot, should startle the silence of the ocean with the cry of land ho!—say, when the day is dawning—and you should see the turquoise mountain-tops of Upolu coming hand over fist above the horizon? Mr. Barrie, sir, 't is then there would be larks! And though I cannot be certain that our climate would suit you (for it does not suit some), I am sure as death the voyage would do you good—would do you *Best*—and if Samoa did n't do, you need n't stay beyond the month, and I should have had another pleasure in my life, which is a serious consideration for me. I take this as the hand of the Lord preparing your way to Vailima—in the desert, certainly—in the desert of Cough and by the ghoul-haunted woodland of Fever—but whither that way points there can be no question—and there will be a meeting of the twa Hoasting Scots Makers in spite of fate, fortune, and the Devil. *Absit omen.*

My dear Barrie, I am a little in the dark about this new work of yours:[1] what is to become of me afterwards? You say carefully—methought anxiously—that I was no longer me when I grew up? I cannot bear this suspense: what is it? It 's no forgery? And AM I HANGIT? These are the elements of a very pretty lawsuit which you had better come to Samoa to compromise. I am enjoying a great pleasure that I had long looked forward to, reading Orme's *History of Indostan;* I had been looking out for it everywhere; but at last, in four volumes, large quarto, beautiful type and page, and with a delectable set of maps and plans, and all the names of the places wrongly spelled—it came to Samoa, little Barrie. I tell you frankly, you had better come soon. I am sair failed a'ready; and what I may be if you continue to dally, I dread to conceive. I may be speechless; already, or at least for a month or so, I 'm little better than a teetoller—I beg pardon, a teetotaller. It is not exactly physical, for I am in good health, working four or five hours a day in my plantation, and intending to ride a paper chase next Sunday—ay, man, that 's a fact, and I havena had the hert to breathe it to my mother yet—the obligation 's poleetical, for I am trying every means to live well with my German neighbours — and, O Barrie, but it 's no easy! To be sure, there are many exceptions. And the whole of the above must be regarded as private — strictly private. Breathe it not in Kirriemuir: tell it not to the daughters of Dundee! What a nice extract this would make for the daily papers! and how it would facilitate my position here! . . .

[1] *Sentimental Tommy:* whose chief likeness to R. L. S. was meant to be in the literary temperament and passion for the *mot propre.*

August 5th. 1894
ÆT. 44

This is Sunday, the Lord's Day. "The hour of attack approaches." And it is a singular consideration what I risk; I may yet be the subject of a tract, and a good tract too—such as one which I remember reading with recreant awe and rising hair in my youth, of a boy who was a very good boy, and went to Sunday Schule, and one day kipped from it, and went and actually bathed, and was dashed over a waterfall, and he was the only son of his mother, and she was a widow. A dangerous trade, that, and one that I have to practise. I 'll put in a word when I get home again, to tell you whether I 'm killed or not. "Accident in the (Paper) Hunting Field: death of a notorious author. We deeply regret to announce the death of the most unpopular man in Samoa, who broke his neck at the descent of Magagi, from the misconduct of his little raving lunatic of an old beast of a pony. It is proposed to commemorate the incident by the erection of a suitable pile. The design (by our local architect, Mr. Walker) is highly artificial, with a rich and voluminous Crockett at each corner, a small but impervious Barrièer at the entrance, an arch at the top, an Archer of a pleasing but solid character at the bottom; the colour will be genuine William-Black; and Lang, lang may the ladies sit wi' their fans in their hands." Well, well, they may sit as they sat for me, and little they 'll reck, the ungrateful jauds! Muckle they cared about Tusitala when they had him! But now ye can see the difference; now, leddies, ye can repent, when ower late, o' your former cauldness and what ye 'll perhaps allow me to ca' your *tepeedity!* He was beautiful as the day, but his day is done! And perhaps, as he was

1894 ÆT. 44 maybe gettin' a wee thing fly-blawn, it 's nane too shũne.

Monday, August 6th.

Well, sir, I have escaped the dangerous conjunction of the widow's only son and the Sabbath Day. We had a most enjoyable time, and Lloyd and I were 3 and 4 to arrive; I will not tell here what interval had elapsed between our arrival and the arrival of 1 and 2; the question, sir, is otiose and malign; it deserves, it shall have no answer. And now without further delay to the main purpose of this hasty note. We received and we have already in fact distributed the gorgeous fabrics of Kirriemuir. Whether from the splendour of the robes themselves, or from the direct nature of the compliments with which you had directed us to accompany the presentations, one young lady blushed as she received the proofs of your munificence. . . . Bad ink, and the dregs of it at that, but the heart in the right place. Still very cordially interested in my Barrie and wishing him well through his sickness, which is of the body, and long defended from mine, which is of the head, and by the impolite might be described as idiocy. The whole head is useless, and the whole sitting part painful: reason, the recent Paper Chase.

There was racing and chasing in Vailile plantation,
    And vastly we enjoyed it,
But, alas! for the state of my foundation,
    For it wholly has destroyed it.

Come, my mind is looking up. The above is wholly impromptu.—On oath, TUSITALA.

August 12, 1894.

And here, Mr. Barrie, is news with a vengeance. Mother Hubbard's dog is well again—what did I tell you? Pleurisy, pneumonia, and all that kind of truck is quite unavailing against a Scotchman who can write—and not only that, but it appears the perfidious dog is married. This incident, so far as I remember, is omitted from the original epic—

She went to the graveyard
To see him get him buried,
And when she came back
The Deil had got merried.

It now remains to inform you that I have taken what we call here "German offence" at not receiving cards, and that the only reparation I will accept is that Mrs. Barrie shall incontinently upon the receipt of this Take and Bring you to Vailima in order to apologise and be pardoned for this offence. The commentary of Tamaitai upon the event was brief but pregnant: "Well, it 's a comfort our guest-room is furnished for two."

This letter, about nothing, has already endured too long. I shall just present the family to Mrs. Barrie—Tamaitai, Tamaitai Matua, Teuila, Palema, Loia, and with an extra low bow, Yours, TUSITALA.

TO DR. BAKEWELL

The following is to a physician in Australia.

VAILIMA, *August 7, 1894.*

DEAR DR. BAKEWELL,—I am not more than human. I am more human than is wholly convenient, and your

1894
ÆT. 44

You are to conceive me, then, sitting in my little gallery room, shaken by these continual spasms of cannon, and with my eye more or less singly fixed on the imaginary figure of my dear James Payn. I try to see him in bed; no go. I see him instead jumping up in his room in Waterloo Place (where *ex hypothesi* he is not), sitting on the table, drawing out a very black briar-root pipe, and beginning to talk to a slim and ill-dressed visitor in a voice that is good to hear and with a smile that is pleasant to see. (After a little more than half an hour, the voice that was ill to hear has ceased, the cannonade is over.) And I am thinking how I can get an answering smile wafted over so many leagues of land and water, and can find no way.

I have always been a great visitor of the sick; and one of the sick I visited was W. E. Henley, which did not make very tedious visits, so I 'll not get off much purgatory for them. That was in the Edinburgh Infirmary, the old one, the true one, with Georgius Secundus standing and pointing his toe in a niche of the façade; and a mighty fine building it was! And I remember one winter's afternoon, in that place of misery, that Henley and I chanced to fall in talk about James Payn himself. I am wishing you could have heard that talk! I think that would make you smile. We had mixed you up with John Payne, for one thing, and stood amazed at your extraordinary, even painful, versatility; and for another, we found ourselves each students so well prepared for examinations on the novels of the real Mackay. Perhaps, after all, this is worth something in life — to have given so much pleasure to a pair so different in every way as were Henley and I, and to be talked of with so much interest by two such (beg pardon) clever lads!

The cheerful Lang has neglected to tell me what is the matter with you; so, I 'm sorry to say, I am cut off from all the customary consolations. I can't say, "Think how much worse it would be if you had a broken leg!" when you may have the crushing repartee up your sleeve, "But it is my leg that is broken." This is a pity. But there are consolations. You are an Englishman (I believe); you are a man of letters; you have never been made C. B.; your hair was not red; you have played cribbage and whist; you did not play either the fiddle or the banjo; you were never an æsthete; you never contributed to —— *Journal;* your name is not Jabez Balfour; you are totally unconnected with the Army and Navy departments; I understand you to have lived within your income — why, cheer up! here are many legitimate causes of congratulation. I seem to be writing an obituary notice. *Absit omen!* But I feel very sure that these considerations will have done you more good than medicine.

By the by, did you ever play piquet? I have fallen a victim to this debilitating game. It is supposed to be scientific; God save the mark, what self-deceivers men are! It is distinctly less so than cribbage. But how fascinating! There is such material opulence about it, such vast ambitions may be realised — and are not; it may be called the Monte Cristo of games. And the thrill with which you take five cards partakes of the nature of lust — and you draw four sevens and a nine, and the seven and nine of a suit that you discarded, and O! but the world is a desert! You may see traces of discouragement in my letter: all due to piquet! There has been a disastrous turn of the luck against me; a month or two ago I was two thousand ahead; now, and for a week back, I have been anything from four thousand eight hundred to five thousand two hundred astern. If I have a sixième, my beast of a partner has a septième; and if I have three aces, three kings, three queens, and three knaves (excuse the slight exaggeration), the devil holds quatorze of tens!—I remain, my dear James Payn, your sincere and obliged friend—old friend let me say, ROBERT LOUIS STEVENSON.

TO MISS MIDDLETON

A letter from the lady to whom this is addressed, and who had been a friend of the Stevenson family in Edinburgh, had called up some memories of the Skye terrier Jura, of whom readers have heard something already.

VAILIMA, SAMOA, *September 9, 1894.*

DEAR MISS MIDDLETON,—Your letter has been like the drawing up of a curtain. Of course I remember you very well, and the Skye terrier to which you refer—a heavy, dull, fatted, graceless creature he grew up to be—was my own particular pet. It may amuse you, perhaps, as much as "The Inn" amused me, if I tell you what made this dog particularly mine. My father was the natural god of all the dogs in our house, and poor Jura took to him of course. Jura was stolen, and kept in prison somewhere for more than a week, as I remember. When he came back Smeoroch had come and taken my father's heart from him. He took his stand like a man, and positively never spoke to my father again from that day until the day of his death. It was the only sign of character he ever showed. I took him up to my room and to be my dog in consequence, partly because I was sorry for him, and partly because I admired his dignity in misfortune.

With best regards and thanks for having reminded me of so many pleasant days, old acquaintances, dead friends, and — what is perhaps as pathetic as any of them — dead dogs, I remain, yours truly,

ROBERT LOUIS STEVENSON.

TO A. CONAN DOYLE

The following refers to the papers originally contributed by various writers to Mr. Jerome's periodical, the *Idler*, under the title "My First Book," and afterwards republished in a volume. The references towards the end are to the illustrations in the pages of the *Idler*.

VAILIMA, SAMOA, *September 9, 1894*.

MY DEAR CONAN DOYLE,— If you found anything to entertain you in my *Treasure Island* article, it may amuse you to know that you owe it entirely to yourself. *Your* "First Book" was by some accident read aloud one night in my Baronial 'All. I was consumedly amused by it, so was the whole family, and we proceeded to hunt up back *Idlers* and read the whole series. It is a rattling good series; even people whom you would not expect came in quite the

1894 ÆT. 44 proper tone — Miss Braddon, for instance, who was really one of the best where all are good — or all but one! . . . In short, I fell in love with the "First Book" series, and determined that it should be all our first books, and that I could not hold back where the white plume of Conan Doyle waved gallantly in the front. I hope they will republish them, though it 's a grievous thought to me that that effigy in the German cap — likewise the other effigy of the noisome old man with the long hair, telling indelicate stories to a couple of deformed negresses in a rancid shanty full of wreckage — should be perpetuated. I may seem to speak in pleasantry — it is only a seeming — that German cap, sir, would be found, when I come to die, imprinted on my heart. Enough — my heart is too full. Adieu.— Yours very truly,

ROBERT LOUIS STEVENSON
(in a German cap, damn 'em!).

TO CHARLES BAXTER

The following was written on hearing of the death of his friend's father.

[*Received 15th September, '94.*]

MY DEAR CHARLES, — . . . Well, there is no more Edmund Baxter now; and I think I may say I know how you feel. He was one of the best, the kindest, and the most genial men I ever knew. I shall always remember his brisk, cordial ways and the essential goodness which he showed me whenever we met with gratitude. And the always is such a little while now! He is another of the landmarks gone; when it comes to my own turn to lay my weapons down, I shall do so with thankfulness and fatigue; and whatever be my destiny afterward, I shall be glad to lie down with my fathers in honour. It is human at least, if not divine. And these deaths make me think of it with an ever greater readiness. Strange that you should be beginning a new life, when I, who am a little your junior, am thinking of the end of mine. But I have had hard lines; I have been so long waiting for death; I have unwrapped my thoughts from about life so long, that I have not a filament left to hold by; I have done my fiddling so long under Vesuvius, that I have almost forgotten to play, and can only wait for the eruption, and think it long of coming. Literally, no man has more wholly outlived life than I. And still it 's good fun. R. L. S.

To R. A. M. Stevenson

Stevenson had received from his cousin a letter announcing, among other things, the birth of a son to the writer, and rambling suggestively, as may be guessed from the following reply, over many disconnected themes : the ethnology of Scotland, paternity and heredity, civilisation *versus* primitive customs and instincts, the story of their own descent, the method of writing in collaboration, education, sex and Christianity, anarchism, etc.; all which matters are here discursively touched on. "Old Skene" is, of course, the great Scottish antiquarian and historian, William Forbes Skene, in whose firm (Edwards & Skene, W. S.) Stevenson had for a time served, irregularly enough, as an unpaid clerk.

1894
ÆT. 44

[VAILIMA, *September*, *1894*.]

DEAR BOB,—You are in error about the Picts. They were a Gaelic race, spoke a Celtic tongue, and we have no evidence that I know of that they were blacker than other Celts. The Balfours, I take it, were plainly Celts; their name shows it—the "cold croft," it means; so does their country. Where the *black* Scotch come from nobody knows; but I recognise with you the fact that the whole of Britain is rapidly and progressively becoming more pigmented; already in one man's life I can decidedly trace a difference in the children about a school door. But colour is not an essential part of a man or a race. Take my Polynesians, an Asiatic people probably from the neighbourhood of the Persian Gulf. They range through any amount of shades, from the burnt hue of the Low Archipelago islander, which seems half negro, to the "bleached" pretty women of the Marquesas (close by on the map), who come out for a festival no darker than an Italian; their colour seems to vary directly with the degree of exposure to the sun. And, as with negroes, the babes are born white; only it should seem a *little sack* of pigment at the lower part of the spine, which presently spreads over the whole field. Very puzzling. But to return. The Picts furnish to-day perhaps a third of the population of Scotland, say another third for Scots and Britons, and the third for Norse and Angles is a bad third. Edinburgh was a Pictish place. But the fact is, we don't know their frontiers. Tell some of your journalist friends with a good style to popularise old Skene; or say your prayers, and read him for yourself; he was a Great Historian, and I was his blessed clerk, and did not know it; and you will not be in a state of grace about the Picts till you have studied him. J. Horne Stevenson (do you know him ?) is working this up with me, and the fact is — it 's not interesting to the public — but it 's interesting, and very interesting, in itself, and just now very embarrassing — this rural parish supplied Glasgow with such a quantity of Stevensons in the beginning of last century! There is just a link wanting; and we might be able to go back to the eleventh century, always undistinguished, but clearly traceable. When I say just a link, I guess I may be taken to mean a dozen. What a singular thing is this undistinguished perpetuation of a family throughout the centuries, and the sudden bursting forth of character and capacity that began with our grandfather! But as I go on in life, day by day, I become more of a bewildered child; I cannot get used to this world, to procreation, to heredity, to sight, to hearing; the commonest things are a burthen. The prim obliterated polite face of life, and the broad, bawdy, and orgiastic — or mœnadic — foundations, form a spectacle to which no habit reconciles me; and "I could wish my days to be bound each to each" by the same open-mouthed wonder. They *are* anyway, and whether I wish it or not.

I remember very well your attitude to life, this conventional surface of it. You had none of that curiosity for the social stage directions, the trivial *ficelles* of the business; it is simian, but that is how the wild youth of man is captured; you would n't imitate, hence you kept free — a wild dog, outside the kennel — and came dam near starving for your pains. The key to the business is

1894
ÆT. 44

of course the belly; difficult as it is to keep that in view in the zone of three miraculous meals a day in which we were brought up. Civilisation has become reflex with us; you might think that hunger was the name of the best sauce; but hunger to the cold solitary under a bush of a rainy night is the name of something quite different. I defend civilisation for the thing it is, for the thing it has *come* to be, the standpoint of a real old Tory. My ideal would be the Female Clan. But how can you turn these crowding dumb multitudes *back?* They don't do anything *because;* they do things, write able articles, stitch shoes, dig, from the purely simian impulse. Go and reason with monkeys!

No, I am right about Jean Lillie. Jean Lillie, our double great-grandmother, the daughter of David Lillie, sometime Deacon of the Wrights, married, first, Alan Stevenson, who died May 26, 1774, "at Santt Kittes of a fiver," by whom she had Robert Stevenson, born 8th June, 1772; and, second, in May or June, 1787, Thomas Smith, a widower, and already the father of our grandmother. This improbable double connection always tends to confuse a student of the family, Thomas Smith being doubly our great-grandfather.

I looked on the perpetuation of our honoured name with veneration. My mother collared one of the photos, of course; the other is stuck up on my wall as the chief of our sept. Do you know any of the Gaelic-Celtic sharps? you might ask what the name means. It puzzles me. I find a *M'Stein* and a *MacStephane;* and our own great-grandfather always called himself Steenson, though he wrote it Stevenson. There are at least three *places* called Stevenson—*Stevenson* in Cunningham,

Stevenson in Peebles, and *Stevenson* in Haddington. And it was not the Celtic trick, I understand, to call places after people. I am going to write to Sir Herbert Maxwell about the name, but you might find some one.

Get the Anglo-Saxon heresy out of your head; they superimposed their language, they scarce modified the race; only in Berwickshire and Roxburgh have they very largely affected the place names. The Scandinavians did much more to Scotland than the Angles. The Saxons did n't come.

Enough of this sham antiquarianism. Yes, it is in the matter of the book, of course, that collaboration shows; as for the manner, it is superficially all mine, in the sense that the last copy is all in my hand. Lloyd did not even put pen to paper in the Paris scenes or the Barbizon scene; it was no good; he wrote and often rewrote all the rest; I had the best service from him on the character of Nares. You see, we had been just meeting the man, and his memory was full of the man's words and ways. And Lloyd is an impressionist, pure and simple. The great difficulty of collaboration is that you can't explain what you mean. I know what kind of effect I mean a character to give — what kind of *tache* he is to make; but how am I to tell my collaborator in words? Hence it was necessary to say, "Make him So-and-so"; and this was all right for Nares and Pinkerton and Loudon Dodd, whom we both knew, but for Bellairs, for instance — a man with whom I passed ten minutes fifteen years ago — what was I to say? and what could Lloyd do? I, as a personal artist, can begin a character with only a haze in my head, but how if I have to translate the haze into words before I begin? In our manner of collaboration (which I think the only possible — I mean that of one person being responsible, and giving the *coup de pouce* to every part of the work) I was spared the obviously hopeless business of trying to explain to my collaborator what *style* I wished a passage to be treated in. These are the times that illustrate to a man the inadequacy of spoken language. Now — to be just to written language — I can (or could) find a language for my every mood, but how could I *tell* any one beforehand what this effect was to be, which it would take every art that I possessed, and hours and hours of deliberate labour and selection and rejection, to produce? These are the impossibilities of collaboration. Its immediate advantage is to focus two minds together on the stuff, and to produce in consequence an extraordinary greater richness of purview, consideration, and invention. The hardest chapter of all was "Cross Questions and Crooked Answers." You would not believe what that cost us before it assumed the least unity and colour. Lloyd wrote it at least thrice, and I at least five times — this is from memory. And was that last chapter worth the trouble it cost? Alas, that I should ask the question! Two classes of men — the artist and the educationalist — are sworn, on soul and conscience, not to ask it. You get an ordinary, grinning, red-headed boy, and you have to educate him. Faith supports you; you give your valuable hours, the boy does not seem to profit, but that way your duty lies, for which you are paid, and you must persevere. Education has always seemed to me one of the few possible and dignified ways of life. A sailor, a shepherd, a schoolmaster — to a less degree, a soldier — and (I don't know why, upon my soul, except as a sort of schoolmaster's unofficial assistant, and a kind of acrobat in tights) an artist, almost exhaust the category.

If I had to begin again — I know not — *si jeunesse savait, si vieillesse pouvait* . . . I know not at all — I believe I should try to honour Sex more religiously. The worst of our education is that Christianity does not recognise and hallow Sex. It looks askance at it, over its shoulder, oppressed as it is by reminiscences of hermits and Asiatic self-tortures. It is a terrible hiatus in our modern religions that they cannot see and make venerable that which they ought to see first and hallow most. Well, it is so; I cannot be wiser than my generation.

But no doubt there is something great in the half-success that has attended the effort of turning into an emotional religion Bald Conduct, without any appeal, or almost none, to the figurative, mysterious, and constitutive facts of life. Not that conduct is not constitutive, but dear! it 's dreary! On the whole, conduct is better dealt with on the cast-iron "gentleman" and duty formula, with as little fervour and poetry as possible; stoical and short.

. . . There is a new something or other in the wind, which exercises me hugely: anarchy,— I mean, anarchism. People who (for pity's sake) commit dastardly murders very basely, die like saints, and leave beautiful letters behind 'em (did you see Vaillant to his daughter? it was the New Testament over again); people whose conduct is inexplicable to me, and yet their spiritual life higher than that of most. This is

1894
ÆT. 44

just what the early Christians must have seemed to the Romans. Is this, then, a new *drive*[1] among the monkeys? Mind you, Bob, if they go on being martyred a few years more, the gross, dull, not unkindly bourgeois may get tired or ashamed or afraid of going on martyring; and the anarchists come out at the top just like the early Christians. That is, of course, they will step into power as a *personnel*, but God knows what they may believe when they come to do so; it can't be stranger or more improbable than what Christianity had come to be by the same time.

Your letter was easily read, the pagination presented no difficulty, and I read it with much edification and gusto. To look back, and to stereotype one bygone humour — what a hopeless thing! The mind runs ever in a thousand eddies like a river between cliffs. You (the ego) are always spinning round in it, east, west, north, and south. You are twenty years old, and forty, and five, and the next moment you are freezing at an imaginary eighty; you are never the plain forty-four that you should be by dates. (The most philosophical language is the Gaelic, which has *no present tense* — and the most useless.) How, then, to choose some former age, and stick there? R. L. S.

To Sir Herbert Maxwell

Vailima, Samoa, *September 10, 1894.*

DEAR SIR HERBERT MAXWELL, — I am emboldened by reading your very interesting Rhind Lectures to put to you a question: What is my name, Stevenson?

[1] *Trieb*, impulse.

I find it in the forms Stevinetoun, Stevensoune, Stevensonne, Stenesone, Stewinsoune, M'Stein, and MacStephane. My family, and (as far as I can gather) the majority of the inglorious clan, hailed from the borders of Cunningham and Renfrew, and the upper waters of the Clyde. In the Barony of Bothwell was the seat of the laird Stevenson of Stevenson; but, as of course you know, there is a parish in Cunningham and places in Peebles and Haddington bearing the same name.

If you can at all help me, you will render me a real service which I wish I could think of some manner to repay.—Believe me, yours truly,

ROBERT LOUIS STEVENSON.

P.S.—I should have added that I have perfect evidence before me that (for some obscure reason) Stevenson was a favourite alias with the M'Gregors.

TO ALISON CUNNINGHAM

For a fuller account of the road-making affair here mentioned, see *Vailima Letters*, pp. 344, 360.

[VAILIMA], *October 8th, 1894.*

MY DEAR CUMMY,—So I hear you are ailing? Think shame to yoursell! So you think there is nothing better to be done with time than that? and be sure we can all do much ourselves to decide whether we are to be ill or well! like a man on the gymnastic bars. We are all pretty well. As for me, there is nothing the matter with me in the world, beyond the disgusting circumstance that I am not so young as once I was. Lloyd has a gymnastic machine, and practises upon it every

1894 ÆT. 44

morning for an hour: he is beginning to be a kind of young Samson. Austin grows fat and brown, and gets on not so ill with his lessons, and my mother is in great price. We are having knock-me-down weather for heat; I never remember it so hot before, and I fancy it means we are to have a hurricane again this year, I think; since we came here, we have not had a single gale of wind! The Pacific is but a child to the North Sea; but when she does get excited, and gets up and girds herself, she can do something good. We have had a very interesting business here. I helped the chiefs who were in prison; and when they were set free, what should they do but offer to make a part of my road for me out of gratitude? Well, I was ashamed to refuse, and the trumps dug my road for me, and put up this inscription on a board:—

"*Considering the great love of His Excellency Tusitala in his loving care of us in our tribulation in the prison, we have made this great gift; it shall never be muddy, it shall go on for ever, this road that we have dug!*" We had a great feast when it was done, and I read them a kind of lecture, which I dare say Auntie will have, and can let you see. Weel, guid-bye to ye, and joy be wi' ye! I hae nae time to say mair. They say I 'm gettin' *fat*—a fact!—Your laddie, with all love,

ROBERT LOUIS STEVENSON.

TO JAMES PAYN

VAILIMA, SAMOA, *Nov. 4, 1894.*

MY DEAR JAMES PAYN,—I am asked to relate to you a little incident of domestic life at Vailima. I had read your *Gleams of Memory,* No. 1; it then went to my wife, to Osbourne, to the cousin that is within my gates, and to my respected amanuensis, Mrs. Strong. Sunday approached. In the course of the afternoon I was attracted to the great 'all—the winders is by Vanderputty—which upon entering I beheld a memorable scene. The floor was bestrewn with the forms of midshipmen from the *Curaçoa*—"boldly say a wilderness of gun-room"—and in the midst of this sat Mrs. Strong throned on the sofa and reading aloud *Gleams of Memory.* They had just come the length of your immortal definition of boyhood in the concrete, and I had the pleasure to see the whole party dissolve under its influence with inextinguishable laughter. I thought this was not half bad for arthritic gout! Depend upon it, sir, when I go into the arthritic gout business, I shall be done with literature, or at least with the funny business. It is quite true I have my battlefields behind me. I have done perhaps as much work as anybody else under the most deplorable conditions. But two things fall to be noticed: In the first place, I never was in actual pain; and in the second, I was never funny. I 'll tell you the worst day that I remember. I had a hæmorrhage, and was not allowed to speak; then, induced by the devil, or an errant doctor, I was led to partake of that bowl which neither cheers nor inebriates—the castor-oil bowl. Now, when castor-oil goes right, it is one thing; but when it goes wrong, it is another. And it went wrong with me that day. The waves of faintness and nausea succeeded each other for twelve hours, and I do feel a legitimate pride in thinking that I stuck to my work all

1894
ÆT. 44

through and wrote a good deal of *Admiral Guinea* (which I might just as well not have written for all the reward it ever brought me) in spite of the barbarous bad conditions. I think that is my great boast; and it seems a little thing alongside of your *Gleams of Memory* illustrated by spasms of arthritic gout. We really should have an order of merit in the trade of letters. For valour, Scott would have had it; Pope too; myself on the strength of that castor-oil; and James Payn would be a Knight Commander. The worst of it is, though Lang tells me you exhibit the courage of Huish, that not even an order can alleviate the wretched annoyance of the business. I have always said that there is nothing like pain; toothache, dumb-ague, arthritic gout, it does not matter what you call it, if the screw is put upon the nerves sufficiently strong, there is nothing left in heaven or in earth that can interest the sufferer. Still, even to this there is the consolation that it cannot last for ever. Either you will be relieved and have a good hour again before the sun goes down, or else you will be liberated. It is something after all (although not much) to think that you are leaving a brave example; that other literary men love to remember, as I am sure they will love to remember, everything about you — your sweetness, your brightness, your helpfulness to all of us, and in particular those one or two really adequate and noble papers which you have been privileged to write during these last years.— With the heartiest and kindest goodwill, I remain, yours ever,

R. L. S.

To Lieutenant Eeles

Vailima, Samoa, *November 24, 1894.*

MY DEAR EELES,—The hand, as you will perceive (and also the spelling!), is Teuila's, but the scrannel voice is what remains of Tusitala's. First of all, for business. When you go to London you are to charter a hansom cab and proceed to the Museum. It is particular fun to do this on Sundays when the Monument is shut up. Your cabman expostulates with you, you persist. The cabman drives up in front of the closed gates and says, "I told you so, sir." You breathe in the porter's ears the mystic name of *Colvin*, and he immediately unfolds the iron barrier. You drive in, and does n't your cabman think you 're a swell. A lord mayor is nothing to it. Colvin's door is the only one in the eastern gable of the building. Send in your card to him with "From R. L. S." in the corner, and the machinery will do the rest. Henry James's address is 34 De Vere Mansions, West. I cannot remember where the place is; I cannot even remember on which side of the park. But it 's one of those big Cromwell Road-looking deserted thoroughfares out west in Kensington or Bayswater, or between the two; and anyway, Colvin will be able to put you on the direct track for Henry James. I do not send formal introductions, as I have taken the liberty to prepare both of them for seeing you already.

Hoskyn is staying with us.

It is raining dismally. The Curaçoa track is hardly passable, but it must be trod to-morrow by the degenerate feet of their successor the Walleroos. I think it a very good account of these last that we don't think them either deformed or habitual criminals — they seem to be a kindly lot.

The doctor will give you all the gossip. I have preferred in this letter to stick to the strictly solid and necessary. With kind messages from all in the house to all in the ward-room, all in the gun-room, and (may we dare to breathe it) to him who walks abaft. — Believe me, my dear Eeles, yours ever,

R. L. STEVENSON.

TO SIR HERBERT MAXWELL

VAILIMA, SAMOA, *December 1st, 1894.*

DEAR SIR HERBERT, — Thank you very much for your long and kind letter. I shall certainly take your advice and call my cousin, the Lyon King, into council. It is certainly a very interesting subject, though I don't suppose it can possibly lead to anything, this connection between the Stevensons and M'Gregors. Alas, your invitation is to me a mere derision. My chances of visiting Heaven are about as valid as my chances of visiting Monreith. Though I should like well to see you, shrunken into a cottage, a literary Lord of Ravenscraig. I suppose it is the inevitable doom of all those who dabble in Scotch soil; but really your fate is the more blessed. I cannot conceive anything more grateful to me, or more amusing or more picturesque, than to live in a cottage outside your own park-walls. — With renewed thanks, believe me, dear Sir Herbert, yours very truly,

ROBERT LOUIS STEVENSON.

To Andrew Lang

The following refers, of course, to *Weir of Hermiston*, the chief character of which was studied from the traditions of Lord Braxfield, and on which Stevenson was working at the full height of his powers when death overtook him two days later.

Vailima, Samoa, *December 1, 1894.*

MY DEAR LANG,—For the portrait of Braxfield, much thanks! It is engraved from the same Raeburn portrait that I saw in '76 or '77 with so extreme a gusto that I have ever since been Braxfield's humble servant, and am now trying, as you know, to stick him into a novel. Alas, one might as well try to stick in Napoleon. The picture shall be framed and hung up in my study. Not only as a memento of you, but as a perpetual encouragement to do better with his Lordship. I have not yet received the transcripts. They must be very interesting. Do you know, I picked up the other day an old *Longman's*, where I found an article of yours that I had missed, about Christie's? I read it with great delight. The year ends with us pretty much as it began, among wars and rumours of wars, and a vast and splendid exhibition of official incompetence.—Yours ever,

R. L. Stevenson.

To Edmund Gosse

The next, and last, letter is to Mr. Gosse, dated also only two days before the writer's death. It acknowledged the dedication "To Tusitala" of that gentleman's volume of poems, *In Russet and Silver*, just received.

1894
ÆT. 44

VAILIMA, SAMOA, *December 1, 1894.*

I AM afraid, MY DEAR WEG, that this must be the result of bribery and corruption! The volume to which the dedication stands as preface seems to me to stand alone in your work; it is so natural, so personal, so sincere, so articulate in substance, and what you always were sure of — so rich in adornment.

Let me speak first of the dedication. I thank you for it from the heart. It is beautifully said, beautifully and kindly felt; and I should be a churl indeed if I were not grateful, and an ass if I were not proud. I remember when Symonds dedicated a book to me; I wrote and told him of "the pang of gratified vanity" with which I had read it. The pang was present again, but how much more sober and autumnal — like your volume. Let me tell you a story, or remind you of a story. In the year of grace something or other, anything between '76 and '78, I mentioned to you in my usual autobiographical and inconsiderate manner that I was hard up. You said promptly that you had a balance at your banker's, and could make it convenient to let me have a cheque, and I accepted and got the money — how much was it? — twenty, or perhaps thirty pounds? I know not — but it was a great convenience. The same evening, or the next day, I fell in conversation (in my usual autobiographical and . . . see above) with a denizen of the Savile Club, name now gone from me, only his figure and a dim three-quarter view of his face remaining. To him I mentioned that you had given me a loan, remarking easily that of course it did n't matter to you. Whereupon he read me a lecture, and told me how it really stood with you financially. He was pretty serious, fearing, as I could not help perceiving, that I should take too light a view of the responsibility and the service (I was always thought too light — the irresponsible jester — you remember. O, *quantum mutatus ab illo!*) If I remember rightly, the money was repaid before the end of the week — or, to be more exact and a trifle pedantic, the sennight — but the service has never been forgotten; and I send you back this piece of ancient history, *consule Planco,* as a salute for your dedication, and propose that we should drink the health of the nameless one who opened my eyes as to the true nature of what you did for me on that occasion.

But here comes my Amanuensis, so we 'll get on more swimmingly now. You will understand perhaps that what so particularly pleased me in the new volume, what seems to me to have so personal and original a note, are the middle-aged pieces in the beginning. The whole of them, I may say, though I must own an especial liking to —

> I yearn not for the fighting fate,
> That holds and hath achieved;
> I live to watch and meditate
> And dream — and be deceived.

You take the change gallantly. Not I, I must confess. It is all very well to talk of renunciation, and of course it has to be done. But, for my part, give me a roaring toothache! I do like to be deceived and to dream, but I have very little use for either watching or meditation. I was not born for age. And, curiously enough, I seem

1894
ÆT. 44

to see a contrary drift in my work from that which is so remarkable in yours. You are going on sedately travelling through your ages, decently changing with the years to the proper tune. And here am I, quite out of my true course, and with nothing in my foolish elderly head but love-stories. This must repose upon some curious distinction of temperaments. I gather from a phrase, boldly autobiographical, that you are—well, not precisely growing thin. Can that be the difference?

It is rather funny that this matter should come up just now, as I am at present engaged in treating a severe case of middle age in one of my stories—*The Justice-Clerk*. The case is that of a woman, and I think that I am doing her justice. You will be interested, I believe, to see the difference in our treatments. *Secreta Vitæ* comes nearer to the case of my poor Kirstie. Come to think of it, Gosse, I believe the main distinction is that you have a family growing up around you, and I am a childless, rather bitter, very clear-eyed, blighted youth. I have, in fact, lost the path that makes it easy and natural for you to descend the hill. I am going at it straight. And where I have to go down it is a precipice.

I must not forget to give you a word of thanks for *An English Village*. It reminds me strongly of Keats, which is enough to say; and I was particularly pleased with the petulant sincerity of the concluding sentiment.

Well, my dear Gosse, here 's wishing you all health and prosperity, as well as to the mistress and the bairns. May you live long, since it seems as if you would continue to enjoy life. May you write many more books

THE HOUSE AT VAILIMA AFTER THE ADDITIONS.

as good as this one — only there 's one thing impossible, you can never write another dedication that can give the same pleasure to the vanished TUSITALA.

1894
ÆT. 44

THE last words were prophetic; and the end came quite unexpectedly two days later. The reader may be glad to remember, what does not appear in the *Letters*, that in these last days, nay, on the last day of all, Stevenson had been once more enjoying keenly the highest pleasure of the artist — a consciousness of perfect command over his subject and his means. This came to him in dictating *Weir of Hermiston* more strongly than it had ever come to him before. On the afternoon of the 3rd of December he had brought his morning's work to his wife, the most exacting of his critics; had asked her whether it was not well done; and in her glow of admiring assent had found, within an hour of his seizure, his confirmation and his reward. The rest cannot be more fittingly told than in the words of the printed letter which was addressed to Stevenson's private friends by his stepson, Mr. Lloyd Osbourne, while his mind was full of the scenes and emotions of the time:

"He wrote hard all that morning of the last day; his half-finished book, *Hermiston*, he judged the best he had ever written, and the sense of successful effort made him buoyant and happy as nothing else could. In the afternoon the mail fell to be answered; not business correspondence — for this was left till later — but replies to the long, kindly letters of distant friends, received but two days since, and still bright in memory.

"At sunset he came down-stairs; rallied his wife

about the forebodings she could not shake off; talked of a lecturing tour to America that he was eager to make, 'as he was now so well,' and played a game at cards with her to drive away her melancholy. He said he was hungry; begged her assistance to help him make a salad for the evening meal; and to enhance the little feast he brought up a bottle of old Burgundy from the cellar. He was helping his wife on the verandah, and gaily talking, when suddenly he put both hands to his head, and cried out, 'What 's that?' Then he asked quickly, 'Do I look strange?' Even as he did so he fell on his knees beside her. He was helped into the great hall, between his wife and his body-servant, Sosimo, losing consciousness instantly, as he lay back in the arm-chair that had once been his grandfather's. Little time was lost in bringing the doctors — Anderson, of the man-of-war, and his friend Dr. Funk. They looked at him and shook their heads; they laboured strenuously and left nothing undone; but he had passed the bounds of human skill.

"The dying man lay back in the chair, breathing heavily, his family about him frenzied with grief as they realised all hope was past. The dozen and more Samoans that formed part of the little clan of which he was chief sat in a wide semicircle on the floor, their reverent, troubled, sorrow-stricken faces all fixed upon their dying master. Some knelt on one knee to be instantly ready for any command that might be laid upon them. A narrow bed was brought into the centre of the room; the Master was gently laid upon it, his head supported by a rest, the gift of Shelley's son. Slower and slower grew his respiration, wider the interval between the long, deep breaths. The Rev. Mr. Clarke was now come, an old and valued friend; he knelt and prayed as the life ebbed away.

"He died at ten minutes past eight on Monday evening the 3rd of December, in the forty-fifth year of his age.

"The great Union Jack that flew over the house was hauled down and laid over the body, fit shroud for a loyal Scotsman. He lay in the hall which was ever his pride, where he had passed the gayest and most delightful hours of his life, a noble room with open stairway and mullioned windows. In it were the treasures of his far-off Scottish home: the old carved furniture, the paintings and busts that had been in his father's house before him. The Samoans passed in procession beside his bed, kneeling and kissing his hand, each in turn, before taking their places for the long night watch beside him. No entreaty could induce them to retire, to rest themselves for the painful and arduous duties of the morrow. It would show little love for Tusitala, they said, if they did not spend their last night beside him. Mournful and silent, they sat in deep dejection, poor, simple, loyal folk, fulfilling the duty they owed their chief.

"A messenger was despatched to a few chiefs connected with the family, to announce the tidings and bid them assemble their men on the morrow for the work there was to do.

"Sosimo asked on behalf of the Roman Catholics that they might be allowed to recite the prayers for the dead. Till midnight the solemn chants continued, the prolonged, sonorous prayers of the Church of Rome, in commingled Latin and Samoan. Later still, a chief arrived with his retainers, bringing a precious mat to wrap about the dead.

"He, too, knelt and kissed the hand of Tusitala, and took his place amid the sleepless watchers. Another arrived with a fine mat, a man of higher rank, whose incipient consumption had often troubled the Master.

"'Talofa, Tusitala!' he said, as he drew nigh and took a long, mournful look at the face he knew so well. When, later on, he was momentarily required on some business of the morrow, he bowed reverently before retiring. 'Tofa, Tusitala!' he said, 'Sleep, Tusitala!'

"The morning of the 4th of December broke cool and sunny, a beautiful day, rare at this season of the year. More fine mats were brought, until the Union Jack lay nigh concealed beneath them. Among the new-comers was an old Mataafa chief, one of the builders of the 'Road of the Loving Hearts,' a man who had spent many days in prison for participation in the rebellion. 'I am only a poor Samoan, and ignorant,' said he as he crouched beside the body. 'Others are rich and can give Tusitala the parting presents of rich fine mats; I am poor and can give nothing this last day he receives his friends. Yet I am not afraid to come and look the last time in my friend's face, never to see him more till we meet with God. Behold! Tusitala is dead; Mataafa is also dead to us. These two great friends have been taken by God. When Mataafa was taken, who was our support but Tusitala? We were in prison, and he cared for us. We were sick, and he made us well. We were hungry, and he fed us. The day was no longer than his kindness. You are great people and full of love. Yet who among you is so great as Tusitala? What is your love to his love? Our clan was Mataafa's clan, for whom I speak this day; therein was Tusitala also. We mourn them both.'

"A meeting of chiefs was held to apportion the work and divide the men into parties. Forty were sent with knives and axes to cut a path up the steep face of the mountain, and the writer himself led another party to the summit — men chosen from the immediate family — to dig the grave on a spot where it was Mr. Stevenson's wish that he should lie. Nothing more picturesque can be imagined than the narrow ledge that forms the summit of Vaea, a place no wider than a room and flat as a table. On either side the land descends precipitously; in front lie the vast ocean and the surf-swept reefs; to the right and left, green mountains rise, densely covered with the primeval forest. Two hundred years ago the eyes of another man turned towards that same peak of Vaea, as the spot that should ultimately receive his war-worn body: Soalu, a famous chief.

"All the morning Samoans were arriving with flowers; few of these were white, for they have not learned our foreign custom, and the room glowed with the many colours. There were no strangers on that day, no acquaintances; those only were called who would deeply feel the loss. At one o'clock a body of powerful Samoans bore away the coffin, hid beneath a tattered red ensign that had flown above his vessel in many a remote corner of the South Seas. A path so steep and rugged taxed their strength to the utmost, for not only was the journey difficult in itself, but extreme care was requisite to carry the coffin shoulder-high.

"Half an hour later the rest of his friends followed. It was a formidable ascent, and tried them hard. Nineteen Europeans and some sixty Samoans reached the summit. After a short rest the Rev. W. E. Clarke read the burial service of the Church of England, interposing a prayer that Mr. Stevenson had written and had read aloud to his family only the evening before his death:

"'We beseech Thee, Lord, to behold us with favour, folk of many families and nations gathered together in the peace of this roof, weak men and women subsisting under the covert of Thy patience. Be patient still; suffer us yet awhile longer; — with our broken purposes of good, with our idle endeavours against evil, suffer us awhile longer to endure, and (if it may be) help us to do better. Bless to us our extraordinary mercies; if the day come when these must be taken, brace us to play the man under affliction. Be with our friends, be with ourselves. Go with each of us to rest; if any awake, temper to them the dark hours of watching; and when the day returns, return to us, our sun and comforter, and call us up with morning faces and with morning hearts — eager to labour — eager to be happy, if happiness shall be our portion — and if the day be marked for sorrow, strong to endure it.

"'We thank Thee and praise Thee; and in the words of him to whom this day is sacred, close our oblation.'"

THE LARGE HALL AT VAILIMA.

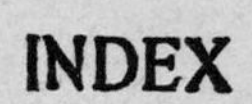
INDEX

INDEX